Breaking Up with Cuba

Breaking Up with Cuba

The Dissolution of Friendly Relations Between Washington and Havana, 1956–1961

DANIEL F. SOLOMON

McFarland & Company, Inc., Publishers
Jefferson, North Carolina, and London

LIBRARY OF CONGRESS CATALOGUING-IN-PUBLICATION DATA

Solomon, Daniel F.
    Breaking up with Cuba: the dissolution of friendly
relations between Washington and Havana, 1956–1961 /
Daniel F. Solomon.
        p.   cm.
    Includes bibliographical references and index.

    ISBN 978-0-7864-5972-8
    softcover : 50# alkaline paper ∞

    1. Cuba — Foreign relations — United States.   2. United
States — Foreign relations — Cuba.   3. Cuba — Foreign
relations —1933–1959.   4. Cuba — Foreign relations —1959–
1990.   5. United States — Foreign relations —1953–1961.
I. Title.
E183.8.C9S67   2011
327.7291073 — dc22   2010049127

British Library cataloguing data are available

On the cover: Vice President Richard Nixon and Cuban Prime Minister Fidel Castro leave Nixon's office in Washington, D.C., April 19, 1959 (AP Images); background © 2011 Shutterstock

Manufactured in the United States of America

McFarland & Company, Inc., Publishers
  Box 611, Jefferson, North Carolina 28640
  www.mcfarlandpub.com

Contents

Preface

The genesis of this book began many years ago, when I was a practicing lawyer in Miami, Florida, living near Little Havana. Although I lived there for more than twenty years, I consider myself a perpetual tourist and in order to better appreciate the local culture, I read widely and attended lectures at Miami Dade College, the Dade County Library, Florida International University, and other local venues. Until then, I was unaware of the pervasive influence that Cuban culture had and continues to have on the United States. I learned that Cuban culture is as diverse as mainstream U.S. culture and that there are innumerable social and cultural conflicts that affect the political climate in Cuba, and to a certain extent in the United States. I kept notes and news clippings, and my inquiry led me to the University of Miami Library, especially the Cuban Heritage Collection and the library at Florida International University.

This book constitutes part of what I have learned, and covers events and issues in U.S. relations with Cuba that have been seldom, if ever, discussed. It is limited to a five-year period after the *Puros*, officers in Cuba's armed services, mutinied against the regime of Fulgencio Batista in April 1956 to the Bay of Pigs fiasco in April 1961. At the time of the 1956 mutiny, there was strict censorship inside Cuba, and the American public was not aware of widespread dissatisfaction within Cuba. By 1956, Cuban society had become largely "Americanized" and commerce was dominated by the United States. At the time, Fidel Castro was living in Mexico, planning to wage armed insurrection. Carlos Prío Socarrás, the last democratically elected president of Cuba, was living in exile in Miami, planning something similar. Batista's government was opposed by student groups, especially from the University of Havana, which were effective and so threatening that Batista closed all state universities. Although some of the Puro leaders had been captured, the Cuban military remained peppered with military officers who wanted to restore democracy. Several important Cuban leaders defected or went into exile, especially to the United States. A clandestine civic resistance movement in Havana, comprising mainly professionals, committed espionage and sabotage, including terrorist bombings of civilian targets. In December 1956, Castro landed with a small group to wage war from the remote mountains in Oriente Province.

Two years later, Batista was pressured to leave the country by many of his former allies, including the hierarchy of the Cuban military. The narrative closely reports the deterioration of the relationship of the Provisional Government, installed in January 1959 with the U.S. government. Although Batista's exit led to great expectations and a period of elation, within the following 28 months, Cuba went from being our closest ally to our enemy. Although the Provisional Government initially comprised a relatively diverse group that reflected a broad spectrum of political, cultural and religious opponents of Batista, Cuba became increasingly nationalistic, defensive and militarized, partly in response to American opposition to the new regime. At onset, the Provisional Government was confronted by a seemingly probable civil war and perhaps an invasion from forces in the Dominican Republic. By 1961, the Provisional Government expected a U.S. invasion. As the U.S. became an enemy, American customs and values became condemned. The U.S. government relied on bad advice and lousy intelligence and had little insight into the Cuban situation.

Among the sources I consulted are numerous news articles, histories, treatises and journal articles. I especially thank the staff at the Library of Congress, Montgomery County Library and George Washington University, where I have been reading for the past ten or more years. My wife, Patricia, accompanied me on quests for information. Many were fruitful, others not, including to museums, bookstores and botanicas (a store devoted to the sale of Santería products) throughout the United States, especially with repeated trips to the Madison Building at the Library of Congress, and did not complain too loudly when we spent much of our family income to purchase books and art objects on the topic. Some of my former associates and colleagues, especially in the Office of Hearings and Appeals, Social Security Administration in Miami, provided me with background for my inquiry. My colleague, United States Administrative Law Judge Pamela Lakes Wood, and her book club provided encouragement and incisive suggestions.

Introduction

During the first half of the 20th century, the United States had a much closer relationship to Cuba, the most "Americanized" country in the region, than to any other Latin American country. However, although we heavily influenced Cuban culture and politics, and although most Cubans greatly admired the United States and our institutions, most Cubans were not completely enamored of the United States' Cuban policy. In fact, most Cubans resented our interference in their internal affairs and this resentment drove much of mainstream intellectual thought.[1]

Perhaps we had been too close. There had been serious discussions about annexation of Cuba to the United States. Most Cubans were aware that more than 70 American expeditions had been attempted to capture Cuba during the 19th century and that we had occupied their country on several occasions. At one time, there had been calls by Cubans to ask for annexation. As recently as the 1930s, there had been requests by some Cuban intellectuals to ask the United States to send in marines to bring order.[2] Although we were not in a position to annex Cuba, we had recently added Hawaii and Alaska, far more distant and no less exotic than Cuba, as states, and Puerto Rico, acquired from Spain at the same time that we had "freed" Cuba, remained one of our "properties," under consideration for statehood. Most Cubans, our friends included, resented our continued presence in Guantánamo, and told us that it was a constant reminder that we had occupied the island on several occasions and could easily do so again.[3]

During World War II the U.S. made a pact with "the Devil." According to President Franklin Delano Roosevelt, we needed a demonic ally* to defeat the amoral, sadistic and lethal Axis — Japan and Germany — that at the start of the war looked like they would prevail. The Axis powers were totalitarian military dictatorships that openly boasted that they would subjugate, enslave and/or exterminate their neighbors. By 1941, they had taken vast swaths of land and had started to execute their agenda. Millions of innocent civilians were killed and millions more were tortured, injured and displaced as eventually tens of millions of people were irreparably damaged by the war.

At the beginning of the war, Germany and the Soviets were allies. However, after the German army had turned on their former ally in a surprise attack, seized the breadbasket of Europe, routed the Red Army, and killed millions of Russians, with our financial and moral support the Soviet Union was able to remove the Germans from Eastern Europe.[4] By doing so, the Red Army was able to spread communist influence in its wake.

The Supreme Commander of Allied Forces in Europe was Dwight David Eisenhower,

---

*In this instance, "the Devil" and demonic ally refer to U.S. cooperation with Stalin and Communism.

3

who would later, of course, become president of the United States. During the war, he and the head of the Red Army, Marshal Zhukov, had become colleagues and friends, although sometimes General Eisenhower directly dealt with Joseph Stalin. Early on, the Allies had determined that they were at war with criminals.[5] Like other Allied commanders, General Eisenhower supported trying "war criminals." As Military Governor of the United States Occupation of Germany, General Eisenhower made the decision to treat former German military personnel as disarmed enemy forces (DEFs), which exempted them from prisoner of war protection under the Geneva Convention. Many DEFs were placed into forced labor.

U.S. State Department policy was supposed to befriend "good neighbors," but many of our diplomats were not very acculturated and often felt superior to our good friends and neighbors. For example, during the 1940s, a United States diplomat stationed at the U.S. embassy in Havana wrote a report on Cuba, in which he described a "state of ferment and license," and an "organized indiscipline," which he described as "a fetish of Cuban life." He did not hold much hope for good government in Cuba.[6] Another American diplomat in the United States embassy in Havana identified vanity as the principal reason why there was social and political ferment:

> Although vanity is a prevailing characteristic of all Latin Americans, ... in the Cubans ... [a] magnified sense of honor of the Spaniards has degenerated in Cuba into excessive and ridiculous vanity. This trait contributed to the uncompromising attitude of the Cubans in certain economic and political matters. Vanity is the root of the Cuban spirit of indiscipline and is followed by some of their political figures merely for the purpose of attracting attention.[7]

The author further described Cubans as a nervous people with liver and stomach problems that made them short-tempered. He described them as good at "bluffing," escapist, obsessed with entertainments like music and dance, excessive spenders, and claimed they spoiled their children so much that as adults they had no ambition.[8]

As a candidate for president, General Eisenhower ran against conservative Robert Taft, who espoused a non-interventionist, if not isolationist, foreign policy. Under General Eisenhower's watch, the United States participated in the Nuremberg Trials. These were tribunals presided over by judges from the Allies, the countries that had won World War II. Taft, "Mr. Conservative," then a Republican senator from Ohio, argued that the charges against the "war criminals" were based on ex post facto crimes, were legally flawed, and that the trials violated the American sense of fair play.

The chief Soviet judge was Major-General Iona Timofeevich Nikitchenko, who had presided at Soviet show trials in the 1930s, in which it was estimated that 681,692 to 2,000,000 Soviet citizens had been adjudicated and "liquidated" for innocuous political "crimes." Millions more were sent to forced labor camps.

President Eisenhower was perhaps the best-qualified expert on international affairs to ever run for the office. Besides his war experiences, he had been the head of NATO forces from 1950 to May 1952, and he had been actively involved in diplomacy. President Eisenhower ran for office while president of Columbia University, a post he held until his inauguration, as U.S. president. At Columbia he concentrated on diplomacy as an academic subject served as a chair of a study group on the Council on Foreign Relations.

However, World War II had not reached Latin America. Many Latin American leaders were seen as close U.S. allies, but some had toyed with becoming part of the Axis.

In Europe and Asia, the United States was confronted by the Soviet Union and, after 1949, by Red China. As a candidate Eisenhower ran on a platform opposing Truman administration policies concerning "Korea, Communism and Corruption." At the time, America was experiencing a "red scare." Accusations were made that the communists were undermining American society. There was a wave of mistrust in American institutions, from education to government to the media. Candidate Eisenhower capitalized on it. His opponent in the Republican primary election, Taft, was more of a hard-liner than Eisenhower on those subjects. Many Republicans considered Eisenhower as an ally of President Truman. Determined to win the primary, Eisenhower took a similar position to Taft's and attacked Truman verbally at every opportunity.

Meanwhile, our ally in Cuba was a totalitarian dictator. Fulgencio Batista had risen to power in 1933 with American help during a violent and bloody revolution, and from that point on he became the most powerful figure in Cuban history before Castro. Batista had a diverse group of allies. If Presidents Roosevelt and Truman and General Eisenhower had made a pact with the Devil to win World War II, Batista was in bed with him to control Cuba. When he ran for office in 1940, Batista ran as a *Socialista*, which can be translated into English as "communist." As president of Cuba from 1940 to 1944, he had communists in his cabinet and they appointed other communists to government positions. Many of President Batista's policies were the same as the communists'. He was out of power for a time, but after he led a military coup in March 1952, Batista disavowed the communists to placate the Truman administration. However, within Cuban politics, the communists had better relations with Batista than they had with his political enemies of the time, the Auténtico and Ortodoxo political parties, which both had a history of anti-communism.

After he lost the presidential race to Eisenhower, Senator Taft agreed not to interfere in foreign policy matters as long as the Eisenhower administration followed a conservative domestic policy.

The U.S. secretary of state became John Foster Dulles.[9] Although he served intermittently in the Roosevelt and Truman administrations, in his 1950 book *War or Peace*, Dulles argued that the U.S. policy of containment should be replaced by a policy of "liberation." As secretary of state in a nuclear age, Dulles urged policies of "brinkmanship" and "massive retaliation." Brinkmanship took the United States to "the verge without getting into war." Dulles argued that nations had to side with the United States: "Neutrality has increasingly become an obsolete and, except under very exceptional circumstances, it is an immoral and shortsighted conception." Dulles and his brother, Allen Dulles, engineered covert operations in Iran and Guatemala to supplant existing governments that they saw as opposing American "interests."

At the same time, President Eisenhower and Secretary Dulles held themselves out to the public as righteous, religious and moral men.[10] However, both expressed a "strident moralism" using a "self righteous and apocalyptic rhetoric" to stake out the U.S. position.[11] As a candidate, Eisenhower led a "crusade," which to most Americans tied notions of Protestantism and missionary diplomacy to the mission of the U.S. State Department. In fact, the Dulles brothers were descended from a family of Presbyterian missionaries and State Department officials. Both of the Dulles brothers were lawyers and partners in the New York law firm of Sullivan and Cromwell, where both had practiced international law. One of their common clients held American interests that would become the centerpiece of U.S. foreign policy in Latin America. In fact, at one time, Allen Dulles served on the client's board of directors. Other members of the Eisenhower State Department also had close ties to that company. That client was United Fruit Company.[12]

During the Eisenhower administration, Alaska and Hawaii were admitted into the Union. The United States acquired Hawaii in 1893, after the native government was overthrown. On July 7, 1898, the United States annexed Hawaii as a territory of the United States. We acquired Hawaii as we were also engaged in the Spanish American War, which primarily dealt with the liberation of Cuba. At the time, the treaty of Paris (1898) also annexed the Philippines, Puerto Rico, and Guam, former Spanish colonies acquired by war. In 1959, the Admission Act made Hawaii a state.

Although our history with Cuba gave us a moral responsibility to ensure that Cuba was well managed, under the Truman and Eisenhower administrations we asserted a "non-intervention" policy, and left Batista in place.

On December 31, 1958, President Fulgencio Batista departed Cuba for good, leaving the country to its fate. After that, relations with the United States became problematical as a period of adjustment occurred. Then relations soured. Cuba, once our solid ally and a valued and trusted customer, became our enemy. But it didn't have to end that way.

Cuba was the fourth Latin American dictatorship to fall within a three-year period. First Argentina, then Colombia, then Venezuela, and finally Cuba changed regimes. By December 31, the first three had become democracies, and throughout Latin America, American democracy was the model for regime change.

Chapter 1

Fast Friends

Cuba and the United States were bosom allies in the 1950s; so close that we were rapidly acculturating to each other. After all, we're only ninety miles apart. We had a lot of common interests and we had won a war together. They might call it the Cuban War for Independence and we might call it the Spanish American War, but it was the same war.

Anyone could have seen from viewing our respective social lives and our popular culture of the era that we were eagerly courting each other. Appropriately, perhaps the most popular couple in 1950s America was Lucy and Desi: Lucille Ball, the vivacious American redhead, and Desiderio Alberto Arnaz y de Acha III, Desi Arnaz, the tall, dark and accented Cuban singer, actor, and straight man, who epitomized the Cuban/American relationship. Each week the *I Love Lucy* television show reminded Americans how close we were to our Cuban neighbors. At a time when most American mainstream culture was directed toward a monolithic, homogeneous, sterile, lily-white majority, Lucy and Desi highlighted their cultural differences and exhibited some good-natured cultural tension to make Americans laugh. Meanwhile, everybody got an education: each of the characters was exposed to a foreign culture and in the process attempted mutual cultural assimilation.[1]

Besides watching Lucy and Desi, we listened and danced to Cuban music, including the rumba, cha-cha,[2] mambo and conga, and Cuban music also greatly influenced American jazz, symphonic and even rock 'n' roll genres. Desi as Ricky Ricardo was a bandleader at the Tropicana Club, later renamed Club Babalu. His band was mostly composed of Cuban musicians wearing frilly costumes, conspicuously thumping Cuban percussion instruments. He would sing and bang out a few numbers on his conga drum, especially his hit record, "Babalú."[3]

Several American nightclubs capitalized on the Tropicana name. It became synonymous with gambling. There was a famous casino in Las Vegas and an infamous roadhouse in Newport, Kentucky, styled after the "Paradise under the Stars," the famous Havana nightclub of the same name.[4] There actually was a Tropicana Club in the Bronx, but it had no connection with the show. Several other popular nonfictional American clubs also had a Cuban ambiance. Founded in 1940, New York City's Copacabana was advertised as the "Hottest Spot North of Havana." Other famous New York clubs that featured Cuban acts were the Latin Quarter and the Palladium Ballroom. Less famous but as authentic were El Cubanacán, El Club Caborrojeño, the Tropicola, La Campana, La Bamba and the Tropicoro. Numerous other venues featured Cuban entertainers, and such venues as Harlem's Apollo and Savoy Ballroom had mambo nights.

Besides Lucy and Desi, another Cuban crossover television show, *The Xavier Cugat Show*, debuted on NBC in February 1957, featuring Cuban music. Over time, Cugat's band

Lucille Ball and Desi Arnaz on the set of America's most popular television show of the 1950s, *I Love Lucy*. The show probably did more to promote Cuban-American goodwill than all of the diplomacy of the period. In 1960, the show was cancelled. Like Cuba and the United States, Ball and Arnaz were soon divorced (photograph from Getty Images).

included a young Desi Arnaz, Miguelito Valdés, Tito Rodríguez, Luis del Campo, Yma Sumac, Cugat's third wife, Abbe Lane, and his fourth, Charo, all of whom would become celebrities. Known as the "Rumba King," Cugat was born in Spain, but he was raised in Cuba and was identified as Cuban in the public mind. He often appeared carrying a chihuahua dog and a pipe, although he didn't smoke. Cugat and his band recorded hundreds of single records and dozens of albums. Among the most famous hit songs were "Perfidia" and "Brazil," recorded in the early 1940s. "Coogie," as he was known, had been a radio favorite and appeared in at least three movies before he was given his own show. After the show was cancelled he and his band continued to appear as guests on other television shows. They toured and were also regulars at major musical venues in Miami and Law Vegas. After Cugat retired, Tito Puente acquired his band.[5]

By the 1950s American jazz had fused with Cuban music to form Latin jazz. At the forefront was avant-garde virtuoso trumpeter Dizzy Gillespie, who recorded "Cubop" with other jazz greats like Charlie (Bird) Parker, Thelonious Monk, and John Coltrane starting in the 1940s. After Cuban conga drummer Chano Pozo became a member of Gillespie's band, other American bands rushed to hire Cubans, especially percussionists. Latin jazz bands like those of Ramón "Mongo" Santamaría, Perez Prado, and Tito Puente were more popular in the United States than they were in Cuba.[6]

Cuban music has a rich history. Over time, dozens of unique musical styles developed from the Cuban tradition. Among the forms familiar to most Americans are the Cuban bolero, the habanera, the danzon and the son. The most famous bolero is the *Habanera* of Bizet's opera *Carmen*, written in 1875. Although Bizet was French and the opera was set in Spain, Cuban music had already become popular. In 1950, Patti Page's "All My Love," a Cuban bolero sung partly in Spanish, was a top-selling recording in the States. The most famous bolero of the 1950s is "Guajiro Guantanamera," which became the anthem of the Cuban Revolution.[7]

The habanera form became popular as American troops were sent to Cuba during the Spanish American War and later occupations. They brought it back to America, where it influenced American music.[8] Musicologists say that the Argentine tango and rock 'n' roll are derived from the habanera.[9] The danzon was at one time the official dance of Cuba, a social dance, similar to a slow dance. The danzon evolved into the son, which incorporates many features of African music. As syncopation was added, the mambo and cha-cha, and later the pachanga, were developed.

The rumba was also popular in the U.S., mostly in the 1930s and 1940s; a rumba craze in the 1930s introduced Cugat and Arnaz to America.[10] The rumba dance form evolved from African dances and from an earlier Cuban dance form, the contradanza. Whereas danzon dancers danced together, the contradazon dancers danced separately. The rumba dance was an extension of Afro-Cuban religious rites, and it incorporated many features of several religious dances.[11]

The distinctive feature of most Cuban music is the *Clave*, a five-beat, 3–2 rhythmic pattern, with a strong first part and an "answering" second part. The term is taken from the instrument used to make the music: *claves* are two sticks used to beat out the rhythm. African and African American music, especially the blues genre, often use a similar call-and-response technique. According to musicologists, the Cuban clave is adaptable to all forms of Cuban music.[12] One of the most identifiable uses of claves is in American songs of the era can be found in the Tempos' version of "See You in September," recorded in 1959.[13] The "Bo Diddley beat" of rock 'n' roll is based on claves, and it is identifiable in many other early rock 'n' roll standards like 1957's "Little Darlin'," by the Diamonds.[14] The Bo Diddley beat would be used later to greater financial success by Elvis Presley, Buddy Holly, the Rolling Stones, Bruce Springsteen and many others.[15]

By the late 1950s Latin jazz had become incorporated into American popular music. American stars like Nat King Cole and Frank Sinatra incorporated Latin jazz elements into their music and paid homage to Cuba by performing there regularly. Cole recorded his 1956 record *Espanole* and the album *Cole en Español* entirely in Spanish in 1958 in Havana.[16]

Cuban influences were evident in America's musical hit parade, the highest-selling records; usually, however, they were performed by Americans.[17] "Mambo Italiano," recorded by Rosemary Clooney in 1954, was the number one single in England in 1955.[18] After song-writer Bix Reichner told popular crooner and television star Perry Como that his newest song couldn't miss because America was "in the midst of a mambo mania," Como recorded "Papa Loves Mambo" in 1954 and it spent eighteen weeks on the charts in 1955.[19] That year, rock 'n' roll pioneers Bill Haley and the Comets recorded "Mambo Rock," and Chuck Berry wrote and recorded "Havana Moon" in 1956.[20] None of these were very authentic.[21]

Some Americans "covered" Cuban music: for example, "The Peanut Vendor," "El Manisero" in Cuba, a classic 1920s Cuban rumba, was recorded in the 1930s by Louis Armstrong, and in the 1950s by Dean Martin. Nat King Cole and later movie star and singer Doris Day and several other Americans recorded "Perhaps, Perhaps, Perhaps," the English version of "Quizás, Quizás, Quizás," written by Cuban songwriter Osvaldo Farrés.[22]

Bandleaders like Machito, Tito Puente, Tito Rodríguez and Jose Curbelo were identified with the mambo dance craze centered in places like the Palladium Ballroom in New York. The mambo fad was closely followed by the cha-cha, also known as the cha-cha-cha. Between 1955 and 1958 the Orquesta Aragon released "Cha-Cha-Cha," "That Cuban Cha-Cha-Cha," "The Heart of Havana" and "Maracas, Bongo y Congas" for RCA Records. In 1955, the "King of Mambo," Perez Prado, recorded "Cerezo Rosa," known in the United States as "Cherry Pink and Apple Blossom White." The ultimate cha-cha, it reached number one on American record charts.[23] In 1956, Prado appeared in the American movie *Cha-Cha-Cha Boom!* which featured Luis Arcaraz and Manny López and their orchestras, and several other Cubans.[24]

Many pop songs of the era were arranged with a mambo or cha-cha beat. For example, the Drifters' 1954 "Honey Love," Peggy Lee's 1958 "Fever," Billy and Lillie's "La Dee Dah" in 1958, and Frankie Avalon's "Venus," released in 1959, all have a Latin beat.[25] Some tunes were morphed: for example, Dean Martin transposed the French "Melodie d'Amour" to Cuban/American "Cha-Cha d'Amour." Cuban composer and bandleader René Touzet's 1956 "El Loco Cha-Cha," would become the form for the rhythm and blues classic "Louie Louie."[26] Alan Dale's vocal version of "Cherry Pink and Apple Blossom White" and "Rockin' the Cha-Cha" both made the pop charts. Among others, Tommy Dorsey recorded "Tea for Two Cha-Cha" and "I Want to Be Happy Cha-Cha" in 1958, the DeCastro Sisters recorded "Teach Me Tonight Cha-Cha" and Edmundo Ros recorded "I Talk to the Trees Cha-Cha" in 1959. Sam Cooke recorded "Everyone Loves To Cha-Cha-Cha" that same year.

The cha-cha dance was almost as prevalent as the jitterbug, as it was spread to the nation on shows like *American Bandstand,* where many of the teenage girls wore shoes with cha-cha heels and other Cuban-influenced clothing, although girls were not permitted to wear their high-waisted, Capri pants on television.[27] Although such songs as Canadian Paul Anka's "Diana," the Everly Brothers' "All I Have to Do Is Dream," the Drifters' rhythm and blues "There Goes My Baby" and "This Magic Moment," and Harry Belafonte's calypso classic "Jamaica Farewell" were not written as Latin songs, people danced the cha-cha to them.

On Broadway, "Mu-cha-cha" was a featured number in *The Bells Are Ringing*, 1956, performed by Judy Holliday and Peter Gennaro.[28] Cuban music was so pervasive in movie scores that Cuba's favorite singer, Benny Moré, was a celebrated featured performer at the Oscar ceremonies in 1957.[29] "Shirl's Theme Cha-Cha," written by Nelson Riddle, was performed in the movie version of *Hole in the Head* in 1959 by Carolyn Jones.

Cuban acts appeared on the popular television variety shows of the era such as Ed Sullivan's *Talk of the Town*, at the time America's number one musical show. To the American audience, virtually everything from Cuba might have been enjoyable. But we didn't get the full story. Sullivan went to Cuba in the fall of 1957. When asked about the ongoing Cuban Revolution, he alleged that he had never even heard of it.[30] After he "discovered" the Revolution, Sullivan interviewed Fidel Castro on January 11, 1959, soon after dictator Fulgencio Batista had fled the country.

In newspaper articles Havana was depicted as a "lovely, busy, exciting capital city, with sweeping views with interesting architecture both ancient and contemporary, with blue skies and a hot tropical sun and a big tropical moon that shines on the Caribbean Sea brighter even than do the neon and winking rum and cigar signs on Havana's streets. The countryside is rich, often lush with the fertile green of tropical crops and year round blossoms."[31] Newspaper articles did not mention the real draws: sex and gambling and prostitution and drugs.

The salubrious climate, the romantic ambiance and the popularity of Cuban entertainment seduced hundreds of thousands of American tourists.[32] Havana was advertised as the "the Paris of the Caribbean," the "gambling Mecca of the New World,"[33] the "crossroads of the world," and the "friendliest city on Earth." Cuba was the "land of eternal spring," the "land of romance" and the "melting pot of races and cultures."[34] In 1957, a $68.80 ticket could buy a passenger a "night club flight," on Cubana Airlines from New York, which included an evening with dinner and drinks at the famous Tropicana nightclub, an overnight stay in a Havana hotel, breakfast, and a return flight.[35] An eleven-day trip from New York to Havana was cheaper by far than a seven-day trip to Miami.[36] Meanwhile, tens of thousands of Cubans visited the States.

Americans went to Havana as tourists, but also with lots of goods to sell. American products dominated Cuban markets. American tourists, American companies and American goods were pervasive throughout Cuba. Most Cubans loved American products and the life style.[37] The U.S. also tried to spread its political system, and Cubans had tried American-style democracy from 1902 to 1952, but Cuban politics always seemed violent and disordered. After that, the new Batista government seemed more reliable and more accommodating and seemed to be closely tied to Washington, so North Americans didn't pay much attention to complaints about the repressive nature of the Cuban government. Latin American countries always seemed to be in bloody revolt, and Cuba was the steadiest and most civilized of them all.

Besides their country's exotic culture, Cubans offered a sunny disposition toward Americans and the conditional use of a land of plenty: fertile soil, valuable raw materials and cheap labor. American companies invested heavily in Cuba.[38] Thousands of American companies owned properties in Cuba. A dozen American industries, including Firestone, Du Pont, Reynolds, Phelps Dodge and Remington Rand built plants in Cuba during the period 1956–1959 and others had building plans.[39] American companies owned Cuban electric and telephone utilities, and thousands of Americans worked in Cuba running American-owned businesses. Americans sold and Cubans consumed Cuban commodities processed in the United States.

Cuba also was seen as necessary to maintain U.S. national security. The United States not only had a military presence at the naval station at Guantánamo, but through most of the period, the U.S, fleet sailed to Havana and other Cuban cities, where thousands of sailors and marines took shore leave, making their uniforms familiar sights to many Cubans.[40]

During that period, Cuba and the United States shared baseball as a national pastime, but to Cubans baseball had become a political and cultural symbol for their independence. Although most people will acknowledge that baseball is an American game, there is a minority view that baseball was actually born in the Caribbean.[41] Whether American or not, modern baseball took shape in the 19th century, and the love of baseball grew in Cuba contemporaneous with rebellion against Spain. The Spaniards never understood the lure of baseball, but they did understand it was not their game. By the last part of the 19th century, all Cuban baseball players were seen by the Spanish rulers as rebels, corrupted by American values.

The Spanish national sport was bullfighting. In Spain primitive bullfighting was fused with religious ceremony, first pagan, later Christian, to became a national obsession. To an outside observer, the parade from the town cathedral to *la corrida de toros*, the bullfight, looked just like a religious procession. Priests and brothers and other church officials often participated in the march of the toreadors to the bull ring. In the most Catholic of countries, the passion of faith was extended to sanctify the formalities of the bloody national sport. Spectators invariably gambled on the outcome. Often driven to great emotion, spectators participated in the spectacle by harassing, teasing and eventually demanding the ritualized killing of the bulls by a matador, translated in English as "killer." It could be bloody for more than just the bull. Sometimes the toreadors and matadors and the horses were gored. In the end, the population got to participate in victory with a communal feast, often on a religious feast day, of the body and the blood of the unfortunate bull.

It could be life-threatening. Sometimes riots erupted. Even today, some bullfight fans risk life and limb to participate in the running of the bulls, such as the religious festival of San Fermin at Pamplona, where at least 13 people have been killed since 1924, with hundreds more injured over the years.[42]

But in late 19th century Cuba, bullfighting was seen as a reminder of the feudalistic dominance of imperial Spain over backward provincial vassals. Before the Cuban War for Independence almost every town of any size had a bull ring surrounded by bleachers. By the end of the war, few bull arenas remained in Cuba and the sport eventually disappeared. Ultimately, Cubans completely displaced the blood lust of bullfighting with baseball. In Cuba, professional baseball became a cultural pageant with political and religious aspects. American fans noted that Cuban players often had a special flair for the game. By 1956, compared to U.S. fans, Cuban fans were insanely fanatical.[43] Cuban baseball was fantastic. Public passion for the nuances of the game extended not only to local teams but to teams in the American major leagues. The fervor extended to all classes and genders. When the World Series was first televised to Cuba that year, business came to a complete stop. True Cubans were engrossed in the national sport: baseball. In 1957, while an armed insurrection was taking place in Oriente Province, all rebel army guerrilla commanders were ordered to halt operations against the Batista forces to give the men an opportunity to listen to the World Series.[44]

In time, American baseball terms became part of the Cuban Spanish language, and other Americanisms soon followed. By the 1950s Cuban Spanish was filled with English words and American-referenced idioms and clichés.[45] In many circles the resulting lexicon is called "Spanglish."

Cuba was a favorite destination not only for Americans and Canadians but for many other foreigners who had been enticed to relocate to Cuba due to the tropical climate, good job prospects and the relatively high standard of living. For example, in 1958, 12,000 Italians and 12,000 more Spaniards applied for immigration visas.[46] By 1957 there was an colony of 12,168 Americans and another 29,848 British/Canadian subjects living in Cuba.[47] There were also approximately 30,000 Chinese who had immigrated to Cuba.[48] Greater still were the numbers of native Spaniards who had emigrated. Some became naturalized Cuban citizens, and their numbers dwarfed other immigrant populations of Cuba many times over.

During the 1950s the most famous person in Cuba was undoubtedly an American: expatriate writer Ernest Hemingway. An avid fisherman, Hemingway had lived in Key West, Florida, for a time with his second wife and had fished in Cuban waters. He stayed off and on in the Hotel Ambos Mundos in Havana, beginning in about 1932, and he wrote many works there. Later his girlfriend Martha Gellhorn discovered a secluded ranch house built in the 1880s that overlooked the lights of the city. They bought it in 1939 for about $18,500 and named it Finca Vigía, "Lookout Ranch." After Hemingway divorced Pauline, his second wife, he and Gellhorn married on November 20, 1940. He wrote *For Whom the Bell Tolls* in 1939 in Cuba and Key West, and finished it in July 1940. The novel is dedicated to Gellhorn, who had served as a correspondent to *Collier's* magazine in Spain during the Spanish Civil War. The story was based on real events and Hemingway's personal experiences.[49] A movie version was made in 1943, starring Ingrid Bergman and Gary Cooper, who later became regular house guests at the *finca*. The movie was the top American box-office hit of 1943, grossing $11 million, and was nominated for nine Academy Awards.

Hemingway affected a distinctive style; a beard and safari clothes, drink in hand. He popularized Cuban products such as the daiquiri, a fruity rum drink. Americans might argue that he invented the "Papa Doble" in Key West at Sloppy Joe's saloon; Cubans say he might have acquired it, perhaps at Sloppy Joe's in Havana, but he perfected it at the Floridita Bar in Havana.

Gellhorn and Hemingway were divorced in 1945, and he soon married Mary Welsh, another war correspondent whom he had met in England during the war. Afterward, he brought her back to Cuba.

Hemingway's *The Old Man and the Sea*, seen as the quintessential novel about Cuba, was completed in 1952 and was a best seller in the United States for 26 weeks. Translated into numerous languages, it earned Hemingway the Pulitzer Prize in 1953 and the Nobel Prize in Literature in 1954. A movie was made in 1958, partly filmed in Cuba, starring Spencer Tracy. The novella was written while Hemingway was living in Finca Vigía, and it describes an epic battle between a crafty old deep-sea fisherman and a giant marlin, potentially the largest catch of his life. He has gone without a catch for a long time, and the protagonist compares his drought to the trials of American baseball hero Joe DiMaggio as an example of persistence and grace under pressure. Here the author explored one of his main themes: tragedy. We all have to die, but a man can be destroyed without being defeated.[50] In the novella, baseball is, in large part, a metaphor for life. As great an athlete as he was during his prime, even Joe DiMaggio had to succumb to age and retire after the 1951 baseball season. In his Nobel acceptance speech, which he did not give personally, Hemingway described the book as about "a man who had gone out too far."[51]

The two most famous people in Cuba, 1959. Nobel Prize–winning American ex-patriate Ernest Hemingway and Comandante Fidel Castro Ruz (Getty Images).

The Old Man and the Sea was first introduced to millions of Americans in full length in *Life* magazine. American readers read it as an adventure yarn, consistent with other Hemingway works espousing manly virtues and a stoic response to a bad outcome, as the protagonist proves his mettle by losing his catch in style. However, there are symbolic references to the crucifixion and other religious images, such as a picture of Our Lady of Charity/the *Virgin del Cobre,* the patroness saint of Cuba. When the protagonist wishes, he says, "I am not religious, but I will say ten Our Fathers and ten Hail Marys that I should catch this fish, and I promise to make a pilgrimage to the *Virgin of Cobre* if I catch him." He catches the fish but loses it, literally and figuratively. After he won the Nobel Prize, Hemingway dedicated his prize to the *Virgin del Cobre,* to be kept at her shrine.[52] Hemingway had to have known that in Santería, an African religion transported to Cuba, the Virgin is seen as *Ochún,* a demigod of love, money and happiness. He also had to have known that his protagonist, an immigrant from the Azores, was not a typical devotee of the *Virgin del Cobre.*

President Batista recognized Hemingway's fame and popularity and awarded him the Cuban Medal of Honor in 1952, and later the Order of Carlos Manuel de Céspedes and the Order of San Cristóbal. Mary Hemingway later said that Hemingway refused to receive awards at the Presidential Palace because he did not want to make it look like he was endorsing Batista.[53]

Hemingway's *The Sun Also Rises* was filmed in 1957. Although Hemingway had initially objected, former swashbuckler Errol Flynn, deteriorating from alcoholism, cancer and depression, was picked for a supporting role. Flynn always had a taste for the exotic, and as soon as he came to Cuba he was hooked. *The Big Boodle* (1957), titled *Night in Havana* in England, was filmed in and around Havana. In it Flynn played a casino croupier falsely accused of counterfeiting. After Batista fled, Flynn made *Cuban Rebel Girls* in 1959.

Besides Ernest Hemingway and Errol Flynn, other writers and celebrities had a presence in Cuba. *Our Man in Havana*, a 1958 novel by British author Graham Greene was a best seller. The hero is an expatriate vacuum cleaner salesman who passes himself off as a British secret agent. Without any real information to send London, he makes up an entire spy network. His fictional atomic weapon looks exactly like a huge version of a vacuum cleaner. The 1959 movie version was filmed in Cuba by British director Carol Reed, starring Alec Guinness, Ernie Kovacs, Burl Ives, Noel Coward, Ralph Richardson and Maureen O'Hara.

Cubans watched American movies and television shows on the island. Some Cuban television shows were designed to sell American products if not American values. Shows like *Reina por un Día* (*Queen for a Day* in the States), *Esta Es Su Vida* (the Cuban version of *This Is Your Life*), *El Hit Parade Cubano* and *El Club Rock 'n' Roll* were knockoffs of American television.[54]

As Cubans were exposed to American advertising, Cuban traditions were influenced. The Spanish Christmas tradition of exchanging gifts on Three Kings' Day, Epiphany, received competition from Christmas traditions popular in the U.S. such as the Christmas tree, Santa Claus and a gift exchange on Christmas Day. Private citizen Fulgencio Batista had lived in Daytona Beach, Florida, and while there, was impressed by the Thanksgiving holiday. As president, Batista decreed Thanksgiving to be a Cuban holiday.[55]

A high proportion of the Cuban business community was bilingual. Ambitious Cubans had attended and sent their children to the many American and English schools on the island or to schools in the States, and worked in firms owned by or in business with American interests. Cubans could shop at American-style stores and supermarkets, and many belonged to American-style clubs and fraternal societies like the Elks, the Moose, the Rotary and the Boy and Girl Scouts. There also was "Americanization" in fashion. Cubans not only bought American-made clothes and appliances, but they manufactured many of their own goods to fit American tastes. Although many Cuban writers were celebrated internationally, most Cubans preferred to read translations of American authors.[56]

Americans were influenced by Cuban styles. Early 1950s women's shoes often had sturdy "Cuban heels." "Cabana sets" of matching shirts and shorts and bathing suits were the mode at the beach and pool. Women were sold Cuban-designed cabana pants and "pedal pushers" in tropical pastel colors. Women's cocktail dresses and formalwear incorporated "sexy," "dramatic," and "shocking" ideas from Cuban designers like Luis Estévez.[57] Although the Cuban guayabera, a men's shirt, never became fully acceptable to the mainstream, American sport shirts were often influenced by them.[58]

Some Cuban designed furniture was in a *moderno movimiento*, "tropical deco" style. During is period, American "modernist" furniture, home decorations, house paints and American cars were also often offered in tropical pastel colors.[59]

By 1958, one of every five Cubans owned a radio, and could listen to 160 local stations, some of them broadcasting in English. At least one Havana radio station exclusively played American popular music. Some Cubans could also pick up American radio stations. By 1958, Cuba had three national networks and 23 television stations that included seven independent local stations in Havana and Camagüey Province.[60] Cuba was the second country to broadcast color television. Although the Minister of Communication tried to ban it, Cuban teenagers loved American rock 'n' roll so much that *American Bandstand*–type shows were introduced in 1956 and 1957 on competing Havana television stations.[61]

Americans acknowledged that Cuban cigars and Cuban rum were the best. Americans also drank other Cuban liquor, and Cuban-style alcoholic mixed drinks were immensely popular. However, the most popular, the Cuba Libre, was supposedly invented by Americans during the Spanish American War. Americans were also addicted to Cuban sugar.

By 1957, Havana was in the midst of a construction boom. The Batista government sponsored extensive highway projects to connect Havana with other large cities, expressways to connect suburban Havana with the old city, hospital and airport construction throughout the island and many other major projects.[62] On January 1, 1958, President Batista and Cuban archbishop Manuel Cardinal Arteaga y Betancourt officiated at the ribbon-cutting ceremony for the unveiling of an imposing Jilma Madera sculpture, *Christ of Havana*, in Casablanca, across the harbor from the old city. A few days later, a new tunnel under Havana Harbor connected downtown Havana with "a new city called 'Eastern Havana,' beautiful, modern and planned according to the latest conception of town planning and landscaping: full of green open spaces, wide streets and magnificent avenues."[63]

Public works reminiscent of U.S. Works Progress Administration projects created jobs for unemployed Cuban workers.[64] School and hospital construction, such as the Topes de Collantes Hospital that specialized in tuberculosis, were initiated in every province, putting tens of thousands of engineers, construction workers and tradesmen to work in high-paying jobs.

Meanwhile, construction of major tourist hotels, casinos and apartment complexes and other private, albeit government-subsidized, projects were also underway. Among these were casino hotels oriented toward the American tourist. The Capri, the Riviera and the Hilton were all completed during the period and all located in the Vedado district of Havana. The avant-garde architecture of these hotels formed a new Havana skyline.

Americans in Cuba had their own English-language newspapers, the *Havana Post*, the *Havana Daily Telegram*, and *The Times of Havana*, established in 1957.[65]

By the 1950s American popular entertainment had become an important part of Cuban society. For example, Cubans were intoxicated by American movies. American film star Tom Mix had been a Rough Rider in the Cuban War for Independence and his vacations in Cuba were publicized throughout the country. Starting in the 1920s, Cuban magazines were devoted to Hollywood movies and movie stars. By 1920, Cuba had over 40 movie theaters with an average seating capacity of 650, or 26,000 seats for a population of 500,000.[66] In the years after that, the number of movie theaters grew even more throughout Cuba.[67] In 1949, the Blanquita theater opened in the fashionable neighborhood of Miramar. It seated more than 7,000. By the late 1950s theaters showing American films were everywhere.

There were American expatriate colonies in and around Havana, but also throughout Cuba. For example, the city of Banes, in Oriente Province, near the homes of both the Batista and Castro families, was an American enclave of the United Fruit Company, where American goods were sold and where English was more prevalent than Spanish. Americans developed golf clubs and tennis clubs and owned beaches that were closed to the Cuban public.

United Fruit began to acquire its property around 1900. It owned two huge sugar mills,

Preston and Boston in Oriente Province, that employed roughly 40,000 people and had an annual payroll of approximately $10 million 1960 dollars. At first, United Fruit hired Jamaicans and Haitians to work the sugar plantations, but eventually used Cuban labor. The company also owned cattle ranches and other businesses, and sponsored a hospital, schools and churches for its employees.[68]

American religious institutions also had a presence in every city throughout Cuba. Before the Spanish American War a few Protestant ministers lived in Cuba. They were seen by the Spanish as conspirators with the rebels. It turned out to be true as several of the ministers, none Americans, were insurrection leaders.[69] After the war, Americans invested heavily in Cuban business and agriculture. As U.S. economic interests developed, American Protestant missionaries descended on Cuba. By 1957 there were more Protestant ministers in Cuba than there were Catholic priests.[70] Several hundred thousand Cubans belonged to more than 500 Protestant churches.[71] By 1957, many of the ministers were Cuban nationals who had attended church schools and seminaries that the major sects had built on the island.

Cuban society became Americanized through advertising. Material values were designed to teach Cubans "modes of behavior, correct dress and proper tastes."[72] Sales of American products soared. Louis A. Pérez, Jr., described this as "the promise of possibilities." Cubans were open to new ways, but due to saturation advertising, transfixed on becoming increasingly American. By 1958, 80 percent of Cuban imports came from North America.[73] Possession and application of American technology became part of the Cuban culture as everything from radio to television to air-conditioning transferred from a luxury to a necessity. With them came "necessary" accessories, such as appropriate clothing and cosmetics.

Lucy and Ricky weren't the only ones acculturating. As early as the 19th century, many Cuban cities had an American appearance.[74] Trade was a major factor in Cuban/American relations, but another was that Cuba and the United States were becoming acculturated. Protestant evangelists started to come to Cuba in the 19th century, ostensibly as tourists but actually to seek converts. This hardened the Catholic clergy to be even more loyal to Catholic Spain. James Thompson, a Baptist evangelist working with the British Bible Society, visited Cuba in 1837 and clandestinely passed out Bibles.[75] Methodists and Baptists brought ideas of abolition with them, and tried to convert slaves. In 1842, David Turnbull, the British ambassador, was expelled for promoting abolition and Protestantism.[76]

The first steamship was brought to Cuba in 1819 and soon weekly service began between Havana and Matanzas. By 1836 routes between Havana and Key West, New Orleans, New York, Baltimore, Philadelphia and Mobile had been established. By 1842, six routes within Cuba were in business.[77] By the middle of the 19th century, Cuba was the third largest American trading partner, after only England and Canada.[78]

Besides sugar, Cuba also had cattle ranching, tobacco, rice and coffee farming, and tropical fruit and mineral commodities to offer to the world. But Cuba became obsessed with sugar. Unfortunately, the sugar plantations only needed workers during the *zafra*, the dry season, November to April, the harvest, when there was plenty of work. However, in *tiempo muerto*, the dead time, or the rainy season, there wasn't much work.[79] The majority population was vastly underemployed. When prices dropped, sugar plantation owners brought in even cheaper labor to cut the cost of production: Haitians, Jamaicans and Chinese coolies.

A national railroad network developed starting in 1837. By the 1850s modern Cuban railroads were second in efficiency only to the United States. The 19th century trains were made in the States, on lines established by and operated by Americans. Unlike the railroads in other countries, those in Cuba were developed to promote links between producers on the island and their foreign markets, rather than to meet the needs of a domestic market and stimulate its growth.[80]

By the middle of the 19th century, Americans owned and worked on sugar and coffee plantations, cattle ranches and tobacco farms. About 2,500 Americans were permanent residents, but some workers were "snowbirds," as they came to winter in Cuba, when construction and manufacture was slow in the States.[81] Even before the U.S. Civil War, about 5,000 annual visitors from the United States went to Cuba, many as tourists.[82]

As sugar went, so went Cuba. By independence, prices dropped so low that outsiders, especially Americans, could buy the sugar plantations at bargain prices. During flush times, such as during World War I, the price of sugar rose and millionaires were made. But by 1920 the price dropped from 17½ cents a pound to almost nothing. Fortunes rose and fell so rapidly that this phenomenon was called "The Dance of the Millions." Many owners had taken out loans based on a 15-cent price and the false assumption that prices were sure to rise. As a result, the worldwide economic depression came early and stayed late in Cuba.[83]

The unpredictability of sugar markets led to attempts to diversify the economy through tourism. After the Civil War, Americans such as former presidents Ulysses S. Grant and Grover Cleveland wintered in Cuba.[84] Steamship travel increased dramatically. The first air service began in 1921, between Key West and Havana.[85] Soon this increased exponentially.

In the States, social legislation gave people more vacation time and post–World War I prosperity gave them increased spending power. Moreover, Americans were becoming more adventurous. Tourism was once exclusively for the wealthy, but it now became an option for some middle-class Americans.

Cuba became a place where Americans could get what they wanted. Pari-mutuel gambling on horse racing had been banned in such states as New York and Pennsylvania, creating a demand for Cuban racing. Venues such as Oriental Park racetrack, opened in 1915, met the demand. After Prohibition, Cuba became famous as the place where Americans could "go wild" (drink openly) in high style. Americans with names like DuPont, Whitney and Biltmore, along with luminaries such as American national hero Charles Lindbergh, socialite Gloria Vanderbilt, actress Gloria Swanson, humorist Will Rogers, New York City mayor Jimmy "Beau James" Walker, and many others ostensibly came for legalized casino gambling, horse racing, golfing and country-clubbing. But they could do all of it while legally imbibing alcohol. Beer halls flourished. Old distilleries expanded. New distilleries and wineries opened, many with American investors. The Havana Distillery Company made Scotch rye and blended whiskey.[86] The Polar Brewery went from a local to an international brand. Bacardi became a world-renowned rum.[87] Cubans had manufactured rum, from sugar, before Prohibition, but afterwards, production skyrocketed and numerous rum concoctions were developed. The Cuban government looked the other way as Cuban liquor was smuggled out of the country. Cubans also began to manufacture bourbon and wine to meet American demand.

The governments of Gerardo Machado (1925–33) and Fulgencio Batista (1940–45 and 1952–58) needed foreign capital, and they turned largely to the United States. In 1924, 30,000 American tourists visited Cuba.[88] The following year, heavy American investments started to bring in many more tourists. There were about 15,000 American millionaires by 1927 and Cuban tourism targeted this market. Representatives of Cuban tourism advertised in American newspapers and magazines and opened tourist offices. Visitors were introduced to Spanish colonial cathedrals and forts, and to the colorful and fragrant tropical flora and fauna, but also to jai alai, dog racing and other exciting sporting events. Luxury tour trains to Santiago and other cities were established. A seaplane service began. Dozens of American-owned hotels and restaurants opened, many catering exclusively to Americans and given American-sounding names. Havana became a convention city. The exclusive Country Club of Havana in Marianao, a suburb, opened in 1920. It had a membership of 1,500, many of them Americans attracted by its championship golf course. Members included a Vanderbilt, an Astor, Milton S. Hershey of the Hershey candy company, the presidents of Coca-Cola and Chase National Bank and numerous American and Cuban sugar barons.[89] A home development adjacent to the grounds targeted and successfully sold mansions to the members. Dozens of other golf courses and similar luxury developments would soon follow.

Other American-style amusements caught on with Cubans. Miniature golf became a fad in the 1930s. Palisades Park, an American style amusement park, named for the park in New Jersey, attracted as many as 15,000 people a day on a good weekend.[90]

In 1937, 178,000 Americans visited Cuba. In 1957, 356,000 visited.[91] So many Americans came and American trade was so lucrative that Cuban-owned businesses were often staffed by Americans.[92] Store shelves were stocked with items that Americans might use, and when Cuban consumers came in contact with them, demand for everyday items like toiletries, cosmetics, and clothing increased.

Famous American entertainers played in Cuba. The leading bands and orchestras of the era, from Paul Whiteman, the "King of Jazz" in the 1920s to John Philip Sousa, the "March King," played in Havana.

When the Gran Casino Nacional opened in 1928, Havana earned numerous nicknames, such as "American Riviera," the "Paris of America," and the "playhouse of the Caribbean."[93] Havana was celebrated in a succession of American movies, starting with 1929's *The Girl from Havana*, filmed by Fox Pictures. A second movie with the same name was made by Republic Pictures in 1940. As early as 1911, Irving Berlin, who wrote "God Bless America" and "White Christmas," wrote "There's a Girl in Havana."

Although Cuba built an unrivaled haven for rich tourists, the Great Depression and the instability generated by the Cuban Revolution of 1933 diminished the flow of tourists to the island to a trickle. After World War II, the Batista government was able to get foreign investment, but Batista turned in large part to American gamblers, reputedly gangsters, some of whom were being prosecuted at home. Casinos were springing up. Whereas Machado targeted wealthy tourists, tourism in the 1950s brought in middle-class Americans. With the advent of low-cost air fare after World War II, even more tourists came.

In *Pleasure Island: Tourism and Temptation in Cuba*, Rosalie Schwartz documents how one movie, *Week-End in Havana*,[94] lured young American girls with its images of archetypal innocent salesgirls enjoying exotic romantic interludes in Cuba. World War II intervened, but because air travel to Cuba became cheaper after the war, the United States in effect subsidized tens of thousands of other young American women, who saved for and eventually took such a vacation.[95] Competition between Pan American Airlines, Cubana Airlines and others drove the prices down. That was why the cost of a round trip in 1957 with amenities was such a great deal.[96]

Cottage industries related to tourism sprang up. Some American lawyers advised their clients on Cuban divorce laws. Clinics for the treatment of "social diseases" flourished; many of the patients were Americans. Many Americans came to teach English.[97] American banks and other financial institutions opened offices in Cuba. The tourist trade and American

Besides sending troops and warships and having a naval base in Cuba, the U.S. occupied Nicaragua, Haiti, and the Dominican Republic, and also sent troops into Mexico, Panama, and other countries.

In 1933 the Franklin Roosevelt administration initiated a "Good Neighbor Policy" toward Latin America designed to overcome hostility to the extension of the Monroe Doctrine. The U.S. declared a complete change of policy, declaring mutual respect rather than dictating terms to U.S. allies and trading partners in Latin America. At the Montevideo Conference in 1933 the U.S. declared a "nonintervention" policy and established incentives to increase trade and spur economic recovery. In 1934 the marines withdrew from Haiti and the U.S. established an export/import bank to grant low-interest loans for Latin American development.

During a period of bloody civil strife in Cuba starting in 1928, after the U.S. threatened to intervene again, the 1903 Reciprocity Treaty was amended and the Treaty of Relations was signed May 29, 1934, by President Roosevelt. Cuba received a guaranteed market for its products, especially sugar, its main commodity, the United States received certain tariff discounts, and American products sold in Cuba received large tax discounts.[8]

Although it was not directly threatened, Cuba joined the U.S. in World War II soon after Pearl Harbor was attacked. After the war, Cuba was an early member of the United Nations, and in 1947 both Cuba and the United States were parties to the Inter-American Treaty of Reciprocal Assistance in Rio de Janeiro, now commonly known as the Rio Treaty, which established a mutual defense system.[9] Both were also charter members of the Organization of American States (OAS), established in Bogotá, Colombia, in 1948. At Bogotá, members pledged to fight communism.[10]

In 1949, President Truman initiated the Point Four program for technical assistance, a "bold new program for making the benefits of our scientific advances and industrial progress available for the improvement and growth of underdeveloped nations."[11] Cuba took advantage of the program, especially after Batista took power in 1952. On March 7, 1952, the U.S. entered into a Mutual Assistance Treaty which would provide Cuba with millions in military hardware. Batista took over three days later. The treaty was amended further in 1955 when the U.S. agreed to provide advisors to the Cuban military.[12]

During the Truman administration, the United States foreign policy was centered on Europe. The Soviet Union had conquered Eastern European territory during the World War II and some feared that Communism would predominate even in Western Europe. The U.S. spent vast sums on the Marshall Plan to rehabilitate Western Europe, and Latin America took notice. During the Good Neighbor period several democracies had been overtaken by dictatorships, although the U.S. had continued to insist that countries should be democratic. Democratic Latin American allies wanted aid and development to combat both fascism and Communism. However, the United States decided to combat Communism with "friendly" dictators.[13] In an address to the Pan American Society in 1949, President Truman "changed the tone" of U.S.–Latin American policy. In a program of what would be called "containment," the U.S. would de facto recognize the dictatorships in order to promote "long term" democracy and ensure that Communism was not spread locally.[14] In order to accomplish this, the State Department under Secretary Dean Acheson established the "Miller Plan," named for Under Secretary Edward G. Miller, Jr. Miller established diplomacy with dictatorships, even those seen as anti–American, such as the Argentine government of Juan Perón. Privately, Miller told people that Latin Americans were "like children, not yet ready to exercise, for themselves, the responsibility of adult nations."[15] During the

Korean War, the Truman administration decided in 1950 to arm Latin America to defend against Communism. Latin American countries would agree not to purchase their military hardware from foreign sources and would have to agree to make their military bases and airfields available to the United States military. In 1950, the United States gave more than $38 million in military aid to Latin America, and in 1951 it gave more than $50 million.[16]

Fulgencio Batista, who had been the *de facto* military leader of Cuba from 1933 to 1940 and the elected president of Cuba from 1940 to 1944, led a coup in 1952. Although he replaced a U.S.–friendly and democratically elected administration, and an election was pending, the Truman administration immediately recognized his government. By that time, almost every Latin American nation that had become democratic during the Good Neighbor Policy era had been overcome by dictatorships.[17]

In January 1952, Secretary Acheson testified to Congress that United States policy had been successful in Latin America. The major trouble spots noted were Argentina and Guatemala. Argentina was anti–American, but "Peronista, and not communist."[18]

As a candidate for president, Dwight D. Eisenhower attacked Truman's Latin American policy as nonexistent and alleged that the Truman administration was "soft on Communism" and supported "containment" rather than confrontation of communists. Although it labeled its foreign policy "The New Look," the Eisenhower administration policy in Latin America turned out to be an extension of the Truman administration's policy.[19] Soon after the inauguration, CIA director Allen Dulles reported to the president that Communism was making inroads in Latin America. In "United States Objectives and Courses of Action with Respect to Latin America," the administration set out a plan of "social evolution without revolution" to quash Communism by offering inducements to governments to do so.[20] Although some of the most influential Latin American allies wanted the United States to address economic development, human rights and democratization in the Latin America, the policy did not address them. President Eisenhower espoused a "trade, not aid" program, and initiated a "fondness" campaign, whereby the president attended luncheons with Latin American leaders, invited leaders to Washington, and addressed Latin American diplomatic corps on Pan American Day.[21] The U.S. awarded the Legion of Merit to such persons as dictators Manuel Odría of Peru and Pérez Jiménez of Venezuela.[22] The administration issued commemorative stamps with Latin American themes and produced and distributed pro-American movies for Latin Americans. The president also sent his brother, Milton Eisenhower, on goodwill trips to Latin America.

At the same time, the U.S. also attacked Communism in Latin America through what President Eisenhower termed "psychological warfare," using advertising and public relations techniques and even resorting to propaganda and "dirty tricks."[23] For example, the U.S. spent more than $5 million per year on United States Information Agency projects such as anti-communist comic books, newspaper comic strips, and radio shows. The CIA operated a radio station in El Salvador. U.S. personnel disrupted communist conferences and meetings.[24] The U.S. also organized the Inter-American Organization of Labor (Organización Regional interamericana de Trabajadores), run by the AFL-CIO, to oppose Peronist and communist infiltration of trade unions.[25] The U.S. also established deals that granted favored treatment if countries agreed not to deal with the Soviet Union.[26]

Covert activities such as secret spying and sabotage missions were authorized after 1948, but they were seldom used or acknowledged. A National Security Council memo stated: "If uncovered the United States can disclaim any responsibility."[27]

Moreover, like the Truman administration, the Eisenhower administration tried to make sure that the United States sold arms to every one of the Latin American states. In order to accelerate the process the U.S. tried to instill fear that the Soviets might dominate the region and that there was an urgent need for mutual defense. Some countries broke diplomatic relations with the Soviet Union in order to qualify for more purchases of weaponry.[28]

In 1954, the U.S. intervened in Guatemala to remove the government with a CIA-trained insurgency. This became an object lesson for the rest of Latin America. Although the government was not Communist per se, Guatemala had recognized the Communist Party and had appropriated American-owned property.[29]

Although Latin American leaders pressed the United States to provide aid and despite rumors that there would be an "Eisenhower Plan," similar to the Marshall Plan, to bail out Latin America, the U.S. did not present any new ideas at the Rio Conference of 1954. In fact, some observers felt that the United States had returned to policies that predated the Good Neighbor policy.[30]

Meanwhile, however, another insurgency occurred in Bolivia, where guerrillas led by Ángel Víctor Paz Estenssoro, head of the Movimiento Nacionalista Revolucionario (MNR), the Nationalist Revolutionary Movement. During the period, the United States provided more aid to Bolivians on a per capita basis than to any other country in Latin America.[31] When asked why the United States supported Bolivia and destabilized Guatemala, especially as the governments of both had been similar and had similar goals, the administration stated that it opposed Communism, not change and reform.[32]

By the mid–1950s Cuba and the United States were also bound by:

- an air transport agreement,[33]
- an agreement that set up the way that shipping was financed and established how supplies would be furnished to naval vessels,[34]
- an agreement to provide notification of private air traffic between the two countries,[35]
- an agreement that permitted visits by warships,[36]
- an agreement that exempted pleasure yachts from entry, clearance, and some customs laws,[37]
- an agreement that would provide for free entry of American non–commissioned military personnel into Cuba,
- a consular convention,[38]
- a general agreement for economic cooperation that extended the Point Four program,
- two treaties that would require return of fugitives from justice, including a full extradition treaty,[39]
- an agreement to suppress smuggling and an agreement to provide information on drugs.[40]

By 1957, the United States and Cuba were so closely allied that Cuba had supported every measure the U.S. supported in the Organization of American States and in the United Nations.

Stated U.S. policy toward Cuba was the same as almost every other Latin American country. The U.S. supported the Cuban government as long as it was secure, stable and protected American investments. However, initially, the State Department under President Eisenhower supported Batista wholeheartedly. In fact, Arthur Gardner, United States ambas-

President Dwight David Eisenhower with Cuban president Fulgencio Batista, July 23, 1956. After a coup in March 1952, the Batista regime was recognized by the Truman administration. The United States provided military and other support to the Cuban government until it concluded that instead of using the equipment and supplies for defense, it was using them to repress a domestic insurrection. Accordingly, the Eisenhower administration stopped shipping military supplies to Batista in spring 1958 and demanded that he democratize his government. Pressured by his own military, Batista fled on New Year's Eve, December 31, 1958 (AP Photo/Byron Rollins).

sador to Havana from 1953 to October 1957, is now seen as a cheerleader for Batista.[41] The U.S. and Cuba had a special relationship. Although Batista promised that he would return Cuba to democracy, the U.S. became impatient after he failed to do so. However, after it was determined that Cuba had violated the Mutual Defense Assistance Agreement of 1952, on March 18, 1958, President Eisenhower announced an arms embargo on Cuba.[42]

Chapter 3

Culture Clash

Although Americans and Cubans were familiar with each other, we did not completely understand each other's culture. It is now clear that Cuban and American officials had misconstrued important matters that eventually would poison our relationship.

For example, almost all Americans assumed that dissent in Cuba came from the dispossessed: We assumed that Batista was opposed by a peasant insurrection. The Cuban Revolution is now symbolized by a picture of a stern, gaunt *guajiro,* a peasant, holding a machete menacingly over his head. Castro would later claim that the revolution was fought for the poor. In fact, dissent against Batista crossed economic lines. Actually, most of the leaders of the revolution had middle-class backgrounds and had become opponents of Batista as students at the University of Havana.[1] Almost all of the leaders of the Rebel Army came from the middle class. None of the Council of Ministers in the Provisional Government installed after the takeover had been *guajiros.* Almost all of the leaders of Batista's opposition had been living "transnational" lives: They spoke English, had traveled and had extensive American and other foreign contacts.[2] Some had been wealthy. For example, the Castros were a nouveau riche landowning family.[3] The richest man in Cuba avidly supported the revolution.[4] The owners of thriving businesses such as Bacardi Liquors did also. Many other well-off Cubans were hostile to the Batista government and supported a takeover of the government.[5] Most opposed Batista on a moral or ethical basis. Some had a legalistic rationale. Almost all had sociological, cultural and even religious grounds to oppose the existing order.

From a longitudinal perspective, the revolution had been ongoing prior to independence in 1902. From the onset, Cubans appeared to have a national inferiority complex. At that time, the United States virtually "owned" Cuba. After independence Cuba seemed unable to manage its own affairs.[6] Although Cuba had been granted independence, the revolution and M–7–26, the Movement of July 26th, the revolutionary organization named for the 1953 date when Castro made his first move, and also the anniversary of José Martí's birth, can be seen as another phase in a continuum of national political turbulence that included the Machadato, a bloody revolt that occurred from the late 1920s to 1934.[7] Among its leaders was Fulgencio Batista, who became the Cuban strongman and the subject of the 1956–1959 revolution.[8]

Although he had been an effective president from 1940 to 1944, Batista had little chance in a national election. He was third in a field of three candidates for president in 1952.[9] The sitting president, Carlos Prío Socarrás, was a lame duck because under the Constitution, he was precluded from succeeding himself. His Auténtico party had been reformist, had been in power after 1944, was well organized and was by far the largest. However, the more reformist Ortodoxo Party, orthodox in that it aspired to follow the tenets of Cuban martyr José Martí, and more reform-minded in that it promised to rid the government of fraud, corruption and outright theft, had ardent followers.[10] But Batista still controlled segments of the military and, urged on by some junior officers, he took over on March 10, 1952. The Cuban public gave Batista the benefit of the doubt at first. Batista alleged that he had led a revolution to rid Cuba of corruption. However, he cancelled the election and began to arrest his political enemies and set about amassing his own largesse.

The coup and the ensuing hostility to the majority political parties enraged even some of Batista's potential supporters. For example, the coup emotionally devastated one Ortodoxo candidate, originally from Batista's home area, who had been a personal acquaintance, but who had been a shoo-in to win a seat representing a Havana district in the Cuban House of Representatives.[11] He was well spoken, well read, and physically imposing, with a charismatic stage presence. As a child he had written a highly publicized letter to Franklin Delano Roosevelt and had written several published letters to the editors of major Cuban newspapers.[12] At one time, his family had even been the subject of a radio comedy show.[13] He had been recognized by newspapers as the best scholar-athlete in Cuba in 1945, and gave the valedictory address for his class at Cuba's most prestigious prep school, where he was trained and praised by Jesuits as the student most likely to succeed.[14] He had married into a famous political family, and he and his bride received a wedding present from Batista which they used in part for an extended honeymoon to the States.[15] His new father-in-law had been mayor of Banes, the Cuban home to United Fruit Company, a large landowner and sugar mill operator, and he was also one of their lawyers.[16] He was a recent graduate of the University of Havana School of Law, and although he had written a treatise on commercial law and could have made a fine living representing corporations and wealthy patrons, he had donated much of his time as a pro bono lawyer representing the downtrodden and dispossessed to further his political career.[17] He had a popular local radio show, wrote controversial newspaper articles and letters to editors, and his exploits had been followed in the Cuban media for years.[18] He had developed a persona as a muckraker, obsessed with rooting out government fraud and abuse. His controversial activities gained notoriety and he and several of his close colleagues had been accused of assault, battery, extortion, gangsterism and even murder by their opponents, although they had never been tried for crimes.[19] Although he had taken almost no salary during his campaign, had he won election, he would have received $4,000 per month in congressional pay in 1952 dollars. At the time, U.S. Congress members received $12,000 per year — an indicator of how devastating the loss of the office was to him, his wife and young child.[20] In addition, among the privileges of office he would have received was immunity from prosecution for most crimes.

Soon after Batista assumed power in 1952, lawsuits were brought against him under Article 148 of the Cuban Constitution of 1940 for performance of an "act aimed at bringing about an armed uprising against the Constitutional Powers of the State. The penalty shall be imprisonment for from five to twenty years, in the event that insurrection actually be carried into effect." The lawsuits were dismissed as the Cuban Cabinet declared a national emergency. However, they did so after the fact. Later a judge would declare that as a result, the revolution was sanctioned by the Cuban Constitution. One of the lawyers who brought the lawsuits was the same young Ortodoxo lawyer who had not been seated in the Cuban House of Representatives: Fidel Castro Ruz. The judge who ruled that the revolution was permitted under Cuban Constitutional law was Mario Urrutia Lleó. In January 1959, Urrutia would replace Batista as president of Cuba under a Provisional Government.[21] Castro would lead his Rebel Army to revolution and eventually would assume power as "maximum leader" of Cuba.

Most Americans assume that the revolution was a military victory by Castro's forces, and Castro would later take credit for a military overthrow of Batista. Actually, Batista fled after enemies within his regime threatened a coup. They had once been loyal and trusted supporters.[22] Castro had only a few hundred armed followers; he had failed to capture any heavily populated areas and the level of combat violence had been "modest."[23] Cuban military officers had mutinied on several occasions against Batista, beginning with a mutiny by "*Puros*," pure, incorruptible mostly junior officers in the spring of 1956 and in a bloody uprising at the Cienfuegos Naval Base in September 1957. The allegation was made that Batista and his cronies had embezzled funds allocated for weapons purchases, that ordinary Cuban service members were being constantly defrauded, and that the rank and file were forced to bear the blame for crimes committed by Batista's men.[24] On leaving, Batista attempted to turn over the government to the military, but the *Puros* considered themselves to have been part of a coalition of groups united to remove Batista, and Castro had been the head of their military operation. He was not a member of the cabinet of the initial Provisional Government.

The United States did not notice that there was an insurgent "generation gap" in Cuba as young people sought their own forms of expression through rebellion. Cuba had a history of violent student rebellions from the late 19th century. Student activism, if not gangsterism, had been rampant in Cuba from the time of Machado.[25] In 1933 and 1934, students and professors from the University of Havana had gained control of the government, but were forced out by the military, led by Batista with the connivance of the U.S. ambassador.[26] Many former students felt that regime's business had not been finished and the revolution to oust Machado had been usurped.[27] In fact, even under Batista, the University of Havana had been declared a place of sanctuary under the Cuban Constitution, because student dissent had led to the formation of a democratic constitution. By 1957, after Batista had been the subject of an assassination attempt by members of a student group, the Directorio Revolucionario, the "DR," he closed the university. Strikes were called at many other schools in support of the students. Most of the students were children of well-to-do parents and had been expected to become the professional class of Cuba. Soon students from the university had their own army in the field. By 1959, the revolution appeared to be a youth movement, and the youthful, charismatic and bombastic Fidel Castro would become a star. Soon Cuban children wanted to be identified with the revolution and adopted a new fad: olive drab fatigues.[28] Although young rebels may have been allied with many older people, such as former president Carlos Prío Socarrás and his Auténtico political party, the largest in Cuba at the time, in fighting against Batista, young activists resented the existing Cuban political parties almost as much as they hated Batista.[29]

Americans also underestimated the resentment that most Cubans had toward the United States. Inside Cuban politics, Yankee-baiting was almost universal. Although Americans thought that the U.S. generously handed Cubans their independence, most Cubans do not agree; they proudly maintain that they earned it.[30] Batista was depicted as a toady of the United States, but he too resented and would eventually blame the United States for his demise. Even José Martí, the "Apostle of Cuba," who laid a philosophical basis for Cuban independence, who had been a resident of the United States through most of his productive intellectual life, and who is venerated by all segments of Cuban political thought, warned that the United States was the menacing "Colossus of the North." Many Cubans were convinced that, regardless of whatever influence Cubans might have over their own affairs, inevitably Americans would dictate government policy. Cubans might have wanted to live like Americans, but they did not, for the most part, want to become American. One symbol of this sentiment was the American sugar policy. Cuba was dominated by a sugar economy. Before independence, the sugar economy required massive use of slaves and vast tracts of land dedicated to sugar at the expense of the ecology of the native flora and fauna. For example, in some areas, mahogany and other valuable forests were felled to make way for sugar. After independence, the United States Department of Agriculture set annual quotas of how much sugar could be exported from Cuba to the States. Americans gained control of much of the production, manufacture and export of Cuban sugar, and because the United States market dominated the Cuban sugar crop, the U.S. dictated how Cuba would manage its affairs. The Cuban economy rose and fell on prices set in the States through production quotas set by the United States Department of Agriculture. A series of boom-and-bust cycles were blamed on the policy and numerous farmers and sharecroppers were forced from their land and lived in a constant state of deprivation. Because the production of sugar is labor intensive and because the Cuban government permitted sugar interests to take advantage of labor, there were also negative sociological ramifications attributed to the way business was controlled by the United States.

American influences were often misinterpreted so that fantasy was taken for reality. For example, historian Louis Perez, Jr., points out that Cuban culture was so enamored of American movies that Cuban newspapers covered them intensely and Cuban literature also referenced them to the extent that Cuba adopted American movies as part of their culture. The U.S. passed on its vision of beauty and glamor, but we weren't necessarily a good example. In the 1930s gangster movies had become extremely popular, and they became "a prominent motif of political warfare" as Cuban gangs practiced what we now call "drive-by shootings," machine gun assassinations and escapes and car chases learned from Hollywood movies.[31] By the 1950s, *pistolerismo*, gang warfare, flourished as political parties and even the government supported "action groups" that engaged in open violence.[32]

Conversely, many Cubans on all sides feared that if Cuba became "too" independent, the United States would intervene in Cuban affairs. Intervention could include sending in the marines to "restore order," as had been done on several occasions. There were many Cubans who wanted it.[33] Had it been up to many of our military leaders of the era, we would have done it again.

During the Spanish American War, hatred of the Spanish army as outsiders fired a Cuban nationalism. The United States allied itself with the Cubans, but, in essence, ruled Cuba from 1989 to 1902, and granted itself a legal right to protect American interests after that, through the Platt Amendment to the Cuban Constitution.

At the same time, most educated Cubans were aware that several prominent Americans had made racist and other derogatory statements about Cubans. Theodore Roosevelt and his successors had little respect for Cubans.[34] American newspapers ran derogatory cartoon caricatures of Cubans. American books and magazines depicted the Anglo-Saxon "race" as superior to the Latin people.

Many Cubans considered their country to have been dominated by the United States, and would have agreed with Martí that the United States as the "Great Colossus of the North" had exerted undue influence on the Cuban economy and culture. Some Cubans were resigned that they would never receive full acceptance by the United States, but were more than willing to accept American culture, mores and economic interests as a pathway to personal success. Others sought to diminish the "intrusion" of American culture in Cuba.

When confronted with Cuban anxiety about potential American intervention in Cuba, Americans were confused. We condescendingly felt that we had done so much for Cubans that they ought to be grateful to us. Although the Eisenhower administration had initiated overt policies of "psychological warfare" and "fondness" in Latin America, especially toward dictatorships, in October 1959 President Eisenhower stated that he was confused as to why Cubans resented the United States. "I don't know exactly what the difficulty is," he remarked. It was "a puzzling matter to figure out."[35] Americans thought that only radical Cubans were oppositional, and speculated that Castro's "revolutionary fervor, his idealism and his emotional makeup," gave him a bad attitude.[36]

Actually, the U.S. did not address the real diplomatic issue of the moment: Cuban sovereignty. Did the United States and United States citizens' private interests have any rights in Cuba? If so, to what extent?[37] Several historians suggest that the Eisenhower administration was more interested in fighting communists than in addressing anti–Americanism, and peg this as the real reason for the two nations' eventual breakup.[38]

Americans also didn't understand the religious fervor of the era. Most Americans considered Cuba to be a Catholic nation in the Spanish tradition. This perception seemed to be substantiated on the evening of January 1, 1959, in Santiago de Cuba, when Fidel Castro, the archbishop of Santiago by his side symbolically sanctifying victory, announced to his nation that Batista had fled. By the time Castro arrived to take power in Havana, it seemed like a religious revival had struck Cuba and the entire population was in a state of rapture. As Castro's January 1959 five-day victory caravan passed from Santiago to Havana, ardent supporters swooned in awe and many held up religious articles in the path and wake of the procession.

Conversely, Batista characterized his opponents as atheistic communists, and this was echoed by some influential American newspaper reporters. However, Americans saw on television that Castro wore a heavy cross on a chain around his neck and that his official entourage included priests. Castro's early speeches could have been taken as homilies, as he passionately railed against the sins of crime, public corruption, gambling, prostitution and alcoholism. Observers would later say that Castro was on a missionary crusade for the revolution. Castro promised to "purify" the country.[39]

In reality, Americans were generally not informed that many of Batista's most influential opponents were Cuban Protestants and that several would become members of the initial Council of Ministers in the Provisional Government of 1959.

Like the United States, Cuba was a sociological "melting pot." At the time, the dominant white American mainstream did not empower others. Not African-Americans, nor Hispanics or Native Americans, nor even Catholics and Jews had much say in our government. Cuba was similar. U.S. leaders identified with the power elite Spanish, Creole, mainly white Cuban culture, and failed to note that the close U.S. ally President Fulgencio Batista was not considered "Spanish" or "Creole" by his countrymen.[40] Actually, Cuba did not have a majority white population, although Creoles dominated society and the economy. Americans didn't know that Batista was often resented by Creoles as a mulatto, if not a black Santería follower, who had risen to rule his "betters."[41] Although he courted the Creole culture, he also enthusiastically pursued Santería political support. For example, in 1958, when he was being pressured by both the rebels and the United States State Department, he paid Santería priests to publicly sacrifice roosters and goats at Guanabacoa, ostensibly to remove

President Fulgencio Batista (1940–1944, 1952–1958) and his second wife, Marta, with Cardinal Manuel Arteaga y Betancourt, ca. 1958. Although Batista publicly held himself out to Catholics to be one of them, and although he received favor from the cardinal, he had been educated at a Quaker school and apparently had been baptized as one. However, to many Afro-Cubans, he also was seen as Santería patron, if not a follower. He publicly paid Santería priests to sacrifice goats for protection (University of Miami Libraries, Cuban Heritage Collection).

the pressure.[42] In some circles he held himself out as a *babalu*, a Santería priest.[43] Santería followers described him as a son of Changó, the Santería god of war.

On one hand, Batista's Creole opposition held his ancestry against him; on the other, his political opponents competed against him on the religious front. Americans were not aware that a war was being fought within Santería, and that eventually, Santería would be seen as revolutionary. We also were not aware that others wanted to bring back the "old time religion": state-sponsored Catholicism. These groups had a common complaint: both were opposed to American religious influence in Cuba.

During the United States occupation, all religious observances in Cuba, including Catholic, had been banned because of the heightened emotional state they produced. Americans were ignorant about the pervasive and seductive African religions of Cuba.[44] For example, Santería was not mentioned in a single article in most major American newspapers throughout the 1950s and 1960s. When it was mentioned, in the 1970s, it was referred to as voodoo and was demeaned as degenerate superstition.[45] Although once misunderstood as a cult and ridiculed both in and out of Cuba, Santería is now recognized as a valid religion. By 1957, Santería was an important part of the Cuban culture. Every Cuban would have known that Desi Arnaz' "Babalú" was a reference to a god, or *orisha*, Babalú Aye, in the African religion known in Cuba as Santería.[46] Santería shamans or faith healers are also called *babalús*. Most Americans didn't learn about such matters until the 1980s, after Florida church members sued to enforce their rights under the First Amendment and opened the religion to full public scrutiny.[47]

The United States Supreme Court eventually recognized that as hundreds of thousands of the Yoruba people had been brought as slaves from western Africa to Cuba, their traditional African religion was integrated into the culture through adaptation of elements of Roman Catholicism. Slave owners denied slaves the right to practice their religion, and characteristics of their gods were attributed to Catholic counterparts. The resulting syncretion, or fusion, is Santería, "the way of the saints."[48] The exact number of adherents in Cuba is unknown, but it is estimated that from one-half to two-thirds of the population are active followers.[49] Thousands of their descendants now live in the United States, especially in Miami, the New York City area, San Francisco, and also in places like South Carolina's Oyotunji Village, founded as a Santería commune.

Yoruba express their devotion to *orishas* through the iconography of Catholic saints; Catholic symbols are often present at Santería rites, and Santería devotees often attend the Catholic sacraments.[50] But they practice ritual sacrifice, accept as reality possession by spirits, and engage in ancestor veneration. In the *Hialeah* case, testimony estimated that there were 50,000 practitioners in the Miami area. This probably was an underestimate.

African religions like Santería were introduced as academic study in the work of Fernando Ortiz (1881–1969) and his sister-in-law Lydia Cabrera (1900–1991). Besides Santería, other African religions are widely practiced in Cuba. Although white, Cabrera was the pre-eminent anthropologist and chronicler of Afro-Cuban culture of her time. Her seminal work, *El Monte*, published in 1954 and a best seller in Cuba, records stories of another African religion, Palo Monte. She was also a social crusader for the rights of women.

Ortiz was an anthropologist and a lawyer, a social reformer and would-be politician, a publisher, a college professor, and essayist. His first published work on the ethnic makeup of Cuba appeared in 1906: *Hampa Afro-Cubana: Los Negros Brujos*. It documented what he called "transculturation," and he was nominated for a Nobel Prize in 1955.[51] He also was a political philosopher, and the Castro regime attributes some of its policies to his ideas. Ortiz wrote the seminal work on what he called *personalismo*, the dominance of sugar in Cuba, in *Contrapunteo Cubano*, or *Cuban Counterpoint: Tobacco and Sugar* in English.[52] Strictly speaking, in Latin America *personalismo* is the practice of glorifying a single leader to the detriment of all other political interests, and Ortiz used the term as personification for the importance of sugar to Cuba.[53] Ortiz compared the production of tobacco, a native crop, with sugar, which had been brought to Cuba by Columbus.

By January 1959, followers of Santería more closely identified with the Rebel Army and Fidel Castro than with the Batista regime as M–7–26 took advantage of the Mambi revolutionary tradition. Troops wore the M–7–26 red and black prayer beads, identified by the faithful with the Orisha Elegua, and as the Rebel Army marched into Havana, Santería priests declared Fidel Castro an *elegido*, a man chosen by the gods.[54]

The 1950s is usually seen as a period of prosperity for both the United States and Cuba. On a statistical basis the United States surpassed Great Britain as the dominant force in the world, not only militarily, but politically and materially. The United States had the greatest industrial capacity in the world. After the GI Bill granted World War II veterans extensive educational and housing benefits, the U.S. workforce was the most educated in the world and the best housed. Almost half the American workforce was unionized, and benefits were given to many other workers. As a result, many Americans had discretionary money to spend. American products were seen as the most modern and the most dependable. Sales of consumer goods like television sets boomed. American music and movies became popular worldwide. American scientists led the world in almost every area. Most symbolic was the elimination of the dreaded disease polio. America also became the art center of the world, displacing Europe. More people were able to buy their own homes, and there was a population shift from urban areas to the suburbs.[55]

Despite sometimes being depicted as a "golden age," the Eisenhower administration economic record was mixed.[56] As the Korean War ended, the economy lagged as a result of reductions in military spending. When faced with a recession, the administration tried to cut federal spending. By 1955, recession was over and the gross national product boomed. However, in 1957 the economy declined rapidly. Industrial production fell 14 percent, corporate profits dropped 25 percent and unemployment rose to 7.5 percent. By 1959 the U.S. had a record $12 billion deficit.[57]

Socially, although depicted as a period of innocence, it probably was more a period of naiveté. During the

Lydia Cabrera and her brother-in-law Francisco Ortiz chronicled the complexity of the formerly undocumented Afro-Cuban culture, which influenced American art, music and politics during the period. Although Cabrera exiled herself to Miami, Ortiz remained and died a national hero in Cuba (photograph from University of Miami Libraries, Cuban Heritage Collection).

era, mainstream "middle American" values were challenged by the youthful Beat Generation, and a nascent sexual and cultural revolution would explode in the 1960s.

During the prim 1950s in America, vice crimes like gambling were prosecuted in most states. Consequently, many famous American gamblers were courted by the Batista government and made their way to Havana. Much of this was documented in American newspapers and magazines. In *Pleasure Island*, Rosalie Schwartz documents how Americans were sold sin and excitement and adventure through public relations and advertising by a succession of Cuban governments that culminated in a massive tourist boom in the late 1950s.[58] Anyone could see that there was a boom; but it turned out to be a bubble. Legitimate American investors were also often "sold" Cuba as the pot of gold, only to find out too late that it was on the wrong end of the proverbial rainbow. Although there was an ongoing revolution at this time, American television and radio shows broadcast from Cuba and tried to depict the glamor and élan of Cuba. An episode of *The Steve Allen Show*, was televised from the Riviera Hotel in Havana on January 19, 1958.[59]

There was some more in-depth reporting. At one point Jack Paar, then the king of late night television as the star of *The Tonight Show* on NBC, reporting from Havana, attacked the Batista dictatorship in Cuba and made claims supporting revolution.[60] José Melis, a Cuban, was the conductor of *The Tonight Show* band from 1957 to 1962 and may have had some influence on Paar's investigation.[61] A few others reached the same conclusion.[62] By January 1958, American papers reported that American gamblers had relocated en masse to Cuba.[63] By March 1958, *Life* magazine had exposed that the Riviera Hotel was mob owned and managed by American gangsters.[64] The hotel reportedly cost $14 million to build, and entered popular culture as the Mafia's headquarters in Havana in Mario Puzo's *The Godfather*.[65] The Havana Hilton, completed in the spring of 1958, was built by loans principally from the Gastronómico, the culinary workers' union.[66] Although it may be true that Batista had a business relationship with the Mafia, aka the "Syndicate," or "the boys," it is also true that by the fall of 1958, a number of American casino owners had cashed out of Cuba.[67]

During this period, Cuban news was not well reported in the States. Cuban émigrés tried to tell the whole story, but in Cuba, the Batista government abolished civil rights and there was strict media censorship. Through much of the period there was only one American newspaper that covered Cuba: the *New York Times*. It had one full-time reporter on the Cuban beat: Ruby Hart Phillips. During the period 1956–1961, she did much of her reporting from her home in Havana, using local news articles and telephone calls to sources for information.[68] The U.S. ambassador to Cuba Philip Bonsal observed that some U.S. media stressed "the freakish or the Communist-potential angles of the Revolution." He also observed that as bad as the American press was on Cuba, the Cuban press was worse on the United States.[69]

It is evident that Fidel Castro read his press clippings from American newspapers. He accused the wire services of defaming him and his policies and repeatedly asked the U.S. government to make them stop, or at least give him an opportunity to rebut the accusations. He was overly sensitive to accusations early on that he was a communist and that he would turn Cuba into a satellite of the Soviet Union. There is some question whether prognostications by some of Castro's enemies in the press were prescient or whether they provided an additional initiative to drive him into the Soviet sphere, as he already was confrontational and suspicious of the aims of the United States.

Sometimes the word did get out. After Batista had maintained that Fidel Castro had been killed, stories and photographs in the *New York Times* and live interviews with CBS News impeached Batista's credibility, and after that, Americans became skeptical. Even when Americans could not get the whole story, sometimes symbols were more important. During the 1958 World Series, the revolution received a public relations coup when three Cubans jumped a fence and unfurled a banner reading, "Castro Frees Cuba," for the American television audience.[70]

Below the surface, the United States had its own troubles. Not everyone in America prospered. There was a wide disparity in incomes among racial and demographic groups. There was civil unrest, especially in the South.

There were five confirmed lynchings of Afro-Americans in 1956 and three in 1957. The Civil Rights movement was just getting started. Racial segregation in public education and public accommodation still reigned.[71] In September 1957, President Eisenhower called out the military to enforce desegregation in public schools in Little Rock, Arkansas. Two southerners, Virginia senator Harry Byrd and newsman James J. Kilpatrick of the Richmond, Virginia, *News-Leader* urged "massive resistance" to stem reported federal intrusion into the "southern way of life."[72] The Civil Rights movement was often met with force. The allegation was made that Communists were behind integration. Starting with Little Rock, clashes over school integration would last well into the 1970s.

Many southerners objected to the federal government "meddling" in their affairs, in social matters, in much in the same way that many Cubans complained that the United States had interfered in their political, economic and social affairs. For example, in early 1960 the *Florida Times Leader* ran an editorial that assorted: "It is fundamental — indeed it is elementary — that there is a point beyond which the Government can not go in meddling in the affairs of a people and their state."[73]

Racial integration problems also were evident in Cuba. In 1956 Nat King Cole, then one of the most popular singers in both the United States and Cuba, was scheduled to sing in Havana. He wanted to stay at the Hotel Nacional de Cuba, a popular tourist destination for Americans, but it was a whites only hotel (primarily to accommodate Americans) and he had to stay elsewhere. Likewise, although they could play in Cuba on integrated teams, African-American baseball players were often refused hotel accommodations in Cuba and some Cuban restaurants refused to serve them.[74]

Integration of schools was seen by some Americans as the beginning of an erosion of personal liberty. These people believed that there was a general breakdown in civility and morals. According to some American groups, such as the John Birch Society, founded in 1958, the American and Soviet governments were controlled by the same "furtive conspiratorial cabal of internationalists, greedy bankers, and corrupt politicians. If left unexposed, the traitors inside the US government would betray the country's sovereignty to the United Nations for a collectivist new world order managed by a one-world socialist government."[75]

Some Americans were afraid that the communists had infiltrated the State Department, the military, and had infected our water.[76] Loyalty oaths were required of government workers, news reporters, and even television and movie stars. We discovered that the Soviets had the nuclear capacity to blow us to smithereens, and we were constantly reminded of that fact as we performed civil defense drills and were subjected to random air raid siren alerts and radio and television tests of the defense warning signal. Movies and television shows played to U.S. fears of the communists and their allies. When the Soviet *Sputnik 1* orbited the Earth in 1957 we were concerned that the technology which made the Commies an external threat could also drop atomic bombs on Americans.

Although the revolution in Oriente Province may not have reached Havana, Cubans visiting the U.S. country learned that Americans had to practice hiding in civil defense shelters to survive an impending nuclear holocaust. To many Cubans, U.S. foreign policy was designed to instill in Cubans the same level of dread of nuclear holocaust that Americans had.

Other purported evidence of the erosion — especially of moral values in the Bible Belt — included jazz and rock 'n' roll music. With origins in African American culture, these genres were known as "race" music. For some opponents of the modern music, "race" music was the Devil's music. Others blamed it as a psychological tool of the communists to weaken American society. For still others it was both.

The civil rights problem was reflected in the popular national pastime. In Cuba, Afro-American ballplayers had an opportunity to play in the Cuban Winter League even when they were barred from play in the U.S. major leagues. Although the major leagues were integrated beginning with the Brooklyn Dodgers in 1947, by 1956 some teams, particularly the Boston Red Sox, the Philadelphia Phillies, and the Detroit Tigers, had never fielded a single Afro-American player in a major league game. The Phillies had played one African-

American player in 1957. The Chicago White Sox integrated its team in 1951 by playing Minnie Minoso, an Afro-Cuban. By 1957, although some teams had acquired a few token players of color, public sentiment assumed that they would not draw fans if more were added to the rosters. However, the Dodgers and the Milwaukee Braves belied that theory. Although the Washington Senators did not take credit for being an integrated team, current scholarship shows that mulatto Cubans had passed as white and played in the major leagues.[77] Afro-Cuban ballplayers played on teams that had defeated barnstorming teams that boasted great American players such as Ty Cobb and Babe Ruth. It was said that Afro-Cuban players could have been the stars of baseball if they only had gotten a chance.

Although black American ballplayers were more upwardly mobile in Cuba than in the States, there was still discrimination. Many hotels and bars would not serve black patrons. Although slavery lasted longer in Cuba than anywhere in the Western Hemisphere,[78] and although Cuba had a race war in 1912, when Afro-Cubans were vilified as "savages" and Afro-Cuban leaders were summarily executed,[79] people of African origin were generally more accepted in Cuba than in the States. The hero of the Ten Years War and the Spanish-American War was Antonio Maceo, an Afro-Cuban who achieved the rank of general of the Cuban Army. Afro-Cuban social clubs, *cabildos*, had supplied much of the manpower that defeated the Spanish. Afro-Cubans served in the armed forces and under Batista were given rights of promotion.

In the States there was ample evidence that prominent Americans had been communists or "fellow travelers." However, whether communists actually had infiltrated government and to what extent, was open to question. Congressional committees held hearings to root out alleged spies and saboteurs. An investigation of Hollywood yielded evidence that some communists and former communists were important actors, directors and producers, and the rush to judgment held that they were brainwashing us with communist propaganda. Professors, union officials, and newspaper reporters also were called on the carpet by the House Un-American Activities Committee. Many former Communist Party members testified and provided investigators with names of suspected communists. In 1953, communists Julius and Ethel Rosenberg were executed for having spied for the Soviet Union.

There was an omnipresent threat of destruction by the Soviets, who now had the hydrogen bomb. The U.S. public was frightened by the dangers of Communism as reported in the news, but also in books, movies, and television. Science fiction was popular, and in many films it was clear that extraterrestrials were symbolic stand-ins for the communists. Aliens could take over the planet. As mentioned previously, after the Soviets sent *Sputnik 1* into space in October 1957, alarmists claimed that the communists now owned space and that it would become a staging area for attack on our defenseless population. It seemed that conflict with the Soviets was inevitable. Feelings of fear and dread intensified.

But some of the anti–communist investigators had become overzealous, and doubt was growing about many of the charges against ordinary citizens. The FBI falsely accused Cord Meyer, a CIA agent, of being a communist. This pitted the agencies against each other.[80] As the CIA was a spy agency, this was not widely reported.

There was also a threat our constitutional First Amendment rights to free speech and free assembly were in jeopardy. Senator Joe McCarthy had brought charges against the military, but in 1954, McCarthy and his chief counsel, Roy Cohn, were accused by the army of trying to coerce preferential treatment for their former aide and friend of Cohn's, G. David Schine. In the dramatic climax to a senate hearing shown on national television, McCarthy was humiliated.

In 1950s America, no one was above suspicion of being a communist or a fellow traveler, including America's favorite television star. In 1936, Lucille Ball registered to vote as a communist. Later, she alleged that she never really was a communist, but did it to please her grandfather, a party member. In 1953, after an investigation by the FBI, Ball testified before the House Un-American Activities Committee. She convinced the committee that she had not really been a communist and was not prosecuted.[81] But that did not stop Walter Winchell and other newsmen from continuing to report that Ball had been a communist. Her popularity actually increased. But she and Desi Arnaz continued to be followed by the FBI.[82]

Ball was in good company, as the same groups accused Presidents Abraham Lincoln, Franklin D. Roosevelt, Harry S Truman, Dwight David Eisenhower, and Secretary of State John Foster Dulles and his brother CIA director Allen Dulles, among others, of being involved in communist conspiracy.[83]

Americans might have "tolerated" Desi and Xavier Cugat and Minnie Minoso, but during the same period, the U.S. had policies to rid the country of illegal aliens. People were convinced that aliens were taking American jobs to the extent that we'd have to start speaking Spanish.[84] Senator Pat McCarran, who introduced legislation to remove illegal aliens, alleged that there were 5 million (5,000,000) in our country, including "militant communists, Sicilian bandits and others."[85] Herbert Brownell, the attorney general under President Eisenhower, asserted that U.S. borders were being penetrated and that the country "was faced with a breakdown in law enforcement on a very large scale." In 1954, the Immigration and Naturalization Service (INS) initiated "Operation Wetback" to round up and deport about 1.2 million illegal Mexican immigrants. The INS estimated that approximately 14,500 aliens had engaged in subversive activities.[86] "Wetback" was a derisive term often applied to all Hispanics. When the INS picked up Hispanics, white agents often had difficulty telling a Cuban from a Mexican.

Americans were so preoccupied with Communists at home and the Soviets abroad that we failed to notice or forgot that the former U.S. ally Batista had been allied with the communists. In 1938, Batista and the leader of the Cuban Communist Party (Partido Socialista Popular, or PSP) Blas Roca agreed to a Batista-Communist alliance that lasted until 1952 when Batista was pressured to outlaw the party and force it underground as a condition precedent to good relations with the United States.[87] When he first ran for president of Cuba, in 1940, he did so under the banner of the "Coalición Socialista Democratica." "Socialista" connoted "communist" in Cuba. His political positions from the period were the same as the communists.'[88] At that time, Cuba recognized the Soviet Union, which opened an embassy in Havana. Batista had communists in his cabinet during his presidency, (1940–44).[89] He was also accused of having Nazi and fascist views at a time when the Nazis and Communists had entered into a non–aggression pact.[90] In 1952, the Soviets broke off diplomatic relations with Cuba after the Cuban government refused to grant diplomatic immunity to two Russian couriers.[91] Due to U.S. pressure, Batista set up BRAC,[92] an investigative police agency designed to root out an estimated 100,000 Cuban communists.[93] Although that was the mission, allegations have been made that by early 1958, Batista actually entered into a secret deal with them.

Many Cubans felt that the United States wanted to export its dread of nuclear holocaust and a need for civil defense to Cuba. However, in some Cuban circles, Americans became the subjects of the same kind of xenophobia that some Americans had to foreigners, aliens and communists.

By November 1957, the State Department Office of Middle American Affairs had issued a memorandum suggesting that the United States act as a "discreet middleman" between Batista and the opposition.[94] According to Julia Sweig, instrumental State Department officials had suggested that all of the parties in opposition, including Batista and the Castros, should leave Cuba until a negotiated settlement could be reached. She also reports that these officials had settled on Felipe Pazos, head of Banco Nacional de Cuba, Cuba's central bank under Prío, as the next president of Cuba.[95] The principal State Department official involved was William Wieland, director of the State Department's Office of Middle American Affairs. Castro had other plans, and although he wanted to talk with the U.S. government, it was too slow to negotiate before Batista fled.[96]

In early 1958, Castro offered a truce. If Batista would remove the Cuban Army from Oriente Province, Castro would agree to an election supervised by the Organization of American States and would abide by the result.[97] He agreed to disband his army as soon as the election ended. On one hand, the offer looked like a publicity stunt. Although there had been battles and although M–7–26 had won some victories, the Cuban Army vastly outnumbered the rebels and controlled all of the important positions in Oriente. It was not as if M–7–26 was offering any territory. But it also showed that Castro was willing to compromise. Batista had argued that Castro was a communist and was taking orders directly from Moscow. The Soviet Union had never accepted democratic elections and the rule of law. Castro stated that his allied organization was willing to let some of the other organizations take the lead. Castro seemed more reasonable than Batista. But, of course, Castro knew that Batista wouldn't agree.

More importantly, by February 1958 a military victory was far from obtainable. Everyone involved on all sides knew that Castro's plan was to enact a general strike followed by insurrection. Although Castro called for general strikes, they never worked.

Although the United States had provided military aid to Cuba under four separate treaties, especially the Mutual Defense Assistance Agreement of 1952, on March 18, 1958, President Eisenhower announced an arms embargo.[98]

To a certain extent, Batista had not wanted to join the U.S. crusade. For example, despite the fact that America was supplying arms and munitions to Cuba under four separate treaties, and despite the Point Four aid, Batista sold sugar to the Soviet Union.[99]

On the other hand, in the public mind, Batista was linked to the United States and to American companies. American ambassadors and generals were seen with him as the Cuban government received American arms. Vice President Richard M. Nixon made a visit in 1955, as did Allen Dulles, head of the CIA.[100]

Some of Batista's relationships with Americans symbolized the lack of control that the Cuban taxpayers had over their own country. For example, Cubans had the highest ownership of telephones in Latin America. However, the telephone company, ITT, was an American-owned monopoly. On March 14, 1957, one day after the attempt on his life, Batista decreed a rate hike of 20 percent and extended the monopoly. The public inferred that he had been bribed. ITT gave Batista a gold telephone as a symbol of its appreciation.[101] Every Cuban telephone represented a symbol of the 20 percent rate hike paid to Americans. The gold telephone became a symbol of Batista's link to corruption and graft. The gold telephone also represented Batista's debt to ITT, the American company that dictated prices to and profited from the Cuban consumer.

By the 1950s sugar, tobacco, coffee and tourism were well-developed industries. Many staples, such as rice, had to be imported, however. Knowing how fragile and vulnerable the economy was, Batista attempted to diversify. By 1958, sugar production was good, but constituted only 56.7 percent of the agricultural economy. Rice, at 6.6 percent, coffee, and tobacco were the next four highest.[102] Cuba also experimented with cotton, one of the agricultural products that had been replaced by sugar during the colonial period.[103] It also tried soybeans, many other varieties of beans, cocoa and corn. At one time Cuban citrus was considered the best in the world, but predatory pricing by American growers, especially from Florida, diminished its importance. Cuba also produced bananas and other tropical fruit, but that market was highly competitive. United Fruit, one of the largest landowners in Cuba, also had huge holdings in Central America and did not consider fruit as the highest and best use of its Cuban holdings.

Although Cuba had two growing seasons that could have supported a massive truck farming capacity to rival California's San Joaquín Valley in output, because of the obsession with sugar and tobacco, and because of problems with spoilage, Cuba chose not to compete in that arena.

During World War II the United States opened a nickel plant in Nicaro, Cuba. After the War ended it was closed, but Batista reopened it after he took over in 1952. Cuba reportedly has the second largest nickel deposit in the world, after Russia. During the period 1957–1959, cobalt and nickel mines and a smelter at Moa Bay were also in full operation. Employment ads in Cuban newspapers noted "work 365 days a year."[104] Cuba became the world's number one producer of cobalt, and was a world leader in the export of magnesium and chromium.[105]

Cuba also has large deposits of copper. In fact, copper is an important mineral in the history of Cuba, as a resource and for spiritual reasons. Cuba had an open pit copper mine in the town of El Cobre that was founded in 1550, worked by slaves and native people. In 1608 two natives and a young slave, Rodrigo, Juan de Hoyos, and Juan Moreno, were in a boat returning from collecting salt on the coast near El Cobre, when a storm arose, threatening to swamp them. But then a small statue of the Virgin Mary, carrying the Christ child and a gold cross, appeared on a raft bearing the inscription, "Yo soy la Virgen de la Caridad," (I am the Virgin of Charity). The waters became calm and the boys were miraculously saved. To many Cubans, the fascination with the Virgin of El Cobre is considered to be a cult within Catholicism. Some Cubans believe that the Virgin recognized young Moreno, whose name in Spanish means "brown," and conclude that his salvation was an affirmation of his culture. His culture includes the religion now referred to as Santería, and in that tradition, the Virgin of El Cobre is seen as Ochún, goddess of the rivers, an Orisha, or god in the pantheon of the Yoruba people. Numerous miracles have been attributed to the Virgin, or her "other path," the Orisha Ochún.[106]

In 1630, the copper mine was closed and the slaves were freed. The statue became symbolic of a spiritual victory over the conquistadores and slavery. However, as sugar became a cash crop, in 1731 an attempt was made to reintroduce slavery in El Cobre. During the 19th century, the Virgin/Ochun became the symbol of emancipation of the slaves and Cuban independence. The Virgin was canonized in 1916 as the patroness saint of Cuba.

There is a similar Catholic cult which surrounds St. Lazarus. But almost all Cubans recognize that for many, in his "other path," he is Babalú Aye, an Orisha in Santería, and the subject of Desi Arnaz's theme song.

Nickel and cobalt were also being mined at El Cobre, and at Moro Bay. In the 1950s Cuba struck uranium in Pinar del Río Province. A Cuban bank worked out a deal in England to set up a nuclear plant in Cuba,[107] and by 1958, a 10,000-kilowatt plant was opened.[108]

The government also ran a national lottery. Every Saturday, there was a televised drawing, *El Premio Gordo*, "the fat prize," worth about $100,000. Batista used the lottery proceeds to buy political support. Some of the money went to bribe newspapers, labor unions, and even the Catholic Church.[128]

There were thousands of phantom government employees known as *botelleros,* who took paychecks for no work or perhaps as a bribe or to pay blackmail. After the revolution, it was determined that the Public Works Department was paying $400,000 per month for ghost workers.[129] It later turned out that the Treasury Department had 800 *botelleros* who had to be removed.[130]

The government also sold "permits," in order to start any kind of business, and these were subjects of bribes and payoffs. With enough bribes in place, businesses could ensure they would have no competition.[131]

The opposition alleged that the Batista regime was the second coming of the Spanish Inquisition. Prisoners were guilty until proven otherwise and could expect torture. Police would allegedly assault prisoners openly; women were gang raped and men had been castrated in front of wives and mothers.[132] One Batista administration police chief inserted a needle directly into the eye of his victim. He was so proud of the procedure that he demonstrated its use to other police officers. Another technique was to insert a high-pressure hose in the victim's mouth and hold the nose until the victim drowned. The police kept track of the numbers of their victims by filing their clothes in manila bundles. The bodies were dropped in public places to instill a sense of terror.[133]

Although capital punishment was prohibited by the Cuban Constitution, Batista carved out an exception for shooting an escaping prisoner in the back, so there were hundreds of such cases. Notable opponents of the regime disappeared, never to be seen again.[134] Some were said to have been dumped into the sea, weighted with anchors.[135] When members of the Cuban College of Lawyers, the bar association, protested against civil rights abuses, many of them were jailed. Batista also removed judges who had ruled against his policies and nullified the pension of Judge Manuel Urrutia Lleó, who had ruled that the insurgents had a right to rebel under the Cuban Constitution.[136] Eventually there were allegations that the Cuban Army had engaged in mass killings in the Sierra Madre and the Cuban Air Force bombed civilian targets using inhumane American "anti–personnel" products like napalm.

Although Batista had been "our man" in Cuba, he had helped to enforce a policy of "Cubanization" to force American and other foreign business owners to divest their properties. In 1935, a report of the American Foreign Policy Association outlined how Cuba should proceed: land reform and the release of the naval base at Guantánamo were suggested.[137] A newly elected president, Miguel Mariano Gómez, outlined an ambitious land reform policy that would convince large landowners to turn over "surplus" holdings for distribution.[138] The 1940 Cuban Constitution, sponsored by Batista, also contained a land reform provision. By 1950, among those divested was Hershey Chocolate, founded by Milton S. Hershey,[139] the Pennsylvania candymaker, who had installed a utopian plantation authority over vast holdings in Cuba used to provide sugar for his products. Hershey modeled his Cuban holdings after his model company town, Hershey, Pennsylvania, with a school for orphans, the Milton Hershey School.[140] However, the largest landowners, such as United Fruit Company (later United Brands and Chiquita Brands), important to the life stories of both Batista and Castro, did not divest.

By 1957, the U.S. ownership share in Cuba had diminished, but Americans continued to be the largest market for Cuban products, especially sugar.

By late 1958 there wasn't any jail space left in Cuba. Because students seemed to be constantly in revolt, Batista closed schools all over the island. Cubans lobbied Washington, hoping that the United States would pressure Cuba to release political prisoners and reopen the schools. The U.S. tried to pressure Batista to appear less totalitarian and to hold democratic elections.[141]

By late 1958, despite the profits that his cronies were amassing, despite comparative economic good times in Cuba, and despite the fact that Rebel Army had not made many gains in the field and combat had not spread to the major cities of Cuba, from the inner circles in the Cuban government things looked bleak. The general mood of the country had been "Batista, leave." His opponents now included the professional class, the trade unions, and even the church.[142] The Rebel Army was threatening to burn the sugar crop, and the harvest was just beginning; fear that Cuba could lose its most important product sent the economy into a downward spiral. Elements of the military had mutinied, some army troops had become lazy, and in the field, army units were actually negotiating surrender or contemplating switching sides.[143] To his supporters, it looked like Batista was subjected to outright hostility with a threat of complete abandonment from the U.S. State Department. The U.S. government had tired of having to cajole him. Eventually Batista got the message: he left. Both friend and foe acknowledge that he and the inner circle absconded with millions of dollars. Castro later accused him of stealing the entire Cuban treasury. Batista's press secretary later acknowledged that Batista was "only" able to take $300 million.[144] The *Washington Post* later published that it was "only" $200 million.[145] Today, many of his former followers call him a coward for failing to go down with his ship of state.

The U.S. State Department did have some trepidation about the opposition. M–7–26 was named for the Castro attack on the Moncada Barracks in 1953, but the organization of opponents to Batista included many different political parties and represented every segment of Cuban society, and most had close ties with the United States, so Castro was not an absolute commander. Batista accused Castro of having communist sympathies if not having direct influence from Moscow. Castro's brother Raúl had been a member of the Communist youth organization and had traveled to communist countries before he joined his brother in the Moncada expedition. On June 26, 1958, Raúl Castro and a band of rebels invaded an Oriente Province mining camp and took 10 Americans and two Canadians as hostages. Fidel Castro maintained that he did not authorize or approve of the raid, and the hostages were soon released. Raúl Castro had been commander in the northern area of Oriente that had been open to outlaws. He captured most of the local bandits and accepted several of them into his unit. Although Fidel Castro did not deny that there were Communists in Raúl Castro's units, he also had over 1,000 ex-bandits and at least one Catholic priest ostensibly tending to his Catholic rebels.[146] However, the allegation of Communist influence on or from Castro remained. There were also reports that the rebels were extremely unhappy with the United States for supplying Batista with bombs and napalm.[147]

Fidel Castro maintained that he, personally, did not hold America responsible. "That is the simple view of simple people," he told the *Washington Post*. "I do not agree. What is happening in Cuba today is the outgrowth of Cuba's own political vices and cannot be blamed on anyone else."[148]

However, there were allegations from large property owners in Oriente Province, where M–7–26 had obtained a measure of control, that M–7–26 compelled "taxes" that sounded a lot more like protection money.[149] Americans held millions of dollars worth in assets that they needed to protect.

Batista's opponents found that anti–American rhetoric was politically useful. For many from the countryside where there actually was shelling and fighting, the national identity issue became paramount. Many of them had supported Batista during his first term (1940–44) and later had expected him to further land reform and other social improvements. To gain support of *guajiros*, the rural people, it was easier to scapegoat Americans as the reason for Batista's decadence than fully blame Batista, a man of the people. For many in Havana and other cities, antagonism against America was often fused with the public sentiment against Batista.[150] For years Americans were accused of controlling 90 percent of Cuba's electrical utilities, and holding the telephone monopoly, dominating the banking system, and dictating sugar prices through the sugar quota. Cubans were reminded that Cuban railroads were controlled by U.S. banks, Bethlehem Steel owned 300,000 acres of Cuban iron ore, and opposing politicians argued that Cuba was nothing more than a colony of the United States. Although he depicted himself as a nationalist leader, Batista was clearly allied with American military support, befriending American companies and American interests. He was more concerned with and deferential to them while he rejected reconciliation with Cuban moderates. He had brought American gangsters like the Mafia and Meyer Lansky into Cuba and even made Lansky a paid government consultant.[151] The Cuban government and Cuban institutions like banks and labor unions helped American gangsters expand the casino industry to make Havana one of the leading gambling meccas in the world. The skyline of resort hotels of Havana was a symbol and testament to a dependence on gambling and other vices to support the Cuban economy. Although Cuba had long advertised itself as a playground to attract tourist dollars, Americans were accused of having corrupted Cuban morals. Prostitution was rife. Although Havana had *fleteras*, streetwalkers of the 16th century who attracted sailors from ships of the Spanish Main,[152] and although prostitution flourished in Cuba long before there was a United States of America, in the common mind prostitution was attributed to American influence, because it was so attractive to American tourists. Of course, prostitution was not only attractive to the marks, it was profitable for the workers; a high-end whore at an institution like the Hotel Casa Marina could earn as much in a night as a white-collar worker could earn in a month.[153] By 1959, 10,000 prostitutes were active in Havana.[154] Profits were shared with high-ranking officers of the army, navy and national police.[155]

Therefore, although Americans profited from vice, Cubans did too. Most of the Americans had Cuban partners, and the casinos, brothels and other enterprises hired Cubans. Most Americans were sure that Cubans would not kill the goose that laid their golden egg. It was expected that a new regime would build on the prosperity and social gains made under the Constitution of 1940. However, over time, disillusionment set in.

Batista had been on a long leash, but the U.S. shortened it to require that he permit honest elections as a prerequisite to further U.S. involvement.[156] U.S. diplomats had threatened him on several occasions. Consensus in Cuba was that if the Cuban insurrection became an all-out civil war, the United States military would step in to bring order. It had been done many times previously. Batista had agreed to resume the constitutional guarantees as a predicate to further grants of military assistance, from not only the United States but also Britain and Canada.[157] But he failed to live up to his promises. Instead, he tried to legitimize his reign as an absolute ruler by having the Cuban Congress declare a national state of emergency, so he could seize full control of the military and take over legislative functions.[158] Even his friends, business partners, and former colleagues could not accept those terms.

Actually, Batista left after a confrontation with his former military commanders who had tried to make a deal with Castro. By that time, he had finally figured out that the United States also wanted him out. Besides M–7–26 in the field, he was also opposed by the Directorio, which had nearly accosted Batista at the Presidential Palace in March 1957, and was still actively pursing assassination. It had its own independent guerrilla army, led by Fraure Chomón in the field in the Escambray Mountains. Yet another guerrilla force operating independently, founded November 10, 1957, was the Second Front, led by Eloy Gutiérrez Menoyo, and William Morgan, an American renegade. In addition, the Communists had a small force led by Víctor Bordón and another, the "Máximo Gómez column" led by Félix Torres in the Escambray. Independently operating in the cities was Civic Resistance, led by José Miró Cardona, former president of the Havana bar association. Among the members of this group were professional people — doctors, lawyers, engineers — committed to urban sabotage.

Batista decided not to stand for reelection in 1958. He knew from September 1957 on that he could not replace himself.[159] His 1958 candidate was another yes-man, similar to the weak puppet presidents of the 1930s, who had been controlled by Batista from behind the scenes. Batista's man, Andres

Former Cuban presidents Carlos Prío Socarrás (1948–1952) and Ramón Grau San Martín (1933–1934, 1944–1948). Both were leaders of the Auténtico Party. Prío was forcibly removed in a coup by Batista on March 10, 1952. Both supported the insurrection and Revolution, but both fell out with the Provisional Government, went into exile and died in the United States. Although the accusation was made that Prío had stolen millions of dollars during his presidency, he died penniless in Miami (photograph from University of Miami Libraries, Cuban Heritage Collection).

Rivero Agüero, represented a coalition of four minor political parties co–opted by Batista. He was opposed by former President Ramon Grau San Martín of the Auténtico Party, Carlos Marquez Sterling, and Alberto Salas Amaro, an ex-friend of Batista and a newspaper publisher. However, Grau San Martín withdrew just before the vote. M–7–26 and all of its components and allies disrupted the campaign, threatened the candidates and discouraged voting. Although most of the Cuban electorate were located within Batista's government's control, Fidel Castro decreed from his hiding place in the mountains of Oriente Province that any candidate who participated would be disqualified for elective or appointive posts for the next 30 years after Batista was overthrown.[160] Reportedly, at least three candidates were killed by the rebels in Oriente.[161]

Rivero Agüero was declared the winner by a landslide. Batista's coalition "elected" six governors of provinces, 72 senators, 166 representatives, 126 mayors and about 1,800 aldermen. But it was apparent that most people did not participate, from protest or fear or conviction that the election was rigged.[162] It is estimated that only about 15 percent of eligible voters actually went to the polls. However, although Rivero Agüero had won, he also had lost, as his brother Nicolas Rivero Agüero, his campaign manager, had been assassinated. In addition, his half brother Luis Conte Agüero, a critic of the Batista government, had to go into exile to Venezuela.

There was massive fraud in the 1958 election. Even the U.S. ambassador Earl E.T. Smith, who was a Batista supporter, called the election Batista's "last big mistake."[163] Batista had been stowing money in foreign accounts and by 1958, had sent over $30 million to Switzerland, the United States, Mexico and elsewhere.[164] In January 1959, Rivero Agüero was to be inaugurated as president and Batista was due to leave the Presidential Palace. But the United States had made it abundantly clear to both Batista and Rivero Agüero that we would no longer accept them as leaders.[165]

By late 1958, leaders of the military threatened a palace coup against Batista.[166] Because Batista continued to violate the terms of treaty to provide U.S. arms shipments to him, and because the U.S. protested profusely, he knew that he was losing U.S. support.[167] On December 9, 1958, Batista received a visit from his friend William Pawley, a private citizen who had lived in Cuba and was an investor in Cuban businesses. Pawley was also a former U.S. Ambassador to Peru and Brazil. Pawley told Batista that it looked like the U.S. government wanted him out immediately and wanted him to hand over the reins of power to a caretaker government. Batista was offered asylum in Daytona Beach, but Pawley could not actually show that he was authorized to act on behalf of the U.S. government.[168] Several days later, Batista was told by Ambassador Earl E. T. Smith that the U.S. would not accept a further Batista-controlled government.[169]

As Batista noted, public opinion was greatly influenced by random, indiscriminate terror that occurred at schools, restaurants, department stores and other public buildings. An urban underground movement was responsible for daily terrorist attacks on civilian as well as military targets. Batista was personally affected. He had been the subject of mutinies in the military and at least one nearly successful assassination attempt at the Presidential Palace. Some of his close allies had been killed or wounded in assassination attempts. In recent years, the myth of military victory has been diminished by the revelation that the rebel underground was as important in Batista's exit as the military myth.

By December 22, Batista was shocked when he discovered that his military leadership had worked out a truce with M–7–26 and Fidel Castro. Ironically, one of the commanding general's sons, Silito Tabernilla, was Batista's confidential secretary. Tabernilla later said that he knew that there were negotiations that led to a deal, but he didn't have the heart to tell Batista.[170] Batista threatened to remove the commanders but was told, "It is a little late, because a truce has been ordered by the Chief of the Armed Forces at Santiago de Cuba, Col. Rego Rubido, and the Chief of the Naval District, Commodore Carnero, so that an agreement can be reached with Fidel Castro."[171] Castro was told that the United States was informed about the truce negotiations.[172] Although the truce did not hold, by that time Batista had to have known that he had as much to fear from his own men as he did from the guerrillas, who were still in the field, hundreds of miles from Havana.

In fact, after Batista fled, the generals tried to take control in Havana and General Eugolio Cantillo, by then default head of the military, tried to turn control of the country over to Colonel Ramón Barquín, who had been one of the leaders of a 1956 mutiny,[173] and who was brought to Havana still dressed in prison garb from internment on the Isle of Pines. The entry of Barquín was ostensibly part of a "third force" attempt at a solution by Montecristi, a group including lawyers, members of medical profession and bankers, most of whom were Catholic and could claim that their group was church supported.[174] They also had some support in the U.S. State Department and CIA.[175] Castro had yet to enter Havana. But Barquín saw himself as a cooperating member of the M–7–26 coalition and would not assume power unitarily.[176]

At the same time that Cantillo was negotiating with Castro, and at the same time that efforts were being made to bring Barquín from prison to head the army, the CIA was working with former president Prío Socarrás's Second Front in Las Villas Province to support the group led by Eloy Gutiérrez Menoyo and another led by Manuel Antonio (Tony) Varona, former vice president under Prío Soccarás, in Camagüey.[177] At the same time the U.S. supported his organizations in Cuba, Prío Socarrás was being prosecuted in Miami for violations of the Neutrality Act.

Batista later alleged that even before the election took place, the U.S. had already decided to support Castro. There is no hard evidence to justify this assertion, but there is a lot of circumstantial evidence. For example, according to several sources, the CIA gave the Rebel Army and Castro's organization M–7–26 $50,000 in mid–1958.[178] The U.S. reportedly took a "neutral" position; cut him off from new shipments of arms; and granted asylum to many of his political enemies, who organized his overthrow from the United States. He also alleged that Castro had ordered that any candidate for office who did not withdraw would be subject to execution. Although the allegation about political assassination is not proven, urban terror did increase dramatically, and dozens of killings occurred.[179] The three killings in Oriente Province certainly appear to have been political assassinations.

On December 31, 1958, the U.S. State Department notified the Senate Foreign Relations Committee that the Batista government would soon fall. Assistant Secretary of State for Inter-American Affairs Roy Rubottom told a subcommittee that if the central city of Santa Clara were taken, the government would fall.[180] This news was not widely published until Batista had actually fled.[181] During a hearing, Rubottom denied that the U.S. government was ready to send in American troops to support Batista. When asked by Chairman Wayne Morse, senator from Oregon, Rubottom said that there was no truth to rumors that Castro was communist or had been influenced by them.[182] He stated that Batista had been weakened by failing to produce a government capable of dealing with the rebels. When questioned about Rubottom's testimony, Nicolás Arroyo, the Cuban ambassador to the United States, denied that the Batista regime was in trouble and stated that the rebels had communist help.[183]

Chapter 4

Bill of Particulars

After he was captured trying to seize the Moncada Barracks in 1953, Fidel Castro asserted during his trial that the Batista regime was illegitimate and that, faced with tyranny, the Cuban people had a legal right to rebel. His closing argument lasted two hours and is now known as the "History Will Absolve Me" defense.[1]

Castro was a student of history whose primary reference was José Martí, the Cuban national hero and martyr, and also its best known writer and philosopher. Although Martí had not been an insurrectionist or a member of the Mambi Army that fought the Spanish army from 1868 and would eventually defeat Spain, in 1892, he became chief delegate of the Cuban Revolutionary Party. On March 25, 1895, Martí and Máximo Gómez, another Cuban national hero, published the *Manifesto of Montecristi*, the Cuban Declaration of Independence. Martí became the spokesman and principal theoretician for Cuban independence. He is now the principal Cuban martyr and his writings have become the "bible" for almost all Cubans, whether in or out of diaspora, by followers of philosophies ranging from anarchy to Communism, and even in the exile community, including Cubans across he political spectrum. His name is on monuments throughout Cuba, and both a city in Cuba and the Havana airport bear his name. He is the subject of a famous statue in Central Park, New York, and less famous ones in Tampa and Miami. The U.S. government named the broadcast organizations directed at Cuba as Radio and TV Martí.

Expelled from Cuba by the Spanish, Martí made a short visit to Spain. He then made a brief return to Cuba, but he was expelled a second time. Martí lived in the States from 1880 to 1895, when his most important works were written and published, including the Cuban declaration. He was also a noted news reporter, translator, playwright, and novelist, and is considered to be a father of the modernist school of Spanish poetry; his work is still revered and studied in almost all Spanish-speaking countries.[2] *Nuestra América* (*Our America*), an essay, is also still read. "Guantanamera," based on a traditional folk tune, is probably the most recognizable Martí work to Americans.

Martí advocated a war of "redemption and redistribution." He advocated racial equality, and envisioned a nation of small farmers and declared that there was so much wasted uncultivated land in Cuba that it should be redistributed to *guajiros*, small farmers.[3] Soon after returning to Cuba, and soon after the *Manifesto of Montecristi* was declared, Martí was killed in combat in a suicide charge. His life as a patriot and his heroic death make him Cuba's most important martyr.[4]

Martí is celebrated as the "Apostle" of Cuba, but he was a very atypical Cuban. He renounced Catholicism, and it is perhaps reasonable to surmise that his patriotism became his religion.[5] He noted that the Spanish government tried to use race to attempt to divide the independence movement. He argued that "textbook races" were "invented" in order to justify expansion and empire.[6] Although he advocated class warfare and workers' rights and probably agreed with Marx about property rights, he was also a Jeffersonian democrat.[7] His principles are espoused by Cubans with political positions from the extreme right wing to the left: from the framers of the proto–United States Constitution of 1902 (the Cuban Constitution was modeled after our Constitution and the Platt Amendment was added to satisfy the Roosevelt administration) to Machado, who was an outright fascist, to military strongman Batista to Castro and Cuban communists to the current Miami exile community.

Reportedly, 70 of Castro's colleagues were killed after they were captured.[8] A lawyer, Castro alleged that he was not permitted to view the indictment against him and he was not able to seek advice from another lawyer.[9] He was originally to have been tried with a hundred codefendants, many of whom were leftists who had nothing to do with Moncada but were tried under general principles used by Batista to pressure the court system to suppress his political enemies. After the full trial began, Castro was falsely certified as too physically ill to proceed, so his case was severed from the rest. His trial took place in a hospital room, closed to the public. Although the law that was being enforced provided a maximum penalty of 20 years, the prosecutor asked for 26.[10]

Castro went on the offense and rhetorically "prosecuted" Batista, accusing him of tyranny,[11] of "cruel and debase despotism," of corruption and cronyism,[12] of usurping the Cuban Constitution,[13] and of outright murder.[14] Castro argued that in such a situation, Cuban law contains a right of insurrection.[15]

Castro invoked legal, historical and religious allusions to identify the Cuban people, including:

six hundred thousand Cubans without work, who want to earn their daily bread honestly without having to emigrate from their homeland in search of a livelihood; the five hundred thousand farm laborers who live in miserable shacks, who work four months of the year and starve the rest, sharing their misery with their children, who don't have an inch of land to till and whose existence would move any heart not made of stone; the four hundred thousand industrial workers and laborers whose retirement funds have been embezzled, whose benefits are being taken away, whose homes are wretched quarters, whose salaries pass from the hands of the boss to those of the moneylender, whose future is a pay reduction and dismissal, whose life is endless work and whose only rest is the tomb; the one hundred thousand small farmers who live and die working land that is not theirs, looking at it with the sadness of Moses gazing at the promised land, to die without ever owning it, who like feudal serfs have to pay for the use of their parcel of land by giving up a portion of its produce, who cannot love it, improve it, beautify it nor plant a cedar or an orange tree on it because they never know when a sheriff will come with the rural guard to evict them from it; the thirty thousand teachers and professors who are so devoted, dedicated and so necessary to the better destiny of future generations and who are so badly treated and paid; the twenty thousand small business men weighed down by debts, ruined by the crisis and harangued by a plague of grafting and venal officials; the ten thousand young professional people: doctors, engineers, lawyers, veterinarians, school teachers, dentists, pharmacists, newspapermen, painters, sculptors, etc., who finish school with their degrees anxious to work and full of hope, only to find themselves at a dead end, all doors closed to them, and where no ears hear their clamor or supplication.

He also alleged that 85 percent of the small farmers in Cuba paid rent and lived under constant threat of being evicted; that more than half of the most productive land was in the hands of foreigners; and that in Oriente, the largest province, the lands of the United Fruit Company and the West Indian Company link the northern and southern coasts. There are two hundred thousand peasant families who do not have a single acre of land to till to provide food for their starving children. On the other hand, ... cultivable land owned by powerful interests remains uncultivated.

He argued that Cuba was primarily a producer of raw materials:

We export sugar to import candy, we export hides to import shoes, we export iron to import plows.

He argued that most Cubans did not have adequate housing, sanitation and electricity. He implicated a poor education system. He invoked Cuban irony to castigate the Cuban health system:

Only death can liberate one from so much misery. In this respect, however, the State is most helpful — in providing early death for the people.

He asserted that 90 percent of the poor children carried painful parasites.

By implication, he accused the wealthy Cubans who had risen to success. "The nation's future, the solutions to its problems, cannot continue to depend on the selfish interests of a dozen big businessmen nor on the cold calculations of profits that ten or twelve magnates draw up in their air-conditioned offices."

Of the 100 defendants, the court found 26 guilty. It rendered mostly lenient sentences. The court found Fidel Castro guilty and sentenced him to 15 years, and gave Raúl Castro a 13-year sentence.

Castro's manifesto implicated only Batista. He did not mention such perceived indignities as "Americanization" of the public schools, the "imposition" of the American holiday of Thanksgiving and the displacement of traditional Spanish symbols and customs other by imported symbols of Christmas, like Santa Claus and the Christmas tree.[16] He did not address the marketing of Cuba as a place where vices that were outlawed in the United States could legally be performed.

Castro was certainly not the first to issue these allegations. Although he mentioned the poor, many of his allegations addressed the wrongs to his class of Creole young professionals.

Most of Castro's defense was taken straight from the philosophy of Martí, who would not have appropriated large estates but would have split up government land to give to small farmers.[17] During the 1930s, the Grau San Martín administration, ostensibly in homage to Martí, had put into place many of the reforms that Castro requested. Although Grau San Martía was anti-communist, ABC was pro-fascist, and its program was modeled after a 1919 Italian Fascist program. Its policies were also similar to Castro's. The ABC Manifesto-Program of 1932 would have split up the *landifunda* (large estates), nationalized public utilities, and placed limitations on holdings of United States citizens in Cuba, but it was not populist or progressive.[18] The accusation was made that ABC stood for Asociación Blanca de Cuba, "Association of Cuban Whites," as ABC argued that only literate people should vote, meaning that most Afro-Cubans would lose the privilege and the white Creoles would control Cuba, like the Fascists controlled Italy and the Falangists would control Spain.[19] The Constitution of 1940 also stood for land reform.

By 1958, most of the Cuban public would agree with Castro on all points. By that time, even the head of Batista's military, Francisco J. Tabernilla, had decided that the Cuban public completely supported revolution.[20] After Fidel Castro's closing argument was published, it became the manifesto of M–7–26, the July 26 Movement. At that time, most of the Cuban people of the era did not trust electoral politics, especially after Batista held phony elections in 1954, 1956 and 1958, and did not trust Batista to peacefully surrender power. In their estimation, and following Cuban history and tradition, all that was left to them was revolution.

Chapter 5

Cuba, the U.S.A.,
and the World, 1956–1959

After the Soviets took over the Baltic countries (Estonia, Lithuania, and Latvia) soon after World War II, Poland, Yugoslavia, Hungary, Czechoslovakia, Albania and other countries fell. Italy, Greece and Turkey were threatened. Soon the mainland of China would become Red China. The Truman Doctrine was designed to contain Communism; In Europe in 1949 the North Atlantic Treaty Organization (NATO) was established, and that same year the Point Four program was inaugurated.

Republican theoretician John Foster Dulles argued that containment should be replaced by a policy of "liberation."[1] When Dwight Eisenhower became president in January 1953, he appointed Dulles as his secretary of state. As secretary of state, Dulles still carried out the "containment" policy, but with the advent of Soviet nuclear capacity, initiated a policy of mutual assured destruction and brinkmanship. Critics blamed him for damaging relations with Communist states and furthering to the Cold War. Dulles was a devout Presbyterian, son of a minister. His brother Allen W. Dulles was the head of the CIA. Their mission appeared to many to be a "crusade" to replace Communism and with the "American" value system.[2]

By 1953, with the Korean War winding down, the Soviets tried to expand into Latin America. Soon after he was elected, President Eisenhower contemplated making a goodwill trip to shore up U.S. relationships in Latin America.[3] Instead, the president sent his brother, Milton, then president of Penn State University, on a fact-finding mission to the area.[4] In March 1954, Secretary of State John Foster Dulles personally pushed through an inter–American resolution at the Tenth Inter-American Conference calling for joint action against Communist aggression or subversion in Latin America.[5] He described the document as the internationalization of the Monroe Doctrine.[6] Three months later, Jacobo Árbenz's government in Guatemala was overthrown with CIA support.

During the Truman administration, the United States had a policy of providing aid to countries to demonstrate how development could foster or perpetuate democracy. During the first part of the Eisenhower administration, U.S. policy was "trade, not aid." The United States determined that countries would best be served by attracting private capital to develop goods that could be used in trade with the United States.[7]

Although the U.S. was officially committed to democracy, we were more interested in "stability" in Latin America, which meant that dictatorships were tolerated. At the time, 15 out of 20 Latin American governments were dictatorships; many had tended toward fascism during the war, but afterward became ardently anti–communist.[8] Demonstrable evidence of how the U.S. could put policy into practice took place in Guatemala in 1954, when the U.S. supported a takeover of the elected government on allegations that it was Communist influenced. Many Latin American countries did have Communist agitation; most also suppressed demands for more freedom.

Guatemala was an example of how far the United States would go to stop perceived Communist incursion into the region. The U.S. used covert activities, and support from the OAS and placed an economic blockade on Guatemala. However, it would later be revealed that the United States State Department may have had an ulterior motive to attack the Árbenz government. As a young lawyer, among John Foster Dulles's first clients at the law firm of Sullivan and Cromwell were companies with investments in Latin America. Dulles was the nephew of Robert Lansing, then secretary of state. Lansing brought Dulles into the State Department in 1917, with a mission to provide for the protection of American properties in Latin America.[9] Later both he and his brother and law partner, Allen W. Dulles, would become lawyers for United Fruit Company. Eventually Allen W. Dulles would be named to the company's board. By 1954 Allen was head of the CIA.[10] Just before President Eisenhower was inaugurated, the Guatemalan government announced that it would expropriate some of United Fruit's Guatemalan holdings by eminent domain. The decision to overthrow the Árbenz government was made in large part by the State Department official with the most inside knowledge about Guatemala: John Moors Cabot. At the time, the president of United Fruit was Thomas Dudley Cabot, brother of the first assistant secretary of state for Latin American affairs. John Moors Cabot recommended the overthrow.[11] At the same time, President Eisenhower's personal secretary was married to United Fruit Company's principal lobbyist.[12]

On his return from a 1955 tour of Cuba, the Caribbean, and Central America, Vice President Nixon recommended that the countries of the region should expend their own resources and join forces to ensure their political stability. "Communist forces," he noted, "although small, are well organized, and present in every country, lurking for the chance to gain ascendency."[13]

Meanwhile, in other continents the U.S. had different positions: the stated policy was to contest communists directly. U.S. nuclear weapons gave us leverage in foreign relations, allowing the States to use the strategy of brinkmanship and the threat of massive retaliation to deter communist expansion. The U.S. could use our "nuclear policy" to force a belligerent country to back down. "Massive retaliation" showed our enemies that we could obliterate them if they defied us.

We also ascribed to a "domino theory"; if one country fell to Communism, a ripple effect would cause its neighbors to succumb as well.[14] This theory was first discussed when the Geneva Accords of 1954 were negotiated, ending France's involvement in Indochina. Neither the United States nor the South Vietnamese supported the accords. Our policy was that to "give" North Vietnam to the communists was to give up the entire region. To counter, we created the Southeast Asia Treaty Organization (SEATO.)

In Europe, NATO established a system of mutual defense to be deployed in response to an attack by any external party. However, after West Germany joined NATO and after NATO demonstrated that it could field perhaps a 100,000 men under arms, the Communist European countries formed the Warsaw Pact, which further solidified the opposing sides in Europe.[15]

Although the U.S. espoused "trade not aid," we strategically installed military bases and coupled them with military sales and foreign aid. For example, in 1953 the U.S. entered

Dominican dictator Rafael Trujillo Molina (second from left). On January 1, 1959, Trujillo provided sanctuary to former Cuban president Fulgencio Batista, and later permitted former Cuban general José Pedraza to recruit and train a Cuban "Liberation Army." He also ran a propaganda campaign, sent spies into Cuba and even attempted an invasion and insurrection within Cuba, but his August-September 1959 plot was foiled when he was tricked by American comandante William Morgan. Trujillo's Liberation Army included fascist "volunteers" from Spain and Nazi World War II veterans. Mysteriously, however, Trujillo had a change of heart in early 1960, when he allied himself with Cuba. He was assassinated in 1961, with CIA help (Associated Press).

into a pact with Spain — still fascist, anti–Protestant, anti-masonic and anti–Semitic — to place military bases there. As a result, the U.S. provided Spain with $45 million in aid in 1960.[16]

In Europe the U.S. also supported the right to revolt in the name of democracy. That occurred in Hungary in 1956. The Hungarian uprising was not planned in advance. It occurred after the Soviets had given Poland, then a Soviet vassal state, a degree of autonomy. A United Nations investigation concluded that events took participants by surprise and there was no single explanation why the outbreak occurred. There had been general resentment about the stifling control that the Soviets had exercised over Hungary. Although the U.S. argued on behalf of the popular insurrection in the United Nations and deplored Soviet intervention, actual policy was not to intervene. After democratic rebels took the government, a large Soviet force invaded Hungary in early November and overran the rebels. Over 2,500 Hungarians and 700 Soviet troops were killed, and 200,000 Hungarians fled as refugees.[17]

In the Middle East, after the Suez Crisis in which Israel, Britain and France attacked

Egypt, then part of the United Arab Republic, the United States and the Soviet Union ended the crisis through negotiations at the United Nations. However, Soviet prestige in the region was on the rise as a result. President Eisenhower issued the Eisenhower Doctrine starting that the United States would use military force if necessary to resist Communist aggression, and sent 14,000 American troops to Lebanon in 1958 at the request of the pro-Western government.[18] After that, the U.S. amended the "trade, not aid" policy, providing development funds to Egypt, in hopes it would encourage strongman President Gamal Abdul Nasser to see things our way.

In Latin America, the United States was part of the Organization of American States and the Committee of Twenty-One, a group of foreign ministers from the member countries. Although the U.S. had an interest in Latin America, it was preoccupied with the Soviet Union, with whom we met at the United Nations and at summit conferences. The first summit conference with the leaders of the United States, the Soviet Union, Great Britain, and France was held in Geneva in 1955, and tensions decreased. However, when Sputnik 1, the first artificial satellite, was sent into space in 1957, the "space race" began, engendered by a "missile gap" between the United States and the Soviet Union.

It seemed that the entire Latin American region was in revolt, especially where the U.S. supported dictators. Although the United States did not administer the day-to-day affairs of dictatorships in places like Nicaragua and the Dominican Republic, we were depicted as codependents and cofounders. The U.S. had intervened in Nicaragua as early as 1909, primarily to protect American mining interests.[19] Our man in Nicaragua was Anastasio Somoza García, who had been raised in Philadelphia, and who had become essential as a translator for the United States Marines that were sent to Nicaragua to fight against a guerrilla army led by Augusto Sandino between 1927 and 1933. Somoza rose through the ranks of the National Guard and, by 1934, after he ordered Sandino's assassination, he become the preeminent strongman of his country. He performed a coup against President Juan Bautista Sacasa, and became president in 1937 after a rigged election. In essence, the U.S. selected him to run his country.[20] Throughout the period, Somoza maintained an intimate relationship with the United States. Nicaragua declared war on Germany during World War II, and was the first country to sign the United Nations charter.[21] Somoza consistently was shipped American arms, although Nicaragua was under no imminent threat. From time to time he would accuse Costa Rica, which had no standing army, of threatening his country, creating a "crisis" to be assuaged by more arms and other aid from the United States. For example, Somoza was opposed to President José "Pepe" Figueres Ferrer of Costa Rica. Nicaragua claimed that members of the Caribbean Legion, a group of political exiles from Caribbean nations, participated in a plot to assassinate him from Costa Rica. In 1955, Somoza supported Rafael Calderón Guardia, a former president of Costa Rica, who led a group of rebels from Nicaragua to take Villa Quesada.[22] The OAS interceded. In 1956 Somoza was assassinated.[23] Although one son, Luis Somoza Debayle, was "elected" president and declared that Nicaragua was democratic, the real power was held by his brother, Anastasio Somoza Debayle, head of the National Guard.

In the Dominican Republic, the U.S. and the Catholic Church supported the dictatorial regime of General Rafael Leónidas Trujillo Molina, who depicted himself as an international leader, despite valid reports of state-directed terror and assassination of his political opposition, massacres of Haitians, and plots against other countries, including Cuba. Trujillo had threatened the regimes of Grau San Martín, Prío Socarrás, and Batista before Castro.[24] As in Cuba and Nicaragua, U.S. Marines had intervened in the Dominican Republic from

1916 to 1924, and the U.S. had "interests" to protect. However, Trujillo was not deferential to American interests — he nationalized electric and telephone companies.[25]

In Venezuela, the U.S. had supported the dictatorship of Marcos Pérez Jiménez, who helped overthrow a constitutional democracy, although he was extremely unpopular. Under Pérez, Americans invested heavily and he awarded generous contracts to American oil companies. After he outlawed the Communist Party and broke relations with the Soviet Union and Czechoslovakia, President Eisenhower awarded Pérez a Legion of Merit medal.[26] After a coup in 1958, Pérez was deposed, and he relocated to the protection of President Trujillo in the Dominican Republic.

In Argentina, a bloody coup deposed dictator Juan Perón in 1955. A democratic government was put in place but unrest continued. Perón had nationalized Argentina's large corporations and co-opted labor unions, permitting the state to rationalize conflicting interests. After he was deposed, Perón moved to the Dominican Republic but his followers remained to undermine democracy. Reports of riots, political assassination and kidnapping continued. Many other Latin American countries also had a history of unrest. A Bolivian revolution in 1952 instituted agrarian reform and nationalization of the country's largest tin mines, many of them American owned. Guerrillas were still seen roaming the Andes.

In British Guyana, the British suspended the colonial constitution and sent in troops in 1953 to "restore order." The government was given to conservative elements, but by 1957 after a new constitution was written and elections held, the British accused the new government of being Communist. Britain governed until 1966.

In Colombia, la Violencia, "the Violence," a period of anarchy, lasted from the late 1940s into the 1950s. On April 9, 1948, liberal presidential candidate Jorge Eliécer Gaitán was assassinated. Riots, known as el Bogotazo, erupted in Bogotá, spread through out the country, and at least 180,000 Colombians were killed. Fidel Castro was present and may have played a significant role. Dictator Gustavo Rojas Pinilla rose to preeminence.

In Brazil, a military junta forced Brazilian strongman Getúlio Dornelles Vargas to commit suicide on August 24, 1954. By 1956, Juscelino Kubitschek took office. His opposition included many members of the military opposed to democracy. Eventually, he was deposed and exiled.

In 1955 the OAS prevented a war between Ecuador and Peru over a boundary dispute.

In Panama, President José Antonio Remón Cantera was assassinated in January 1955. Panama surrounded the United States Canal Zone, and in essence the U.S. created Panama by encouraging the areas surrounding the canal to secede from Colombia. Remón had been in negotiations with the United States. A 1955 treaty bears his name, but by then he had already passed away.[27] Subsequent Panamanian politicians described the United States as the "big bad wolf," as there were accusations that we controlled their government and there were intermittent anti–American riots.[28]

The United States had its own problems with Puerto Rico. Under Pedro Albizu Campos, a chemical engineer and a graduate of Harvard Law School, the Puerto Rican Nationalist Party stressed the use of terror and assassination to gain independence. In 1950, 33 people were killed in a failed insurrection in Puerto Rico, where there was an aborted assassination attempt on Governor Luis Muñoz Marín.[29] Later, an attempted assassin and a police officer were killed in an attempted assassination of President Truman in Washington.[30] In 1954, four Puerto Rican nationalists opened fire from the gallery of the U.S. Capitol and wounded five congressmen. Albizu called the attack called the attack on Congress "an act of sublime heroism." Albizu was jailed from 1937 to 1943, 1950 to 1953 and 1954 to 1964.[31]

While Abrizu was in prison in 1955–1956, his wife, Laura Meneses, was living in Mexico City. Among her acquaintances at the time were fellow expatriates Che Guevara and his first wife, Hilda Gadea, and Fidel Castro; they compared complaints and he discussed the "Yankee penetration" of Cuba as de facto colonialism.[32]

Although a Puerto Rican constitution was approved in 1952, there were still other legitimate grievances. There had been another nationalist plot on President Eisenhower's life.[33] While on another "Goodwill Mission" in May 1958, Vice President Nixon was harassed by law students in Montevideo, Uruguay, stoned by university students in Lima, Peru, and assaulted by a mob in Caracas, Venezuela.

On the trip, Nixon first attended a swearing-in ceremony of Argentine president Arturo Frondizi as riots took place outside the building. As soon as he arrived in Uruguay, Nixon was "showered with anti–U.S. pamphlets as he passed the University of Montevideo Law School. Next day, against the cautious advice of U.S. embassy and Uruguayan police officials, Nixon paid a spur-of-the-moment visit to the Law School, was asked to talk with Ricardo Yelpo, 26-year-old leader of the Communist-front Student Federation. Nixon agreed. 'We reproach the U.S. for its passive policy towards dictatorships in Latin America.'"[34]

In Paraguay, Nixon was greeted at the airport with a warm *abrazo*, a hug, from President Alfredo Stroessner, cheers and a 21-gun salute. Stroessner had taken power in a coup on May 4, 1954, declared "a state of siege" and was the only candidate in a special rigged "election." He was reelected seven times — in 1958, 1963, 1968, 1973, 1978, 1983, and 1988. However, Stroessner was a military dictator and ran a fascist police state he euphemistically called "guided democracy." Nixon must have recognized that the soldiers in his honor guard were wearing Nazi-style uniforms. They goose-stepped and gave him a "seig heil" salute. Nixon's CIA report must have noted that the president, the son of German immigrants, was openly pro-German during World War II and gave aid to Nazi war criminals.[35]

In Peru, Nixon was blocked from visiting San Marcos University by a crowd of demonstrators chanting "Go home, Nixon!"

Next Nixon visited Venezuela. Hostile crowds spat at him as he arrived. Until that year, the U.S. had supported Venezuelan dictator Marcos Pérez Jimenez, president from 1952 to January 1958, when he was deposed by a coup. Like Batista, Pérez rose from a captain in the army to lead a coup. From 1945, he had been the military strongman behind several governments. In 1952, he was a member of a ruling junta that called for open elections. But after it looked like Pérez could not win, the junta suspended the election and appointed Pérez as president. Pérez employed a "National Security" police force that was as oppressive as any in Latin America.[36]

With rioting in the streets, and under threat of an insurrection, Pérez fled to the Dominican Republic, and later Spain, where he retired on an estimated $250 million that he had taken from the government. Murder charges were pending, but later Venezuelan president Hugo Chavez, an admirer, lifted them in 1999.[37]

In Caracas, Nixon's motorcade was blocked, and for 12 minutes a hostile crowd rocked the cars back and forth and tried to bash in the windows From all accounts, Nixon barely escaped.[38] Scenes of the riot were shown on American television and the incident was widely reported in the newspapers. As a result Latin America finally got President Eisenhower's attention. A thousand U.S. Marines and paratroopers were sent to the Caribbean.

Before 1958, two violent revolutions had succeeded in overthrowing existing Latin America governments: Mexico, 1910–1940, and Guatemala, 1944–1954. The U.S. opposed both of them. They both were nationalistic and expected that land reform would improve the lot of an impoverished majority. Both were socialistic. The U.S. did not overtly attempt to overturn the Mexican Revolution, but were successful in Guatemala.

Point Four aid was administered by the Technical Cooperation Administration, a unit within the Department of State. Under a 1951 agreement, the United States sent scientific "experts" to Cuba.[39]

By March 1958, Nikita Khrushchev had become the Soviet premier, and the Soviet Union had undergone a period of de-Stalinization and promised to coexist and maybe even cooperate with us. Although the Soviets had toned down their militancy, President Eisenhower described "the new Communist line of sweetness and light [as] perhaps more dangerous than their propaganda in Stalin's time."[40] By 1958, the Soviets purchased 100,000 tons of Cuban sugar, as did communist Czechoslovakia.[41]

Fresh from his Latin American experience, after conferring with Dulles and Eisenhower, Vice President Nixon announced a new concentration on the region.[42] But in Cuba, Nixon was identified with Batista. In February 1955, Vice President Nixon had praised "the competence and stability" of his regime, awarded him a medal of honor, and compared him to Abraham Lincoln. Nixon hailed Batista's Cuba as a land that "shares with us the same democratic ideals of peace, freedom and the dignity of man."[43]

Today there is a perception that U.S. problems with Cuba stem from a history of imperialist domination and colonization of the island. There are reasons for this perception. The U.S. coveted Cuba virtually from the founding of the United States as a nation and had even threatened to grab it from Spain several times.[44] The Monroe Doctrine asserted rights in all of Latin America.[45] The U.S. tried to buy Cuba from Spain.[46] The U.S. intervened in the Cuban War Independence and labeled it the Spanish American War. Privately we discussed taking Cuba, either by acquiescence or by force. Theodore Roosevelt reported that after the Spanish American War, generals on the ground had reported "that in two or three years they [the Cubans] will insist upon being part of us."[47] We had inserted the Platt Amendment into the Cuban Constitution of 1902 to give us a right to intervene in Cuban affairs even if Cuba were not kept clean from "dangerous diseases," and we took navy base rights on Cuban soil.

American diplomats like General Enoch H. Crowder in the early 1920s and Sumner Welles in the 1930s were seen as the powers behind several Cuban administrations. Threats of using American warships and sending in the Marines forced several governments to follow U.S. wishes regarding renegotiation of the lease for Guantánamo and the Platt Amendment.

This had to be galling to the Cubans who had fought for their independence. But from the Cuban standpoint, Americans were a lesser threat than the former Spanish rulers. After all, Spain actually had been the imperial force that colonized, occupied, bled and tyrannized the Cuban people for centuries. Spain had actually set up concentration camps and had a relocation policy to move tens of thousands of mostly tenant farmers to the cities. That turned the descendants of Spanish colonists into Cuban rebels in the same way that British tyranny turned its American colonists into revolutionaries in the 18th Century. This precipitated a failed insurrection, the Ten Years' War,[48] and the revolutionary 19th century Spanish American War.

Cubans complained that Spanish citizens immigrated to Cuba and took Cuban jobs. There was a continuing concern about Spanish influence in culture, politics and education. There were 184,374 Spanish citizens were registered in Cuba as Spanish aliens in 1956.[49] The number of Spanish aliens does not count those who had become naturalized Cuban citizens. During World War II, between 30,000 and 50,000 Spanish Falangists lived in

Cuba.[50] Many more were allied with Basque separatists, who continued to fight in Spain, and refugees from the Spanish Civil War included Communists and anarchists as well as Republicans and aristocratic monarchists, all opposed to the Falangists.

British and Canadian citizens also had extensive Cuban investments and were deeply involved in Cuban national security. Uranium had been discovered in Pinar del Río Province in 1957 and the Cubans were negotiating with the British to build a nuclear facility on site.[51] Although the plot in Graham Greene's comedy[52] *Our Man in Havana*, written during the same period, involves a supposedly preposterous idea that the British were worried about a nuclear weapon being built in Cuba during the period, it is possible that the British did send an MI-6 agent to Cuba to check on it. During the Spanish Civil War and World War II, Greene had been such an agent. Britain continued to sell tanks and planes to Batista for nearly a year after the U.S. had stopped.[53] Cuba was strategically important, and when Greene was in Cuba researching his book, Cuba had been negotiating in England to set up its nuclear plant. After January 1, 1959, Greene accused Britain of complicity with Batista.[54]

After independence, both the Cuban military and Cuban economic leaders chose to collaborate with the United States. They needed the security and the capital from the States. Successive Cuban governments were so unstable that on some occasions the government requested American troops. Stated U.S. policy toward Cuba was "nonintervention." The U.S. has aware that it appeared that we were closely associated with Batista and that he had some failings. By March 1958 the U.S. determined that the Batista government had violated the terms of the Mutual Assistance Treaty as the Cuban military used weapons provided under the treaty for offensive rather than defensive purposes. Among the weapons provided by the U.S. were land mines and other controversial weapons, including napalm bombs, known as liquid fire. Although Batista would no longer receive weapons, he remained free to use those he already had.

During the period, U.S. diplomats were presented with numerous reports of state-directed terror. Opponents to the regime would "disappear." Bodies would later be found beside highways and in alleyways, a warning not to cross the regime. A rebel woman held in police custody was reportedly brought one of her brother's eyeballs on a platter to her cell.[55] Other rebels reportedly were forced to watch as their wives were raped.[56] Thousands of Cubans immigrated to the U.S. with reports that Batista was a tyrannical totalitarian dictator. They reported incidents of brutality. For example, after the head of military intelligence was killed in 1956, agents led by Rafael Salas Canizares, head of the National Police, stormed the Haitian embassy to capture nine students who had been granted asylum there. Seven of the nine were shot on the spot. The other two were wounded. While they were in treatment, police officers cut their throats in front of several witnesses.[57] There were reports of hundreds if not thousands of explosions and other instances of sabotage in Havana and Santiago. Although it was not widely reported, the U.S. government knew that Batista barely withstood the 1956 mutiny by one of his most trusted officers, and 30 more were arrested and sentenced.[58] Batista also narrowly escaped the attempted assassination in March 1957 by students from the University of Havana.[59] Elements of the Cuban military mutinied the following September against Batista. Many more defected. Although the Cuban Constitution had outlawed the death penalty, many of the accused held in police custody were tortured and killed.

Despite reports of human rights abuses by the Cuban government, U.S. preoccupation with developments behind the Iron Curtain, the Mideast, China, the former Indochina, Korea, and Africa diverted our attention.

Chapter 6

Happy New Year 1959

January 1, 1959, rang in a happy new year for most Cubans. The population was optimistic that a tyrant would be replaced by a popular government that most probably would be democratic and restore the Cuban Constitution of 1940. The Constitution was in force during Batista's first presidency, 1940–1944. It was modeled in part after the U.S. Constitution, with three branches of government and a bicameral legislature, but the Cuban government also had aspects of a parliamentary system, partly due to the fact that Cuba had far more than two active political parties, and the government could be formed from a majority coalition of several political parties. In addition to the president, Cuba also had a prime minister. Half of the Cuban cabinet could simultaneously vote as legislators. The constitution incorporated social goals such as the elimination of discrimination by race, land reform, union rights, public education, minimum wage and other progressive ideas. Although Batista allegedly took over the government to protect the Cuban people from a dictatorship by the outgoing President Carlos Prío Socarrás, he immediately suspended portions of the same Constitution that he had taken credit for sponsoring and enforcing during his first regime. Batista's first act after taking power in 1952 was to increase military pay and the pay of the national police.[1] His authority came from them; he needed them more than they needed him. His leather jacket and his pistols became the symbols of that authority.[2] To most Cubans, Batista had fouled his own nest. A typical comment was that Batista's displacement "replaced indecency with decency."[3]

When Batista took over on March 10, 1952, the United States was engaged in the Korean War and the Cold War with the Soviet Union. The year 1952 was a presidential election year in the United States but at the time, it was not clear who the candidates would be. Incumbent president Harry S Truman had wintered in Key West, Florida, but that was as close to Cuba as he had ventured.

Besides Korea, his administration was also preoccupied with hot wars in French Indochina and North Africa that were on the verge of erupting into a worldwide conflict. The Soviets were believed to be making inroads in Latin America, especially in Guatemala, and Egypt and Syria appeared to be trending toward the Soviets. The U.S. was uncomfortable with the nationalism of an elected democracy in Iran. Truman was considering a run for reelection in the face of extremely low approval ratings. Factions in both parties attacked him for what they saw a the unchecked spread of Communism abroad and perceived influence, if not infiltration, spying and sabotage, at home. His administration did not pay much attention to Cuba. Truman's government recognized Batista within a few days. The Republican opposition, led by conservative senator Robert A. Taft of Ohio and retired general Dwight David Eisenhower, did not discuss Cuban policy during their primary campaigns, so it is perhaps reasonable to infer that both approved of Truman's policies regarding Cuba.

Although the Cuban Constitution may have been modeled after the U.S. Constitution, by 1940 it was tailored to fit a Cuban political reality that included aspirations of social justice and social welfare. Although Cuba maintained a congress and had the appearance of an independent judiciary that was supposed to represent a separation of powers, for all intents and purposes, democracy had ended in March 1952, with the military takeover by the second Batista regime. Batista depicted his coup as a "revolutionary movement."[4] After he regained power, Batista cancelled pending elections and jailed and exiled some of his adversaries. He governed as a despot, so that Cuba no longer had a balance of power between three branches of government. Acts of the Cuban Congress became mere formalities. Although Batista purportedly promoted open elections after the takeover, they were a sham, all form with little substance, as the general population did not support limited elections of candidates approved or tolerated by Batista. Almost all of the major political opponents of Batista refused to stand for election so long as he was in charge.

Although some of the Cuban political parties may have appeared to resemble the American political parties, in reality they were uniquely Cuban. They were far more parochial than U.S. parties, more issue oriented, and more uncompromising than the "big tent" parties in the States. Cuban politics and political parties consisted of active groups of true believers who ran the gamut from anarchists to communists,[5] to several varieties of socialists, to liberal republicans, to even monarchists and outright fascists, who needed to make alliances to become part of the government. Although most Cuban businessmen dressed like Americans and drove American cars and although many Cubans may have spoken English for business reasons and educated their children in English, as English was a path to success, the native language was Spanish. The native dialect was Cuban. There is a high degree of circumstantial evidence to show that although many Cubans of the period spoke English, they thought in Spanish, and were steeped in local culture, stewed in a cultural melting pot. This mix produced a communal inferiority complex that made them fiercely nationalistic. Many Cubans had a low threshold for indignities to their culture, such as attempts to Americanize them. Many Cubans were outraged that their country was openly sold by advertising Cuban hedonism, especially sexually oriented "adult" tourism, or that their country was perceived as open to American gangsters, gambling and prostitution.

Many Cubans considered their culture to be more refined and fully developed than U.S. culture. They were proud of Cuban style and considered U.S. culture too rigid, bland and simplistic. For example, although Cuban cuisine resembled Spanish food to an outsider, and may have been influenced by American tastes, it fed a uniquely Cuban appetite derived from local flora and fauna, seasoned for a spicy Cuban palette. Although Cuban music was also popular in the United States, Cubans naturally had a greater identity and understanding of it proudly extolled the fusion of the music of several cultures: classical European symphonic music, Afro-Cuban music, Spanish music ranging from folk songs to flamenco to Gypsy music, fused with American jazz and popular music. Most symbolic was that although the two countries shared baseball as a national pastime, in Cuba baseball was a symbol of independence from Spain, but it was also a symbol of dependence on the United States.

Moreover, most Cubans felt that Batista could not have taken over the government and retained power without U.S. support. Batista's last act as president was to hand power to a junta of generals, led by General Eulogio Cantillo.[6]

At that time, Fidel Castro was in Oriente Province, hundreds of miles away, and was upset that the revolution might have been undermined by a military coup.[7] On the radio from Santiago, Castro shouted, "Revolution, yes! Military coup, no!" He announced a general strike.[8]

Meanwhile, in Havana, Carlos Piedra, Chief Justice of the Supreme Court and next in the line of succession, published a notice of a cease-fire and offered the position of leadership to Colonel Ramón Barquín, who had led the failed Puro mutiny against Batista in 1956, and who was fresh from prison.[9] General Eulogio Cantillo, military chief of staff, also issued a cease-fire order to the Cuban military and political prisoners were released.[10] Cantillo then tried to appoint Barquín to head the military. However, Barquín, still dressed in his blue prison uniform, arrested Cantillo and announced that he supported M–7–26.[11] The revolution had succeeded.

It really was a most joyful 1959 New Year for most Cubans. In Havana, church bells pealed and car horns tooted the news. People rushed into the streets, set off fireworks and shot guns into the air. Flag-waving, cheering residents wore red and black, the colors of M–7–26. Some marched through the streets while others danced in mile-long conga lines. It was a carnival-like atmosphere, as drummers beat out Afro-Cuban rhythms and other musicians appeared to be playing "Guantanamera" almost everywhere. Some revelers got carried away, and some glass windows were shattered and there was some looting. Havana's entire inventory of parking meters was destroyed by decapitation, and a couple of the large casinos were ransacked. Most people were gleeful though, and despite the absence of the police, order was soon restored.[12] As soon as the people were told that Castro had decreed a general strike, all commerce stopped and the crowds diminished.[13]

It would take five days for Fidel Castro to travel to Havana from Santiago. By that time many Havana residents had been whipped into an ecstatic frenzy. The *barbudos* (bearded troops), who preceded him into Havana were peaceful and were there to restore order. Castro's followers had spread his myth and his presence was anticipated. Thousands of copies of the formerly underground M–7–26 newspaper *Revolución* were distributed throughout Havana. They featured a portrait of Fidel Castro that used an artistic light effect sometimes used to depict Catholic sainthood, captioned in part, "May God continue to illuminate him."[14] Castro was physically imposing: he was more than six feet tall and he had an athletic demeanor and a stage presence. Radio and newspapers amplified tales of his intellect, cunning and courage. Every day, his arrival appeared imminent and anticipation increased. During his journey, he had been followed on television and had addressed the public several times on *Radio Rebelde,* the short-wave radio station run by and for M–7–26; he had been seen and heard by almost the entire population of Havana. To some, the trip to Havana was like a religious procession.[15] A *Washington Post* editorial compared him as David to Batista's Goliath.[16] His speeches expressed a need for peace and calm. As Fidel Castro made his first address after his arrival in Havana to the people of Cuba on January 8, 1959, three white doves fluttered into view and one landed on his right shoulder.[17] By that time, there was sufficient evidence to show that Fidel Castro had become the greatest hero in the history of Cuba.[18]

Although President Eisenhower and the State Department also tried to express calm, U.S. Ambassador Earl E. T. Smith told the press that the United States was ready to evacuate Americans from Cuba. There had been assertions that if Batista were ousted, there would be a certain bloodbath against his collaborators and a civil war. Smith arranged for a cruise ship to travel to Havana, and he had car pools arranged to get passengers to the docks. Smith also arranged with M–7–26 to obtain permission for Cubana Airlines to take American passengers from José Martí Airport.[19] Although there had not been significant bloodshed at that point, and although the State Department had sent William Wieland, an Office of Middle American Affairs officer who had issued a November 1957 memorandum suggesting the U.S. mediate between Batista and the opposition to the scene to assess the matter, Smith said that he was considering evacuating 40,000 Americans from Cuba.[20] But consensus was that the U.S. would not evacuate if it meant a loss of assets in Cuba. Meanwhile, however, five navy vessels, three destroyers and two submarine tenders were sent to waters off Cuba as a precaution.[21]

Cubans were exhausted by war, corruption, and outright tyranny. A historic wave of emotion swept Cuba at the time. It is difficult to describe the passionate ecstasy of most Cubans at the departure of Batista. It was as if there was a rebirth of patriotism and for some, rapture, as revolution was promoted as a fulfillment of the prophecies of José Martí, Cuba's apostle and martyr. For many Christians, it was an epiphany comparable to Easter in January. Castro wore a cross and was Jesuit trained. One of his comandantes, a major in the Rebel Army, who was apparently in the high command, was a priest, Father Guillermo Sardiñas. Castro also had a personal chaplain, Angel Rivas Canepa.[22] As Castro gloried in his ascension from rebel outlaw to leader of his nation, the archbishop of Santiago, Enrique Pérez Serantes, stood on the victory platform with him in Céspedes Park in Santiago and blessed the proceeding, the gathering and the new government.[23]

For the many followers of the predominant religion, Santería, New Year 1959 is seen as a *bembe*, a ritual party celebrating the culmination of the ascendency of their philosophy if not their culture. Besides the cross, Castro and his men wore red and black armbands and red and black beads, colors associated with Changó, a Santería *orisha*. And to accentuate the point, Castro also wore an emblem of the Virgin del Cobre, Cuba's patroness saint, who is also viewed in Cuba as a Santería symbol.[24]

Castro had advertised that M–7–26 would restore the rule of law to Cuba. He maintained that he would accept the will of the people as long as democracy was restored. He emphasized that he did not want to lead. "Once we finish this war," Castro told Huber Matos, one of the other comandantes, "the military commanders cannot occupy political positions. We have to remain the moral guardians of the revolution. Our duty is to ensure that the promises to the people are kept."[25]

Under the Constitution, Castro was too young to become president anyway. Castro announced that the first provisional president would be Manuel Urrutia Lleó, a righteous judge who had to flee to New York for his life after having ruled against Batista many times, including issuing the release of several Granma survivors on the basis that those opposing Batista were doing so within rights to rebel granted by the 1940 constitution.[26] Urrutia's prime minister was José Miró Cardona, who had been president of the Cuban bar association and Cuba's most famous criminal attorney.[27] Neither was actually a member of the M–7–26 movement. Both had been affiliated with Civic Resistance, another anti–Batista, prodemocracy group. Their ascension symbolized a return to justice. By naming Urrutia and Miró, Castro dispelled some of the accusations that he was too close to the Communists. It was assumed that the 1940 constitution would soon be restored. It looked like elections would soon follow.

By 1958, the trend was that Latin American dictators were being removed by revolution. Prices of staples like coffee had been falling, which led to less political stability. Because the United States supported many of the dictators, it was often seen by the new regimes as opponents to democracy and reform. In order to combat that attitude, the U.S. State Department emphasized promoting American democracy. By January 1, 1959, the only Caribbean and Latin American countries still ruled by dictators were the Dominican Republic, Nicaragua, Haiti and Paraguay.[28]

Despite all the signs that the Batista government was finished, the White House was not ready for the new regime. Although the U.S. wanted Batista out, and although a change in leadership was expected, and although the State Department had made some plans for a peaceful change in leadership, the events did not turn out as anticipated.[29] The United States had been advocating for installation of a democratic regime after early 1957, but Batista refused to take warning. In November 1958, the State Department was supposed to tell the Cuban government that continued support would depend on support from most of the political groups in Cuba, including some nonviolent opposition groups who acquiesced to leadership by M-7-26, the Castro-led coalition group.[30] That group ascended to power on New Year's Day pretty much by default. Batista turned power over to a military junta, and in turn they also fled. Had the U.S. State Department executed a final, unequivocal timely challenge to Batista or Roberto Rivero Agüero, Batista's handpicked successor, things might have turned out differently. However, the news was not immediately relayed by Ambassador Earl E. T. Smith, who went back to Washington for clarification after he read his instructions.[31] It is now clear that he favored Batista and failed to carry out his duty as directed. But Batista had also received pressure from many other sources, including his own military high command. This will be discussed later. By the time Batista fled, there were several contingencies planned for Batista's succession, but none of them addressed what actually occurred.

Most of the Cuban population was also unprepared. On December 31, the *New York Times* stated that Batista would hold on until February 24, when he was to cede power to Agüero, but noted this was problematical.[32] There had been a report that two Kentucky schoolteachers were arrested and roughed up by the Batista government for having shouted pro-Castro slogans while at the airport. The teachers were released after protests by the U.S. government.[33] The State Department also announced that although there had been some calls to mediate the Cuban Revolution, we would keep a "hands off" policy.[34] But the *Times* also reported that Batista had sent two of his sons to New York.[35] By the time that this news was delivered to Havana, Batista had already fled. Although there was fighting in the provinces, there were no reports of any fighting in Havana, although a powder magazine had been blown up across the bay from Havana.[36]

The U.S. had mediated when President Gerado Machado, the would-be "Mussolini of Cuba," was in power (1925–33) and Cuba was threatened with civil war. In reality, the U.S. used its position as an intermediary between opposing Cuban political groups to dictate Cuban domestic policy, and forced Machado to step down. This followed the ascension of Batista and the Sergeants' Revolt. After the U.S. installed a government more amenable to U.S. policies, the U.S. instituted the Treaty Between the United States of America and Cuba, signed on May 29, 1934. Although the treaty ended the U.S. right to directly intervene in Cuba, it extended the U.S. rights to the naval station at Guantánamo.[37] On January 1, 1959, that treaty was still in force and Guantánamo was seen as an entré into further American intervention in Cuban affairs. On March 7, 1952, the U.S. entered into a military assistance treaty with Cuba.[38] Millions of dollars would soon be forthcoming. Batista initiated his coup a few days later. It is reasonable to assume that the timing was not mere coincidence. Although the U.S. had been supplying the Batista regime with millions of dollars' worth of arms and munitions under that treaty, in early 1958 Batista had violated the terms by using supposed defensive weapons during offensives against Cuban rebels. As a result, the U.S. insisted he relinquish power. Given that history, neither Batista or the rebels wanted the U.S. to mediate.

Although President Eisenhower probably had been given the news on New Year's Day, he had other matters of state to consider. He was watching a football game on television at his farm in Gettysburg, Pennsylvania, when he received a telegram from Nikita Khrushchev, the Soviet premier, wishing him a happy new year and world peace. He returned the message, but discussed the issue of the day: containment of Communism. There is no indication whether Cuba was discussed. The Soviets wanted to make Berlin a "free" city. The Cold War was on; Germany was divided into two countries. Berlin stood alone, and the United States, Great Britain, France, and the Soviets had been administering zones under treaties negotiated at Yalta, Potsdam and by the United Nations. If the people of Berlin had free elections, the Soviet proposals would most probably have meant that Berlin would come under Communist control and eventually would become part of Communist East Germany. Eisenhower sent a reply cable. He diplomatically told Khrushchev that peace was not consistent with taking over Berlin.[39] He then suggested a conference to discuss Berlin.

By New Year's Day, most American residents of Havana rode out the revolution like it was a typical tropical hurricane: they had stored supplies of food and water, remained shuttered at home and waited for the storm to pass. When Machado was toppled, there was a threat that United States would intervene.[40] Workers' strikes broke out. All over Cuba, armed gangs popped up, fought with each other for turf, and mobs looted and robbed at will. Thousands were killed. Machado supporters were summarily executed by impromptu firing squads. Lynched Machado officials hung from trees and light posts and cadavers rotted on the streets. Workers took over sugar mills and set up their own governments.[41] It seemed very possible that Cuba would turn to Communism.[42] In fact, in 1933, field and mill workers expropriated several dozen sugar mills and estates and set up 36 peasant councils, or soviets, modeled after the Russian model.[43] In many circles, it was assumed that if Batista left, the same kind of devastation would occur.

On January 1, 1959, an Associated Press headline trumpeted, "Agonizing Hour Has Come for Cuba After 50 Years." William L. Ryan predicted a "wave of bloodshed," fueled by "thousands of hotheads in Havana thirsting for revenge." "There are others, namely Communists, who could deliberately touch off the riots."[44] The Associated Press also ran a companion article by Ruben Batista, then age 25, son of President Batista, also alleging that without resistance, the Communists would prevail. He said he did not know what he would do, "but I will not sit around with folded arms and do nothing."[45] It was assumed that a civil war was imminent. At the time, the Associated Press was the largest news service in the world, and its articles ran in at least 1,500 American newspapers, including the influential *Washington Post*. The other wire services ran similar articles.[46]

Although there were some incidents of violence and damage, it wasn't anything like the repercussions from the fall of Machado or anything like the "bloodbath" or reign of terror predicted by Ryan and other American reporters. However, news articles accentuated the negative.[47] The Associated Press stated that the rebellion "may become [a] bloody riot in Havana."[48] Although the article reported that "Castro's troops" were rapidly moving into Havana, the first *barbudos* were actually from the "Second Front," which comprised mainly former students at the University of Havana, led by Eloy Gutiérrez Menoyo.[49] The next to arrive were from the DR, the Directorio Revolucionario, also mainly ex-students, who

Rebel leaders Ernesto "Che" Guevara and Camilo Cienfuegos flank incoming Provisional President of Cuba Manuel Urrutia Lleó in early January, 1959. Urrutia had been a judge who had ruled in favor of revolution, who had to flee to exile in New York. Installed by a coalition of anti–Batista groups, after an ecstatic period of social change, Urrutia Lleó was forced to resign his presidency in July 1959, after he accused the Communists of trying to take over the government (photograph from Getty Images).

encamped at the Presidential Palace and at the university.[50] These *barbudos* made a point of being courteous and friendly, and order was soon restored.

The American press did not discern that the *barbudos*, who wore olive drab fatigues and beards, were not under Castro's command. They did not have the same political orientation and did not have the same marching orders. In fact, the Second Front and the DR army, the Thirteenth of March Movement, might have acknowledged Castro as supreme commander, but only in a sense that he was the titular military leader. When it came to who was the *comandante* in the Escambray Mountains where the Second Front operated, Gutiérrez Menoyo and Chomón did not subject themselves to M–7–26's orders. Moreover, although Gutiérrez Menoyo and Chomón had once been close allies and both represented student-based organizations, they had broken with each other and were as jealous of each other as they were of Castro.

Eloy Gutiérrez Menoyo, el Gallego, then 24 years old, was born into a political family in Spain and spoke with a distinct accent. His father had been a founding member of the Spanish Socialist Worker's Party. A brother, José Antonio, was killed as a soldier in the Republican Army in Spain. Carlos, his older brother and mentor, was killed in the failed assassination attack on Batista at the Presidential Palace by student members of the Directorio in March 1957. Carlos was a veteran of the Spanish Civil War and had fought with the United States Army in World War II, as a tank commander in General Patton's Third Army, before coming to Cuba to become a student at the University of Havana.[51] Chomón was also one of the attack leaders, and although most of the DR leadership was killed, he was able to escape.[52] "Gallego" refers to Galicia, a province in Spain that produced, among others, Francisco Franco and Castro's father. The charismatic Gutiérrez Menoyo owned a popular bar in the Vedado area of Havana near some of the American owned hotels. Despite his young age, he was recruited as a leader by the underground. Although he had no military background, by the fall of 1957 he established the Second Front in the central part of Cuba, hundreds of miles from Castro's Rebel Army, which was then limited to the Sierra Maestra mountains in Oriente Province.[53] One reason that the DR chose the Escambray Mountains was to divide the Cuban Army's attention and make it send resources from Oriente. Another was that the area was remote, and particularly suited to wage a guerrilla war; it had few roads, and a mountainous topography filled with crevices, ravines and caves.

Chomón led a boat landing on the north coast of Cuba in February 1958. Eventually his force worked its way into the Escambray Mountains and joined with Gutiérrez Menoyo.[54] Chomón returned to Havana to work in the underground. He was the acknowledged secretary general of DR, and requested that some of the Second Front's weapons should be used in Havana. Gutiérrez Menoyo resisted, and after Chomón supported Rolando Cubela as leader of the Second Front, the two groups parted ways. Chomón, then age 29, remained the head of the DR and its army in the field, while Gutiérrez Menoyo led an independent group, the Secundo Frente Nacional de Escambray (SNFE), primarily funded by the Auténticos and former President Prío Socarrás.[55] Both of these groups were geographically much closer to Havana than the Rebel Army and that is why they were the first to enter the city.

Although it was not highly publicized, Gutiérrez's troops of the Second Front had also taken Trinidad and Cienfuegos, two of Cuba's principal and most strategic cities, from the Cuban Army.[56]

After New Year's Eve, tourists in Cuba for the holidays were anxious to leave. All of the stores and casinos were closed. On January 2, the ferry *City of Havana* carried 500 Americans to Key West.[57] On arrival some of the tourists complimented the revolution. "That was the most courteous revolution I ever heard of," said former Miami Beach mayor Abe Abramovitz. No Americans were killed or injured.[58] A *New York Times* editorial recognized that the policies of the United States had built up anti–American sentiment and noted that Cuba would need U.S. help desperately and it must be given with generosity and understanding.[59] On that day, Fidel Castro told the *Times* that his organization, M–7–26, had been fighting for "a democratic Cuba and an end to dictatorship."[60] U.S. newspapers and television were full of stories about Castro. In movie clips, he was photogenic, spoke soft accented English, and dressed for his role as a guerrilla in battle fatigues. He added, "We have no animosity towards the United States and the American people."[61] The next day, another *Times* editorial described Batista's government as full of "sadists and crooks" fattened on "graft and corruption." It asked for a "free, clean and democratic" replacement.[62]

On the other hand, the wire services interviewed Batista from the Dominican Republic. Batista denied that Castro and M–7–26 had forced him out. Batista actually passed the reins of power to a military junta, but they, like he, fled. He later said it was the Cuban Army that forced him out, but still later said that his aides had defected to Castro.[63] Associated Press stories told how three Associated Press employees were arrested and detained for 30 minutes for questioning by the rebels.[64]

For most Cubans, the revolution was an opportunity for celebration and self-expression, if not for self-determination. That meant less dependence on the U.S., despite close ties. For many it also meant an immediate lifestyle change. Suits were out. Fatigues were in. There was a promise of better times when people and businesses would operate free from institutional bribes, graft and corruption, but it also meant that every *bolita* (numbers racket) was out of business. It meant that the five largest *bolita* bankers went into hiding or were arrested.[65] It meant that the 20 percent "commission" taken by Batista cronies for every ticket and every prize was over.[66] Slot machines and other forms of gambling ceased immediately. And after *barbudos* arrived in Havana, and started to keep the peace, streetwalkers also disappeared.

After Castro entered Havana, Secretary of State John Foster Dulles remarked, "I don't know whether this is good for us or bad for us."[67] But on March 26, Allen Dulles informed the president that CIA information indicated a steady movement toward complete dictatorship on the island, with Communists "operating openly and legally in Cuba," although Castro's government was not Communist.[68]

Chapter 7

The Provisional Government

In their *Manifesto Against Tyranny*, written in 1957, Fidel Castro and Faustino Pérez called for a national strike followed by military action to overthrow Batista. Because they needed to promote a sense of unity among groups opposed to Batista, the manifesto argued that independent Judge Urrutia Lleó, who had ruled that insurrection against Batista was authorized by the 1940 constitution, should be selected as the provisional president of Cuba as soon as victory was won.[1] None of the other anti–Batista groups openly objected to Urrutia. At the time, M–7–26 was fighting for its survival, and any talk of victory was extremely problematical. They needed moral, but more importantly, monetary support, just to fight against far superior forces. At the time, Judge Urrutia was in New York, and could potentially raise funds for the cause.

By mid–1958 many of the erstwhile leaders of all of the other important opposition groups had been exiled to the diaspora.[2] Leaders of those groups met in Caracas, Venezuela, in July, to chart the future course of the insurrection. The communists were not part of the concerted opposition and did not send a representative. The coordinator or secretary was José Miró Cardona, dean of the Cuban bar association, professor of criminal law at the University of Havana, and the lawyer who had represented Colonel Barquín after his ill-fated mutiny attempt in 1956.[3] By the summer of 1958, Miró Cardona had been to Washington and was lobbying the State Department. He had an excellent reputation as a lawyer and as a scholar, made a good appearance, was well spoken, and had many well placed friends in the United States, and therefore his presence at the conference represented influence on Washington. He and Justo Carrillo Hernandez also aspired to be named provisional president, but after negotiations, the parties agreed on Urrutia.[4] The plan was to promote a general strike throughout Cuba followed by an armed insurrection, as described by Castro and Pérez in their manifesto, and because M–7–26 was still in active insurrection within Cuba, it would take the lead in forming a government. The parties agreed to establish a "brief" provisional government before returning to a constitutional democracy. The parties also produced a document requesting that the United States terminate all assistance to Batista.[5]

As a result, M–7–26 received financial support from the other groups, including the Auténticos in exile and deposed Auténtico president Carlos Prío Socarrás, who consensus said had enough resources to support a war by himself.[6]

On December 31, 1958, Batista fled to exile in the Dominican Republic.[7] On January 1, 1959, Urrutia was in Oriente Province conferring with Fidel Castro when he got the news. He had been living in Woodside, New York, and his wife and 14-year-old son were still there.[8] At first, Fidel Castro was concerned that the revolution had been undermined. Batista might have fled, but his Rebel Army had not won the guerrilla war.[9] In Havana, General Cantillo attempted to find someone to take Batista's place, according to rule of succession in the Cuban Constitution.[10] Although Chief Supreme Court Justice Carlos Piedra was next in line, he refused to cooperate.[11] On the radio from Santiago, Castro announced a general strike.[12]

Simultaneously in Havana, Justice Piedra and General Cantillo issued a cease-fire order to the Cuban military, and political prisoners were released.[13] Cantillo then tried to appoint Barquín to head the military. However, Barquín arrested Cantillo and announced his support for M–7–26.[14]

That day, the Cuban army ceded the city of Santiago to the Rebel Army. That evening Castro, Urrutia and Archbishop Enrique Pérez Serantes addressed a crowd in Céspedes Park in Santiago and proclaimed victory and the establishment of a new government.[15] Members of the Cuban military were told that as long as they had not committed crimes against the people of Cuba, there would not be reprisals.[16] Fidel Castro stated that the new revolution would not be like 1898, "when the North Americans came and made themselves masters of our country."[17] He told the audience that even if he remained head of the army, he would subjugate himself to the provisional president.[18] He took the title "Commander of the Cuban Land, Sea and Air Forces," and gave himself the rank of major. The national strike order was rescinded on January 4.[19]

A *New York Times* article said that Castro wanted an orderly change and speculated that one reason some of the casinos may have been ransacked was because M–7–26 opposed gambling.[20] The plan was to decentralize the government. Castro would move cabinet departments from Havana to provide an economic boost to the provinces. He would also lessen the power of cabinet officers in patronage and in influence over national affairs. He would have placed the Ministry of Mining in Oriente Province, the Ministry of Tobacco in Pinar del Río, the Ministry of Cattle in Camagüey, and the Ministry of Sugar in central Cuba. Newspapers speculated that decentralized power would make the government less prone to corruption, and any economic policy would be conservative.[21]

In Miami, Cuban exiles celebrated. At the airport 500 Rebel sympathizers demonstrated against arriving Batista government officials.[22] Demonstrators also protested arrivals in New Orleans and in Linden, New Jersey. In New York, a pilot alleged that he had been ordered to fly Batista cronies at gunpoint.[23]

U.S. Secretary of State John Foster Dulles was then age 70 and wracked with cancer. He was preoccupied with the Soviet Union and events occurring in such places as Berlin, Vietnam, Egypt and Iraq. The deputy undersecretary of state was Loy W. Henderson, who relied on the expertise of the undersecretary for Latin American affairs, Roy Rubottom, Jr., who relied on the experience of William Wieland at the Caribbean desk. Wieland had lived in Cuba on several occasions, was fluent in Spanish and had many local contacts.[24] The State Department did not have a clear indication of what was happening on the ground. Ambassador Earl E. T. Smith was seen as pro-Batista. The head of the CIA was John Foster Dulles's brother Allen. His chief expert on Cuba was Lyman B. Kirkpatrick, Jr., inspector general of the CIA, who had made three visits to Havana in 1956, 1957 and September 1958. He eventually determined that Fidel Castro was a revolutionary who originally had no precise political philosophy and, moved by circumstances, "turned Communist when the Communists seemed to offer him the most support."[25] However, at the time, the U.S. was uncertain of Castro's position.

Rubottom told the Senate Foreign Relations Committee on December 31, "It has been

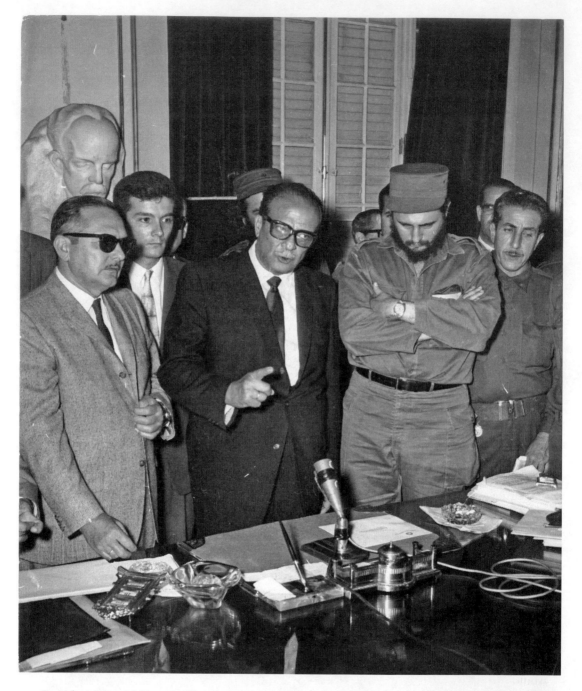

President Manuel Urrutia Lleó (left), Premier José Miró Cardona and Head of the Cuban Military Fidel Castro soon after installation of the Provisional Government in January 1959. Urrutia had been a judge and Miró, Cuba's most famous lawyer. Among his clients had been Ramón Barquín and several of the defendants from the Moncada uprising. Neither Urrutia or Miró had been members of M-7–26, Castro's insurrection organization, but they had been selected in mid–1958 when allied insurrection groups met in Caracas, Venezuela., They were installed in office by M-7–26 after Batista fled (University of Miami Libraries, Cuban Heritage Collection).

hard to believe that the Castros alone, that the 26th of July Movement alone could take over."[26] Later that day, at the White House, Rubottom met with Christian Herter, former governor of Massachusetts and now number two man at the State Department, and Admiral Arleigh Burke of the Joint Chiefs of Staff. During a heated argument with Admiral Burke, who argued that Castro was a Communist, Rubottom took the position that whatever Castro might be, American interests required a "third force" in Cuba "to defeat Castro politically."[27]

What Rubottom meant was that the United States should invest in seeing that an opposition party, friendly to "American interests," should immediately be cultivated. On January 2, former president Carlos Prío Socarrás arrived in Havana from exile in Miami. Colonel Barquín and Colonel Manuel Varela y Castro, acting heads of the Cuban military, arrested several "pro-Batista" members of the armed forces as a precaution. Both had been jailed by Batista early in his second regime for inciting mutiny and were fresh from prison themselves. Both alleged that they, like Fidel Castro, had no political aims.[28] Although it was assumed that there would be some resistance within the military, no incidents occurred. Soon Barquín and his fellow "incorruptible" military mutineers ceded power to M–7–26.

Castro told the press that "war criminals" had to be punished, that the U.S. military mission in Cuba should be withdrawn, that he opposed gambling,[29] and that Cuba should subsidize the Havana Sugar Kings, Cuba's baseball team in the International League that was heavily in debt and was threatening to leave for Jersey City, New Jersey.[30] He said that baseball would remain in Cuba, "even if I have to pitch."[31]

The leaders of the revolution all opposed corruption in government and opposed excesses in Cuban society, although they did not agree politically, as their allegiances ranged from radical to liberal to conservative. They also all brought a missionary zeal and a puritanical presence with them. For example, both President Urrutia and Premier Miró Cardona were staunchly opposed to gambling. Urrutia said that when he was in the United States, he had been offered $400,000 to lobby on behalf of continued gambling in Cuba. He turned down the offer.[32] A group within the Provisional Government was opposed to American tourism, because it thought that Americans came primarily for the gambling, prostitution and drugs — all opposed by the revolution, especially because young Cuban virgins from the country were reportedly enticed to wind up as prostitutes for tourists.[33] Castro made similar statements about the vices of gambling and even drinking alcoholic beverages. He contemplated banning both.[34]

Castro brought up the military mission issue repeatedly.[35] The missions were composed primarily by advisors who trained Cuban military troops how to use weapons the U.S. had supplied them. At most, 34 men were involved. Castro later would say that the mission was unnecessary, but "it would be discourteous for Cuba to ask anyone to leave the country."[36] By the end of the month, the missions were recalled.[37]

Archbishop Arteaga immediately rushed to visit Colonel Barquín at Camp Columbia military headquarters. It was apparent that he hoped that Barquín, rather than M–7–26, would ascend to power. In Washington, Ernesto Betancourt took control of the Cuban embassy for M–7–26, but when he asked to obtain the diplomatic files from Batista's ambassador, Nicolás Arroyo, Arthur Gardner, former U.S. ambassador to Cuba (1953–57), intervened, although he had no authority to do so.[38] As ambassador, Gardner was an open Batista advocate, and he was replaced by Earl E. T. Smith although he had asked President Eisenhower to remain.[39] But Betancourt was installed. "I have been too close to the [Batista] government," Arroyo told the *Washington Post* on leaving. Some Cuban ambassadors in other nations, such as Argentina and France, publicly congratulated M–7–26.[40]

Among those on hand to help requisition the embassy were exiled M–7–26 leader Javier Pazos, who had been captured by Batista but escaped to exile, and his 14-year-old brother, Felipe,[41] sons of Felipe Pazos, perhaps Cuba's foremost economist and the head of Banco Nacional de Cuba, Cuba's central bank under Prío Socarrás. Batista alleged that Javier was a terrorist who had bombed the Tropicana on New Year's Eve in 1956.[42] Both father and son were leaders of the underground, closely associated with Faustino Pérez, then Castro's principal man in Havana. The Pazos family had to go into exile after Felipe Sr. had openly associated himself with M–7–26. Pazos was generally considered conservative and pro-American, and some Americans ventured that Pazos should become the next president of Cuba.[43] Young Felipe, a celebrity in his own right, had been featured as the young boy in the movie version of Ernest Hemingway's *The Old Man and the Sea*, and was a student at Sidwell Friends School in Washington, Javier's alma mater.

Also present at the embassy to support the takeover were Cuban exiles Nicolás Rivero and George Perramon, who were interviewed by the press. Rivero had been a high-level diplomat removed by Batista and Perramon had been a Cuban air force officer jailed by Batista for refusing to bomb civilians during the September 1957 Cienfuegos mutiny. Perramon had been released after seven months in prison.[44] Later, Betancourt divulged that M–7–26 had had a spy at the embassy for several years.[45] A couple of weeks later, Ernesto Dihigo was named ambassador by President Urrutia. Dihigo had been minister of state in the Prío administration, and was well known in Washington.[46]

On January 3, Urrutia took the oath of office as provisional president at Oriente University in Santiago and swore in five of seven new ministers. Fidel Castro was sworn as commander in chief of the Cuban armed forces, and said that the constitutional guarantees suspended by Batista and the freedom of the press would immediately be restored. As his first act, he ordered the arrest of General Cantillo as a war criminal for permitting Batista to escape.[47]

Urrutia said that Cuba would file claims with the Organization of American States (OAS) against countries that sold arms to Batista.[48] The president said that, due to a history of coups and coup attempts, in the future the Cuban military would not be involved in Cuban politics. He reminded the country that Batista had led the Sergeants' Rebellion, and had taken power in 1952 by a *golpe de estado*.[49] He told a television interviewer that he had faith in the Cuban people and "the job of the new government won't be has hard as everyone believes."[50] Urrutia also added a new position to the cabinet: Minister of Recovery, in charge of confiscating stolen property. Dr. Faustino Pérez was given the assignment.

Although Urrutia was the president, Castro remained the center of attention. Whenever the press needed copy, Castro was available. He gave speeches, wrote letters and articles, and appeared on radio and television daily. He was especially accessible to the American press. Besides important reporters like Jules Dubois and Herbert L. Matthews, he was interviewed by Ed Sullivan, Jack Parr and Edward R. Murrow on CBS's *People to People*, and he appeared on NBC's *Meet the Press*, CBS's *Face the Nation* and many other American news programs. After he was frustrated by some negative reporting in the American press, he took his arguments directly to the American people. Despite protests like "I am not the Cuban government," and "I am a man, not a god," he soon became the petulant authority on all subjects.[51]

One persistent rumor was that Batista had stolen the entire Cuban treasury. There were reports that records showed that Batista had control over 40 domestic Cuban companies worth between $30–40 million.

Another rumor was that Castro enemy Rolando Masferrer had been stopped by United States Customs agents on his yacht in Key West and was found to be in possession of $17 million.[52] This was denied by the authorities, however. After a few days, the Immigration Service reported that Masferrer would be given a "hard look." He had been accused of murder and torture and the Cuban government requested extradition. In all, 312 Batista cronies had entered the United States and 172 had been granted visas by the embassy in Havana. Of these, 140 had no papers, 83 had been admitted on probation, and most were women and children.[53]

Castro named Argentine Ernesto "Che" Guevara as comandante of La Cabaña prison, which was filled with Cuban air force officers who had refused to bomb their fellow Cubans during the September 1957 Cienfuegos mutiny. Throughout the time that M–7–26 was engaged in the mountains in Oriente Province, allegations had spread that Guevara was a communist. He denied that he had ever been a communist. He addressed these concerns to Herbert Matthews of the *New York Times*. "Dictators always say that their enemies are communist and it gives me a pain to be called an international communist all the time. When a thing is said often enough, people begin to doubt and believe, as I think your State Department did."[54] However, Guevara openly advocated nationalization of Cuba's utilities and distribution of large estates to the *guajiros*. Although he was a foreigner, the Fundamental Law of Cuba was soon amended to grant Guevara full citizenship rights.[55]

Within the month, however, communists tried to take some credit for the success of the revolution. Severo Aguirre, a Cuban, told the Soviet Party Congress in Moscow that Communists were in "the first rank" of the revolution.[56]

Guevara was not alone on the defensive. Batista repeatedly had accused the entire revolution, Castro and M–7–26 of being communist. At the time, many Cubans saw the allegations as fuel to stoke the United States to send more arms. Several American congressmen and several American news sources continued to attack Castro on this basis or accused him of being manipulated by communists and the Soviet Union. On his way to Havana, Fidel Castro had reportedly told his close advisor Celia Sánchez that he was tired of Americans "twisting everything" he said.[57] In a discussion over whether there was a chance that the United States would militarily intervene, he reportedly said that if this occurred, "Two hundred thousand gringos would be killed."[58] A few days later, after he said the same thing in the presence of reporters, Castro had to acknowledge that he had made harsh statements against the United States, and he apologized. On January 15, in a speech at the Havana Rotary Club, Castro said that he did not believe that the United States would intervene in Cuba.[59] Castro later told NBC's *Meet the Press* that the U.S. should not have intervened in 1898. He said that the U.S. intervention took advantage of Cuban Independence. Had the U.S. lifted a ban on arms, Cuba would not have needed the United States to free itself from Spain. U.S. intervention gave "traitors," who had sided with Spain, an opportunity to save their property and become part of the government. Likewise, the U.S. gave Batista military support. Castro said that the United States perpetually threatened Cuba economically, most apparently through the sugar quota.[60]

Guevara was quoted by the *Washington Post* saying that "while the American government was giving arms to Batista, many members of the Communist Party were fighting Batista." He said that the communists had earned the opportunity "to be one more party in Cuba."[61]

Soon Camilo Cienfuegos arrived to take command of the Cuban Army at Camp Columbia, where his men were outnumbered by the incumbents by five to one. However, no incidents were reported. By day four after the revolution, it was reported that after

Batista fled, at least one naval officer was executed in Cienfuegos, site of the 1957 mutiny against Batista, and one army officer had been killed trying to escape.[62]

Police officers had been arrested but the Provisional Government said that most would be released after an investigation. However, those charged with killing and torture would be held for trial.[63] It was rumored that Juan Salas Canizares of the Cuban National Police had been executed for war crimes such as murder and torture of political prisoners. Searches were underway for officials of the Batista regime believed to be in hiding. Reportedly, at least three had been tried and executed.[64] The rebels were also rounding up candidates who had stood for election in November 1958 against orders from M–7–26 not be complicit with Batista by doing so. Several days later Urrutia announced that Cuba would honor a treaty of asylum and permit 300 former Batista government officials who were at foreign embassies the right to exile.[65] Batista's brother, Paciano Hermolindo Batista, had voluntarily turned himself in to the *barbudos*, but he was not charged and was released.[66]

Also named to posts in the Provisional Government were two Americans who had fought in the Rebel Army, William Morgan and John Spiritto.[67] Morgan was a comandante in the Rebel Army, and he was named military chief of Cienfuegos. Spiritto was named chief of Cumanagua. Morgan was an Ohio native who had served in the United States Army. After being dishonorably discharged, he led a colorful life as a drifter, and once was a fire eater in a carnival. After he arrived in Cuba he made his way into the mountains and eventually led a group of guerrillas attached to Gutiérrez Menoyo in the Escambray Mountains in central Cuba who were not under the direct command of Fidel Castro. Under Gutiérrez Menoyo, Second Front attacked the city of Cienfuegos. After a siege of several weeks, the Cuban naval command surrendered Cavo Cayo Loco Naval Base and the rebels took the city. In December 1958, Morgan's command joined forces with Guevara's M–7–26 column in the attack on Santa Clara. He and Guevara were the only foreigners to be given the rank of comandante by Castro.[68] However, he and Guevara had a history of competition, confrontation and threats.

Spiritto had also been in the Escambray with Gutiérrez Menoyo, and had served as a Captain in the Rebel Army. According to later reports, John Maples Spiritto, aka John Meckpless Espiritto, had been a CIA spy who infiltrated Cuba in 1958.[69] While serving as head of the highway patrol, he was convicted of murder by the Provisional Government for shooting a soldier who was firing a machine gun in a park.[70] However, he was given a suspended sentence with the provision that he remain in Cuba for one year.[71]

There were several other Americans in the Rebel Army. For example, Herman Marks, then 37-years-old, had been promoted to captain but was wounded late in 1958 and returned home for medical care. On January 5, 1959, Marks returned to Havana from Milwaukee, where he had been recuperating, and immediately went to see Che Guevara, his former comandante. He slept overnight at Guevara's house. The next day Guevara escorted Marks to General Headquarters and Captain Marks was assigned to take over the corps of guards and the security of the Rebel Army at La Cabaña Prison.[72]

Also, Neil Macaulay was a lieutenant in the Rebel Army. In *A Rebel in Cuba: An American's Memoir*, Macaulay describes his time as an officer, serving mostly in Pinar del Río Province. Another Rebel Army lieutenant, former United States Marine Gerry Holthaus, had deserted from Guantánamo, and took with him a jeep, rifles and ammunition. After serving in the Cuban National Police, he would later turn himself in to United States authorities.[73]

Other Americans, such as bush pilot Jack Youngblood, helped supply the Rebel Army.

Fidel Castro with American television impresario Ed Sullivan in early 1959. Castro appeared on television news shows like *Meet the Press* and *Person to Person* with broadcasting icon Edward R. Murrow. When he had difficulty impressing the U.S. government, he hired a New York public relations firm to improve his public image in the States (Getty Images).

"I have no loyalties. I just work for money," he later told *Time* magazine.[74] Several militant Catholics, such as Evans Russell, who worked under Raúl Castro in a clandestine munitions factory, also served.[75]

The *New York Times* noted that President Urrutia had not been part of Castro's organization per se; that he was "anti–Red" and was actually a member of the Civil Resistence Movement; that M–7–26 was not a homogeneous organization, but was composed of several different political groups; and that the revolution was not "the poor against the rich."[76] A couple of days later, the *Times* called Urrutia a man of ideals, honesty and courage.[77]

When asked about Cuban-American relations, Castro said that Cuba would respect the United States if the United States reciprocated. He also denied that the M–7–26 had any association with communists.[78] The communists took over a newspaper, *Replica*, but were ousted after complaints to M–7–26. They also took over headquarters of the construction workers and barbers' unions and several others but decided to vacate after they were physically confronted by armed *barbudos*.[79] According to an American who served in the M–7–26 underground, the communists had "no weight as a party." This American indicated that although some communists were in the Rebel Army, they "come as Cubans, not as communists."[80] It was assumed that the party had about 8,000 members.[81] Although the Soviet Union had made overtures, Urrutia later announced that Cuba had no plans to recognize the Soviet Union.[82] When Castro was asked, he said that the Soviet Union was a dictatorship and that Cuba should not have diplomatic relations with any dictatorship.[83]

Although the Provisional Government had not decided how to proceed with the United States, it had decided to sanction Britain for dealing with Batista. Castro told the press that the British would "pay dearly" for selling war planes to Batista to use against the rebels. The British said that the deal with Batista was only "partly completed."[84] However, by January 7, the British government recognized the Provisional Government,[85] and within a few days, Castro said that although he did not like the fact that the British government had sold arms to Batista, the Provisional Government would pay off any debt owed for them.[86]

On January 3, Carlos Prío Socarrás also arrived. He still considered himself as head of the Auténtico Party, and told members to "follow orders" of the Provisional Government. He noted, however, that no members of his party would become part of the government.[87] Castro and other M–7–26 leaders remarked that the party did not cooperate in driving out Batista. Within days, the Provisional Government decreed that all political parties were abolished. It was assumed by some in the U.S. press that this was directed to Prío.[88]

Although Castro had initially stated that Santiago would become the capital and that Urrutia would sit there, Urrutia arrived in Havana on January 5 and moved into the Presidential Palace. He was soon visited by Earl E. T. Smith, the U.S. ambassador, and by the Papal Nuncio.[89] The meeting between Smith and Urrutia turned "frigid" when Smith asked for an assurance that *Batistianos* would be given safe passage out of Cuba. When no assurance was given, and he was told that international law would be followed, Smith left abruptly.[90]

While en route to Havana, Castro gave daily speeches and press conferences and even appeared on Ed Sullivan's television show.[91]

In Havana, there was dissension reported within M–7–26 as members of the Directorio Revolucionario (DR), the students' organization led by Faure Chomón, who had objected after Castro had tried to name Santiago as capitol, objected to Castro unilaterally calling a strike after Batista fled. The DR was deployed at the University of Havana with 1,000 men and heavy arms and armored cars.[92] They also held the Presidential Palace. Although Castro recanted his positions on both issues, he ordered all groups, including the Directorio, to turn in their arms to the Rebel Army.[93]

Chomón had been one of the student leaders who attempted to assassinate Batista in March 1957, and he later was involved in espionage in Havana and in military operations in central Cuba.[94] Both the Second Front and the Directorio had been closely linked to Prío and the Auténticos for financial and moral support, but the operation in the Escambray Mountains had internal dissension.[95] However, DR was an integral ally with M–7–26, especially in Havana, its base of operations. According to Macauley, although Chomón was a leader of the DR he was never acknowledged as a comandante by Fidel Castro. Macauley describes how the Rebel Army and the students in Havana were in competition for power and says that Batista's greatest mistake was to close the University of Havana because this gave the students time to organize.[96] The students' uprising failed, but pressure from the underground was a factor in the abdication by Batista on New Year's Eve.

Castro accused Chomón of appropriating 500 rifles and machine guns and 80,000 rounds of ammunition from an armory at San Antonio de los Baños. He ordered Chomón and Gutiérrez Menoyo to disband their armies. All Cubans were expected to give up their weapons. They were also not to organize further at the University. Both Chomón and Gutiérrez Menoyo complied on the following day in the name of unity.[97] After Urrutia arrived in Havana, he made an appearance at the University in a gesture of unity. In his speech, he attacked "factionalism" but said that political groups were free to present their positions to the new government, and if the position was "in line" with the government's aims, the position would be deemed acceptable.[98]

The DR alleged that it had stopped an attempted assassination of Castro by five men, one of whom was the son of Mugardo Martín Pérez, head of Batista's National Police.[99]

Although they gave up control of the Presidential Palace and gave up their arms, some of the students complained to the *New York Times* that Castro was taking unfair advantage of the Cuban people's emotional state of patriotism and nationalism and his position as national hero.[100] "We are afraid that Fidel wants to run the show all by himself," an anonymous student asserted. "He has reached a stage of exaltation where he won't accept criticism and can't stand anyone disagreeing with him."[101] Students said that they wanted to work with the new regime, but that Castro was centralizing power in the military. "If he does this, he will be a military dictator, and we did not fight for this."[102]

Although the rebels maintained that they would soon restore the Constitution of 1940 and that the government would be democratic, all of the elected members of the government had run for office in the 1958 elections. The Provisional Government soon announced that it would be in place for 18 months. Castro had threatened that anyone who had cooperated with Batista in those elections would be barred for life from obtaining public office. Therefore, on January 6, 1959, the two houses of the legislature were dissolved and all provincial and local officials, including all governors and mayors, were removed from office.[103] Urrutia also abolished the Urgency Court, where he had been a sitting judge.

There were soon reports that some of Batista cronies and Cuban army officers had been executed. Ambassador Smith appealed to Camilo Cienfuegos to save General Cantillo. After a trial before a military tribunal, Cantillo was sentenced to 15 years' imprisonment.[104]

After Smith made a round trip to Washington, the United States recognized the Cuban Provisional Government on January 7, 1959.[105] The U.S. State Department told the press that usually it waited until a new government is viable before granting recognition. However, the State Department said it had been assured that Cuba's Provisional Government was stable because it contained representation from a broad range of anti-Batista groups, and recognized that some of the leaders were "men of stature" in their professions.[106]

Among those in the Provisional Government were:

- José Miró Cardona, Premier (Prime Minister). Besides his many personal accomplishments and the fact that he had been the coordinator of the Caracas Conference, Miró had been one of Castro's professors at the University of Havana and had been one of his mentors.[107] It was important that Miró was perceived as having influence in the United States.[108]
- Roberto Agramonte, Minister of Foreign Relations. Agramonte had been Ortodoxo candidate for president of Cuba in 1952 and may have been leading at the time of the Batista *golpe*. He was dean of the School of Philosophy and Letters at the University of Havana and was also a noted lawyer and law professor seen to be friendly to the United States.
- Justo Carrillo Hernandez was named president of the Agricultural and Industrial Development Bank. He held a similar position in the Prío government.[109] Carrillo had led the Montecristi movement, the Catholic moderate group that tried to negotiate with Batista, but by mid–1958, Carrillo became a cosigner of the Caracas Pact, and provided M–7–26 with needed financial help.

- Angel Fernández, Minister of Justice, was a lawyer and a close friend of Urrutia.[110] He had been a district attorney in Santiago.
- Luis Orlando Rodríguez, Minister of the Interior, had been an anti-communist student leader at the University of Havana, and later had joined M–7–26 in the field. He was the editor of the M–7–26 publication *Cubano Libre*.[111]
- Julio Martinez Páez, Minister of Health, had been a student leader opposed to Machado, and was part of the Havana underground until 1958, when he became a physician with M–7–26 in Oriente Province. He was a comandante in the Rebel Army.
- Raúl Cepero Bonilla, Minister of Commerce, had been a law student at the University of Havana at the same time that Fidel Castro was there. In 1948, while still a student, his book, *Sugar and Abolition,* was published. He had been a member of the underground in Havana and had been arrested several times. Cepero died at age 42 in a plane crash in 1962.
- Manuel Fernández García, Minister of Labor, was an accountant, a former follower of Antonio Guiteras Holmes, a former member of Joven Cuba, and a former follower of García Barcena, but by 1959 was a Social Democrat.[112]
- Armando Hart Davalos, Minister of Education, was 28 at the time. His grandfather was born in Georgia, and his father was a judge. Removed by Batista in June 1958, Davalos's father eventually on the Cuban Supreme Court.[113] Hart had been a follower of García Barcena and was closely aligned with Faustino Pérez in the Havana underground. By 1956 he was the titular head of the M–7–26 underground. He had been arrested several times and had served a year in prison but escaped. Soon after his appointment, he announced that surplus personnel would be dismissed and all textbooks would be revised.[114]
- Enrique Oltulsky, Minister of Communications.
- Faustino Pérez, Minister of Recovery of Stolen Property.
- Manuel Ray Rivero, Minister of Public Works.
- Rufo López Fresquet, Finance Minister. López Fresquet, a graduate of Columbia University, had positions in the Grau and Prío regimes and had been a columnist in the *Diario de la Marina* newspaper.
- Regino Boti, Treasury.

José Rego Rubio was named head of the army and Major Efigenio Ameijeiras was named chief of the National Police. *Barbudo* comandante Camilo Cienfuegos was named to head the army in the Havana region. He told the press that the military would be reformed, but that current members of the Cuban army who were innocent of crime would be retained.[115] Also named as heads of military regions were Raúl Castro in Oriente Province, Huber Matos in Camagüey, Calixto Morales in Las Villas, Dermitio Escalona in Pinar del Río and William Galvez in Matanzas.

Raúl Chibás, Angel Fernández Rodríguez, Humberto Sorí Marín, Agusto Martinez Sánchez, Elena Mederos, Luis Buch Rodríguez, and Gaspar Buch were named as advisors to President Urrutia.

Later a new Supreme Court was named, with Emilio Menéndez Menéndez as chief justice and Armando Hart Davalos's father, Enrique Hart, as one of the associate justices. The operation of the court system was suspended for 30 days so the new government would have a chance to choose new judges. In the interim, disputes were heard by military tribunals, under a procedure established when M–7–26 operated in "free" territory in Oriente Province that had been taken from the Cuban army during the two years of revolution.[116] Although the Constitution of 1940 had eliminated the death penalty, it was "amended" to permit executions for "repression and espionage" in wartime.[117] It would later add "war crimes," extortion, expropriation of government funds, and racketeering as capital offenses.[118]

The Provisional Government was filled by many professional men who had served in the underground in Havana and or had to flee, principally to the States. The FBI investigated and reported that Urrutia was anti–communist and anti–gambler.[119] Many of the members of the cabinet were appointed because they had influence in the United States. The Provisional Government was the latest in a long line of other "revolutionary" regimes, and it was hoped that they would rise to the occasion, but the conventional wisdom in Cuba maintained that the Americans were behind everything, and without U.S. support, this Cuban government would just become a footnote to history. As mentioned above, this was not mere paranoia, as the U.S. had intervened militarily. In the view of most Cubans, the U.S. made a good scapegoat for the corruption of the Batista regime.

Urrutia stated that foreign investments in Cuba would be protected because they were made to the benefit of the entire Cuban people. However, when Urrutia was asked whether gambling would be restored, he responded, "Absolutely not."[120]

Urrutia also formed the Department of Purification to root out "informers, grafters and others who lined their pockets under Batista." Because so many of the national police and other peace-keeping forces were in jail, the Ministry of the Interior set up a military police organization under Luis Orlando Rodríguez.[121]

On January 7, the Vatican recognized Cuba.[122]

The next day Castro arrived riding on a tank with fellow *barbudo* comandantes Camilo Cienfuegos and Huber Matos, his general staff. Church bells rang, guns were fired, including a 21-gun salute from the cannon at La Cabaña fortress and guns from warships in the harbor. Planes from the Cuban air force flew overhead, car horns sounded, and people shouted in glee.[123] After a confetti-filled triumphal trip from Camp Columbia to the Presidential Palace, Fidel Castro gave an emotional and inspiring two-hour speech from a balcony overlooking the plaza, accompanied by white doves perched on his shoulders. It was the first time he had ever been inside the palace. He said that there would be only one revolutionary organization, and that members of other anti–Batista groups should join with him. Any attempt to "break the peace is the greatest crime that can be committed now." He again asked all armed groups to disband and join forces with the Provisional Government. Regular army soldiers would remain at their posts, but "those who had committed crimes will face a firing squad."[124]

After his speech, Castro walked unescorted by security at the head of the procession for 10 miles from the palace to Camp Columbia, to show that Cubans were a disciplined people and "to show that not a single soldier is needed to keep me from the public."[125]

Although Urrutia and the Provisional Government were in power, Castro continued as the main attraction for the American media. He appeared on CBS on January 10 to again say that most Cubans were complying with his request that they give up arms. When asked whether American business would be adversely affected by new regulations, he said that American businesses would have no problem, "if they agree with the law."[126] However, he again stated that American gambling interests "would encounter trouble."[127]

Although Castro and Urrutia had condemned factionalism and asked political parties to disband, the Communist Party was recognized.[128] When asked, *barbudo* Camilo Cienfuegos, now commander of the Cuban army in Havana Province, said that although Communism was not a crime, he had three or four communists serving under his command, "if the Communists violate democratic principles or threaten the interests of the nation, we would have to take proper action."[129] Castro said that the communists were recognized when all of the freedoms that existed prior to Batista were restored. He said that Cuba has nothing "to fear from the Communist Party as long as it adheres to the laws."[130]

The *New York Times* reported that the Communists would form an opposition party to challenge the Provisional Government (that is, Castro) for power and that some of the older students were talking of forming a "liberal" opposition party.[131] Within days, the National United Labor Front was formed, supposedly representing 1.2 million Cuban workers. Although the head of the organization was David Salvador, who was seen as anti-communist, Communists immediately became a part of it and received three seats on a 15-man board.[132] After the party was recognized, the first communist rally drew about 130 people.[133]

Tourism had fallen off, and Castro said that he wrote a letter requesting a resumption of tourism from the United States. He said that he wanted tourism to benefit all Cubans, "and not just a few businessmen." Although some gambling might have been necessary to attract tourists, he felt it must be kept out of the hands of gangsters. He signed a letter to American businessmen, "to come back to Cuba with the assurance that they will be welcomed by all citizens of our country."[134] Rofo López Fresquet, minister of finance, appeared on ABC television with Castro and stated that American investments in Cuba were safe, but that businessmen should come to Cuba with a "democratic spirit." Both stated that Batista ha stolen huge sums of money. Fresquet put the figure at $500,000,000 and Castro said it might have been even higher.[135]

A *Washington Post* editorial on January 10 objected to postponing elections for 18 months and to "a program of vengeance" against members of Batista's military. The newspaper also congratulated the U.S. State Department for recognizing the Provisional Government, but said that it should remove Earl E. T. Smith as ambassador because of his close tie to Batista.[136] The same edition showed two pictures of a man who had been chief of police under Batista being executed in Santa Clara: in one panel he is marched to the firing squad, in a second, his hat flies off as he is shot.[137] The *New York Times* and its reporter Herbert L. Matthews compared the Cuban revolution after 10 days with other Latin American revolutions and found that the Cuban version was conservative, which was noted as ironic because Batista and his supporters had accused Castro and his followers of being communists.[138] Matthews reported that Castro did not ask for a position in the Provisional Government and recited the life accomplishments and political positions of Urrutia and his ministers. Matthews also noted that Castro started as a radical but was educated while he was alone fighting the Cuban army in the mountains. He determined that the communists would become an opposition party: "They tried to get on the Fidelists bandwagon toward the end [of the Revolution] but were rebuffed and they will be given no chance ... to be an important part of the Provisional Government."[139]

Matthews noted that the Cuban people had never seemed so unified. However, he warned that "Cubans are a fickle and volatile people in a political sense, and this honeymoon will not last forever."[140]

Many American businessmen in Cuba had benefited from Batista and believed stories that Batista had spread naming Castro and his followers as communists. Matthews determined that if the Provisional Government were able to eliminate much of the graft and corruption that persisted under Batista, some of the American business community would be "unhappy. Moreover, a democratic government is never so easy to deal with as a dictator whose sole word is law."[141]

Matthews further noted that reports of the executions were "exaggerated." He noted that they were proportionately few, and known "torturers and wanton killers" had been executed, "but this has nothing to do with opposition to the new government."[142] However, the next day, his paper ran a front page story alleging otherwise. So did the *Washington Post*, which alleged that 75 people had been executed in Santiago.[143] The *Post* reported that most of the trials had been held in secret, and occurred in two groups: one of 14 and the other 61. Unidentified eyewitnesses said that bulldozers had built a 40-foot trench at a rifle range, and after receiving their last rites from priests, the condemned stood at attention without blindfolds to be mowed down by automatic weapons and rifles. The report also stated that all of the executed were men, and that Batista government police executives, secret agents and police informers had been executed. As of January 12, 1959, about 130 executions had occurred.[144]

On American television, a uniformed Castro stated that although thousands of prisoners had been captured during the war, "We never killed anyone, never tortured anyone," he told the American audience in English.[145] There had been accusations that 75 executions had been performed at one time, and there had been some congressional protests over executions.[146] Senator Wayne Morse of Oregon, chair of the Senate Foreign Relations Committee, asked Cuba to suspend the executions until emotions cooled. Morse had been a vocal critic of the "fascist" Batista regime.[147]

Castro spoke in English, but at times conferred with an interpreter. He maintained that all executions had followed fair trials. "We would never punish anybody without a trial," he told the American public on CBS's *Face the Nation*. He tried to appear as friendly as possible; he may have been wary that the United States could intervene militarily.[148] All of the executed had been tried by military tribunals; according to Castro, every one of the executed had been easily proven guilty. After 3,000 cheering spectators turned the execution of six men by firing squad into a spectacle, the Cuban army decided that spectators would be banned, as such spectacles did not "conform with our culture."[149]

Castro made a point of distinguishing the American people from the United States government. He said that he was impressed by the Americans he had met and was also impressed with American's stated aims of democracy, but that the government "forgets about the democratic feeling of the people of Latin America." He reminded the audience that the U.S. had provided arms to Batista until March 1958, but also said he was grateful for recognition of the Provisional Government by the U.S. government.[150]

The military tribunals held trials in lieu of revolutionary courts which had yet to be established. President Urrutia sanctioned the military tribunals until that time. The courts consisted of two Rebel Army officers and one civilian, and all defendants were represented by counsel. Urrutia admitted that executions had occurred but alleged that all were for war crimes. Although some of Batista's cronies were in custody and some political arrests had been made, no civilians had been executed. The president said that about 1,500 members of Masferrer's private army, the Tigers, accused of torture and murder, were being hunted in Oriente Province. Approximately 100 others were killed while trying to evade capture.[151]

Likewise, the head of the Cuban army in Havana Province, Camilo Cienfuegos, invited American newsmen to witness the trials for themselves. He also said that the only executions were for torture and killing.[152]

Castro later told the press that despite the U.S. protest, the trials and executions would continue. He said that the people who protested the executions did not protest when Batista tortured and killed innocent Cubans. He reminded the Havana Lions Club and the assembled press that 53 demonstrators were killed by the police in Havana's Central Park, 450 innocent people were killed in Bueycito, Oriente Province, and hundreds more in Ojo de Agua.[153]

A *New York Times* article described a trial in Santiago, where four defendants were tried and convicted. The prosecution presented witnesses, and the accused were given an opportunity to testify and to call defense witnesses.[154] The next day, Castro said that 100 more trials would take place at La Cabaña prison in Havana. All would be open to the public, including the American press. He said that after conviction, "We have given orders to shoot every one of those murderers, and if we have to oppose world opinion to carry out justice we are ready to do so."[155] A few days later, he told the Rotary Club that the military tribunals were the same as war crimes trials that the United States had participated in after World War II and that the U.S. had also participated in hanging the guilty.[156] He later estimated that eventually there would be a total of approximately 450 executions.[157]

Minister of Interior and Minister of Defense Luis Orlando Rodríguez told the press that there had not been any mass executions as reported in the American news, and accused the U.S. media of issuing false reports.[158] It was reported that over 100 defendants held in La Cabaña prison in Havana had admitted their crimes and more than 600 would come to trial. Carlos Franqui, press coordinator, said that in order to show that the rule of law was being carried out consistent with the Nuremberg trials after World War II, the press and television crews would be given full access to the trials, and that full access to interview all of the parties would be given, including the accused and their families.[159] Within a few days, people stayed peaceful demonstrations urging Urrutia to continue to support the trials and executions.[160]

Father Jorge Bez Chabebe, a Catholic priest who had been part of Civic Resistance in Santiago, told the press that there was an urgency for quick executions: "To avoid a return of these people to power."[161]

Castro reiterated to Matthews that he had no plans to run for president of Cuba. He also said that he planned to cut the Cuban military from 39,000 troops to 20,000. He later said that he planned to relieve the army from having to provide police protection, and that he would bring in the Royal Canadian Mounted Police to train the National Police and the Rural Guard.[162] He told Matthews that his job would be daunting. He had no privacy. "I haven't had a minute to myself. They won't leave me alone. There are thousands of things I know nothing about." As they spoke, several constituents from Santa Clara had waited 32 hours outside his apartment at the Havana Hilton. "These are my comrades in arms whom I've been trying to see," he told Matthews.[163] He was obviously pressured.

The same day, Ambassador Smith resigned. President Eisenhower accepted it "regretfully." However, a number of complaints had been filed against Smith and the United States embassy in Havana for their apparent support of the Batista regime. Two congressmen had demanded the resignation, one describing Smith as "100 percent pro-Batista."[164] In his letter accepting the resignation, President Eisenhower stated, "We all earnestly hope … that the people of that friendly country, so close to us in geography and sentiment, will through freedom find peace, stability and progress."[165]

On January 13, it was announced that Philip Bonsal would be named ambassador to Cuba. He had been a vice consul in Havana in the 1930s and had been ambassador to

Bolivia.[166] After he was appointed, a *Washington Post* editorial asked the United States to be patient with Cuba.[167]

Meanwhile, Castro had decided that Cuba needed cash flow and that moral objections to gambling were outweighed by the need for cash.[168] Within a few days, Castro announced that the casinos could reopen, but that only foreigners would be permitted to gamble, gangsters could not manage the casinos, and the casinos were subjected to a "high tax."[169] This position was not unanimous, because Premier Miró Cardona told the press at the Rotary Club that "if tourism depends on gambling, we do not need tourism."[170]

In order to avoid the appearance that the U.S. was fortifying Guantánamo, the U.S. Navy decided to forgo an exercise that would have brought 3,000 Marines to Cuba.[171] Simultaneously, former Batista ministers and allies who were given amnesty in foreign embassies were permitted to leave the country. President Urrutia told the press that human rights would be respected. By the end of February, almost all had been given safe conduct.[172]

However, the Provisional Government named Osvaldo Dorticós Torrado, another former president of the Cuban bar association, as minister to "consider the authority of the Laws of the Revolution." Among other laws that were "amended" were the death penalty — reinstated for certain crimes; ex post facto applications of criminal violations were suspended to exclude collaboration with "the tyrant"; confiscation of property from certain criminals was authorized; and candidates who participated in Batista's phony elections were banned forever from holding public office.[173] Dorticós Torrado and his committee approved the amendments. Miró Cardona and Urrutia both argued against the amendments but were outvoted. Miró Cardona threatened to resign, but was talked out of it.[174]

On January 13, there were calls in Congress for an investigation of the executions in Cuba. Representative Benjamin Celler of New York, asked for a United Nations investigation of the executions, and Representative William L. Springer of Illinois stated that there had never been "such a bloodbath" when a dictator rose to power. Representatives Charles O. Porter and Adam Clayton Powell argued that there was no proof of any bloodbath and asserted there had been no due process violations.[175] During the debate, Representative Powell charged that the U.S. was sending Marines to Haiti in a deal with Dominican dictator Rafael Trujillo, who was afraid that Haiti would be the source of an attempt to attack his country.[176]

On January 18, the *New York Times* ran an editorial stating that although the paper still supported the revolution, the luster was lost due to the executions.[177] On the same day, the *Times* described the executions in Santiago as a "purge," evoking the era of show trials and executions in Soviet Union in the 1930s.[178] The article described the five-hour trial of a former Batista aide presided by three *barbudos*. "Spectators crowded into a makeshift courtroom. Witnesses for the prosecution and defense testified…. Then the judges rendered their verdict: 'Guilty!' The prisoner was immediately escorted to a field outside. He confessed to a Catholic priest; he was given a lighted cigarette. Then he was shot. His body toppled backward into an open pit." The nature of the crime was not mentioned in the article, but stated that the scene represented "scores" more and repeated the "bloodbath" language. It did say that the U.S. State Department, through Roy Rubottom, Jr., assistant secretary of state for interamerican affairs, did not want the United States to appear to interfere in Cuba.

The *Times* also ran a headline that read: "rabbi deplores Castro revenge," and an article quoting a rabbi, who inferred that the trials and executions showed that Castro might be another Batista, and who called for leaders of other American religions to protest to Castro "grave errors of the infant regime."[179] The *Times* reported that newspapers in Argentina,

Ecuador, Brazil, Peru, and Costa Rica had called for a halt to the executions and that Uruguay had brought the matter to the United Nations.[180] However, Cuban Catholic priests and Protestant ministers protested the protests and asked that the trials and executions continue. They sent a telegram to President Eisenhower, stating: "The international press has paid no attention to the moral reforms, the order, and the renewed faith in the government which has surged forth with the new regime."[181] The Cuban Knights of Columbus and the Catholic magazine *La Quincena* published an editorial espousing the same view.[182] Castro said that he would like to send Cuban mothers who had lost children to reported Batista torture to Washington to show the need for justice and closure, and many black-clad women supported his appearances in appearing in force in the audiences.[183] Almost all of the accused in trials in Havana had been charged with murder.[184]

Castro asserted that the objections from Congress were a first step in an attempt to re-institute the Platt Amendment.[185] Although Castro invited several congressmen to Cuba to see things for themselves, almost all refused. Senator Morse accused Castro of "perpetrating jungle law" and Senator Homer Capehart of Indiana accused Castro of asking him to participate in a "stunt." He said, "The fellow [Castro] is getting more ridiculous all the time."[186]

On January 21 Castro held a huge rally in Havana. Standing with him on the podium were United States representatives Charles O. Porter and Adam Clayton Powell, who had accepted his invitation to come to Cuba. About 250 newsmen also had come to Cuba as guests of the Cuban Army, 90 of whom were American. Schools, factories and most business establishments had closed for the day and there were perhaps a million spectators. Although the crowd was friendly, some communist banners read "Down with Yankee Imperialism" and "No to Foreign Interference," and there were hundreds of other signs supporting trials and executions.[187] Castro told the vociferous crowd that Batista had been Cuba's Hitler and that he would ask the Dominican Republic to extradite him for war crimes. Castro also told the crowd that Cuba would not have to answer to the United States for the execution of convicted war criminals. His statement, "Our explanation will be given to the people of Cuba," was met with thunderous shouts of approval. The inference was that it was none of the United States' business. "One million Cubans of all ideals and all classes have voted as a jury," he responded. He asked the United States to return war criminals for trial: "These are not political refugees, but common criminals." Specifically named were: Rolando Masferrer, whose private army, the Tigers, was charged with thousands of crimes; Esteban Ventura, a former police colonel and reputedly the most hated man in Cuba; Pilar García, former head of the National Police; and General Francisco Tabernilla Doltz.[188]

The next day, the first public trial in Havana was held. Three defendants accused of 200 murders were brought before a military tribunal and 18,000 "frenzied," screaming justice fans in the Sports City Stadium. The military tribunal consisted of *barbudo* comandantes Humberto Sorí Marín, Raúl Chibás, and Universo Sánchez. Sorí Marín had been a distinguished Catholic Auténtico lawyer and Sanchez had been a small businessman before they joined M–7–26.[189] Chibás was Ortodoxo founder Eddy Chibás's brother. As the accused were led into the dock in handcuffs, the fans booed and jeered, some chanting "kill them" in unison. Although *barbudos* tried to provide security, some of the crowd made moves to attack the defendants. The court officers spoke over microphones, but the shouts from the crowd drowned them out. The prosecutor was a *barbudo* and the defense attorney, appointed by the court, was a former member of Batista's Cuban army.[190]

The first defendant, Major Jesús Sosa Blanco, was accused of 108 crimes in Oriente

Province. He told reporters that his captors had treated him well. Hundreds of witnesses had been brought from Oriente Province and were available to testify. The first witness testified that the major had killed a family of nine people; the second that he had killed another 43 people in one day. The prosecutor read the major's military record into evidence: while in service he had been accused of numerous murders but had never been found guilty, and was promoted despite the charges. Sosa Blanco had been a member of the Rural Guard, a national police force, who had received promotion to general. He had been accused as the leader of "massive attacks" against civilian targets, including wiping out the town of Levisa.[191] A parade of 42 other witnesses testified accordingly. Periodically the crowds were so threatening that the court had to send *barbudos* into the stands to restore order. When one witness was asked by Attorney Acosta if he had actually seen the killings, he replied that he had not, because if he had, he would have been one of the dead.[192] In his defense, Major Sosa Blanco testified that he had been a mere soldier performing his duty. However, eyewitnesses saw him shoot 19 people. A woman testified she saw him shoot her husband. Sosa Blanco was guilty, but there was a question as to what law should be applied and whether the evidence was sufficient to warrant a death penalty.

Although the American papers did not publish it at the time, Sosa Blanco actually admitted to killing 108 people, and said that he would do it again given the opportunity. His defense was that he was merely following orders from his command. Among the witnesses was an 11-year-old boy who had escaped death only because his parents and siblings had covered him in a pile of bodies, and he had been left for dead. He identified Sosa Blanco as the man who had come to his hut and set his house and the family on fire.[193]

Acosta argued that Sosa Blanco could not be tried under the recent modification of the Constitution, because the alleged dates of the crimes predated the Fundamental Law. Section 25 of the Constitution of 1940 had eliminated the death penalty and Section 21 barred ex post facto application of law. That would make prosecution via ex post facto laws unconstitutional or at least unenforceable. The court ruled that the operative law was military law passed by M–7–26 in early 1958, which provided for the death penalty in certain cases such as war crimes, and the Constitution had been amended by the Fundamental Law.[194] The defendant objected that the law had not been the announced basis for the prosecution prior to trial, and a sentence of death was not universally applicable at that time. At 6:00 a.m., the verdict of guilt was rendered and Sosa Blanco was sentenced to die. A rowdy crowd of about 4,000 remained, cheering wildly. As Sosa Blanco was removed, some of the crowd tried to encircle him, but *barbudos* held them off. The trial of the two co-defendants was postponed. They, too, needed to be protected from a crowd that looked like a lynch mob. Major Sosa Blanco called the trial a circus, and the American press and several important members of Congress agreed.[195]

Castro objected to the reporting. Castro would say later that Congress "vilified" Cuba and would have to change its policies and the American press "engaged in a criminal campaign to defame" Cuba.[196] Congressman Porter told the press that Sosa Blanco "deserved it," and that the United States' reaction was "half cocked."[197] Congressman Chester Bowles, a former governor of Connecticut and ambassador to India, wrote a letter to the *New York Times* echoing Porter's sentiments.[198] Sosa Blanco appealed his case to a five-man Supreme War Council, but it was a foregone conclusion that the sentence would be affirmed.[199]

Later, Castro said in a press conference before 350 foreign news reporters that the executions would be suspended as soon as the major war criminals were tried. He circulated pictures of mutilated bodies of Cubans killed during the Batista regime.[200]

On January 23, Castro traveled to Venezuela where he received a hero's welcome from General Wolfgang Larrazabel, one of the members of the junta that overthrew Marcos Pérez Jiménez, the former dictator. Castro thanked the crowd for the welcome. He told them, in part, that progress in Cuba was impossible as long as the United States had the power to intervene in Cuban affairs. He also told them that freedom should be extended to other Latin American countries, and "dictators should be expelled" from the Organization of American States. In particular, he stated that Rafael L. Trujillo of the Dominican Republic was attempting to form a "Continental Dictatorship" and that dictatorships in the Dominican Republic, Nicaragua and Paraguay should soon fall.[201] When asked whether he would be willing to lead actions against the three dictators, Castro said he was willing to help, but would not lead. He later met with enthusiastic university students and a labor group. He suggested that Venezuela and Cuba should mutually waive visa requirements. Castro met privately with president-elect Rómulo Betancourt and asked him to loan Cuba $300,000,000, and also asked him to provide oil for Cuba in order to play "a game with the *gringos*."[202]

Cuba would soon formally ask the Dominican Republic to extradite Batista, and he asked the Organization of American States to expel the Dominican Republic because its charter admits only democratic nations. However, Cuba and the Dominican Republic continued to maintain diplomatic relations.[203]

After his tour of Cuba, Representative Powell told the press that he did not watch any of the trials, but reported that Castro told him that he regretted holding them in a sports stadium.[204] The trials were removed to Camp Columbia (renamed Camp Liberty, military headquarters) and although they were open to observers and to the press, television and radio were no longer permitted to broadcast them.[205] Soon, the Supreme War Council, acting as the appellate court, announced that Sosa Blanco had won a new trial. It was assumed that the circus atmosphere and the bad press might have had something to do with it.[206]

Moreover, Archbishop Pérez Serantes, Castro's longtime benefactor who stood on the victory platform with him on January 1, asked him to reduce the penalties that were being administered by the military tribunals in the war crimes trials.[207]

As noted above, on February 7, the cabinet passed a "Fundamental Law" that gave it certain wartime powers to permit action without regard to civil rights or due process of law.[208] The right of habeas corpus, which grants prisoners a right to know the charges brought against them, was suspended.[209] This was not widely reported. Internally, Urrutia and Miró Cardona protested after a discussion over whether to resume gambling, and when it looked like they would not prevail, they tried to tender their resignations. The resignations were rejected.[210]

A few days later, the Fundamental Law was used to amend the law that governed eligibility for candidates for political offices so that the minimum age for the position of President of Cuba was reduced from 35 to age 30, ostensibly to make Castro eligible.[211] The law also granted "native born" status to Che Guevara. Newspaper reports were full of rumors that there would be changes and that Guevara might be named a cabinet member, although there was speculation that the "native born" status under the Fundamental Law would conflict with the constitutional requirement that a cabinet member actually be native born.

Three days after that, February 14, 1959, Premier Miró Cardona and the entire Provisional Government tendered their resignations.[212] President Urrutia was reported to have been too sick to attend the prior two cabinet sessions. Although the other ministers were supposed to clear all government business with the prime minister, most of them had bypassed Miró Cardona for direct meetings with Fidel Castro, then staying in the Havana Hilton, and therefore Miró Cardona was prime minister in name but not in function.[213] Interior Minister Luis Orlando Rodríguez and Castro went to Urrutia to make the suggestion that the resignation be accepted, and he appointed Castro as premier.[214] Under the Cuban parliamentary system, the premier had the power of appointment of the cabinet; the other sitting ministers remained in place until it was decided how Castro was to proceed. News articles speculated that there had been friction between Castro and Miró Cardona and Urrutia over opening of casinos, as all were opponents of any kind of gambling.[215] Again Urrutia tried to resign, and wanted to be named to the Supreme Court, but was talked out of it.[216] In his letter of resignation, Miró Cardona suggested that Castro replace him.[217]

Meanwhile, in Santiago, a mass trial of 16 pilots, 19 bombardiers and five air force mechanics was ongoing, and the prosecution asked for the death penalty for 35 of the 43 for bombing and strafing innocent civilians. Aristedes Acosta represented 10 of them.[218]

In Honduras, an attempt was made to overthrow a democratically elected government. In the States, news articles appeared accusing Castro and Betancourt of Venezuela of plotting to overthrow the Nicaraguan dictator, Luis Anastasio Somoza Debayle, who had become president after his father, Anastasio Somoza, was assassinated in 1956. Although Somoza denied having anything to do with the Honduran situation, the president of Honduras, Ramón Villeda Morales, accused Somoza of initiating the attempted coup.[219] In Paraguay there were disruptions and protests invoking Castro's name against dictator Alfredo Stroessner.[220] Cuba considered withdrawing its representative to the Organization of American States to protest against the inclusion of Somoza, Trujillo and Stroessner as active members, on the basis that membership should be limited to democracies.[221]

On February 16, Castro, dressed in fatigues, was sworn as premier. Ruby Phillips wrote that in accepting the position, Castro promised to solve all the problems of the Cuban people.[222] The *Washington Post* quoted Castro saying the job was the "toughest test of my life."[223] About 500 black-clad women, many holding placards, stood across the street separated by a ring of *barbudos*, protesting further executions. During his address, Castro said that executions would probably end in a month. He asked for patience.[224] A *Times* editorial opined that Cuba had no alternative to Castro.[225] Miró Cardona told the press that Castro was the man "most fitted for the job."[226]

The retrial of Sosa Blanco resumed. This time the room held only 300 people and there were no television cameras, although the proceedings were broadcast on radio. Most of the spectators were newsmen, lawyers and members of the Havana Rotary and Lions clubs. The same judges heard the case.[227] The trial court reached the same result as before, and Sosa Blanco was sentenced to death.[228] An appeal was immediately rejected by the Supreme War Tribunal, and after he asked the firing squad to forgive him, he was shot.[229]

Also, jails were packed with about 3,000 "civilian" prisoners, mostly tied to the Batista regime. Some of them had been "gangsters," like Santos Traficante, Jr., but others had been involved with companies accused of graft.[230] At one point, 13 Americans were held.[231]

Some observers, like Ruby Phillips, began to observe that the people considered Castro to be "supreme leader."[232] The inference was that Urrutia was nothing but a figurehead. Likewise, Jules Dubois of the *Chicago Tribune* and the Associated Press, had already submitted a draft of a book titled *Fidel Castro: Rebel, Liberator, or Dictator?* Both authors were highly influential. Castro accused the Associated Press of bias for Batista and against him. Accusations were made that reporters had taken bribes from Batista and that the new regime cut them off and the reporters sought retribution.[233] However, Castro was the public face of the Provisional Government, and whatever he wanted, he got. Castro continued to promise democratic changes, but when asked about elections, he said that immediate elections would be unfair as "we have an overwhelming majority at present and it is in the interest of the nation that political parties be developed." As of February 1959, democracy would not arrive for another 18 months.[234] Moreover, at the time, it looked like the Cuban Revolution would spread throughout Latin America.[235] If Castro was not behind widespread revolution in Latin America, he was the role model for it.

The regime continued to direct its attention to the United States. Castro continued to speak to the American press, and appeared on American radio and television, even as he was complaining that Americans distorted his statements and were hostile to his policies. Castro hired a New York fund-raiser.[236] Castro was invited to visit the United States by the American Society of Newspaper Editors in April. He said in late February that "I shall be glad to see President Eisenhower," if they had time for each other.[237] Cuban officials made several goodwill trips to the United States. For example, two Cuban war heroes, army chief of staff Comandante Camilo Cienfuegos and Pedro Miret, now underminister of defense, made an uninvited visit with a delegation of 10 in late February to Washington and Miami. Wounded while a student at the University of Havana in 1953, Cienfuegos had fled to New York. He had lived several places in the United States, working in entry-level jobs before returning to fight in the Sierra Madre. He was still only 27-years-old and made a favorable impression wherever he went.[238] Almost the entire delegation were *barbudos*, which seemed to be the most interesting factor for the press, which also commented that the *barbudos* did not drink alcoholic drinks as a matter of discipline. A *Washington Post* article described how Cienfuegos would not drink a soda in a glass, but requested to drink directly from a bottle.[239]

Although the State Department was aware that Castro had been invited to come to the States, they considered it a diplomatic embarrassment, because protocol dictated that heads of state were not supposed to be invited by private organizations. Although Representative Powell had asked the president to invite Castro, the president did not do so. Powell reiterated the request, stating that Castro was "now ready to accept your invitation."[240]

On March 2, the military tribunal hearing the case in Santiago against the 43 airmen accused of bombing and strafing civilians returned a "not guilty" verdict. Batista's bombers killed at least eight and injured 16 in 600 attacks. The prosecution submitted flight reports of the attacks signed by the pilots themselves. Defense attorneys did not deny that innocent people had been killed. However, their defense was that the prosecution had tried the wrong men. The actual perpetrators had escaped and were not tried. In addition, they argued that genocide was not defined by Cuban law. Moreover, although some of the airmen had dropped 6,080 bombs and fired 5,000,000 machine-gun bullets, they allegedly deliberately missed and dropped their bombs outside the target area, sabotaged bombs so they would not explode, and falsified their flight reports. The three-man tribunal made two main points: Many of the attacked villages were legitimate military targets, since "our forces were in most of them," and "it has not been possible to identify which of the accused on trial here were those who produced the deaths." As a not guilty verdict was read, spectators rioted in the courtroom and *barbudos* had use force to bring order. Street demonstrations followed.[241] The prosecution appealed. Castro told the press that the acquittal was a great injustice, and that the verdicts were caused by "counter-revolutionaries" and "vested interests."[242]

Within days the Provisional Government ordered a review. No new evidence would be considered, but a new prosecutor, Agusto Martinez Sánchez, was sent to Santiago to plead the case before a five-man military tribunal. The defense, aided by the bar association, also protested.[243] In the U.S., the *New York Times* published an editorial excoriating Castro for failing to follow the rule of law.[244] The Fifth Amendment to the U.S. Constitution contains a "double jeopardy" clause: an accused cannot be tried twice for the same crime. However, the Cuban Constitution did not contain a similar clause, and the enactment of the Fundamental Law gave the cabinet wartime powers. Moreover, Castro probably considered the "review" as something akin to appellate review. Castro argued that the trial was part of an attempt to split Cuba and was used as a pretext by counter-revolutionaries and "certain lawyers in Santiago" to attack the Provisional Government.[245]

During the trial, Carlos Peña Justiz, one of the defense attorneys, argued that the outcome could determine whether Castro would be seen as democratic or would turn out to be just another *caudillo*.[246] Peña Justiz had been one of the lawyers who had defended the Moncada attackers. Although he was asked by his opponent to withdraw his argument about Castro, he later compared Castro to Trujillo and to Porfirio Díaz of Mexico, dictators who had good intentions as they rose to power, "but they used force to keep themselves on top for thirty years."[247] The prosecution accused both Peña Justiz and Acosta of treason. At one point, Acosta was sent to counsel with Raúl Castro.[248]

Although Castro had estimated that about 400 would eventually be executed, that number was exceeded in early March.[249] Castro was quoted as saying that the military tribunals had been forced to sentence on "moral conviction," because "legal proof" was impossible to obtain.[250] *Time* enumerated the number of executions, but did not detail the actual records of the tribunals.

Ambassador Bonsal arrived in Havana on February 19 and immediately called on Agramonte.[251] In March, Castro sat down on the side porch of his villa outside Havana one afternoon to get acquainted with Bonsal. "Friendly, cordial and knowledgeable about Cuba," said Castro. "A good ambassador."[252]

Although Castro's attitude over the acquittal of 43 airmen left the impression that the military tribunals would rubber stamp the indictments, the fact that the airmen had been acquitted refuted that assumption. There had been acquittals in other cases, as in the 25 other war crimes cases that were on trial at the same time as the retrial of the 43. All of the accused faced the death penalty. Of those, three had been condemned to death, 12 were sentenced, and 10 were acquitted. The sentences ranged from one to 30 years; one person got a 30-year sentence.[253]

On March 11, Castro announced that the Fundamental Law would be amended so that embezzlers and others who stole public funds would be subject to the death penalty. He had a case in mind; it was someone that he knew. The next day, Castro announced that René Ray Rivero, a member of the government and brother of Minister of Public Works Manuel Ray Rivero, had committed suicide at police headquarters in Havana. The allegation was that he had stolen $400,000 from a seized bank account of $900,000 held by René Ray Rivero's employer, the Ministry for Recovery of Stolen Property.[254] An intellectual, Rivero had edited a book, *Libertad y Revolución*, published in Havana in 1959. Like his boss, Faustino Pérez, and his brother, René Ray had been a member of the First Presbyterian Church in Havana. There had been no arrest and no trial.

On March 13, five Americans were arrested at the José Martí Airport for trying to bring large amounts of pesos into Cuba.[255] At the time, there was an ongoing black market of Cuban pesos in the United States. Although it was supposed to be valued on par with the

American dollar, pesos were selling at a 20 percent discount in the United States, and the Cuban government was afraid that the country would be flooded with contraband currency taken by Batista and his allies when they fled or by counterfeit currency.

On March 19, the official M–7–26 newspaper, *Revolución*, called for an end to executions.[256] By that point, 483 people had been executed.

On March 21, in front of a huge crowd assembled to commemorate the March 1957 DR attack on the Presidential Palace and to honor the students who had been killed by Batista, and to support Cuban labor, Castro shared a podium with former Costa Rican president José Figueres Ferrer, who had been invited to Cuba as an ally. Like Castro, Figueres was considered to be a hero in his own country and throughout Latin America. Like Castro, he had led a victorious peasant revolt against both a Costa Rican dictatorship and Communist rebels, and formed the Caribbean Legion, a guerrilla army, dedicated to remove three Central American dictators. During 1945 and 1946 he tried but failed to initiate a general strike throughout Central America. However, his army prevailed in Costa Rica and as the key member of a Junta Fundadora, Founding Council. By 1948 Costa Rica abolished its army, disarmed its population, and initiated a constitution and a program of social legislation similar the Cuban Constitution of 1940. It gave women the right to vote and nationalized the country's banks. Figueres was president of Costa Rica from 1953 to 1958, when he waged war, without an army against Somoza of Nicaragua. In 1958, as president of Costa Rica, at a time when other nations were embargoing arms shipments, Figueres had sent M–7–26 a planeload of weapons.[257] After Vice President Nixon's 1958 trip to Latin America, Figueres appeared before the United States Congress. He testified that United States policy toward Latin America had to change:

> With all due respect to Vice-President Nixon, and with all my admiration towards his conduct, which was, during the events, heroic and later noble, I have no choice but to say that the act of spitting, however vulgar it is, lacks a substitute in our language to express certain emotions.... Our poverty does not diminish our pride. We have our dignity. What we want is to be paid a fair price for the sweat of our people, for the impoverishment of our land, when we provide a product needed by another country. That would be enough to live, to raise our own capital and to carry on with our own development.[258]

Castro and the crowd had expected Figueres to express similar views on the podium. However, he encouraged all of Latin America to side with the United States and all other democracies in the Cold War. If there a real war, he said, Latin Americans would fight along with the United States. Labor official David Salvador grabbed the microphone from Figueres to protest that the United States was oppressing Cuba. Castro asked, "Why should Latin America be on either side?" He said that Figueres was too heavily influenced by bad press reporting about Cuba and that big trusts and vested interests had killed more people in Cuba than even Batista.[259] Figueres later said that the goal between rich and poor nations was to seek justice, and he admonished Cuba for the executions.[260] He also told Ruby Phillips that Latin Americans felt "resentment, not hatred" toward the United States. Although the United States seemed like it was an "accomplice" to Latin American dictators, Figueres told Phillips that the threat of Soviet Union imperialism was even more dangerous.[261]

But soon Castro told his countrymen that Cuba had to mobilize every man, woman and child to defend the country against external threats from the Dominican Republic and the United States.[262] He did not directly accuse the U.S. government of planning an invasion, but he told a crowd of 100,000 that when Costa Rica, a country without a military, had been attacked by Nicaragua, which was led by a dictator, the United States had sold Somoza's jet planes for one dollar apiece, and the Dominican Republic had the same kind of deal. Batista was in the Dominican Republic, and he and "some" Americans and some news agencies were behind a plan of counter-revolution.[263] Although Figueres did not disclose it at the time, he had been receiving payments from the CIA.[264] Castro's views obviously were discussed in Washington. The State Department said that no arms were licensed for shipment to Batista, and that no clandestine arms shipments originated from U.S. soil.[265] Representative James G. Davis of Georgia soon announced that he would protest Castro's impending visit to the United States.[266]

In the American press, Castro was depicted as a would-be Simón Bolívar, fomenting further Latin American and Caribbean revolutions. The American public was told he would speak nightly to other Caribbean people to wage revolt, and that he had designs on capturing the Panama Canal.[267] They were told that he permitted Latin American rebels who had plans to attack Haiti, the Dominican Republic and Nicaragua to reside in Cuba.[268] He denied that Cuba would participate, however. On March 31, Drew Pearson told his readership that Castro was a communist.[269] He repeated charges that Castro had led an attempted takeover of Colombia in 1948 and stated that Castro would never have risen to power without support from the *New York Times* and CBS News.[270] A few days later, Pearson revealed the source of his information about Castro: He had interviewed Batista.[271] In a nutshell, according to Batista, Castro was a "madman."

Other widely circulated columnists, among them Westbrook Pegler, of King Features Syndicate and Hearst newspapers, had depicted Castro as communist from the outset. However, Pegler had said the same about President Franklin Delano Roosevelt and depicted President Eisenhower as a "pinko."

Castro continued to press the United States to extradite war criminals and accused the U.S. government of permitting former Batista supporters to buy arms to oppose his government. The United States and Cuba had entered into an extradition treaty in 1904. The State Department sent Castro a list of American citizens in Cuba whom it wanted. However, Castro noted that many of the people requested were running Cuban casinos and thus providing work to Cubans, so extradition was "unreasonable."[272]

Ironically, the press reported that the man in charge of Cuban executions was American Captain Herman Marks, then age 37. A picture showing him giving an execution order was published extensively.[273]

As all of this was happening, the price of sugar dropped precipitously, to 2.91 cents per pound from a high of seven cents a pound in 1957. A *New York Times* editorial related the drop to politics and stated that Castro had frightened investors.[274] The next day, Castro asked the United States to restore a higher sugar quota and said that the Cuban government would seek aid from the United States and Canada.[275] Neither the *Times* editorial nor Castro's response noted that the Cuban Revolution had raised sugar prices, and when instability in Cuba ended, prices dropped.[276]

A military tribunal ordered the execution of a marijuana seller, sentenced under Article 16 of the Rebel Criminal Code. Although the code didn't directly establish a death sentence for the sale of drugs, an interpretation by the tribunals extending the code to the Fundamental Law made it a capital crime.[277] A few days later, the body of the president of the military tribunal who had heard the retrial of the 43 airmen was found in a car. Major Félix Peña had just been named military attaché to West Germany. He left a note stating that his suicide had nothing to do with politics.[278]

On April 10, an airline pilot was killed over Haiti by six Haitian rebels, who forced the copilot to take them to Cuba. On landing in Santiago, the rebels shouted "Viva Fidel Castro!" The rebels were part of a force opposed to François "Papa Doc" Duvalier, whose government immediately requested extradition. The plane was immediately turned over to the Haitian authorities.[279]

A few days before his planned trip to the United States, Castro told an audience that Cuba was under imminent threat and that elections would be possible only after corruption was eliminated and the threat was diminished. Elections would be held "when all the people know their rights and duties." He told his audience that anyone who wanted elections was trying to stymie the revolution. The crowd broke into a cheer: "No elections! No elections!"[280] Castro also attacked the press, especially United Press International, and said that local newsmen were highly influenced by foreign sources.[281]

Castro had asked to see Vice President Richard M. Nixon on his trip to Washington, and Nixon extended an invitation to Castro.[282] The press reported that Castro would press for an increase in the sugar quota, and for aid. It was reported that Castro would have to submit a list of projects. The State Department acknowledged that there were serious threats against Castro and that tight security would be needed. Among the organizations that were identified was the "Anti-communist Movement of the Americas," led by Rafael del Pino, described as a former Castro associate. Cuban government sources alleged that del Pino had been a traitor since 1956 when he took a bribe of $10,000 to betray M–7–26 in Mexico and was seen with Batista agents.[283] On April 14, Cuban baseball's opening day, Castro threw out the first pitch for the International League at Gran Stadium in Havana. With him was Philip Bonsal, the United States ambassador to Cuba, and ambassadors from Mexico, Canada and Venezuela.[284] It is reasonable to expect that they talked about baseball, but it also possible that they discussed Castro's pending trip to the United States. He called it a "truth mission" to dispel anti-revolutionary propaganda.[285] He told the crowd he hoped "that the Sugar Kings might win this year and that eventually Cuba would have a major league franchise."[286] As Castro was on his way to the United States, the Havana Rotary Club submitted a request that habeus corpus be restored so that prisoners could get a speedy trial.[287]

Chapter 8

Role Reversal

Within a month after Batista fled, anti-civilian terror returned to Cuba in full force. As Cubans celebrated the one-month anniversary of the revolution in a religious procession, two women and one man were killed and 50 were wounded in a hand grenade attack. The attack occurred along a mountain road as pilgrims traveled to a sunrise service honoring *El Cobre*, Our Lady of Charity, Cuba's patroness saint. Although the perpetrators were not identified or caught, they were thought to be renegades, former Batista men, who had been in hiding in Oriente Province near the scene of the crime.[1]

There also were reports of attempts to assassinate Castro. In December, a 31-year-old pilot from Chicago, Alan Robert Nye, a navy veteran of the Korean War, had been sent into Cuba. He was living in Coral Gables, Florida, when he was hired, and allegedly volunteered in the Rebel Army but was arrested December 26, 1958, accused of an attempt to assassinate Fidel Castro. His rifle, a telescopic sight, and a .38 caliber handgun were found at a farmhouse in Oriente Province, on a route Castro was supposed to have taken. The report of the arrest wasn't released until February 2, 1959, and by February 5, he reportedly "confessed," although he told American newsmen another story. The government version was that he had been hired by a Batista agent in Miami and was to be paid $100,000. His version was that he had offered to fly bombing missions on behalf of the Rebel Army.[2]

On the same day of the Nye announcement, the Cuban army also announced that it had arrested a 20-year-old soldier for organizing a group to take to the Sierra Maestre to start a counter-revolution to oppose Castro.[3] Many similar arrests would follow.[4]

Castro had been wary of earlier attempts on his life. While he was being held for trial in the Moncada attack, he was certain that his food would be poisoned.[5] After he was released from prison, others given amnesty were murdered or beaten and Castro was certain that he would be next.[6] While he was in Mexico in 1955 and 1956, Castro learned that Batista had paid assassins $20,000 to kill him.[7] Soon after the Granma landing, Eutimio Guerra, a member of M–7–26, was offered $10,000 and the rank of major in the Cuban Army in return for assassinating Castro.[8]

Later in the Sierra Madre, Batista placed a "dead or alive" bounty on him of $100,000, and up to $5,000 for information leading to the capture of Raúl Castro, Cresencio Pérez and Guillermo González.[9] But Castro had taken the position that he wanted to contrast himself with Batista and to appear more honorable, humane and less vengeful than his opposition.

Although he had been the subject of reported attempts on his life, Castro decried the use of assassination to evoke regime change. During his time in the mountains, Castro had adamantly opposed political assassination as an illegal means to end the Batista regime.

When the DR, initially under Echevarria Bianchi, tried to assassinate Batista and members of his high command, Castro objected publicly.[10]

On January 13, exiled former President Fulgencio Batista had issued a statement from exile in the Dominican Republic alleging that Castro had initiated a "river of blood" in Cuba, which he attributed to Castro's "vengeance and savagery." He denied that his government had tortured or killed 20,000 people. He said he wanted only wanted what was best for Cuba.[11] The next day, the Provisional Government alleged that Batista allies were recruiting an army in the Dominican Republic to attack Cuba.[12] They produced a witness, a driver for former general Francisco Tabernilla Doltz, who had escaped to Jacksonville. He said that the aim was to fund a force of 10,000 to attack Cuba from the Dominican Republic. There were also threats that Batista hired assassins from the Dominican Republic and Guatemala to kill Castro.[13]

Accusations of threats from the Dominican Republic seemed substantiated when Trujillo established the Foreign Legion, ostensibly to defend Haiti. Haiti was ruled by dictator "Papa Doc" Duvalier, and the coast of Haiti is only 50 miles from Cuba across the Windward Passage. Although Haiti had only a 5,000-man army, the legion would have 25,000 men, and Trujillo would requisition 25,000 machine guns, 25,000 machetes and 3,000,000 bullets.[14] Castro anticipated (probably reasonably) that they were to be used against Cuba. This was probably further confirmed when Trujillo told the press that aggressors should avoid the Dominican Republic, unless "they want to see their beards and brains flying about like butterflies."[15]

Moreover, holdovers from the Cuban army, from Rolando Masferrer's Tigers and from the National Police were in hiding and were reconstituting their forces in Oriente and in Las Villas Provinces. Many were the same people the Provisional Government had accused as potential candidates for trial for torture and murder. It was estimated that about 400 of these were in the Sierra Maestre, which had been the lair of the M–7–26 Rebel Army, and 80 were in the Escambray Mountains, where the Second Front operated during the revolution. The Provisional Government dispatched Raúl Castro and his forces to the Sierra Maestre and Che Guevara and his men were sent to the Escambray to root out these groups. There were also reports that the groups constituted a guerrilla army, were receiving supplies from Batista, and would soon represent a challenge to the new government.[16]

Several days later, terms of sales of jet fighters to the Dominican Republic from Canada were reported, needed "in the wake of the Cuban revolt."[17] General Trujillo also said he needed the planes to fend of any internal "Cuba-like" revolt. Although the United States supposedly had nothing to do with the sale to Trujillo, it permitted the planes to be shipped across the United States. At the same time, demonstrators in the United States protested against Trujillo.[18]

There were also reports that 10 army men and one civilian were arrested for treason against the Provisional Government. Details were not given.[19]

In early March 1959, a new radio station, known as "the Voice of Free Cuba," announced that a "democratic" military presence was operating to oppose the Provisional Government in Oriente Province.[20] The members included some former members of the Cuban army and some former exiles. Castro alleged that his enemies were openly buying arms in Miami, unimpeded by the United States.[21]

Meanwhile, Castro invited refugees from Latin American dictatorships to come to Cuba.[22]

On April 11, Nye appeared for trial in the ballroom of the Officers Club at La Cabaña

Fortress before a military tribunal and 200 spectators. He looked tall and gaunt and was dressed in his prison uniform. His first attorney abruptly resigned, alleging that he had just received the indictment and did not have enough time to prepare an adequate defense. At trial, Nye was represented by Arturo Quintana Cabrera. Also present were his stepfather and a family friend, a lawyer from his hometown, and representatives from the U.S. State Department. After the prosecution presented 11 witnesses to tie him to Batista's General Francisco Tabernilla Doltz and to arms that were intended to ambush Castro, Nye called the American lawyer as a character witness.

Before the trial, Nye's mother had visited Cuba, asked for mercy, and asked to see Premier Castro, and it was rumored that even if Nye were guilty, Castro would release him rather than provoke the United States. That was exactly what happened. Although he still protested that he was innocent, Nye was convicted of conspiring to murder Castro, but with a few hours was released to exile.[23]

Chapter 9

The Balance Sheet

Castro laid out an ambitious plan to improve Cuba's economy. He planned to provide about 200,000 landless *guajiros* with enough land to provide subsistence, announced that the tariff system would be improved, and said he would initiate a merchant marine to stimulate the economy. He also wanted to support the Cuban motion picture industry and establish a Latin American news agency. He also asked unions to hold immediate elections.[1]

Batista had planned to start a government-owned, 17-ship merchant marine, and the Provisional Government established the Merchant Development Commission to attempt to foster a private shipping industry.[2]

Although Castro depicted Cuba as independent and sharply criticized the United States, it was evident that the government was aware that it needed our financial support. For example, in February the Provisional Government promoted a "welcome tour." A parade of 30 floats included Castro's ship, the Granma, marching bands and drill teams including some from the United States, a Miami police motorcycle squad, and waves of schoolchildren and athletes. All marched before Premier Castro and President Urrutia, and the assembled Provisional Government and the *barbudo* heads of the military at the Capitolo. Tourists also were entitled to free attendance at an air and water show and a performance at the amphitheater at the University of Havana. Included in the special tour package was plane fare, three nights in a top hotel, sightseeing tours, round trip ground transportation to and from the airport, and free drinks at participating Havana restaurants and cabarets. By that time, the casinos had reopened. The cost was only $55.50 from Miami, $59.50 from Fort Lauderdale and $29.50 from Key West.[3] The United States was asked to supply economic and technical support to eliminate poverty in Oriente Province.[4] Representative Porter said that he would support the request.

Expectations were high for a recovery of the Cuban economy. The government announced that the Cuban peso remained at the same value as the dollar. Although some rail lines in Oriente Province had been damaged in the war, they were being repaired and it was expected that the sugar crop worth $600,000,000 to $700,000,000 would be "assured." The Cuban government had established crop restrictions limited to almost 5,800,000 tons to stabilize prices, and would continue to do so. Of that, it was expected that the United States, Cuba's largest customer, would buy about 3,400,000 tons. Cuba's national debt as of January 1 was almost $770,900,000, most of it owed to Cuban investors. The revolution cost the Cuban government about $7,000,000 in 1958. Prior to that the country's budget had a surplus, but as a result a deficit was expected. The national reserves had declined by $600,000,000, and foreign trade was down but because imports especially from the United States had declined, the balance of trade was expected to increase. Tourism was down appreciably. Although trade in most commodities was reduced, nickel produced by the United States government's Nicaro Plant had increased.

Felipe Pazos, president of the National Bank, said that there would be a continuity from the old regime, but he was looking for ways to diversify the Cuban economy. Pazos later stated that the national debt had risen from $200,000,000 in 1952 to $1,500,000,000.[5] Another problem was that foreign companies were restricted on how much money they could send out of the country. These regulations were imposed to keep followers of Batista from slowing down commerce, and this would have to be fixed.[6]

However, the price of sugar declined, not because of overproduction, but because the war had increased prices. Once the war ended, prices declined.[7] World sugar crops were not solely on a free market, as virtually all producers were governed by the International Sugar Agreement. In the United States, the Department of Agriculture set the amount of sugar permitted to be sold. In Cuba, a council set sugar quotas and prices, and if sugar dropped below 3.25 cents per pound for 17 consecutive days, the quota would have to be cut 2.5 percent. The price had dropped to 3.1 cents. In the United States, if cheap sugar were sold, under the Sugar Act the quota of sugar permitted from Cuba would have to be cut.[8] If that were to happen, the net effect would be that there would be less need to buy as much Cuban sugar and sugar mills and plantations would lay off Cuban sugar workers. Cubans had accused the United States of manipulating the sugar quota for political rather than economic purposes as a means to intimidate the Cuban government.[9]

Minister of the Treasury Rufo López Fresquet stated that although taxes were being paid, cash flow was a problem He stated that eventually, "ghost" employees would be removed from the government rolls, and the cost of supplies would be cut to remove the graft imposed by the Batista regime. These measures would help balance the budget.[10] However, behind the scenes, Castro complained that López Fresquet had retained two-thirds of the old treasury employees. It later turned out that the Treasury Department had 800 *botelleros* (sinecures), paid for doing nothing, who had to be removed.[11] Other agencies also had similar problems. The Ministry of Communications had 600 *bolleteros* who were removed.[12] But the government was able to stop the practice of paying bribes to newsmen and to eliminate another $400,000 paid monthly for sinecures at the Department of Public Works.[13] Moreover, the government was able to recover $40,000,000 in stolen items such as hidden cash, securities jewelry, and the like mainly from émigrés. Titles to property of people connected to crimes were also being traced.[14] López Fresquet later said that the sugar quota agreement with the United States was being renegotiated, and the personal income tax exemption would be increased from $100 per month to $200. Given that most Cubans did not make that much, most would no longer have to pay any income taxes.[15] The idea was that the decrease would permit more people to spend more of their income, thus stimulating the entire Cuban economy.

However, the Cuban peso dropped on foreign exchanges from equal parity to a dollar on December 31, 1958, to 75 cents by mid–February 1959. Most international sales were made in dollars, so commercial transactions were probably not affected. The Provisional Government had been wary of an attack on the currency by Batista, either by use of counterfeit money or by excessive withdrawals of currency. The Cuban government had warned American banks not to honor large denominations, and the government had initiated a program to replace large bills with smaller ones, and also changed the color of the bills. The government estimated that Batista associates and American "gangsters" had absconded with between 50 million to 70 million pesos that they were trying to cash in the States. Travelers were restricted to bringing in or taking out a maximum of 50 pesos. American banks were refusing to buy pesos and many foreign traders refused to accept them, but a large black market in pesos developed where pesos traded for as low as 40 cents per dollar.[16] Soon the government required companies trading in dollars to exchange all of them for pesos.[17]

The Cuban government asked for special import restrictions for 175 American luxury items. The Provisional Government was in a perilous situation because Cuba's reserves of gold, which backed the currency, had been depleted, and Cuba needed U.S. cooperation to avoid spiraling into bankruptcy.[18] Cuba also had to diversify its exports, as it had been mired in a sugar economy. Exports of tobacco, cattle, rice, nickel, cobalt, manganese, copper and petroleum needed promotion.[19]

As a matter of good faith, many American companies doing business in Cuba made approximately $3,000,000 in advance payments on taxes in order to support the Provisional Government and provide it some cash flow.[20] American oil companies Texaco and Esso ran ads in *Revolución*, the voice of the new government.[21] Domestic companies such as Bacardi and Hatuey Beer also paid taxes in advance as a patriotic gesture.[22]

Newspapers in the States began to promote Cuba. The *New York Times* ran articles asserting now that the revolution was over, Cuba was safer and more inviting than ever.[23] The *Washington Post* reprinted an invitation to Americans to visit Cuba.[24]

One major concern was the viability of Cuba's largest electricity and telephone utilities, American-owned monopolies valued at $400 million. The electric company was valued at $256,942,000. Besides electricity, it also distributed natural gas. It had grown rapidly during the Batista regime partly through favored loans from the Cuban government and from the United Stated Export-Import Bank.[25] The companies had been attacked as monopolistic and graft-ridden by anti–Cuban nationalists like Eddy Chibás and the Ortodoxos, and the press reported rumors that Castro had said that they should be nationalized.[26] The Cuban Electric Company, owned by American and Foreign Power, said that it had suffered about $600,000 in damages in Havana alone during the revolution. About half of that was covered by insurance. The telephone company, owned by International Telephone and Telegraph Company, was extremely profitable and needed to expand to keep up with demand. The company had a poor reputation: in 1956, it received applications for 60,000 new telephones but only installed 1,371 phones.[27] The accusation was made that both had sweetheart contracts with the Batista regime that needed to be renegotiated.[28] Soon employees of the electric company staged a strike for higher wages and a "takeover of management."[29] Rates in Havana were 9 cents per kilowatt hour, and in Pinar del Río, 13 cents; the average household paid approximately $35–38 per month. The cabinet cut the postal rate in half, and the electric rates were set at Havana rates.[30]

Meanwhile, despite the "labor action" at the electric company, Manuel Fernández, the minister of labor, announced that the 1,600,000 strong Cuban Confederation of Labor had agreed to be more cooperative with the Provisional Government than it had been with the Batista regime. The minister told the press that the confederation had agreed to be run democratically and that none of its officers were communists. He said communist union members were "small, although loud voiced, and active."[31] In Oriente Province 50,000 workers demanded 20 percent pay raises and four work shifts instead of three. David Salvador, for the Confederation, said that negotiations were ongoing, but that the right to strike would be protected. Sugar mill owners had agreed to postpone disputes to get the harvest on its way and the government imposed a freeze on strikes, but there were still some walkouts.[32] Castro would later say that such demands were justifiable, but all within a capitalistic framework, and what Cuba needed was new jobs, not more work out of the old jobs.[33] One demand was for a six-hour workday; employers alleged that the demands would raise the cost of doing business by 70 percent.[34] At Moa Bay Mining, 3,200 workers walked off the job.[35] Hotel and restaurant workers walked out to demand reopening of the casinos.[36] There also was a strike against eight ships that the Batista government had bought from the Canadian government and had intended to use in its merchant marine fleet. The Seafarers' International Union picketed in Havana, Canada, and even in Baltimore, where one Cuban ship was at drydock.[37] When Shell Oil workers threatened to strike, Castro told them that they should cooperate with the government, inferring that a strike would make them his "enemies." However, he negotiated the workers a 50 percent pay increase and Shell Oil agreed to contribute $250,000 to a fund to provide housing. "We did not carry out the Revolution to defend the interests of the powerful, but of the humble," Castro stated.[38]

Each of the new cabinet members had patronage rights, and some started to replace workers from their agencies with friends, relatives and members of their own political parties and cliques. It soon became apparent that because so many had been dismissed that government continuity and government operations were adversely affected. But it was apparent to M–7–26 members that many of the new employees were not loyal to the "Revolution," meaning to them. Many had been Auténticos or Ortodoxos. Also, thousands of "excessive" employees had been wrongfully removed from their jobs. As soon as he was sworn in as premier, Castro pledged to reform the practice. He said that the ministers could replace employees in high positions, or who were known Batista collaborators, but not rank-and-file employees. He said that as soon as the Provisional Government were more fully established, it would set up a civil service system, and he would consider giving the employees severance pay and pensions.[39] Salaries of ministers were cut from $1,350 per month to $900. Some ministers kept a "secret expense" account that may have been used for personal gain, and Castro stated that ministers shouldn't profit from public service.[40] After elections, as Congress was suspended, salaries for congressmen would be cut from $4,000 to $500 or $600 per month.[41]

On January 28, Castro announced a land distribution policy, based on a provision in the Cuban Constitution of 1940, that gave the state a right to distribute public land and expropriate "excess" land that was not being cultivated. Many Cubans had objected that the titles to many of the properties came from Spanish land grants, and that many of the properties were taken by adverse possession or by force from state lands.[42] Also, large landowners had been given the privilege to set their own value on land for tax purposes, and it was assumed that taxes were based on artificially low values.[43] Squatters in Oriente Province could receive parcels of 33 to 100 acres. Castro later stated that about 7 million acres had been stolen but would be recovered constitutionally.[44] The land would be owned by the *precaristas* (squatters) but the recipient could not transfer the property except through rights of inheritance.[45] Although some *precaristas* had taken it upon themselves to appropriate land from some coffee plantations, Castro told them that the government would not honor such conduct and those who had acted would forfeit their rights to receive government distributions.[46]

The government passed a law confiscating land owned by collaborators with the Batista government. There was some question about who was considered to have been a collaborator. Some property was seized, but property not "acquired through collaboration" would be returned. Legal proceedings were planned and the courts to handle complaints were not yet in place.[47] The government also passed a law forcing owners of vacant lots to sell to anyone wishing to construct a building on them. The value of residential property was placed at 15 percent over the cost of the property plus reasonable expenses for maintaining it to date of sale. The value of commercial property was set at 12 percent plus expenses. Since much of the land had been inherited, there were complaints that the law was unfair.[48]

Castro also asked foreign investors to come to Cuba, but there were reports that he also had said that after the investments made a fair return, they would be turned over to Cuba.[49]

The first land given to the *precaristas* was property in the tobacco area of Pinar del Río Province, partly formerly owned by the Cuban Land and Tobacco Leaf Co., an American firm. However, the land was bought by Batista's Bank of Agriculture and Industrial Development in 1955. The Provisional Government would take title and then transfer it. The new owners were 70 sharecropper families who had been living on the land for generations.[50]

The notion of Latin American agrarian reform was not new and the United States had a lot of experience in the field. For example, after Mexico had nationalized industries and expropriated American owned property in 1938, the U.S. secretary of state, Cordell Hull, demanded and American oil companies received "prompt, adequate and effective" compensation.[51] There was so much regime change in Latin America that companies often inserted a "Calvo clause" in contracts, whereby foreign businesses agreed not to seek diplomatic protection from their native countries, to protect new governments from having to pay damages due to civil wars.[52] By 1959, the United States "good neighbor" foreign policy was in flux. In 1947 the U.S. determined that Latin American foreign policy was apparently based on whether a government could maintain law and order. After the 1952 Batista *golpe* (coup), the U.S. continued to give Cuba aid under the Point Four program, just as we did with other Latin American countries we deemed compliant with this policy.

However, in Guatemala, the democratically elected government of Jacobo Árbenz Guzmán had appropriated land and recognized the Communist Party as Castro was prepared to do. At that time, American-owned United Fruit, the same company that owned estates in Oriente Province, established an "American" city in Banes, and the Castro family's benefactor or competitor, depending on how the story was told, was Guatemala's largest landowner.[53] Under the Árbenz law, United Fruit was subject to lose all of its uncultivated land. By March 1953, 209,842 acres of United Fruit Company's uncultivated land was taken by the government, which offered compensation of $525,000. The company wanted $16,000,000. The U.S. put pressure on Guatemala through import policies and isolated Guatemala within the OAS, but the government persisted in its nationalization program. The CIA established Operation PBSUCCESS to remove Árbenz in favor of a more compatible government. Eventually, after the Truman administration was replaced by the Eisenhower administration, an operation headquarters was established in December 1953 in Miami and the CIA set up a clandestine insurrection force. Árbenz was confronted with a possible invasion. After he could not buy arms from the West, he bought arms from Czechoslovakia, a Communist country. This increased CIA pressure, and the U.S. set up a blockade of Guatemalan ports. On June 7, 1954, the U.S. sent a "contingency evacuation" force, five amphibious assault ships plus an "anti–submarine warfare" aircraft carrier to the Caribbean off Guatemala. On June 18, 1954, a "liberation army" led by former Árbenz ally Carlos Castillo Armas prevailed, and Árbenz resigned and fled to Mexico.[54]

At the time, it was common knowledge that United Fruit had been represented by John Foster Dulles's law firm prior to his selection as secretary of state. His brother, Allen

W. Dulles, was head of the CIA, and also had a lengthy history with the company. The company president's was an undersecretary of state, John Moors Cabot. When the State Department investigated Guatemala, it sent Cabot. He reported that Árbenz was a Communist. President Eisenhower's personal secretary's spouse was the principal United Fruit lobbyist, Ed Whitman, who produced a movie, *Why the Kremlin Hates Bananas.*[55] The CIA established a propaganda campaign in Guatemala to instill fear rather than educate the population — to make people think that the government was worse than it actually was. For example, the CIA inverted a phony militant group as a threat to set up a totalitarian dictatorship. It accused Árbenz of planning to ban Holy Week and of planning to send the archbishop of Guatemala into exile. Other accusations included planning to set up re-education centers for all Guatemalan children, confiscate bank accounts and expropriate all private land. The CIA also established a sabotage campaign through leadership of an underground CIA-led cadre.[56]

Although the Castro brothers were in jail in the Isle of Pines during the period that regime change occurred in Guatemala, they knew all about it. Fidel Castro included a reference to United Fruit in his "History Will Absolve Me" speech. Che Guevarra had been personally involved and openly discussed his Guatemalan experience.[57]

Roberto Agramonte, Cuba's foreign minister, said that he was gratified by remarks by Senator John F. Kennedy of Massachusetts, who spoke in favor of better relations with Cuba. The Cuban government was still working on unfreezing assets to accommodate better trade and was also recalling large currency bills and replacing them with smaller ones. But the government sealed bank vaults and deposit boxes of Batista allies. He also said that he was negotiating the extradition of war criminals from the United States and thanked the United States embassy in Havana for facilitating discussions. Agramonte also said that Cuba would work to observe the right to asylum of those in foreign embassies, but Cuba wanted to make sure that asylum was not offered to common criminals.[58]

Beginning in mid–January 1959, Cuba participated in talks with other Western Hemisphere nations in Operation Pan America, a program to promote development in Latin America.

On February 19, most of the large American-owned casinos were permitted to reopen.

The minister of communication, Eugene Oltulsky, told Ruby Phillips that although it had a hundred radio stations, Cuba needed more channels. He also said that advertising time would be cut and advertising for "sex" would be eliminated.[59]

Medical students at the University of Havana replaced the dean with one of their favorites and fired 145 professors. At Calixto Hospital, affiliated with the medical school, the Board of Governors was removed.[60]

Former president Ramón Grau San Martín, who was held in low regard by the new regime, stated that the United States should cede Guantánamo to Cuba as a matter of goodwill, for the purpose of adding the land to the agrarian reform program.[61] Grau had been a faculty member of the medical school at the University of Havana, but one of the first demands by returning students was his removal. Apparently, his statements were made to try to better relations with the new administration.

Also in February the Provisional Government announced that telephone rates would be reduced on April 1, and that it had taken over management of the phone company. An interim director was named to manage the company until it could be determined how its affairs would be handled.[62] During the revolution of 1933–34, workers had intervened to run the electric company. At the time, during the first Grau San Martín Administration, this procedure was approved.[63] In 1957, Batista had extended the monopoly and the company initiated a $65 million investment program. The government was in the process of investigating how much the rates would be, but the exclusive contract was rescinded.[64] It is clear that the public remembered that Batista had received a gold telephone in appreciation of having granted the company a 20 percent rate hike.

The Provisional Government also cut rents on existing rental properties from 30 percent to 50 percent. In order to stimulate building, newly constructed owner-occupied properties would be exempt. Existing rentals of $150 or less were cut by 50 percent.[65] The vast number of rentals at that time cost well under $150 per month. Government employees' wages were raised from $60 per month to $85 per month.[66] Soon taxes were cut and mortgage interest was set at 4 percent to help landlords cope with the cuts.[67] Castro told the press that he envisioned that no new apartment complexes would be constructed and that the government would try to help everyone to own their own homes.[68]

The government also established a special program to stimulate the economy and rebuild the infrastructure in Oriente Province, where entire villages had been destroyed during the war.[69]

When Castro was asked whether private land would be parceled out, he said that some undeveloped land would be. He said that the government had no interest in productive land that was currently under cultivation. He said that much of the "excessive" land had been inherited and had not been put to use for years.[70]

Cuba intended to drain the Cienega de Zapata, a huge swamp. Castro asked the Japanese government to send 50 families to Cuba to show Cubans how to grow rice. Cuba was a rice-importing nation, and Castro wanted it to become a net exporter.[71]

Cuba transformed the National Lottery, and reconstituted it to benefit housing for poor Cubans.

Castro told sugar mill owners that they had to reform and conform. "We do not wish to harm anyone," he said, but he thought sugar mills should offer year-round work and have a social conscience. Companies should turn over land parcels not used for export to small planters and use profits from exports to create new industries because the country must industrialize if the revolution were to be successful. He maintained that in effect, the revolution had rescued the "rich" and the sugar industry, because if Batista had remained in power, the peso would have become worthless.[72]

On March 31, the government fired or laid off thousands of its workers.[73] Several newspapers and radio stations objected. They also complained about slowing growth and growing inflation.[74]

In 1934, the United States Congress passed the Jones-Costigan Act, which permitted Congress to set quotas on surplus agricultural products. Sugar was designated as a surplus crop. Most domestic sugar was produced by beet farmers in the mountain states, in Hawaii, Puerto Rico and in the southeastern part of the U.S. The Sugar Act of 1937, which was extended in 1948, permitted restrictions on domestic production and limited exports to protect domestic sugar producers, but also gave preferences to the Philippines and Cuba, because of longterm U.S. interests in those countries. Price supports made American sugar prices the highest in the world, about one and a half times the world price. In 1958, Cuba shipped 3,500,000 tons of sugar to the United States. The U.S. used a total of 9,000,000 tons, the most in the world. Some 3,000,000 tons were domestically produced, so Cuba sold more sugar to the United States than was produced and Cuba was the largest U.S. supplier. Castro requested that the United States take a larger share than in prior years. Much of the sugar produced in Cuba used land owned by American interests. It was refined by American-owned mills and transported to the United States mainly on American ships. However, a 1956 amendment to the Sugar Act reduced the ability of Cuban shippers to sell in the United States. Formerly, Cuba could sell 96 percent above the quota set by the Department of Agriculture for a given year. The department usually set the price in December, before the harvest, and established an initial low quota to raise the price of sugar.

The effect was that after 1956, Cuba was getting a lower proportional share of the market and thus other countries were able to get a higher market share. Because world sugar prices fell, the Cuban economy was in dire straits. Therefore the only hope for a higher market share would be if Congress revoked the 1956 amendment to the Sugar Act.[75]

Meanwhile, the Americans in the Rebel Army looked to other pursuits. Morgan remained military commander of Cienfuegos for a time, and was given a $125 per month salary as an honorary comandante.[76] Eventually, he became a rancher of sorts: He ran a frog farm.

Morgan and his former commander, Eloy Gutiérrez Menoyo, had planned a series of public relations trips to the United States beginning in February, arranged through the American embassy. Their contact at the embassy, Paul Bethel, later was discovered to be a CIA agent. Bethel initially had thought that Gutiérrez Menoyo would become a principal advisor to Castro, and also thought that he could use them to make more contacts and set up FBI contacts for speeches in several major cities.[77] However, the trips were postponed.

Neill Macaulay also went into agriculture. He initially returned to the States, but returned to Cuba, registered as a landless *guajiro* under the Agrarian Reform Law and was granted 66 acres. He planted tomatoes and cucumbers and netted about $3,300 from sales at the farmer's market in Pompano Beach, Florida.[78]

Chapter 10

The 1959 Castro Visit
to the United States

The April trip to the United States would take 11 days. President Urrutia and Ambassador Bonsal saw the diplomatic contingent off at the military airfield at the former Camp Columbia. Agusto Martinez Sánchez was appointed to serve as premier while Castro was out of the country.[1] Castro told the cabinet ministers that the trip would give Cuba a chance to explain "revolutionary justice" to the people of the United States. He received advice on how to proceed by hiring an American public relations agency.[2] He had appointments with leaders of government, industry, academia, and the media. Castro had been invited by the newspaper organization, but had also been invited to meet with Vice President Nixon, appear on television shows, and to give speeches at Princeton, Columbia and Harvard universities. Although he tried to make arrangements to visit with American labor leaders, he wasn't able to meet with any.[3] In flight, Castro was given a manicure and read comic books. Although some of his companions wanted to discuss economics, he declined.[4]

There was some question whether Castro could make the trip. On March 26, 1959, the National Security Council debated whether to grant Castro an entry visa. However, Ambassador Bonsal sent a telegram advising that if Castro were to fail, it must not look like the United States had anything to do with it. A visa was granted.[5]

Castro and his entourage were met at the airport by Wiley Buchanan, head of protocol for the State Department; Roy Rubottom, Jr., undersecretary for Latin America; William Wieland of the State Department Caribbean and Mexican Affairs Office; and the president of the American Society of Newspaper Editors. He was also met by a security detail of more than forty agents.[6] He was to lunch with Christian Herter, who was the de facto Secretary of State and have dinner with Nixon. He would later meet Dag Hammarskjold, Secretary-General of the United Nations. Although he spent 11 days in the States, he did not meet with President Eisenhower.

Although Castro made big news in the American press, religion also made front page news. The new pope, John XXIII, issued an edict forbidding Catholics from voting for candidates who support or give comfort to communists. As the Communist Party was especially active in Italy, this was surprising. This also meant that Catholics were instructed not to participate in coalition governments, where the Communist Party took part in democratic elections, as they did in much of Latin America. This edict would apply to potential Cuban elections.

Also, the Dalai Lama, then age 23, fled from China into India and accused the communist Chinese of failing to acknowledge Tibet's autonomy, interfered in religious affairs, destroyed monasteries, murdered priests and sent many more into slave labor camps. As a result, the Tibetans had staged a doomed uprising.

Another insurrection failed, this one from right-wing Falangists seeking to take over Bolivia. In French Algeria, elections were marred by killing and guerrilla warfare, similar to M–7–26's insurrection. The incidents took place in the Kabylia region, east of Algiers. In Iraq, the premier, Abdul Karim Kassim, had come to power after the assassination of King Faisal and Premier Nuri Al-Said after a bloody revolt. Within Iraq, a pan–Arab group wanted to ally itself with Gamal Abdel Nasser of Egypt, and groups of Kurds and others opposed. The Kurds were also fighting Turkomans. In the bedlam, there was a strong threat that the country would ally itself with the Soviet Union.

During the week, the newspapers also reported that talks between the United States and the Soviet Union in Geneva over a proposed nuclear test ban were on the verge of collapse, and the United States had determined that although problems related to Berlin had been front page news, communist aggression would more likely erupt in the Middle East than anywhere else. Eisenhower proposed a step-by-step plan for disarmament. However, by the end of the week Khrushchev rejected the plan and the Soviet Union accused the United States of sabotaging any hope of peace by arming West Germany with nuclear weapons. The U.S. was also going to attend upcoming NATO talks in Paris and which would be attended by Undersecretary Christian Herter.

There were also stories that an African American prisoner was murdered by a lynch mob in Poplarville, Mississippi, two miners were killed in shootings, and an arsonist started a fire in a coal mine in Hazard, Kentucky, during a long and bloody strike.

On arrival, Castro's plane was met by Ambassador Ernesto Dihigo and a crowd of 1,500, mostly Cubans but some Dominicans, all shouting encouragement to Castro. The Cuban entourage of 30 included cabinet ministers and Cuban economic experts, including Felipe Pazos, head of the National Bank; Rufo López Fresquet, treasury minister; Regino Boti, chief economist; and José "Pepin" Bosch, head of Bacardi Liquors.

Castro walked through the crowd, shaking hands as he walked to a microphone. "I have come to speak to the people of the United States," Castro told audience.[7] He spoke softly, in English. He told news reporters that he would answer questions later.

Normally, the White House would invite a head of state to come to the U.S. As premier, Castro was not the official head of state, but he was very important. From early March, it was apparent that President Eisenhower would rather play golf at Augusta National Golf Club in Georgia than meet Castro. According to some sources, Eisenhower had been told that Castro had begun to act like a dictator, and so decided not to greet him personally.[8] However, as Cuba was not a major foreign concern at that time, it is just as likely that golf interested him more. Eisenhower golfed during the entire five days that Castro spent in Washington.

On the way to the States, Castro told his advisors that Cuba had to stop the executions and the "*infiltrado,*" communist infiltration.[9] There had been a scene at the March M–7–26 convention when several members asked for an immediate halt to all executions. Raúl Castro attacked them. Fidel issued an order for them to cease. Later it turned out that Raúl had permitted a couple of executions after the order, but alleged that he had not yet received the news.[10] As soon as he got to Washington, Castro learned that Panamanian authorities had protested that Cuba was fomenting a revolt in their country.[11]

A *New York Times* editorial acknowledged that the American press had been harsh on Cuba and that Castro had resented it. However, it described him as "hypersensitive" and opined that he should become more statesmanlike.[12] The *Washington Post* and approximately 600 other newspapers ran Drew Pearson's "Washington Merry-Go-Round," where he quoted Rafael del Pino's description of Castro as a Communist.[13] Meanwhile, the U.S. press covered Eisenhower's golfing exploits.

On the first day, Castro had lunch at the Statler Hilton with Herter, soon to be named secretary of state to replace the ill and dying John Foster Dulles. Herter invited 25 dignitaries to the lunch, and Castro brought eight *barbudos* as a security detail. The *barbudos* were unexpected but Castro demanded that they be served with everyone else. There were no seats for them, so they had to sit on the floor. After Wieland was introduced to Castro as the "man in charge" in Cuba, Castro quipped that he thought that he was in charge.[14] Reportedly Rubottom told Castro that the United States would consider economic aid to Cuba as it was in the U.S. interest to see that the Cuban economy got off to a good start.[15] Herter called Castro an "enigma" who "confused the roar of mass audiences with the rule of the majority," and he sent a memorandum to Eisenhower advising that the United States should "watch and wait." Eisenhower wrote, "File, we should check in one year," on the memo.[16]

Castro met with waves of reporters, answering questions in several languages. Castro seemed at ease, but he also stated that because of misreporting, "The world is against us now." He said he would provide the whole truth. He again alleged as fact that the Batista government had committed approximately 20,000 murders and other war crimes and that the culprits had been given a right to trial and were legally subject to execution. He said that allegations that the executions were retaliation for political crimes was entirely false. "Bodies pushed into rivers, the killings hidden…. These men have robbed and killed the people … since when are robbery and murder political crimes?" He alleged that all of the trials were open to the public and to the press and that the executions were a lesson to future governments.[17]

There were 35 picketers at the White House. When questioned by reporters, some said that they had been paid as much as $35 to picket Castro.[18] The papers did not report who had paid them.

The next day, Castro told his host, the American Society of Newspaper Editors, that he and his *barbudos* were humanists, "We are not Communists."[19] Speaking in English, he told them the basic rights of Cubans were "the right to live, the right to eat, [and] the right to work." He said that the number of unemployed in Cuba was proportionally greater than the amount of unemployed Americans during the Great Depression. He alleged that 95 percent of the Cuban people had supported a removal of Batista and thus supported the revolution, and that included all ranks of Cuban society, from the wealthy to the poor. When asked about executions, he alleged that Cuba had executed only those guilty of war crimes. When asked about existing treaties with the United States, Castro said that he would honor all of them, including the agreement to maintain the U.S. naval base at Guantánamo, and he recognized that Cuba was legally bound to the agreement to defend the Western Hemisphere from outside aggression and said that Cuba would fulfill its commitments. Although Cuba would support the overthrow of dictators, it would not intervene in the foreign affairs of any nation. He told the editors that Cuba was not a beggar nation, rather it wanted more trade with the United States.[20]

Castro again chided the American press for failing to report that there had been 20,000 victims of torture and assassination under Batista. He alleged that this was partly due to government censorship during the Batista regime. "The first thing that dictators do is finish off the free press. There is no doubt that the free press is the first enemy of dictatorship."[21] This brought a standing ovation.

Castro did not mention that a war crimes tribunal sentenced former *Pueblo* columnist Fernando Miranda to 10 years' hard labor in the Zapata swamps for calling the Castro rebels "thieves and bandits."[22]

In his speech and in questioning, Castros aid that Cuba would not expropriate private property and said, to the contrary, that Cuba sought industrial investments. He extolled free trade, saying "We must have a market for our goods." He hoped that the United States would revisit its sugar quota.[23]

Between scheduled visits, Castro toured Washington. He and the entourage visited the Lincoln and Jefferson memorials, and Mount Vernon, George Washington's home. Dozens of newsmen followed, took pictures of Castro posed at our national shrines and reported how Castro spoke knowledgeably and highly of the founding fathers and American democracy. He told the newsmen that Cuba would like to become more democratic, but he estimated that the Cuban people needed about four years before free elections would serve their interests.[24] He said that the words of the Declaration of Independence "support the ideals of the Cuban Revolution."[25] Castro told the Senate Foreign Relations Committee: "The July 26 movement is not a communist movement. Its members are Roman Catholics, mostly." On investment, he said: "We have no intention of expropriating U.S. property, and any property we take, we'll pay for." Although all of the senators seemed cordial, and newspapers reported that most senators felt that Castro had reassured them, *Time* magazine pointed out that Florida's Democratic senator George Smathers later stated: "Castro hasn't yet learned that you can't play ball with the communists, for he has them peppered throughout his government." He also said that serious trouble was "brewing" in Cuba and suggested that the Organization of American States form a voluntary police force to keep the peace in Latin America.[26]

That night, Castro attended a reception at the Cuban embassy. The papers noted he wore a white shirt and black tie under his fatigues. Although Castro had chastised the American press for its reporting, he awarded medals to newsmen who had interviewed him while he was in the mountains.[27] Among those he honored were Herbert L. Matthews, Robert Taber and Georgette "Dickey" Chapelle of *Reader's Digest*, who had spent about three weeks in the Sierra Maestras. Ruby Phillips and wire service reporters were not among them.

In a *Meet the Press* television interview on NBC, Castro was asked whether Cuba would support the United States in conflicts with the Soviet Union.[28] The United States and Cuba had entered into mutual defense treaties, and Castro said that Cuba would honor them. When asked point-blank whether he was a communist, he said: "Democracy is my ideal, really ... I am not a Communist." When asked whether Raúl Castro or Vilma Espín, his loquacious American-educated wife, were communists, Castro said they were not. Although there were some Communists in the government, he alleged that "their influence is nothing."[29] The *Washington Post* quoted Castro as saying when asked about Khrushchev: "We are against all kinds of dictatorship ... that is why we do not agree with Communism."[30] Arguing that the war crimes trials were fair, Castro said that more than 1,000 people tried before military tribunals had been exonerated.[31]

Meanwhile, Castro had police protection, as rumors of an assassination plot were rife.[32]

Immediately after the *Meet the Press* interview, Castro met privately with Vice President Nixon in his office. Nixon had preconceived notions that Castro was the enemy, although Castro characterized the talks as "friendly, informal and positive."[33] It is reasonable to believe

Fidel Castro meets Richard Nixon, April 1959 in Washington. "I talked to him like a Dutch uncle," Nixon would say. He and Gerry Droller, aka Frank Bender, a CIA operative, provided Castro with detailed surveillance information about his own organization. Droller/Bender did not believe Castro was a communist, but Nixon would soon lobby for a covert CIA operation, similar to ones deployed in Iran and Guatemala, to unseat the new regime (photograph from Getty Images).

that the suspicions were mutual. Allen Dulles, head of the CIA, had told the National Security Council that the Cuban government "had to be treated more or less like children. They had to be led rather than rebuffed. If they were rebuffed, like children, they were capable of almost anything."[34]

Nixon had a lengthy history with Cuba and with Charles "Bebe" Rebozo, who he met in 1950, and with whom he was extremely close. Rebozo was a native-born United States citizen, but his parents were Cuban immigrants and he spent a lot of time in Cuba. According to several sources, Rebozo was a Nixon fund-raiser and had covered Nixon's gambling losses at the Hotel Nacional in Havana.[35]

In 1952 Rebozo campaigned for Nixon and was with Nixon in Key Biscayne, Florida, as they celebrated the 1952 election victory. Another Nixon fund-raiser had been involved in a scandal over "razzle dazzle," a notorious rigged dice game, in 1953, and Nixon and Rebozo intervened with Batista directly on his behalf.[36] Beginning in 1954, Nixon spent vacations with Rebozo at his house in Key West, Florida.[37]

Several internal government memoranda from the period list Rebozo as a source of information about Cuba.[38] CIA documents show that both Rebozo and Nixon held investments in Cuba in February 1959.[39] Meanwhile, Rebozo was also closely associated with Havana casino owner Santos Traficante, Jr., also originally from the same neighborhood in Tampa, who by April 9, 1959, was in jail in Cuba.

In February 1955, Nixon had come to Havana to discuss "problems" with Batista. At that time, Batista told him that "communists" would demonstrate against him, and Nixon was heavily guarded everywhere he went.[40] He and Batista openly discussed the Cuban sugar quota, and Batista complained that American beet and cane farmers wanted to cut the quota, to their benefit and Cuba's detriment.[41]

Nixon also made a stop in Cuba on his 1958 Latin American trip, when angry crowds stoned him and spat upon him as a symbol of "Yankee imperialism." From all accounts, Nixon barely escaped from Latin America. Scenes of the riot were shown on television and widely reported in the newspapers, and Nixon was described as a hero for standing up to anti–Americanism.[42] When he returned, 40,000 people met him at the airport. Some carried signs that said "Remember the Maine."[43] In fact, while Castro was in Washington, the Senate held hearings resulting from Nixon's trip, and that is the reason given for Castro's testimony before the Senate.

Nixon started the meeting by showing to Castro CIA files indicating that some of his associates had a connection to the Soviet Union.[44] Nixon then told Castro that the executions had a negative public relations effect in the United States.[45] Castro switched the subject, described his vision for Cuba and told Nixon that Cuba was not interested in U.S. military aid, but only in U.S. investment and business development. Nixon told Castro that the United States was attempting to balance its budget and thus was short on funds. He told Castro that if Cuba needed money, it should seek aid from private industry rather than the government.[46] After Castro said he wanted the U.S. government to invest in Cuban industries, Nixon and Castro reportedly discussed the nature of private investment and Castro offered that he favored state-licensed industry, rather than permitting private companies the right to develop on their own.[47]

Nixon later alleged that he hoped to urge Castro to move "in the right direction," but thought Castro was naive, childish or both.[48] He used Puerto Rico as an example, which must have infuriated Castro. Castro had been the head of a student movement interested in Puerto Rican independence, and Castro was a social acquaintance of the wife of the now jailed Puerto Rican independence leader Albizu Campos. More importantly, Puerto Rico was an American possession without sovereignty.[49]

"I talked to him like a Dutch uncle," Nixon stated patronizingly.[50] In a memorandum of the meeting, Nixon reported:

> I was convinced Castro was either incredibly naive about Communism or under Communist discipline and that we would have to treat him and deal with him accordingly—under no illusions about "fiery rebels" in the "tradition of Bolivar." My position was a minority one within the Administration and particularly so within the Latin American branch of the State Department. Trying to "get along with" and "understand" Castro continued to be the State Department line despite my own strong recommendation to the contrary.[51]

As soon as the meeting ended, Nixon immediately suggested that the United States enable Cuban exiles to establish a CIA-sponsored army to overthrow Castro.[52]

At the time, Nixon was preparing for a summer trip to the Soviet Union. He had been contemplating a run for the presidency and the trip would, he hoped, give him the same if not more good publicity than his Latin American trip had given him.

Castro again met with Herter privately and met with "Frank Bender" of the CIA, who was an expert on communist infiltration in Latin America. At the time, communists from all over Latin America had come to Cuba, offered as a refuge against dictators by Castro and the Provisional Government. Bender described how the communists would try to infiltrate, then overcome the Provisional Government. Castro reportedly told "Mr. Bender" that he was aware, but that the best tactic was to permit the communists to expose themselves, so there would be public proof of any deception.[53] After three hours, Mr. Bender reported that not only was Castro not a communist, he was avidly anti-communist.[54] "Bender" was actually Gerry Droller, then age 54, who later would be one of the CIA officers responsible for the Bay of Pigs operation.[55]

Castro also met with Henry Luce, publisher of *Time* and *Life* magazines, both of which were highly critical of Castro. Luce's wife, Clare Boothe Luce, considered herself an expert on Latin America, and Luce and his wife had lobbied John Foster Dulles to ask Eisenhower to replace Earl E. T. Smith as ambassador to Cuba with Mrs. Luce rather than Bonsal.[56] Instead, Eisenhower named Mrs. Luce ambassador to Brazil. *Time* had run weekly reports describing the executions in Cuba as vengeance rather than justice. Despite the meeting, *Time* continued to run articles inferring that Castro was a Communist.[57] The title of the ensuing edition of *Time*, "The Other Face," implied that Castro was two-faced—that he was deceptive and manipulative. The article began,

> With 100 cases of good-will rum in his baggage and a permanent grin on his bearded face, Prime Minister Fidel Castro flew into Washington last week and spared neither energy nor charm in putting a good face on his revolution and trying "to understand better the United States." He even kissed a baby in a Washington park.

The article reminded readers that while Castro was schmoozing in Washington, trials of dissidents were ongoing in Cuba.[58] In a follow-up article, *Time* reported that Castro wasn't fooling anybody, even the "*New York Times*, one of his warmest U.S. press friends all through the revolution, [which] abruptly shifted its news line with a 1,400-word story on growing Communist influence in the Castro regime. In pursuit of 'revolutionary justice,' noted the *Times*, 'it has become customary to arrest members of the Batista armed forces, publish their pictures in the newspapers, including *Hoy*, the Communist organ—asking if anyone has an accusation against these men.'"[59] The Associated Press ran similar articles,

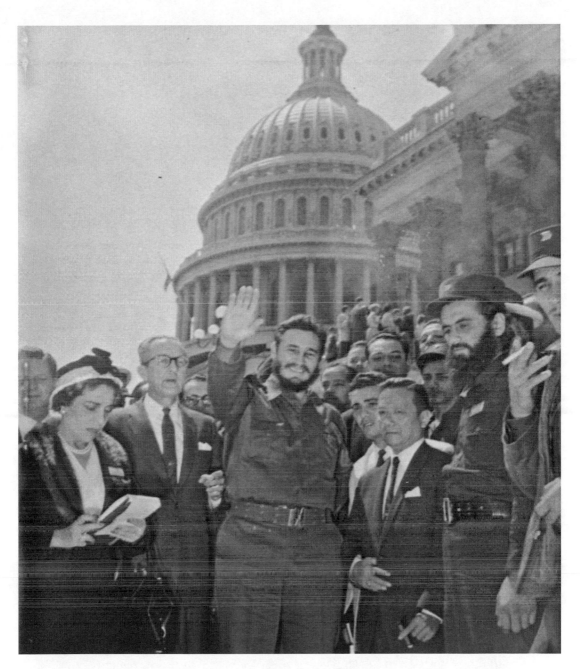

Fidel Castro in Washington. Castro was not invited as a head of state, but came at the invitation of the Society of Newspaper Editors. Although he stayed several days in Washington and met with government officials, President Eisenhower conspicuously took a golfing trip to avoid him (Associated Press).

alleging that Communists ran the Cuban army information program, the fine arts commission and the National Institute of Culture. But it also noted that the Communists had once been cozy with Batista and did not support Castro's calls for strikes when he was fighting in the mountains. It said that Cubans were waiting to see whether Castro would crack down on Communists.[60] Castro also met with another critic, Frank Bartholomew, president of United Press International.

While Castro was in the States, the Provisional Government arrested members of a "Carribean Legion" at a Nicaraguan rebel training camp in Pinar del Río Province that was planning a guerrilla military attack on Panama. At the time, Panama was among four countries ruled by dictatorships that had been marked for revolution. The others were Nicaragua, Haiti and the Dominican Republic, where Batista had fled. Although the Provisional Government could not deny that groups of exiles from other Latin American countries were living in Cuba and plotting the overthrow of their governments, and although the Cuban government empathized with the plight of the people of those countries, it decided that it would not permit émigré rebels to involve Cuba in the internal affairs of those countries. Cuba, like the United States, would permit dissident exiles to immigrate and reside peaceably, but could not let them wage war from its territory.[61] Although there was no evidence that Cuba was about to attack any neighbor, the president of Guatemala issued a statement saying Guatemala would defend any country if attacked.[62] But when a group of several Haitians and 28 Cubans was stopped at sea by the Cuban navy, although it looked like an invasion force, the leaders denied that they would abuse Cuban hospitality to attack Haiti.[63] Soon after that, a group of black uniformed mercenaries known as "the shadows," training for an invasion of Nicaragua, were arrested by the Cuban government. Among those arrested was Lawrence Eugene Hall, age 29, of Wichita, Kansas, an army veteran.[64]

Before leaving Washington, Castro left a wreath at the Tomb of the Unknowns at Arlington National Cemetery and also visited an elementary school. Castro told the press that he had achieved everything he wanted to do when he came to Washington, and he would miss it and the "many good people" he had met.[65]

After a train trip to Princeton University, Castro spoke at the Senior Conference of the American Civilization Program on "The United States and the Revolutionary Spirit." Castro said that democracy was "the most beautiful political and social idea." He told the audience that the Provisional Government would allow minority parties to develop in opposition to his regime, and that while there were "no plans to nationalize any lands," his government would "expropriate legally" any "idle or unproductive lands." *The Newark Evening News* reported that Castro had said that Cuba "asked for nothing" from the United States, only "understanding." Charges of communism leveled against the regime, he claimed, were part of a campaign by opposition leaders outside of Cuba." His government was pledged to "satisfying the people's material needs without sacrificing any freedoms." "There is little room in Cuba for communist ideas," he declared. In response to an implied accusation that his motives were less than altruistic, Castro reportedly rejoined with the following assertion: "I could be rich…. You know how? By writing the history of our revolution for Hollywood."[66] Castro also visited Lawrenceville Prep, a private school, where he told the students in halting English to learn foreign languages.[67] At a reception in his honor at Princeton, Castro met with former secretary of state Dean Acheson.

The next day, thousands of well-wishers came to see Castro. The streets were jammed with people shouting "wild cheers," chanting his name in unison, and waving Cuban flags and signs as his motorcade drove a block from Penn Station to his hotel. "This is just the way it is in Cuba," Castro stated. At times, he waded into the crowds. There were about six picketers carrying pro-Batista signs and a brief scuffle ensued.[68] As Castro entered New York to a "tumultuous" reception, the *New York Times* ran an article describing a Cuban government plan to raise taxes by imposing high import duties and by requiring half of all cargo entering Cuba to enter on Cuban registered ships. At the time, the United States required half of all aid shipped to be sent on United States ships. However, the State Department pointed out that Cuba would set that requirement on all cargo. The article also described a plan to require any Cuban shipping that was not wholly maintained by private capital to sell 60 percent of its ownership to a government-owned shipping company.[69]

That afternoon, Castro appeared at a seminar at Columbia University (where President Eisenhower had been employed prior to election), and he met with the university president and with students to discuss agrarian reform. Castro said that the goal was to make Cuba more self-sustaining and that he hoped that by reducing the average size of the estates, they might be able to produce at a much higher rate. He said that Cuba needed to build its industrial base and was not interested in American aid. He also said that Cuba would not seek to extradite Batista, but hoped that the United States would censure Trujillo for harboring him.[70]

After the seminar, Castro met with the editorial board of the *New York Times*. That evening, he addressed a group of women lawyers at a dinner at his hotel. He told them that he was a lawyer "who took arms defending the law."[71]

Although Castro continually denied that Cuba needed economic aid from the United States, the *New York Times* continued to publish articles asserting that Cuba's economy was in dire straits and that the only resolution was a drastic austerity program and the infusion of massive aid from the United States. The article referred to unknown government sources who concluded that the Cuban government would last to, at best, September 1959. According to experts, the Cuban economy would have had the same fate under Batista, as world sugar and other commodity prices drove down the value of the Cuban peso. Without U.S. aid, Cuba would "have to adopt a controlled economy, with restrictions on imports and foreign exchange transactions, ... internal subsidies and deficit financing." The article also stated that the United States had two choices: to give Cuba an infusion of aid or let it go "through the wringer." The article suggested that Castro had a good financial team and that the United States should aid Castro, or else he might be "overthrown by communists or extremists on the right."[72]

Cuba had participated briefly in Operation Pan America, but the Provisional Government was just getting organized by the time that other Latin American countries had agreed to 24 proposals to further economic development in Latin America. The plan was to establish a billion-dollar Inter-American Development Bank. Also, many Latin American governments had agreed to a process of "stabilization" of their economies, by permitting the U.S. government to provide standards to send aid and trade ... in essence making the dollar the currency for the Western Hemisphere. Unnamed sources were quoted as saying that unless Cuba agreed to the same type of program, it was doomed.[73]

Conversely, the *Times* also ran articles quoting Rufo López Fresquet, the Cuban minister of the Treasury, saying that 1959 would be Cuba's best year. López Fresquet was a Columbia University graduate and was married to an American. He said that there was a recession, that there was regime change and that Batista had stolen much of the national treasure, and he said he was speaking as an economist and not as a politician, and claimed the Cuban economy would improve. The key would be the potential recovery of over $100,000,000 in back taxes, money that would be plowed into the economy. He also said that by eliminating graft, a tremendous drain on the budget was ended. Tourism, trade and domestic commerce were picking up and Cuba did not seek aid, only more trade.[74] A few days later, the Cuban government announced that tax evasion would be treated as a counter-revolutionary activity.[75]

On April 22, Castro made a three-hour visit to the United Nations. As he arrived,

President Eisenhower (seated left) and Secretary of State John Foster Dulles (seated right) meet with Soviet deputy premier Anastas Mikoyan (seated center) during a 1959 visit to the United States. The two men standing are unidentified. Vice President Nixon visited the Soviet Union in July, and Premier Khrushchev visited the United States for two weeks in September, signaling a thaw in tensions and an indication of a willingness to negotiate. However during a January 1960 Mikoyan visit to Cuba, which formerly did not have diplomatic relations with the Soviet Union, a trade deal was announced. That deal would lead to the end of United States and Cuban diplomatic relations (photograph from Getty Images).

there were about 100 picketers protesting his appearance, but his admirers far outnumbered them. He received a standing ovation from most of the Latin American ambassadors. He repeated that the Cuban people did not want elections until the country had stabilized, there were no communists in the government, the revolution was "not ready for export" to any other nation, the Cuban United Nations delegation would be independent of any bloc, and civil courts were being reestablished in Cuba as the military tribunals existed only to hear war crimes trials. He also talked to Secretary-General Dag Hammarskjold privately for about 30 minutes, and invited him to visit Cuba.[76]

After a lunch with the Overseas Press Club, he visited the New York City mayor, the owner of the *New York Post,* and the editor of *La Prensa,* a Spanish-language newspaper published in Argentina. He later gave a press conference at his hotel. As Castro traveled throughout Manhattan, his security had to be increased as there were reports of threatened assassination attempts. One rumor was that the Mafia and Meyer Lansky had placed a contract on Castro's life.[77]

In Washington, Herter was officially sworn in as secretary of state. John Foster Dulles was in Walter Reed Hospital, and President Eisenhower visited him on his return from his golf trip and swore him in as a presidential consultant on foreign affairs.

While Fidel Castro was visiting the "Colossus of the North," his brother and potential successor was contemplating how he could consolidate his power. Raúl Castro was not personally a member of the Provisional Government but he was in charge of the army. Many of his fellow comandantes had become his adversaries. He was in competition with other M–7–26 officers and his popularity was eclipsed by Cienfuegos and even Matos. During his brother's trip to the United States, Raúl Castro became worried that Fidel had been seduced by the Americans. He telephoned him, but Fidel told him he should not worry.

However, Raúl actually considered splitting the movement to demonstrate that Fidel Castro could not govern without the help of the communists.[78] He decided that he would develop his own cadre and place his own men into power. To do it, he sent Lazaro Peña, a longtime communist, to ask the Soviet Union to send him a few Spanish graduates of the Soviet military academy as advisors, "to help the Cuban Army on general matters ... and for the organization of intelligence work."[79] Raúl had been a member of the Socialist Youth, but after he had joined with his brother in the Moncada attack, he had been expelled from the Communist Party. However, he obviously kept his connections with them.

On April 24, a day after Castro met with the editorial board, the *New York Times* ran another article by Ruby Phillips questioning Castro's ties to Communism. She reported that despite the allegation that there were no communists in the government, Castro was "applauded daily" in *Hoy* (Today), the communist paper run by Carlos Rafael Rodríguez, a Communist *barbudo* with close ties to Castro, who had been a minister in the 1940–44 Batista regime but served in the mountains in the Rebel Army with M–7–26. The M–7–26 newspaper, *Revolución*, was run by Carlos Franqui, who at one time had worked for *Hoy*. *Hoy* ran an editorial denying that communists had influence, "in the sense that you understand and propagate it in the *Times*." However, Phillips responded that Juan Marinello, president of the Cuban Communist Party, had gone to Moscow to tell the Soviets how communists had been an integral part of the revolution and that experienced Communist leaders were back in power in Cuba. She also repeated the allegations that Che Guevara was a communist and that Castro's brother and heir, Raúl, and his wife, Vilma Espín, had been accused of being communists.[80]

Phillips also alleged that many Cubans, including Castro's allies against Batista, were worried that the country was turning to Communism. She said that there were executions of people who were not war criminals; there were mass arrests for counter-revolutionary activities; and there was concern about how these people would be treated. She told how the middle class was squeezed by social programs like reductions in rents, reduction of land values and forced sales of vacant lots. "Meanwhile," she said, "the Communist Popular Socialist Party is organizing every town and village. The influence on unions is rising. Leaders of the 26th of July movement are combating these efforts, but the youthful rebels are amateurs at organization compared to the communists."[81]

William L. Ryan of the Associated Press attended the lunch at the Overseas Press Club. Although he remained critical of Castro, Ryan acknowledged that Castro appeared to have become more polished, if not more humble, since his early appearances in Havana. He "captured and cultivated his audience." He defended his ideas of revolutionary justice "eloquently." But he also said that Castro "appeared to be a man way off on cloud 9, a man far removed from politics, economics, government, and life." However, he admitted that Castro's uniform was an image that connotes a "military government." He noted that Castro's enemies outside the country have far more money than he, and inside Cuba there were still large numbers of well trained military from the old regime.[82]

That morning, Castro lectured the Council on Foreign Affairs, a New York-based group of private citizens and former government officials. He had a prepared speech, but became confrontational with his audience during the session. He alleged that Cuba would never beg the United States for economic assistance. Angered by some of the questions, especially about executions, Castro left abruptly.

He also visited the Coffee and Sugar Exchange and the Bronx Zoo, where, to the consternation of security, he jumped a fence to pet a tiger. He said that he and the tiger had a lot in common; they both had experienced jail.[83]

That evening as Castro was addressing 30,000 people at a rally on the Mall in Central Park, a man was arrested with a bomb.[84] Castro spoke mostly in English to the huge crowd for more than two hours to numerous ovations. The press described the scene as "one of dark shadow and bright glare. Police searchlights roved continuously, picking out the hills of the park, the thousands of flags, the thousands of faces." On duty were 500 policemen on foot and 33 mounted on horseback.

Later that evening Castro announced that Cuba would retain its professional baseball team after he conferred with Roberto "Bobby" Maduro, owner of the Havana Sugar Kings in the International League, who flew from Havana for the occasion.[85] While he was in New York, baseball scout Joe Cambria asked Castro to return to Washington to pitch against Hall of Famer Mickey Mantle, the Yankees' center fielder, who was scheduled to play against the Washington Senators, then loaded with Cuban players. However, Castro's schedule would not permit it. Cambria also hoped that Castro could be present when fellow Cuban Pedro Ramos was scheduled to pitch against the Yankees.[86]

The *Times* published another article, relying on unnamed government sources, reporting that Cuban American relations were uncertain. Again noting that the experts said that Cuba must go "through the wringer," it stated that although no one could predict the outcome, it was reasonable to expect that the Provisional Government would collapse. If that were to happen, the article reported, from an American perspective the best result would be a right-wing takeover and the worst would be Communism.[87]

In Boston, 2,500 police officers were detailed to avert threatened assassination attempts.[88] Castro spent much of his time at Harvard with his host, dean of the Faculty of Arts and Sciences, McGeorge Bundy. Castro told Bundy that although he had applied for admission to Harvard, he had been rejected.[89] When Castro was introduced, Bundy told the crowd that Harvard was now ready to admit him. By the time Castro spoke to Harvard law students and faculty in Cambridge, the estimated number of police present had increased to 4,000. However, Castro evaded security as he walked into the crowd of students to shake hands and to talk to them directly. Castro spoke on several subjects and received "tremendous applause and cheers," and took questions, which were mainly concerned with the executions.[90]

By the time Castro left the States, he had been given an opportunity to explain his opinions on every subject from the executions to baseball. Even the formerly jaded Associated Press ran an article saying that as a result of the trip, Castro had been able to convince skeptics that he was not an ogre, as had been previously reported.[91]

In Montreal, a cheering crowd of 5,000 people surrounded him as he arrived. However, there were more death threats.[92] He cut short the welcoming speech from Montreal's mayor as he waded into the crowd of admirers. He also upset the plans of the Cuban consul as he and his entourage left a planned lunch before eating anything. The press called him a "creature of impulses" as he was late to several appearances, including a press conference.[93]

Meanwhile, an invasion of Panama had failed. Fifty armed men from Cuba said Castro had sent them to liberate the country. Among those arrested in Panama were two Cubans. The leader was a Panamanian, Roberto Arias, husband of Margot Fonteyn, a British ballerina, who was seeking asylum in the Brazilian embassy.[94] Rumors had been circulating for weeks that Arias would lead an attempted insurrection in Panama,

After Montreal, Castro spent a night in Houston, Texas, on his way to a meeting of the Committee of Twenty-One, a political organization representing 21 republics in the Western Hemisphere. Castro was the representative of his country. In Houston, Raúl Castro was waiting for him. There is no record of what transpired, but it is safe to assume that Castro received reports on the state of the Provisional Government. Castro later drove to Wharton, Texas, to take a look at a colt that a Texas oilman had given to him.[95]

He also stopped in Brasilia, where he met with the Brazilian president. On his arrival, May 1, riots were ongoing as groups of Peronistas, right-wing followers of deposed Argentine dictator Juan Perón, now in exile in the Dominican Republic, clashed with Communists.

Both Fidel and Raúl Castro stated that any member of the Cuban armed forces who was assisting the invasion of Panama would be discharged. They sent representatives from Cuba to ask the rebels to lay down their arms, and Raúl held the head of the Panamanian rebels, still in Cuba, under house arrest.[96]

It was also reported that although a military tribunal had ordered the death penalty for a convicted marijuana seller, the sentence was rescinded as there was no basis for it under Cuban law, and a new trial was ordered.[97] The military tribunal had exceeded its authority.

In Buenos Aires, undersecretaries Thomas Mann and Rubottom represented the United States. They were ready to acknowledge that the region needed new investment. Between 1945 and 1959, Latin America had received about 2 percent of United States foreign aid. In 1955 Latin America led the world in private United States investment; by 1959 it was last.[98] Mann spoke of the establishment of the $1,000,000,000 Inter-American Development Bank as the key to Latin American development. The first order of business was to seat the committee chairman. Venezuela and Cuba objected to the naming of the Nicaraguan representative, on the basis that Nicaragua was a dictatorship.[99]

It took several days before Castro could address the conference. On May 2, he sat two seats away from Undersecretary Mann, who had spoken before Castro arrived. Several speakers before Castro drew no reaction from the audience. Castro "nervously jiggled his legs, stroked his mustache, chewed at the end of his pencil and made asides to photographers" and to other delegates.[100] When Castro rose to speak, he was the center of attention as every point brought cheers from almost the entire audience. However, the representatives from the Dominican Republic, Panama and Paraguay did not applaud. Castro said that the bank was a good idea but was not funded well enough and called on the United States to supply Latin America with $30 billion of economic aid over a 10-year period. The delegate from Venezuela had proposed that the United States grant priority to Latin American products. Castro reminded the members that the United States had graciously come to the aid of Western Europe after the devastation of World War II, and through its investment in the Marshall Plan, Europe had prospered and no longer needed American aid. He said that like Western Europe after the War, Latin America experienced political instability of governments and poverty in Latin America was the *result* of underdevelopment, "and not the cause of underdevelopment as some maintain." In fact, Latin America was in worse shape. If Latin

America received similar treatment, it would soon be in a position of parity with other countries and would no longer need help. He warned that the recent overthrow of dictators in Latin America could be an "illusion" and that democracy would be only temporary unless economic progress were achieved.

Castro said that in order to rise from poverty, Latin American countries needed national savings, private capital investments and foreign assistance with public funds. He asserted that import restrictions like the United States sugar quota prevented Latin American countries from exporting sufficient quantities of product to accumulate savings. If the United States and Canada removed all restrictions on the importation of Latin American raw materials, and withdrew all subsidies being paid to domestic producers of competing raw materials, the Latin American countries could earn enough dollars to undertake their own development. According to Castro, private capital investment would not solve Latin American economic problems, primarily because private capital would seek the best investment climate and would thus tend to bypass those countries where social conditions were most turbulent and where development was most needed. He recommended encouraging the investment of capital by national enterprises by making credits available to them which would be secured from international credit agencies. He preferred investment by national firms, but he said he would not exclude international investors and would offer them the equal rights and guarantees.

Castro advanced governmental financial aid (*financiamento publico*), as the best way to solve the problem. He said that technicians of the Cuban delegation had calculated that $30 billion was needed over a period of 10 years for the full economic development of Latin America. However, although the program might cost a lot in the short run, the United States had made similar financial sacrifices before to aid Europe and the Middle East. Castro declared that this policy would be the easiest for the United States to implement, much easier than eliminating restrictions against the importation of Latin American products, and would redeem to the mutual benefit of the United States and Latin America. Castro said that he had support for the proposed aid program in American public opinion and referred to statements by three United States senators which gave some support to his ideas.[101]

Although the United States was expected to reply to Castro's remarks, it declined. Rubottom was quoted as saying, "We don't feel that Castro speaks for all Latin America and we don't intend to engage in polemics."[102]

Castro visited Uruguay and Brazil before returning to Cuba. While in Brazil, Castro withdrew the plan. Although he was aware the plan had been withdrawn, Undersecretary Mann released a reply that attacked Castro's plan, in favor of "moderation."[103]

Ambassador Bonsal later wrote that Castro could have made the speech in Washington and returned to in Havana in one day, but Castro's ego drove him to self-deception about the value of the trip.[104] Had there been better diplomacy and less ego on both sides, Castro's ego and Mann's pride of authorship could have accommodated discussions on points of conflict at the time. These conflicts were trivial compared with the consequences for Cuba, United States, and for Latin America.

By the time the trip ended, Castro was convinced that the United States was considering an invasion.[105] He sensed that Nixon had been hostile.[106] He had circumstantial evidence that the CIA was involved with an insurgent army in the Dominican Republic preparing to attack Cuba. He set up contingency plans to return to the mountains to fight a guerrilla war in case the U.S. Marines took the major cities, and Cuba bought small arms and munitions in Europe to give to its population a means to resist.[107]

Chapter 11

May Day

On May 1, 1959, Cuban workers observed the first May Day program after the revolution. Premier Fidel Castro was not present as the Cuban Confederation of Labor presented a 14-hour parade in front of the Capitolo involving thousands of workers. On the reviewing stand, President Urrutia Lleó was presented a list of demands and said that after full consideration, he would recommend all that were not "materially impossible."[1] Workers demanded 20 to 30 percent increases in wages, requested a workers' armed militia, and demanded that the government invoke more restrictive work laws on foreign workers, increase import tariffs, and protect certain domestic industries like liquor and shoe manufacturing. Cuban artists and musicians demanded that all movie theaters should also be required to present vaudeville shows and that television broadcasters air more live entertainment and fewer movies. Cuban transport workers demanded they unload and reload at point of entry U.S. boxcars being shipped through Cuba rather than allowing the boxcars to be sent directly to their destination. The printers union requested a 40-hour workweek at 44 hours of pay and requested a ban on importing all foreign publications. The sugar workers demanded that half of all sugar produced in Cuba be refined in Cuba. They also demanded reinstatement of all workers who had been dismissed during the Batista regime. Workers at *Excelsior* and *El País,* daily newspapers in Havana, demanded that they be given control of editorial policy and demanded that all "enemies of the revolution" should be dismissed.[2]

At that time millions of Cubans were still living in crushing poverty, unemployment was between 12 and 15 percent, Cuba's asset values had fallen with the declining price of sugar, the value of the peso had caved, much of the arable land was still unproductive, the tourist trade was down and much of the treasury had been taken overseas. News articles also highlighted problems in government transition; there was still some of the old corruption, there was anxiety among large landowners and foreign investors, and there was an acknowledged rise in Communist influence.[3] Despite these domestic problems, Castro had concentrated on Cuban foreign policy, and apparently had assumed responsibility for the problems of all of Latin America. He had been away for more than two weeks.

While Castro was still in Argentina and Uruguay, CBS ran a program alleging that Cuba was becoming a "communist beachhead." Correspondent Stuart Novins had spent two months in Cuba and reported on the CBS news program *Studio 56* that the new government was rife with Communists. He alleged that if anything happened to Castro, there would be a "bloodbath." He said that there could be a bloodbath in any event because anticommunists "feel they have no course to take but violence." Novins said that the only way to avoid bloodshed was to hold free elections. Castro said he was for them but changed his mind as to when they might occur.[4] Castro was told what Novins had said, and he replied that Cuba was a true democracy, where all viewpoints are respected. He accused the United States of attempting to incriminate and imprison Communists.[5]

On May 7, Jules Dubois's article titled, "Red Power in Cuba Held Exaggerated" was run nationally. Dubois alleged that although there was Communist infiltration, there was not domination. He noted that although there were Communists in the Cuban labor movement, they were few, and they had lost "thumping" defeats in recent union elections. The only alleged Communist in a "dominating" position was Che Guevara, commander of the La Cabaña prison. Dubois noted a "wide line" between being a leftist revolutionary and a communist, and noted that the official M–7–26 newspaper, *Revolución*, and its editor, Carlos Franqui, opposed communist infiltration in the labor movement. He also noted that the fact that Raúl Castro visited behind the Iron Curtain at age 20 "does not make him a communist."[6] However, on the same day, the *New York Times* reported that American labor groups alleged that free trade unions suffered "setbacks" in Cuba and cited to "domination of infiltrating communists."[7]

On May 8, Castro returned to Cuba after 23 days.[8] Three members of his group had contracted smallpox during the trip, so the party was quarantined. However, that night, he told a crowd of tens of thousands in the Plaza de la República that Cuba had the respect of all of Latin America. He privately told Urrutia that he had been warned that the communists wanted to oust him from the government. Urrutia said that "this was indeed the opinion of some people."[9]

The next day, the University of Havana opened for classes for the first time in two and a half years. About 30 professors had been purged, and had to be replaced. Students who left the country after Batista had closed the school were considered to be deserters, and their foreign credits and degrees were nullified. Among the 18,000 returning students were thousands of war veterans.[10]

That evening, Castro gave a six-hour televised interview and told his fellow Cubans that he had been pleasantly surprised by the warm reception he received from the American people, despite what he viewed as a negative press campaign against the Revolution. The American people, Castro said, "know nothing of dictatorship and terror." He outlined his proposal made to the Committee of Twenty-One and told Cubans that conditions in all of Latin America were getting worse, and that a huge investment in the region could save it. He described the Inter-American Development Bank, but said that it would not be a large enough investment. He also stated that the military tribunals would come to an end and that civil courts would soon be reestablished, along with the right of habeus corpus.[11] By that time, 621 prisoners had been executed. When he was told that workers at the newspaper *El País* wanted the right to set editorial policy, Castro said that workers have no rights over such matters. Within a few days, former President Prío Socorrás, speaking as head of the Auténtico Party, asked for immediate restoration of civil rights and elections.[12]

A few days later, Castro addressed some of the demands that labor had been making and which Urrutia had discussed on May Day. He said that wage demands were out of the question because Cuba had to reduce labor costs to make products less expensive. He said that labor unions should have asked for wage increases when Batista was in power and that wage increases would be addressed only after production increased. Labor agitation must end, he warned, or the government would take steps to end it.[13]

On May 12, the *New York Times* ran an editorial, "Red Embrace in Cuba," in which it described how Communism would apply the "kiss of death" to Castro unless he repudiated it immediately as "neutrality or detachment ... is impossible."[14] A couple of days later, the official M–7–26 newspaper, *Revolución*, again attacked the communists as "divisionists." The article noted how the communists took credit for issuing government announcements. "We are neither with Communism or Capitalism as Fidel Castro has said. This is a humanist revolution against right and left dictatorships."[15] CBS ran the second part of its series *Is Cuba Going Red?*, and three Cuban diplomats testified that it was not. However, a poll was taken of people who recognized Fidel Castro, and only 31 percent found him well regarded.[16]

The *Washington Post* noted that things were improving in Cuba upon Castro's return. For one thing, the military tribunals ceded power to civilian courts. For another, the government newspaper *Revolución* had taken on the communists.[17] Castro said that the Cuban Revolution was an "olive green" revolution and not a "red" revolution. He stated that "extremists" would not have a place in the revolution. When asked whether the extremists he had referred to were communists, he stated, "Perhaps there is much coincidence in this."[18] He was quoted as calling the communists "counter-revolutionaries."[19]

While Castro was away, the price of sugar started to rise dramatically.[20]

Although Castro and the government had ordered that any illegal appropriation of property would not be tolerated, squatters had taken some land, mainly in Oriente Province.[21] Meanwhile, the Provisional Government issued an order seizing property from 117 companies and 18 individuals, mostly developers and contractors, who had unjustly enriched themselves under the Batista regime.[22]

Within a few days the front page of the *New York Times* featured a story by Ruby Phillips about the Provisional Government's finally amending the Fundamental Law to provide for land reform.[23] Under the Agrarian Reform Law, only companies owned entirely by Cubans would be permitted to grow sugarcane. The article stated that American-owned sugar companies like United Fruit would lose their plantations unless they met a requirement that companies could only sell cane if it was entirely owned by Cubans. The law set maximum estate sizes at a little less than 1,000 acres; it established a system of profit sharing; it expropriated *latifundia*, large landed estates; set up a system of distribution of land to small farmers; and also expropriated certain cattle ranches.[24] Soon the story was carried throughout the United States. Newspapers reported that there would be "grave economic repercussions."[25]

Actually, there were a lot of loopholes. The government could exempt large estates held by large companies if they were deemed to be held in the national interest. It did not apply to rice or sugar plantations if the yields were greater than one and a half times the national average, and in that case, a company could hold up to 3,333 acres.[26] Therefore, the huge American companies were exempt.

The law would affect about 40 percent of Cuba's land. Foreign companies would have until the harvest of 1960 to comply and there was no reason why companies could not establish a sale and lease-back arrangement with Cuban nationals for the properties to avoid confiscation. Payments would be made based on tax appraisals for confiscated land by 20-year bonds paying 4.5 percent. The National Institute of Agrarian Reform (Instituto Nacional de la ReForma Agraria, or INRA) was established to oversee and administer the provisions of the law. INRA would act as trustee and in some cases would operate cooperatives and in others would distribute land, mainly in 67-acre parcels. *Precaristas* and sharecroppers would have first priority on the parcels.[27]

However, INRA kept complete control, as property could never be sold or mortgaged if it had been held by INRA, and INRA could determine what crops had to be grown and set the price for them.[28] It also paved the way for state ownership of most of the best land.

José Martí had envisioned land reform, as had Grau San Martín and later Batista. It was written into the Cuban Constitution of 1940. Batista had enforced some measures that required foreign investors to sell to Cuban interests. In fact, General Douglas MacArthur had established a similar system in post World War II Japan during the U.S. occupation.[29] Castro sometimes alleged that his version of land reform was devised by General MacArthur. By 1959, American ownership of land in Cuba had dropped from a peak of 65 percent to about 35 percent.[30] Castro had announced a need for land reform in his "History Will Absolve Me," speech. While M–7–26 was in the mountains, it enforced Law Number 3 of the Sierra Maestra, enacted in fall 1958, and applied it to the "liberated territories" of eastern Cuba that were under its control.

Castro told the *guajiros* that land reform was "*de los humildes, por los humildes and para los humildes*" of the poor, by the poor and for the poor. Castro referenced Abraham Lincoln as well as the Bible in support of land reform.[31] He maintained that when Cuban farmers had income, they would no longer be a drain on the Cuban economy because they would use their income to buy machinery and this would stoke industrial growth.

Despite the anxious tone of Ruby Phillips reporting on agrarian reform, the *New York Times* asked for calm. It determined that land reform was overdue in Cuba and noted that the real test was whether Cuba would pay "adequate, just and prompt compensation for expropriated land."[32]

Castro said that he did not think that loss of some cane fields would be "worth disruption of the friendly relations between Cuba and the United States."[33] He also said that the American companies would be well compensated, but Phillips pointed out that before the Revolution, land had been far more valuable.[34] Castro suggested that if the United States had enforced the return of money stolen from the Cuban treasury by the Batista regime, there would have been funds to pay for compensation. He later offered to sell to the U.S. futures contracts of 8,000,000 tons of sugar for 1961, at what he considered to be a low rate. He made the offer as Congress was considering an extension of the Sugar Act.[35]

In a follow-up article, Phillips again connected Castro to Communism. She said that the government was a "one-man show," and the one man was Fidel Castro. Although Castro continued to castigate communists, she said that because Castro used an allusion to respond to the question of whether communists were extremists when he said that extremists should not be in government, and although he directly answered Jules Dubois, she accused him of avoiding the issue. She equated the Agrarian Reform Law to Communism and to communist tactics, and alleged that INRA was being run by a communist.[36] She also stated that there was generational warfare among members of M–7–26 as the young members were pushing out the older members.[37] The same day, President Urrutia Lleó announced that it had taken over most of the country's airlines and air facilities after a finding that their ownership violated rules of collaboration with the Batista regime or ownership by Batista cronies.[38] In a later article, Phillips quoted Faustino Pérez, referred to as Castro's right-hand man, who stated that the distribution of property to the *precaristas* and sharecroppers was Cuba's best weapon against Communism.[39] Several days later, a *Times* editorial said the same.[40]

However, there were protests by some landowners, principally in Pinar del Río Province, who said that they would never deliver title to their properties. Some *precaristas* and peasants also protested that they would never "own" the land they were to receive; they would just get a license to use it.[41] The Provisional Government refused a sugar mill owners' offer to give the government $2,5000,000 and 10,000 heifers to change the law.[42] "We do not wish the aid of these counter-revolutionists," Castro was quoted as saying. He also said that neglect of the properties would be considered as sabotage. The mill owners had a year to dispose of their sugarcane holdings.[43]

The communists knew that when Castro referred to "extremists," he referred to them. Blas Roca, the head of the Communist Party, accused Castro of running an anti-communist campaign and endangering national unity by doing so.[44]

Despite the public disputes between Castro and the communists, the *New York Times* continued to run Ruby Phillips's articles restating her earlier allegations that "Castro has yet to take a firm stand on [the Communists'] role in politics."[45] She also reported "sweeping" changes in taxes including a 40 percent profits tax, and personal income tax taxed at a rate of 4 percent for the lowest category and 50 percent for those making more than a $1,000,000 a year.[46] At the time, most American corporations in the United States were subject to a higher rate, and the maximum personal income tax rate was 91 percent.[47]

Castro also announced that Che Guevara would be sent to meet with Gamal Abdel Nasser in Egypt.

In Nicaragua, President Luis Somoza suspended the Constitution as there were threats of armed invasions from Cuba and Costa Rica and reports that anti–government guerrillas were operating within the country. Although Cuba and Venezuela opposed it, the OAS voted to investigate the matter.[48] Castro said the charges were groundless. The invasion of Panama and an insurrection in Paraguay remained simmering issues. Martial law was declared in Ecuador after rioting. In Peru, opposition leaders were jailed and the constitution was suspended. There were also riots in Colombia, Brazil, and Argentina. Although there was not a central theme behind the conflicts, Radio Moscow determined that the theme was evidence of "active nonconformism of the proletarian and intellectual classes with North American imperialism."[49]

In Haiti and the Dominican Republic, Cuban exiles tried to assassinate the Cuban ambassador to Haiti, and in the Dominican Republic, two Cuban diplomats were accosted at a bank and a mob of exiles tried an assault on the Cuban embassy.[50] In Cuba, a bomb was discovered but diffused inside the Haitian embassy. Tensions among Cubans in the States started to fray. In Miami, a bullet was fired at an alleged Castro supporter's restaurant.[51] Also in Miami, seven Batista supporters were arrested attempting to run a planeload of guns and munitions.[52] In Cuba, the police continued to arrest anti–government plotters.[53]

Ambassador Bonsal reported ongoing nightmares. In one scenario, Castro would be assassinated and the United States would be blamed. Armando Hart told him that the Cuban government had been warned that there was a plot to assassinate Bonsal.[54] There may have been some truth to the threats. Batista told reporters that Castro would not last the year.[55]

If Nixon later found that Castro was a communist, others saw Castro as an idealist who used Communism as a tool to support a deep hatred of the United States.[56] Nixon issued a memorandum to the CIA, the State Department and the White House that rejected attempts to "get along with" and "understand" Castro.[57] He also suggested that the United States immediately organize a force of Cuban exiles to overthrow him. At that time, the only way to do it would have been to use Batista, as many future anti–Castro Cubans were still in a honeymoon period with Castro.[58]

Herter also wrote a memorandum, deriding Castro as childlike[59] and further advising that as an evaluation of Castro was uncertain, the U.S. should be cautious.[60]

After Castro returned to Cuba, he announced that if Cuba would seek any aid for development, it would do so through the Organization of American States and not directly through the U.S. State Department. The 1959 Provisional Government knew that the United States used the sugar quota to try to keep Batista in line.[61] The allegation is that Batista left Cuba with an $801,000,000 deficit and that he stole $400,000,000 from the national treasury.[62] American banks reportedly held $424,000,000 in Cuban National Bank reserves.[63] Cuba looked to the States for an infusion of cash. There were renewed threats that Batista and his allies would inflate the currency to cause a panic.

Chapter 12

Decline of the Moderates

On May 2, 1959, Cuba and the United States signed a Point Four Agreement providing for technical cooperation in agrarian reform. On May 17, the Provisional Government signed an Agrarian Reform Law. One aspect of the law required companies that sold sugarcane to sugar mills to be owned entirely by Cubans by 1960. Land owned by foreigners would be confiscated, subject to payment of just compensation. Another aspect was that confiscated land would be turned over to a new agency, INRA, to distribute plots to landless peasants, tenants and sharecroppers, or to hold the land as a public corporation and to manage the properties. On June 5, Senator George Smathers of Florida, a close friend of former ambassador Earl E. T. Smith and a vocal critic of the new government, and especially of Castro, sponsored a bill in the Senate to reduce Cuba's sugar quota. On June 12, Ambassador Bonsal presented a note from the State Department to the Provisional Government objecting to certain aspects of the Agrarian Reform Law.[1] Within a few hours, five Provisional Government ministers resigned or were replaced.[2] Most conspicuous was Humberto Sorí Marín, minister of agriculture, judge advocate general of M–7–26, and the chief judge of the military tribunal that tried Sosa Blanco and twice sentenced him to be executed. Sorí Marín had run-ins with DR over his theories while in the Sierra Madre, and had overcome an attempt by Armando Hart, then representing the DR, to remove him as an M–7–26 theoretician and head of legal affairs.[3] However, he remained in the Castro inner circle, and was an M–7–26 Rebel Army comandante.

Sorí Marín had ostensibly been the author of the Agrarian Reform Law, and under his 1958 interim Law Number 3 of the Sierra Maestra, land in "liberated" territory was given to whomever farmed it. After January 1, as minister of agriculture he put his plan into action and appointed fellow Catholics and M–7–26 veterans Manuel Artime Buesa, a young physician, and Rogelio Gonzalez Corso as deputies in charge of the Commandos Rurales, Rural Commandos, most of them Catholic students from Havana who had gone to the mountains dedicated to working with and improving the lives of *guajiros*.

Sorí Marín was supposed to draft an extension to his plan, but Castro and Che Guevara modified it. Although the preamble to the new law stated "Those who work the land shall own it," Castro had determined that ownership of small lots would lead to consolidation and trading of land by cash-starved subsistence farmers. If the land were distributed into small plots, the productive capacity from large plots would decrease.[4] Sorí Marín's plan was changed so that the land was owned not by the individual but rather the state, as the owner could not sell or mortgage it. In order to reduce the threat of subsistence farming, and to ensure that most crops would be sold rather than consumed by the farmer, the plot sizes were also increased.[5] Although the language of the Agrarian Reform Law was "moderate," in practice the net effect of agrarian reform was that so long as INRA controlled the land, the large plots were subject to becoming cooperatives, which could easily turn into collectivization.[6] In this way, the plan was more radical than even the Communist Party of Cuba had envisioned.[7]

Sorí Marín did not object when the law was passed, and also did not object when Castro credited him as the principal drafter. But he soon resigned. His version did not include cooperatives and agricultural corporations, added ostensibly by Castro just before the law was signed.[8] While Sorí Marín was busy preparing his version of the law, Castro was meeting with Che Guevara, Carlos Rafael Rodríguez, and Antonio Núñez Jiménez to develop the final plan. Although Sorí Marín was a trusted and loyal colleague, he was not included, because Castro felt that his plan was too "moderate."[9] He needed a "radical" plan.

Although Castro viewed his revised plan as radical, it was praised by the Catholic Church.[10] Castro later said that the land reform program was outlined in "History Will Absolve Me," in which he discussed cooperatives, reforestation and industrialization. However the main reason to change the law was to provide land to hundreds of thousands of people who lived in rural areas without land, tens of thousands of renters and even more sharecroppers.[11] Conversely, some of the *latifundios* were comprised of a half million acres, much of which was not in cultivation. Castro says that he did not want to destroy the sugar industry and did not want to confiscate productive land.[12] However, he wanted to distribute as much land as he possibly could.

Foreign Minister Roberto Agramonte was replaced by Raúl Roa García, who had been the Cuban delegate to the United Nations. Teresa Casuso replaced Roa at the UN. Many considered that Agramonte would have been the rightful president of Cuba had the election of 1952 transpired, and he was also seen as head of the remnant of the Ortodoxo Party. Ambassador Bonsal said that he had dinner with Agramonte on the evening that the new cabinet was announced, and that his resignation must have been a shock.[13] Minister of the Interior Luis Orlando Rodríguez was replaced by José Ose Naranjo. Minister of Health Julio Martínez Páez was replaced by Serafín Ruiz de Serate. Minister of Social Welfare Mederos was replaced by Rachel Raquel Pérez. American newspapers reported that the ministers resigned over the valuation and compensation of foreign property. The main objection was the payment of bonds instead of cash.[14] A *New York Times* editorial reminded Castro that "Cubans should not underestimate the importance of the United States. Policies that are mutually beneficial are the only ones that make sense."[15] Speaking for the cabinet, Castro said that the agrarian law was within Cuban jurisdiction and reminded the United States that Cuba was a sovereign nation.[16] Speaking for himself and the Auténtico Party, Antonio de Varona, former president of the Cuban Senate, said that the law was unreasonable and violated the Constitution of 1940 that protected property rights. De Varona spoke on behalf of the party because Prío was on a tour of Europe at the time. The *Times* editorial said that criticism from the Auténticos showed that there was a "loyal opposition," and therefore elections were warranted.[17]

In his book, *Fidel Castro & Company*, President Urrutia Lleó did not mention the agrarian reform issue as a basis to object to Castro. He signed the law. He also did not indicate whether the five ministers resigned over the issue of just compensation. According to Castro, during the discussion of agrarian reform, President Urrutia was entirely preoccupied with the issue of gambling and continued to demand that all casinos be closed.[18]

In a television interview, Urrutia expressed the view that the government was anti–communist. Castro's position was that the government was neutral, and that communists

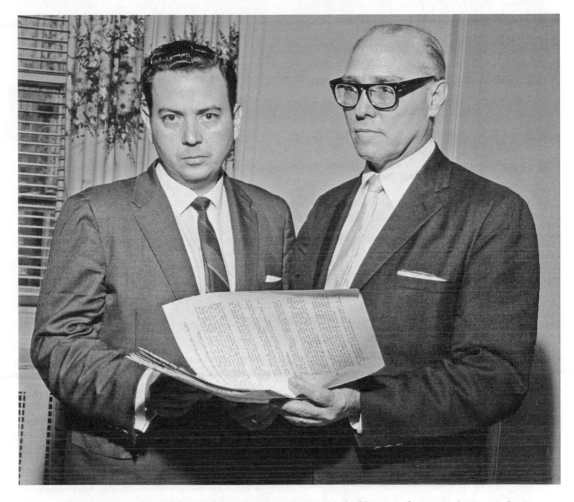

Manuel (Manolo) Ray Rivero (left) and Antonio (Tony) de Varona planning the Bay of Pigs invasion. Ray had been minister of public works in the Provisional Government and Varona had been premier of Cuba in the Prío government. Ray secretly had been head of Civic Resistance, in charge of clandestine sabotage in Havana, and was most probably the most knowledgeable person concerning Cuban defense philosophy and the location of installations. He was one of three members of the First Presbyterian Church of Havana named a minister in the Provisional Government after Batista fled. A graduate of the University of Utah and former head of the Cuban engineers association, he had taught at the University of Havana and also had taught military tactics at the Cuban War College, and had a following within the Cuban military. However, on the eve of the Bay of Pigs invasion, Ray and his men were dismissed, ostensibly because he favored "Castroism without Castro" and was a Protestant and was therefore considered too liberal for the Armada hierarchy and for the CIA (Associated Press).

were free to be part of the government, in the name of unity.[19] In return, Anibal Escalante attacked Urrutia on behalf of the party. Castro took the position that there was freedom of speech and assembly and that "we proclaim everyone's right to write as he thinks."[20]

Soon after the resignations of Urrutia and Sorí Marín, Rogelio Gonzalez Corso, director of agriculture and Dr. Manuel Artime Baesa, the 27-year-old, head of the Manzanillo zone of INRA, who were Sorí Marín's trusted subordinates in the Ministry of Agriculture, formed the Movimiento de Recuperación Revolucionaria (MRR), the Movement to Recover the

Revolution, to oppose the new Provisional Government.[21] Although Artime Buesa was the son of a Cuban communist, he was an ardent Catholic. A physician, he had taught military tactics at the Cuban Military Academy. During the revolution, he organized a group of about 4,000 Catholic Action students to support Castro, and after the Provisional Government was formed, he continued to try to maintain their loyalty. His youth division used the name Revolutionary Student Directorate (Dirección Revolucionaria Del Estudiante, or DRE) the same name once used by the group that came to power in 1933. In retrospect, he has been accused of having been planted into M-7-26 by Jesuits.[22] Artime's group was joined by Jorge Sotús, a colleague of martyr Frank País and several other highly placed Provisional Government officials, including Higinio Díaz, who had served under Raúl Castro and who was operating in the mountains as an insurgent leader.[23]

There are competing versions of why Artime Buesa resigned. The Cuban version is that Artime was accused of expropriating 100,000 pesos from a cattle cooperative, which was proven by Humberto Sorí Marín, Artime's mentor. He was also accused of having been a spy.[24]

On November 7, 1959, Artime's letter of resignation was published on the front page of *Avance* in Havana. He accused Castro of wanting to "communize Cuba," and referred to the Cuban Army as the "Red Army."[25] The letter substantiated many of the accusations that were made about communist infiltration into the Provisional Government. It made Artime a fugitive. Disguised as a priest, Artime was able to escape from Cuba on a Honduran freighter, aided by a CIA man from the American embassy.[26]

At the same time, another former Rebel Army officer who had been passed over for jobs in the Provisional Government, Captain Manuel Beatón, who had served under Che Guevara in the Rebel Army, led a band of about 20 bandits.[27] The government accused him of having killed Major Cristino Naranjo, an aide to Comandante Camilo Cienfuegos, soon after he went missing. He was held for trial, but escaped to the Sierra Maestra, near where Castro and his men had waged revolution.[28]

The note that Ambassador Bonsal took to the Provisional Government did not object to agrarian reform, per se.[29] From the American perspective at the time, Cuba was entirely dependent on the United States. Cuba had a sugar economy and had to sell its sugar, and the United States dominated its sales. Cuba also sold petroleum products, rare minerals, and many other commodities to the United States. It appeared as if there was no other place to sell these products. Eighty percent of all commercial transactions were with the United States.[30] The U.S. State Department considered this as leverage on Cuban domestic policy.[31] Moreover, it was clear that some American politicians such as Senator Smathers, took the position that the only reason the U.S. bought so much of Cuba's sugar was that the ownership was primarily American. There also was some question whether Cuba would continue to have the capacity to meet the sugar quota.

As soon as the law was announced, the values of stocks of Cuban companies and American companies doing business in Cuba plummeted and American corporations started to protest to the United States government.[32] Cuban ranchers protested that only way that cattle ranching was profitable if one had *latifundio*-sized holdings.[33]

If the awards for compensation were based on tax assessments, common knowledge in Cuba was that they were set by the landowners at a fraction of their actual value. Moreover, the Provisional Government did not have cash to pay the potential awards. If the awards were paid in scrip, or "chits," as the bonds were backed by the speculative full faith and credit of a Provisional Government, they probably would not, even under the Cuban Constitution of 1940, approach just compensation. This method of payment was similar to the method that the Árbenz government used in Guatemala in 1952. Guatemala issued 25-year government bonds with a 3 percent interest rate. The valuation of the land was to be determined from its declared taxable worth as of May 1952.[34]

But it was clear that agrarian reform was the centerpiece to Castro's vision for a social revolution in Cuba.[35] Castro met with Ambassador Bonsal the next day and appeared to be cordial.[36] The visit from Bonsal was probably as symbolic as it was unfortunate diplomatically. Bonsal was only following orders. However, in the mind of most Cubans of the era, the visit conjured up images of United States ambassador Sumner Welles dictating Cuban domestic policy to Batista. The Provisional Government sent Bonsal a response, stating that it was impossible to pay awards in cash, and said that it hoped that the United States would "understand and appraise the powerful reasons which justify the form of payment of the indemnities."[37]

The United States would have negotiated further. Wayne S. Smith, who was an embassy employee at the time, says that the United States could have offered loans to pay the awards, so the use of Cuban notes to pay the awards would not have been necessary.[38] Moreover, both Wayne Smith and Ambassador Bonsal say that initially Castro was also willing to negotiate. At the time, Castro described the United States' approach as "respectful."[39] In fact, all of the American interests that would have been affected took steps to comply with the law.[40]

However, the issue of agrarian reform became the major impasse between Cuba and the United States.[41] Castro soon accused all opponents of the plan as enemies in a "life and death battle" and accused them of a "reactionary campaign" against the revolution. He said the note from Bonsal was "an insinuation which served to awaken our people."[42] As time passed, he would tell his country that the agrarian reform issue was the best opportunity the Provisional Government had to bring socialism to Cuba. Castro would wait another three months before he would again meet with Bonsal.[43]

At the same time it tackled agrarian reform, Cuba initiated other social reforms. It presented a stimulus program by funding public works.[44] It initiated an industrialization program: the Development Bank could loan money to people starting or expanding businesses, and protective tariffs were established. It also expanded and reorganized the public education system. At that time, the government still considered English to be an important part of the curriculum.[45] The Tax Reform Law, authored by Treasury Minister López Fresquet, was introduced.[46] The effect of lowering rents and raising the minimum wage stimulated the economy and some sectors improved dramatically.[47] However, there were still complaints from landlords and large estate owners. As the law was being signed, López Fresquet reportedly joked that by the time tax reform would become effective, Cuba wouldn't have any taxpayers left.[48]

While all of this was happening, Che Guevara was on a trip to Egypt, India, Indonesia, Yugoslavia, and Ceylon.[49]

On June 13, Carlos Herrera, a Baptist chaplain to the Rebel Army toured the United States to witness that the climate for a religious resurgence had never been better in Cuba, and the Cuban government was backed by an "immense" majority of religious people who also backed complete separation of church and state. Communism in Cuba, he said would be defeated by "bread and democracy."[50]

On June 18, four explosions occurred in Havana. They were apparently directed against civilian targets, and at least one person was killed and several others were severely injured.

Although there had been other attacks, the newspapers reported that this was the first act of terror since the revolution. On the same day, the Provisional Government announced that 26 members of the Cuban air force had been removed from the service. The American press called it a purge.[51] Among those removed were the head of the air force, Major Pedro Díaz Lanz, and his brother, Captain Marcos Díaz Lanz. Juan Almieda, the new chief of the Air Force, reported that they would stand trial for treason, desertion, robbery and conspiring with the enemy.[52] Within hours, the Díaz family was on a small boat to Key West. According to Castro, Díaz was the Benedict Arnold of the Cuban Revolution. Cuban witnesses declared him to have been nothing more than a mercenary, if not a spy.[53]

A few days later, 31 people were arrested in Cartagena for attacking an army post.[54] In Havana, conspirators were arrested and vast amounts of munitions and equipment were discovered. There were several accounts of gunfire. In Pinar del Río armed guerrilla bands were seen roaming in the Organo Mountains. Others were in Oriente Province. Forty-one people were arrested in Banes, the company town of United Fruit Company, and there were also reports of guerrilla bands of Batista supporters sighted in the Escambray Mountains in central Cuba.[55]

The charter of OAS, formed in 1948, stated: "An act of aggression against one American State is an act of aggression against all American States."

There were valid reports that Cuba and the Dominican Republic were arming against each other. In fact, one United Press International report said that Cuba had launched a failed invasion against Trujillo.[56] Actually, there were three. Ambassador Bonsal later called it Castro's "Bay of Pigs," because it was so inept.[57] On June 14, a group headed by Delio Gómez Ochoa was captured. Some Cubans were murdered, although Gómez was able to escape, only to be recaptured.[58] Trujillo admitted that he had "exterminated" a number of rebels. The Dominican government also alleged that Castro had bought arms from the Soviet Union to use in an invasion and that Castro was pro-Communist.[59] On June 26, the Provisional Government formally broke diplomatic relations with the Dominican Republic.[60] Venezuela also had broken relations with the Trujillo government. Raúl Roa García, Cuba's new foreign minister, alleged that Trujillo was murdering native insurgents, who should have been treated as prisoners of war.[61] In Miami, members of the Teamsters Union and its president, Jimmy Hoffa, were charged with trying to send arms to Batista in the Dominican Republic.[62] In Havana, residents were told that there was a possible threat of attack by the Dominican Republic, and air patrols were organized.[63] The Cuban ambassador to Britain accused the Dominican Republic of having agents actively obtaining weapons and recruiting mercenaries throughout Europe, North Africa and the Middle East. A Dominican spokesman replied that he was unaware of a network of agents, but it would be logical for a threatened nation to buy weapons.[64] Trujillo had an estimated 25,000-man standing army with 600,000 in reserve. He also had an anti-communist "volunteer" foreign legion that included veterans of the Spanish Blue Division, Germans and Eastern Europeans.[65] The Spanish mercenaries were sent by Generalissimo Francisco Franco, and ostensibly, the others were mostly fascists and ex-Nazis.[66] These estimates do not include the Cuban, Argentine and Venezuelan forces training in the country at the time. Radio broadcasts from the Dominican Republic into Cuba called for sabotage of power and transportation facilities. Other broadcasts came from an organization opposed to both Castro and Batista in support of former Cuban general Pedraza to lead a "just and Holy war against Communism in Cuba."[67]

Castro has never denied that he had sent men into the Dominican Republic during this period.[68] Some of them turned out to be Puerto Rican mercenaries recruited in New

York.[69] There were other groups detained in Cuba for attempting to invade Nicaragua and Panama. Some of the alleged principals were American and British citizens.[70]

On July 4, the Cuban consul in Miami was beaten by a mob.[71] The next day, the Cuban news was full of anti–American stories and editorials, and the mood in Havana seemed less friendly. For the first time, foreign residents of Cuba were required to obtain army intelligence papers. The lines in Havana were over a block long.[72]

After the Dominican Republic brought charges against Cuba and Venezuela for attacks, the OAS had decided to thoroughly discuss how to temper the revolts, invasions and brush wars that seemed to be spontaneously erupting throughout Latin America. In Washington, President Eisenhower said that the United States should defer to the OAS to investigate the matter. However, Castro said that Cuba would never relinquish any rights of sovereignty. "No one is going to investigate [on] Cuban soil," he stated.[73] He also reminded the United States that it had granted asylum to "war criminals" and to people who had allegedly stolen the national treasury. To complicate the issue, the Dominican ambassador to the United States denounced Trujillo and asked for political asylum in the States.[74]

Meanwhile, although the five cabinet ministers had been replaced, squabbles were ongoing within the Provisional Government. On July 13, President Urrutia was again interviewed on television and again asked about communists in the Provisional Government. Urrutia prefaced his remarks by saying that although it was true that there were internal disputes in the cabinet, he and Castro were on "the same road." However, he told the interviewer, the viewing public and the world that in his opinion, "the communists were creating a second front against the Revolution.... I reject communist support."[75]

In Washington, the Senate Judiciary Committee, Internal Security Subcommittee held hearings. Appearing as the star witness was Major Díaz Lanz, who accused Castro of being a communist. In Cuba, Díaz Lanz was not considered a major figure, but his stature grew in the media.[76] Díaz Lanz and his brother, Sergio, appeared under tight security as credible threats had credible threats made against them. Also testifying was the chief of naval operations, Admiral Burke, who said the threat that communists would take Cuba was great.[77] Díaz Lanz alleged that Castro had told him that the government would take over the banks, take private land and give Cuba "a system like Russia has." He also said that Cuba had made military assaults on the Dominican Republic and Nicaragua.[78]

To most Cubans, the fact that Díaz Lanz appeared before a United States government committee was almost universally taken as interference in Cuban domestic affairs.[79] President Urrutia chastised the United States for giving asylum to Díaz Lanz, a "traitor and a deserter." He said that whereas the Díaz Lanz testimony made it look as if Cuba was interfering in the internal affairs of the United States, Cuba was "not interested in the internal affairs of other countries." He also said that he was strongly opposed to Communism and said that there was no communist infiltration in the Provisional Government. He also said that the antidote to Communism in Cuba was agrarian reform.[80] However, in attacking Communism, by implication Urrutia had left an impression that Díaz Lanz might have been correct about communist intentions on Cuba.[81]

In a press conference, President Eisenhower stated that the United States did not ratify the Díaz Lanz charges. The Senate is not part of the executive branch of government, and only the president could speak for the country: "The United States has made no such charges."[82] The *New York Times* ran an article by Herbert L. Matthews that disputed Díaz Lanz's testimony.[83] Matthews's logic was that Castro was such an egotist that he would not share power, let alone take orders from Moscow.

News reporters, among them Drew Pearson, continued to report that the Castro government was on its last legs.[84]

In July, Santos Traficante, Jr., was released from prison for deportation to the United States.[85] However, because he was wanted for questioning involving charges in the States, including his involvement in the 1957 murder of mobster Albert Anastasia in New York, he remained in Cuba.[86]

Cuba held an Agrarian Reform Forum from June 28 to July 10. Although they were initially involved in the discussions, the Cuban Cattlemen's Association and the Sugar Mill Owner's Association pulled out.[87]

On July 17, the M–7–26 newspaper *Revolución* ran a huge red headlines: "Fidel Resigns!" He actually had no intention of resigning. Castro had reportedly told Carlos Franqui, the editor, that instead of resorting to a *golpe* to remove Urrutia, he devised a "coup de television" to do it.[88] He had planned a celebration in Havana to commemorate July 26 and to celebrate the Agrarian Reform Law. Tens of thousands of *guajiros* who had received parcels of land and hundreds of thousands who were waiting for the law to go into full effect were invited. Arrangements had been made for them to stay with Havana residents. Havana was packed with them.

On July 18, Castro publicly attacked Urrutia. Although Urrutia alleged that the resignation was entirely based on reactions to his anti-communist message, there had been accusations that he used his position to obtain an extravagant home in the Biltmore section of Havana. In fact, Urrutia brought a defamation suit against a reporter who alleged some kind of undue influence in obtaining the house. If Urrutia prevailed in his lawsuit, the reporter could have been charged with a crime for showing disrespect to the president. Urrutia would later say that Castro was behind the attack on his integrity and credibility.[89] In the televised speech, Castro brought up the house controversy. He also alleged that the presidential salary, $40,000 per year, the same as Batista had awarded himself, was too high and that Urrutia had prevented the cabinet from lowering it. According to the logic, Urrutia was using the bogeyman of Communism to provoke the North Americans, (the United States), to intervene in Cuba; and if and when they did, Urrutia planned to become an absolute ruler. Castro also alleged that Urrutia had corrupted the judicial nomination process, wanted to take personal control of the judicial system, and even had removed the name of God from the language of the Fundamental Law. Moreover, Urrutia was slow to implement revolutionary priorities such as maximizing the sugar harvest and promoting Cuban tourism Despite the fact that tourist dollars were necessary, he still objected to casino gambling. Castro did not accuse Urrutia of outright treason, but he accused him of opposing his own regime.[90] By the time Castro completed his speech, loud, rowdy, threatening crowds had formed outside the Presidential Palace, chanting in unison for Castro to stay and for Urrutia to resign.[91] Urrutia reportedly stated, "Fidel Castro is the Maximum Leader of our revolution and its power is in the people. If the people ask him not to resign, he will listen to them." The cabinet accepted President Urrutia Lleó's fourth resignation.[92]

Castro would later say that Urrutia was a good judge and was picked for the position due to exigent circumstances. However, he was "inexpert and unfortunately incapable" and the position "went to his head…. The man had decided that this [Cuba] was some kind of a banana republic."[93] He said, "He wasn't a traitor, he was an opportunist, a mediocre individual."[94] It is clear that Urrutia avoided arguments and had attended few cabinet meetings after the five ministers were removed in June. He had alienated not only Castro but also most of the other cabinet ministers, even those he had appointed.

Throughout the crisis at the palace, Urrutia was alone in his office, and was visibly reduced to tears.[95] He had tried to resign before, when he had wanted to place himself as chief justice of the Supreme Court. He had no recourse but to acquiesce. After he resigned, he left immediately and went home.[96] He would later visit the Venezuelan embassy, where he was granted asylum.

The cabinet elevated Osvaldo Dorticós Torrado, then age 40, described by the press as a quiet, bookish workaholic, from minister overseeing the Fundamental Law to president of the Republic. Castro initially told Dorticós that Miró Cardona should be elevated to president.[97] However, Dorticós was a more logical choice. Skeptics find that Dorticós was the most loyal and trusted "yes man" in the cabinet at the time. However, Dorticós Torrado was from a wealthy Cienfuegos family and had been a famous lawyer. He had been Dean of the Cuban bar association, a country club member, and was probably the wealthiest member of the cabinet. During the revolution, active in Civic Resistance, he was arrested and briefly exiled to Mexico but was not part of the M–7–26 hierarchy. However, he had also been a member of the Communist Party as a student and at one time had been secretary to Juan Marinello, then head of the party.[98] He later became a prosperous corporate lawyer in Cienfuegos.[99] It turned out that he also had once accepted a sinecure from Batista.[100]

As soon as he was sworn, Dorticós Torrado rejected Castro's resignation and restored him as premier. However, Castro waited a couple of days to respond. Dorticós Torrado told the press that although no legal charges would be brought against Urrutia, "moral charges" remained.[101] He kept the remainder of the cabinet intact, and he voluntarily reduced the president's salary to 2,500 pesos per month. In order to reduce expenses, Dorticós Torrado and his wife did not live in the palace; Dorticós Torrado said any savings would be donated to an orphanage.[102]

A *Washington Post* editorial concluded that Castro ran the government and that Urrutia was not the man for the job, but the tactics in removing Urrutia discouraged Castro's friends as well as his enemies.[103] Later analysis alleges that Dorticós Torrado was part of a parallel secret cabinet that had been meeting to determine how to implement socialism in Cuba. Among the others were Che Guevara, Alfredo Guevara, Raúl Castro, Antonio Núñez Jiménez, and Camilo and Osmani Cienfuegos. As Urrutia became more vocal, the need for a "face man" less offensive to the ownership class and to the United States became less important. At some point, Castro invited the Communists to attend the meetings.[104] This theory substantiated some of Urrutia's claims. On the other hand, he signed into law every one of the first steps: reestablishment of the death penalty, increase in the numbers of crimes punishable by death, and such measures as the Agrarian Reform Law and the Tax Reform Law.

At the same time, Castro was able to manipulate public sentiment and to replicate the public euphoria in Havana similar to when he arrived on his trek from the Sierra Maestras in January. Massive demonstrations took place and labor unions went on strike in support of his return to government. David Salvador, the head of the union, asked a million people to strike for one hour to demonstrate support for Castro. Hundreds of thousands of straw-sombrero-wearing, machete-carrying *guajiros* roamed throughout Havana.[105] On the evening of July 24, Castro was decked out in a baseball uniform, emblazoned with *Barbudos* across the front, as he pitched an inning in a Sugar Kings game for the benefit of the Cuban Agrarian Reform Fund. He struck out each of the batters. The newspapers commented, however, that the umpire seemed to give Castro deference when calling strikes.[106]

At the same time that the controversy swirled over the Castro-Urrutia dispute, Foreign

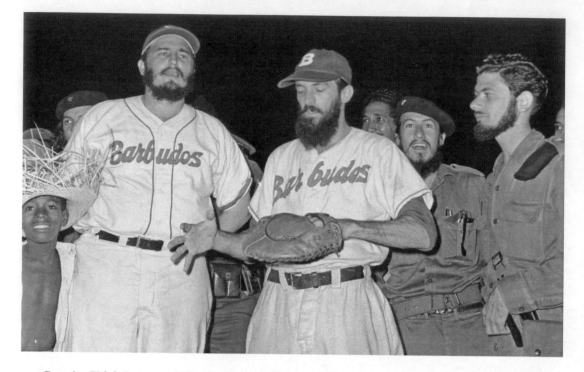

Premier Fidel Castro and Major Camilo Cienfuegos in baseball uniforms, July 24, 1959, while attending an International League baseball game. Baseball was considered the Cuban national sport, and Cubans were considered the most fanatical fans in the world. Castro once said that Cuba would retain professional baseball "even if I have to pitch." At the time, the barbudos were celebrating the anniversary of an attack on the Moncada Barracks, July 24, 1953. The Provisional Government had come to power on January 1. Castro had no position in the new government but assumed the position of head of the military, and Cienfuegos was military governor of Havana Province. However, after the first premier, José Miró Cardona, resigned, Castro assumed power as premier. Under the Constitution of 1940, Cuba had a hybrid form of democracy, in part similar to the United States Constitution and in part a parliamentary form, but due to the exigency of the revolutions, the new government suspended the Congress and assumed total power with an expectation that elections would soon follow. During a crisis when former allies were declared traitors, Cienfuegos's airplane disappeared in October 1959 and his body was never recovered (Associated Press).

Minister Raúl Roa García accused several United States congressmen and the Dominican Republic of conspiring to diminish Cuba and break the Cuban government by reducing the sugar quota.[107] The price had fallen to an 18-year low, and there were reports that Cuba was dumping sugar to make up for lost reserves taken when Batista fled.[108] Roa also alleged that the Dominican Republic was going to invade Cuba. Meanwhile, Batista had apparently tried to enter the United States from the Dominican Republic, but he had no exit visa, so the Trujillo government denied him the right to leave. He also did not have a valid United States entry visa.[109] Although there had been credible reports that Batista feared for his life in the Dominican Republic, he denied that he had tried to leave. The Trujillo government did not deny that there was a Cuban "liberation army" formed in the Dominican Republic that was headed by General Pedraza.[110]

Within Cuba, a secret anti–Castro organization was forming, called the White Rose, after a Martí poem made famous by the song "La Guantanamera." Former Batista officers established cells throughout Cuba.[111] Meanwhile, Rafael del Pino, who had been living in the United States, was involved in a gun battle at the airport and had to be pulled out of a burning airplane. It turned out that he was a leader of the White Rose organization, and he was arrested. The Provisional Government also announced that four other White Rose members had been rounded up.[112] While del Pino was hospitalized, Castro visited him. Although del Pino was a naturalized United States citizen, and although Castro questioned him for about two hours, their discussions were not reported.[113]

On July 26, thousands of rifles were shot into the air, church bells rang, and white pigeons and balloons were released to announce the M–7–26 holiday. A midnight mass was held at a stadium at the University of Havana to commemorate the deaths that occurred during the revolution. Castro used a helicopter to attend ceremonies at several locations, including the Martí Monument. Later, after a mile-long parade of *barbudos*, students and marching bands, perhaps a million Cubans celebrated the anniversary of Martí and Moncada at the Plaza Civica as millions more watched on television. Dorticós Torrado was first to speak. When he announced that Castro would resume his office as premier, the crowd cheered wildly. The crowd became thunderous as Castro appeared. After telling the crowd that he had returned to office, "by the will of the people," Castro spoke for several hours. He said that Cuba's first priority was its poor, and that the symbol of the revolution was the machete. In response, more than 100,000 *guajiros* raised their machetes, which glistened in the sun. He said he wanted to have good relations with the United States and sent greetings to the U.S. people. He also said, "Tell them that we want the best relations between the people of Cuba and the people of the United States." He later gave the same speech in English for the benefit of the American NBC television audience.[114]

Although Castro used the American media, he was still sensitive to press criticism. In a news conference, Castro compared himself to President Franklin Roosevelt, who was challenged by "trusts and monopolies," and stated that Cuba had not "investigated" Americans such as Senator Eastland, who he alleged had a relationship with Trujillo and who had brought Major Díaz Lanz to Washington to appear before an American committee of inquiry.[115] He said that the same media which criticized Roosevelt also criticized him.

At Gran Stadium, as the Havana Sugar Kings played the Rochester Redwings in an International League baseball game, Sugar Kings shortstop "Chico" Cardenas and Rochester coach Frank Verdi were shot by stray bullets. Verdi wasn't injured severely, but he was knocked down, and the game had to be suspended in the 11th inning when the game was tied, four to four.[116] As part of the ceremonies at the plaza, Faustino Pérez, minister for the recovery of stolen property, handed Castro a check for 20,000,000 pesos. David Salvador, secretary general of the Confederation of Cuban Workers, also spoke. Also present was former Mexican president Lazaro Cardinas.[117]

During the festivities, Huber Matos, military governor of Camagüey and member of the general staff of the Rebel Army, submitted his resignation. Matos was considerably older than Castro and had been a teacher at an agricultural college, like Castro had been an Orto-doxo, and was extremely popular in Camagüey across all sectors, including the cattle ranchers who held large tracts in the province. He was also a Mason, and so were some of his followers.[118] Although he was one of Castro's most trusted advisors on military matters, he was not considered a political leader. He candidly told Castro that too many communists had been given positions in the military, and he wanted no part of it. Castro replied that he was aware that Raúl Castro and Che Guevara had flirted with Communism, but claimed that the matter was under control. The resignation was refused.[119]

An OAS fact-finding committee investigated Nicaragua's charges of Cuban interference, and determined that Che Guevara had urged Cuban authorities to provide "all forms of cooperation and help" to Nicaraguan rebels. However, the report did not substantiate charges that Cuba was planning three more invasions.[120] Castro later stated that there was no unrest in the Caribbean, and that "hunger, poverty and underdevelopment" should be investigated.[121] After the OAS refused to add underdevelopment to the proposed agenda for its next meeting, the Cuban delegate walked out. Cuba received eight votes for the resolution, but it needed 11. Nine countries, including the United States, abstained.[122]

Castro stated that the "acclamation of the masses" was more accurate than any election tally. He stated that the most voters that could be expected in an election in Cuba was about 1,300,000, and on July 26 more than a million people came out in support of his government. He estimated that each of the people in the crowd represented more people who not only agreed with government policy but felt strongly in favor of it. The M–7–26 newspaper, *Revolución*, called the crowd "the greatest plebiscite of our Republic's history."[123]

This popularity sparked a new fad for kids: wearing olive drab uniforms and playing *barbudo*. The National Police started the Juvenile Patrol, which performed close order drill during the July 26 parade. Members were trained by the local police departments and the Red Cross, fire departments and the Cuban navy. However, in addition to organized playtime, children were also given political indoctrination.[124]

Cuba declared July 30, the date when Frank País was killed in 1957, as the Day of the Martyrs and held a ceremony in Santiago.[125] País had been a Baptist and so were many of his followers, who were celebrated. The Cuban Council of Protestant Churches issued a statement "in support of Cuba" and denied that the Provisional Government was communist influenced.[126]

Chapter 13

The Sting

From some reports, by August 1959 all of Cuba was in turmoil. Cuban exiles in Mexico reported that air and sea sorties from the Dominican Republic had tried to land in Cuba, at the Isle of Pines, to free prisoners held there. There were also reports of underground activities and even assassination attempts: sporadic shots sprayed at Fidel Castro's home and in other parts of the country, and a menacing gunman was arrested at a wedding that Raúl Castro had attended. Later there were rumors that somehow Fidel Castro had been injured. It was difficult to determine the truth.

One insurgent anti–Castro guerrilla force sent from the Dominican Republic was led by Armentino Fería, a former communist and Spanish Civil War veteran who was a Batista ally. His group was immediately detected by the Cuban army and annihilated.[1] Trujillo's agents were allied with disgruntled cattlemen from Camagüey who were about to lose their livelihood, guerrilla bands operating in Oriente and Las Villas Provinces, and others opposed to government policies. Trujillo supplied about $500,000 to people who opposed agrarian reform to develop an underground. Under the Trujillo plan, the "liberation army" would release Batista allies from the prison on the Isle of Pines, supply them with 25 heavy machine guns and other automatic weapons, and march on Havana. Clandestine operatives in Havana would assassinate Castro and other high-ranking figures. In order to accomplish this, Trujillo, his foreign legion and the liberation army relied on two ambitious high-ranking comandantes of the Rebel Army, men who were jealous of Castro and craved power for themselves, men who had led their own loyal cadres in guerrilla warfare outside of Castro's command and men who had publicly opposed some of his policies. By all accounts, one of these men could rival Castro tactically in the field and in charisma, demeanor and popularity. In theory, once they were in the field and openly opposed to the government, many *barbudos* in the military would defect to their command.[2]

However, Trujillo's plans never came to pass. From August 8 to 10, over 4,000 people, including over 1,000 veterans of Batista's Cuban army, were arrested for insurrection. Twenty-eight more airmen and mechanics in the Cuban air force were held for questioning about antigovernment activities. According to these reports, the invasions were led by General Pedraza and Emilio Núñez Portuondo, in conjunction with the White Rose. The newspapers reported that a group of 15 gunmen had been captured by Eloy Gutierrez Menoyo after a firefight in Cienfuegos. There were reports of another two dead and 15 wounded after an attempted assault. The government also arrested several politicians and the president of the Cuban Association of Cattle Growers.[3]

Rumors continued. Fidel and Raúl were reportedly seen on their way to the front at the Isle of Pines. However, the news reports were confusing. Gutiérrez Menoyo and the second Front of the Escambray had been the first *barbudos* to enter Havana after the revolution. They saw themselves as the vanguard of the new government, but had not been given important positions. Castro had publicly challenged them in January, and they had stood down. They had not been celebrated by Castro as conquering heroes as he made his way to Havana, and they had not been asked to take part in the ceremonies on his arrival in Havana or to stand with him on the podium on January 8, although they had contributed to the victory. To an outsider, Castro's tone toward them appeared insulting and demeaning. However, despite outward appearances, they remained allies with Castro.

Gutiérrez Menoyo and his associate, the American renegade Comandante William Morgan, had effectively passed themselves off to Trujillo and his allies as envious, disgruntled and ambitious. Morgan had made public statements against Communism, and although he had been scheduled to make public appearances in the U.S. on behalf of the revolution courtesy of the State Department, it seemed he had decided to leave public life. But he had been in contact with the Dominican Consul in Miami, and told the Dominicans that he would cooperate to remove Castro.[4] Trujillo and his allies were told that Morgan was a mercenary who "would do anything for money." Morgan told the conspirators that he could take the airfield, hold it and make it available as a drop zone for the invasion. Morgan let the CIA know that he was involved in a plot to assassinate Castro.[5] He received $100,000 in advance from General Pedraza, through a priest acting as a go-between with Trujillo and Morgan. This information was relayed to J. Edgar Hoover of the FBI, who sent two men to interview Morgan in Miami on July 31, but Morgan was able to evade them. However, Ambassador Bonsal discovered that Morgan had told embassy officials of the plot, and Bonsal, fearing that the United States would be blamed in complicity if Castro were killed, told Foreign Minister Roa García as much as he knew.[6] Ambassador Bonsal described Morgan as a double agent.[7]

As planned, Morgan took the airfield and sent a personal message to Trujillo that he had taken it. Soon troops, arms and other supplies arrived, including a "government in waiting," comprised of Arthur Hernández Telleheche, president, and Arnaldo Caiñas Mílanés, minister of agriculture. Morgan's men reportedly shouted slogans like, "Down with Castro! Death to agrarian reform!" as the invaders assembled. As approximately 2,000 gathered, Castro reportedly walked from under a nearby mango tree and personally arrested all of them, including the pilot who had taken Batista to the Dominican Republic on December 31, 1958. The priest, Father Ricardo Velazco Ordóñez, a Spanish national, had met with Morgan in Miami and had also smuggled in bazookas and other weapons, and was among those put on display for the media.[8] After their capture, Castro displayed his prisoners in what Ambassador Bonsal described as a "television spectacular."[9]

During the flight from Cienfuegos to Havana, Castro was accompanied by Father Rosario Maxilliano, whose father had been executed by Batista's police, whose three brothers and a brother-in-law had been tortured, and who had been jailed during the Batista regime. Father Velazco had just been captured and his role within White Rose and the connection to Trujillo was public. At this time, the Christian Democratic Movement had been founded by José Ignacio Rasco, a former classmate of Castro at both Belen Academy and at the University of Havana, to promote a Catholic opposition.[10] Castro asked Father Maxilliano whether he would support a national church and if so, would he head it.[11] A similar allegation was also made by Father Eduardo Aguirre García and Father Ramón O'Farril soon after they defected in December 1959.[12] The Archbishop of Havana, Evelio Díaz, denied this, and also stated that the church had a good relationship with the revolution.[13]

As the episode in Cienfuegos was unraveling, the Committee of Twenty-One was meeting in Santiago, Chile. Castro initially said that he would attend, but he decided not to, especially as the threat of invasion was imminent. At the beginning of the meeting, Cuba's foreign minister Roa accused the Dominicans of threatening to kill him. U.S. Secretary of State Herter spoke, and asked for calm. His prepared remarks condemned Communism and condemned the invasions of Panama, the Dominican Republic and Nicaragua. "[A]ny effort to promote democracy ... through outside intervention was 'self-defeating' and 'history has shown that attempts to impose democracy on a country by force from without may easily result in the mere substitution of one form of tyranny for another.'"[14] Castro told the press that the Santiago meeting was a "farce" and that most of the problems in Latin America could be traced to intervention by the United States. He reminded them that Herter didn't discuss 30 years of dictatorship in the Dominican Republic or discuss poverty in Latin America.[15] He also did not discuss the Dominican Republic's attempt to invade Cuba. Venezuelan president Rómulo Betancourt told Herter that nonintervention should not be used as a shield to protect dictatorships.[16] Privately, however, Betancourt told other ministers that Castro was becoming "an evil influence" in Latin America.[17]

For Secretary Herter, the Committee of Twenty-One was only one of his problems. Although the U.S. was concerned about invasions in Panama, Honduras, Nicaragua, Haiti, the Dominican Republic and Cuba, and although there were serious internal disruptions in Paraguay, Argentina, Venezuela and Bolivia, Herter had been tested globally as soon as he was sworn. The U.S. had discussions within NATO and SEATO about nuclear disarmament and was concerned that there might be a nuclear strike at any moment. Some U.S. allies, especially France, confronted with wars in North Africa, decided to withdraw from the alliances. The U.S. was discussing nuclear matters in Geneva. The Soviet Union accused the United States of arming neighbors such as Pakistan, Afghanistan, Iran and Turkey, and attempting to encircle the country. The U.S. disputed the status of Berlin and an insurgency in Laos. The Soviets and the North Vietnamese accused the United States of setting up military posts in that country. We also were concerned that the United Arab Republic, Syria and Egypt, had become Soviet allies, and that Iraq would also fall to the Soviets. The U.S. still had troops in Germany and in Korea manning armed borders. And at home, although Joseph McCarthy was dead, we were still seeking out communists in government and especially in the State Department. When Wieland told the State Department that after a thorough review, he still thought that Castro was not a communist, one military attaché accused *him* of being either a fool or a communist.[18]

Near the close of the conference, Castro sent his brother, Raúl, to Santiago. At first, his plane was delayed at the airport. But eventually he made a grand entrance, still in fatigues, with an entourage of *barbudos*. Despite the fact that Roa García had committed Cuba to a position that OAS would "inspect" the Dominican Republic due to the recent invasion, Raúl said that Cuba would refuse any similar inspection.[19]

In the States, there were news reports that Latin American communists had been meeting in Santiago, and the implication was that was actually why Raúl Castro had attended.[20] There were reports that the Soviet Union had sent an agent to Havana to train Cuban communists to infiltrate the Provisional Government.[21] News reports about Latin America included allegations that the Soviet Union was actively trying to capitalize on unrest; others said that the Soviets were the cause of it.[22]

The instability in Cuba had one positive effect for the Cuban economy: sugar prices jumped.[23]

Chapter 14

Hard Nose

After the Santiago meeting, Secretary Herter decided to take a "hard nosed attitude" toward Cuba. He accused Castro of continually blaming the United States as an aggressor, and of inciting anti–American paranoia as if we had been part of the assassination attempts and the aborted invasion by Trujillo and his allies.[1]

As a result, the American press became even more critical of Castro. Privately Ambassador Bonsal told Washington that he was afraid that Castro's tirades would cause mob attacks against Americans.[2] Publicly, he told the press that he had not been able to meet with Castro for over three months, and that Cuba would not negotiate.[3] Herter urged President Eisenhower to "encourage within Cuba and elsewhere in Latin America, opposition to the extremist, Anti-American course of the Castro regime."[4] At the White House, Vice President Nixon had been advocating that the CIA "provide arms, ammunition and training for Cubans who had fled the Castro regime and were now in exile in the United States and various Latin American countries."[5] It is not clear whether President Eisenhower approved at that time.

Bonsal had to have advised his superiors about the Trujillo relationship to Morgan. Castro had imputed direct knowledge of the Invasion Trick to the State Department when he accused the United States and OAS of complicity with Trujillo.

The U.S. knew that there were attempts to overthrow some of Castro's enemies. There had been an invasion attempt of Haiti by 30 *barbudos* from Cuba, some of whom had been captured. The Cuban ambassador to Haiti had survived assassination attempts in May and accusations had been made that Trujillo was behind them. The Cuban prisoners reportedly admitted that they had been trained by Che Guevara, who had told them that as soon as they landed, a spontaneous revolt would take place. A remnant of the invasion force was still in the mountains of Haiti, but there had not been any sign of a widespread revolt.[6] After several days of impasse, on August 29 Cuba closed its Haitian embassy. Haiti accused the Cuban ambassador of inciting revolution.[7] Cuba accused Haiti and the Dominican Republic of conspiring to remove Castro and also alleged that the United States had approved it.[8] *Revolución* ran an article describing Haitian execution of prisoners that described the rounding up and massacring of peasants. It also ran an editorial accusing the United States of protecting Haitian dictator François "Papa Doc" Duvalier.[9] According to reports, approximately 15 Cubans were waging a guerrilla war within Haiti.

Likewise, similar charges of outside interference by Cuba had been made in Nicaragua. A Cuban-backed invasion by Nicaraguan exiles had landed in Honduras by mistake. After their capture, the exiles complained that Raúl Castro had offered to help them only if they would join with a popular front that included communists. The leader also alleged that he was told that Che Guevara was in charge of the Caribbean insurgencies and that he was a communist.[10] At the time of the invasion attempt, Guevara was on a goodwill trip to Africa and Asia, so there was some question about the credibility of the information.

While all of this was occurring, Cuba announced that it had negotiated close ties with the United Arab Republic, another country that did not have good diplomatic relations with the United States.[11]

As further evidence of the hard-nosed approach, the State Department entered a Certificate of Loss of American Citizenship to Morgan. It instructed the U.S. embassy in Havana that "any United States Citizen who entered either the regular or irregular forces of Cuba shall be considered to have lost United States Citizenship."[12] It was estimated that another 20 Americans had entered Cuban service and would lose their citizenship. Neil Macaulay and Herman Marks were among them. Morgan was determined to keep his at first. Trujillo had issued a bounty against Morgan, but he survived several drive-by shootings and a potential kidnapper sent by Trujillo was captured.[13]

Castro soon announced that Morgan had decided to renounce his American citizenship and become a naturalized Cuban citizen.[14] Unlike many other countries, Cuba does not recognize dual citizenship, so Morgan had to renounce his United States citizenship.

On September 3, Ambassador Bonsal met with Fidel Castro for six hours at Foreign Minster Roa Garcia's apartment. There is no indication whether the insurgencies in Haiti and Nicaragua were discussed or the issue of citizenship came up. Bonsal said they had a cordial meeting. After Castro complained that the American press was overly critical, Bonsal tried to explain to Castro that the State Department had nothing to do with the press and told him that the American press did not speak for the government. He also commented on Che Guevara's trips and remarked that the United States was aware that Guevara was telling diplomats that Cuba had nothing to fear from Communism and that the real aggressor in Latin America was the United States. Castro told Bonsal that the remarks were "exuberances of a young and inexperienced" revolutionary.[15]

At the same time, Cuba had tried to buy weapons from Britain to replenish its arsenal. The United States had placed an embargo on the sale of arms and military hardware on Cuba beginning in March 1958, and kept it in place after the Provisional Government took power. The Cuban military acquired millions of dollars' worth of weaponry that was in disrepair or needed upgrading. The United States, however, did not want to send military aid to Cuba as it considered the country to be in an unstable condition, and U.S. policy was not to provide aid that could be used for an offensive campaign. Apparently, the State Department did not feel that external threats to Cuba from the Dominican Republic warranted the need for a viable military defense. However, Castro and the Provisional Government were sure that there was a need to be armed and began to search for places to buy small arms, despite American policy. Although the Belgian government was able to sell some arms to Cuba, the U.S. put pressure on Britain not to sell.[16] Britain acquiesced, and in response Cuba put trade pressure on them. The British were concerned that the Provisional Government would initiate an anti–British boycott.[17] During the period from January 1958 to October 1959, 190 people were convicted of gun running in United States courts. The government estimated that it had captured about 40 percent of the actual traffic.[18]

Plotting and resistance to the Provisional Government continued.[19] The group centered around the Jesuit Catholic University Association, led by *barbudo* physician Manuel Artime Buesa, *barbudo* lawyer Emilio Martinez Venegas, psychiatrist Lino Fernández and civil engineer Rogelio González Corso, actively recruiting counter-revolutionary guerrillas.

Although Artime had fought alongside Castro and was an official and supporter of INRA and agrarian reform, his group was more militant than Rasco's organization.[20] In late September, 40 armed insurgents were arrested trying to take an airfield in Oriente Province and another 30 were arrested at a sugar mill in Pinar del Río.[21] Included among the prisoners were two American pilots.[22] There were also several domestic fights hijacked to Miami and an aerial bombing or two. The Provisional Government placed restrictions on the use of Cuban air space. Accusations were made that the United States was involved or that we let planes take off from U.S. airports in the States.[23]

However, after the Castro-Bonsal meeting, the strident tone against America became somewhat reduced. By that time, Cuba's position was that although communists could act freely, they would not be permitted to undermine the Provisional Government. Although he had initially delegated most financial matters, Castro exerted an interest in economic affairs and during this period he maintained regular meetings with his "moderate" advisors. Although Cuba continued to seek expropriation of sugarcane properties, and continued to pressure the American-owned utilities, public statements seemed to be more accommodating to Americans. *Revolución* ran articles reminding readers that the communists were late to accept the leadership of M–7–26, and at least one editorial alleged that had General Cantillo performed his *golpe* in mid–1958, the communists would have recognized it and joined in his government.[24]

Conversely, while Castro appeared to be open to some compromises with the United States, the American press continued to report that there was widespread unease in Cuba and that the population was turning against him. Castro was accused of giving the people "spectacles and side shows" but failing to aid anyone economically; for every gain, there was a retrenchment. Most symbolic was a decline in American tourism. Many reports had already written off Cuba and depicted the Provisional Government as communist-leaning, if not communist-controlled.[25] These articles appeared as there were reports of external invasion and domestic insurrection.[26] There also were reports that Castro had begun to stifle free speech. Ruby Phillips reported that charges were brought against the *Diario de la Marina*, which considered itself the unofficial voice of the Catholic Church. The paper had argued that although the life of rural Cubans might have been improved, "civilization" for the middle class would be ruined by import quotas as Cuba did not produce "luxury" items such as cars and a long list of other products, such as diesel engines, typewriters, cameras and television sets.[27] Castro continued to state that American newspapers and reporters, like Dubois, were trying to undermine his regime. However, Phillips's reports were premature.[28]

At the time, charges were made that the United States government had a censorship policy. The administration had determined that the Hennings-Moss Act of 1958 gave the President "executive privilege" not to disclose American matters of state. Newspapers accused the administration of obscuring, clouding or even blacking out news to further a political agenda.[29]

There also was dissension regarding diplomacy. Democratic Senator John F. Kennedy published a book called, *The Strategy of Peace*, in which he accused the Eisenhower administration of fueling antipathy toward Cuba, making it an easy target for communist intervention. He noted that Castro followed the legacy of Simón Bolívar, and speculated that had the Eisenhower administration given a "warmer welcome" to Castro when he visited in April, Castro might have been more open to American interests. He also wondered whether Castro would have taken "a more rational course" had the United States not backed

Batista.[30] Senator Kennedy would later become President Kennedy. He made several trips to Cuba and spent three days in Havana in December 1957, hobnobbing with Ambassador Smith and Senator Smathers.[31] According to several sources, he was also friendly with Meyer Lansky and Santos Traficante, who set him up with prostitutes.[32]

About this time, Finance Minister Rufo López Fresquet began to negotiate with representatives of the U.S. embassy.[33] He described his position as engaged in "conspiratorial activities." He was a double agent, if not a mole in the Provisional Government.

CIA records revealed that by this time, President Eisenhower agreed to support Cuban groups opposed to Castro, with a view that they would make it seem that Castro had created his own downfall.[34] The CIA also either authorized or condoned sending raiding parties to Cuba from the United States.[35] At this time WH/4, Task Force 4 of the Western Hemisphere Division, was directed to plan to carry out the policy.[36]

Castro hoped to increase American tourism and tout the successes of the revolution. Cuba brought in American travel agents so they could see for themselves. However, the news descriptions of the tourism program were more than cautionary, citing to the possibility of the lack of food, potential crime and high prices.[37] However, the government made sure that the agents were impressed. When the travel agents arrived, the Provisional Government displayed how orphans and other deprived children had been relocated to palatial estates formerly owned by Batista cronies.[38]

In Pinar del Río Province the Provisional Government established a single cooperative that mainly comprised uncultivated or abandoned land. Most of the best land in the province was dedicated to tobacco farming, but as this land was unsuitable for it, it would be used to grow cotton, peanuts, castor oil plants, beans, onions, potatoes, and corn, with a plan to also build a factory. This land was sparsely settled, so the government moved in landless people and gave each of them control of a 66-acre plot. It was estimated that it would take about five years to make the land become profitable.[39]

Minister Armando Hart announced that the Cuban education system would be revamped. Three thousand new schools would be opened in September, with 2,000 more in the planning stage. Teacher salaries would be increased. Eighteen "scholastic cities" would be built, each accommodating several thousand children. The school day, normally a half day, would be increased to a full day. A campaign was initiated to eliminate illiteracy. Books and school supplies would be provided without cost. Conservatives complained that the hierarchy was comprised mostly of leftists. Among other new texts was a history authored by Antonio Núñez Jiménez, head of INRA, which incorporated the assertion that Cuba had already won its war for independence when the United States entered in 1898 to support its "imperialistic policy."[40]

On bonds, Castro said that Cuba had no dollars to pay for land, and had "no alternative and we are going to pay for the land with the means that we have."[41] Castro alleged that any money that the Provisional Government might have was in United States banks, in the name of Batista and his cronies. He characterized the bonds as future dollars.

The American newspapers continued to stress objections to Provisional Government economic policies. Things had been going well until the Castro resignation on July 17. After that, the price of sugar went to a new 20-year low. There was high unemployment, foreign reserves were low, and Cuba had a reduced balance of payments to drag down the economy. There was no foreign investment and imports from the United States were declining rapidly. As a result, experts predicted that the Provisional Government would have to place strict price and wage controls on the Cuban economy to survive. Experts said that measures to help the employment situation could hurt the balance of payments and vice versa. One measure would have been to devalue the peso. However, all anticipated measures had draw-backs, and the best remedy, according to these experts, would be a loan from the United States with a stabilization program directed by the International Monetary Fund. Julio Lobo, one of Cuba's leading financiers, was amassing small banks although he reportedly lost $25 million from his land holdings. According to an unnamed treasury official, banking could have become the most profitable business under Castro. Prospects for sugar and other agricultural investments were dim. Real estate and construction were dead.[42]

American mining and petroleum holdings were exempted from the Agrarian Reform Law. Among the largest were nickel and cobalt factories at Moa Bay (then still under con-struction) and Nicaro Nickel, owned by Freeport Nickel Company and National Lead Com-pany, respectively. Despite an episode of kidnapping at the plant in 1958 by M-7-26 *barbudos*, and despite strikes, owners reported that relations with Castro were "very good." Oil companies also reported good relations. However, the American-owned telephone com-pany was controlled by an intervener and the American-owned electric company was still under study by the government. It was estimated that there were about $850,000,000 in American investments in Cuba.[43] Castro would later discuss buying the nickel mining oper-ations.[44] The United States had said that it was interested in selling the properties it owned in Cuba.

Approximately 95 percent of Cuban land was covered by petroleum claims, but little actual drilling had been done. Cuban wells produced only 600 to 700 barrels per day while Cubans consumed 50,000 barrels per day, mostly American oil. The law would soon be amended to cover petroleum holdings.[45]

In August, the Provisional Government announced that because the United States had failed to cooperate on sugar quotas and prices, it was hoping to find new markets. The Sugar Stabilization Institute sold about $9,500,000 worth to the Soviet Union at 2.58 cents per pound. The Soviets had purchased sugar from the Batista government in previous years, but they needed significantly less in 1959 than in past years.[46]

In September, the Provisional Government doubled the tax on liquor. It had contem-plated outlawing all liquor sales, but needed revenue.[47]

More importantly, Cuba started a trade war with the United States, as taxes on imports increased dramatically. Cuba presented its program to the International Monetary Fund, which approved it as an emergency measure. Castro said that because Cuba had domestic problems and had an imbalance of trade, "temporary" restrictions were needed immediately. The 1959 trade deficit was estimated at $175,000,000. The law precluded sellers of imported goods from raising prices accordingly, so it was feared that all imports would cease. The press was told that Cubans needed to invest in machinery and equipment, like tractors, rather than luxury items, like American cars. Violations of the law would bring jail sentences of six months to three years.[48] The measures were taken without consultation or prior notice to the United States, then Cuba's major trading partner. Cuba imported $546,000,000 in goods from the United States. Cuba did seek approval from the International Monetary Fund to ensure that the peso would not come under attack.[49]

At the time, there wasn't an international organization to monitor trade, and the United States and Cuba had entered into GATT, the General Agreement on Tariffs and Trade. GATT's main objective was the reduction of barriers to international trade through the reduction of tariff barriers, quantitative restrictions and subsidies on trade through a series of agreements. There was an argument that the imposition of predatory tariffs singled out the United States, that it was politically rather than economically inspired, and that it was a violation of standing GATT treaties. When asked, Roa García told the press that Cuba would trade with anybody, including the Soviet Union, on its own terms. Cuba needed to industrialize and the tariffs were designed to promote Cuban self-dependence. Although there is some question about a causal relationship, the United States increased the sugar quota.[50]

On September 26, the Provisional Government decreed the bond issue: 100,000,000 pesos at 4.5 percent for 20 years. Americans protested that the use of bonds was not "prompt, adequate and fair compensation."[51]

As this was happening, Soviet premier Nikita Khrushchev was visiting the United States. During his first election campaign, President Eisenhower was depicted by leaders of his party as too accommodating to the Soviets. They had been U.S. allies in World War II, but soon became depicted as evil enemies, who would do anything to destroy the American way of life. During the first part of the Cold War, conservatives in the Soviet Union depicted the West in the same way.

Khrushchev was a reformer. His speech "On the Personality Cult and its Consequences" to the closed session of the Twentieth Soviet Communist Party Congress, February 25, 1956, denounced Stalin's totalitarian rule and cult of personality. Khrushchev freed millions of political prisoners. "Khrushchev's Thaw" relaxed the use of terror and improved the economic situation for the majority of Soviets. Although hard-line communists within the Soviet government reacted against reform, Khrushchev defeated Stalinist attempts by an "Anti-Party Group" to remove him. He was able to purge the government, but unlike Stalin, he did not eliminate his enemies. Instead, his enemies were demoted.[52]

Most of these reforms were not well reported in the United States, which was still reeling psychologically from the McCarthy anti-communist panic. Americans continued to view any Soviet policy as anti–American. Khrushchev's reputation suffered when he revealed that he had sent in Soviet troops to subdue revolts in Hungary in 1956.[53] He had shared power at that time. After he became premier of the Soviet Union on March 27, 1958, Khrushchev promoted coexistence and a domestic reform program concentrating on the production of consumer goods rather than on heavy industry, "to catch up and overtake the West." He replaced traditional defense spending with a new emphasis on technology, especially rocket based defense. Internally, Khrushchev continued to be opposed by the military, which would eventually oust him. However, Khrushchev was not completely open to outside values, and he cracked down on religious groups and had many churches closed or destroyed.

With the Nixon visit to the Soviet Union in the summer of 1959, Khrushchev publicly took the position that the U.S. and the Soviets were not doomed to an epic battle; we were mere economic and political rivals, which might be able to eventually have a normal relationship with each other through "peaceful coexistence."

Khrushchev spent 13 days in the United States. Khrushchev had two requests: to visit Disneyland and to meet John Wayne, the movie star. He wasn't able to do either, but he did visit Hollywood and tour the country. During the trip, he was threatened, and at least two assassination plots were foiled. Khrushchev was deeply offended.

The State Department leaked news that the United States would officially protest confiscation of American properties in Cuba. Also implied were threats to whether the United States should continue to buy Cuban sugar or whether we would "expropriate" part of the price differential that Cuba was receiving in sugar sold in the United States.[54] Cuba continued to maintain that the use of bonds was the same policy that the United States had imposed in Japan. However, the U.S. took the position that in Japan, bonds were given to Japanese landowners, not Americans, and therefore the Cuban bond issue was different.[55]

The Provisional Government realigned several departments. Raúl Castro was named Minister of the Armed Forces. The Ministry of Defense was abolished and its minister, *barbudo* comandante Agusto R. Martinez Sánchez, was named Minister of Labor, replacing Manuel Fernández Garcia.[56] It was reported that soldiers complained that they were required to perform manual labor on public works projects. However, it was also reported that Raúl Castro personally commanded 1,200 soldiers in Pinar del Río Province who were looking for insurgents. The news reports speculated that the new alignment reduced the authority of Comandante Camilo Cienfuegos, who had been an influential insider in the Provisional Government and who had been critical of Raúl Castro. It was also speculated that the military would be cut by an added 18,000 men.[57]

When Raúl's promotion was considered, several high-ranking military officers vociferously protested. *Barbudo* comandante Huber Matos, military governor of Camagüey Province, and one of Castro's most trusted advisors in the Rebel Army, submitted his resignation. Matos was eight years older than Fidel Castro and had been a teacher and owned a rice plantation prior to the revolution. He had delivered a planeload of arms donated by Costa Rican president Figueres in March 1957 at a time when the Rebel Army was extremely vulnerable.[58] He had not been in the inner circle prior to his promotion to command the Antonio (Tony) Guiteras Column Number 9, named for the anti-communist martyr killed by Batista's men in 1935, but he established himself as a military genius and held the same rank at the same level as Raúl Castro and Che Guevara.[59] He was an expert on agriculture and had friends among the cattlemen whose lands were to be confiscated.

Among the first acts of the revolution, a military cultural school was established under Che Guevara at La Cabaña prison.[60] The military also participated in the literacy campaign. Matos was afraid that his men were being subjected to propaganda when pro-Marxist articles were published in the army magazine *Verde Olivo*. He complained to Fidel Castro about it. He also complained that Raúl Castro had named known communists to his general staff, and he had submitted his resignation in protest in July, but Fidel Castro had talked him out of it.[61] On October 19, he sent a second letter of resignation to Castro. Twenty other military officers also resigned.[62]

On that morning, Castro spoke to the travel agents to tell them how much he and his government loved Americans.[63] By that afternoon, Castro had received the Matos letter, and by that evening, his demeanor and attitude toward Americans had changed.[64]

Castro's demeanor was probably also affected by another incident. At the same time that Castro received the text of Matos's letter, there was another bombing. However, the "bombs" dropped by a single aircraft were probably only propaganda leaflets, but the Cuban civil air defense panicked after seeing the aircraft, and two were killed and at least 20 more were wounded by antiaircraft fire and in sporadic shooting incidents. The bomber was able to escape. There were other simultaneous reports of sabotage, including at least two bombs directed at civilian targets, drive-by shootings and a grenade attack in Havana.[65] The American Society of Travel Agents convention was ongoing in Havana as the panic and violence was occurring.

On the same day, Castro's former best friend and ex-brother-in-law, Rafael Diaz-Balart, announced through the news media that he was the head of the White Rose organization, and related that his organization had cells in every town and city in Cuba, consisting of "thousands" of guerrillas in the field. None, he said, were aligned with the "Liberation

Army" of General Pedraza in the Dominican Republic or with any groups supported by Batista. The cells were set up independently, so even Diaz-Balart could not know who the members were. Another anti–Castro organization was actively recruiting in New York, but White Rose had nothing to do with it. Diaz-Balart alleged that all of his units were inside Cuba and that Castro would be removed without any outside help.[66]

Matos was open about his feeling that the communists had infiltrated the army. In the public mind, Matos was closely associated with Castro. He had ridden on the tank with Fidel Castro and Camilo Cienfuegos as they made their flower-strewn triumphal arrival into Havana on January 8. During the war Matos was the "hero of Santiago" as his unit besieged the city with only about 100 men, keeping Batista's army pinned down without a chance to fight in Oriente Province. In the Provisional Government, he was a military governor of one of the most influential provinces in Cuba. At the time, he was one of the most popular men in Cuba.[67]

Matos also had some objections to the agrarian reform issue. Camagüey was a province of large *latifundas*, like the King Ranch, rich in livestock. It had few sugar mills, few *guajiros*, and only a few Afro-Cubans. A majority of the citizens were Creoles. Former agriculture professor Matos was able to maintain production levels in his province, primarily because it was unlike the rest of Cuba.

However, it looked like reform practices from other provinces would extend to Camagüey. For example, in Oriente Province, INRA had become the middleman for buying and selling fruit, potatoes, milk, eggs, coffee and eventually all minerals. INRA also set up approximately 400 "stores of the people," operated at a 15 percent margin. Prices at these stores were much less than at competing groceries, and many of the established stores had to ask for bankruptcy protection. Unnamed government officials said that the grocery stores had "robbed" the people for years and deserved to be put out of business.[68] These stores would eventually replace *bodegas* all over the rest of Cuba.

"Fidel, you are destroying your own work," Matos wrote. "Great men begin to decline when they cease to be just."[69] He also said, "Everyone who has had the frankness to talk to you about the communist problem should leave, before he is removed."[70] Castro was obviously offended. A radio station had spread a rumor that Matos was going to issue a manifesto, and there was some question whether his followers were involved in a conspiracy.[71] Castro thought that an insurrection was occurring and ordered a takeover of the airport and the radio stations in Camagüey.[72] Castro sent fellow comandante Camilo Cienfuegos to arrest Matos and his men, most of whom had served with him in the Antonio Guiteras Column.[73] During the subsequent meeting between Cienfuegos and Matos, who had grown close during the revolution, Matos said he believed Cienfuegos had been sent to make the arrest so that forces allied with Matos might kill each other off, because Cienfuegos had become so popular that Castro needed to eliminate any competition, and could eliminate two competitors at the same time.[74] Matos reportedly also told López Fresquet that Raúl Castro was such a communist ideologue and so ambitious that he would kill Fidel to take over the government, if necessary.[75]

Based on an assumption that the airplane that had dropped the leaflets had originated in the United States, the next day a loud anti–American rally and a one-hour strike took place in Havana. By this time, the familiar refrain was "¡Castro Sí¡ ¡Yankee No¡" As thousands marched on the American embassy, Ambassador Bonsal issued a statement that the airplane's origin would be investigated.[76] Within hours, the FBI announced that not only had the flight originated in Miami, but the pilot was a former head of the Cuban air force, Major

Díaz Lanz, and it was a military aircraft.[77] Castro appeared on television and in a four-hour diatribe attacked the United States. Castro reminded the United States that Cuba permitted the use of Guantánamo, while "they give war criminals bases from which to bomb us." He said that the threats of further incursions required mobilization of the entire country.[78] The Cuban government published *Havana's Pearl Harbor*, a pamphlet describing an attack emanating from the United States, with an altered photograph depicting an air war over Havana on its cover. Cuba also brought charges against the United States at the United Nations.[79] The U.S. embassy protested against anti–American rhetoric. However, two more planes appeared to drop more leaflets, inciting the matter further. Cuba also requested the extradition of Díaz Lanz, but it would take another month to do so.[80]

In the United States, Cuban workers at Idlewild Airport staged a one-hour strike to protest the bombing.[81]

A couple of days later, after Castro called for another rally against the bombings, and after all work was halted so that the public could attend, Castro appeared before a crowd of 300,000 to 400,000 to protest American "aggression" against Cuba. He alleged that he had hard evidence that seven or eight airplanes had been cleared by United States Customs at Miami to fly to Cuba and back. Castro told the crowd that military tribunals needed to be reinstituted. In his fiery speech, Castro used a call-and-response technique to offer the names of his opponents. "¡*Paredon!*," "firing Squad," or "to the wall" was the response to each of them, including to the name of former hero of the revolution, the Hero of Santiago, Comandante Huber Matos.[82]

Several other terrorist incidents were reported, including one stating that when a grenade was thrown into the *Revolución* newspaper office, one person was injured. Castro reminded the crowd that Batista had used American-made bombs, including napalm liquid fire incendiary devices, on innocent civilians and on his rebel forces during his insurrection.[83]

In Miami the head of customs denied that American airports were used as bases to raid Cuba. A federal judge refused to issue a warrant for Díaz Lanz on charges of attempted murder, as the government did not supply sufficient proof.[84]

Ambassador Bonsal would later say that the bombing episode was a "providential diversion" to permit Castro to avoid having to explain the Matos episode. He was able to rally his "mobs" to change the issue. Castro denied that he was a communist, denied that the Provisional Government was being overtaken by communists, and denied that his brother was a communist. But he maintained that as Matos took the same position that Díaz Lanz and Urrutia had taken, that he was oblivious to a communist takeover and refused to address it, and had convinced another 20 members of his staff to take the same position. This was "treason."[85] Bonsal was probably not aware that President Eisenhower said privately that instead of protesting flights from Miami to the United States, Castro should "just shoot the planes down."[86]

Within the Provisional Government Council of Ministers, Faustino Pérez, Manuel Ray and Enrique Oltulski spoke in favor of Matos: There was no hard evidence that he was leading an insurrection. Raúl Castro said that Matos should be shot. Fidel Castro said: "Either Huber Matos is a traitor or I am a liar."[87] Felipe Pazos had glibly told President Dorticós that if Matos were a traitor because he opposed communism, then he was also. Dorticós reported this to the council as if Pazos had tried to recruit him to treason.[88] Raúl Castro said he wanted to execute him also.

Meanwhile, among the first *latifunda* that was confiscated was the Castro family property in Birán. Although Fidel and Raúl Castro both had an interest in the 21,650 acres, only 1,000 acres would remain family property managed by Ramón Castro. The rest was distributed to tenants and *precaristas*.[89]

American landowners complained that they weren't given adequate notice. Although there was no hard evidence that *campesinos* demanded a quick takeover, *barbudos* "intervened" in sugar mills and large estates. Between July and December 1959, over 40 "interventions" were reported against American properties, including some properties that weren't covered by the law.[90] Americans reported that the INRA employees were often rude and threatening. There were accounts of workers paid not to work. Although the law did not address equipment or machinery, they were often taken with the land.[91]

After the loophole exempting mining from the reform and tax imposition was closed, and after taxes of 5 percent on severance and 25 percent on exports of minerals were imposed, nickel production in Cuba came to a halt. Although Cuba had the capacity to become the second largest nickel producer in the world, and although there were large deposits of iron ore and cobalt also to be mined, there was no demand for Cuban minerals.[92] There was also a 45 percent tax imposed on corporate profits. The United States owned the Nicaro nickel plant, the largest in Cuba, and Freeport Nickel, an American-owned company, also owned a large plant that it was expanding, but that would soon end. Most Cuban nickel had been sold to the United States. Canada was a producer of nickel and was the largest beneficiary of the industry's demise in Cuba.[93]

The Provisional Government announced that it would establish an agency in Oriente Province that would be solely charged to buy and sell minerals. The agency would ensure the "rapid sale of minerals, immediate payment and the best possible economic condition for a sale."[94]

The *Times* reported the complaint of Florence Steinhart, whose father had established the first electric company and streetcar system in Havana in 1906. Her vacant land in Cojimar was assessed at $2700, although the family had paid $5,000 for it years before and she said the actual value was $100,000.[95]

Actually, although Americans had owned most of the Cuban sugar interests, no new sugar mills had been constructed after 1929 and American firms began to divest in the 1930s. Legislation favoring domestic ownership had been passed during the first Grau administration, and American companies had to comply with strict Cuban labor laws and powerful Cuban labor unions.[96] The largest landowner at the time was the American-owned Cuban Cane Corporation, which was sold in 1934. By 1959, although many mills were titled as American companies, ownership included Cubans. For example, Batista owned 10–15 percent of American Cuban Atlantic Company, and Julio Lobo, the largest Cuban shareholder, sometimes was able to control the company.[97] Moreover, although profit margins had been extremely high, by the late 1950s there were only modest profits to be made. Lobo also controlled several other large properties, including the former Hershey properties. The largest landowner was the American-owned Cuban Atlantic Gulf Sugar Company; the second was the American-owned Cuban-American Sugar Company; and third was the American-owned United Fruit.[98]

Lobo was ostensibly the wealthiest man in Cuba. He had been opposed to Batista and had lent his support to M–7–26. He provided employees with housing, schools and churches, and had a good relationship with the unions. He was a free-trader, and opposed Batista's national price fixing program. Although his family had lived in Cuba since 1902, they had come by way of Venezuela and Curaçao, and he was seen in Creole circles as a *moro*, as he was born in Venezuela and his family origin were Sephardic Jews. A graduate of the sugar institute at Louisiana State University, he worked his way up from a low level employee to owner of 11 sugar mills in Cuba, and he controlled another 15–20 mills. He also had interests in the Capri and Riviera hotels, broadcasting, and many other industries in Cuba, Puerto Rico, the Philippines and in the United States.[99]

The second largest landowners were the progeny of Laurencio Falla Gutiérrez, who had emigrated from Spain to amass 300,000,000 acres.[100]

During this time, the Council of Ministers also banned the Thanksgiving holiday, which had been a Batista innovation, implemented after his stay in the United States. Rules also were established requiring the use of Spanish on labels of all products brought into the country.[101]

Although U.S. foreign policy had hardened, some Americans were quite satisfied with the progress of the revolution. Presbyterian missionary leader E.A. O'Dell issued a press release saying that despite reports of repression, 95 percent of the Cuban people experienced a "genuine sense of freedom and liberty" and that the church was an integral part of successes since the Provisional Government was installed. He cited the Presbyterian role in developing literacy programs, led by the Reverend Fernández Ceballos, pastor of the First Presbyterian Church of Havana and secretary of the Council of Evangelical Churches.[102]

Barbudo comandante Rolando Cubelo was elected president of the DR, defeating Pedro Luis Boitel in a student election at the University of Havana.[103]

Cuba invited Egyptian president Nasser to visit after Che Guevara had introduced himself to him on his "goodwill" trip.[104] At the time, Egypt and Syria were nonaligned nations, but they leaned trending toward the Soviet Union. The Provisional Government would soon threaten to remove itself from the western bloc of nations, led by the United States. Castro wanted to form a worldwide bloc of neutral, nonaligned nations, and planned to hold an organizational meeting in Havana.[105]

Until World War I, Egypt had been part of the Ottoman Empire, although British and French companies built the Suez Canal on Egyptian territory and had a presence in the country. After a period under the British mandate, Egypt became a constitutional monarchy in 1923, using the British parliamentary model. However, Britain retained a measure of control. In the 1952 revolution, military officers led by Nasser forced King Farouk of Egypt to abdicate in support of his son Fuad. On June 18, 1953, the Egyptian Republic was declared, with General Muhammad Naguib as the first president of the Republic. In 1954 Nasser ousted Naguib in another coup, and he declared independence from the United Kingdom on June 18, 1956. Although the British maintained a military presence at the canal, the Egyptians stopped traffic, especially that which carried goods to and from Israel. Under Nasser, Egypt supported demonstrations and groups opposed to Britain throughout the Middle East, and in 1955 the country entered into an arms deal with communist Czechoslovakia. Nasser nationalized the Suez Canal on July 26, 1956.

Israel, Britain and France attacked Egypt in 1956. Israel captured the Gaza Strip and Sinai and the joint force, Operation Musketeer, took the Suez Canal. The United States executed the Eisenhower Doctrine to negotiate a cease-fire and a truce.

Starting in 1952, Egypt began a program of agrarian reform. Between 1955 and 1957, Nasser executed a program of nationalization, similar to the Cubanization laws first enacted in 1934 and revisited by the Provisional Government.

After the Suez Crisis, Nasser moved Egypt politically closer to the Soviet Union, as the Soviets agreed to provide approximately one-third of the cost of the Aswan High Dam and sent 400 construction engineers to Egypt. The United States initially agreed to fund the dam. Although not a member of the Soviet bloc, Nasser was the leader of the Arab world, representing Pan-Arabism. In 1958, Syria and Egypt formed the United Arab Republic, which became a military force in the region. Most of its weapons were purchased from the Soviet Union. After the purchase of arms from Soviet bloc countries, the U.S. withdrew its offer.

Like Nasser, Castro probably saw himself as a nationalist. He probably was encouraged that Nasser had withstood the attack of two of the major powers, Britain and France, and had stood up to the United States. He also probably noted that Egypt also had a similar land reform. Both men were tall, had a military bearing and were charismatic leaders. By 1959, Nasser proved so appealing to other Arabs that several other nations asked to join his program.

At the same time, a similar form of nationalism was taking place in Venezuela and Brazil. American companies were subjected to seizure in Brazil, and American companies were leaving Venezuela. Several other Latin American countries had, for the first time, voted against United States positions at the United Nations. Brazil was negotiating trade with the Soviet Union.[106] However, although Venezuela opposed the United States on some issues, the majority party also remained anti-communist, and relations with Cuba had gone from close support to outright animosity. Raúl Castro was to have made a visit to Venezuela, but the government would not grant him an entry visa, on the basis that he could incite Venezuelan communists. In response, Cuba ceased diplomatic relations with Venezuela.[107]

As all of this was occurring, Ambassador Bonsal presented a bluntly worded letter to President Dorticós. On one hand he expressed regret that inter-country relations had been reduced to "distrust and hostility," but on the other he complained about some of Castro's statements about the United States and about the publication of the *Pearl Harbor* pamphlet. For some reason, although Castro did not explicitly threaten to do it, the United States attributed complaints about the Guantánamo Treaty as a direct threat to recover it.[108]

However, the letter restated United States policy against intervention in Cuba, citing the Neutrality Act and other laws that prohibited Cuban residents in the United States from taking actions against the Cuban government. The letter stated that allegations against Cuban émigrés would be investigated, but noted that they were entitled to due process. It noted that although the United States had asked the Provisional Government for sufficient information to bring charges against the accused émigrés, necessary information was not provided, and specifically noted that William Morgan claimed to have information, which was not provided.

The letter also indicated that Díaz Lanz was under investigation, but as of that date there was no evidence that bombs had been dropped on Cuban targets from airplanes based in the United States. It also stated that the United States had nothing to do with any acts against Cuba. The letter also denied that there was a press campaign to discredit Cuba. Lastly, the letter restated American policy to oppose Communism but stated that the United States did not oppose reform in Cuba.[109] Bonsal would eventually say that the United States and United States' private interests evidently had no rights, whatever, in Cuba but this was not stated in the letter.[110]

In response, President Dorticós told Ambassador Bonsal that the protest was "without foundation." He also announced that the military tribunals would be reestablished. The *New York Times* reported that although the letter didn't mention Castro by name, it was a "sharp answer" to Castro's allegations about United States intervention in Cuba.[111] The *Washington Post* called it a "rare slap" voicing "shock and amazement" at Castro's statements.[112]

The next day, President Eisenhower gave a short statement on Cuba at a news conference. He said that he was confused why Cubans would not want to have a good relationship with the United States: "I don't know exactly what the difficulty is." He said that he would do all that he could to ensure that the United States was not used as a base of operations by hostile émigrés. It was "a puzzling matter to figure out."[113] News articles speculated that the confusion stemmed from Castro's "revolutionary fervor, his idealism and his emotional makeup."[114] A *Washington Post* editorial suggested that there were problems and "freebooting aviators and disgruntled exiles" should not be able to use the United States "to stir up hostility."[115] Within a few days, the pilot of the plane that had dropped leaflets over Havana, Frank Fiorini, better known later in American history as Frank Sturgis, described as a former American civilian military advisor to Cuba, admitted his role and said that Díaz Lanz had accompanied him.[116] Several days later, the Justice Department and the Federal Aviation Agency ordered close surveillance of flights to Cuba, including a requirement that pilots would have to file a detailed flight plan.[117]

Ambassador Bonsal would later say that Castro's performance at the October 26 speech "spelled the end' of good Cuban/American relations.[118]

A few days later, the constitutional right to habeus corpus was suspended by the Provisional Government and the military tribunals were reinstated with a new focus: counter-revolutionary activity. Three Americans were held subject to trial: Austin Young and Peter Lamberton, who had been captured in Pinar del Río, and del Pino.[119]

At the same time, Comandante Camilo Cienfuegos was missing. He had been in Camagüey to arrest Matos and to take over his governorship. He was to fly 300 miles from Camagüey to Havana as a passenger in a small airplane.[120] According to Franqui, who was his close friend, Camilo Cienfuegos Gorriarán was the "nicest and most Cuban of all the barbudos."[121] Cienfuegos had been an art student. After he was wounded in a student protest, he had lived for a time in the United States. He met Fidel Castro in Mexico, and took part in the Granma expedition. Eventually he became a comandante and the head of the Cuban military in Havana Province. He was closely associated with Fidel Castro but was not on friendly terms with Raúl Castro.[122] Although he was also close to and influenced by Che Guevara, Franqui described him as a "helter skelter" thinker, implying that he was not a communist. On the other hand, he had "let" the communists into the Rebel Army at the end of the war and had permitted Félix Torres, a controversial communist, to become a comandante. Cienfuegos's parents were Spanish anarchists and his brother Osmani Cienfuegos became a devoted communist. In August 1958, he had given Franqui all of his manuscripts from the war: His mental state at that time was that he did not have long to live. Despite their friendship, after he arrested Huber Matos, Cienfuegos accused him of treason at a press conference.[123]

Search parties tried to find the airplane. Rumors spread that Cienfuegos was kidnapped or he had defected. There were also rumors that he had quarreled with Raúl Castro. A *New York Times* article implied he had been "eliminated."[124] Castro suspended all of his other responsibilities to spend almost two weeks looking for him. *Barbudo* comandante Juan Almeida Bosque, a veteran of Moncada and Granma, was named to replace Cienfuegos as army chief of staff.

The Dominican Republic confirmed that it had spent $50 million on arms purchases to help defend against potential threats from Cuba and Venezuela.[125]

On October 24 and 28, Soviet radio, which had not reported on Cuba for a long time, stated that Castro was "ready to die" in his fight against foreign and domestic enemies, and described the accusation that flights to bomb Cuba originated in the United States and were a violation of Cuban sovereignty. It also said that because the United States was using its sugar quota to undermine the Cuban economy, the Soviet Union would buy sugar from Cuba.[126] Further, rumors were rife that Cuba was negotiating with Czechoslovakia to buy Soviet MiG jet fighters, as Cuba had failed to purchase airplanes from Great Britain.[127]

On November 1, Díaz Lanz was arrested by the FBI and threatened with extradition to Cuba for the murder of a Cuban and injuring 24 others during the bombing.[128]

On November 4, three men were seen fleeing after shots were fired at Morgan's house.[129]

The American press reported that although many of his followers remained loyal to Castro and were sympathetic to his regime, some (even members of M–7–26) felt that they were no longer insiders. People were afraid to speak their minds, fearing that they would be labeled as traitors.[130] Castro brother Ramón attacked brother Fidel in a letter to *Prensa Libre*, the newspaper condemned by Castro as anti–revolutionary. Ramón defended *Prensa Libre's* right to freedom of speech and also criticized agrarian reform. In response, the M–7–26 newspaper *Revolución* attacked Ramón Castro's character, asserting that he had refused to join the Revolution due to "a lack of courage and the permanent desire to make money."[131]

In New York, the White Rose announced that it had selected a Cuban government in exile, despite warnings from the U.S. government that it would be a violation of the Neutrality Act to do so. Domingo Gómez Gimeranez, M.D., a professor of medicine at Columbia University was chosen as provisional president in exile, while Morab Sosa, a former Batista colonel, now a textile worker, was selected as chief of the armed forces. Secretary General Díaz Balart told the press that White Rose had 300 cells and 2,700 militarily trained members in Cuba. Rolando Amador, a lawyer, and Alonso Martinez, a former soldier, were named to the "executive cell."[132]

At least one American company that had lost most of its holdings decided to stay in business in Cuba. Cuban Land and Leaf Tobacco Company of Trenton, New Jersey, operating from Pinar del Río, decided to stay in business and agreed to buy the crops that its former sharecroppers, now landowners, would sell to them. The Provisional Government took 2,633 acres valued at $2,500,000 that the company owned and another 333 acres it had under lease. The company received Cuban government 4.5 percent 20-year bonds for the land.[133]

The next day, the Hearst Headline Service raised the question of whether the Soviet Union had supplied Cuba with rockets, although it noted that there was "no corroboration" to date.[134] The Hearst papers had run several similar articles, predicting that if the United States did not stop Castro, other Latin American countries would confiscate American-owned properties.[135]

Although the U.S. State Department publicly aired concerns about the method of repayment for confiscated land through government notes, privately the State Department had determined that it would not contest the Agrarian Reform seizures. United States taxpayers would pay as much as $1,000,000,000 in losses written off by United States taxpayers who lost property in Cuba. The United States was confronted with similar situations in other countries such as Brazil, Bolivia and Venezuela, and it did not want to act impetuously and turn Castro into a martyr, which it feared could tilt Latin America directly toward Communism.[136]

In union elections, the communists were soundly defeated as the M–7–26 candidates won 90 percent of the vote and the communists only received 5 percent.[137] Former member of the M–7–26 underground David Salvador was challenged by two candidates who were seen as more accommodating to the communists, and who had not supported his calls for strikes during the revolution. Salvador was viewed as anti-communist, although he had once been a party member. He was expelled in 1951. After a rowdy and sometimes bloody election, during which Fidel Castro pleaded for "unity," Salvador prevailed by a landslide, as did his entire slate of candidates for the executive committee. Behind the scenes, Raúl Castro was incensed, as none of his favorites won. There was still tension between Raúl Castro and the veterans of the underground. As an accommodation, Salvador selected at least two "unity" members to serve on the executive board. Both Fidel Castro and Salvador asked the convention to support Cuba's right to purchase arms, especially jet aircraft from other countries, and condemned the United States for interference in deals with European countries. Castro also said that property owned by counter-revolutionaries would be confiscated.[138]

To try to control labor, Minister Manuel Fernández was replaced after the Matos incident by Agusto Martinez Sánchez, who had been legal advisor to Raúl Castro, then Minister of Defense. Like Matos, Fernández had been a follower of Guiteras and was considered to be a revolutionary.[139] Cuban labor had been independent, socialist, but anti–Batista and anti-communist. No one had challenged Fernández's loyalty or criticized his work as minister of labor, and, in fact, he had been able to neutralize some of the demands that might have caused more economic friction. However, he was not as close to Raúl Castro as his successor. Labor leaders remembered that Batista had sided with the communists in the late 1930s. The Cuban Federation of Labor, CTC, took credit for ending the Batista regime. It had initiated strikes in 1956, 1957, 1958, and on January 1, 1959, (which shut down Havana), and which labor felt had crushed any claim that the military junta and General Cantillo might have had to retain power. Of course, this narrative did not fit the myth of a military victory. Although the executive committee of the CTC were all M–7–26 officials, and none were communists, Castro was able to manipulate the organization to seat leaders more amenable to him.[140] Communists tried but failed to disrupt the meeting, as fights broke out on the floor. Although the communists received no seats on the executive committee, the CTC withdrew from a regional labor organization that was seen as supporting dictators like Trujillo and Somoza and was depicted as pro-American and anti-communist. The organization was supported by the AFL-CIO, which had refused to meet with Castro when he visited the United States in April. The CTC planned to start its own "revolutionary" regional labor organization.[141]

Some American reports noted that Fidel Castro's pleas for "unity" were meant to include all labor organizations, including communists in CTC leadership. Three members of the executive board were seen as supporters of "unity." However, communist labor leaders condemned the vote.[142]

Soon after the conference the Provisional Government passed a new law giving the minister of labor the right to intervene in strikes or in any company whose production was hampered "for labor reasons."[143]

Representatives of the Soviet Union and East Germany spoke at the convention to a mixed reception. Calls of "propaganda" were heard by American reporters. A resolution censoring the newspaper *Prensa Libre* for attacking Castro was passed. Workers for the paper were to appear before a CTC committee investigating the matter.[144] A press organization called this "censorship by terror," accusing high ranking Cuban government officials.[145]

The National Bank of Cuba announced that all permanent residents in Cuba had to convert dollars into pesos on a one-to-one basis. This had to be accomplished within 72 hours of the receipt of the dollars.[146] The rule targeted exporters, and the purpose was to try to stabilize the value of the peso. Cuba also initiated a new savings bonds program, patterned after the War Bonds program of the United States during World War II. The bonds were needed for industrial investments to displace foreign investment, because the government was sure that no outside help would be coming.[147]

In a statement before the United States Chamber of Commerce, President Kubitschek of Brazil said that Brazil was "bitter" about being ignored and that it should be at the same level of interest to the United States as Britain or France. He said that the level of anti–American hatred had remained the same or had increased since Nixon made his 1958 trip to the region. He asked the United States to "do something dramatic soon, not necessarily in economic terms," to change the sentiment. The Brazilian foreign minister told the chamber that he was tired of learning about American foreign policy in the newspapers, implying that Brazil was not important enough to enter into a dialogue with the State Department. The *Washington Post* reported that Brazilians believed the difficulties between the United States and Cuba would seem like a "mild squall" compared with the problems that American diplomacy and policy would cause in Brazil. "We are sick and tired of being treated as a banana republic," one unnamed Brazilian was reported as saying.[148]

After he had discontinued his search for Cienfuegos, Fidel Castro gave a major television speech. According to Ruby Phillips, he looked exhausted. He accused the United States of extending open arms to war criminals and sarcastically asked the United States to account for the derivation of Díaz Lanz's airplane. He castigated the American press for spreading wild rumors about the disappearance of Cienfuegos, but said that his airplane probably had gone down over the ocean, making recovery difficult. He also accused the press and "vested interests" of carrying out attacks against Cuba.[149] The speech lasted eight hours, into the next morning when Cuba published a 29-page white paper responding to the two State Department notes. Cuba denied any attempt to instill "distrust and hostility" in the relationship between Cuba and America. It objected to the American version of the Spanish American War as fact. It objected to the positive characterization of American investments in Cuba. It reminded the State Department that the sugar quota system served only to limit exports into the United States, and that reductions in the quota cost the Cuban economy $200 million. It reminded the United States how Cuba sacrificed itself to benefit of the United States in World Wars I and II. It repeated the bombing charges, and objected to the American arms policy. It did not directly accuse the United States of complicity, but it did accuse the United States of negligence in failing to take account of "war criminals" in our midst. Cuba said that the United States had not responded to the charges that in addition to the Díaz Lanz flight, there was no action taken as to evidence of the bombing of two sugar mills, and although the United States may have had the right to deny licenses to sellers of arms from the United States into the Caribbean, it did not have the right to stop sales of arms from other countries such as Britain to Cuba. It alleged that Cuba needed to defend itself from an invasion from the Dominican Republic. It also asked whether the United States endorsed "insults, falsehoods and other insidious propaganda" generated by the American press. It also objected to the language on Communism in the second note, alleging that Communism was used as a ruse to encourage foreign intervention. In conclusion, the United States was asked to reconsider and revise its policy toward Cuba. The note was signed by Raúl Roa García, foreign minister of Cuba.[150]

Ambassador Bonsal did not discuss the note in *Cuba, Castro and the United States.* Apparently, the white paper was not taken as an added affront, and therefore, he was not asked to counter the new charges. At home, several newspaper columnists considered the white paper to be a direct challenge to the United States, and called for a break in relations with Cuba.[151] The United States Chamber of Commerce and the American Legion had been on record urging a break with Cuba before that. Actually, agricultural interests encouraged reduced Cuban sugar quotas, consistent with the allegations made about the use of quotas. Sugar beet farmers in the West expected record profits. Bad relations with Cuba would signal a need for a larger domestic crop.[152] President Eisenhower established a National Advisory Committee on Inter-American Relations, chaired by Secretary Herter.

Other columnists renewed the attack on Castro. For example, Jules Dubois, once a supporter, wrote a widely circulated series of columns in the *Chicago Tribune* that attacked Castro and said that Cuba was ruled by a military triumvirate. Although he published a book, *Fidel Castro: Rebel, Liberator or Dictator?*, supporting the revolution, his change in tone had been noticed, and he had been threatened by mobs on his last visit to Cuba. Dubois called Castro a "Red Robin Hood," robbing from the rich to give to the poor. He said that, despite Castro's promise during the revolution that he would not expropriate American property, under the influence of his brother Raúl and Che Guevara he was trying to destroy the free enterprise system. The "presents" given to the poor, however, had "knots" with "red bows" on them that amounted to slavery in the mode of a Chinese communist takeover of the land. *Campesinos* who received land were "told to produce and keep on producing or they will lose the land. They do not get full title and are being organized into cooperatives under control of 'tactical forces' under the command of Che Guevara." He said that the middle class would have only the "kind of freedom" that INRA supervisors under Che Guevara would give them.[153] He also described a "hate America" campaign, class warfare and reeducation programs. He accused Castro of "smearing" Díaz Lanz and newspaper editors, and of censoring the news in Cuba. A recent amendment to the law imposed a six- to 18-year sentence for publications tending "to impair the independence of the nation or provoke the non-observance of the laws in force."[154]

The Soviet Union initiated a $100 million publicity campaign in Latin America. Soviet deputy premier Anastas Mikoyan was on a tour, starting with Mexico, to "capture" Latin American markets. Juan Marinello, longtime communist leader and cabinet minister in the first Batista administration, had been in Moscow, where he attended the February Communist meeting, and reportedly stayed to receive about four months' "training." Dubois also alleged that the Soviets would use Cuba as their base in Latin America.[155]

Che Guevara was interviewed by Karl Meyer of the *Washington Post*, who had a year earlier interviewed Fidel Castro in the Sierra Madre. Guevara was pictured as soft spoken and amicable but naive. At the time, Guevara was head of the industrial section of INRA. He would soon be named president of the National Bank of Cuba. He denied he was a communist. He was a leftist, however, and had a "hidden resistance" toward the United States, stemming from his experiences in Guatemala. He praised the U.S. State Department in its relations in Egypt and Ghana, where the United States had provided assistance. However, he asserted that the United States did not act similarly in Cuba because of the large American investments in Cuba.[156]

At this time, Havana hosted a National Catholic Conference. A torch relay from the shrine to Our Lady of Charity in Oriente Province to Havana — 640 miles — carried a flame symbolizing the power of Cuba's patron saint.[157] Thousands of pilgrims came to Havana to see the statue, and there was a torchlight parade of 30,000 marchers to the Civic Plaza. The Communist Party claimed that counter-revolutionaries had made up placards that read,

"Down with the Catholic Congress," attributed the signs to communists, and displayed them in the crowd to stir up resentment against them. Pope John XXIII delivered a radio speech in Spanish to the crowd and blessed the Cuban people. Although he attended a mass with his mother and two sisters, Castro said that the conference was used by the privileged class as a "cloak" for attacks on the revolution. "Our people ... pray for Cuba and the Revolutionary laws." Although President Dorticós and the majority of the Council of Ministers attended, Raúl Castro and Che Guevara were conspicuous in their absence.[158]

In Boston, a Catholic cardinal accused Castro of "acting like a communist." He accused the Cuban government of impounding church funds.[159]

In Puerto Rico, an independence assembly passed resolutions supporting Castro and the Revolution.[160] However, in the Dominican Republic, Premier Castro and 113 others were tried in absentia for bringing an invasion in June. Castro was convicted and sentenced to 30 years' hard labor, as was President Rómulo Betancourt of Venezuela. The court also levied fines of a $100 million.[161]

At the same time that the announcement was made that Che Guevara would be the new head of the National Bank, an announcement was made that Faustino Pérez and Manuel Ray Rivero were replaced in the Council of Ministers. Headlines in American newspapers said that the moderates in the Provisional Government were being replaced by leftists. Pérez, of course, had been a medical student at the University of Havana at the same time Castro had been a law student, had been involved in the Ortodoxo movement with Castro, had been one of the founders of the directorate of M–7–26, was one of the survivors of the Granma expedition, was a *barbudo* comandante, a head of the underground who had brought hundreds if not thousands of supporters into active insurrection against Batista, had helped draft some of the most important revolutionary documents, including the *Manifesto Against Tyranny*, and from outward appearances was still one of Fidel Castro's closest advisors. He continued to debate privately with Castro, but the Matos matter apparently was the last straw. Although he was doing a good job, and had brought millions into the treasury, he was replaced by Rolando Díaz Restarain, a navy captain seen as more loyal to Fidel Castro as well as Raúl Castro, Chief of Staff of the Cuban military. Ray was appointed head of the Superior Institute of Science and Technology at the former Camp Colombia, Batista's military headquarters.[162] He also was a professor at the University of Havana.

Guevara replaced Felipe Pazos, who was named economic ambassador to Europe. Pazos had been meeting with Ambassador Bonsal on a regular basis.[163] According to López Fresquet, President Dorticó's denounced Pazos as a traitor in a cabinet meeting. He said that Castro had turned Cuba over to the Soviet Union.[164] After surveying his options, Castro chose Che Guevara for the position, probably due to the fact that he was the only person in the room he could be assured was loyal to him.

Soon after the public announcement was made that Guevara would be the head of the Cuban National Bank, there was a run on all the banks in Cuba.[165] Speaking at a program to honor the martyred medical students killed by the Spanish in 1871, Guevara said that the run on the banks was "logical" when Felipe Pazos, viewed as "moderate," was replaced by "a person who enjoys the fame of being extremely radical."[166]

After Guevara replaced Pazos, Ruby Phillips wrote an article summarizing her feelings about the recent developments. In "Castro Actions Suit the Communists' Aims," she noted that when the revolution began, almost all segments of society had been involved. However, first the "conservatives" and then the "moderates" were removed from the Provisional Government. She accused the Provisional Government of trying to eliminate all class distinctions and, in so doing, destroying the middle and upper classes. Although she said that she did not believe that Castro was a communist per se, she accused Castro of "supporting actually and effectively the Soviet Union's long time objective — to destroy United States influence in Latin America and to create a hostile group below the Rio Grande."[167]

Behind the scenes, CIA deputy director General C. P. Cabell reported that Castro was far more radical than the communists, who apparently feared that Castro was capable of destroying the entire revolution with his appositional behavior. They also would not accept him because he came from a bourgeois family, and he had suppressed the communists who were in the M–7–26 during the war. At the time, Ambassador Bonsal agreed with this position, except he concluded that by confronting the United States, Castro was "making Castroites out of his communist compatriots" rather than being co-opted by them.[168]

Faure Chomón, recently returned from communist China, led a four-hour parade to the shrine of the martyred medical students. Chomón said that China was interested in opening discussions with Cuba, soon to be a leader in the world. Castro referred to the marching students as a "wall" in defense of Cuba. Although they were not in the march, the *Chicago Tribune* described Cuba's juvenile patrol as "Hitler like," referring to the Hitler-Jugend, *Bund deutscher Arbeiterjugend* (Hitler Youth, League of German Worker Youth), a youth organization of highly indoctrinated, and often fanatical students, used to enforce the tenets of the Nazi Party, such as anti–Semitism, and which eventually was called to fight in World War II.[169]

Afraid that he would be captured, Manuel Artime Buesa, now head of MRR, resigned his position at INRA. He decided to leave Cuba, and was eventually relocated from Cuba by the CIA via a Honduran freighter.[170]

A highly publicized trial of two Americans for "taking arms against the state" was ongoing in late November and early December. Austin Young and John Lamberton had been arrested with 37 Cuban nationals after they had been surrounded by the army in the mountains in Pinar del Río Province. Several of the Cubans admitted that they were part of an anti–government insurrection, and testified that Young and Lamberton were leaders of the group. Young and Lamberton maintained that they were there merely to photograph the guerrillas for American newspapers and magazines. However, photographs showed both of the Americans in combat gear carrying rifles.[171] It would later turn out that both were members of the Movement of Democratic Recuperation (MRD), an anti–Castro group.[172]

Young, then 38, was a pilot who had served in the Royal Air Force and in the Flying Tigers in China during World War II. In March 1959, he was arrested in Cuba for trying to smuggle Batista followers to Florida. He was tried, convicted, and assigned a lengthy sentence. However, in August, he was deported. By September, he was back in Cuba and was arrested again. After a trial before a five-judge military tribunal, he was convicted on December 8. He was sentenced to a lengthy prison term, 30 years at hard labor, although the prosecution had requested the death penalty. Lamberton was also found guilty and was given 25 years.[173] The military tribunal did not accept the allegation that they were news reporters. A guerrilla organizer, former Cuban senator Fernando Pruna, a graduate of Columbia University, also was sentenced to 30 years at hard labor. Seventeen accomplices were sentenced to from two to 25 years. Twenty accused Cubans were acquitted. Young told reporters that he would have preferred to be sentenced to death rather than serve 30 years, but added that he would never serve out his sentence, because "the Castro government won't last more than a few weeks."[174]

Castro's former friend Del Pino was also tried, convicted and sentenced to 30 years for attempting to help war criminals escape, despite a prosecution demand for the death penalty. A companion was acquitted before the military tribunal, but was turned over to civil courts, charged with illegal possession of firearms and unlawful flight. In sentencing Del Pino, the military tribunal noted that no life had been lost and that he was a naturalized United States citizen.[175]

The next day, however, Young and another prisoner escaped through a hole in a guardhouse. Although they also could have escaped, another six did not, including Pruna. [176] A day later, Young was recaptured. Also arrested was James Buchanan, a *Miami Herald* reporter, accused of aiding Young's escape.[177] The *Herald* said that Buchanan had been in Miami on the day Young escaped, and merely interviewed Young while he was in hiding. Cuban police maintained that Buchanan had paid Young's hotel bill, and therefore was an accomplice after the fact.[178] After a trial in which Young appeared as a defense witness, Buchanan was convicted and sentenced to 14 years of hard labor. However, the Provisional Government deported him just before Christmas.[179]

The Cuban government had published a pamphlet in English saying that Cuba had been bombed by airplanes originating from the United States. Cuba did "not accuse the United States government with connivance with the Batista elements that are planning the overthrow" of the Cuban government. "It merely wishes to point out to the American people the existence of these criminals in their midst and the unpardonable acts they are bent upon executing." The State Department charged that the pamphlet was inaccurate and offensive because it charged that planes piloted by war criminals had flown from Florida and killed two people and injured 45. In Miami, five Cubans were caught loading bombs on a rented airplane at a remote airport.[180] In the Council of OAS, Guatemala accused Cuba of helping communist insurgents.[181]

At the same time, the British finally rejected the Cuban attempt to buy jet fighters. *Revolución* sarcastically said the decision was "Made in the USA" and that golf was more important to President Eisenhower than good relations with Cuba, referring to the failure of President Eisenhower to personally meet Castro during his April visit to Washington.[182] However, Cuba announced that France, the Netherlands and Germany had extended $100 million in loans, despite pressure against them. According to Antonio Núñez Jiménez, head of INRA, the money would be used to buy agricultural and industrial machinery. Cuba was a net importer of beans, corn and potatoes and an import tax on them was being used for the "stores of the people," ostensibly eliminating middlemen to reduce prices.[183]

In addition, greater restrictions were imposed on imports and on the right to take currency out of the country. Cubans had been able to take $500 out of the country per year, but that was reduced to $150 per year. Cuban students abroad were limited to $1,000 per semester for tuition and $150 per month for expenses. Tourists leaving Cuba could exchange up to two hundred pesos for two hundred dollars; if the traveler could prove that more than $200 was brought into Cuba.[184] At the time, a thousand dollars per semester exceeded most United States college tuition.[185] There were several other limitations on sending money out of the country, and imports were further restricted.

However, at the same time that the trade restrictions were announced, Cuba asked the United States to negotiate a trade agreement. Secretary Herter responded that Cuba had "rebuffed" negotiations, as "we have had a great difficulty in communication."[186]

As part of its overture to American tourism, Cuba was also working with American horse racing interests to revive the sport in Cuba.[187] There was some thaw when the United

States Department of Agriculture increased the Cuban sugar quota in December to an amount that would take about half of the anticipated crop.[188]

Paraguay announced that it had defeated an invasion and insurrection attempt in a matter of hours. The invaders came from Argentina, but wore armbands similar to the Cuban M–7–26 armband.[189] However, there were reports of a "liberation army" of about a thousand Paraguayans still fighting to remove General Stroessner.[190] Stroessner accused Cuba of funding the rebels.[191]

Comandante Matos and his codefendants were brought to trial on December 11. The chief judge of the court was a known communist who also was the commander of the Cuban air force. President Dorticós attended the entire trial. Matos could not deny that he had tried his best to delay implementation of Agrarian Reform and that he had appointed known anti-communists to positions in his government. However, neither of these actions constituted a crime. He was charged with treason: insurrection. One of the first witnesses was Raúl Castro, who Matos had accused of being a communist. Under oath, Raúl Castro testified that he was not a communist but that he would not lend himself to "the dirty business of anti-communism." He testified that Matos had used the "phantom of Communism" to divide the Cuban people. Several days later, Fidel Castro testified that Matos's resignation was part of a "prepared plot" to overthrow the Provisional Government. Fidel Castro testified that he would not discriminate against communists, some of whom had served in the Rebel Army.[192] As the trial was ongoing, *Revolución* ran an accusation that Matos's attorney, Francisco Lorie Bertot, had been a Batista "collaborator."

Matos testified that there was no counter-revolutionary intent in his resignation, but that the Castros had lied about communist infiltration of the army and INRA. The court ruled that closing arguments would begin at six o'clock in the morning. "All I wanted to do," he told them, "was to save the Revolution." He railed at the court and argued that the trial violated the terms of the Cuban Constitution and the United Nations Declaration of Human Rights, as he said that he had been held in solitary confinement in a tiny cell and could not assert a defense, since the prosecution did not tell him what the charges were until after the trial began. He insisted he was innocent: "They have done me the injustice of calling me a traitor." Matos was convicted. Although the prosecution requested the death penalty, Matos was sentenced to 20 years.[193]

As Matos was being tried for treason in Havana, the first trials for counter-revolutionary activity before the reinstated military tribunals took place in Pinar del Río. Two men were executed for insurgency and 38 others were given sentences from five to 30 years. Thirteen others were acquitted. One of the executed men was convicted of killing a family of five during the war and of joining counterinsurgency guerrillas later.[194] In Santiago, Waldo Pérez Almaguer, former governor of Oriente Province, and 12 navy officers were accused of similar offenses, and in Havana another 15 sailors were arrested.[195] Several days later, another American, John Martino, was sentenced to 13 years for attempting to smuggle out the family of former Batista administration police chief Esteban Ventura, described as a war criminal. Martino maintained that he was a telephone salesman, and while in Cuba, he was to have taken a message to a friend of a friend, but had nothing to do with Ventura.[196]

The Matos trial unsettled the middle class, and there was a resulting aura of suspicion as a result.[197] Consensus was that the government had not proved that Matos was a traitor. It seemed that any form of criticism of the Provisional Government was deemed unpatriotic. The revolution had stated that its main aims were to provide dignity for the Cuban underclass and in so doing provide full employment to them. In the first year, the

Provisional Government passed over 700 new laws and rules interpreting them that were designed to level society and purge foreign influences. But the nature of the government changed, as moderate groups, even those who were part of M–7–26, were replaced by Castro loyalists. The government had a network of paid informers, and some innocent people had been detained under suspicion of counter-revolutionary activities. Laws were passed reinstituting the death penalty and permitting confiscation of properties of counter-revolutionaries.[198]

By December 1959, Cuba had also weaned itself from all alliances with the United States. The Cuban Revolution and Fidel Castro were seen throughout Latin America as an inspiration for rebellion. Cuba was involved, if not directly, in insurgencies in Panama, Nicaragua, Guatemala, the Dominican Republic and even Paraguay.[199]

The new leaders in the Council of Ministers all scapegoated the United States as a matter of course. Americans often felt that it was due to personal hatred, but American policies were easily exploited for domestic political reasons and anti–Americanism became increasingly popular.[200] The *New York Times* declared that in Latin America every nationalistic revolution was "inescapably anti–Yankee." The solution, it suggested, was that the United States should not act unilaterally. The United States should join with all of the countries in the rest of the region for a solution.[201]

The Provisional Government took advantage of the moment to purge Cuba of a most pervasive and symbolic American imposition and intrusion into Cuban culture: Santa Claus. Santa Claus was not part of the Spanish tradition, and marketing Christmas American style had been introduced during the Machadato, in the early 1930s. Christmas trees were derived from a northern European tradition. The Provisional Government banned imported Christmas trees, and discouraged importing Christmas decorations and treats.[202] The Provisional Government would venerate the holiday by distributing money to the poor and by reducing the prices of the traditional Christmas *noche buena*.[203] A new figure, Don Feliciano, was installed as a substitute for Santa Claus.[204]

Castro predicted that 1960 would be difficult. The first order of business was a threat that Batista would seek to return to power and that Cuba would be invaded. He told sugar workers on December 16 that they would have to defend themselves and the revolution and would have to be armed and trained to fight.[205]

He told the workers that Cuba's enemies would institute a boycott, "to encircle us with hunger." Castro told people to wear only clothes made from Cuban cotton, to buy nothing but Cuban products and to sacrifice all luxuries. The profits from Cuban sugar would be used to buy "machinery, not perfume." If bank withdrawals continued, Castro said Cuba would print new currency.[206] After that the Cuban police and armed forces were placed on 24-hour alert for invasions and for internal insurrections.[207]

After a tour of Cuba, Arthur Miller, a Presbyterian minister from Denver, and moderator of the general assembly of the Presbyterian Church of the U.S.A., said that after traveling more than 1,000 miles and after speaking to hundreds of Presbyterians in Cuba, "the United States should do everything possible to maintain friendly relations with the people of Cuba." At the time, the Presbyterian Church was Cuba's third largest Protestant denomination, after Baptists and Methodists. He told the press that the States should be more eager to aid a "next-door neighbor," "than Pakistan." He estimated that 95 percent of the population supported Castro and that he was told "every time the United States pushes Castro, they push him to the left." When asked about agrarian reform and the accusation that the United States companies such as United Fruit had been hurt, Reverend Miller said they knew the risks involved when they decided to do business in Cuba and that they had made huge profits over the years. He noted that the majority of Cuban land had been held by a small number of people, and added that even in the United States there was redistribution of wealth, albeit through mechanisms like inheritance taxes.[208] Other Protestant religious leaders agreed with Reverend Miller, some saying that the cause of religious freedom was expanded under the Provisional Government.[209]

The government had banned all gambling, and the old lottery had been converted into an "investment plan." The government sold "bonds," formerly known as lottery tickets, which hypothetically could be redeemed in five years with interest. The money collected was spent on public housing, through the National Institute of Savings and Housing. Reportedly, hundreds of homes had been built and delivered by the end of 1959.[210]

The government had built approximately 5,000 new schools, and had built new roads and paved old ones. Some of the work was performed by "labor brigades" from the Cuban Revolutionary Army.[211]

Soon after his talk to the sugar workers, and after a drive-by attack on Minister of Labor Agusto Martínez Sánchez in which three of his bodyguards were wounded, Fidel Castro told a mass meeting of workers that they had a duty to spy on anyone opposing the revolution and to report them to the police.[212] There were some reports that the new government had already replaced the spy system of paid *chivatos* with its own Departmento Investigacion Exercito Revolutionario (DIER).[213] There were accusations that people were arrested and their property was confiscated on flimsy evidence generated by enemies who might have had a grudge or who might have been envious and that many members of DIER were nothing more than teenage hoodlums.[214]

The government confiscated six henequen plantations, paying half of the value in pesos and the remainder in bonds.[215] The government said that the remaining henequen plantations, including one owned by American company International Harvester, would also be acquired.[216] There were also reports of other businesses being seized by the Ministry of Labor on the grounds that they could not be managed due to labor disputes.[217]

Former president of Cuba Carlos Prío and four others pleaded guilty to violations of the Neutrality Act in the United States District Court for the Southern District of Florida for having run weapons to Cuba during the Revolution. All were placed on five years' probation.[218]

On December 28, *Revolución* ran a huge headline with accompanying article saying that an armed invasion was imminent. The article claimed that the attack was being planned in Guatemala, Haiti, Honduras, the Dominican Republic, Mexico and Miami by former Batista allies and by Trujillo. It was reported that Díaz Lanz and other pilots in Miami had disappeared five days earlier. The article accused United Fruit of helping to raise an invasion army and navy by hiring mercenaries, including former German soldiers. At the same time, there were reports of arrests of conspirators and of arms shipments from the U.S. to antigovernment forces.[219] The Provisional Government soon required all Cuban high school students to learn to use weapons.[220]

At the same time that the country was girding for war, it attempted to instigate another type of invasion: tourists. In order to bring more Americans to Cuba, the Provisional Government initiated a "giveaway plan" offered by the Cuban tourist commission. More than 2,000 Americans took the offer.[221] On New Years' 1960, Americans filled Havana's night clubs and casinos.[222] The Provisional Government ordered people not to fire weapons to celebrate. Ruby Hart Phillips reported that everything was peaceful. Fidel Castro hosted a party at the Havana Hilton that included American boxing champion Joe Louis and his wife and French authors Gisèle Halimi and Claude Faux. American baseball stars Jackie Robinson, Willie Mays, and Roy Campanella and owners of Afro-American newspapers were also invited, but Phillips didn't report on whether they attended.[223]

The Provisional Government also released over 1,200 common criminals on Epiphany, the day when Cubans shared their Christmas presents.[224]

In 1960, after only a year in power, the Provisional Government planned to head a "third bloc" conference of underdeveloped nations not committed to either the United States and the Soviet Union. The idea was to create a voting bloc in the United Nations to promote the interests of countries that had little power individually.[225]

Chapter 15

Hardball

After an emotional celebration of the first anniversary of the revolution, Ruby Phillips reported that Cuba exhibited an atmosphere of fear and uncertainty.[1] The impression was that elation became gloom. She highlighted threats of continued violence and continued tightening of state control over all aspects of commerce. Moreover, there continued to be increasing reports of arrests of counter-revolutionaries.

After a vacation and after conferring in Washington, Ambassador Bonsal returned to Cuba on January 10, 1960, and brought with him a diplomatic note protesting violations of the "basic rights of ownership" of American citizens' property and the method of payment for expropriated American property.[2] Hundreds of millions of dollars' worth had been taken. Castro publicly stated that the note was an affront and that it had been designed to stir counterrevolutionary activities.[3] The Cuban Foreign Ministry replied that Cuba would accelerate the seizure process.

Soon, Allen Dulles, head of the CIA, began to call for the overthrow of Castro.[4] Within the White House, the 5412 Committee had been established to oversee covert CIA activities, and on January 13, Dulles suggested to the president and to the committee that covert activities should be used to overthrow the Provisional Government.[5] Colonel J. C. King, chief of the CIA's Western Hemisphere Division, had drafted a report in which he described the Provisional Government as a far-left dictatorship.[6] President Eisenhower agreed. He accused Castro of being a "madman" and discussed instituting a blockade to make the Cuban people "hungry," to force them to "throw Castro out." However, he decided not to institute the policy at that time.[7]

The National Security Council was sent Colonel King's report, and established "Operation 40" to monitor and set up "alternative solutions to the Cuban problem." Among those who were part of the group were Vice President Nixon, Admiral Burke, Allen Dulles, Livingston Merchant of the State Department, and National Security Advisor Gordon Gray.[8] Soon, the CIA group that had overthrown Árbenz in Guatemala was reconstituted. Among those who met on January 18, 1960, as the CIA Cuban Task Force were Tracy Barnes, who acted as chair, E. Howard Hunt, Jack Easterline, David Phillips and Gerry Droller, aka Frank Bender, the same man who had met with Premier Castro in April.[9] Barnes told the group that Vice President Nixon was the "case officer" running the operation and he had enlisted two Texas oilmen, George H. W. Bush and Jack Crichton, to be the money men for the Cuban operation.[10] The group's mission was to come up with a plan to destabilize the Cuban government. The CIA assigned WH/4, Task Force 4 of the Western Hemisphere Division, to carry out the policy.[11]

A study by the *New York Herald Tribune* showed that Americans had not been paid "one penny" of compensation for their expropriated properties. The largest reported losses were to the Cuban Electric Company, which had to pay a retroactive rate rebate and lost the ability to maintain a bond issue, therefore losing millions of dollars. The Cuban telephone company, owned by ITT, had a similar fate. The American employees were let go and the Cuban replacements were immediately given a pay raise. Companies like United Fruit, Bethlehem Steel and Freeport Sulphur lost tens of thousands of acres, livestock, physical plants and equipment.[12]

Meanwhile, American newspapers continued to report that the United States was attempting to help Cuba by providing charitable projects and continued use of technical advice under the Point Four program. For example, thanks to advice given on how to manufacture bags for sugar and other commodities, Cuba would no longer have to import $300 million worth of bags each year. Americans continued to aid in agricultural research, helped modernize the air traffic control system at Havana Airport and helped establish a chemical engineering school at Santa Clara.[13] However, Cuba received far less Point Four aid than any other Latin American government.

In Washington, there were complaints that the U.S. was subsidizing Castro by charging American consumers more than world prices through our sugar policy.[14] Vice President Nixon echoed those sentiments and "hinted" that if there was expropriation without compensation there might be serious economic consequences to Cuba.[15] In Congress, H. Allen Smith, closely associated with Nixon, said that Castro was taking Cuba to Communism and that the United States should act to stop the Soviets from establishing a base so close to the United States. Castro soon reacted to Nixon's statement. He accused him of threatening Cuba and alleged that 90 percent of Cubans were prepared to die to protect their country.[16] It seemed that the entire nation was mobilizing. Students and workers were being trained as a new militia.[17]

INRA began expropriating sugarcane fields six months earlier than expected, as the harvest was ongoing. The first fields taken were from Vertientes-Camagüey Sugar Corporation, which was American owned, and from the Cuban-owned Agramonte mill, also in Camagüey Province.[18]

Mysteriously, radio attacks against Cuba from the Dominican Republic ceased during mid–January.[19] Soon broadcasts on *Voz Dominicana*, Dominican state radio, began to praise Cuba and even touted Castro as an international leader. It was speculated that the Dominican Republic wanted to ease tensions or, because there was an upcoming trial of the men involved in the Morgan and Gutiérrez Menoyo "trick," the Dominican Republic hoped that the government would go easy on the perpetrators.[20] It was later reported that Dominican liberation fighters who had been given sanctuary in Cuba had left for Venezuela after the Cuban government put pressure on them not to attack from Cuba.[21] Reports from within the Dominican Republic noted that Trujillo had arrested more than 100 people and that 40 prominent Dominicans had been sentenced for 30 years each for endangering state security. Demonstrators protested at the Dominican consulate in New York, and the story made the front page exposure of the *New York Times*. Many of the jailed were reported to be "moderate" politically, held because they favored democracy for their country. The Venezuelan government asked OAS to investigate for possible human rights abuses, but the U.S. State Department said that the OAS could condemn Trujillo but did not have the power to stop Trujillo from arresting and jailing Dominican citizens.[22]

The publisher of *Avance* took refuge in the United States.[23] He would later tour the country to tell and write articles how he had been a supporter of the Revolution, but after he determined that Castro was leading to a "Communist dictatorship," and expressed those views, he was "terrorized" and had to leave the country. As soon as he left, the newspaper was seized. He had been accused of being a counter-revolutionary.[24]

After a public row at a television station, the ambassador from Spain, Juan Pablo de Lojendio, Marquis of Vellisca, was asked to leave the country. There are several versions why the Spanish ambassador might have been incensed. Castro had attacked Spanish priests for being more loyal to Spain than to Cuba. He said publicly that Spain was ruled by "a tyranny of more than twenty years," meaning Francisco Franco. There also was an allegation that the Spanish embassy had contacts with anti–government guerrillas and was trying to help some Batista followers leave the country. Ambassador Bonsal recounts that the Spanish ambassador told him that Castro said that he was too stupid to have dreamed up coming onto a television set by himself, and that the American ambassador must have put him up to it. Ambassador Bonsal stated in his book that he considered it an unmatched act of defiance.[25] After the ambassador was removed from the studio, Castro indicated on television that the United States, Spain and others were part of a conspiracy to undermine the Provisional Government. Although the U.S. State Department and congressional leaders scoffed, a letter from a sister-in-law of Pedro Díaz Lanz surfaced alleging that counter-revolutionaries were helped by the Spanish and American embassies in Cuba and by the Roman Catholic Church.[26]

In response to the incident, Secretary Herter said that the speech that Castro gave after the Spanish ambassador was removed was the "most insulting" yet. Most damaging was a charge that Ambassador Bonsal or the American embassy were intervening on behalf of Cuban opposition groups. The letter, read by Castro on the air, was used to show how the "war criminals"—the big landholders—were linked to the Spanish and American embassies.[27]

Secretary Herter asked Ambassador Bonsal to return to Washington for talks. At the same time, the Eisenhower administration asked Congress to give it the power to raise or lower sugar prices and production quotas. The United States had other sources for sugar: Argentina, Brazil, the Dominican Republic, Mexico, Peru, Philippines and Taiwan.[28] An editorial in the *Washington Post* speculated that Castro really wanted the United States to end buying its sugar to make it a scapegoat for the Cuban economy.[29] At the time, there was no Cuban ambassador in Washington. Ambassador Ernesto Dihigo had been recalled to Havana for consultations at the same time that Ambassador Bonsal had been in Washington, so it looked like the United States was retaliating.[30]

It would later be revealed that the Spanish embassy had held a meeting of almost all Catholic orders in Cuba to organize resistance to the Provisional Government.[31] It is interesting that Secretary Herter did not directly admit or deny that the American embassy was supporting the opposition within Cuba. Some sources said that the recall of Bonsal made it look like the United States was complicit with Spain in contesting Cuba and that there was some truth in Castro's allegations.[32]

A Cuban journalists organization accused the United States Information Agency, the Associated Press, the United Press and another agency known as "USIS" of sending propaganda into Cuba.[33]

On January 26, President Eisenhower stated in a news conference that the United States would not initiate any reprisals against Cuba. He again stated that he was "concerned and perplexed" at the anti–American sentiments expressed by Fidel Castro and other Cubans.[34] American policy was not to intervene in Cuban affairs. The president also said that the United States tried to prevent gun-running and anti–Cuban acts in U.S. territory and was as effective as Cuba in stopping attacks on other foreign countries. The president recognized that Cuba had a right to effect social and economic reforms, and he acknowledged that the United States was sympathetic, but said that the U.S. would continue to point out violations against its citizens in Cuba. While the United States did not object to confiscations of property, it did object to the method of payment. Eisenhower said that if the matters could not be negotiated, the United States would bring the matter to the International Court of Justice. He stated, finally, that he hoped that the people of Cuba would "recognize and defeat the intrigues of international communism which are aimed at destroying democratic institutions in Cuba and ... friendship between the Cuban and American peoples."[35] The warning was also directed at other Latin American countries.

The State Department publicized that the United States would:

1. Give the Cuban people time to establish a government that would restore friendly relations with the United States,
2. Avoid any action that would hurt the Cuban people,
3. Give no support to Batista or to Trujillo or their allies,
4. Insist on fair treatment for Americans in Cuba,
5. Defend U.S. leaders from verbal attack, "but in a dignified way."[36]

In response to the statement, President Dorticós Torrado said that he objected to the "insinuation" that Cuban American friendship could be destroyed by "intrigues" of international Communism. He said the United States misunderstood the goals of the Revolution.[37]

Responding to several letters to the editor and editorials commending the United States hard-nosed Cuban policy and attacking the Provisional Government as communist, a Presbyterian minister wrote a letter to the *New York Times*. The writer had been on a "preaching mission" and had visited the central provinces of Cuba. He said that communists had "little sway" in Cuba. The amount of repayment "is based upon the owners own evaluations for tax purposes.... If the evaluations are low, it is because our American investors have attempted to avoid payment of full taxes in the past." He responded to other letters that the U.S. treat Cuba like Puerto Rico, which had territory status. He pointed out that Puerto Ricans were citizens of the United States, yet "Cuba is ... an independent nation." He also noted that Cuba had constructed 10,000 new schools, and housing projects and public beaches. "The Cuban people remember well that Batista did none of this."[38] However, the president of the United States Beet Sugar Association urged the United States to cut the sugar quota to curb what it viewed as the anti–American acts of Fidel Castro.[39]

Within a few days, Robert Taber, the CBS broadcaster who had filmed Castro in the mountains in the spring of 1957 and dispelled the Batista allegation that Castro had died, wrote an article published in *The Nation* magazine stating that the Provisional Government was not getting a "fair play" in the American press and in Congress. On February 9, he wrote letters to several other Americans to ask them to organize a "Fair Play for Cuba Committee."[40]

Observers in Cuba noted that the anti–American tone had decreased. Castro spoke on the anniversary of Martí's birth without any sarcastic remarks about the United States or Americans. They attributed it to Dorticós' reply.[41] However, in New York an observance at Martí's statue in Central Park turned into a riot where three were injured and six were arrested, including Fidel Castro's ex-best friend and ex-brother-in-law Rafael Díaz-Balart.

After he was released, Díaz-Balart gave a 90-minute speech at a hotel where he alleged that his organization, the White Rose, would free Cuba from tyranny and Communism. Another riot broke out, and at least one innocent bystander was injured.[42]

On February 4, Anastas L. Mikoyan, first deputy premier of the Soviet Union, visited Havana to open a Soviet science exhibition. On the way, Mikoyan had dinner with Allen Dulles, and told him that he was on a trade mission.[43] As this was happening, raids on Cuba by the White Rose and other anti–Castro groups were ongoing from the United States. The day after Dorticós's reply, bombs landed in two places in Cuba. Another raid from Florida was made by a pilot tied to Rolando Masferrer.[44]

After the Soviet Union had a falling out with Cuba in 1952, Cuba had no diplomatic relations with the Soviet Union. However, Mikoyan had toured Mexico in November 1959, and he had spoken favorably about the Cuban Revolution. Soon after Mikoyan left Mexico, the two countries began a cultural exchange. Soviet authors, performers, and musicians toured Mexico, including the Bolshoi Ballet Company. After Mikoyan toured the United States, the United States and the Soviet Union exchanged exhibitions, Vice President Nixon toured Russia, and Premier Khrushchev toured the U.S.[45] Mikoyan was met at the airport by Castro and other dignitaries, including Che Guevara, then president of the National Bank of Cuba. Also at the airport were Juan Marinello, Lazaro Peña and Carlos Rafael Rodríguez, longtime high-ranking Cuban communists.[46]

The next day, there were riots when Deputy Premier Mikoyan arrived for the opening ceremonies at the exhibition. During the riots, three people were wounded by gunfire and seventeen were arrested. The riots began when students carrying signs that read, "Viva Fidel" and "Down with Communism" were attacked. Police reportedly fired guns into the air. After order was restored, it was announced that the Soviet Union would buy 345,000 tons of Cuban sugar.[47]

At that time, Cuba sold half its crop to the United States at what were considered to be inflated prices. Thirty percent of the sugar used in the United States came from Cuba. Cuba had been looking for a way to reduce U.S. influence on the sugar market. At the time, sugar was selling at five cents per pound under the Sugar Act. The Soviets would pay only 2.78 cents per pound. The worldwide sugar markets immediately began to rise. The Soviet Union would buy a million tons of sugar per year for five years at a lower price than the United States was offering at the time. In return, the Soviet Union would pay 20 percent in cash and the rest would come in the form of Soviet products. The Soviets also extended low-interest loans to Cuba for the purchase of machinery and equipment.[48] While Mikoyan was in Cuba, an East German trade mission also arrived, along with agricultural equipment. While in India, Premier Khrushchev stated that the Soviet Union would aid Cuba and other Latin American countries in their struggle against "foreign enslavement." He told the Indian Parliament that the Soviet Union was the strongest military power in the world.[49] Like Cuba, in 1960 India was a nonaligned nation.

After a trip with Castro to visit rural Cuba, Mikoyan announced that the Soviet Union was willing to sell Cuba the aircraft that the United States and Britain had refused to sell.[50] At the same time, the United States delivered two airplanes to Argentina to track a "mystery" submarine off its coast.[51]

Brazil offered to mediate between Cuba and the United States, but the State Department refused, stating that there was no need for mediation. Although the White House said there was nothing to mediate, it continued to seek congressional authority to give it permission to manipulate the sugar quota without needing further congressional action.[52] Cuba announced that it would not need American sugar purchases: sugar contracts with Japan amounted to 700,000 tons; China, 500,000 tons; and 200,000 would cover the lost United States market.[53] As soon as the deal was announced, world sugar prices rose significantly.[54] Cubans would receive pig iron and rolled steel, aluminum ingots and rolled aluminum, newsprint, fertilizer, sulfur, machinery and other items as barter for sugar.[55]

In an interview, Che Guevara, then president of the bank, said that Cuba would not seek foreign investment unless it were closely regulated. Cuba would control its own "basic" industries, like metals, combustibles, food products, heavy chemicals, and sugar and sugar by-products. He said that Cuba would not participate in the Inter-American Development Bank because it was mostly funded by the United States and Guevara felt the U.S. would set bank policies.[56] At the same time, Guevara was making other plans. In addition to his position as head of the national bank, Guevara also was head of INRA's Department of Industrialization, which had been making an inventory of American products imported to Cuba. The organization had been searching for substitutes. All of these moves were part of an ambitious plan to transform the Cuban economy. The search for substitutes ended on February 13, during the Mikoyan visit. Later, Guevara traveled to Soviet bloc countries to order the substitute products. He would soon receive offers from the Soviets for $100 million to fund a steel industry, to produce a geological survey of Cuba, and to build an oil refinery and electric plants. Funding to build an automobile factory came from Czechoslovakia, and Romania, Bulgaria, Poland and East Germany also offered funding for several projects. China offered $60 million in funding for 24 factories.[57]

Meanwhile, Brazil, Venezuela and Ecuador told Cuba that they would not attend a summit of nonaligned nations, planned for September 1960.[58] However, Nicaragua, which had accused Cuba of trying to overthrow its government, entered into diplomatic negotiations with Cuba and announced it would send an ambassador to Havana.[59]

At the same time, in Miami, Rafael García Navarro told the press that there was a 4,000-man anti–government underground army operating in Cuba led by former head of the Cuban air force Pedro Díaz Lanz.[60] The MRR and Manuel Artime Buesa released a statement of moral position: "To overthrow Castro; but to permanently fight for an ideology of Christ; and for a reality of liberating our nation treacherously sold to the Communist International."[61] It was assumed that Artime could rely on many of the M–7–26 veterans who had served under him as well as his former Catolica Acción followers, many of whom were still working for INRA or were still in the army.

To some observers, Castro was playing the United States and the Soviet Union against each other to try to get Cuba the best deal. Some believed that Cuba was moving more toward a system of national socialism than Communism.[62] Under Secretary of State Rubottom met with business leaders. Among the areas of discussion were whether to isolate Cuba among other Latin American countries, to redraft the Sugar Act, to impose an added tariff on Cuban sugar to pay for the properties expropriated by the Cuban government, to submit the American property claims in Cuba for mediation by other Latin American countries, and to set up a powerful radio transmitter to broadcast American views and news to the Cuban people.[63]

Rumors were rife. Although it was widely reported that Cuba had purchased from the Czech 12 MiG jet fighters, Castro denied that he would receive airplanes and he also dispelled other rumors, such as that the Soviets would build a rocket base in Camagüey.[64] He reminded the Cuban people that the United States had stopped sales of airplanes from Great Britain and that the Cuban air force was unable to defend itself, even "from attacks by small airplanes."[65] Unsubstantiated rumors suggested that Castro did not like the terms of the sugar deal, especially since Cuba would receive a lower price from the Soviets and whereas the Americans paid in cash, the Soviets preferred to barter. The fact that Cuba was in a position to purchase military hardware sealed the deal.[66]

Later analysis showed that the Soviet Union actually had received the benefit of the bargain, so much so that the deal with the Soviets could be seen as a low-interest loan given by the Provisional Government to the Soviet Union. The terms permitted the Soviet Union to set any price, no matter how exorbitant, that it wanted for its products.[67] However, in the Cuban press and in the public mind, the Iron Curtain shrouding the Soviet Union was lifted and the Soviets were transformed from enemies to close friends. "I never knew Russia was such a great industrial country and so up to date," an unidentified source told Ruby Phillips. She noted that many of the crowd at the exhibition hall drank Coca-Cola during the tour.[68]

During January and February, Cuba continued to accuse the United States of harboring anti–Provisional Government insurgents, and there continued to be reports of bombing raids on sugar mills and sabotage on civilian targets. On February 17, an airplane bombing a Cuban sugar mill exploded. Two bodies were found: both turned out to be Americans. The pilot was identified as Robert Ellis Frost. On his body, maps and other documents were found showing that he had taken off from Tamiami Airport in Miami. A passenger's cadaver was later identified as Robert Kelly, a member of the United States Civil Air Patrol. That evening, during a television appearance, Fidel Castro accused the United States government of either granting "immunity" to saboteurs or showing negligence in letting the airplane fly to Cuba. He noted that the route to Cuba from the airport passed Homestead Air Force Base and the Key West Naval Air Station. The Cuban government alleged that there had been about 30 such raids that had caused Cuba to lose about 225,000 tons of sugar.[69]

A couple of days later, President Eisenhower announced that the FBI would enforce the Neutrality Act, and could seize any boat or airplane carrying arms to Cuba. Until that order, the FBI had to obtain a warrant to arrest the suspected offenders.[70] Moreover, the United States investigated the bombing incident and determined that the airplane had originated in Miami, and issued a formal apology to Cuba. Records showed that the pilot had filed a flight plan for a domestic flight. The apology alleged that the airplane had evaded United States government attempts to eliminate such flights.[71] The Cuban government accepted the apology as vindication for previous charges Castro had made about an American role in attacks on Cuba.[72]

Chapter 16

The New Cuba

In January 1960, labor unions began to purge themselves of all anti-communist officials. The head of the unions was David Salvador, an important member of the M–7–26 alliance, who had at one time been a communist himself. He also had often been at odds with them, but he managed to weather internal union dissension after Fidel Castro interceded on his behalf.[1] However, he was unceremoniously replaced. Within a year, over 1,000 union secretaries-general of Cuba's more than 2,000 local unions would be removed. Many of these officials had been involved in revolution with M–7–26 actively or as part of the underground, and many of them would be not only removed from their positions but expelled from union membership.[2]

Jesús Soto, the new secretary of the Executive Committee, had been a member of Che Guevara's troops, and was favored by the cabinet.[3] By April, Soto would oust Salvador, who had been one of Fidel Castro's earliest supporters and who had a wide following himself.[4] The union movement had been controlled by the communists during the first Batista regime. However, the communists lost power and prestige during the Auténtico regimes of Grau San Martín and Prío Socarrás, and after Batista took power, he outlawed the party at the behest of the Truman administration.[5]

On February 20, the Provisional Government announced that it instituted central planning through the Central Planning Board, which comprised Fidel Castro, Che Guevara, and a delegate from INRA. Foreign products would have to be repackaged in Cuba before they could be sold to the public. All advertising of foreign products was banned, unless the advertising was prepared in Cuba.[6]

At about the same time, President Eisenhower embarked on a tour of four Latin American countries: Argentina, Brazil, Chile and Uruguay. Cuba simultaneously asked the United States to negotiate, and notified the United Nations it wanted a seat on the Security Council.[7] Chile also wanted a Security Council position. Cuba had told the United States that it wanted to set a date to negotiate diplomatically in December, but actual negotiations never took place. As the president landed in San Juan, Puerto Rico, to initiate the trip, he was shielded from Puerto Rican nationals who supported Puerto Rican independence carrying signs saying "Liberty or Death."[8]

After reports of a bombing attack on Cojimar, a suburb of Havana where Fidel Castro had a home, and after an airplane was seen heading north, unnamed officials in the U.S. State Department said that it would welcome diplomatic talks with Cuba. The officials alleged that the United States was trying everything it could to eliminate attacks on Cuba.[9]

As the president landed in Brazil, he told a cheering crowd that United States policy was to honor "the right of people everywhere to choose their form of government, their method of progress ... but we would consider it intervention in the internal affairs of any American state if any power, whether by invasion, coercion or subversion, succeeded in denying freedom of choice to the people of any of our sister republics." As the president's caravan passed one building, a group of students held up a sign that read, "We love Fidel Castro." The president reportedly laughed.[10]

President Kubitschek of Brazil had an "Operation Pan-America" plan for the economic development of all of Latin America that he wanted the United States to endorse. He told Eisenhower that if the economies were sound, there could be no Communist threat in Latin America.

A letter to the *New York Times* signed by Charles Santos-Buch protested *Times* articles written by James Reston that depicted an American foreign policy designed to isolate Cuba from other Latin American countries. The letter writer argued that the United States overreacted to the Mikoyan visit, saying that the Soviet-Cuban agreement was only an attempt to diversify the Cuban economy — to change Cuba from a "'supplier colony' to an affluent social democracy."[11]

In a television interview, Fidel Castro made a "diplomatic retraction" of accusations he had lodged on January 21 against the United States ambassador, Philip Bonsal, of plotting to overthrow the Provisional Government. Although the State Department had taken the statement as an affront, Castro said that he merely read the letter from Díaz Lanz's sister-in-law without suggesting that the contents were accurate.[12]

Castro told the Cuban Federation of Labor that in the future all private foreign investment would be made through the government. He told a cheering crowd that private foreign capital was not premised on generosity or what is best for the people. Anti-communist groups wanted to demonstrate at the rally but were not permitted to do so because of fear of riots.[13]

Among $15 million worth of property seized from former Batista "collaborators" were the Casa Grande Hotel in Santiago and docks in Baracoa. The government had taken control of companies for three reasons. It had intervened on behalf of the public to manage utilities such as the American-owned telephone and electric companies. Some employers asked the government to intervene to head off strikes, and in some cases it was unable to tell who actually owned the business. Finally, INRA controlled surplus property as *latifundas* were broken into smaller estates.[14] Some of property owners objected to intervention, as it may have led to outright expropriation. In some cases, INRA did expropriate land for distribution to *guajiros*. But in other cases, the state kept the land. Besides working in agriculture, INRA was involved in industrialization and in setting up a nationwide oil distribution network, and had by March 1960 established 1,300 "people's stores," mostly in rural areas. Che Guevara told cane planters that small operators could keep their plots, to "work [them] as they wish, when and where." However, he also said that Cuban agriculture would be driven by a series of cooperatives established by INRA.[15]

As Castro was speaking, anti–Castro airplanes bombed and burned 50,000 tons of sugar near Santa Clara.[16] There were reports that although 13 percent of all sugarcane fields had been bombed during the first two months in 1960, none of the sugar had been lost.[17]

An editorial in the *New York Times* noted that Castro said that Cuba would invest $150 million, but that actually Cuba would need $500 million to get its people out of poverty. As a result, Cuba would continue to need foreign aid to prop up its economy.[18]

On February 25, the Provisional Government announced that 34 members of the Revolutionary Army would be court-martialed for attempting an invasion of the Dominican Republic.[19]

Members of the United States Senate protested that the United States was sending one-third more military aid to Latin America than it had authorized.[20] However, the big story was that both Cuba and the Dominican Republic were still receiving United States military aid.[21]

On March 1, 1960, the United States responded to the Cuban request to negotiate only if U.S.–Cuban relations were kept at status quo during bargaining. The U.S. decided that sugar quotas would not be set. Rather, it asked to negotiate and stated that the United States must "remain free in the exercise of its own sovereignty, to take whatever steps it deems necessary."[22] A *New York Times* editorial stated that this approach was reasonable, citing the State Department position that the U.S. government's separation of powers meant that quotas were within the legislative province and that the executive branch could not bind the House and Senate.[23] However, the State Department and the *Times* failed to note that U.S. treaties can bind the legislative branch as treaties rise to the same level of authority as the Constitution.[24] The United States had imposed the quota system on Cuba in the 1934 Reciprocity Treaty. George Sokolsky, writing for the Hearst newspaper syndicate, called the Cuban request for negotiations an example of Cuba's "new impudence," asserting that the Eisenhower administration was too weak in dealing with Castro. He asked for a reduction in the sugar subsidy and an elimination of the two cent per pound sugar subsidy. "[W]hat would Castro do? Would he hurl a bomb at Miami?"[25] Soon Republican leaders proposed legislation that would give the president authority over sugar quotas.[26]

Meanwhile, France and Italy filed formal objections to restrictions on their citizens and businesses in Cuba. Cuba intervened against properties owned by Amadeo Barletta Barletta, an Italian national with reputed ties to Batista. He owned 43 businesses valued at approximately $40 million. Barletta had been granted amnesty by the Italian embassy in Havana.[27] One French company had refused to pay a higher rate for maritime workers than those working on land and lost a lawsuit for back pay to Cuban maritime workers for over $3 million.[28] Barletta was accused of having been an agent for Mussolini during World War II. Forced into exile in Venezuela during the war, he was able to return afterward to Cuba. By 1959, he was the exclusive Cuban dealer for General Motors and owned the newspaper *El Mundo* and the television station Telemundo.[29] According to several sources, he was a Mafia boss, and ran dozens of businesses through the Trust Company of Cuba, which had been a beneficiary of BANDES, the development bank run by the Batista administration.[30]

While President Eisenhower was on his Latin American trip, he was met with protests, especially in Uruguay, where crowds had to be subdued by tear gas. Eisenhower, too, was teary, and he was wet from the spray from water cannons. Although he would describe the incident as a "very small thing," he could not miss that fact that some of the protesters carried signs supporting Cuba, some proclaiming "Death to Yankee Imperialism." One protester was shot and another was stabbed. While the president was in Montevideo, Uruguayan students signed pledges to fight for Cuba in case of war.[31] However, the president repeatedly told Latin American leaders that the United States "had no thought of intervention."[32]

When he returned from his trip to Latin America, some in the U.S. press extolled American prestige as the highest in the region after World War II. In the Declaration of Montevideo, U.S. policy in American policy was described as:

1. A repudiation of dictatorships "on the left and the right,"
2. Assistance in development in the region,
3. Opposition to "subversion" and a restatement of mutual assistance as expressed by the 1947 Rio Treaty,
4. Curtailing sales of arms in the region.[33]

However, privately many other Latin Americans said that United States policy and attitude continued to disappoint them.[34] The *New York Herald Tribune* attributed the demonstrations in Uruguay to Cuban "agents."[35] The Cuban government had established Cuban friendship committees through diplomatic missions in almost every Latin American country.[36]

As the 1960 sugar harvest was culminating, the *New York Times* ran an item predicting that as soon as the harvest was over, the Cuban government would intervene on the United Fruit Company's holdings, estimated by the company as worth $32 million.[37]

Cuba planed a conference on hunger, but many Latin American leaders refused to attend. There was no indication whether they did this independent of pressure from the U.S. State Department.[38]

On March 4, 1960, at least 75 people were killed and 200 were injured when *La Coubre*, a French-owned ship unloading cargo from Belgium, exploded in Havana harbor, less than a mile from where the battleship *Maine* had exploded in 1898. Cuba was placed on a military alert.[39] During a funeral service, Premier Castro said that the explosions could only have been the work of "enemies of the Cuban people," and claimed they were part of a plot to keep Cuba from receiving arms shipments. He noted that the arms shipment was from Belgium and that the United States had tried to persuade Belgium not to sell arms to Cuba. He stated that although he had no proof, he believed that the explosion was caused by people who did not want Cuba to defend itself.[40] The United States embassy issued a note regretting the loss of life, and a few days later denied any involvement. An American passenger on the ship, Donald Chapman of North Bend, Nebraska, was arrested for allegedly taking pictures of the ship, but was released within two days. Among his interrogators was Premier Castro.[41]

Although he did not directly implicate the United States, the American newspapers attacked Castro for implying that the United States might have been behind the blast. A *New York Times* editorial derided "paranoia" and noted that munitions were made to explode.[42] The *Washington Post* attributed the reaction to Castro's "neurosis."[43] Ambassador Bonsal was not on the scene, but he said that not only had the ship exploded, but Castro exploded also, and that his remarks displayed "shamelessness and venom."[44]

Secretary of State Herter "upbraided" a Cuban official for the "baseless, erroneous and misleading" Castro "insinuation" of United States of involvement in the *La Coubre* blast.[45] Cuba immediately objected to Herter's "derogatory" tone, asking the State Department to show "absolute respect."[46] The next day, the *New York Times* ran an article justifying and defending Herter's remarks saying that any deal with Cuba was far off.[47] However, Secretary Herter later apologized for the "severity" of his remarks but maintained that he had not been "insulting."[48]

According to an American eyewitness, Jack Lee Evans, the explosion was set off by anti-communist Cuban dockworker as part of a plot. Evans said he was working for Comandante William Morgan and was staying at his house and had accompanied him to the ship.[49] Soon after the explosion, Evans returned to Miami and told the *Miami Herald* that he had learned about a plot to blow up the ship two days before the explosion, and saw the perpetrator burn a three-inch length of fuse to time it.[50] Although Evans had also placed Morgan on the boat, Morgan denied it.[51]

None of the major American wire services mentioned the Evans allegations, and the *New York Times*, which issued several articles about the blast, did not report the story. However, the *Washington Post* reported that a defecting naval attaché, in Venezuela at the time, speculated that the heat of the water in Havana harbor set off the explosives.[52] Cubans still maintain that the explosion was the result of a CIA operation.[53]

At the same time, Cuban militias were mobilizing and strict censorship was ordered. Another attack on a Cuban sugar mill burned more than 3,000 tons.[54] Cuban newspapers were filled with anti–American rhetoric.[55] There were rumors that the United States would start to evacuate American citizens.[56] At the same time, the United States and several Latin American countries began naval maneuvers in Panama and the Canal Zone.[57] Soviet documents now show that Castro told Soviet agents he was convinced by this time that the United States would attack Cuba. He anticipated the following:

1. Terrorist acts against him and his associates
2. A break in diplomatic relations
3. Economic sanctions
4. Attack. To justify it, there would be an explosion in the American embassy or the murder of American citizens.[58]

Castro said that his statements at the funeral had been misconstrued and he did not actually accuse the United States of direct sabotage, but stated that he did have "the right to wonder." "The United States does not order, but does permit," he stated, and added that any improvement in relations would have to come from Washington.[59] He also told the Cuban people to be ready for an attack.[60] Anti-American protesters carried signs reading "Death to Eisenhower;" "*Patria o Muerte*" ("Nation or Death") and "Let the Americans Come — We Will Show Them How to Fight."

At a meeting of the CIA Branch 4 Task Force on March 9, 1960, Colonel J. C. King predicted that unless Fidel Castro and Che Guevara were eliminated, "This operation can be a long, drawn-out affair, and the present government will only be overthrown by the use of force." He estimated that Castro was supported by 60–70 percent of the Cuban people.[61]

A few days later, purported American embassy official Mario Lazo discussed a possible solution with Finance Minister Rufo López Fresquet: The United States would offer Cuba airplanes and technical assistance.[62]

It was revealed that despite the Eisenhower administration's diplomatic position that it wanted to end arms sales in the Caribbean, the U.S. had sold five B-26 bombers to the Dominican Republic. The government arrested a Chilean arms salesman in Miami for filing a false document alleging that the airplanes were destined for Chile, rather than the Dominican Republic.[63] Besides American airplanes, the Dominicans also owned British Vampire jets and Mustang propeller-driven fighter planes. There were about 24,000 men in the Dominican military forces.[64] After the deal was publicized — after the embarrassment of permitting a deal that violated stated U.S. policy — we asked Trujillo to return the five airplanes.

Almost simultaneously, the Commerce Department revoked transport licenses for four helicopters to Cuba which had been previously purchased.[65] Premier Castro called the action, "a new act of aggression."[66]

On March 17, 1960, Fresquet was instructed by President Dorticós to tell Mario Lazo that the American offer to negotiate had been rejected.[67] Dorticós told López Fresquet that the United States was not bargaining in good faith and that as soon as Cuba reached a deal on paper and stated publicly that the United States was friendly, the deal would never be put into effect. "They will give us nothing," he told López.[68] It would later turn out that Lazo was not an American citizen. He was not authorized to speak for the American embassy, and the proposal was entirely his idea.[69]

On the same date, the State Department rejected an offer from President Kubitschek of Brazil to formally mediate between the United States and Cuba. The State Department thanked President Kubitschek for his interest, but told him that the U.S. would proceed through normal channels.[70]

At the same time, Cuba announced the sale of 100,000 tons of sugar to Great Britain and 50,000 more to Poland.

After he was told that the Lazo offer was rejected outright, López Fresquet resigned his position as treasury minister. Rolando Díaz Astarian, formerly with INRA, was named the new finance minister.[71] With López Fresquet's resignation, none of the moderates were left in the Provisional Government. The loss of López Fresquet was greater for the United States than for the Provisional Government, because López Fresquet actually had been an American spy, and without him the United States lost any chance it might have had to get detailed insider information from within the government.

A naval attaché defected and made a speech at OAS against Castro, accusing him of turning over the government to communists. The Cuban government accused him of treason, of theft of more than $100,000, and alleged that the Americans were paying him $1,500 per month and had provided him with a $40,000 house.[72]

After an extradition hearing in Miami, a United States District Court ruled that the Cuban government had failed to prove that Major Díaz Lanz, charged with the murder of a Cuban and injuring 24 others during a bombing in Cuba, had committed a crime.[73] Although Díaz Lanz had admitted that he had flown from Miami to Cuba to drop leaflets on several occasions, the court and the U.S. State Department determined that violations of the Neutrality Act were not considered a sufficient crime to warrant extradition. In the end, Díaz Lanz was not prosecuted for violating the Neutrality Act.

In early March, Freeport Sulphur Company, owner of the Moa Bay Mining Company, announced that it would close its Cuban plant on April 1.[74] The properties were valued at about $75 million. However, the Cuban government "intervened" to keep the plant open, ostensibly to protect 1,000 Cuban workers from losing their jobs.[75] Other mining companies, such as Bethlehem Cuban Iron Company, were confronted with high taxes, went out of business, and failed to pay their registrations for business fees. As a result, the Provisional Government considered the claims to have been abandoned.

The government also intervened on properties held by the Hedges family, primarily used for tobacco production. One family member, Burke Hedges, had become a Cuban citizen and for a time was Cuba's ambassador to Brazil, appointed by Batista in 1958.[76] INRA had already established a number of cooperatives on tobacco plantations. For example, 120 sharecroppers had been given an ownership interest in properties formerly owned by Senator Pedro Menéndez, minister of agriculture in the Batista administration.[77] Many of the relocated people came from unsanitary housing — thatched, dirt-floored *bohios* without running water or electricity. The new community had new homes, paved streets and landscaped lawns and would soon have a school and a medical clinic. Furniture and other accouterments were being made on site by members of the Cuban military.[78] After the properties of American-owned Cuban Land and Leaf Company were intervened, the American managers stayed. The company produced corona tobacco and processed it in its New Jersey factory, which it maintained generated the best cigars in the world. Seventy-five former sharecroppers became members of a cooperative on the property. The owners presented a claim for $2,600,000 to the Cuban government as just compensation for seizure. They expected to receive bonds from the government paying 4.5 percent, which, according to the company, would exceed the current return on investment on the property. Moreover, the Cuban government had already reimbursed ownership for the annual cost of production of the tobacco.[79] Some of the sharecroppers had made as much as $20,000 a year in a good year, and one had made $14,000 the previous year. At the time, this was as much as pay for members of the United States Congress. When Premier Castro examined the books, he was incredulous that a sharecropper could earn so much.[80]

By early March, the Provisional Government and INRA had also intervened 32 sugar mills and plantations, and on three sugar mills owned by the Guantánamo Sugar Company, of New York, investigated regarding a relationship with the prior regime. A railroad that supplied the mills was also intervened. The company maintained that it had no dealings with the Batista administration and, to its knowledge, no shareholders had either.[81]

In the Dominican Republic, President Trujillo called Premier Castro and President Rómulo Betancourt of Venezuela "practically madmen," and said that in order for the Cuban Revolution to succeed, the Dominican Republic would have to be destroyed. In a CBS interview he said that since the presidency of Franklin Roosevelt, the United States had been an enemy of the Dominican Republic. He did not deny that he was a dictator but said that he would permit municipal and national elections starting in mid–1961. However, Trujillo said that he would never retire. His personal wealth was estimated as more than $800 million.[82]

When it was announced that Ambassador Bonsal would return to Cuba after a two-month absence, Senator Smathers rose in the Senate to state that the return of the American ambassador to Cuba was an "act of appeasement." Smathers said the sale of five million tons of sugar to the Soviet Union at half the price sold to the United States was the "worst capitulation we could ever engage [in] in the Western Hemisphere," and called Cuba a communist-controlled country. He maintained that the Cuban sugar quota should be reduced and the balance given to Mexico, Brazil and El Salvador. His remarks were seconded by Senator Russell Long of Louisiana.[83] However, a majority of the Senate Foreign Relations Committee supported returning the ambassador, who determined that there was political posturing involved in the face of an impending presidential election.[84]

At the same time that the decision was made to return Ambassador Bonsal to Cuba, the administration decided to accept Vice President Nixon's urging to permit the CIA to recruit and train Cuban exiles for "military service."[85] A covert war called Operation Pluto, similar to the operations in Iran and Guatemala, was envisioned. Reportedly, assassination of Castro was not expressly discussed, but it was implied.[86]

By April, the CIA started to recruit for the International Anticommunist Brigade, led by Frank Sturgis.[87] The CIA broadcast anti–Castro radio programming to Cuba and anti–Trujillo programming to the Dominican Republic from Swan Island, off the coast of Honduras.[88] Navy Seabees were to build the pier on Swan Island.[89] However, the first priority was Cuba.

The CIA named David Atlee Phillips, who owned a public relations firm in Havana and who had been a contract CIA employee, and a veteran CIA operative who had worked on the removal of Árbenz from Guatemala, as chief of propaganda for the task force. He was told that the operation would be similar to the Guatemalan action.[90] He had developed the use of radio propaganda, and had used the CIA radio signal to overtake the Guatemalan government radio frequency, hired groups of Guatemalan newspaper reporters to place propaganda in their news items, and hired Guatemalan housewives to bang on pots and pans in protest demonstrations. A Catholic archbishop was convinced to write an anti–government pastoral letter. Using psy-ops (psychological operations, Phillips's tactics), the CIA was able to neutralize the population and even convince some Guatemalan army members to switch sides.[91] E. Howard Hunt was named as head of political action, assigned to set up a government in exile.[92]

Soon the CIA would acquire Southern Air Transport, financed through a CIA holding company, Actus Technology, and use it to run the CIA operation into Cuba.[93] Fifty-four marine sales companies, gun shops, travel agencies, real estate companies, and detective agencies opened as CIA fronts in Miami.[94] Phillips was already hard at work recruiting students, women and professional groups in and out of Cuba.[95]

Rafael Rivas Vasquez, an associate of Artime, sent a confidential memorandum encouraging a psychological warfare campaign to demoralize the Cuban military "based on terror." He also suggested using sabotage, including blowing up an INRA radio station that had a signal that interfered with Radio Swan.[96]

As Ambassador Bonsal and his wife returned to a warm welcome at the airport in Havana, the *New York Times* front page headline reported "Cuba's Bank Chief Views U.S. as Foe in Economic Fight."[97] The *Washington Post* and most other newspapers used the same theme but did not necessarily run it as front page news.[98] The *Post* reported that many of the people who cheered the U.S. ambassador also shouted "¡*Viva* Castro!" No Cuban government official was in the welcoming party. The article stated that Havana was more hostile to Bonsal than when he had left, two months earlier, and referred to Che Guevara's comments about economic issues confronting the two countries. He stated that Cuba did not need private foreign capital, as it "comes here only for profit and does nothing for the people of Cuba."[99]

On March 21, two Americans were shot down while reportedly trying to help a former Batista official and his family escape from Cuba.[100] The *New York Times* acknowledged that unauthorized flights from Florida were an everyday event in Cuba, and that some made the trip to drop bombs. It noted that there was no air patrol to monitor the situation and that there were limited resources allotted to monitor airfields. It stated that Cuban-American relations were bad enough without letting "adventurers" use the United States as a base of operations.[101]

During March and April, American newspapers ran almost daily accounts of defections of Cuban government officials and military officers. Some were paraded on publicity tours throughout the United States and even to foreign countries. Artime Buesa, touted as a defecting former official in the Cuban Ministry of Agriculture, made a tour of Latin America where he predicted that Castro would be deposed within a year.[102]

In Cuba, the nation was girding for an invasion. By that time, Cuba had a 50,000-man militia in addition to its regular military, which was expanding also. In addition, every student in Cuba was being instructed how to fight. Castro invoked speeches of Winston Churchill during the bleak period of World War II when Britain stood alone against Nazi Germany. Castro said, "We shall fight in the mountains and in the fields and in the cities.

We shall fight by street and block by block and house by house. We shall fight everywhere because not even an inch of our soil can be taken away."[103] After a broadcast by Luis Conte Agüero, a friend of Castro, in which he stated that he opposed the influence of Communists, riots erupted at his television station.[104] By that time, the government had intervened in five of eight television stations and in 85 radio stations.[105] School students collected money for arms and ammunition. Workers agreed to give part of their salaries and government workers were urged to tithe to buy munitions to save their country.[106] Although there were daily reports of the dispute between the United States and Cuba, and the U.S. was obviously the "aggressor" that Cubans were preparing to fight, no reports of attacks on even slights against American citizens were recorded.[107]

However, the Baltimore Orioles baseball team cancelled a series of exhibition games against the Cincinnati Reds that were to have been played in Havana. The owner of the team denied that the U.S. State Department had anything to do with the decision.[108]

Cuba continued to file formal diplomatic protests that the United States was interfering with its sovereignty. Secretary Herter continued to allege that Cuba had communists and communist sympathizers in its government. Castro objected that General Pedraza, a reputed war criminal and the head of an army in the Dominican Republic, was permitted entry into the United States.[109] Moreover, there were still open issues involving whether workers at Guantánamo were governed by Cuban law. Castro said that he accepted American jurisdiction under our mutual treaty, but objected to allegedly harsh treatment of workers at the base. He also protested a State Department refusal to permit shipment of helicopters, already purchased from an American company, which Castro said were to have been used for agricultural purposes.[110]

In a March 30 news conference, President Eisenhower said that the United States was willing to discuss all of the Cuban complaints, and said he was disappointed that Cuba and the United States could not work out their differences.[111]

Meanwhile, Jorge Sotús, a former friend of Premier Castro, a colleague of Artime's in MRR, a Rebel Army veteran, early M–7–26 supporter, and the former head of Cuban army intelligence in Matanzas, was captured, tried, convicted and sentenced to 20 years for conspiring to commit treason.[112] At the University of Havana, communist students asked the university to set up disciplinary tribunals to purge it of "counter-revolutionary elements."[113]

During this period the cost of living was increasing while shortages of staples were noted, and the government decided to institute an austerity program. For example, the government ordered a "chicken-less Wednesday." Items such as pharmaceuticals and automobile parts were starting to become scarce, which many attributed to the restrictions on imports.[114] Ruby Phillips reported that dockworkers in Santiago were idled because of the curb on imports, and after the "wealthy" were taxed at high rates, domestic workers were let go. As in Havana, shortages in necessities and slowdowns in public construction were noted. She said that many of the people she met in Santiago were formerly avid supporters of Castro who had donated money and even their children to M–7–26 during the insurgency, and felt "cheated" by recent developments.[115] She also said that there were rumors of armed revolt in the country.

Phillips reported that managers of United Fruit Company holdings said they were besieged by the government. Company-owned equipment like tractors, cement mixers, bulldozers and trucks were "borrowed," never to be returned, and government officials tried to tell managers how to run the business. United Fruit owned two huge mills in Oriente Province, Boston and Preston, both operating year round. There were about 2,000 squatters on

United Fruit property, and the government started to build houses for them. The government had seized 30,000 acres of cattle land and almost 7,000 cattle as of March 25, 1960, but had been paid only a nominal amount for them. Two hundred seventy thousand acres of sugarcane land had not been expropriated.[116]

Within days of Ruby Phillips's article, United Fruit was advised that it would receive $6,118,407 in 20-year bonds and 4.5 percent for 272,472 acres. The company estimated the actual value was $38,000,000.[117]

The *New York Times* ran an editorial, in effect asking Premier Castro to remove communists from his government. "It never makes sense to nurse a viper at one's bosom, even if it behaves placidly," it stated.[118] In a follow-up article, the *Times* noted that there were several avenues that the United States could take:

1. Recall of our ambassador and isolation of Cuba in world politics;
2. Military incursion;
3. Government restriction of tourism;
4. Government restriction of exports to Cuba.
5. Government restriction of Cuban imports;
6. Freezing Cuban dollar balances in the U.S.;
7. Severing all communications with Cuba in conjunction with OAS;
8. Termination of diplomatic relations.[119]

Even if the United States did not threaten Cuba with the options directly, members of the Provisional Government read the *New York Times*.

On April 1, the Cuban government announced a trade deal with Poland that would reportedly bring airplanes, helicopters, ships, and plant machinery and equipment to Cuba. The deal would also send Polish technicians to Cuba. The deal included many of the same items that Cuba had tried to obtain from the United States. Cuba had few reserves remaining, and the United States and Western European countries refused to extend credit, in effect forcing Cuba to look to Soviet-aligned countries.[120] Although the American press said that MiG jets were included, Polish officials denied this. The airplanes were allegedly all small crop dusters.[121]

At the same time, columnist Jack Anderson alleged that the Cuban government was able to buy B-25 and B-26 airplanes from the United States Air Force and ferry some of them to Cuba. Several fighter planes with Cuban markings were seen at Miami International Airport, guarded by Cuban soldiers. Some had been damaged "with homemade bombs" by anti–Castro Cubans. There had been rumors of smuggling of small arms and ammunition, but these were not substantiated.[122]

After Dominican dictator Trujillo was accused by Venezuelan president Betancourt of civil rights violations, OAS voted to investigate. However, Trujillo refused to permit the investigators to enter his country. It was the first time in the 12-year history of OAS that a member nation failed to cooperate.[123] The United States would not intervene.

The United States was considering broadcasts to Cuba to counter censorship and anti–American propaganda.[124] In the States, an American group called the Fair Play for Cuba Committee ran an ad in the *New York Times* headed "What Is Really Happening in Cuba." This ad generated tremendous publicity after it was reported by other news media and eventually led to congressional hearings. Among the signers of the ad were several famous authors. Waldo Frank was listed as chair and Carleton Beals was listed as co-chair of the sponsor. The ad said that although there was bargaining between Cuba and the Soviet

Union, there was "not a shred of evidence" that Cuba was seeking military weapons from the USSR. In effect, the ad said that although Cuba was depicted as a land of terror, chaos and dictatorship, Cubans were freer "in many respects" than Americans.[125]

After the Cuban Supreme Court ruled in favor of two American companies in INRA claims, the head of INRA said that the court needed more members, and that verdicts not in accord with revolutionary principles must be overturned.[126]

At the same time, Neil Macaulay had problems with the U.S. government. After his discharge from the Rebel Army, he received a land grant in Pinar del Río and stayed to farm tomatoes and cucumbers, which he sold at a farmer's market in Pompano Beach, Florida. Macaulay was friendly with Fidel Castro, and when they saw each other, Castro always was interested in the farm's progress. After Macaulay registered with the American Consulate and showed them a copy of his discharge papers, he was accused of having been a member of the armed forces of a foreign nation and therefore subject to loss of his American citizenship.[127]

Ambassador Bonsal had not met with Premier Castro after his return and had only one meeting with Foreign Minister Roa. In a letter to some Chilean students, the U.S. ambassador to Chile stated that there was repression of civil rights in Cuba. This was followed by a press conference in which Secretary Herter described attacks on anti-communists as repressive. He also said that the United States was upset that Cuba said it was not bound to mutual defense under the Rio treaty because the government had not signed it.[128] President Eisenhower stated that Latin America had nothing to fear from the United States, and that all we wanted was for all nations to prosper. He reminded them that had Communism been allowed in these countries, liberty and freedom "would have been utterly destroyed."[129] The next day, President Eisenhower's and Secretary Herter's statements were labeled "an attack on the people" in the Cuban press.[130]

Some anti–government activities were reported when a *guajiro* in Oriente Province was killed. It was known that Manuel Beatón, considered a bandit, was operating near where the man had been killed. Another group was led by Nino Díaz.[131] There had been a near-riot in a movie theater after a showing of *The FBI Story*, as a few people applauded when the American flag was shown.[132] The *New York Times* and Tad Szulc reported that besides Beatón and Díaz in the field, MRR actively opposed Castro and comprised disaffected former Castro supporters who wanted representative democracy and individual liberties like freedom of expression. It was noted that former M–7–26 officer Sotús had been captured, but the group had disavowed terrorism and also supported reforms, including land reform, "that hands the peasants true land ownership, and that establishes true cooperatives and not collective farms."[133] Szulc mentioned that although the aspirations sounded rational, the Cuban "masses" were not fully aware of the controversy over Communism and still identified with Castro.

David Salvador, the fiery former head of Cuban labor, returned to the sugar plantation from where he had started.[134] After losing their union membership, many other former labor leaders could not find a job.

As diplomatic relations continued to deteriorate and as the American press noted the terrorism and the impending conflict with Cuba, tourism from the United States was almost nonexistent. The Tropicana nightclub closed in February. As a result of continuing losses and layoffs of employees, Cuba expropriated several hotels, including the American-owned Riviera, Capri and Deauville.

Diplomatically, in the face of Cuban criticism over the president's and secretary of state's statements that Castro had betrayed his revolutionary ideals, the United States continued to file protests over what could be considered minor matters. Among them were an attempt to reinstate a union official who had been fired from a job at Guantánamo naval base, the request for helicopters and other armaments. The United States also had withdrawn Department of Agriculture inspectors. The tone of the three diplomatic notes was consistent with the hardball approach that the administration took toward Cuba.[135]

On May 1, 1960, a United States U-2 spy plane, was shot down by a Soviet surface-to-air missile. Although the U.S. initially denied it, pilot Francis Gary Powers had been on a top secret CIA mission in a program approved by President Eisenhower in 1954.[136] By May 9, 1960, the *New York Times* had announced that the United States had a "spy crisis," and asked where it was leading. Although it lambasted the Soviet Union for its spy operations, it noted that the United States committed a serous intelligence failure coupled with "political stupidity." There was no mention of Cuba.[137] Two days later, President Eisenhower admitted that the U.S. had spied on the Soviets, but alleged, in essence, that they made us do it in retaliation for a Soviet "fetish of secrecy and concealment" and a need to protect the country. "Nobody needs another Pearl Harbor," he was quoted as saying.[138] However, privately, he was so upset that he told his secretary, "I would like to resign."[139]

In early May, E. Howard Hunt made a secret visit to Cuba to assess the situation. Hunt found that the CIA had been able to recruit, but that neighborhood watches identified his contacts who, for the most part, had been "lined up against a wall and shot." Hunt determined that the bulk of the population was either enthralled with Castro or scared to death by him, and that there was little hope of an internal uprising.[140] The only hope seemed to be an external impetus. He suggested that all communication, including radio and television, should be cut at the time of invasion.[141]

During the time that Hunt was in Cuba, Cuba reported that its navy had fired on a United States submarine in its waters. It reported that at least nine subs had been seen in Cuban waters between May 6 and May 11, and that an American light cruiser, the *Norfolk*, had come precariously close. In a speech, Castro said that the "United States will not do here what it did in Guatemala, Nicaragua and Haiti."[142] However, when Castro proposed José Miró Cardona as new Cuban ambassador in the United States, American newspapers reported that the appointment would improve relations between the two countries.

In mid–May President Eisenhower attended a summit meeting in Paris, which, in the wake of the U-2 incident, turned out to be a disaster. Khrushchev asked Eisenhower to punish those responsible, and after Eisenhower did not respond, Khrushchev walked out of the conference.[143]

On May 19, a small group of anti–Castro exiles met at a motel in Fort Lauderdale with Artime Buesa and two operatives known as "Jimmy" and "Karl." Jimmy was introduced as the head of the operation to invade Cuba. Within days the group was transported to Useppa Island, near Fort Myers, Florida, for guerrilla training.[144]

In Cuba, David Salvador, former head of Cuban labor, formed the 30th of November Movement, named for the date that Frank País's organization had started the revolt in anticipation of the Granma landing.[145] Among the several former M–7–26 leaders, others who joined him included former Rebel Army captain Hiram González. Former cabinet member Manuel Ray Rivero founded the Revolutionary Movement of the People, and among its members was Pedro Luis Boitel, an influential student leader at the University of Havana and also a former M–7–26 veteran. Ray's slogan was *Fidelismo sin Fidel*, "Castroism without Castro."[146] Salvador's and Ray's organizations would eventually unite.

CIA manager E. Howard Hunt (left) and former Bay of Pigs Brigade 2506 Commander Manuel Artime Buesa in 1977. The incident is generally considered among the most incompetent military exercises in American history, and both are deemed partly responsible, but the White House and the CIA were responsible for conception and execution. (Associated Press).

Besides the Artime Buesa group that was still mostly within the Cuban army, other dissidents included former Auténtico Tony Varona, who formed Revolutionary Rescue and the Frente Nacional Democratico Triple A, led by Aureliano Sánchez Arango, the controversial former minister of education in the Prío Socarrás government. Moreover, remnants of the Catholic inspired Montecristi movement led by Justo Carrillo also were active.[147] Catholic students started the Directorio Revolucionario Estudrantil (DRE), named after the student group from the 1930s, led by Alberto Müller, Juan Manuel Salvat and Ernesto Fernández Travieso.[148] Smaller groups were headed by Orlando Bosch, Rafael Díaz Hanscom, and Laureano Batista.[149] Bosch was another physician who had been a member of M–7–26, and had been governor of Las Villas Province until he defected.[150]

The CIA tried to establish a single front, the Frente, to consolidate all of the opposition forces, except those of Batista. The group held a press conference June 22 in Mexico City to announce its plans. Mexico City was probably chosen because the Frente hoped to replicate the successes of the M–7–26 in removing Batista. Many of the leaders had been officers in the Rebel Army and the Provisional Government, and many of them stated that the only thing wrong with the revolution was its leader, Fidel Castro.

During this period, Cuba needed oil to run its industry and supply its military. After it stopped receiving oil supplies from the United States, most of the oil refined in the three oil refineries — Texaco, Esso and Shell — came from Venezuela. However, Cuba received oil under the terms of the treaty with the Soviet Union. The Mineral and Fuel Act of 1938 required foreign refineries to process Cuban oil, which American companies defined as oil taken from within Cuba. However, the Cuban government did not see it that way.[151] On

May 23, all three companies were ordered to refine Soviet oil. Shell Oil was a British sub-sidiary of Royal Dutch Shell, and the British government had not been using hardball diplo-macy with Cuba. The local management of Shell Oil, however, failed to consult with the British consulate and took the same legal position as Esso and Texaco.[152] Initially Ambassador Bonsal and the U.S. embassy took the position that the refinery matter was contractual between Cuba and the companies and that the United States had no say in the matter.[153] After deliberating, all three companies refused to refine Soviet oil.

At about the same time, American embassy legal attaches Edwin L. Sweet and William G. Friedemann were arrested at a private home and charged with encouraging terrorist acts, granting asylum to enemies of the state, financing subversive publications and smuggling weapons. They were immediately deported. The State Department said that Sweet and Friedemann were liaisons to local police departments to keep track of people in Cuba wanted for crimes in the United States.[154] Within hours, the United States expelled two Cuban diplomats for "acts incompatible with their status as consular officials." The acts included espionage, running a network of agents, and "racial agitation."[155] Later, Cuba arrested two other embassy employees, both secretaries, who didn't have diplomatic immunity. However, after the women were accused of espionage, they were deported immediately.[156] Many other Americans were detained for questioning during this period.

Although Cuba expropriated the Hilton, the Nacional, and other Cuban-owned hotels, despite the lack of tourists Premier Castro told employees that no worker would lose a job, because the government would open hotels as "tourist centers" with swimming pools and other amenities, open to the public at nominal cost.[157] The Havana Hilton was renamed the "Havana Libre."

On June 25, the United States formally announced the end of its "patience" with Cuba and threatened a new policy.[158] At the time, the terms of the policy were not expressly stated.

In retaliation, Cuba expropriated the three oil refineries because the companies refused to refine Soviet oil. At the time, it was thought that Cuba had no oil fields in its territory and the American refinery companies had a monopoly.[159] Cuba had so little oil that the Esso refinery would had to close, pending an attempt to obtain oil from Venezuela. The Cuban Petroleum Institute estimated that it had only about 59 days' worth of oil left.[160] The United States filed a formal protest, accusing Cuba of using "economic aggression" against American interests.[161]

The American press reported that the recent events in Cuba were further signs that the Castro regime was attempting to become a Soviet satellite and to rectify the Soviet record in Hungary and the communist Chinese record of repression in Tibet.[162] At the same time, there were reports that a student was killed in disruptions at the University of Havana.

During this period, Cuba, the United States and the Soviet Union entered into a heated diplomatic exchange which invoked all sides to institute policies that culminated in a dis-solution of the economic ties between Cuba and the United States. On June 22, Secretary of State Herter appeared before the Senate, seeking authority to cut the sugar quota. Imme-diately Cuba reacted, asserting that a cut in the quota was "economic war." For every cut in the quota an American sugar mill would be nationalized.[163] On June 27, the House Agri-culture Committee voted to cede power over sugar to the president. On July 5, 1960, Cuba announced that it would nationalize all American industry on the island. After the Eisen-hower administration assumed authority over the quotas, on July 6, the United States announced that it would not buy 7,000,000 tons of sugar that remained in the 1960 quota. As the first Soviet ambassador was assigned to Cuba, President Eisenhower accused Soviet premier Khrushchev of transforming Cuba into a Soviet vassal state after Khrushchev stated that the USSR would help Cuba overcome an "economic blockade."[164]

Throughout much of this time, the United States and the Soviet Union were also embroiled over developments in the Congo, which had just gained independence from Belgium. United Nations troops had been sent to the Congo to secure peace. Almost as soon as the Belgians left, Katanga Province declared itself independent and as a civil war erupted, the Soviet Union threatened to intervene.[165] Some critics said that Premier Khrushchev took this position at this time because elections in the United States were looming, and the prospect of a new administration made United States confrontation less likely. By the end of July the American political parties had chosen their candidates: Vice President Nixon for the Republicans and Senator John F. Kennedy for the Democrats. Their views differed on Cuba policy.[166]

About this time, the CIA negotiated with one of its operatives to assassinate Raúl Castro for $10,000. However, after the initial offer was made, the CIA reversed its position and retracted the offer.[167] The anti–Castro brigade that had been training in Useppa, Florida, was sent to Finca Helvetia, the Swiss Farm, a coffee plantation in Guatemala, where "Mr. Karl" would be in charge of further training.[168] The farm was owned by the family of the Guatemalan Ambassador to the United States. Approximately 1,500 guerrillas would be trained there.

The U.S. exerted pressure on every conceivable front. On July 8, 1960, the president of the International League, Frank Shaughnessy, announced that the Havana Sugar Kings ball team would be moving to Jersey City, New Jersey, and be renamed the Jersey City Jerseys. "We have to protect our players," he stated.[169] However, the decision was actually made by Secretary Herter.[170] The team owner, Bobby Maduro, told the press he had not been consulted: "Baseball was a strong link between the Cuban and American peoples and should never have been broken."[171] Castro stated that American players were respected in Cuba and protested that "violating all codes of sportsmanship they now take away our franchise. It is another aggression against us. We've never told our players not to play in the United States in spite of attacks against us there."[172] When the team was relocated, several of the players and manager Tony Castaño refused to go. When Castaño was replaced by Napoleón Reyes, Reyes was called a traitor and needed security protection.[173]

On July 11, former Rebel Army officer Neil Macaulay and his wife and daughter were able to return to the United States. In order to avoid losing some of his possessions, because the authorities were confiscating "Cuban" property and his car and was registered in Cuba, he traded cars with a fellow American, loaded the car, and sent it on the ferry to Key West while he and his family flew on to Miami.[174] Although Macaulay had been a United States Army officer, and a graduate of the Citadel, a military college, and although he had registered in good faith at the U.S. consulate to retain his passport, he was accused of having served in a foreign army. He was able to retain his United States citizenship only at the intercession of Senator Strom Thurmond, who represented his home state, South Carolina.[175]

Rafael Cepeda, a Presbyterian minister, published an article in *Bohemia* titled, "Fidel Castro and the Reign of God," extolling Christian work through "word and example" and favorably comparing Castro's goals to Christian teaching.[176] Reverend Fernández Ceballos, by then a government official as well as a pastor, also wrote articles in support of the government, noting a common Marxist and Christian attitude toward property, poverty and helplessness. Reverend Daniel Alvarez, who had been head of a government program designed to eradicate prostitution and begging, would leave Cuba in August and begin preaching against what he saw as Cuban government tyranny in his pulpit at the First Spanish Presbyterian Church of Brooklyn, New York. However, other pastors would object to his remarks.[177]

On July 23, CIA director Dulles briefed presidential candidate John F. Kennedy on Cuba. Over two and a half hours, Kennedy was told about the training of an exile brigade and invasion plans.[178]

In August, Richard Bissell met with Colonel Sheffield Edwards, head of the CIA Office of Security. Edwards suggested using the Mafia, which had been exiled from Cuba, to eliminate Fidel Castro. After Bissell agreed, Edwards began to plan a series of operations using Mafia CIA assets, especially through former FBI agent Robert Maheu, an employee of tycoon Howard Hughes.[179]

After learning the *Miami Herald* was going to publish a story about Cuban exile guerrilla groups training near Homestead, Florida, the CIA quashed it.[180] The CIA hired a public relations firm, Lem Jones Associates, Inc., to handle publicity for the anti–Castro groups.[181]

On August 18, President Eisenhower signed a $13 million budget for Cuban covert operations, but asserted that no American personnel were to be used.[182]

On August 25, the OAS met in San José, Costa Rica. The primary issue was an allegation that Dominican dictator Trujillo had contracted for the murder attempt on Venezuelan president Rómulo Betancourt. A vote supporting Venezuela passed. However, the United States also requested that the OAS censure Cuba for failing to institute representative democracy and for bringing Communism to the Western Hemisphere. Cuba vociferously objected, but this request was ruled out of order and was replaced by a resolution against intervention in the hemisphere by an "extra-continental power." Everyone knew that phrase was a euphemism for the Soviet Union. By the time of that vote, however, after Foreign Minister Roa protested by leaving, Cuba resigned from OAS.[183]

The next day, presidential candidate John F. Kennedy stated that Fidel Castro was an enemy of the United States and that Cuba was a satellite of the Soviet Union. After Vice President Nixon told the Veterans of Foreign Wars that the United States was invincible militarily, Kennedy alleged that U.S. "security and leadership" in the world was "slipping away."[184]

After Carlos Rodríguez Santana, a trainee, was killed in an exercise in Guatemala, the brigade renamed itself in his honor after his identification number, 2506.[185]

As the vocal confrontations between the respective governments heightened, allegiances became stressed. Rumors within the Presbyterian Church were that the Cuban church would separate itself from the American church. However, these rumors were dispelled.[186]

Both President Eisenhower and Premier Khrushchev attended meetings at the United Nations. President Eisenhower spoke first, asking for disarmament and offering reciprocal inspections. Khrushchev brought Castro, Presidents Nasser, Tito, Nehru of India and Sukarno of Indonesia with him to demand an end to colonialism throughout the world. At the time, there was civil war in the former Belgian Congo and an insurrection in French Algeria. Although Khrushchev indicated he would agree to inspections, he criticized the U-2 flights and other "provocations." Khrushchev also was critical of the United Nations and asked Secretary-General Dag Hammarsjköld to resign because he favored "colonialists." He also asked to move the United Nations out of the United States. The *New York Times* called the meeting a "propaganda circus."[187]

The Soviet Union reaped another propaganda bonanza when two U.S. National Security Agency employees defected to the Soviet Union and denounced the United States. President Eisenhower called them traitors; the Defense Department called one "mentally sick" and both "confused."[188] However, in the States, José Paz Novas defected from Cuba and brought with him the names of 120 Cuban agents in New York and Miami.[189]

On September 19, Premier Castro came to New York to attend the United Nations meeting. After staying one night in the UN hotel, Castro complained that there was tight security and he moved to Harlem to the Hotel Theresa.[190] The Fair Play for Cuba Committee held a reception in his honor. In an address before the United Nations, September 26, 1960, Premier Castro alleged:

1. That Cuba had been a virtual colony of the United States;
2. That the U.S. government was allied with monopolies that controlled Cuba's natural resources;
3. That cession of the U.S. naval base at Guantánamo had been forced upon Cuba;
4. That the Batista dictatorship was chosen by the monopolies to protect their interests;
5. That the Batista regime had U.S. military support;
6. That the balance of payments between the United States and Cuba was so unfavorable that the U.S. was "sucking the blood" of Cuba;
7. That reduction of the Cuban sugar quota was "economic aggression" against Cuba;
8. That the United States had given sanctuary to murders and "bloodthirsty criminals";
9. That the United States had either permitted or was complicit in sabotage of *La Coubre*;
10. That the U.S. permitted bombing of Cuba from United States territory;
11. That the United States had taken over Swan Island to set up the radio base given to war criminals;
12. That the U.S. "smeared" the government of Cuba by accusing it of Communism;
13. That the United States was inciting labor problems at Guantánamo to set up a pretext for an attack;
14. That the United States had denied Puerto Ricans the right to self-determination; and most importantly,
15. That the United States refused to renegotiate with Cuba.

Castro also complained about the security and hotel accommodations in New York for the Cuban delegations and claimed that the anti–Cubans were permitted to get so out of hand that an innocent nine-year-old girl was killed.[191] A Cuban immigrant, Francisco Molina, who turned out to be a Castro supporter, was tried for the shooting. Although Castro had to have seen sure by that time that the United States was planning an invasion of Cuba, he did not mention it.[192]

As the drama was occurring at the United Nations, Robert Taber and Richard Gibson were forced to resign at CBS, reportedly due to their membership in the Fair Play for Cuba Committee.[193] CBS issued a statement denying that they were discharged.

The next day, Castro and his entourage discovered that his airplane had been seized because they owed debts to American creditors. Although the United States delegation to the United Nations said it would bring a restraining order because the airline was entitled to sovereign immunity, Castro and his delegation returned to Cuba on a Soviet airplane.[194]

On September 28, the CIA tried to drop weapons to guerrilla units in Cuba, but the

Above and following page: By 1960, Castro envisioned himself as "neutral" in the dispute between the United States and the Soviet Union for world leadership. He visited the United Nations in September 1960, where he met with Sukarno of Indonesia (above), Prime Minister Nehru of India (in white hat on p. 191) and Krishna Menon, chief Indian delegate to the United Nations, and Nasser of Egypt. All expressed a desire to form a third body to confront both the United States and the Soviets (Associated Press).

plane bringing them missed its target by seven miles, and the Cuban military wound up with the weapons. The CIA agent on site in Cuba was killed. Then the CIA airplane missed its landing zone in Guatemala and landed in Mexico, where it was impounded.[195] At the same time, a pleasure boat delivered 300 pounds of cargo and picked up two émigrés.[196] Increased bombing and other sabotage was reported; for example, on one night, bombs exploded in three different Havana neighborhoods, and a communist statue was destroyed on the campus of the university. There were reports of firefights in the mountains and arrests of public officials accused of collaboration with the counter-revolutionaries.[197]

    At this same time, Cuba initiated Committees for the Defense of the Revolution, with

stated goals of ensuring that revolutionary decrees would be carried out.[198] Citizens would systematically provide the same kind of information that the *chivatos* performed during the Batista regime. Files were kept on every individual.

On September 30, 1960, President Eisenhower advised all Americans working in Cuba to send their families home.[199]

In preparation for the second television debate with Vice President Nixon, presidential candidate John F. Kennedy linked Nixon to a "glaring failure" in United States foreign policy, and accused him of having, in essence, been identified with the Batista government and having been in a position to cut off the problems in Cuba before Castro acquired any power. Nixon's campaign slogan was "Experience Counts." Kennedy stated that the American people could not afford any similar experiences.[200]

On October 4, several assault boats landed in Cuba but the occupants were immediately captured. Three of them were Americans. All were tried and executed.[201] Eight others, who landed at Bahía de Navas and Baracoa, were captured, including another American.[202] On October 12, they were also tried and executed.[203]

On October 7, Cuban foreign minister Raúl Roa García stated that a "CIA army" was being formed on an estate belonging to the brother of the Guatemalan ambassador to the United States, and he identified CIA bombers in hangars at La Aurora Airport.[204]

In late October the CIA-Mafia deal was almost exposed. Chicago mob boss Sam Giancana's girlfriend Phyllis McGuire was said to be having an affair with comedian Dan Rowan. A team hired by Robert Maheu was caught trying to bug Rowan's hotel room, but, fearing exposure, the CIA asked the local authorities not to prosecute.[205]

On October 17, 1960, Comandante William Morgan, his wife, and Cuban army major

Jesus Carreras were arrested for attempting to smuggle arms to anti–Castro guerrillas in the Escambray mountains. Morgan and Carreras were taken to La Cabaña prison.[206] By some accounts, Castro had told Morgan to leave Cuba, but Morgan resisted.[207] He had lost his United States citizenship and had become a Cuban citizen.

Several prisoners escaped from Morro Castle, the fortress prison overlooking Havana Harbor. Credit for the escape would later be taken by the Revolutionary Movement of the People.

On October 19, the United States began a trade embargo against Cuba under the Export Control Act of 1949, which was directed against communist countries as retaliation for policies against the U.S. government and against American interests.[208] At first there were exceptions for medical supplies and food, but within a few months, these were also banned. The next day, the U.S. withdrew its ambassador.[209]

As the 1960 presidential election grew closer, the candidates continued to attack each other over Cuba. Senator John F. Kennedy stated that his administration would aid anti–Castro groups in exile. Nixon, who had been privately doing just that through Operation 40 and CIA groups, took the public position that Kennedy was reckless, risking World War III.[210] However, in so doing, Vice President Nixon referenced Guatemala as a good example of Eisenhower administration foreign policy. In Latin America, both views were highly criticized. The Brazilians stated that they remained willing to mediate. One Brazilian newspaper stated that there was no worse example of bad policy than Guatemala.[211]

During the course of the presidential campaign, Castro ridiculed both candidates, calling them "illiterate" and "monopolistic." After the election, Premier Castro said that he hoped the United States would change its policy toward Cuba. He told students at the University of Havana that an American attack on Cuba would be "suicidal." As he spoke, at least two bombs exploded, one close enough to shake the building where he was speaking.[212] During the period, explosions were heard almost nightly, and the population of Cuba was depicted in the American news as in constant fear of an invasion.[213]

There were approximately 1,000 guerrillas in the Escambray. However, because there were so many sectarian disputes and ego problems, focusing the Frente on a single result was impossible. Richard Bissell declared that the Cubans were "incorrigible."[214] First Sánchez Arango quit, then Justo Carrillo. Despite the assertions that Batistianos would not be welcome in the Frente, some obviously were, driving the defections. Some of the Catholics did not want to work with liberals like Manuel Ray Rivero, whom they equated with communists. Some of the Frente complained because Gerry Droller spoke English with a thick German accent, could not speak Spanish and could not relate to or communicate with the guerrillas. Some said that he treated the Cubans "like peons." His cover was as a steel magnate and he played the part.[215]

Other support in the Escambray did arrive as former M–7–26 officers such as William Morgan and his colleague Major Jesús Carreras joined the Frente.[216] Catholic priests sold war bonds to support the insurgents. The bonds were endorsed "With God and With Cuba ... to fight the red revolution."[217] A stash of dynamite was found in a church.[218] However, most of the new arrivals were soon caught.

Former Castro ally David Salvador, now head of the November 30th Organization, was caught and arrested with six others as they tried to escape to Miami on a yacht. Arrested with him was Juaquín Agramonte Molina, who had once been coordinator of M–7–26 in Camagüey Province. After a trial, Salvador was convicted, and although there were calls for his execution, he was sentenced to 30 years at hard labor.[219]

Meanwhile, guerrilla training expanded beyond Guatemala, as guerrillas were seen training in the Everglades and in the Florida Keys. On November 19, *The Nation* magazine ran an article titled "Are We Training Cuban Guerrillas?"[220]Although a press release was issued by *The Nation*, the wire services ignored the story and only one or two papers mentioned it.[221]

In late November, CIA director Allen Dulles and deputy director Bissell briefed President-elect Kennedy on Cuba. President Eisenhower met with Kennedy on December 6 and January 11, and recommended planning a "military operation" against Cuba.[222]

In December, the Presbyterian Church in Cuba announced that its membership was growing. However, it also began to have financial problems. Pastors and other church employees in Cuba could no longer afford to make their pension payments, as there was an embargo.[223] Americans were leaving Cuba, yet the same period was ironically a "peak time" for the Cuban Presbyterian Church, as its board approved $50,000 for a Presbyterian camp and school, planned a radio program, and saw four Cuban pastors ordained by the divinity school in Matanzas. The Synod of New Jersey contemplated holding its convention in Cuba.[224] However, at the same time, many Presbyterians had immigrated to the United States and there were few American citizens left in Cuba.

Soon after Europa, the largest department store in Havana, was nationalized, a fire broke out and it was burned to rubble.

Chapter 17

Trial Separation

During the celebration of the second anniversary of the revolution, January 1, 1961, a bomb exploded near Plaza Cívica, in downtown Havana. The next evening, speaking to a mass audience estimated between 100,000 and 250,000, Castro accused the United States of having set it or having provided his enemies an opportunity to do so, and he declared that the United States embassy had 48 hours to reduce its staff to 11 people, the same number as staffed the Cuban embassy in Washington. Castro alleged that the U.S. embassy was the source of counter-revolutionary sabotage: "It is the American Embassy that is paying the terrorists to put bombs in Cuba." He later would state that the Cuban people needed to be ready to repel an invasion.[1]

In his recounting of the events, Ambassador Bonsal did not mention the bomb in the Plaza Cívica, but did speculate that "Castro's words [demanding the reduction in force] came to him while he was orating; once the words were out of his mouth he could not retreat."[2] He also alleged that by that point the United States had no other choice than to close the embassy.

Cuba was placed on a national alert, in panic over an impending attack by the United States. A commemoration parade included Soviet-made tanks, artillery and anti–aircraft guns, units of the military and militia, some of whom were from youth work brigades and cadres of women teachers, carrying Czechoslovakian-made automatic rifles. Also displayed were the remnants of the "Yankee rocket" that had been fired from Cape Canaveral on November 30.

In the reviewing stand were Soviet, Chinese and other foreign dignitaries, including members of the Fair Play for Cuba Committee. At a later reception, Castro stated that if an invasion did come, the United Stares could lose more men than at Normandy or Okinawa in World War II.[3]

Within hours, the United States announced that it would withdraw its entire embassy staff and that we had broken relations with Cuba. Ambassador Bonsal speculated that Castro could not have expected that the lame duck Eisenhower administration would take the initiative to invade Cuba.[4]

Privately, the president was told by National Security Advisor Gordon Gray and General Lemnitzer, the chairman of the Joint Chiefs of Staff, that the Cuban exiles in training were "the best Army in Latin America." Assistant Secretary of State Mann told the president that support for Castro had diminished from approximately 95 percent to about 25–30 percent. The original CIA plan called for in invasion near the city of Trinidad, in central Cuba near the Escambray Mountains, to link with anti–Castro guerrilla units. After listening to his advisors, President Eisenhower stated that the invasion should occur before January 20 "if the Cubans provided him a really good excuse." Without an excuse, he ventured that the CIA "could think of manufacturing something that would be generally acceptable."[5]

There was an immediate surge in the exodus of Americans and of Cubans closely identified with the U.S. Among those leaving in a hurry was Francis Bartes, owner of the Guantánamo Railroad, who told the *New York Times* that although he had been a follower of Castro, he had abandoned his family and left over $7,000,000 in Cuba to escape. On the same flight was Lincoln Rodon, former Auténtico and speaker of the Cuban house of representatives. The implication was that Cuba was in a state of war and that anyone with ties to the United States would be arrested.[6]

Within Cuba, rumors were spread that the communists would exterminate their enemies, especially Catholic leaders. Rumors also spread that children of Catholics would be sent to the Soviet Union or other Soviet bloc countries for communist indoctrination. In Operation Pedro Pan, run clandestinely from December 1960 to October 1962, more than 14,000 Cuban children were sent to live apart from their parents in the United States. Placement of the children was made by the Miami Catholic Diocese and Monsignor Bryan O. Walsh.[7] Castro would later condemn the accusation that his government would take children from parents as "an appalling lie," and he alleged a conspiracy between the church and the United States.[8]

Crowds of Cubans tried to seek visas to emigrate, but the Cuban government stopped issuing them. Visas were given to the 120 Cuban employees of the embassy. Hysterical crowds rushed the empty American embassy, holding out hope to leave. Government photographers took their pictures for future reference, as radio reporters called them traitors. The Cuban government guaranteed safe passage to the Americans, but not necessarily to the Cubans wishing to emigrate.[9]

That evening, President Dorticós addressed a massive crowd shouting anti–American slogans at the Capitol. Wearing a military uniform with a pistol in a conspicuous holster, he told the people to be ready for the "Yankee invasion."[10]

On January 4, a day after the national security meeting at the White House, senior CIA officials prepared a memorandum "to outline the status of preparations for the conduct of amphibious/airborne and tactical air operations against the Government of Cuba and to set forth certain requirements for policy decisions which must be reached and implemented if these operations are to be carried out."[11] The concept was as follows:

> The initial mission of the invasion force will be to seize and defend a small area.... There will be no early attempt to break out of the lodgment for further offensive operations unless and until there is a general uprising against the Castro regime or overt military intervention by United States forces has taken place. It is expected that these operations will precipitate a general uprising throughout Cuba and cause the revolt of large segments of the Cuban Army and militia.... If matters do not eventuate as predicted above, the lodgment ... can be used as the site for establishment of a ? [question mark in original], provisional government that can be recognized by the United States.... The way will then be paved for United States military intervention aimed at pacification of Cuba, and this will result in the prompt overthrow of the Castro Government.
>
> It is considered crucial that the Cuban air force and naval vessels capable of opposing the landing be knocked out or neutralized before amphibious shipping makes its final run into the beach.[12]

Apparently the Cubans were surprised by the American reaction.[13] The *New York Times* said that President Eisenhower had no other choice, but stated there was hope that the breach would be healed. However, the *Times* also noted an "awkward state" because the Eisenhower administration left resolution of the problem to the incoming Kennedy administration.[14] The *Baltimore Sun* and most other American newspapers agreed with the last part. However, the *Louisville Courier Journal* asserted that the break accomplished little and forced Cuba to accept aid from the Soviet Union. The *San Francisco Chronicle* commented that the United States had not created a policy and said there was "an element of failure" in that the way to halt Castroism was to declare war on "hunger, ignorance and economic injustice."[15] British newspapers accused President Eisenhower of panicking in his final days in office.[16]

Cuba announced that four Americans had been tried and convicted for espionage, including the wiretapping of the Chinese embassy. Three received 10-year terms and the fourth was deported.[17] Cuba tried to bring the threat of an invasion to a United Nations Security Council vote, but it could not obtain a quorum. In rejecting the petition, diplomats noted that the new administration was not yet in place.[18] The United States denied that there were any plans for invasion. "We don't know what they're talking about," James Hagerty, President Eisenhower's press secretary, told the media.[19] At the same time, anti–Castro Cubans protested against President-elect Kennedy, asking for weapons to attack Cuba. At the airport as he was leaving New York, Kennedy said he would not address Cuba until his inauguration.[20]

On January 5, Tony Varona, speaking for his group, denied that the United States was backing the invasion, although his group was "almost ready" to invade.[21] The Fair Play for Cuba committee accused the CIA of training anti–Castro Cubans in Florida, Nicaragua and Guatemala.[22] Other anti–Castro groups led by General Pedraza and Rolando Masferrer were also planning to invade Cuba.[23] At the same time, the United States Navy was planning war games in the Caribbean. Two U.S. destroyers and one submarine were already in Guantánamo Bay; the aircraft carrier *Franklin D. Roosevelt* was on its way, and 11 destroyers, an assault vessel and a reinforced regiment of U.S. Marines were scheduled to be involved.[24]

The combined effect of the news of naval maneuvers and the recall of the entire American population of Cuba to the States fueled the sense of panic. Rumored bombings of oil refineries and impending landings were also fueled by news that *The Nation* had published a report that a Cuban exile army in Guatemala was ready to strike, and six bombers at an undisclosed Guatemalan airstrip were ready to bomb Havana. There were also charges that the United States would provoke an attack or use a dispute at Guantánamo as a pretext to stage an all-out attack on Cuba.[25]

Columnist Marquis Childs opined that it was too late for an invasion to work. The Castro government had infiltrated the insurgents and the Cuban army had been tipped off several months earlier that the anti–Castro groups planned an invasion. Castro was able to gain equipment enough to arm a 150,000-man army. According to Childs, Castro would only have needed about a tenth of that, 15,000 troops, to stave off the planned invasion. Childs also reported that the leadership of the Cuban groups was divided. In one camp were democratic leaders and in the other were former Batista followers, "secret police and the torturers."[26]

As Americans were leaving, militia units poured into Havana. Barricades and ramparts were built along the seawall; anti-aircraft guns and other heavy weapons were deployed everywhere.[27] Premier Castro placed the blame for the split on the Eisenhower administration, leaving hope for discussions with the incoming Kennedy administration. Brazilians still held out hope that President Kubitschek could mediate a resolution.[28] The government announced that 10 "terrorists" had been arrested near Havana with a cache of explosives and chemical charges, all supposedly working for former Minister of Public Works Manuel Ray Rivera, who was now in the United States.[29] Ray had been head of Civic Resistance and was an expert in the use of explosives. As head of Public Works, he had access to the building plans of most of the government facilities in Cuba. Military installations, public buildings and nationalized businesses were all placed under heavy guard. Military and militia units were on patrol in almost every part of the country. In Havana, gun crews were stationed behind sandbags along the seawall, as anti–aircraft and antitank cannons pointed northward. There was an ongoing blood drive and food was collected for storage in case of a siege. The government reported that it had arrested hundreds of suspected counter-revolutionaries in other parts of Cuba.[30]

However, Cubans celebrated Three Kings Day as usual on January 6. Ruby Phillips reported that children received "war toys" for Christmas, as depicted in newspaper stories and as seen throughout Cuba. Children were pictured in fatigues, armed with cap guns of all types, especially rifles and machine guns. Phillips noted that instead of playing "cowboys and Indians," Cuban children now played "Cubans and Yankee invaders." She noted however, that the children had trouble finding players who would fill the Yankee invader role.[31]

The cabinet passed a law that saboteurs would be subject to the death penalty. The government took over the Knights of Columbus headquarters and the Catholic Workers Association.[32]

On January 7, six Americans were arrested in Havana Harbor in a yacht and charged with insurgency. All six alleged that they had come to Cuba to join Castro. By the end of January, all were convicted, and although the prosecutor requested the death penalty for each, they were sentenced to 30 years for crimes against the security of the state.[33]

In a front page article in the *New York Times* on January 10, it was asserted that expenses for the Fair Play for Cuba Committee ad had been paid by the Cuban government through the Cuban consulate.[34] However, the Cuban deputy consul, Raúl Roa Kouri, son of the Cuban foreign minister, denied the allegations.

In an improbable turn of events, the press reported that Cuba and the Dominican Republic had reconciled their differences. Both countries had been sanctioned at the OAS meeting in January in San José, and both opposed the United States and Venezuela. Radio Caribe, owned by the Dominican government, began to compliment Cuba and attack the Catholic Church and especially "Yankee imperialists."[35] There were also reports that Delio Gómez Ochoa, the former M–7–27 major who had been captured in June 1959, in an incursion into the Dominican Republic, was seen in Havana.

On January 11, the Joint Chiefs of Staff were told that an invasion was imminent. A working committee comprising staff from the CIA, Department of State, Department of Defense, and the Joint Chiefs was established.[36] The Defense Department produced a memorandum setting out a plan already approved by the Joint Chiefs that included an invasion by an American-trained and -supported volunteer army.[37]

The Guatemalan government denied that the United States or anyone else was using its territory to mount an attack; it maintained that the only military training that was taking place was for defense purposes. The U.S. State Department and Defense Department were asked to comment, but refused. Lincoln White, the State Department press officer, said "I know absolutely nothing about it."[38] However, the president of Guatemala acknowledged that there were several guerrilla training camps in his country but denied that an invasion of Cuba was planned. In the *Washington Post* version of the story, the invasion scare was traced to a trainee who defected to Cuba, and reported "to Castro" on the size and strength of units he had seen.[39]

Because of the mobilization for civil defense in Cuba, the sugar harvest was affected, and Cuba was not be able to produce its usual crop.[40] Eventually, the government had to seek volunteers to harvest the crop.[41]

On January 12, the Cuban government arrested MRR guerrilla commander Ramon Carvajal for conspiring against the state.[42] An American citizen, John Gentile, was sentenced to 30 years in prison for sabotage and assassination attempts against Cuban leaders.

On January 16, the State Department limited American travel to Cuba. Articles depicting a large guerrilla force operating within Cuba were published in major American newspapers. The *New York Times* version quoted Tony Varona as saying that there were no longer plans for an invasion of Cuba, and that reports of training of guerrillas outside of Cuba were "exaggerated and largely untrue." Reports and pictures showed that the rebels depicted looked just like the M–7–26 rebels of 1956 to 1959, except that they did not have beards. Priests were conspicuous in the *Times* pictures.[43]

President Eisenhower and President-elect Kennedy met a day prior to inauguration, and Kennedy was told that the Cuban project was going very well. "Senator Kennedy asked the President's judgment as to the United States supporting the guerrilla operation in Cuba, even if this support would implicate the United States. The President replied, 'Yes, as we cannot let the present government there go on.'"[44]

Chapter 18

Bay of Pigs

On January 20, 1961, President John F. Kennedy was inaugurated. In his speech, Kennedy asserted that the United States was willing to "begin anew the quest for peace":

> To our sister republics south of our border, we offer a special pledge — to convert our good words into good deeds — in a new alliance for progress — to assist free men and free governments in casting off the chains of poverty. But this peaceful revolution of hope cannot become the prey of hostile powers. Let all our neighbors know that we shall join with them to oppose aggression or subversion anywhere in the Americas. And let every other power know that this Hemisphere intends to remain the master of its own house.[1]

The Cuban government responded that the new administration was following the same "aggressive" policy as the Eisenhower administration.[2]

The next day, Premier Castro quoted President Kennedy's address in part and told the press that Cuba was willing to "begin anew." He said that the troops and militias on alert would stand down. Addressing 50,000 militia members, Castro said that the new administration held out "hope for peace," but he alleged that the American people had been "fed on lies" and said that he wanted the new administration to tell the truth. He also announced that trials of anti–government rebels would be suspended, including the trial of six Americans arrested as spies. Two Cuban guerrillas had just been executed and 10 others given 30-year sentences after trials that day. At the same time, Raúl Castro was in Santiago, Chile, railing about "Yankee imperialism." Meanwhile, there were reports that approximately 10,000 to 15,000 troops were in the mountains fighting anti government guerrillas.[3]

On January 25, the president was asked whether relations with Cuba could be restored. He indicated that the United States would make no move as long as Cuba was aligned with the Communist bloc.[4] There had been rumors that the president would restore consular offices in Havana, if for no other reason than to permit Cubans still in Cuba to obtain a visa to leave the country. President Kennedy could have asked another country to relay a message to Cuba to initiate a discussion, but apparently there was no interest. There is also no indication that Castro had tried to do the same. At the time, U.S. interests were handled by the Swiss embassy in Havana, and other than Castro's speech, there is no indication that he tried to "begin anew" diplomatically.

On January 28, President Kennedy received his first official briefing on Cuba. Also present were Vice President Lyndon B. Johnson, Secretary of State Dean Rusk, Defense Secretary Robert McNamara, National Security Advisor McGeorge Bundy, General Lemnitzer (chairman of the Joint Chiefs of Staff), Assistant Secretaries Mann and Nitze, and Director Allen Dulles and Tracy Barnes of the CIA. The Defense Department advised the president that there was no plan that could overthrow the Castro regime. The State Department told the president that without OAS cooperation, Latin Americans would oppose invasion. After listening, Kennedy instructed the CIA to increase propaganda and political action and sabotage, and to continue overflights. He ordered the Defense Department and CIA to establish plans for internal guerrilla warfare and he ordered the Department of State to try to isolate Cuba in OAS.[5]

In his State of the Union address, President Kennedy stated the following:

> In Latin America, Communist agents seeking to exploit that region's peaceful revolution of hope have established a base on Cuba, only 90 miles from our shores. Our objection with Cuba is not over the people's drive for a better life. Our objection is to their domination by foreign and domestic tyrannies. Cuban social and economic reform should be encouraged. Questions of economic and trade policy can always be negotiated. But Communist domination in this Hemisphere can never be negotiated.
>
> We are pledged to work with our sister republics to free the Americas of all such foreign domination and all tyranny, working toward the goal of a free hemisphere of free governments, extending from Cape Horn to the Arctic Circle.[6]

Soon Brigadier General David W. Gray, chief of the Joint Subsidiary Activities Division of the Joint Chiefs of Staff, reviewed the "Trinidad Plan." Gray's group determined that the brigade "could last for up to four days, given complete surprise and complete air supremacy. Success will depend on uprisings in Cuba. Gray estimates the chances of success at about 30–70 but no figures are used in the Gray committee's report."[7] In a report from the Joint Chiefs, an analysis found that the invasion plan had "a 'fair' chance of ultimate success and, even if it does not achieve the full results desired, could contribute to the eventual overthrow of the Castro regime."[8] The CIA and Defense Department were "quite enthusiastic." "At worst, they think the invaders would get into the mountains, and at best they think they might get a full-fledged civil war in which we could then back the anti–Castro forces openly." The State Department was "cooler," primarily because it determined that "the political consequences would be very grave both in the United Nations and in Latin America."[9]

Richard Bissell of the CIA reported to the president that with the Joint Chiefs' estimated fair chance of success, an invasion force might still have an ability to survive, hold ground, and attract growing support from the population, "and that at worst, they should have been able to fight their way to the Escambray and go into guerrilla action."[10] However, after hearing the State Department assessment, President Kennedy demanded alternatives to a full-fledged invasion, supported by American planes, ships and supplies. "Could not such a force be landed gradually and quietly and make its first major military efforts from the mountains ... not as an invasion force sent by the Yankees?"[11]

The *New York Times* reported that the Guatemalan government accused two members of an anti–Castro Cuban organization of setting up guerrilla bases and asked them to leave the country. The Cubans, José Miguel Tarafa and Orlando Núñez Pérez, reportedly were leaders of the Revolutionary Democratic Front, but both denied that any camps existed.[12] The brigade was in turmoil as almost half of the men, including the entire second and third battalions, resigned. Brigade Commander "Pepe" Perez San Roman attempted to resign, but the CIA agent known only as "Frank" who was running the operation reinstated him. Twelve "troublemakers" were detained until after the invasion was over.[13]

At the United Nations, the Guatemalan representative was adamant that there were no anti–Castro guerrillas training in his country.[14] The Cuban ambassador, Manuel Bisbe, had a heart attack and passed away during the debate, but controversy over the threat of invasion continued.[15]

On February 17, President Kennedy met with representatives from the State Department, CIA, and Joint Chiefs of Staff. After a presentation from the agencies, he decided that he favored a more moderate approach, such as mass infiltration. The president requested an examination of all possible alternatives. The planned invasion date of March 5, 1961, was cancelled. In a memorandum to the president the next day, National Security Advisor McGeorge Bundy noted: "[CIA Assistant Director] Bissell and [Under Secretary of State] Mann are the real antagonists at the staff level." He noted that President Kennedy favored the State Department view of the situation. Bundy recommended "a trade embargo first, let internal opposition build for several months and then launch "Bissell's battalion ... [so that] the color of civil war would be quite a bit stronger."[16]

Eloy Gutiérrez Menoyo had been arrested in Belgium, accused of plotting revolutions in Spain and Portugal. Another plot, against the Portuguese colony of Angola in West Africa, was also reportedly quashed.[17] Gutiérrez Menoyo was released and returned to Cuba. However, on January 26, 1961, he defected and was picked up in Key West by the United States Immigration Service. He spent the spring and early summer in an Immigration Service holding facility in McAllen, Texas.[18]

Within Cuba, as it developed that several members of the Second Front had joined the counter-revolution, Castro and Che Guevara publicly disputed that Gutiérrez Menoyo had actually been a Rebel Army leader, or that the Second Front had played a role in the Revolution. Guevara wrote an article titled, "The Escambray: A Sin of the Revolution," in which he labeled Gutiérrez Menoyo and his men as "pseudorevolutionaries" who deserved no credit.[19]

On March 10, Morgan, age 34, and 12 others were tried for treason for sending arms to insurgents in September and October 1960. Reportedly Morgan also had called Premier Castro and other government leaders "Communists." Morgan and Major Carreras were convicted and sentenced to death. Three were acquitted, seven were given 30-year sentences and another, who had given evidence against Morgan, received a 15-year sentence. Morgan reportedly maintained that he still believed in the revolution. He asked his mother to care for his Cuban wife, refused to take an appeal and was shot within a few hours.[20]

Several years later, Frank C. Emmick, age 49, of Rossford, Ohio, who was president of the American Club of Havana, would later be tried, convicted and sentenced to 30 years as an accomplice of Morgan and as a CIA spy. Sentenced with him were three Cuban associates.[21]

After a speedboat attack on the former Texaco refinery in Santiago, Cuba filed charges at the United Nations against the Kennedy administration, alleging that the United States was planning "illegal, perfidious and premeditated" armed aggression.[22] Cuba alleged the attack was from "a pirate ship." Also at that time, two Woolworth's stores in Cuba that had been nationalized were burned.[23]

During February and early March, United States military maneuvers took place in the Caribbean, attended by 60 Latin American military officials. The president of the Interamerican Defense Board, H. H. Fischer, announced that military force would remain in the Caribbean on conclusion of the maneuvers. This force would consist of five naval units and an infantry battalion of U.S. Marines.[24]

During the lead-up to the invasion, the CIA tried to keep the details as secret as possible. At Francisco Molina's trial for the riot killing of the bystander during Castro's September visit to the United Nations, the government asserted privilege from any testimony concerning an "unidentified agency" and Cubans in South Florida preparing for an invasion.[25] Molina's lawyers argued for a mistrial, alleging that without the testimony, their defense was impaired. Nevertheless, Molina was convicted.[26]

However, the dispute within the White House over invasion became public. James Reston reported the controversy in a *New York Times* article. Cuba had amassed 30,000 tons of weaponry valued at $50,000,000, and its military was estimated as between 250,000 and 400,000 troops. On one hand, the anti–Castro opposition had a right to resist, and if there were no restrictions to Cuba internationally, there was an imminent threat that Cuba's influence would extend throughout Latin America and destabilize the entire region, which would further encourage the communists to attempt to come to power in several other countries. On the other, American involvement would violate American treaties, especially the OAS's Bogotá Treaty. The U.S. had similar problems elsewhere, with "proxy armies" in Laos and Vietnam. Invasion of and concentration on Cuba could weaken U.S. positions there, and the use of force could damage our prestige with our allies. As a matter of fact, the U.S. had exactly the same difficulty in Laos, where we were accused of trying to destabilize the government.[27] Some of President Kennedy's advisors wanted the U.S. to wait until Cuba attacked Haiti or another vulnerable country. In that event, we would not have violated any of our treaties and we would not incur opposition from other Latin American countries, which would have to follow us under the terms of the Rio Treaty.[28]

Colonel Jack Hawkins had worked out a plan to destroy the Cuban air force prior to invasion that made it appear more palatable, although Bundy had been skeptical about Bissell's plan. He told the president he was more amenable to invasion in a meeting documented by a memorandum to President Kennedy dated March 15.[29] On the same date, Arthur Schlesinger, Jr., noted that the United States was going to issue a "demarche," a demand on Castro that we would hold off any attack if he accepted certain terms. Among those considered were free elections: "It does seem to me that setting up free elections as a test might give Castro a show and give him an opportunity to recover his prestige."[30]

In Miami, Masferrer and seven other men were indicted for violating the Neutrality Act in a bungled attack Masferrer sponsored to Cuba on October 4, 1960. Three Americans had been captured and executed. He sponsored another bungled attempt on September 26, 1960.[31]

In Cuba, people were told to get ready for the invasion. The Committee for the Defense of the Revolution had been established in every municipality and workplace to root out opposition to the government. People were told to find out "whatever everyone you know is doing, who their contacts are and if they are against the Revolution. The only obstacle possible to the crimes of the counter-revolutionaries is the firing squad."[32] Castro announced that if Cuba were invaded, other Latin Americans would support Cuba. In Mexico, former president Lázaro Cárdenas had said that "not a single monopolist or Yankee official could feel safe" in any Latin American country if the United States attacked Cuba. Castro said that Mexicans would be willing to "take up arms and go to the mountains" to defend Cuba, and Cardenas agreed that was true throughout Latin America.[33]

In a March 26 article Ruby Phillips, still in Havana, reported that although the Cuban government had accomplished more in two years than other socialist governments had done in many years, the Cuban mood had gone from joy in January 1959, to "a state of sullen resentment."[34] She stated that the Castro government no longer had time to savor its accomplishments because "equally dedicated enemies are placing bombs, setting fires, and sabotage

... hotly pursed by the Castro police and militia and apparently without any connection to the revolutionaries abroad ... making life extremely precarious on this island."[35]

On April 3, the State Department issued a brochure accusing the Cuban leadership of betraying its own revolution. The brochure was a counterpoint to the view that Cuba accepted communist help only after it was shunned by the United States.[36] The Cuban United Nations delegation immediately protested and continued to predict an invasion.[37]

On April 7, the *New York Times* reported in a front page article that approximately 5,000–6,000 men were training for an invasion, some in the Florida Keys and in Louisiana. Former Cuban premier José Miró Cardona held a press conference as the Cuban president in exile and as president of the Cuban Revolutionary Council to state that the exiles were waging an "imminent" revolution against a betrayal of the revolution by Fidel Castro from within Cuba. "I reject the idea that it is a counter-revolution," he stated. Former Cuban director of public works Manuel Ray was introduced as a military leader of the Frente. Miró had met with Ambassador Bonsal and presidential advisor A. A. Berle. Ray was reported to have taken a position against outside military intervention because it would open charges of "collusion" with the United States. According to CIA estimates there were about 3,000 insurgents in the mountains in Cuba and another 20,000 sympathizers.[38] Other members of the government in exile were former Cuban premier Tony Varona, former Cuban president Carlos Hevia, Justo Carrillo and Dr. Antonio Maceo. All of them had opposed Batista, had supported the revolution and many of Castro's social initiatives. All were well known in Cuba as moderates, and Miró and Ray were former close associates of Castro who had been displaced. Before he defected, Miró had been Castro's choice for ambassador to Spain and later ambassador to the United States. Manuel Artime was noted as Miro's personal representative in Guatemala. Ray acknowledged that some former Batista followers had infiltrated the Frente, but he said that they would be removed.[39] Other reports said that factions within the Frente were trying to purge Ray and his group, who supported "Fidelisimo without Fidel."[40] Tony Varona and Justo Carrillo complained that naming Artime as commander was a coup against them by the CIA.[41] There were reports that internal disputes within the Frente were so violent that Artime was accosted, beaten and seriously injured by some of his opponents on the streets of Miami.[42]

Although the Cuban leaders denied it, CBS and many other sources reported that an invasion was coming, and that mobilization orders had been issued. After CBS reporter Stuart Novins reported that Miró Cardona was said to head the entire operation, the next day Miró issued a call for an insurrection inside Cuba. However, he told the *New York Times* that no invasion was forthcoming and that no United States aid was involved.[43]

In a letter to the editor of the *New York Times* dated April 8, Taylor Adams reminded the *Times* and President Kennedy that overthrowing the Castro regime had a "slim chance" for the U.S. He directed their attention to the American Expeditionary Force incursion into Russia in 1918–1919 as an "ill fated foray."[44] A similar letter was also published from Raymond D. Higgins, the assistant editor of *Hispanic American Report* and Martin B. Travis, a Stanford University professor.[45] On April 12, Brigade 2506 in Guatemala received orders to mobilize, and began to relocate to the disembarkment point, Puerto Cabezas, Nicaragua.[46] Within Cuba, there was some insurrectionary activity as one bomb damaged stores in Old Havana and another went off next to the Pepsi-Cola factory in Havana.[47]

At a meeting attended by the president, the secretary of state, the Joint Chiefs and other officials, Richard Bissell outlined the latest changes. The invasion was finally scheduled for April 17:

D-7 (seven days prior to invasion), Commence staging main force;

D-6, First vessel sails from staging area;

D-2, Diversionary landing in Oriente (night of D-3 to D-2);

D-2, Limited air strikes; two fake defector Brigade pilots in B-26s land in Florida to create the impression that the air strikes originate in Cuba;

D-Day, main landings–limited air strikes; two B-26s and liaison plane land on seized airstrip;

D-day to D+1, vessels return night of D to D+1 to complete discharge of supplies;

D+7, diversionary landing in Pinar del Río.

President Kennedy did not give final approval at this meeting; he was informed that the decision had to be made within a day or two.[48]

Meanwhile, guerrilla groups in Cuba were reported to be on the move and the government was sending in Cuban army troops to catch them. A possible insurrection was reported mounting in the Organos mountains in Pinar del Río Province, the westernmost part of Cuba. In central Cuba, about 100 guerrillas under Osvaldo Ramirez were reported to have smashed through a line of government troops and headed from the Escambray Mountains to the plains in Las Villas Province. A force of about 200 rebels remained in the Escambray under Major Evelio Duque.[49]

At a State Department press conference, President Kennedy ruled out, under any condition, an intervention in Cuba by the United States armed forces.[50] However, he told Bissell to let the air strikes go forward. When told that 16 planes would be sent, he ordered Bissell to keep it "minimal." Eight planes were authorized.[51]

On April 15, eight bombers from Nicaragua with Cuban air force emblems attacked three Cuban air force bases near Havana and Santiago. They destroyed several aircraft, but one of the attack planes was hit by anti–aircraft fire and had to land in Key West, Florida.[52] A Cuban pilot landed at Boca Chica Naval Air Base near Key West. The aircraft had bullet holes in it. Two other planes also landed in Key West and Miami. The pilot stated that he was a Cuban air force officer who had defected from Cuba, and he turned over his aircraft. Although Cuban leaders accused the United States of the attack, few of the diplomats in Havana believed it.[53] In the States, newspapers ran front page stories with such headlines as, "Castro's Pilots Bomb Their Own Bases." News reports listed that seven were dead and 29 wounded, and claimed that most of the Cuban air force was in ruins.[54] It would later be revealed that the "captured" airplane had come from Nicaragua, the "defecting" pilot had been a CIA contract agent, and the entire episode was a CIA psychological warfare trick.[55]

As the invasion boats were leaving Nicaragua, dictator Somoza from the dock asked the troops to bring him "a couple of hairs from Castro's beard."[56]

Former premier Miró Cardona, spokesman for and president of the Revolutionary Council, told the press that he had been in contact with the pilots, but again denied that there was an invasion.[57] The U.S. government denied that it had anything to do with the bombings. At the same time, the U.S. announced more naval maneuvers involving fourteen navy ships off of Mayport, Florida.[58]

A diversionary force was supposed to land in Oriente Province, near Guantánamo. However, three boats were lost. Another attempt was thwarted when heavy activity from the Cuban army and militias was noted and problems with another boat slowed down the landing attempt. The men reported that they could see "cigarettes glowing in the dark and stationary lights ready to shine on them." The group, led by Nino Díaz, were told to join the main force, but were too late. The invasion was underway.[59]

Another force landed near Baracoa: a Catholic organization led by Fidel Castro's former classmate José Ignacio Rasco. However, they were detected almost immediately, and retreated, leaving their arms and ammunition.[60]

From April 15 to April 17, the police rounded up as many as 100,000 suspects, including most of the CIA's 2,500 agents and 20,000 alleged anti–Castro sympathizers.[61] On April 16, the Cuban police and army rounded up 27 men for conspiring to assassinate Fidel Castro.[62] Government agents raided churches and arrested several priests; even Archbishop Pérez Serantes was placed under house arrest.[63] At another location state security agents arrested 15 people and found eight tons of hidden arms consisting of 40 cases of rifles, 12 cases of automatic weapons, 18 cases of Thompson machine guns, mortars and plastic explosives.[64]

Soon after the invasion fleet left the dock, Castro was aware that Cuba would come under attack. He probably expected a full invasion, with U.S. Marines landing on the beachhead.[65]

Just before the invasion, the president decided that the D-Day air strikes should be canceled to avoid accusations that the United States was directly involved in the invasion. The CIA protested, but the president would not relent. Secretary of State Rusk told General Cabell and Bissell that the U.S. must avoid the appearance of any interference. Secretary Rusk offered to let the CIA representatives speak directly to the president, but they decided otherwise.[66]

On the morning of April 17, former premier Miró Cardona announced to the press that an invasion was underway in Oriente Province, where, he said, his troops encountered no opposition. He also said that an internal uprising had been ordered. Cuban radio reported that there was fighting in Matanzas and that landings had been made at three places on Cuba's southern coast, one only about 90 miles from Havana.[67]

On that date, four transport ships carrying 1,297 members of Brigade 2506 traveled from Nicaragua to Cuba.[68] However, the Cuban air force was alerted, and the troops and their equipment were attacked as they were being loaded on landing craft and as they headed for the "Blue Beach" at the Bay of Pigs. The order canceling the air strikes was dispatched to Nicaragua, just as pilots were in their cockpits ready for takeoff, leaving the armada without air cover. Two of the four boats were sunk or grounded on the beach after being hit by bombs and strafing by Cuban air force planes. By the evening of D-Day the situation was so grim that the president contemplated sending in the Navy and Marines to extricate the brigade.[69] The next day, Allen Dulles met with former vice president Richard Nixon. Dulles told him, "Everything is lost. The Cuban invasion is a total failure." He blamed everything on the Kennedy administration.[70]

Committees for the Defense of the Revolution were mobilized in every neighborhood in Cuba, and anyone "suspicious" was detained.[71] During the fighting, an auxiliary Catholic bishop, Monsignor Eduardo Boza Masvidal, was arrested for hiding American currency and medical supplies for the Americans. Unconfirmed reports stated that the landing force had broken out and was moving into Matanzas Province. Reports that Raúl Castro had been captured or committed suicide were unconfirmed. The Revolutionary Council was standing by, ready to send the government in exile into Cuba.[72] Other reports said that the invasions were taking place at four locations in four provinces.[73] At the United Nations, Cuba accused the United States of aggression. This was denied by U.S. Ambassador Adlai E. Stevenson.[74] In a press conference, Secretary of State Dean Rusk stated that the United States would not intervene in Cuba. He said that only about 200 to 300 men were involved in the landings

José "Pepito" Miró Torra as a prisoner after the failed Bay of Pigs invasion. Pepito's father, José Miró Cardona, was the head of the Frente (Cuban Revolutionary Council), which attempted both an invasion and a domestic overthrow of the same Provisional Government that he had served as its premier. The following week, Miró Cardona made the cover of *Time* magazine under the caption "The Cuban Disaster." Later a law professor at the University of Puerto Rico, Miró Cardona would blame the CIA for the defeat at the Bay of Pigs (University of Miami Libraries, Cuban Heritage Collection).

and that the landings had been designed to get supplies to the anti–Castro underground already in place inside Cuba.[75]

At the United Nations, the Communist bloc and the Latin American countries pressed for resolutions to stop the insurgency.[76]

By April 21, 1961, 104 men from Brigade 2506 had been killed in action and the remainder were captured. One American paratrooper attached to the unit was among the dead. Four American and 10 Cuban exile airmen were also killed. In total, 1,204 Cuban exiles and two Americans were captured.

Among several executed immediately after the Cuban victory at the Bay of Pigs was Humberto Sorí Marín, the M–7–26 legal officer who had drafted the agrarian reform plan used in the occupied territory prior to the initiation of the Provisional Government. He had been an advisor to President Urrutia Lleó at the onset of the new government, was the chief judge in the first "show trial" of Major Jesús Sosa Blanco, and had been minister of agriculture until his version of agrarian reform was rejected.[77] Some news accounts noted that Sorí Marín, ironically, had been responsible for legalizing the executions.[78] Shortly after a Cuban tribunal sentenced Sorí Marín to death, his mother asked Fidel Castro to spare his life. Sorí Marín and Castro had fought as comrades in the mountains, and after the revolution they often met at Sorí Marín's house.[79] He might have been a close friend, but to Castro he was a traitor, and he was executed.

Thousands of potential enemies of the state were now in custody. There were reports that prisoners were being whisked from Havana to be warehoused elsewhere. Jails were so overcrowded that the Sports Palace was used as an extra jail. The government had arrested more than 100 Catholic priests for conspiring with the insurgents.[80]

After the defeat became known, there was sufficient blame to go around. From the view of most of the members of Brigade 2506, the Kennedy administration should have unleashed the might of the United States to support the assault. If not the Marines, the United States could have at least provided competent air cover. Most historians now say that Kennedy was "forgivably disposed" to permit subordinates to proceed despite many indications that the risk was great.[81] Many, including the CIA inspector general Kirkpatrick, accused the CIA of gross incompetence.[82] Some also accused it and Bissell of gross arrogance, functioning as a law unto themselves.[83]

Although the leadership and the Revolutionary Council had emphasized that the Bay of Pigs was not an invasion but a landing, the expected internal insurrection never took place. Although Manuel Ray was supposed to have been in charge of the insurrection, by the time the ships from Nicaragua disembarked, due to internal dissension his men were purged from the brigade. One demolitions expert, who was supposed to have been infiltrated into Cuba to wreak devastation in coordination with the landing, was left in Miami. Another 100 or so were left on the dock when they did not receive word in time.[84] Leaders complained that Manuel Artime was named brigade leader only because of politics: he was more conservative than Ray. In fact there were other well qualified and respected candidates for brigade commander, such as Ramón

Ramón M. Barquín was a Cuban army colonel who led a failed mutiny against President Fulgencio Batista in April 1956. He was captured, tried, sentenced and jailed with a number of his fellow officers. The CIA encouraged the Cuban military and Cuban Supreme Court to elevate him to the position of president when he was released from prison January 1, 1959. While he was in prison, his followers, Cuban military officers who opposed Batista, staged a second failed mutiny in Cienfuegos in September 1957, which led to a brutal retaliation by Batista. However, Barquín considered his organization to have been allied with M-7-26, the organization led by Fidel Castro, and he declined the presidency and recognized the Provisional Government led by Manuel Urrutia Lleó (Associated Press Photograph).

Barquín, who had a sterling reputation as a *Puro* and had been offered the position of president when Batista fled, but who had turned the matter over to M-7-26.[85]

Ray was almost universally considered the most competent and charismatic leader and had an organization on the ground in Cuba, in guerrilla groups and in the underground. As a former head of Civic Resistance and a former director of public works, he would have had the most gravitas in Cuba. Unlike Artime, he also spoke excellent English and could communicate with his CIA handlers.[86] Ray was a well-respected college professor who still had a following at the University of Havana as well as in the Cuban army with his former students at the military college. He could undermine much of Castro's base of support. He had been a Presbyterian lay leader with hundreds of influential allies throughout Cuba — a completely different line of support — and was the single best logistics expert in the brigade. He also had expertise in potential sabotage to the Cuban inventory of plant and equipment, yet he was considered too leftist for U.S. tastes. It was evident that Artime had not been able to inspire many of the former M–7–26 officers who were still in Miami and who wanted to return to Cuba to freelance, as guerrillas in the mountains, just as they had done in 1958.[87]

The invasion was defective in formation, design, and in execution. Most historians now say that the concept and design were risky at best.[88] Critics note that the brigade had been sent to an improbable site; the attack was not coordinated with opposition groups on the island, and the leadership of the invasion was unknown to most of the Cuban people. More importantly, as long as the Batistianos were involved in the brigade, "the people would rather live under Castro," even with all of his faults.

Chapter 19

The Alienation
of Affections Theory

Clearly, the Cuban-American affair deteriorated from a symbiotic relationship in 1898 to a love-hate relationship after the Platt Amendment was attached to their constitution in 1902–1903. Then we became amiable "good neighbors," next had a more businesslike relationship, and finally there was outright hatred that engendered a complete separation in 1961.

American policy toward Cuba was based in large part on the theory that Cuba had been infiltrated and controlled by the Soviet Union in its quest for world domination. The primary reason for the dissolution was reaction to the Soviet presence.

The prototypical Cuban/American couple, Desi Arnaz and Lucille Ball were also feuding at about the same time that the United States and Cuba were squabbling. The *I Love Lucy Show* ended in 1959, and after 20 years of marriage, Lucy and Desi were divorced in 1960. Although the show didn't engage in ethnic jokes per se, historians now note that Ricky "acculturated imperfectly and oblivious to the imperfections." He "mispronounced English and used idioms incorrectly, mangled syntax and routinely employed bad grammar," all of which made him a perfect target for satire and ridicule. In arguments Ricky could hold his own only by reverting to Spanish, and in Spanish, to monolingual Americans he sounded like he was angry, profane and overexcited.[1]

Actually, Desi Arnaz had become an entrepreneur and an innovator. His success can be seen as an American example of the kind of transculturation that Fernando Ortiz observed among various identity groups in Cuba. Among his many achievements was the creation of ancillary television rights, as the Arnaz family company, Desilu, filmed each episode, making them available later for syndication. In 1953, Lucille Ball and Desi Arnaz were paid an unprecedented $8,000,000 by CBS and their principal sponsor, the Philip Morris cigarettes company. The deal covered *I Love Lucy* for two and a half years. Under this agreement, the couple retained all of the residual rights to their program, which had the highest television viewership at that time.[2] By late 1957, Desilu had become the largest film producer in Hollywood after it acquired the former RKO Studios. By the time Lucille bought out Desi in 1962, the company's hard assets were valued at $20 million.[3] Desilu and Arnaz also produced other television series, such as *Our Miss Brooks*, *Make Room for Daddy* (also known as *The Danny Thomas Show*), *The Real McCoys*, *The Dick Van Dyke Show*, *The Untouchables* and *Wyatt Earp*.[4] All were huge successes.

Desi Arnaz had been accused of having a "roving eye" and was depicted of having strayed outside his marriage often and openly. Tabloids and magazines reported him in the company of other women. Lucille Ball had filed for divorce in 1944, when she accused him of having a girlfriend, but they reconciled. Rumors of other affairs persisted, and they finally divorced in 1960. Soon after the divorce, Desi married Edith Mack Hirsch, a younger red-head, a former cigarette girl at Santa Anita Racetrack, where Desi had been hanging out for years.[5] At the time, the couple had two children (Lucy, then 8; Desi IV, 7), and the company was reportedly grossing more than $20 million a year.[6] However, matters of the heart often take precedence, even over economic concerns.

In syndication, the character of Ricky Ricardo and his Cuban persona persist in U.S. culture. Because of immigration to our country from Cuba, there are other cultural points of contact.

Perhaps both sides needed a period of adjustment. Perhaps both needed to be educated; or perhaps there was a necessary period of maturation. For example, when Batista fled, Ernest Hemingway, who before Castro had been the most famous man in Cuba, quipped: "*Sic transit hijo de puta*," "There goes the son of a whore."[7] In April 1959, he told the press: "I believe in this movement.... It was a historical necessity to clean up things."[8] On his arrival back in Cuba in from a European tour in November 1959, Hemingway told the press that he still had "every sympathy" with the Castro regime.[9] However, within a year, Hemingway would relocate to the States, never to return; he never tried to retrieve his Cuban property. On July 2, 1962, he committed suicide. After her husband died, at a dinner at the White House in honor of American Nobel Prize winners with President Kennedy, Mary Welsh Hemingway offered to intercede with Castro. "I could jump into Cuba, you know. The Cubans liked my husband, and I know Fidel."[10] President Kennedy declined the offer.

Since 1959, Cuban-American relations first cooled and then froze as we parted company on almost every level. Cubans now argue that as early as February 12, 1959, U.S. hostility was evident when we refused to return to Cuba $424,000,000 in Cuban National Bank reserves that were held in the United States.[11] Despite our mutual extradition treaty, we also refused to extradite "war criminals" who had been granted asylum in the U.S. country. From the Cuban perspective these people were Batistiano torturers and murderers, seeking to return to power, who were disrupting the administration of orderly government and were indiscriminately bombing, sabotaging and terrorizing their country. Although the extradition treaty remains in force, neither country has extradited a single person since then. We could not deny that some of the raids on Cuba had originated in Florida and they violated their sovereignty. Despite these facts, the two nations still had relatively good relations until late 1959, but the relationship finally dissolved in 1961. Since then, Cuba and the United States have opposed each other on almost every front, from human rights to trade to terrorism.[12]

Many "experts" alleged that the breakup of Arnaz family and the breakup of Cuba and the United States were clear cases of alienation of affections: that Arnaz and Cuba had both been seduced. The U.S. State Department assumed that it was a clear case of seduction. At the time, there was a healthy competition between the United States and the Soviet Union for moral and economic authority. For a while, this theory appeared credible. With recent information, however, it is more rational to think that Cuba wanted merely to get the best deal it could get, and as the United States refused to deal, Cuba became more and more belligerent and hostile.[13] It was an emotional breakup.

To put the lover's triangle analogy in perspective, in the period 1956–1961 the Soviets were reeling from their intervention to crush the 1956 nationalistic insurgency in Hungary. Stated U.S. policy was to contain the Soviet Union. To do so, we placed military installations in strategic locations. The Soviets objected to the United States establishing military bases on their borders. We had at Guantánamo a military base inside Cuba. Likewise, we had not recovered from the McCarthy era, when some viewed every setback as a result of the presumed communist conspiracy. Even if the Cuban Revolution had been a popular nationalistic overthrow of a tyrant, Cuba was experiencing an anti–American "spasm" because we had refused to deal with it on its terms.[14]

Soon after victory, the Provisional Government requested that the United States sell Cuba parts and other military equipment to replenish the table of operations and equipment in the Cuban military inventory, most of which had been manufactured in America and had been serviced by advice from our military "advisors." We flatly refused to do so. Cuba then asked Britain, which had sold planes and other equipment to Batista even after the United States had refused to do so, to sell it munitions. After several months, and after the United States pressured Great Britain, that country also refused to sell to Cuba. Cuba tried to buy arms from several other countries, mostly in Western Europe. After a lapse of about six months, the Soviets announced that they would be willing to provide the sales during the Mikoyan trip. At the time, Cuba and the Soviet Union had not yet established diplomatic relations. There was time for the United States, Britain or France, for that matter, to have negotiated with Castro. The offer was announced on February 12, 1960.

At the same time, the Cuban government had been secretly negotiating with the Dominican Republic, viewed from within Cuba as a major threat to sovereignty. The "Liberation Army" that had been waiting a year to invade Cuba was soon dissolved. It might have become a Cuban "second front" a year later, when the U.S. did invade Cuba at the Bay of Pigs. Apparently Fidel Castro and Trujillo hated each other, but both had a potential common enemy in the United States.[15]

The Provisional Government was following an established negotiating pattern for Latin American countries dealing with the U.S. When Juan Perón was the dictator of Argentina, he articulated a "Third Way" foreign policy, to pit the United States and the Soviet Union against each other. He restored diplomatic relations and sold grain to Soviet Bloc countries. In 1948, Perón organized a student congress contemporaneous with the OAS organizational meeting in Bogotá. He sent Diego Luis Molinari, head of an Argentine Senate committee, to Cuba to recruit students to attend and to agitate against the United States. One of the students he recruited was Fidel Castro.[16]

Although he had opened Latin America to the Soviet Union, Perón agreed to vote with the United States at the United Nations, especially over Korea. For complying, he received a $125,000,000 credit from the United States.[17] After Perón was deposed, the United States provided approximately $287,000,000 in aid to Argentina. During the same period Argentina also received about $104,000,000 in trade from the Soviet Union. During the same period, Cuba received about $19,000,000 from the United States.[18]

By late 1959, Perón's fellow Argentine, Che Guevara, was head of the National Bank of Cuba and also was head of INRA's Department of Industrialization. His subordinates made an inventory of American products imported to Cuba and searched for substitutes. The search ended after the Mikoyan visit opened trade with the Soviet Union.[19] Soon after, Guevara traveled to Soviet bloc countries to order the substitute products.

Meanwhile, President Eisenhower continued to negotiate intermittently with Premier Khrushchev on variations of the themes of coexistence and confrontation. At the time, the Khrushchev Doctrine presented a more conciliatory position, which was to extend socialism through trade rather than revolution. The U.S. reciprocated. Vice President Nixon visited the Soviet Union, Khrushchev had visited the United States and Deputy Premier Mikoyan had visited the United States and Mexico, in an attempt to defrost the Cold War. When asked point-blank whether the Soviets were trying to seduce Cuba, Mikoyan stated: "There are many people who say that we are trying to disturb relations between Cuba and the United States. How could we, who are trying to improve relations with the United States, try to destroy your relations with them?"[20]

However, the U.S. did not believe a word. We were preoccupied with the Soviet Union. The Soviets were ahead of us in the space race.[21] We had a 2,500,000-man army, but they had a 3,900,000 man army.[22] We feared potential confrontations with the Soviets and the Red Chinese globally. In early 1960, the U.S. engaged in a covert war in Laos, where we had a "secret" army.[23] We were contemplating another in Vietnam,[24] and were managing similar operations in the Middle East, Africa and in Europe. In the Congo, the Soviets had threatened to send in troops to support a nationalistic leader that the U.S. clandestinely opposed.[25] Although the U.S. engaged in discussions with the Soviets about disarmament and reducing tensions, and had East-West Summit talks scheduled for May 1960, behind the scenes we maintained "cloak and dagger" spy operations worldwide, and the CIA had its Soviet equivalent, the KGB.

On a theoretical level, the U.S. State Department continued to maintain the foreign policy of John Foster Dulles, even after he passed away. Secretary of State Herter continued to issue policy statements reasserting U.S. philosophy on mutual assured destruction on every front. There was a pending summit between the Soviet Union and the United States. There were also pending talks on a nuclear test ban.

The U.S. did not have the complete confidence of its allies. We had not backed Britain, France and Israel in the Suez Crisis. Although France had been our ally, despite our protests it became the fourth nuclear power, after the United States, the Soviet Union and Great Britain.[26] At home, France was in crisis as its war in Algeria was not going well. The De Gaulle government faced an insurrection by Europeans living in Algeria, who had supporters within the French government and military. It needed to concentrate on its own problems rather than U.S. international interests.[27] In Germany, the U.S. opposed elections in Berlin, on the grounds that elections would be manipulated and Berlin would be swallowed up inside East Germany.[28]

Domestically, the U.S. was still routing out suspected communist agents and investigating anyone who might be a fellow traveler. It was an election year, and Democrats called for the Eisenhower administration to stimulate the economy. They controlled both houses of Congress, and the president threatened to veto every piece of legislation that differed from his policies.[29]

With the enormous complexity of the Eisenhower administration's problems at the time, Cuba was not considered to be very important. Even in early 1960, it was clear that both sides had misconstrued many of the pertinent facts, were emotional and impetuous, and had made costly "miscalculations."[30] The U.S. tried to squeeze Cuba diplomatically and economically. Because we objected to Cuban arms purchases, they had to pay double the actual cost to obtain weapons.[31] However, Cuba only hurt itself in its hasty January 1960 deal with the Soviet Union.[32] The Soviets got a below-market-rate, low-interest loan that allowed it to charge high prices for its products against a worldwide price for sugar, appreciably lower than Cuba could have gotten under the existing trade policy according to the U.S. Sugar Act. The Soviets also forced Cuba to buy big ticket items such as machinery at whatever prices they wanted to set. Under the terms of the agreement, there was no reason why the Soviets could not buy cheap Cuban sugar and trans-ship it to get world market prices.[33]

By early February, congressional leaders such as J. W. Fulbright, chairman of the Senate Foreign Relations Committee, questioned State Department policies and the U.S. diplomatic stance toward Cuba.[34] Fulbright argued that if we did not change the conditions that led Cuba to revolution, the rest of Latin America would revolt.[35] In hindsight, the United States could have given Cuba a far better deal than it got from the Soviets. However, it is clear that neither side even tried to deal.

From a Cuban perspective, the U.S. forced them to spend a high proportion of their domestic product on military expenses. Those monies should have been used to invest in their economy and social revolution. The U.S. embargoed their economy after October 1960,[36] attacked their country in 1961, came within a whisker of having to use nuclear force in 1962, and threatened their leaders with assassination. We have kept them in a state of fear of invasion and perhaps near starvation since.

Initially, Fidel Castro was actually not actually a member of the Provisional Government, although as head of the military, he was the most influential person in the country. The U.S. could have negotiated with Cuba from the outset and brought President Urrutia and his cabinet to the forefront to deal directly with them. We had done the same with our former enemies after World War II at the same time we were prosecuting some of their former leaders for war crimes. It would later be revealed that at least one cabinet member, Minister of Finance Rafo López Fresquet, was our agent, by act if not in contract, and most of the rest were "moderates" with deep ties to the United States.[37]

As soon as the Provisional Government came to power, traditional economists in the Cuban government had proposed establishing deals with the United States.[38] When Castro came to the United States, approximately 100 days after the Provisional Government gained power, he was told by no lesser authority than Vice President Nixon that the United States policy was trade, not aid, at a time when the United States was aiding practically every other Latin American country by providing them arms. At the time, Cuba needed help with its infrastructure. It also faced a perceived threat from the Batista followers still in Cuba and in the "Liberation Army" in the Dominican Republic, by the hostile Dominican dictator Trujillo, and in a group of exiles organizing within the United States.

The prototype for negotiations would have been the U.S. relationship with Bolivia. Under Ángel Víctor Paz Estenssoro, Bolivians exhibited the same kind of nationalism, had the same kind of revolution, undertook the same kind of agrarian reform, nationalized the mining industry, and instituted the same kind of provisional government as Cuba had. Between 1953 and 1961, although the U.S. espoused "trade, not aid," we supported Paz with $192,000,000 in aid. In 1957, the U.S. supplied more than 40 percent of the entire Bolivian national budget. This kept Bolivia, with leadership as radical as Cuba's, within the Western sphere of influence.[39]

As noted, Argentina tried to strike a similar bargaining stance under Juan Perón. Perón had been accused of fascist and Nazi leanings, and the U.S. also accused him of being too cozy with communists. The U.S. tried to undermine his election as president and afterwards tried to isolate him in the same way we would later try with Cuba.[40] But in the end, the Eisenhower administration sent him aid and we supported him on a quid pro quo basis.[41]

At the same time Brazil was trading with both the United States and the Soviet Union and we treated Brazil as an ally.

Egypt under Gamal Abdel Nasser took the position that it was a "neutral" nation, apparently to play the Western bloc against the Eastern bloc for economic advantage. Castro had sent Che Guevara on a mission in May 1959 to the United Arab Republic. At the time,

Cuba was negotiating with the United States exclusively. Soon Cuba would also deal with the Soviets.

Some writers have observed that the U.S. missed other possible ways to take advantage of Castro's ascension to power. He could have used us and we could have used him. For example, Carlos Alberto Montaner points out that Castro would have loved to have American encouragement to fix his sights on the Trujillo regime in the Dominican Republic or the Somoza regime in Nicaragua.[42] The U.S. could have ingratiated itself by being Cuba's sponsor and patron. Had we done so, Castro might have become a democrat and Cuba might not have become a despotic totalitarian Communist dictatorship.

Most historians now agree that it would have been better policy to butter up Castro than to alienate Cuba. Although Cuba and the United States had good relations in 1959, when Castro came to visit the United States, President Eisenhower, an avid sportsman like Castro, decided he'd rather play golf at Augusta National Golf Course than greet Castro. In exploring Castro's psyche, Peter I. Bourne, a psychiatrist and historian, emphasizes that Eisenhower conspicuously and conveniently left town, and Castro reacted to this apparent rejection with frustration and anger.[43] The U.S. had already recognized the Provisional Government and the two nations were still bosom allies. By that time, Castro had most probably already personified the Cuban national identity as his destiny. In all probability, Castro took Eisenhower's decision as a diplomatic and personal affront. Montaner accurately points out that Castro considered himself a sportsman in all matters, including diplomacy, and thus had a heightened sense of competitiveness. "His ideal formula for 'settling' the problem of Cuba versus the USA is shutting oneself up in a room or going on a shark hunt with the Yankee chief and Indian wrestling like two old savage leaders until one of the two gives up."[44]

At the same time the U.S.-Cuba relationship with Cuba was dissolving, U.S. allies such as Great Britain were reluctantly doing so also. The British government believed that hardball U.S. policies created a self-fulfilling prophecy, making Cuba more susceptible to communist influence than it might have otherwise been. However, the British considered the United States' special relationship with Britain and acquiesced.[45]

Most of Castro's biographers, as well as Wayne S. Smith, a former head of the United States Interests Section in Havana and a longtime American diplomat in Cuba, believe that Castro has a "messianic complex," and had a compulsive interest in fulfilling a "second liberation" of Latin America.[46] The U.S. had every reason to know that. There is evidence to show that CIA inspector general Lyman Kirkpatrick met with representatives of M–7–26 in Venezuela in August 1958, when plans were made to replace Batista with a government headed by Urrutia.[47] Therefore, the U.S. had time to plan for his ascendency. As soon as he became provisional president, Urrutia petitioned the OAS rather than the United Nations or the United States for help.

Moreover, both Wayne Smith and Ambassador Bonsal relate that Castro was initially willing to negotiate. At the time, Castro described the United States' approach as "respectful."[48] After he was rebuffed several times, Castro accused all opponents as enemies in a "life and death battle" and accused them of a "reactionary campaign" against the Revolution.

The OAS could have acted as a mediator, whereby the parties could air grievances privately rather than in public through position statements and press releases, and through mutual assent both sides could have presented a public perception that each could claim as a negotiation victory. However, the OAS was incompetent. Both sides were fixed in their

Premier Fidel Castro and Comandantes William Morgan and Eloy Gutiérrez Menoyo announce that they had tricked Dominican dictator Rafael Trujillo to foil an invasion and attempted takeover of the Provisional Government in September 1959. At the time, the most immediate threat to Cuba came from Trujillo and his allies, including the leaders of a would be provisional government who were captured. Later, however, Morgan, an expatriate American, would-be tried and convicted for treason and executed. Gutiérrez Menoyo would defect, but later return to be captured and imprisoned for 20 years (University of Miami Libraries, Cuban Heritage Collection).

diplomatic positions. The United States failed to take advantage of the situation to bargain with Cuba rather than attempt to humiliate Cuba over Castro's perceived role as "liberator" at an OAS meeting in Santiago, Chile, in August, 1959.[49]

The United States used baseball terms to describe its diplomatic position with Cuba and, by early 1960, moved into the "hardball" phase. Although Cuba had been politically fragmented when the revolution occurred, by August 1959 Castro had become the metaphorical field manager and was close to taking over as general manager in charge of Cuban foreign policy. Castro's destiny had become Cuba's destiny.

Most of the Americans involved in diplomacy probably were not aware that if baseball is the national sport of Cuba, the second most popular is chess, and every Cuban leader was considered a master tactician. Seemingly every crossroads in Cuba has a Capablanca chess club, named for José Raúl Capablanca, world chess champion, who lost only one game over a 10-year period. In 1959, Fidel Castro was eager to bargain, but soon figured out that the Eisenhower administration was more interested in undermining his government than in actual negotiations.

Castro was aware of the Eisenhower Doctrine in the Middle East. Castro's view of a Latin American movement was similar to the Pan-Arab movement, which was seen by Pres-

Fidel Castro (front right) playing Cuba's second favorite sport, chess (other persons not identified). Castro could not pass up an opportunity to compete, whether it was baseball, track,
basketball, chess or diplomacy. As a student, he gave his school's valedictory address and was
selected Cuba's best scholastic athlete by newspapers. As premier, he would miss cabinet meetings
because he stopped to play in sandlot baseball games. In 1959, he won the Hemingway fishing
tournament. However, persistent rumors that he was a major league baseball prospect are exaggerated (University of Miami Libraries, Cuban Heritage Collection).

ident Eisenhower and Secretary Dulles as susceptible to Communist influence. The president
received congressional authority to send in the Marines to protect Lebanon's Christian
Falange president, who had extended his power over the Moslem Lebanese minority, in
contravention of the Lebanese Constitution. Castro knew that President Eisenhower did
not seek a similar authorization from Congress vis-a-vis Cuba, and could assume, therefore,
that he had plenty of time at the diplomatic level. He also was aware that the United States,
despite its "trade, not aid" position, had provided $200,000,000 in economic and military
aid to the Middle East.

However, Castro had not anticipated attacks on Cuban culture. The elimination of
Cuban professional baseball represented one of the most symbolic blows to the Cuban
national pride. At the time, baseball was our common national pastime. Cubans are perhaps
even more passionate about baseball than Americans, and baseball remains part of their
national persona. Like many other Cubans, Fidel Castro had an emotional attachment to
the game. Castro had said that professional baseball would continue in Cuba, even if he
had to pitch.[50] He threw out the first pitch on opening day of the International League season.[51] When there was a financing crisis for the Havana Sugar Kings, he brought the team

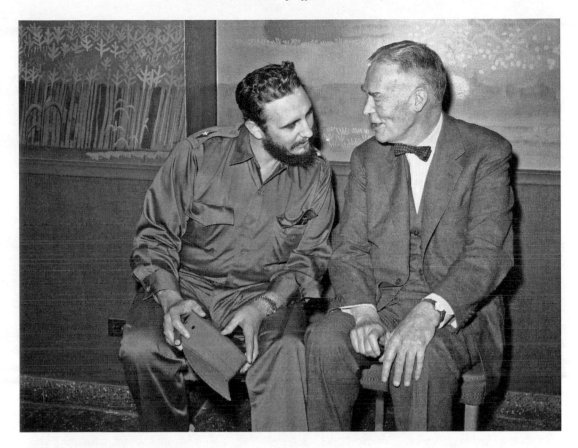

Fidel Castro meets Christian Herter in Washington, April 1959. Later as secretary of state, Herter would play "hardball" with Castro. Among the policies was to order the president of the International Baseball League to cancel the franchise of the Havana Sugar Kings as part of a show of strength to Cuba (Associated Press).

owner to the United States to confer and agreed that the government should subsidize the sport and the franchise, if needed.[52] He played in exhibition games bedecked in a baseball uniform, and the pictures were widely disseminated.[53] Castro cancelled cabinet meetings to play or attend games.[54] After the Sugar Kings won the Junior World Series in October 1959, the victory was a national celebration and a source of national pride. The decision to relocate the minor league Havana Sugar Kings, seen as "Cuba's team," a privately owned team playing in a privately owned league, from Cuba in the summer of 1960, less than a year after the team had won the Junior World Series, was a foreign policy decision by the U.S. State Department.[55] Castro protested the move as a violation of "all codes of sportsmanship."[56] It was perceived as an act of retribution.

At the time, a new professional league was being contemplated, and instead of "hardball" diplomatic tactics, baseball should have been a matter for diplomatic negotiations.[57] Castro dearly wanted Havana to become a major league city.[58]

If life imitates art, and the Arnaz problem was similar to the Ricardo problem, then the problem was either a lack of communication, an abundance of acrimonious misinterpretations or both. The result, in any case, was divorce.[59] Although parents may divorce, the children remain a constant reminder that divorce is only a legal procedure. The parties may have continuing commitments to the children and to each other for other contractual reasons. By 1961, the United States and Cuba had the same problem.[60]

Land Reform

Another reason given for the breakup was objection to the "legal theft" of American property by the Cuban government. Although the United States had a lot to lose in Cuba, it did almost nothing to protect its interests. Actually, the concept of land reform was initially popular with most Cubans. Moreover, anti–American sentiment did not reside entirely with the Castro family and with the communists; it existed in some degree among almost every class of Cuban society and across the Cuban political spectrum during the period 1957–1961. For example, the CIA-backed insurrectionist counter-revolutionary organizations, led by Artime Buesa and Ray Rivero, supported land reform.[61]

From onset, the Provisional Government was attempting "revolution" domestically by diversifying its economy and consolidating power. To do that, it threatened "American interests" in Cuba, not just in terms of trade, but in terms of property rights. The American interests issue was nothing new to Latin America. It had arisen in Cuba in the 1930s and also had precedents in Mexico, Argentina, Venezuela, Bolivia, Guatemala and others. It had also arisen in Japan, where land reform provisions were contained in a constitution devised by General Douglas McArthur. Other countries, such as Iran, Egypt and Indonesia, had similar policies.[62] Secretary of State John Foster Dulles (deceased in 1959), had been an international lawyer for many years whose job was to represent American companies in dealings abroad. He had to have been acutely aware of the Act of State Doctrine, which dictates that decisions of other countries relating to their internal affairs would not be questioned by the United States.[63] But we were locked into our foreign policy of confronting to Communism, and were applying it to Cuba. When President Eisenhower took his 1960 trip to Latin America, the U.S. was attempting to freeze Cuba diplomatically at the same time that there was an implied threat of invasion. The U.S. lobbied other OAS members to vote against measures that Cuba considered to be important and sought Latin American allies to take our position, to isolate and confront Cuba, using a "hard line" taken right from the John Foster Dulles playbook: We were pushing Cuba diplomatically "to the brink."

The late secretary of state's brother, Allen W. Dulles, was an international lawyer in the same law firm, with the same background. As head of the CIA, he had supervised the overthrow of elected governments in Iran and Guatemala. On March 17, 1960, he was officially delegated the responsibility of doing the same in Cuba.

The Dulles brothers had saved intervention of United Fruit property by overthrowing the Árbenz regime just six years earlier. It would later be revealed that some of the ships used by Brigade 2506 were supplied by United Fruit.[64]

Had the U.S. actually contemplated land reform and considered the risk-reward relationship inherent in covert war, we could have made sure that American companies were given just compensation, and probably saved many American companies from expropriation. After the losses occurred, American taxpayers had to foot the bill for tax write-offs and insurance companies had to pay claims arising from expropriations. At the time the issue was not so much the amount of the losses, but how they would be repaid.[65] Cuba offered bonds. The U.S. could easily have negotiated loans to pay the amount of judgments due American landholders, saving the American taxpayers and insurance companies full exposure for losses.[66] The U.S. also could have negotiated ways to minimize the judgments, by transfer of some of the properties to Cuban interests, as some American companies had done previously.[67] However, as a result, many American companies and individuals lost everything and many Cubans and Americans suffered even more in the pain and agony of displacement and separation.

From a commercial standpoint, the U.S. lost the entire Cuban market, and Cuba lost its number one customer. It would take several years to replace the loss of jobs and revenue.

The Cuban government did not begin to expropriate all American property until after the U.S. government imposed the trade embargo, months after the Cuban/Soviet trade deal.

Retribution and Retaliation

Any reconciliation of affections probably was doomed when the Cuban government entered into a trade agreement with the Soviet Union early in 1960. At that time, in the midst of the Cold War, the U.S. took the position that any cooperation with the Soviet Union was a pact with the Devil: appeasement to dark, evil forces hostile to U.S. security interests. In Latin America interference by the Soviet Union was viewed as a subversion of U.S. status under the Monroe Doctrine and a violation of the Rio Treaty, which required all Latin American nations to support one another militarily.[68]

Despite the potential interference of the Soviets into the U.S. sphere of influence, we had interests to protect, beyond resentment over our displacement as a trading partner with Cuba. However, at that time, the U.S. had military commitments to 48 other countries, and U.S. experts said that we did not have the manpower to fulfill them.[69]

During the time that Cuba negotiated with the Soviet Union to strike the trade deal, the respective ambassadors from the U.S. and from Cuba had been withdrawn, and Cuba and the United States were mostly talking about each other and past each other rather than to each other. The Mikoyan visit to Cuba occurred on the same day that the United States rejected an offer from the Brazilian government to mediate our disputes.[70] At the same time, although the U.S. was ostensibly concerned by Soviet intrusion into "our" domain, Premier Khrushchev had visited the United States and met personally with President Eisenhower at Camp David in September 1959. A summit meeting was planned for later in the year, and the U.S. sought to soften its confrontational position. However, as to Cuba, the State Department was doing more hardball posturing. Confrontation did not work and probably hardened the Cubans position: Despite threats from proponents of the military might of the United States to pulverize the Provisional Government, they did not back down. By that time, they knew all about U.S. negotiating tactics such as "brinksmanship," which was referenced for sarcastic, comedic effect in the Cuban newspapers.[71] Had the U.S. known that there was a deal brewing, we could have easily upped the ante, making any potential deal too expensive for the Soviets. During the "trade, not aid" period, the U.S. gave over $53,000,000 in aid in 1959 to Latin American countries, mostly for military expenses. In 1960, military aid rose to over $68,000,000.[72]

Americans claimed more than $1 billion in tax losses in Cuba.[73] American businesses lost an estimated $42,000,000 a year in 1960 dollars in shipping to Cuba. United Fruit estimated it had lost $60,000,000. Even before the Bay of Pigs, First National City Bank of New York estimated its Cuban losses as $45,000,000, and it had already written off tax losses of $36,000,000.[74] American Tobacco Company had already taken more than $16 million worth of deductions.[75] American oil companies lost $130,000,000.[76]

By early 1960, tourism had declined to a trickle. Airline service was down substantially and Cuban Airlines announced it was losing $10,000 a day to maintain service to New York.[77] Soon air passengers to Miami would be threatened with skyjackings, where passengers would be taken to Cuba at gunpoint.[78] Skyjackings lasted into the 1970s.

By early 1960, many of the expatriates from the American country club communities in Havana and similar enclaves had already returned to the United States. Almost all would have relocated soon after September 30, 1960, when President Eisenhower advised all American nationals to leave. For some Americans the "return" was really an exile: Some of them had been born and raised in Cuba.[79] By early 1960, the United States had become the "other," a scapegoat, in much the same way that foreigners were used as boogeymen by medieval Spain and the way Muslims, Jews and Protestants continued to be used in Franco's Spain. By early 1960, the Cuban government changed school textbooks to delete references to the United States as a benefactor of Cuba. Students were taught that the United States was an imperial power which had, in effect, colonized Cuba to rob it of its wealth without consideration of the economic and social needs of its population. English-language textbooks and English teachers in Cuban schools became extremely rare. Attendance was down at the Protestant churches,[80] and Santa Claus had been sent into exile. Customs such as the Christmas tree and Christmas carols like Cuban favorites "Jingle Bells" and "Rudolph the Red-Nosed Reindeer" were banned in public places. If Cubans wanted to decorate a tree, it would have to be a palm or a sturdy Cuban hardwood, as all materials had to be made in Cuba.[81] Guayabera-clad Don Feliciano, "Sir Friendly" in English, had been elevated to take Santa's place to pass out gifts on Three Kings Day, which was returned to preeminent status.[82] Popular gifts were toy rifles and cap machine guns.[83] Instead of cha-cha dresses and cha-cha boots, teenage girls would prefer unisex combat fatigues. Cuban kids gave up playing at cowboys and Indians and instead played Cubans and Yankee invaders.[84]

By that time, the Batista-decreed Thanksgiving holiday had been eliminated. Radio stations had stopped playing American music, and American-style television broadcasting had been replaced. Advertising for American products and services had almost been eliminated. In 1959, the Ministry of Commerce passed a regulation that all packaging should use only Spanish words. The government intended to purify Cuban Spanish to eliminate Spanglish, as baseball terms were changed to create a Cuban argot: for example, *el pitcher* became *el lanzador*, a term that sounds like it has its antecedents in the bullrings of Cadíz, rather than the playing fields of Cooperstown, New York.[85]

Many of the enclaves and mansions of the wealthy had become multifamily homes for the dispossessed. Many American businesses in Cuba had been intervened, and almost all would eventually be nationalized. Many companies had relocated. Most of the American newspapers had closed. *The Times of Havana* published its final edition in November 1960. It relocated to Miami to join the numerous Cuban Spanish-language publications that emigrated with their ownership.

Miami was now transformed from a tourist haven to a "city of intrigue."[86] The CIA presence extended to planning and executions of other projects throughout the Western Hemisphere. Many of the former members of the Provisional Government and M–7–26 became CIA "assets." However, soon these were accusations that the Cuban government and/or the communists had infiltrated the CIA and anti–Castro organizations. In Miami, a federal grand jury heard such charges just days after the Bay of Pigs incident.[87] Among the Cubans living in the diaspora were former president Urrutia Lleó, former premier Miró Cardona, and many other high-ranking former friends and colleagues of Castro. Miró Cardona would become the titular leader of the Bay of Pigs invasion and the spokesman for Brigade 2506. Almost all of the former leaders in exile had ties to the CIA and few would ever see Cuba again. Many of them had expected to return to Cuba within a matter of days and presumed the United States would invade Cuba. By August 1963, former premier Miró Cardona would speak for many when he accused President John F. Kennedy of breaking a "promise" to invade.[88] During the 1970s groups opposed to dialogue with the Cuban government terrorized their opponents in the exile community by intimidation, bombing and assassinations.[89]

By early 1960, as many as 250,000 Cubans had immigrated to the United States.[90] By late 1961, 125,000 more were in Havana waiting eagerly for visas. Approximately 1,350 Cubans arrived in Miami daily.[91] The population of Cuba in 1960 was about six million. About a tenth would leave.

Since then, 114 provincial and municipal governments in exile ("*municipios*") wait in Miami to return. For a number of years, a government in exile was in place, ready to return to Cuba on a moment's notice. Almost none of the émigrés considered themselves to be immigrants; many came to this country on a tourist visa and most expected to return in a few weeks or so.

Although Cuban immigrants would be relocated to 49 states, in Miami there were soon complaints from African American and other groups that Cuban immigrants were taking their jobs and that the public school and other government services were overwhelmed.[92]

Although commerce and diplomacy ceased, Americans still listened to Cuban-inspired music, if not authentic Cuban music. The cha-cha would remain popular. In 1960, Elvis Presley's "It's Now or Never," with a cha-cha beat and the *claves* conspicuously in the background, was a number one hit record. In 1962, Bobby Rydell still sang that everybody loves "The cha-cha-cha." Ray Barretto sang the most authentic Cuban song to ever hit the American charts "El Watusi," entirely in Havana street slang.[93] It made no difference to the American music audience that Barretto was a native New Yorker of Puerto Rican heritage.

However, interest in Cuban inspired clothing and styles declined.

American churches were no longer be able to send large numbers of missionaries to Cuba. The Presbyterian Church, which had three members in the cabinet of the Provisional Government, attempted to continue an amicable relationship with the government in Cuba. However, one of the former cabinet members, Manuel (Manolo) Ray Rivero, became a leader of anti–Castro organizations while the others, José Antonio (Pepin) Naranjo and Faustino Pérez, remained in Cuba as influential government officials and became members of the Communist Party. Their pastor, Raúl Fernández Ceballos, remained a government official as well as an official of the church. Once part of the United Presbyterian Synod of New Jersey, in 1967 the Presbyterian-Reformed Church in Cuba became an autonomous denomination. By that time, the membership in Cuba had dwindled to about a third of its former size.[94] At the First Spanish Presbyterian Church of Miami, the membership of "golden exiles," mostly professionals such as physicians and lawyers, grew from 87 in 1958 to 105 in 1960. The pastor, Martín Añorga, began to disseminate anti-communist materials.[95]

The counter-revolution was now depicted by many of its members and by the Catholic Church as a religious crusade against the government.[96] By early 1960, many of the non–Cuban Catholic clergy had left Cuba. After the Bay of Pigs incident, they were expelled. Several Catholic institutions, such as Universidad Católica de Santo Tomás de Villanueva in Havana and Fidel Castro's alma mater, Belen Jesuit Preparatory School, would relocate

President Kennedy meets representatives from Brigade 2506 on December 27, 1962, in Palm Beach, after they had been released from prison by Fidel Castro after negotiations were reached with Donovan, Sanchez and Ruiz-Williams. Left to right in the garden of the "Winter White House"; Robert Perez San Roman, who escaped by boat during invasion; José Perez San Roman; President Kennedy; Manuel Artime; Erneido Oliva; and Enrique Ruiz-Williams (AP Photo/William J. Smith).

to Miami and reopen. Santo Tomás reopened in 1961 as Biscayne College, and is now St. Thomas University. Eventually, the archdiocese of Miami built a shrine to Our Lady of Charity, *El Cobre*, and her Saint's Day, September 9, was celebrated by hundreds of thousands of Cubans in Miami.[97] The Shrove Tuesday carnival also transported to Miami, and was observed as El Paseo.

Santería made inroads into American culture. Besides the Church of the Lukumi Babalu Aye (documented in the United States Supreme Court case), similar churches and botanicas, stores selling Afro-Cuban religious articles, opened in many major cities. Santería is practiced not only in Cuban enclaves like Miami, Hialeah, and Union City, New Jersey, but Oyotunji Village, South Carolina, is an entire Santería community.[98] It is unclear how many of the hundreds of thousands of worshipers who observe El Cobre day in Miami are followers of Santería, but Chango's birthday and Babalu Aye's birthday are observed in Miami.[99]

In Cuba, Russian tourists could not replace the Americans in number, or in other ways. "No ride taxis, no chew gum, no shoe shine, no beer, no bird food, no shave blades, no chase the Cuban señoritas," one immigrant told the *Washington Post*.[100] Some experts say (perhaps hyperbolically) that Cuba lost its entire professional class in the greatest brain drain in the history of civilization.[101]

With the demise of professional baseball in Cuba, most of the professional Cuban players under contract to American teams would remain in the States. As intercountry relations were dissolving, in a game on July 23, 1960, the Washington Senators baseball team executed an all-Cuban triple play.[102] With two runners on base, the batter, Whitey Herzog, hit to pitcher Pedro Ramos, who threw to first baseman Julio Bécquer, who threw to shortstop Jose Valdivielso to complete the play, the only triple play in the American League that year. The odds of that occurring with three Cuban players in the American major leagues is astronomical.

Many of the few players who were able to remain in professional baseball distinguished themselves. After the Bay of Pigs and the Cuban Missile Crisis, immigration of Cuban baseball players completely stopped. Among the expatriated players were Tony Pérez, who would be named to the Baseball Hall of Fame, and players like Camilo Pascual, Tony Oliva, Luis Tiant, Jr., and Bert Campaneris, should probably also be given consideration. The first Cuban inducted into the Hall of Fame was Martín Dihigo, who never played a day in the major leagues because of his race. Called by some the greatest all-around player who ever lived and perhaps the greatest Latin ballplayer of all time,[103] he most probably was the first avowed communist ever inducted. After his playing career ended, he was a sports reporter for *Hoy*, the communist newspaper. Reportedly, Dihigo was exiled in Mexico in 1955 when he met Fidel Castro and Che Guevara and donated money for the Granma expedition. He relocated to Cuba in January 1959, was briefly minister of sports, and died in 1971. He is venerated in Cuba.[104]

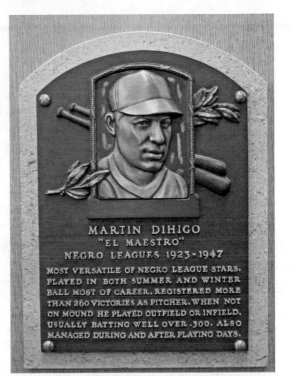

Cuban Martín Dihigo was posthumously inducted into the United States Baseball Hall of Fame in Cooperstown, New York, in 1977. Generally considered one of the greatest all around players in baseball history, he never played in the major leagues because of segregation. After he retired as a player, he wrote articles for *Hoy*, the Cuban Communist newspaper, and reportedly helped sponsor the 1956 Granma invasion of Cuba. After Batista fled, Dihigo returned to Cuba, where he served as minister of sports until his death in 1971. He is probably the only Communist in the American Baseball Hall of Fame.

Although the stands at Gran Stadium, home to the Havana Sugar Kings, had been mostly empty before 1959, baseball in Cuba was rejuvenated. The pipeline of talent to the United States was soon clogged, but elite players remained in Cuba as hometown heroes, to play professionally for local teams in new government-sponsored leagues, before fanatical fans in packed stadiums where the ushers were *barbudos* and the beer ads on the outfield fences were replaced by communist slogans while Afro-Cuban drummers beat out rhythms in support of their favorites.[105] By that time, we had already started to go our way, and they theirs.

By that time, because most of the Cuban opposition leaders had immigrated to the United States, there was little opposition to the Castro regime remaining in Cuba.

At War with Socialism

Although the U.S. often described the Cold War as a dispute between private enterprise and socialism, in 1959 and 1960 almost all U.S. allies invoked socialism in one form or another. For example, Great Britain had nationalized its coal production, health care, the Bank of England, almost the entire British transport industry, and the iron and steel industries. In theory, the means of production, distribution and exchange of necessary industries were acquired because the managers of many of these industries had not performed well. The British Labour Party could say that any profits from these industries benefited the entire British population.

Under Batista, the Cuban government had been mixed, but it granted licenses and permits, and some entities, such as the monopoly electric and telephone companies, were owned by American companies. In his political campaigns, Batista called himself a socialist.

The Provisional Government originally comprised members of several different political parties, men who had among them several political philosophies. Some of them were "liberals," meaning that they supported the free market system in most things. Almost all would, however, have accepted that land reform and nationalization of the utilities were necessary. Some, like former Minister of Public Works Ray Rivero, did not object to any of Castro's economic reforms; they did, however, object to a dictatorship.

Most U.S. allies that had nationalized many of their industries had done so in a democratic framework. However, in Cuba, there were no democratic elections. Many Cuban Americans on the scene at that time felt the Revolution was hijacked. Many of the leaders and officials of the Provisional Government did not survive the period or eventually went into exile.

The positions and policies of the Castros have not always been consistent. At first, Castro supported elections. However, he kept putting them off, and in the interim, the cabinet enacted all of the laws. After he forced most of the moderates from office, only his followers remained in the cabinet.

Fidel Castro now says that he was a communist from the onset of the revolution, but the facts do not fully support this assertion. It is more likely that he is merely an opportunist.[106] The CIA and State Department thoroughly investigated an alleged communist connection but failed to establish that he was ever a true believer.[107] Although he produced a body of written work, none of his early documents make a single reference to Marxism or quote communist sources.[108]

Another view is that American foreign policy forced Cuba "into the arms of Communism."[109] Although there is ample evidence to support this theory, the U.S. was not the catalyst for the Cuban Revolution, which had many different aspects. The U.S. is a huge and mighty country, but Castro has been able to resist everything we have thrown against his regime. If a favorable Castro legacy remains viable in Cuba, it is because of the attention given to domestic issues. The U.S. does, however, make a good boogeyman for the regime.[110]

Batista was opposed by the communists until the late 1930s, when he began negotiating with them. By that time, the Cuban communists were among the most subservient and obedient to the Soviet Union in the world. The Soviets dictated policy to the Cuban party. In the Soviet Union, former party leaders who may have had a minor disagreement with party policy were executed after show trials as an object lesson to anyone who would not completely submit to party discipline. As World War II approached, the acid test for party loyalty became whether Cuban communists could accept the Treaty of Nonaggression between Germany and the USSR. Signed in Moscow, August 24, 1939, it established an alliance with the Nazis. Most Cuban communists acquiesced, and followed the party line. In many other countries, like in the United States, the Communist Party lost about half of its membership over the treaty and over Moscow's insistence of blind obedience to party discipline.

The communists openly supported Batista and he gratefully accepted their support when he ran for the presidency of Cuba in 1939.[111] At the beginning of World War II there had been accusations that Batista's affinity with the communists was so strong that, like the Soviet Union, Cuba would accept an alliance with Germany.[112] Communists occupied influential cabinet posts in his 1940 administration.[113] In their 1945 book *En Defensa del Pueblo* (In Defense of the People), communists Carlos Rafael Rodríguez and Blas Roca stated that "the people's idol, the great man of our national politics" was Fulgencio Batista.[114] When Batista performed his coup in 1952, the leadership of the Communist Party (Partido Socialista Popular), endorsed the coup in the name of returning order and stability, by displacement of the democratic regime with Batista, an old ally.[115]

Castro allegedly led the 1953 Moncada attack to restore democratic principles.[116] The communists denounced the attack as foolish, "putschist and adventurist."[117] They called Castro a gangster and a madman.[118]

Although the Communist Party was supposedly banned, members actively supported former president Grau San Martín during a phony presidential election set up by Batista in 1954. The Castro brothers were in jail at the time and opposed the election. When asked directly whether he was a communist, Fidel Castro emphatically denied it: "If I were a communist, I would belong to that party and not to the July 26 movement."[119]

While he was in Mexico preparing an invasion of Cuba, Castro was arrested by the Mexican police. During that time, Batista accused Castro of being a communist. There is some evidence that Castro had made contact with the Soviet embassy in Mexico City and that some of his close associates were allegedly communists. Raúl Castro had belonged to the Socialist Youth but was excommunicated by the Communist Party because he participated in the Moncada attack. But Castro publicly rebuked the allegations. In fact, he accused Batista of being closer to the communists than he was. Castro wrote in a lengthy letter published in *Bohemia*: "What moral authority ... does Mr. Batista have to speak of communism, when he was the Communist Party Presidential candidate in the election of 1940, when his electoral posters were sheltered by the hammer and sickle ... if half a dozen of his present ministers and collaborators were well known members of the Communist Party."[120]

When Castro and his men traveled to Cuba on the Granma to fight a guerrilla war, the communists did not approve. In a letter of the National Committee of the Popular Socialist Party to the 26th of July Movement dated February 28, 1957, Castro was told that armed struggle was not the correct answer.[121] A similar position was taken by Juan Marinello, then the head of the party, in a letter to Herbert Matthews dated March 17, 1957, which called for civil action, such as strikes, demonstration and civil protests, and not for violence.[122]

While he was in the mountains, Fidel Castro published a "Political-Social Manifesto" July 12, 1957. In it he planned for free elections and a restoration of the 1940 Cuban Constitution. When the rebels used slash-and-burn tactics, communists objected as "sabotage and the burning of cane fields principally affects workers and small or medium-sized farmers." The party committed itself to waiting until "objective and subjective" conditions made overt challenges to the regime viable and not self-defeating.[123] The communists believed that Castro was too strident and couldn't reach unanimity with the other Cuban opposition groups and revolutionary organizations and therefore could not defeat Batista.[124] He was also considered too anti–American. The consensus at the time was that any threat to American interests would bring on a military attack. After all, America had intervened in Cuba over less important issues.

Although there were probably tens of thousands of communists in Cuba during the period, they certainly did not rush to join M–7–26 in the field.[125] Castro could have overtly or covertly asked them to join M–7–26, but there is no evidence that he ever did. In May 1957 the communists openly rejected Castro and his tactics.[126] During 1957 and 1958 the communists gave only tepid support to general strikes planned by M–7–26, and Castro accused them of actively undermining M–7–26.[127] A Spanish journalist accompanied Castro for four months in 1957 and 1958. He decided that although Castro was anti–American, he was not a communist. When asked, Castro stated: "I hate Soviet imperialism as much as I hate Yankee imperialism!"[128] He criticized Communism for "wiping out man's freedom."[129]

When communists did enter the fray against Batista, they often had their own units, like Víctor Bordón's unit in the Escambray, that marched to another drummer, because it refused to serve under M–7–26 leadership. In the ranks, there was outright animosity against the communists. For example, in late 1958, Bordón's unit was captured by Eloy Gutiérrez Menoyo's unit.[130] The communist-led units were small, and not all members were Communists. When some communists were permitted to join M–7–26, they were suspect. The M–7–26 veterans called them "melons": watermelons, green like the olive drab *barbudo* uniform on the outside but red on the inside.[131]

Although there is some evidence that rebel soldiers and *guajiros* in freed areas were subjected to communist propaganda, there is more evidence that M–7–26 *barbudo* Catholic priests provided public baptisms, masses and public education.[132]

After Batista fled, Castro derided the communists as "divisionists."[133] Some historians note a period of ambivalence early 1959 toward the communists.[134] Soon, Lyman B. Kirkpatrick, Jr., the CIA inspector general during this period who was sent to Cuba to investigate, determined that Fidel Castro was a revolutionary who originally had no precise political philosophy and who "turned communist when the communists seemed to offer him the most support."[135] As stated earlier, the record shows that instead of the communists infiltrating Cuba, it more probable that Castro infiltrated and manipulated the Communist Party as a means to overcome and displace dissidents in the Provisional Government.

It is more reasonable that had Castro been given an opportunity to enter into real negotiations with the United States, he would not have had to take a defensive posture and would not have become a dictator. As it became clear that the U.S. would intervene, one way or another, in Cuba, Castro became suspicious to the point that he feared almost any dissent. He knew from his days in the mountains that Batista had put a price on his head. He knew that the CIA had been active in Cuba before Batista's fall. In 1957 and 1958, the CIA paid at least $50,000 to various elements of M–7–26.[136]

He knew that some of his men had mixed loyalties, or could be bribed, or even had personal plans to overtake him as a leader. In the mountains, he had to confront desertion in the ranks, and from the onset of the Provisional Government, personality conflicts often trumped patriotism and loyalty. It is now clear that his brother, although not a member of the cabinet, was really the only person he could trust. Raúl Castro, however, was not entirely subservient to Fidel, as he wanted to have his own men in control of his fiefdom. As early as April 1959, Raúl sought to install outsiders, entirely beholden to him, as his cadre. It was obvious that the other comandantes all had a personal agenda and had personality conflicts. For example, Che Guevara and Faustino Pérez, both loyal to Fidel Castro, did not get along and could have been pitted against each other.[137] To ensure that his followers were loyal only to him, Raúl Castro recruited his cadre from the Soviet Union.[138] These people would be loyal to him before God, country and even Fidel Castro.

Castro also could tell that his opponents were flush with money. Determined to be able to defend Cuba, he first asked the United States to replenish the Cuban arsenal. Most of it had been provided to Batista. Almost all of it came from American manufacturers and many of the armaments were no longer useful without parts to repair them. The United States flatly refused. If the United States had been playing for time, it could have asked to inventory them or to assess them. The Eisenhower administration could have placed conditions or made a counteroffer to every one of the Cuban government requests, but chose not to do so. It could have offered agricultural equipment or plants and machinery to help Cuba restart its economy, but did not choose to do so.

Soon after President Eisenhower returned from his Latin American trip, Mario Lazo took it upon himself to talk to the Cuban finance minister, Rufo López Fresquet. Lazo was not even a diplomat. The principal U.S. diplomat, Ambassador Bonsal, had been in Washington for two months. Dan Braddock was the diplomat in charge of the American embassy, and he had been dealing with the Cuban foreign minister at the time, Raúl Roa. López Fresquet later turned out to have been a double agent, from September 1959.[139] It would take several years for the U.S. to discover that almost every agent we had employed in Cuba had turned out to have also been reporting to the Castro regime.

As the possible deal was contemplated, President Eisenhower was pressured by Vice President Nixon, then a candidate for president, to initiate a takeover of Cuba in the same way that the U.S. had intervened in Iran and in Guatemala.[140] As early as October 1959, President Eisenhower clandestinely agreed to support Cuban groups opposed to Castro, with a view that they would make it seem that Castro had self-destructed.[141] Although they were not aware of these developments, Democrats from sugar-producing states and conservative leaders of the Republican Party had taken the position that U.S. foreign policy was not tough enough. Nixon's Democratic opponent in the general elections had not yet been selected, but Senator Stuart Symington of Missouri, Senator Hubert Humphrey of Minnesota, and Senator John F. Kennedy of Massachusetts all decried the policy of nonintervention.

On March 17, 1960, President Eisenhower gave the CIA the go-ahead, to, in effect, wage war on Cuba. Whether the decision was made before or after he heard from López Fresquet, his man in Cuba at the time, is unclear.

Objectively, had the U.S. actually wanted to open negotiations with the Cuban government, we would have done so through diplomatic channels, and especially not through someone who would soon be considered to have been an admitted traitor by the sitting Cuban government. Moreover, as we were planning to enter into a covert war at the time, our credibility must have been suspect.

Personal Animosity

The dissolution was probably was less due to ideological conflicts or policy issues as to the clashing personalities of our leaders. President Eisenhower tried to maintain an image as the national grandfather, wise, patient and restrained; but in reality he was resistant to any criticism of himself or his country.[142] Premier Castro was mercurial, loud and dramatic.

National interests are supposed to predominate over personal interests, but the break-down appears now to have been as much a matter of the heart as a matter of public policy. To Eisenhower, Castro's language probably sounded inflammatory. Conversely, Castro should have had reason to know that his statements about America would have been deeply resented. However, anti–American demagoguery was a staple not only of Cuban politics but the politics of almost every Latin American country, and even if Castro used the U.S. as a totem, by early 1959 he was not involved in a political campaign and had nothing to gain by the rhetoric. He also taunted President Eisenhower. In the days leading to the Bay of Pigs incident, he told the press that the United States would lose more men in battle than we did at Normandy or Iwo Jima in World War II if we attacked.[143]

On the other hand, there was some truth to many of his allegations. The U.S. took a patronizing view that Cuba was a dependent of the United States. We also still maintained a variant of the Monroe Doctrine to the extent that we felt that only we could protect such a small country from external aggression.[144] By April 1959, Castro needed assurances the United States would not oppose him. He craved a "state visit," but came to the United States at the request of newsmen, rather than the U.S. State Department. Among the people that represented the U.S. government to Castro were Vice President Nixon and Gerry Droller. By that time, Droller, a/k/a Frank Bender, supposedly our best CIA man, had personally discussed overthrowing Castro with Dominican dictator Rafael Trujillo and Johnny Abbes García, head of Dominican intelligence, who had established a "Caribbean Legion" to achieve the overthrow.[145]

Many, if not most of "our" CIA "assets" turned out to have been double agents.[146] By the time that Castro met with Gerry Droller aka Frank Bender, Batista and former general José E. Pedraza y Cabrera were both living in the Dominican Republic and Pedraza publicly had announced plans to lead a liberation army to free Cuba. Pedraza had been second in command during the Sergeants' Rebellion in 1933. Later he was the head of the Cuban National Police force, and when Batista was elected president, he was elevated to the chief of staff of the military. In 1941, Batista removed him after Pedraza attempted a military takeover of the government, and he was exiled to Miami.[147] He had been convicted in 1945 for trying to remove newly elected President Grau San Martín by a *golpe de estado*, ostensibly to take over in the same manner that Batista later did in 1952.[148] After Batista regained power, Pedraza returned to the army, and was promoted to major general. Pedraza was a member of the junta which would have replaced Batista on December 30, 1958, and taken over Cuba. He was able to escape on December 31.[149]

Presumably, the ranks of Pedraza's troops included enough double agents to let the Cuban government know that Gerry Droller (Frank Bender) had met with their benefactor, Trujillo, who was hiring mercenaries from Europe, including Fascists sent to him by Franco and former Nazi troops, and was admittedly planning to send them to invade of Cuba. Even if Castro had not received direct evidence that the CIA was involved with Trujillo, there was circumstantial evidence simply in the fact that Pedraza was recruiting part of his army in the States. Cuba put pressure on Trujillo when on February 26, 1959, Cuba formally asked the Dominican Republic to extradite General Pedraza and seven others.[150] In combination, with the use of Trujillo's troops, Pedraza's legion would have outnumbered the Cuban army.

During this period, Cuba was engaged in executions of "war criminals." In the States, these executions were seen as an attempt by the victors to kill the opposition from the prior regime. The Cuban Constitution of 1940 forbade the death penalty, but during the Batista era, an exception was made for "escaping" prisoners, and it is estimated that hundreds were killed in this manner. The death penalty was first imposed in military areas that came under the control of M–7–26, and the power to execute for war crimes was extended by a Provisional Government edict to military tribunals. By the time that Castro arrived in the United States in April 1959, Castro's position was that the executions were an object lesson: Those in power would have to stand trial for crimes against humanity like murder and torture of political prisoners and political opponents.[151] By that time, approximately 550 prisoners had been tried and executed.[152] Castro announced that Cuba would consider itself "neutral" in world politics, which added fuel to Eisenhower's resentment.

President Eisenhower was deeply affected by the executions, and in the middle of the Cold War, to be "neutral" was to be opposed to the West. Although U.S. military tribunals had tried and executed German spies during World War II, and although President Eisenhower had a hand in the creating the Nuremberg trials, some U.S. news organizations described the Cuban executions as a bloodbath and labeled Castro as a murderer and a madman. The record shows that the State Department and the CIA substantiated this image in their presentations to the president, and he accepted the description.[153] The U.S. filed formal protests. At the time, President Eisenhower was concentrating on the Soviet Union and many other issues, but Fidel Castro was concentrating on the United States. The president's attention was scattered, and his inability to turn Cuba around led to bewilderment, frustration and anger.[154]

In reliance on an assumption that U.S. foreign policy was correct and viable to "save" Cuba, and in reliance on CIA information and advice, President Eisenhower gave the go-ahead to, in effect, wage war on Cuba on March 17, 1960. The United States did not sever diplomatic relations with Cuba until January 3, 1961, only days before Eisenhower left office.

It is reasonable that had Eisenhower sought out Premier Castro, the course of both nations would have taken a different turn. Diplomatic relations had ceased, but within a month after the Bay of Pigs incident, although our government would not acknowledge any involvement, after Cuba made a demand for a trade, negotiations began over the return of the members of Brigade 2506, held captive in Cuba. The initiative came from Fidel Castro. He proposed a trade. Cuba would return the brigade members in exchange for tractors, and would "throw in the Falangist priests for nothing."[155] Ruby Phillips thought that Castro was only being sarcastic, and the article was not run on page one of the *New York Times* as so many of her earlier scoops had been.[156]

However, it wasn't a joke.

Cuba permitted private negotiations and even paroled some of the members of the brigade to the States to help in the negotiations. The U.S. initially attempted to negotiate through the "Tractors for Freedom Committee," comprised of former First Lady Eleanor Roosevelt, Milton Eisenhower, and others. That initial attempt failed, and eventually James B. Donovan, the president of Pratt Institute, a lawyer and unsuccessful Senate candidate from New York, took it upon himself to negotiate with Fidel Castro. Donovan was able to obtain the release of the entire brigade and 35 Americans who had been held in Cuba.[157] The press reported that Donovan represented the families of the prisoners and did not have any government guarantees or government sanction. He eventually determined that Castro needed the deal to become more independent of the Soviet Union. Although Donovan was supposedly acting purely as a private citizen, Republicans in the U.S. House of Representatives

Alvaro Sanchez, Jr., left, and Enrique Ruiz-Williams are shown with attorney James Donovan, right, at Donovan's office in New York during a press conference as Sanchez and Ruiz-Williams reported on their negotiations in Cuba for the release of anti–Castro Cuban fighters, November 20, 1962. Sanchez was chairman of the Cuban Families Committee working for freedom of prisoners; Donovan was the committee's general counsel. It was announced at the meeting that most of preliminaries had been agreed upon by Cuban premier Fidel Castro and the committee to arrange an exchange of Bay of Pigs invasion prisoners for food, medicine and drugs (AP Photo/Anthony Camerano).

eventually accused him of violating the Logan Act, which bars private citizens from dealing with foreign governments, or being an "agent" for the Kennedy administration, and conducting diplomacy with an enemy.[158] The brigade went on trial in March 1962, but due to Donovan's intercession, a deal was brokered on December 1962, and within days the brigade was returned to Miami.[159]

On December 30, 1962, the brigade stood at the Orange Bowl in Miami, as President Kennedy addressed them. He did not tell them that they would probably have been freed a year earlier if he had been willing to negotiate directly with Castro. Although the troops had to be happy to be free, they still shouted "¡Guerra, ¡Guerra, ¡Guerra¡," "War! War! War!" at the end.[160]

Conclusion

Dissolution benefited the Castro regime politically as many of the once viable opponents relocated from Cuba into the diaspora. Using its own version of "hardball" diplomacy, the Cuban government was able to consolidate power and simultaneously to humiliate and repel an outside invader. It also maintains that it has opened Cuban society to all and has established humane social programs. However, the government became increasingly repressive, and because of isolation, and due to the loss of its largest trading partner, Cuba is a poor country with a low standard of living.

Both the United States and Cuba lost in most respects. Today, the dissolution of this relationship looks like a phase in a continuum of application of a rigid policy and a failure of diplomacy, and is a case study in how not to deal with foreign governments. During the Batista regime, despite reports of human rights abuses by the Cuban government, U.S. preoccupation with developments behind the Iron Curtain, in China, in the Middle East and Africa obscured our attention, and we allowed ourselves to become identified as an oppressor. In the past 60 years, the U.S. has been replicating the politics and foreign policy of confrontation left over from the Truman administration and John Foster Dulles, and we have lost American interests in Cuba along with our prestige in the region as a result. We never expected that Soviet communism would implode, and that the most formidable of our former enemies would succumb to entropy. For a while, it looked as if there would peace on earth and goodwill toward all men. However, standing against us today are countries where we tried to effect regime change: North Korea, Iran, and Cuba. In Vietnam, where we failed to institute regime change covertly and overtly, we are now trying conciliation instead of retribution and retaliation, and it looks like it is working. The jury is still out on others such as Iraq, Afghanistan, Venezuela, Honduras and Bolivia.

Notes

Introduction

1. Among the most influential Cuban intellectuals who had espoused this attitude were Hermino Portell Vila, Ramiro Guerra, and Fernando Ortiz. See Hugh Thomas, *Cuba; Or, the Pursuit of Freedom.* (New York: Harper & Row, 1971), p. 1058. Several other Latin American writers expressed the same sentiments; see Leslie Bethell, *Cuba: A Short History* (London: Cambridge University Press, 1993), p. 49. Cuban president (1944–1948) Ramón Grau San Martín, a former professor of medicine at the University of Havana and another leading intellectual of the era, ran an anti–imperialist campaign in the 1930s that appeared to be anti–American at the time. Later, however, he was identified by his political opponents, especially the Ortodoxo Party, as too pro–American. However, polls showed that the public at large were less apprehensive of the United States. Jorge I. Domínguez, *Cuba: Order and Revolution* (Cambridge, MA: Belknap Press of Harvard University Press, 1978), pp. 114, 142.

2. For example, the ABC, a middle-class semi-secret organization, wanted Americans to rout out their opponents in 1932–1934. They wanted to instill enough terror to cause a breakdown in civility such that the United States would have to intervene. Richard Gott, *Cuba: A New History* (New Haven, CT: Yale University Press, 1964), p. 134; Thomas, *Cuba; Or, the Pursuit of Freedom*, pp. 595, 661. Although they sought American intervention, they were also for agrarian reform, nationalization of utilities, and restriction of Americans' property rights. Ibid, p. 594.

3. Like former president Grau San Martín. See "2 Condemned Cubans Make Escape as Firing Squad Pauses to Reload," *Washington Post and Times Herald*, March 6, 1959, p. A7.

4. At the onset of the war, the Germans and the Soviets had been allied, under the Molotov-Ribbentrop Non-Aggression Pact of August 1939, with a covert agreement to take Finland, Estonia, Latvia, Lithuania, Poland, and Romania. Both were ruthless. In Poland, the Soviets perpetrated the Katyn Massacre, killing thousands of Polish military officers, police, intellectuals and civilian prisoners of war. However, the Germans attacked the Soviets in June 1941.

5. After the war, Georgy Konstantinovich Zhukov (1896–1974) was military commander of the Soviet Occupation Zone when Eisenhower was head of the American Zone.

6. H. Bartlett Wells, "A Study of Cuban-American Relations," State Department Document, September 8, 1947, quoted in Lars Schoultz, *Beneath the United States.* (Cambridge, MA: Harvard University Press, 1998), pp. 328–329.

7. James Cortada, "Component Elements of Cuban Temperament," quoted in Schoultz, *Beneath the United States*, pp. 329–330.

8. Ibid.

9. Born February 25, 1888, died May 24, 1959.

10. Before his appointment, Dulles also served as the chairman and cofounder of the Commission on a Just and Durable Peace of the Federal Council of Churches of Christ in America (succeeded by the National Council of Churches), the chairman of the board for the Carnegie Endowment for International Peace, a trustee of the Rockefeller Foundation from 1935 to 1952, and was a founding member of the Council on Foreign Relations. Dulles believed in a "kingdom on Earth" in which Christianity was the "antidote to national and international pathologies." Immerman, *Piety, Pragmatism and Power in U.S. Foreign Policy*, p. 3. *Time* (January 3, 1955) named Dulles its Man of the Year for 1954 and called him a "practical missionary of Christian politics."

11. See Townsend Hoopes, *The Devil and John Foster Dulles* (Boston: Little, Brown, 1973), p. xiv.

12. Stephen E. Ambrose, *Ike's Spies: Eisenhower and the Espionage Establishment* (Jackson: University Press of Mississippi, 1999), pp. 217–232; Dan Koeppel, *Banana: The Fate of the Fruit That Changed the World* (New York: Hudson Street Press, 2008), p. 128; Greg Grandin, *Empire's Workshop: Latin America, the United States, and the Rise of Imperialism* (New York: Metropolitan Books/Henry Holt, 2007), pp. 42–44; Richard H. Immerman, *Pragmatism and Power in U.S. Foreign Policy* (Wilmington, DE: SR Books, 1999), p. 109; Schoultz, *Beneath the United States*, pp. 337–343. Under Secretary John Moors Cabot's brother was president of United Fruit, and the State Department relied on John Cabot's assessment of the Guatemalan situation and his advice to characterize Árbenz as a communist and to remove him. Ambrose, *Ike's Spies*, p. 223; Schoultz, *Beneath the United States*, p. 337.

Chapter 1

1. According to the A.C. Nielsen ratings service, *I Love Lucy* was the number one television show in the United States for the period October 1952 to April 1957 and was first in four of six seasons. The series originally ran from October 15, 1951, to May 6, 1957, on CBS. For a short period of time in 1956, the *$64,000 Question* was number one and *Lucy* was number two, but that was a

brief anomaly. During that time, Arnaz and Ball also starred and produced feature films, including *The Long, Long Trailer* (1954) and *Forever, Darling* (1956). Their production company, Desilu, produced *Our Miss Brooks*, *The Untouchables*, *Star Trek*, and *Mission: Impossible*. Other popular classic TV series, like *Make Room for Daddy*, *The Dick Van Dyke Show*, *The Andy Griffith Show*, and *I Spy*, were filmed by Desilu Studios.

2. Otherwise known as the cha-cha-cha. Some also danced the rumba, the pachanga, and boogaloo. Ray Barretto's "El Watusi," recorded in 1961, is the quintessential boogaloo song.

3. Released in 1946, written by Margarita Lecuona. The instrumental component is an example of conga, which is associated with Arnaz's music, and he is credited with inventing the conga line.

4. The Havana club is memorialized in Rosa Lowinger and Ofelia Fox, *Tropicana Nights: The Life And Times of the Legendary Cuban Nightclub* (Orlando, FL: Harcourt, 2005). The Kentucky club was located in the Glenn Hotel, 928 Monmouth Street, and was reportedly owned by "the Cleveland syndicate" headed by Morris Kleinman, Lou Rothkopf, Moe Dalitz and Sam Tucker, who had been chased from Ohio by Governor Frank Lausche. The hotel and casino were destroyed by a mysterious fire on February 28, 1962. For more details see Bill Davidson, "The Great Kentucky Scandal," *Look*, October 24, 1961. Jeff Ruby's Tropicana at Newport club, which opened in 2002 and is now closed, was apparently modeled after the Tropicana casino on Newport's Monmouth Street. It had no ownership connection to the old Tropicana or to the Las Vegas casino. There is also a Tropicana hotel and casino in Atlantic City

5. Although a New York native Puerto Rican lineage, Ernest Anthony "Tito" Puente, "El Rey del Timbal," is generally identified with the mambo, cha-cha-cha and other Cuban music. A virtuoso Latin jazz percussionist, he was also closely associated with Dizzy Gillespie. Puente was born on April 20, 1923, and died on May 31, 2000. His mambo recordings include *Barbarabatiri* (1951), *Oye Como Va*, *El Rey del Timbal*, *Mambo la Roca*, *Elegua Change*, and *Mambo Gallego* (all 1955).

6. Among the most important Cuban musicians of the era was Ignacio de Loyola Rodríguez Scull, aka Arsenio Rodríguez, who was born in Cuba on August 30, 1911, and died in Los Angeles on December 31, 1971. He is generally known as the father of the mambo, but also developed the *son montuno*. Americans were usually not aware of the historical and political implications of this music. For example, *Adorela como Martí* was dedicated to the Mambi fighters in the Army of Liberation during the Spanish American War and would be used to venerate the Rebel Army. Others included Benny Moré, Prince of Mambo, and Celia Cruz, who would become known as the Queen of Salsa.

7. Written in 1928 by Josieto Fernández, the lyrics are from a poem, *Versos Sinceros*, written by José Martí, known as the apostle of Cuba. See Ed Morales, *The Latin Beat*, p. 122.

8. Several musicologists attribute a direct influence to jazz. For example, W. C. Handy was deeply influenced by the habanera form. John Storm Roberts, *The Latin Tinge: The Impact of Latin American Music on the United States.* 2nd ed. (New York: Oxford University Press, 1999), pp. 30, 40–41, 48; Ed Morales, *The Latin Beat: The Rythms and Roots of Latin Music from Bosa Nova to Salsa and Beyond* (Cambridge, MA: Da Capo Books, 2003), pp. 14–15, 277. American composer George Gershwin incorporated Cuban themes in his music and made musical pilgrimages to Cuba. Roberts, pp. 56, 80.

9. Roberts, *The Latin Tinge*, pp. 133, 136 167, 180, 198. Morales, *The Latin Beat*, pp. 28–281, 284, 285.

10. Roberts, *The Latin Tinge*, p. 49.

11. Morales, *The Latin Beat*, pp. 5–8. As to the relationship to contradanza, see Jory Farr, *Rites of Rhythm: The Music of Cuba* (New York: Regan Books, 2003), pp. 24–25.

12. Morales, *The Latin Beat*, pp. 6–8; Roberts, *The Latin Tinge*, pp. 4–5. Roberts says that Afro-Cuban musicians added a "lift," syncopation using clave, to the other forms.

13. Written by Sherman Edwards, Donald Meyer and Sid Wayne.

14. Written by Maurice Williams, originally performed by The Gladiolas.

15. See Neil Strauss, "The Indestructible Beat of Bo Diddley," *Rolling Stone*, August 11, 2005. Strauss does not mention the clave.

16. See ad in *The Washington Post*, August 10, 1958, p. A18.

17. The program *Your Hit Parade* was broadcast from 1935 to 1955 on radio, and 1950 to 1959 on television. It presented the top single records and sheet music sales products played and sung by the program's own band and vocalists. A Cuban version was *El Hit Parade Cubano*.

18. "Mambo Italiano" was written by Bob Merrill based on an traditional Italian folk song.

19. Perry Como, "A Hit Is Born: The Story of 'Papa Loves Mambo,'" *Coronet Magazine*, February 1955.

20. "Mambo Rock" was written by Mildred Pressman of Philadelphia in 1955 using the pen name Mildred Phillips.

21. Several musicologists attribute the development of rock 'n' roll music and rockabilly music to the habanera, reportedly acquired during the Spanish American War. Musicologists also attribute some of the habanera patterns to the Charleston and the jitterbug. See Roy Brewer, "The Use of Habanera Rhythm in Rockabilly Music," *American Music* 17 (1999), pp. 300–317; Roberts, *The Latin Tinge*, pp. 133, 136, 167, 180, 198. See also Morales, *Latin Beat*, pp. xx–xxl. Morales attributes such songs as early rock great Buddy Holly's "Not Fade Away" to the influence of the Afro-Cuban clave. He also notes that Latin forms were a major influence in rock 'n' roll, especially in the formative years. pp. 276–291.

22. The English lyrics were written by Joe Davis.

23. Although Pérez Prado performed it as an instrumental, over 20 vocal versions were recorded. Among those who covered it were Pat Boone, Georgia Gibbs, and Alan Dale, whose version stayed in the charts for 30 weeks.

24. See generally Roberts, *The Latin Tinge*, pp. 127–159; Ed Morales, *The Latin Beat*, pp. 34–63.

25. "Fever" was written by Otis Blackwell and Eddie Cooley, and the Lee version is heavily percussive and is usually danced as a cha-cha-cha. It was originally recorded as a blues record by Little Willie John. "Honey Love" was written by Clyde McPhatter, then lead singer of the Drifters, and Jerry Wexler of Atlantic Records. "Venus" was written by Ed Marshall.

26. *El Loco Cha Cha* was originally *Amarren Al Loco*, "Tie Up the Lunatic," by Rosendo Ruiz Jr. It was also performed by Ricky Rillera and the Rhythm Rockers, and in 1955, band member Richard "Chuck" Berry reworked it. He recorded it as "Louie Louie" in 1957. A 1963 version by the Kingsmen sold millions of records.

27. "Cha-cha heels" were remarketed Cuban heels. A variation, cha-cha boots, would also become popular. Cha-cha skirts and tops were marketed in the 1960s and

1970s. Longer in back than in front, the cha-cha skirt was considered "too sexy" to be seen on television.

28. A scene in the 1950 Broadway classic *Guys and Dolls* takes place in Havana, where "Havana Dance," including *La Cumparsita*, a tango, is performed. However, it is an Argentine rather than Cuban form.

29. By 1957, Moré led his Banda Gigante (Big Band), and was a frequent act in the States but especially at the Tropicana in Havana. Moré had recorded earlier with Pérez Prado and Orquesta Aragón. In Cuba and in most of Latin America he was dubbed the "Prince of Mambo." He died in 1963 at age 43 in Havana.

30. When Sullivan reported to the CIA, he reportedly asked: "Revolution? What revolution?" *Report on Cuba 1957*, December 1957, Box 146, IHALBSP, quoted in Thomas G. Paterson, *Contesting Castro: The United States and the Triumph of the Cuban Revolution* (New York: Oxford University Press, 1995), p. 103, note 22.

31. Paul J. C. Friedlander, "Castro's Cuba and Tourism," *New York Times*, November 1, 1959, p. XX25.

32. Cuba was the principal tourist destination in the Caribbean, attracting 300,000 visitors a year, 80 percent of them Americans. Larry Rohter, "Cuba Eager for Tourist Dollars, Dusts Off Its Vacancy Sign," *New York Times*, October 19, 1995.

33. Henry Durling, "Gambling Mecca of the New World," *Cabaret Magazine*, December 1956, pp. 33–34, 45. According to Durling, two reasons for Havana's rise are (1) the decline of Miami as a gambling center, as reform elements cracked down on the profitable enterprises there; and (2) the resulting willingness of Americans to move to greener pastures elsewhere. According to Lefty Clark, the United States could not compete with Havana. "[Waning] Las Vegas is purely a resort, while this is a metropolitan center. We are tapping a new market, not the same one."

34. See, for example, *Gente Magazine* (American Edition) 1, no. 1 (January 5, 1958), p. 11.

35. "Night Club in the Sky, Cubana Airlines' Tropicana Special," *Cabaret Magazine*, January 1957, pp. 32–36, 45. Also see Rosalie Schwartz, *Pleasure Island: Tourism and Temptation in Cuba* (Lincoln: University of Nebraska Press, 1997), p. 125.

36. An 11-day trip to Havana cost $207. A seven-day trip to Miami: $232. Diana Rice, "What the Trip Will Cost," *New York Times*, April 13, 1958, p. xx17.

37. Often described as an attraction to materialism and morals. See Louis A. Perez, Jr., *On Becoming Cuban: Identity, Nationality, and Culture* (New York: The Ecco Press, 1999), pp. 242–255.

38. "Scene of Revolt Is a Lush Green Island, Largest and Most Populous of Antilles," *New York Times*, January 2, 1959, p. 7. The article cites $1 billion in 1959 dollars. The largest holdings, $221 million, were owned by American & Foreign Power Company. Others were Moa Bay Mining, a subsidiary of Freeport Sulphur Company; Nickel Processing Corporation; ESSO Standard Oil; Republic Steel and Texas Corporation.

39. "The Vengeful Visionary," *Time*, January 26, 1959; Batista, *The Cuban Republic*, pp. 184–189.

40. After June 1958, when some Americans were kidnapped by the rebels, leave from Guantánamo was limited.

41. Although most Americans believe that baseball was invented by Abner Doubleday at Cooperstown, New York, in 1839, there is an argument that the game of *batos* was invented by the Taino in Jamaica and is the antecedent of baseball, cricket and jai alai. Some say that Columbus discovered baseball. George A. Aarons, "The Lucayans: The

People Whom Columbus Discovered in the Bahamas," *Five Hundred Magazine* 2, no. 1 (April 1990), pp. 6–7. The Lucayans were Tainos who introduced *batos* to civilization. See also Gonzalo Fernandez of Oviedo, *General and Natural History of the Indians* (Spain, 1547). According the the principal authority, the first organized Cuban baseball game was played at Palmar Del Junco, Matanzas, in 1874. Wenceslao Galvez, *El Beisbol En Cuba* (Havana, 1898). Others believe baseball was actually introduced to Cuba in 1866 by American sailors. Roberto González Echevarría, *The Pride of Havana: A History of Cuban Baseball* (New York: Oxford University Press, 1999), p. 75; Mark Rucker and Peter Bjarkman, *Smoke: The Romance and Lore of Cuban Baseball* (New York: Total Sports Illustrated, 1999), p. 12.

42. Paul Winston, "America Not Yet Ready for Running of the Bulls," *Business Insurance*, July 23, 2007, p. 30.

43. "Best Seat in the House," *Time*, October 14, 1957, describes an attraction to "beisbol-slappy Cuba."

44. Perez, *On Becoming Cuban*, p. 266. Castro also recounted this to Dan Rather in the CBS television documentary "The Last Revolutionary," July 7, 1996.

45. Perez, *On Becoming Cuban*, pp. 276–277. Pérez lists dozens of Americanized sports terms, including some from boxing and basketball. For example, a home run is *jonron*, a knockout is *el knockout*, and in basketball the coach is simply *el coach*. Cuban Spanish borrowed from the native population, from Haiti, and especially from African languages prior to the arrival of American culture.

46. Carlos Alberto Montaner, *Journey to the Heart of Cuba: Life as Fidel Castro* (New York: Algora Publishing, 2001), pp. 76–77; Louis A. Pérez, Jr., *Cuba and the United States: Ties of Singular Intimacy*, 2nd ed. (Athens: University of Georgia Press, 1990), pp. 226–227.

47. *The Times of Havana*, September 16, 1957, p. 1.

48. See R. Hart Phillips, "Chinese in Cuba Plan Red Paper," *New York Times*, July 10, 1959, p. 8.

49. The title is taken from John Donne's *Meditation XVII*.

50. James R. Mellow, *Hemingway, A Life without Consequences* (Reading, MA: Addison Wesley, 1992), pp. 579–581.

51. Ibid., pp. 580, 590.

52. Jeffrey Meyers, *Hemingway: A Biography* (New York: Harper & Row, 1999), pp. 511–512.

53. Mary Hemingway, *How It Was* (New York: Alfred A. Knopf, 1976), pp. 405, 427.

54. Pérez, *On Becoming Cuban*, pp. 334–335.

55. "Day Decreed in Cuba," *New York Times*, November 28, 1952, p. 15.

56. Luis, *Culture and Customs of Cuba*, p. 113; Pérez, *Cuba and the United States*, pp. 226–227.

57. See Evelyn Hayes, "Debut for Designer from Cuba," *The Washington Post*, May 3, 1955, p. 31; "A Cuban Way of Styles," *Life*, May 5, 1958; Winzola McLendon, "His 'Sexy Styles' Are 'Good Taste,'" *The Washington Post*, October 2, 1957, p. D3, and "A Success Story in Necklines: Luis Estévez is a One-Year Wonder," *Life*, April 2, 1956.

58. "Banana Pants, Rainbow Shoes Latest Florida Fads for Males," *The Washington Post*, November 20, 1951, p. B4.

59. See John Pile, *A History of Interior Design*, 3rd ed. (Hoboken, NJ: John Wiley and Sons, 2005), pp. 383–387. Pastel colors seemed to be everywhere. In this writer's parents' home, designed by them and built in 1953–1954 in Pennsylvania, there were several "shocking" pastel interior walls, and they bought a 1956 coral pink and white

Oldsmobile and a coral-colored 1957 Ford hardtop convertible.

60. *U.N. Statistical Yearbook, 1958* (New York: United Nations, 1958) p. 580; Manuel A. Alvarez, "A History of Cuban Broadcasting," www.oldradio.com/archives (archived in 2001).

61. Perez, *On Becoming Cuban*, p. 393. In 1957, the Cuban minister of communications, Ramos Vasconcelos, attempted to ban rock 'n' roll from radio and television on the grounds that it was "indecent," but his attempt failed. Donald R. Browne, *Historical Journal of Film, Radio and Television*, Vol. 14 (1994), p. 92. Also see *The Times of Havana*, February 14, 1957.

62. For example, see "New Public Works Projects of the Batista Regime," *Gente Magazine* (American Edition) 1, no. 1 (January 5, 1958), pp. 42–57.

63. "Havana's New Tunnel," *Gente Magazine* (American Edition) 1, no. 1 (January 5, 1958), pp. 66–66A-E.

64. The WPA was also known for a time as the Works Projects Administration.

65. Pérez, *Cuba and the United States*, p. 140.

66. Pérez, *On Becoming Cuban*, p. 289.

67. Ibid., pp. 283–308.

68. R. Hart Phillips, "Castro Increasing Pressure on U.S. Sugar Mills in Cuba," *New York Times*, April 2, 1960, p. 8.

69. Marcos A. Ramos, *Protestantism and Revolution in Cuba* (Miami: University of Miami, North-South Center for the Research Institute for Cuban Studies, 1989), p. 23.

70. Pérez, *On Becoming Cuban*, 254–255.

71. Ibid.; Ramos, *Protestantism and Revolution in Cuba*, p. 23.

72. Perez, *On Becoming Cuban*, p. 309.

73. Ibid., pp. 325–343.

74. Gott, *Cuba: A New History*, pp. 67–68.

75. Ramos, *Protestantism and Revolution in Cuba*, pp. 20–21.

76. Ibid.

77. Perez, *On Becoming Cuban*, p. 18.

78. Ibid., 20.

79. Francisco Ortíz, *Contrapunteo cubano del tabaco y el azúcar* (Cuban Counterpoint: Tobacco and Sugar), trans. by Harriet De Onis. (Durham, NC: Duke University Press, 1995. First published in 1940), pp. 51–54, 61; Pérez, *On Becoming Cuban*, p. 258. Also see the March 1961 CIA report "An Appraisal of the Cuban Sugar Industry."

80. Oscar Lecuona Zanetti, Alejandro García, Franklin W. Knight, Mary Todd, *Sugar & Railroads: A Cuban History, 1837–1959* (Chapel Hill: University of North Carolina Press, 1998), p. xx.

81. Perez, Jr., *On Becoming Cuban*, pp. 19–22.

82. Ibid., 22–23.

83. Thomas, *Cuba: Or, the Pursuit of Freedom*, pp. 544–555.

84. Perez, *On Becoming Cuban*, p. 22.

85. Ibid., 166–167.

86. Ibid., 169.

87. Schwartz, *Pleasure Island*, pp. 67–70.

88. Ibid., p. 3.

89. Ibid., 5–6, 49–50; Pérez, *On Becoming Cuban*, p. 175.

90. Perez, *On Becoming Cuban*, p. 177.

91. Ibid., p. 167.

92. Ibid., p. 173.

93. Ibid., pp. 179–180.

94. 1941, starring Alice Faye, Carmen Miranda, John Payne and Cesar Romero.

95. Schwartz, pp. 103–111, 119.

96. "Night Club in the Sky, Cubana Airlines' Tropicana Special," *Cabaret Magazine*, January 1957, pp. 32–36, 45. Also see Schwartz, *Pleasure Island*, p. 125.

97. Ibid.

98. The full title is *Havana Nocturne: How the Mob Owned Cuba and Then Lost It to the Revolution* (New York: William Morrow, 2008).

99. Thomas, *Cuba; Or, the Pursuit of Freedom*, p. 800.

100. English, *Havana Nocturne*, p. 236.

101. Schwartz, *Pleasure Island*, p. 185.

102. Perez, *Cuba and the United States*, pp. 230, 266. According to Perez, the per capita income of Cubans was $334 per year, compared to $2000 in the United States. Thomas said that per capita income rose to $400 per year. *Cuba; Or, the Pursuit of Freedom*, p. 911.

Chapter 2

1. In the Treaty of Paris, Spain relinquished all claim of sovereignty over Cuba; it was to be occupied by the United States, and the United States would assume and discharge any obligations under international law.

2. The Cuban-American Treaty was signed on February 17, 1903, by the first president of Cuba, Tomás Estrada Palma, and on February 23, 1903, by the president of the United States, Theodore Roosevelt.

3. See "Roosevelt Corollary to the Monroe Doctrine, 1904," *United States Department of State*, Office of Electronic Information, Bureau of Public Affairs, http://www.state.gov/r/pa/ho/time/ip/16324.htm (2007).

4. The Monroe Doctrine is a United States policy dated December 2, 1823, designed to keep European countries from colonizing Latin America or in interfering in the internal affairs of Latin American nations. Through the Roosevelt Corollary to the Monroe Doctrine the U.S. intervened to "restore order" in Cuba, Nicaragua, Haiti, and the Dominican Republic, where we sent intermittently in the Marines. See "Roosevelt Corollary to the Monroe Doctrine, 1904," United States Department of State, Office of Electronic Information, Bureau of Public Affairs, http://www.state.gov/r/pa/ho/time/ip/16324.htm (2007).

5. Charles Edward Magoon, governor of Cuba 1906–1909, was born on December 5, 1861, and died on January 14, 1920. In 1902, Magoon published *Reports on The Law of Civil Government in Territory Subject to Military Occupation by the Military Forces of the United States, etc.* His scholarship and experience in Panama led to his appointment. Although highly regarded by Americans, he was generally detested in Cuba. See Thomas, *The Cuban Revolution*, pp. 403–404, 482–488, 491–492; Gott, *Cuba: A New History*, pp. 117–128, 127.

6. "Dollar Diplomacy, 1909–1913," United States Department of State, Office of Electronic Information, Bureau of Public Affairs, http://www.state.gov/r/pa/ho/time/ip/16324.htm (2007).

7. See "The Negro Protest," in Thomas, *Cuba: Or, the Pursuit of Freedom*, pp. 514–524. The ships were the USS *Prairie*, USS *Nashville*, and USS *Paducah*. The first reported incident involving Americans occurred when an American refused to serve drinks to two Afro-Cuban members of the Cuban Congress. "Negroes Win in Havana," *New York Times*, January 4, 1910, p. 4. Although rioters burned a couple of sugar mills, the "war" was probably more aptly called a "massacre," as Afro-Cuban political leaders were hunted down and executed. Gott, *Cuba: A New History*, pp. 122–125; According to Aline Helg,

Our Rightful Share, The Afro-Cuban Struggle for Equality, 1886–1912 (Chapel Hill: University of North Carolina Press, 1994), pp. 2, 161–226, the "war" was actually a series of one-sided assaults by white racists against Afro-Cubans. Many of the racists were white veterans of the Spanish American War.

8. Perez, *Cuba and the United States*, p. 204; Domínguez, *Cuba: Order and Revolution*, pp. 84–87; Thomas, *Cuba: Or, the Pursuit of Freedom*, pp. 694–695. The United States passed the Jones-Costigan Act in 1934, which established higher prices for Cuban sugar in the United States. In 1937 Cuba passed the Sugar Coordination Act, which tied them to the U.S. act.

9. Twenty-one Latin American countries were charter members of the U.N., and pressed for en end to colonialism and a human rights policy. Grandin, *Empire's Workshop*, p. 37. They brought the same attitude to Rio and to OAS. Ibid.; Stephen G. Rabe, *Eisenhower and Latin America: The Foreign Policy of Anti-Communism* (Chapel Hill: University of North Carolina Press, 1968), pp. 7, 13, 21, 25.

10. Grandin says that the effect was to establish Latin America as a sphere of influence apart from the United Nations. *Empire's Workshop*, pp. 39–40.

11. The program was announced in President Truman's inaugural address, January 20, 1949. The Point Four Program of Technical Assistance to Developing Nations, Harry S Truman Library and Museum. Prepared by Dennis Bilger and Randy Sowell (February 1999). Also see Rabe, *Eisenhower and Latin America*, p. 19.

12. See United States State Department, "Bilateral Treaties in Force as of November 1, 2007," pp. 29–30. The military missions were established in 1950–1951. See p. 30.

13. In Schoultz, *Beneath the United States*, a chapter is titled "Combating Communism with Friendly Dictators," pp. 332–348.

14. This policy is seen as an extension of the Cold War and the red scare that was occurring within the United States during the period. Schoultz, pp. 332–333; Grandin, *Empire's Workshop*, pp. 39–46.

15. Rabe, *Eisenhower and Latin America*, pp. 19–21. Rabe also states that Acheson said Latin America's problems were due to a "Hispano-Indian culture — or lack of it," citing CIA and National Security Council sources. See also Schoultz, *Beneath the United States*, pp. 333–335.

16. Rabe, *Eisenhower and Latin America*, pp. 22–23.

17. Grandin, *Empire's Workshop*, p. 42.

18. Morris H. Morley, *Imperial State and Revolution: The United States and Cuba, 1952–1986* (New York: Cambridge University Press, 1987), p. 41. Acheson testified before the Senate Committee on Foreign Relations, 82nd Congress, Second Session. Juan Perón was the dictator of Argentina. He was seen as a fascist who had been "neutral" during World War II, and opposed the United States' attempts to organize the OAS. In 1949 Perón articulated a "Third Way" foreign policy to pit the United States and the Soviet Union against each other. Diplomatic relations with the Soviet Union were restored, and Perón and Argentina traded with the Soviet Union and other Soviet Bloc countries. He was overthrown in 1955.

19. John Lewis Gaddis, *Strategies of Containment: A Critical Appraisal of Postwar National Security Policy* (New York: Oxford University Press, 1982), pp. 127–197.

20. Rabe, *Eisenhower and Latin America*, pp. 26–41. "United States Objectives and Courses of Action with Respect to Latin America" is a National Security Council document dated March 6, 1953, number 834, found in

Documents of the National Security Council, Third Supplement, academic.lexisnexis.com/documents/upa_cis/11144_DocsNSC3rdSuppl. The phrase "social evolution without revolution" is attributed to Assistant Secretary of State John Moors Cabot. Rabe, *Eisenhower and Latin America*, p. 31.

21. See "Trade Not Aid," *Time*, January 5, 1953.

22. Rabe, *Eisenhower and Latin America*, p. 39.

23. Gaddis, *Strategies of Containment*, pp. 154–157, 177; Grandin, *Empire's Workshop*, pp. 43–44; Rabe, *Eisenhower and Latin America*, pp. 162–163.

24. Rabe, *Eisenhower and Latin America*, p. 33.

25. ORIT was organized in 1951 and headquartered in Havana. Alexander, *A History of Organized Labor in Cuba*, pp. 122–123, 147; Morley, *Imperial State and Revolution*, pp. 92–93; Rabe, *Eisenhower and Latin America*, p. 34.

26. Thomas Zoumaras, "Eisenhower's Foreign Economic Policy: The Case of Latin America," in Richard A. Melanson, and David Mayers, eds. *Reevaluating Eisenhower: American Foreign Policy in the 1950s* (Urbana: University of Illinois Press, 1987), p. 161. Zoumaras reports how Chile was given a special deal in 1953.

27. Gaddis, *Strategies of Containment*, p. 157, quoting from a National Security Council memorandum.

28. Rabe, *Eisenhower and Latin America*, pp. 34–35. For example, dictator Marcos Pérez Jiménez of Venezuela, p. 36.

29. See Grandin, *Empire's Workshop*, pp. 42–44; Schoultz, *Beneath the United States*, pp. 337–343. Schoultz says that Allen Dulles misrepresented the nature of Guatemala's government to President Eisenhower. Regardless of whether any misrepresentation might have been intentional, the beneficiary of regime change in Guatemala was United Fruit Company, which had been a client of both Dulles brothers when they were in the private practice of law. Under Secretary John Moors Cabot also had a relationship with United Fruit.

30. Rabe, *Eisenhower and Latin America*, pp. 76–77.

31. Ibid., pp. 77–83. Rabe notes that between 1953 and 1961, the U.S. gave Bolivia $192 million in aid. In 1957, the U.S. supplied more that 40 percent of the entire Bolivian national budget, p. 77.

32. Ibid., p. 78. Rabe points out that Bolivia had tin, which President Eisenhower said was more valuable than gold, and that Paz Estenssoro was not as radical as some members of his own party, whom he restrained. The president's brother also had a close relationship with Paz. Ibid., pp. 77–83.

33. 1953. See "Bilateral Treaties," p. 29.

34. Entered in 1956. See "Bilateral Treaties," p. 30.

35. 1953. See "Bilateral Treaties," p. 29.

36. Entered in 1949, extended in 1951 and 1956. See "Bilateral Treaties," p. 30.

37. Entered in 1951. See "Bilateral Treaties," p. 30.

38. Entered in 1932.

39. Entered in 1905 and 1926. See "Bilateral Treaties," p. 29.

40. Entered in 1926 and 1930. See "Bilateral Treaties," p. 30.

41. Perez, *Cuba and the United States*, pp. 234–235; Paterson, *Contesting Castro*, pp. 81–84; Thomas, *Cuba: Or, the Pursuit of Freedom*, pp. 845, 947. Thomas says that Gardner thought Batista was Cuba's savior, freeing Cuba from Prío Socarrás.

42. Under the terms of the treaty, weapons were to be used only against targets identified by both countries under established defense plans. In 1957 Batista had been caught using weapons intended for hemispheric defense against

Castro and other opponents, such as the student Revolutionary Directorate. Hugh Thomas, "Cuba: The United States and Batista, 1952–58," *World Affairs* 149 (1987), p. 170. He also used them against his mutineering military at Cienfuegos in September 1957. Also see Paterson, *Contesting Castro*, pp. 125–126.

Chapter 3

1. In fact, Castro's organization was only one of several student/faculty groups opposed to Batista. For example, one of Castro's old professors at the University of Havana, Rafael García Barcena, organized a 1953 plot to take Camp Columbia, the headquarters of the Cuban military. A similar tactic had worked in 1933 as students and noncommissioned officers joined to oust the Machado regime in the Sergeants' Revolt. Castro says that García Barcena had an excellent plan and many well-placed inside operatives; with his large following, he did not need the Ortodoxo youth's help. García Barcena organized the Movimiento Nationalista Revolucionario (MNR), and heavily recruited college and high school students. Among them were Armando Hart Dávalos and Faustino Pérez, who would eventually join with Castro. Although he might well have succeeded, García Barcena tried to enlist over 20 organizations, and in so doing tipped off Batista operatives. Fidel Castro with Ignacio Ramonet, *Fidel Castro: My Life*. Translated by Andrew Hurley (New York: Scribner, 2007), pp. 104–105.

2. The term "transnational" is taken from McPherson, *Yankee No!* Many Cubans learned "Americanism" in school, and Cuban émigrés were found in the United States and in most Latin American countries. See, generally, Perez, *On Becoming Cuban*, pp. 34, 159–160.

3. When Angel Castro died, each of his children received a "sizable fortune." Herbert L. Matthews, *The Cuban Story* (New York: George Braziller, 1961), pp. 29, 137. Each supposedly received $80,000 and a share of the land holdings. Robert E. Quirk, *Fidel Castro* (New York: W.W. Norton, 1995), says the estate was worth $500,000, p. 9.

4. Julio Lobo, the "Sugar King." Thomas, *Cuba: Or, the Pursuit of Freedom*, pp. 1148–1150; "Sugar King," *Time*, July 28, 1958. He provided employees with housing, schools and churches, and had a good relationship with the unions. He was a free trader and opposed Batista's national price fixing program. Although his family had lived in Cuba since 1902, they had come by way of Venezuela and Curaçao. He was seen in Creole circles as a *moro* because he was born in Venezuela into a Sephardic Jewish family. A graduate of the sugar institute at Louisiana State University, he worked his way up from a low-level employee to owner of 11 sugar mills in Cuba (he controlled another 15 to 20 mills. He also had interests in the Capri and Riviera hotels, broadcasting, and many other industries in Cuba, Puerto Rico the Philippines and the United States.

5. In 1959, Castro's trade delegation to the United States included Juan "Pépin" Bosch and Daniel Bacardi, two Bacardi Liquors executives. Because of unrest, the company moved its trademark from Cuba to the Bahamas in 1955. Ian Williams, "The Secret History of Rum," *The Nation*, November 22, 2005. Among those with a relationship with Bacardi were the families of Desi Arnaz and Vilma Espín Guillois, the late wife of Raúl Castro, whose father was a lawyer for the company. She was a chemical engineer who attended Massachusetts Institute of Technology. As Fidel Castro was not married, she was the First Lady of Cuba after January 1, 1959, until her death in 2007.

6. Del Aquila says that frustration was the national mood. *Cuba: Dilemmas of a Revolution*, p. 24.

7. The Machadato is named for Gerardo Machado y Morales, fifth president of Cuba, who became a dictator and was later deposed. An estimated tens of thousands died during this period, and the residual effects on Cuban politics remain even today. See Jaime Suchlicki, *Cuba: From Columbus to Castro and Beyond* (Dulles, VA: Pergamon-Brassey's, 2002), pp. 109–111.

8. Suchlicki says that the entry of the military on September 4, 1933, into the Machadato was the turning point that placed Batista into power. Ibid. See also "The Sergeants' Revolution" in Thomas, *Cuba: Or, the Pursuit of Freedom*, pp. 634–649; Frank Argote Freyre, *Fulgencio Batista: From Revolutionary to Strong Man* (New Brunswick, NJ: Rutgers University Press, 2006), pp. 53–58, 65–70.

9. Montaner, *Journey to the Heart of Cuba*, p. 21. Montaner says that Batista polled barely 10 percent of the vote. Also see Georgie Ann Geyer, *Guerrilla Prince: The Untold Story of Fidel Castro* (Kansas City: Andrews McMeel Publishing, 2003), p. 95. In a survey taken in 1951, Batista polled about 14 percent of expected candidates. Domínguez, *Cuba: Order and Revolution*, p. 113.

10. Actually, the *Partido del Publo Cubano*, the Cuban People's Party.

11. Peter Bourne, *Fidel: A Biography of Fidel Castro* (New York: Dodd, Mead & Company, 1986), p. 64. Bourne, a psychiatrist, says he was "personally devastated" by the coup.

12. Patrick Symmes, *The Boys from Dolores: Fidel Castro's Classmates from Revolution to Exile* (New York: Pantheon, 2007), pp. 65–66; Quirk, *Fidel Castro*, p. 14; Geyer, *Guerrilla Prince*, pp. 32–33; Thomas, *Cuba: Or, the Pursuit of Freedom*, p. 808. Castro's letter to Roosevelt is in the National Archives in Washington, DC. A notation indicates that the president acknowledged its receipt in December 1940. He also publicly criticized a former Batista cabinet member, Juan Marinello, who was then president of the Communist Socialist Popular Party and a senator. The letter defended private schools like the Jesuit Belen Academy from government intrusion, characterizing further government regulation on the private sector as totalitarian. Although he was only a high school student, Marinello wrote a fiery retaliation in *Hoy*, the Communist newspaper, accusing him of elitism and being a divisionist in a time of war. F. Lennox Campello, "The Cuban Communist Party's Anti-Castro Activities," http://members.tripod.com/~Campello/castro.html (1987).

13. In the early 1940s, his half brother Pedro Emilio Castro Argota produced a radio program, *The Castros of Birán*. He depicted an unruly, petty, envious and argumentative family, with little sense of family love or family pride, far more detached and independent than most other Cubans. Pedro Emilio had broken with the family and became a minor Auténtico politician in Oriente Province. His Castros were a family without a Cuban identity. They were not religious people. They did not listen to Cuban music or eat Cuban food. They did not discuss their family history and their ties to Galicia. Whether Fidel was a character in the situation comedy is not reported. According to Georgie Ann Geyer, the program embarrassed Angel Castro so much that he paid Pedro Emilio to have it cancelled. Geyer, *Guerrilla Prince*, p. 21; Bourne, *Fidel: A Biography*, pp. 25–26.

14. Matthews, *The Cuban Story*, p. 137; Gonzalez, *The Pride of Havana*, p. 144; Quirk, *Fidel Castro*, p. 19. The 1945 Colegio Belen Year Book stated:

> 1942–1945. Fidel distinguished himself always in all the subjects related to letters. His record was one of excellence, he was a true athlete, always defending with bravery and pride the flag of the school. He has known how to win the admiration and the affection of all. He will make law his career and we do not doubt that he will fill with brilliant pages the book of his life. He has good timber and the actor in him will not be lacking.

15. Several sources state that Batista gave them $1,000. Antonio Rafael de la Cova, *The Moncada Attack* (Columbia: University of South Carolina Press, 2007), p. 27; Thomas M. Leonard, *Fidel Castro: A Biography* (Westport, CT: Greenwood Biographies, 2004), pp. 13–14. Rafael Díaz-Balart later denied that they had received $1,000; Batista was cheap and gave them only a table lamp. Ann Louise Bardach, *Cuba Confidential: Love and Vengeance in Miami and Havana* (New York: Random House, 2003), p. 40.

16. Rafael Díaz-Balart, Sr., Banes's mayor in 1933, was deposed after Communist-inspired takeovers of some of the mills in the area. Barry Carr, "Mill Occupations and Soviets: The Mobilisation of Sugar Workers in Cuba 1917–1933," *Journal of Latin American Studies*, February 1996, p. 129.

17. Most of his time was spent on pro bono public interest cases, and he took indigent clients that other lawyers referred to him. His brother, Ramón, apparently supported him. Montaner, *Journey to the Heart of Cuba*, p. 19. He took cases against the Cuban Telephone Company and cases against *el forrajo*, a system of semi-official graft, without much chance of success or a fee, probably to gain notoriety. Leycester Coltman, *The Real Fidel Castro* (New Haven: Yale University Press, 2003), pp. 51–52. The Cuban Telephone Company was a subsidiary of International Telephone and Telegraph Company, the American-owned monopoly, and was seen as a symbol of Cubans' lack of control over their own affairs. Castro does not mention his law partners in his autobiography and they are not mentioned by most of his biographers. However, during this period, he proved the depth of his empathy for the underdog and demonstrated his veracity.

18. He was his own publicist, describing his exploits on his daily radio program, and he was published in *Alerta*, an avant-garde newspaper. Thomas, *Cuba: Or, the Pursuit of Freedom*, pp. 819–821; Coltman, *The Real Fidel Castro*, p. 53. When a client sued a man who later would become chief of police under Batista, he generated a lot of publicity. Coltman, *The Real Fidel Castro*, p. 53. See also Thomas, *The Cuban Revolution*, p. 817. In November 1950, he was involved in a melee representing some Santa Clara high school students who were trying to organize. He was arrested and charged. Eddy Chibas reported the incident on his national Sunday-night radio show and again he became national news. Castro represented himself, and after making a passionate closing argument, was acquitted. He also was active in the Cuban Peace Committee and was a spokesman against American intervention in Korea. *Alerta* also ran articles about some of his other cases, especially a labor case involving a company that displaced an established workforce with lower paid workers, in violation of Cuban law.

In 1950–1951, he also had his own daily radio show on Radio Alverez, station COCO. Castro and Ramonet, *Fidel Castro: My Life*, p. 86; Thomas, *Cuba: Or, the Pursuit of Freedom*, p. 817. He had an ardent following but the station had limited power and was heard in only a few Havana neighborhoods. After the suicide, he wanted to assume Chibas's Sunday night program to try to reach a national audience, but was rejected. Castro and Ramonet, *Fidel Castro: My Life*, p. 87.

19. In December 1946, he apparently shot and wounded UIR leader Leonel Gómez, supposedly to prove his depth of commitment to the cause and to curry favor with Manolo Castro, an MSR leader. Manolo Castro was not related to Fidel. Thomas, *Cuba: Or, the Pursuit of Freedom*, pp. 811–812; Tad Szulc, *Fidel: A Critical Portrait* (New York: William Morrow, 1986), p. 144; Coltman, *The Real Fidel Castro*, pp. 23–24. One version is that he was provoked by Gómez. In another account, he shot at Gómez and missed, hitting Fernando Freyre de Andrade, a close friend. Bourne, *Fidel: A Biography*, Instead of holding it against him, Freyre was later an enthusiastic Castro supporter, p. 36. In February 1948, Manolo Castro was murdered. Fidel Castro was accused of committing the crime. Although Castro was arrested, he was not charged, but he was named as the primary suspect in *Tiempo en Cuba*, published by Masferrer, who by that time had become an Auténtico senator. Masferrer's nephew also spread rumors that Castro was the murderer. Szulc, *Fidel: A Critical Portrait*, pp. 172–173. Hugh Thomas says that Grau's adopted son, then aged 20, was actually accused of this killing; if true, the government needed to name a patsy. Thomas, *Cuba: Or, the Pursuit of Freedom*, p. 761.

20. In 1952, the president received $100,000 per year; members of the cabinet received $22,500 per year, associate justices of the Supreme Court, $25,000.

21. See "An Idealistic Cuban," *New York Times*, January 3, 1959, p. 2. Thomas, *Cuba: Or, the Pursuit of Freedom*, p. 870; Gott, *Cuba: A New History*, p. 164; Bourne, *Fidel: A Biography*, p. 153.

22. Fulgencio Batista, *Cuba Betrayed* (New York: Vantage Press, 1962), pp. 62–66. See also Lissner, "Batista Asserts Army Ousted Him," *New York Times*, January 10, 1959, p. 1. Batista said that the joint chiefs asked him to resign because the army would not support him. The joint chiefs had been negotiating a truce with Castro and would install an interim government. He also said that he was told that his resignation would save lives. Paterson, *Contesting Castro*, pp. 204–205; Thomas, *Cuba: Or, the Pursuit of Freedom*, pp. 1022–1024, 1026; Theodore Draper, *Abuse of Power* (New York: Viking Press, 1966,1967), pp. 5–6. On April 4, 1956, Colonel Ramón Barquín López and 29 other officers were arrested in the "Batista Day Plot." Barquín had been a Batista favorite who was named director of the Cuban Military Academy and later chief of intelligence of the Cuban Army. He had also been military attaché to Washington and received the Legion of Merit from the Eisenhower administration. Batista planned a visit to Daytona Beach, Florida, his home in the States, for a "Batista Day," and the plotters must have figured that once the invasion was underway, they would take over the military and he would never return. Thirty officers were caught and sentenced but hundreds more probably were involved. Those who were caught were court-martialed and imprisoned for conspiring with Prío, Fidel Castro and Dominican dictator Rafael Trujillo and elements of the "Caribbean Legion," reportedly allies of Prío, who were planning an invasion of Cuba from Santo Domingo, Dominican Republic. Batista, *Cuba Betrayed*, pp. 44–46. Among the others were: Major José Orihuela of the Military Academy; Rios Morejón, commander of La Cabaña Fortress; Captains Hugo Vázquez, Despaigne and Travieso

of the Division of Infantry; Captains Bernal and Villafaña and Lieutenants Travieso and Michel Yabor, all active pilots in the air force; and Lieutenant José Fernández of the military academy. In 1959, Barquín stated that others who were not caught included: Léon Dediot, Lieutenant Colonel Vicente Léon, Justo Carrillo, Felipe Pazos, Vicente Tejera, Fernando Leyva, Roberto Agramonte and Raúl Chibás. Also see Thomas, *Cuba: Or, the Pursuit of Freedom*, p. 884; Paterson, *Contesting Castro*, p. 31. In September 1957, a group of junior naval officers also mutinied against Batista. Thomas, *Cuba: Or, the Pursuit of Freedom*, pp. 784, 884; Montaner, *Journey to the Heart of Cuba*, p. 66; "Not Afraid to Die," *Time*, March 25, 1957. Eventually the generals in charge usurped Batista and tried unsuccessfully to turn over the government to Barquín. Others say that it was the United States that forced Batista to resign. Former ambassador Gardner testified before Congress that the United States "pulled the rug out" from under Batista, and there was a there was a "cult of Castro worship" in the U.S. State Department that included Under Secretary Rubottom. "Communist Threat to the United States Through the Caribbean," Hearings before the Subcommittee to Investigate the Administration of the Internal Security Act and Other Internal Security Laws, Committee on the Judiciary, United States Senate, Eighty-sixth Congress. Testimony, May 27, 1960. Some historians accuse the United States of forcing Batista to leave and organizing a plot within the military to foreclose a Castro military victory. Samuel Farber, *The Origins of the Cuban Revolution Reconsidered.* Chapel Hill: University of North Carolina Press, 2006, pp. 74–75. Suchlicki says that the work of the underground in causing terror in Havana "more than anything else" brought down Batista. *Cuba: From Columbus to Castro and Beyond*, p. 151.

23. Hugh Thomas,"Cuba: The United States and Batista, 1952–58," *World Affairs*, 149 (1987), p. 171; Montaner, *Journey to the Heart of Cuba*, pp. 81–83. Ambassador Earl E. T. Smith testified that the "Batista regime was disintegrating from within. It was becoming more corrupt, and as a result, was losing strength. The Castro forces themselves never won a military victory. The best military victory they ever won was through capturing Cuban guardhouses and military skirmishes, but they never actually won a military victory." However, Smith later blamed the State Department, the press, other government agencies, and members of Congress for helping Castro take power. "Communist Threat to the United States through the Caribbean," Hearings before the Subcommittee to Investigate the Administration of the Internal Security Act and Other Internal Security Laws, Committee on the Judiciary, United States Senate, Eighty-sixth Congress. Testimony, May 30, 1960.

24. For instance, "Fidel Castro Speaks to Citizens of Santiago," *Revolucion*, January 3, 4, 5, 1959, http://lanic.utexas.edu/project/castro/db/1959/19590103.html.

25. See generally Jaime Suchlicki, *University Students and Revolution in Cuba, 1920–1968* (Coral Gables, FL: University of Miami Press, 1969).

26. The U.S. representative was Sumner Welles. Welles actually asked President Franklin Roosevelt to send in troops to remove the government, but after American warships encircled the island and Batista moved on the government, it acquiesced. See Domínguez, *Cuba: Order and Revolution*, p. 58; Thomas, *Cuba: Or, the Pursuit of Freedom*, pp. 669–672; Paterson, *Contesting Castro*, p. 5; Suchlicki, *Cuba: From Columbus to Castro and Beyond*, 105–107, 113–114; Juan M. Del Aquila, *Cuba: Dilemmas of a Revolution*, 3rd ed. (Boulder, CO: Westview Press, 1984,

1988, 1994), pp. 21–22; Samuel Farber, *Revolution and Reaction in Cuba 1933–1960* (Middletown, CT: Wesleyan University Press), 1976, pp. 49–61.

27. Ibid; Thomas, *Cuba: Or, the Pursuit of Freedom*, pp. 650–655; Suchlicki, *Cuba: From Columbus to Castro and Beyond*, pp. 108–109, 111–114; Domínguez, *Cuba: Order and Revolution*, 58–59, 65–66, 77–79, 100–104; Gott, *Cuba: A New History*, pp. 139–141; Farber, *Revolution and Reaction in Cuba 1933–1960*, pp. 41–45, 59–61; Del Aquila, *Cuba: Dilemmas of a Revolution*, pp. 20–24.

28. R. Hart Phillips, "Castro Movement of Children Rises," *New York Times*, August 7, 1959, p. 6.

29. During the 1952 election, Fidel Castro accused President Prío of paying $18,000 a month to armed gangs at the university to use violence and threats to intimidate political opponents. Thomas, *Cuba: Or, the Pursuit of Freedom*, pp. 820–821. He probably had insider information because he had been involved with student gangs while a student himself. There was student activism in the United States in the 1950s, but it did not become a major force in American politics until the Vietnam War.

30. Raúl Castro told students at the University of Havana that the Spanish American War was an act of "international piracy" as it permitted Americans to steal their country. "Raul Castro Attacks U.S.," *New York Times*, February 25, 1960, p. 12.

31. Ibid, p. 297.

32. Del Aquila, *Cuba: Dilemmas of a Revolution*, p. 30; Thomas, *Cuba: Or, the Pursuit of Freedom*, pp. 741–743; Suchlicki, *Cuba: From Columbus to Castro and Beyond*, pp. 122–124. Among the most famous gangs was Los Tigres, a private army that ruled part of Oriente Province. It was led by Rolando Masferrer, who had been a student leader of action groups at the University of Havana after World War II. Among the *pistoleros* who opposed him at the university and later was Fidel Castro Ruz. Montaner, *Journey to the Heart of Cuba*, 14–16. Montaner says that Ernest Hemingway used Castro as a model for an assassin in "The Shot," a short story published in 1951. *True: The Men's Magazine*, April 1951, pp. 25–28.

33. United States ambassador Bonsal would later say that many Cubans left for exile because they preferred that the United States do the work of restoring Cuba over risking their own lives, and they expected the United States to do it promptly. Philip W. Bonsal, *Cuba, Castro and the United States* (Pittsburgh: University of Pittsburgh Press, 1971), pp. 112–113.

34. See Jason M. Yaremko, *U.S. Protestant Missions in Cuba: From Independence to Castro* (Gainesville: University Press of Florida, 2000), pp. 38–39, quoting racist statements of Roosevelt, General Leonard Wood and Charles E. Magoon. Also see Rabe, *Eisenhower and Latin America*, pp. 19–21, documenting racist statements of Truman administration officials.

35. "Ike Puzzled by Castro's Bitterness," *Washington Post and Times Herald*, October 29, 1959, p. A18; William J. Jorden, "Eisenhower Acts to Bar Illegal Flights — Castro Enmity Puzzles Him," *New York Times*, October 29, 1959, p. 1; "Transcript of President's News Conference on Foreign and U.S. Matters," *New York Times*, October 29, 1959, p. 19. In 1960, Eisenhower maintained the he was still confused. Warren Unna, "Ike, 'Perplexed' by Cuba, Opposes Any Reprisals," *Washington Post and Times Herald*, January 27, 1960, p. A1.

36. For instance, Jorden, "Eisenhower Acts to Bar Illegal Flights — Castro Enmity Puzzles Him," *New York Times*, October 29, 1959, p. 1.

37. See Bonsal, *Cuba, Castro and the United States*, p. 109.

38. Paterson, *Contesting Castro*, pp. 7–9, 150–159, 174, 177, 178, 192, 246; Alan McPherson, *Yankee No! Anti-Americanism in U.S.–Latin American Relations* (Cambridge, MA: Harvard University Press, 2003), p. 59; Rabe, *Eisenhower and Latin America*, pp. 173–178; Schoultz, *Beneath the United States*, pp. 377–378. Lloyd Free and Associates polled Cubans in early 1960 and found that anti-American sentiment was not overwhelming at that time. Domínguez, *Cuba: Order and Revolution*, pp. 118, 142. However, Domínguez admits in *To Make a World Safe for Revolution: Cuba's Foreign Policy* (Cambridge, MA: Harvard University Press, 1989), that United States policy toward Cuba during 1958 angered all sides in Cuba. See p. 12.

39. For example, Tad Szulc, "As Castro Speaks: 'The Wall! The Wall!'" *New York Times*, December 13, 1959, p. SM11; Coltman, *The Real Fidel Castro*, pp. 140–141; Susan Eva Eckstein, *Back from the Future: Cuba under Castro*, 2nd ed. (New York: Routledge, 2003), p. 17; "Castro at Floodtide," *Washington Post*, January 3, 1959, p. A6. Paterson, *Contesting Castro*, p. 233. Paterson reports that the British ambassador called him a combination of José Martí, Robin Hood, Garibaldi and Jesus.

40. "Creole" originally referred to Spaniards born in the New World, but is now more closely associated with "white."

41. Several authors argue that Castro was the "white hope" of the Castilian class to remove Batista, seen as "colored." See, for example, Thomas, *Cuba: Or, the Pursuit of Freedom*, p. 1121, citing Carlos Moore. Batista was the butt of racist jokes. See also Moore, *Castro, the Blacks and Africa* (Los Angeles: Center for African American Studies, UCLA, 1988).

42. Thomas, *The Cuban Revolution* (New York: Harper & Row, 1971), p. 340, and Thomas, *Cuba: Or, the Pursuit of Freedom*, p. 1122.

43. Geyer, *Guerrilla Prince*, p. 168; Ramón L. Bonachea and Marta San Martin. *The Cuban Insurrection 1952–1959* (New Brunswick, NJ: Transaction Books, 1974), p. 132; Migene González-Wippler, *Santería: The Religion, Faith, Rites, Magic* (St. Paul: Llewellyn, 1994), p. 69.

44. Thomas, *Cuba: Or, the Pursuit of Freedom*, p. 517.

45. "Fla. Death Linked to Voodooism," *Washington Post*, October 16, 1973, p. D16; Edward Tivnan, "Voodoo That New Yorkers Do," *New York Times*, December 2, 1979, p. SM46.

46. In Cuban Santería, Babalú Aye has been syncretized with Saint Lazarus.

47. Formerly secret Santería rituals, especially animal sacrifice, became public as a subject in the United States Supreme Court decision in *Church of the Lukumi Babalú Aye v. City of Hialeah*, 508 U.S. 520 (1993). Although an ordinance banned ritual slaughter, the Supreme Court protected Santería practices as a religious rite under the First Amendment to the U.S. Constitution.

48. Ibid. See also Thomas, *Cuba: Or, the Pursuit of Freedom*, pp. 516–523.

49. One author estimates that there are 300,000 in New York alone. J. E. Holloway, *Africanisms in America: Blacks in the Diaspora* (Bloomington: Indiana University Press, 1991), p. 122. A web site purporting to determine religious populations notes that it is difficult to determine worldwide numbers of "Santeríans": "Estimates of Santeríans include 800,000 in the U.S. and one million in Brazil, plus 3 million in Cuba (although many Cuban practitioners identify themselves officially as Catholics or Communists/atheists)." "Major Religions of the World Ranked by Number of Adherents," Adherents.com, http://www.adherents.com/Religions_By_Adherents.html, 2005.

50. See discussion in *Church of the Lukumi Babalú Aye v. City of Hialeah*.

51. See Edna M. Rodríguez-Mangual, *Lydia Cabrera and the Construction of an Afro-Cuban Cultural Identity* (Chapel Hill: University of North Carolina Press, 2004).

52. Published in 1940.

53. See Suchlicki, *Cuba: From Columbus to Castro and Beyond*, pp. 88, 148.

54. Sevando González, *The Secret Fidel Castro: Deconstructing the Symbol* (Oakland, Calif.: Inteli Books, 2001), pp. 264–265. See also Bonachea and San Martin, *The Cuban Insurrection 1952–1959*, p. 329.

55. See generally Halberstam, *The Fifties* (New York: Random House, 1993).

56. In the popular memory, the 1950s are often recalled as a time of boundless prosperity.

57. See "The Budget: Deficit Up," *Time*, June 16, 1958; John F. Kennedy, State of the Union Address, Washington, DC, January 30, 1961.

58. *Pleasure Island: Tourism and Temptation in Cuba*. See also Pérez, *On Becoming Cuban*, pp. 191–194, 469–470; English, *Havana Nocturne*, pp. 214–216.

59. Schwartz, *Pleasure Island*, p. 161. The 1955 movie *Guys and Dolls* depicts gangsters vacationing in decadent Havana. Schwartz notes that like *Guys and Dolls*, *I Love Lucy* was good advertising for Cuba.

60. Paar's report was attacked by Batista supporters and even some members of the United States House of Representatives. "Parr, Jack," *The Museum of Broadcast Communication*. http://www.museum.tv/archives/etv/P/htmlP/paarjack.htm. Also see "The Tonight Show: Jack Paar," http://www.timvp.com/jackpaar.html.

61. José Melis Guiu was born on February 27, 1920, in Havana and died on April 7, 2005, in Sun City, California. Although some of the musicians in his band were jazz greats, most of his albums were schmaltzy.

62. Columnist and television celebrity Dorothy Kilgallen reported that television producer Mark Goodson related that the casinos had full-time protection and that American newspapers were heavily censored to keep out news of the revolution. He also stated that the Ted Lewis show at the Riviera had 25 performers on stage in front of an audience of 15. "Judy Keeps Bodyguards Busy," *Washington Post*, March 25, 1958, p. B8.

63. Edwin A. Lahey, "Gamblers Find Cuban Paradise," *Chicago Daily News*, Jan 9, 1958.

64. "Mobsters Move In on Troubled Havana."

65. *The Godfather, Part I* (1972) was directed by Francis Ford Coppola from a screenplay by Mario Puzo and Francis Ford Coppola, as was *The Godfather, Part II* (1974).

66. Schwartz, *Pleasure Island*, pp. 154–155.

67. Moe Dalitz, Wilbur Clark, Hyman Adams, Morris Kleinman, and Thomas "Black Jack" McGinty all sold out their Cuban interests because of pressure from the Nevada Gambling Commission. Schwartz, *Pleasure Island*, p. 162; English, *Havana Nocturne*, p. 270.

68. George James, "R. Hart Phillips, Times Reporter Who Covered Castro's Revolution," *New York Times*, p. D27. See R. Hart Phillips, *Cuba, Island of Paradox* (New York: McDowell, Obolensky, 1959; New York: Astor-Honor Inc., 1960); *The Tragic Island: How Communism Came to Cuba* (Englewood Cliffs, NJ: Prentice-Hall, 1961). See also "Their Man in Havana," *Time*, January 19, 1959; "Reporting a Revolution," *Time*, February 9, 1959. Phillips was born in 1902 and died in 1985. A magazine profile

about her noted, "Ruby does most of her reporting from her desk, gets many of her leads from her radio, which blares steadily in competition with a tape recorder, a television set, and a green parrot, all in the same room." *Time*, January 19, 1959. She was born in Oklahoma and lived in Cuba from 1923. After her husband was killed in a traffic accident, she became the *New York Times* correspondent on Cuba and served from 1937 to 1961. She left the *Times* in 1963.

69. Bonsal, *Cuba, Castro and the United States*, pp. 82–83.

70. Shirley Povich, "This Morning..." *Washington Post*, October 7, 1958, p. D1

71. By law in the south, by default in the north.

72. Kilpatrick later recanted his segregationist views, but spent nine years as a conservative advocate on CBS TV's *60 Minutes*.

73. Cited in "Opinion of the Week: At Home and Abroad," *New York Times*, February 28, 1960, p. E11. Also quoted in that article is this, from Senator Strom Thurmond (R–SC): "We're going to fight to the finish [over civil rights legislation.] It's not going to be any sham battle." Later, critics would allege that the Republican Party invoked a "southern strategy" to "convert" southern voters by extending de jure integration in the south to de facto integration in the north.

74. Today there is a bust of Cole in the Hotel Nacional.

75. Robert Welch, *The Blue Book of the John Birch Society* (Belmont, MA: Self-published, 1959).

76. In 1957, Oliver Kenneth Goff alleged to the House Un-American Activities Committee that Communist Party leaders had encouraged fluoridation as a method to "keep the general public docile during a steady encroachment of Communism." According to Goff, the party discussed using fluoridation as a tool to "either kill off the populace or threaten them with liquidation, so that they would surrender to obtain fresh water." So far, there is no evidence to substantiate this, but controversy remains. In the 1964 film *Dr. Strangelove*, which satirizes Cold War politics, the character General Jack D. Ripper suffers from paranoid delusions regarding fluoridation.

77. There is some evidence that Roberto "Tarzan" Estalella actually broke the American major league baseball color line. According to Roberto Gonzáles Echevarría in *The Pride of Havana*, pp. 45, 185–186, 191, 255, 264–265, 289, and in Bjarkman, *A History of Cuban Baseball*, p. 330, he was a "light mulatto." This is also documented by Lenny Campello, *The First Black in Baseball*, http://blogcritics.org/archives/2004/08/25/122255.php (2004). He was born Roberto Estalella Ventoza in 1911 in Cárdenas, Cuba, and died January 6, 1991, in Hialeah, Florida. Estalella played for the Washington Senators (1935–36, 1939, 1942), St. Louis Browns (1941) and Philadelphia Athletics (1943–45, 1949). He was one of the players who jumped to the Mexican League and then was suspended by American baseball commissioner Happy Chandler in 1946. Estalella was permitted to return to the A's in 1949. Not only Estalella, but Tomas de la Cruz, another mulatto Cuban player, who played for Cincinnati in 1944, preceded Jackie Robinson. Peter J. Bjarkman, *A History of Cuban Baseball, 1864–2006* (Jefferson, NC: McFarland, 2007), p. 327.

78. The Treaty of Zanjón ended the Ten Year War in 1878 freed slaves who had fought on either side of the Ten Years War Spain enacted an abolition law in 1880 that established a *patronato*, a period of indentured servitude for freed slaves. Slaves were required to spend eight years under the *patronato* working for their masters at no charge, to work off their slavery. The system was abolished in 1886

by a subsequent Spanish edict. Many Cubans saw abolition of slavery as a last-ditch effort by the Spaniards to avert use of the slaves against them in a war for independence.

79. The war started on May 23. By June 27, Evaristo Estenoz, a cofounder of the Partido Indepediente de Color, a black nationalist political party, and 50 others were summarily executed near Alto Songo and their bodies were publicly displayed. "Cuban Rebel Chief Slain in Skirmish," *New York Times*, June 28, 1912, p. 5. That ended the race war.

80. Evan Thomas, *The Very Best Men: Four Who Dared* (New York: Simon and Schuster), 1996, p. 98.

81. Kathleen Brady, *Lucille: The Life of Lucille Ball* (New York: Billboard Books, 2001), pp. 215–222.

82. Ball and Arnaz both have FBI files, which are now available to the public on the Internet via the FBI's Freedom of Information Act website: http://foia.fbi.gov.

83. Welch's *The Politician: A Look at the Forces That Propelled Dwight David Eisenhower to the Presidency* (Belmont, MA: Self-published, 1954, reprinted 1961), asserted that Eisenhower was "a dedicated conscious agent of the communist conspiracy" (p. 210). In *The Actor: The True Story of John Foster Dulles, Secretary of State, 1953–1959* (Belmont, MA: Western Islands, 1968), Allen Stang accused Dulles of the same. FBI files show that Hemingway, who called the FBI the "American Gestapo," and Graham Greene were also accused in some circles of being Communist agents.

Besides Lincoln and Roosevelt, everyone in the State Department was accused by the John Birch Society of being a Communist. Milton A. Waldor, *Peddlers of Fear: The John Birch Society* (Newark, NJ: Lynnross, 1966), p. 5.

84. "Alien Labor Bar Urged," *New York Times*, July 15, 1950, p. 17; Gladwin Hill, "Peons Net Farmer a Fabulous Profit," *New York Times*, March 26, 1951, p. 25.

85. Quoted in editorial, "M'Carran and the Alien," *New York Times*, August 23, 1951, p. 21.

86. *Washington Post*, July 21, 1955, p. 20.

87. Argote Freyre, *Fulgencio Batista: From Revolutionary to Strongman*, pp. 254–255.

88. Ibid. See photograph fronting p. 219.

89. Juan Marinello and Carlos Rafael Rodríguez, both members of Batista's cabinet, later became members of the *barbudo* government. Marinello was also president of the Cuban senate under Grau, 1944–1948.

90. In the early part of World War II, Batista was accused of supporting Germany and the Soviet Union when those countries were allies. "'Down with Batista!' Shout 15,000 Cubans," *New York Times*, January 30, 1940, p. 16. "Batista Is Accused of Having Red Aides," *New York Times*, August 28, 1940, p. 4. Batista's accuser was Eduardo Chibas, later a founder of the Ortodoxo Party. In 1941, after an aborted military coup against the government, Cuban Communist Party president Juan Marinello called Batista "the Savior of democracy in Cuba." R. Hart Phillips, "Democracy Saved, Batista Tells Cuba," *New York Times*, February 5, 1941, p. 1. See also Argote Freyre, *Fulgencio Batista: From Revolutionary to Strongman*, p. 253.

91. See R. Hart Phillips, "Castro's Course Still a Puzzle," *New York Times*, February 7, 1960, p. E5.

92. *Buro de Represion Actividades Comunistas*.

93. According to the U.S. ambassador. Paterson, *Contesting Castro*, pp. 184–185. However, others place that figure at much less, as few as 9,000. Juan De Onis, "Anti-Nixon Drive Found Concerted," *New York Times*, May 10, 1958, p. 1. R. Hart Phillips reported that a 1951 census

counted 60,000 active members. "Reds' Cuban Base Reported Crushed," *New York Times*, September 27, 1953, p. 32. In 1947, the PSP, the Cuban Communist Party, listed its membership as 157,000. Mary Spargo, "Mere 14 Million Communists Are Altering Globe," *Washington Post*, May 23, 1948, p. B1.

94. Julia E. Sweig, *Inside the Cuban Revolution: Fidel Castro and the Cuban Underground* (Cambridge, MA: Harvard University Press, 2002), pp. 84–85.

95. Ibid., pp. 85–86.

96. For example, see "Castro Seeking U.S. Talks on Cuban Political Issues," *New York Times*, December 11, 1958, p. 1. Citing reporter Andrew St. George, the *Times* said that because the U.S. government had failed to act, large American companies with holdings in Oriente Province, such as the Texas Company, had begun their own negotiations with the rebels.

97. Homer Bigarts, "Rebel Chief Offers Batista Plan to End Cuban Revolt," *New York Times*, February 26, 1958, p. 1.

98. In 1957 Batista had been caught using weapons intended for hemispheric defense against Castro and other opponents, such as the Revolutionary Directorate. Hugh Thomas, "Cuba: the United States and Batista, 1952–58," *World Affairs* 149 (1987), p. 170.

99. "Soviet Will Get Cuban Sugar," *New York Times*, August 8, 1953, p. 3.

100. Thomas, *Cuba: Or, the Pursuit of Freedom*, p. 862; "Guns Guard Nixon; He Sees Batista," *Washington Post and Times Herald*, February 8, 1955, p. 2; "Governmental Stability in Cuba Impresses Nixon," *Washington Post*, February 9, 1955, p. 9.

101. Paterson, *Contesting Castro*, p. 45.

102. Batista, *The Cuban Republic*, p. 164.

103. Ibid., p. 163.

104. *The Times of Havana*.

105. Batista, *Cuba Betrayed*, p. 187.

106. George Brandon, *Santería from Africa to the New World: The Dead Sell Memories* (Bloomington: Indiana University Press, 1993).

107. *The Times of Havana*, October 11, 1957, p. 2, and October 21, 1957, p. 3.

108. Batista, *Cuba Betrayed*, p. 187.

109. In more recent times there have been two Canadian joint ventures with Geominera S.A., a Cuban state company. Miramar Mining of Vancouver, British Columbia, developed an open-pit copper mine in eastern Cuba, and Joutel Resources of Toronto is to prospect for gold, lead, silver and zinc in central and eastern Cuba. See James Brooke, "For U.S. Miners, the Rush Is on to Latin America," *New York Times*, April 17, 1994, and John M. Kirk, Peter McKenna, *Canada-Cuba Relations: The Other Good Neighbor Policy* (Gainesville: University of Florida Press, 1997), pp. 161–162.

110. See R. Hart Phillips, "Castro Opposes Alien Ownership," *New York Times*, June 11, 1959, p. 14.

111. Edison Manufacturing Company and the American Mutoscope & Biograph Company both sent cameramen to Cuba in 1898 to shoot the war. Cameramen Billy Bitzer and Arthur Marvin were sent almost immediately by Biograph to Cuba to film events related to the increasing tensions. They filmed the wreckage of the *Maine* and other scenes in Havana. The Edison Manufacturing Co. sent William Paley to cover the Cuban crisis. "Remember the Maine"— The Beginnings of War, Library of Congress, http://memory.loc.gov/ammem/sawhtml/sawsp2.html.

112. *La Habana en Agosto* 1906; *El Parque de Palestino*, and *Un Turista en la Habana*.

113. Luis, *Culture and Customs of Cuba*, p. 90.

114. Produced by Enrique Díaz Quesada, they were propaganda for the political career of Mario García Menocal.

115. Luis, *Culture and Customs of Cuba*, p. 81.

116. It has been since independence in 1902. See "Pearl of the Antilles," *National Geographic Magazine* XVII, no. 10 (October 1906); O. P. Austin, *Commercial Cuba in 1905*, Washington, DC: Bureau of Statistics, Department of Commerce and Labor, 1905.

117. Domínguez, *Cuba: Order and Revolution*, pp. 12, 35–36.

118. Bonachea and San Martín, *The Cuban Insurrection 1952–1959*, pp. 31–34; Schwartz, *Pleasure Island*, p. 138.

119. Bonachea and San Martín, *The Cuban Insurrection 1952–1959*, p. 31.

120. Ibid., pp. 33–34.

121. Thomas, *Cuba: Or, the Pursuit of Freedom*, p. 1027; Perez, *Cuba*, p. 230.

122. Perez, *Cuba*, p. 230. Perez cites the magazine *Carteles*, May 26, 1957. See also R. Hart Phillips, "Castro Regime Strikes at Graft through Drastic Cuban Reform," *New York Times*, January 28, 1959, p. 1.

123. English, *Havana Nocturne*, pp. 131–132. English alleges that banks controlled by reputed Mafia dons Amletto Battisti Lora and Amadeo Barletta Barletta were incorporated into proprietary interests of the Cuban government and into many other investments in Cuba.

124. See C. Wright Mills, *Listen Yankee: The Revolution in Cuba* (New York: McGraw-Hill, 1960), pp. 58–59.

125. English, *Havana Nocturne*, pp. 132–133.

126. Ibid., p. 132.

127. For a discussion of how things changed after the revolution see Phillips, "New Cuba Invites Tourists," *New York Times*, January 18, 1959, p. XX22.

128. Domínguez, *Cuba: Order and Revolution*, p. 94.

129. See, for example, Phillips, "Castro Regime Strikes at Graft through Drastic Cuban Reform," *New York Times*, January 28, 1959, p. 1.

130. Thomas, *Cuba: Or, the Pursuit of Freedom*, p. 1068.

131. Mills, *Listen Yankee*, p. 59.

132. See Ruth Lloyd, "Batista's Trail of Blood," *Washington Post and Times Herald*, April 19, 1959, p. AW6.

133. Ibid.

134. Thomas, *Cuba: Or, the Pursuit of Freedom*, p. 975.

135. Ibid.

136. "Cuba Ousts Judges Who Scored Army," *New York Times*, June 13, 1958, p. 3.

137. Franklyn Waltman, Jr., "Cuba's Choice — Rapid Social Reform or Complete Chaos and Terror," *Washington Post*, January 27, 1935, p. B1.

138. Russell B. Porter, "Gomez Promises Freedom in Cuba," *New York Times*, July 4, 1936, p. 1.

139. Hershey died in 1945.

140. He also set up an orphanage in Cuba called Hershey Agricultural School at Rosario. The first students were boys whose parents had been killed in an accident on the Hershey Cuban Railroad. The school was set up to train boys for jobs on the farm or in industry. See Michael D'Antonio, *Hershey: Milton S. Hershey's Extraordinary Life of Wealth, Empire, and Utopian Dreams* (New York: Simon & Schuster, 2006).

141. Paterson, *Contesting Castro*, pp 112–113, 125–126.

142. Perez, *Cuba*, p. 234; Montaner, *Journey to the Heart of Cuba*, p. 77; Thomas, *Cuba: Or, the Pursuit of Freedom*, pp. 932, 982, 983, 1014.

143. For example, see "Castro Seeking U.S. Talks on Cuban Political Issues," *New York Times*, December 11,

1958, p. 1. According to Andrew St. George, Raúl Chibás led an M-7-26 cadre that contacted Cuban army commanders to convince them to surrender.

144. Thomas, *Cuba: Or, the Pursuit of Freedom*, p. 1027.

145. Ruth Lloyd, "Batista's Trail of Blood," *Washington Post and Times Herald*, April 19, 1959, p. AW6.

146. Thomas, *Cuba: Or, the Pursuit of Freedom*, pp. 993–995.

147. Jules R. Benjamin, *The United States and the Origins of the Cuban Revolution*. (Princeton, NJ: Princeton University Press, 1990), p. 147.

148. Karl E. Meyer, "Neutrality Difficult in Castro's Revolt," *Washington Post and Times Herald*, September 19, 1958, p. A5.

149. Ibid.

150. Dick Cluster and Rafael Hernández, *The History of Havana* (New York: Palgrave Macmillan, 2008), pp. 211–212. The authors cite Carleton Beals, an American news reporter who had covered Cuba from the 1930s.

151. English, *Havana Nocturne*, pp. 98–99; Robert Lacy, *Little Man: Meyer Lansky and the Gangster Life* (New York: Little Brown), 1991, pp. 285, 289–291.

152. See Cluster and Hernández, *The History of Havana*, pp. 11–14.

153. Ibid., *The History of Havana*, p. 194.

154. Schwartz, *Pleasure Island*, p. 122.

155. Ibid., p. 138.

156. Paterson, *Contesting Castro*, pp. 195–196.

157. Ibid., pp. 188–191.

158. "Batista Seeking Absolute Power," *New York Times*, December 8, 1958, p. 1.

159. After the Cuban air force put down the mutiny at Cienfuegos using American arms in violation of the Mutual Defense Treaty, Batista was placed on notice that the United States had lost confidence in him.

160. R. Hart Phillips, "Cuban Voting Set amid Wide Curbs," *New York Times*, October 26, 1958, p. 17.

161. Batista, *The Cuban Republic*, p. 46; Phillips, "Cuban Voting Set amid Wide Curbs."

162. Domínguez says the election was "obviously fraudulent." *Cuba: Order and Revolution*, p. 124.

163. From Senate testimony: "The last big mistake he made was when he did not hold honest elections, which he had promised me on numerous and many occasions that he would have."

164. Thomas, *The Cuban Revolution*, p. 245.

165. See, for instance, Paterson, *Contesting Castro*, pp. 212–213.

166. To be replaced by General Cantillo. Castro says that he met with "the operations chief," Cantillo, and although they had worked out a deal, the army reneged. Paterson, *Contesting Castro*, pp. 216–217; Frei Betto, *Fidel and Religion: Castro Talks on Revolution and Religion with Frei Bretto* (New York: Simon and Schuster, 1987), pp. 260–261. See also Batista, *Cuba Betrayed*, pp. 110–113.

167. Thomas, *The Cuban Revolution*, 183–184.

168. See Pawley testimony of September 2, 1960, "Communist Threat to the United States through the Caribbean," Hearings before the Subcommittee to Investigate the Administration of the Internal Security Act and Other Internal Security Laws, Committee on the Judiciary, United States Senate, Eighty-sixth Congress; Thomas, *Cuba: Or, the Pursuit of Freedom*, pp. 1015–1018; Earl E. T. Smith, *The Fourth Floor: An Account of the Castro Communist Revolution* (Washington, DC: Selous Foundation, 1962, 1987), pp. 166–168. Pawley had a checkered history in Cuba. He was accused of having a sweetheart arrangement with President Prío Socarrás in 1950 when he put

together a deal to replace the trolley system with buses. He received 4 percent of the gross sale of the deal and became president and general manager of Havana's transportation agency. "Wizard at Work," *Time*, March 20, 1950.

169. Earl Smith, *The Fourth Floor*, pp. 170–174; Thomas, *Cuba: Or, the Pursuit of Freedom*, p. 1018; Paterson, *Contesting Castro*, pp. 212–213.

170. Thomas, *Cuba: Or, the Pursuit of Freedom*, p. 1019. Silito was the son of Francisco J. Tabernilla.

171. Batista, *Cuba Betrayed*, p. 111.

172. Castro was told of American involvement by rebel Pepe Echemendia. Paterson, *Contesting Castro*, p. 216. Castro alleged later that he had three reservations to the truce: First, no American involvement. Second, there would not be a coup in Havana. Third, Batista would have to remain and stand trial. Betto, *Fidel and Religion*, pp. 201–202.

173. La Conspiración de los Puros de 1956 (the conspiracy of the pure) also known as Agrupación Montecristi. The group was named for José Martí's and Maximo Gómez's *Montecristi Manifesto*, the Cuban declaration of independence from Spain, written in 1895.

174. The organization was created soon after Batista's coup in 1952. The leaders were Justo Carrillo, an economist, former student activist and president of the Bank for Reconstruction and Development in the Prío administration, and Barquín. Carrillo had been in exile in Miami and had tried to finance an expedition to free Barquín from prison and install him as head of the army. Paterson says that had Barquín been successful in 1956, or even in 1958, Carrillo might well have become president of Cuba. Paterson, *Contesting Castro*, p. 217.

175. Kornbluh, Peter, ed., *Bay of Pigs Declassified: The Secret CIA Report on the Invasion of Cuba* (New York: New Press, 1998), p. 67. The United States probably would have supported Justo Carrillo Hernández, head of Montecristi, as president, and he ostensibly had the support of Venezuela and was prepared to assume power. Carrillo flew to Washington to get support, but he was too late. Washington also did not approve of permitting Venezuelan interference into Cuban affairs. Thomas, *Cuba: Or, the Pursuit of Freedom*, pp. 994–995. Also see Paterson, *Contesting Castro*, p. 217.

176. Paterson, *Contesting Castro*, p. 230; Thomas, *Cuba: Or, the Pursuit of Freedom*, pp. 1027–1028; Earl Smith, *The Fourth Floor*, pp. 200–101.

177. Paterson, *Contesting Castro*, pp. 217–218.

178. Montaner, *Journey to the Heart of Cuba*, p. 78.

179. Batista, *The Cuban Republic*, pp. 45–47.

180. Rubottom would become a controversial figure. In "Communist Threat to the United States through the Caribbean," Hearings before the Subcommittee to Investigate the Administration of the Internal Security Act and Other Internal Security Laws, Committee on the Judiciary, United States Senate, Eighty-sixth Congress, Second Session, Part 9, August 27, 30, 1960, former ambassadors to Cuba Arthur Gardner and Earl E. T. Smith accused Rubottom and William Wieland of facilitating a Communist takeover of the Cuban government. See also "Diplomatic Intervener," *New York Times*, February 20, 1960, p. 12.

181. Russell Baker, "Batista Is in Peril, U.S. Aide Reports," *New York Times*, January 1, 1959, p. 1.

182. Ibid.

183. Ibid.

Chapter 4

1. Editorial de Ciencias Sociales (La Habana, Cuba, 1975). Translated by Pedro Álvarez Tabío and Andrew Paul Booth. http://www.marxists.org/history/cuba/archive/castro/1953/10/16.htm.

2. Nicaraguan poet Rubén Darío also has a claim to be the father of this school.

3. Pérez, *Cuba*, pp. 145–147; Gott, *Cuba: A New History*, pp. 84–90.

4. Luis, *Culture and Customs of Cuba*, p. 103.

5. Carlos Alberto Monataner, *Cuba, Castro and the Caribbean* (New Brunswick, NJ: Transaction Publishers, 1985), pp. 63–70.

6. José Martí, "Mi Raza" ("My Race"), *Patria*, April 16, 1893, trans. and reprinted in *José Martí: Selected Writings*, ed. and trans. Esther Allen (New York: Penguin, 2002), pp. 318–320.

7. For example, Martí reported on the May 1, 1886, Haymarket riot in Chicago, when police were bombed as they were en route to break up a strike. A gun battle ensued. Eight anarchists were arrested, and they were later tried for the murder of seven police officers. Dozens of strikers and bystanders were killed in the melee. Four of the strikers were executed, and another committed suicide in prison. By 1887 Martí had concluded that democracy in the United States was merely a myth. Although he formerly considered himself a member of an enlightened bourgeoisie, after the execution of the Haymarket strike leaders, Martí espoused a distrust of economic elites and wrote that on each May Day, the working class of the world would bring the memories of executed Haymarket strike leaders back to life. See Christopher Conway, "The Silent Hero," *A Contra Corriente* 4, no. 1 (Fall 2006), pp. 155–162; Conway, "The Limits of Analogy: José Martí and the Haymarket Martyrs," *A Contra Corriente* 2, no. 1 (Fall 2004); Monataner, *Cuba Castro and the Caribbean*, pp. 63–70.

8. Gott, *Cuba: A New History*, p. 150. Thomas says that 68 were killed. *Cuba: Or, the Pursuit of Freedom*, pp. 838–839. However, in *The Moncada Attack: Birth of the Cuban Revolution,* Antonio Rafael de la Cova disputes the figures and disputes that there was widespread torture of prisoners.

9. The Havana bar association appointed Jorge Pagliery, its dean, to represent the Castros, but Pagliery was not permitted to interview Castro in private and was given only 10 minutes to prepare, so Castro decided to represent himself.

10. Article 148 of the Cuban Constitution of 1940 read: "A penalty of imprisonment of from three to ten years shall be imposed upon the perpetrator of any act aimed at bringing about an armed uprising against the Constitutional Powers of the State. The penalty shall be imprisonment for from five to twenty years, in the event that insurrection actually be carried into effect."

11. "One day eighteen hoodlums got together. Their plan was to assault the Republic and loot its 350 million pesos annual budget. Behind people's backs and with great treachery, they succeeded in their purpose. 'Now what do we do next?' they wondered. One of them said to the rest: 'You name me Prime Minister, and I'll make you generals.' When this was done, he rounded up a group of 20 men and told them: 'I will make you my Cabinet if you make me President.' In this way they named each other generals, ministers and president, and then took over the treasury and the Republic."

12. Castro accused Batista and his cronies of using the government and its employees for private gain. For example, Batista henchmen replaced civilian labor with soldiers and "put them to work as doormen, chauffeurs, servants and bodyguards for the whole rabble of petty politicians." He accused Batista's pals of having made fortunes using the military at no cost instead of hiring private labor.

13. The cabinet voted to supersede the Constitution, asserting that Cuba was in a state of crisis: "Since these changes may be brought about by a vote of two-thirds of the Cabinet and the Cabinet is named by the President, then the right to make and break Cuba is in the hands of one man, a man who is, furthermore, the most unworthy of all the creatures ever to be born in this land. Was this then accepted by the Court of Social and Constitutional Rights? And is all that derives from it valid and legal?"

14. Castro alleged after Moncada that Batista's army was told not to give any of the conspirators a chance to stand trial. Troops were told to kill 10 prisoners for each dead soldier. He told how an unarmed physician was shot dead. He told how one of his comrades was tortured: Soldiers had captured Haydee Santamaria, and brought her a bloody human eyeball. "This eye belonged to your brother. If you will not tell us what he refused to say, we will tear out the other," she was reportedly told. Two others, hospital patients, were killed while receiving transfusions. "In the early morning hours, groups of our men were removed from the barracks and taken in automobiles to Siboney, La Maya, Songo, and elsewhere. Then they were led our — ried, gagged, already disfigured by the torture — and were murdered in isolated spots. They are recorded as having died in combat against the Army. This went on for several days, and few of the captured prisoners survived. Many were compelled to dig their own graves. One of our men, while he was digging, wheeled around and slashed the face of one of his assassins with his pick. Others were even buried alive, their hands tied behind their backs. Many solitary spots became the graveyards of the brave. On the Army target range alone, five of our men lie buried. Some day these men will be disinterred. Then they will be carried on the shoulders of the people to a place beside the tomb of Martí, and their liberated land will surely erect a monument to honor the memory of the Martyrs of the Centennial." Castro outlined Batista's "treachery of January, 1934, the crimes of March, 1935 and the forty million dollar fortune that crowned his first regime. He had to add the treason of March, 1952, the crimes of July, 1953, and [the theft of] all the millions that only time will reveal." He accused Batista of a history of similar murders of political opponents: "It is common knowledge that in 1933, at the end of the battle at the National Hotel, some officers were murdered after they surrendered. *Bohemia* magazine protested energetically. It is also known that after the surrender of Fort Atarés the besiegers' machine guns cut down a row of prisoners. And that one soldier, after asking who Blas Hernández was, blasted him with a bullet directly in the face, and for this cowardly act was promoted to the rank of officer. It is well-known in Cuban history that assassination of prisoners was fatally linked with Batista's name."

15. Castro cited Professor Infiesta, author of a book on constitutional law: He "differentiates between the political and legal constitutions, and states: 'Sometimes the Legal Constitution includes constitutional principles which, even without being so classified, would be equally binding solely on the basis of the people's consent, for example, the principle of majority rule or representation in our democracies.'" Ramon Infiesta, *The Right of Resistance to Oppression in the Cuban Constitution.*

16. Batista lived in the United States in the late 1940s and liked the Thanksgiving holiday so much that he decreed it a Cuban national holiday. Batista, *The Cuban Republic*, p. 210; also see "Senator from Daytona," *Time*, April 12, 1948. "When Strong Man Fulgencio Batista's candidate lost the presidency to hollow-eyed Ramon Grau San Martin in 1944's free elections, Batista promptly and discreetly took a plane for Miami. Since then, backed by a jumbo-sized bank roll, he has sat out a pleasant exile in some of the New World's toniest suites." He later moved to Daytona Beach. "Every fortnight, Batista drives off to Palm Beach, Orlando or Fort Pierce for secret meetings with aides who bring the political word from Cuba and take back his instructions. Only when the Cuban government discovers an arms cache and shouts 'Batista plot!' are Floridians reminded that their guest is dynamite."

17. Suchlicki, *Cuba: From Columbus to Castro and Beyond*, pp. 76–77.

18. Gott, *Cuba: A New History*, pp. 133–134; Suchlicki, *Cuba: From Columbus to Castro and Beyond*, p. 104; Thomas, *Cuba: Or, the Pursuit of Freedom*, p. 594.

19. Gott, *Cuba: A New History*, p. 134. Their motto, "Cuba First," and their scapegoating of minorities and foreigners reflected similar nationalist-socialist regimes of the period.

20. See testimony of Francisco J. Tabernilla, "Communist Threat to the United States through the Caribbean," U.S. Senate Subcommittee to Investigate the Administration of the Internal Security Act and Other Internal Security Laws, of the Committee on the Judiciary, May 6, 1960. When asked whether the Cuban people would take Batista back, the general responded: "The Cuban people would not take Batista any more; I am sure of that."

Chapter 5

1. In *War or Peace*, published in 1950, Dulles lays out his political philosophy.

2. Besides being a politician, an author, a lawyer and a diplomat, Dulles was a lay leader of the Presbyterian Church. He wrote several articles and gave important speeches outlining his religious views. In time, his opinions on religion merged with his world view. See, generally, Immerman, *Piety, Pragmatism and Power in U.S. Foreign Policy*; Dulles, *The Spiritual Legacy of John Foster Dulles;* Hoopes, *The Devil and John Foster Dulles*.

3. Drew Pearson, "Ike Ponders Trip to Latin America," *Washington Post*, November 20, 1952, p. 51.

4. See "Text of Address by President Eisenhower at Pan American Union," *New York Times*, April 13, 1953, p. 13.

5. Dana Adams Schmidt, "Dulles Applauds Caracas Results," *New York Times*, March 15, 1954, p. 1; John Lewis Gaddis, *The Last Years of the Monroe Doctrine, 1945–1993* (New York: Macmillan and Company, 1995), p. 81; Immerman, *Piety, Pragmatism and Power in U.S. Foreign Policy*, p. 111.

6. Guatemala's delegate called it the internationalization of McCarthyism.

7. See "Trade Not Aid," *Time*, January 5, 1953; Rabe, *Eisenhower and Latin America*, pp. 73–77.

8. Cuba included.

9. Ronald W. Preussen, *John Foster Dulles: The Road to Power* (New York: The Free Press, 1982), p. 22; Immerman, *Piety, Pragmatism and Power in U.S. Foreign Policy*, p. 109; Schoultz, *Beneath the United States*, p. 340.

10. Schoultz says that company records show that Allen Dulles had been billing United Fruit for trips to Guatemala when he was a lawyer for Sullivan and Cromwell. *Beneath the United States*, p. 338.

11. Gaddis, *The Last Years of the Monroe Doctrine*, pp. 79–81.

12. Ann Whitman, married to Ed Whitman. Schoultz, *Beneath the United States*, p. 338.

13. "Caribbean Bloc Urged by Nixon," *New York Times*, March 5, 1955, p. 1.

14. John Lewis Gaddis, *The Cold War: A New History* (New York: Penguin Group, 2005), pp. 123–124; Immerman, *Piety, Pragmatism and Power in U.S. Foreign Policy*, pp. 92, 93, 95–96; Hoopes, *The Devil and John Foster Dulles*, pp. 214, 446.

15. Warsaw Pact members were the Soviet Union, Hungary, Czechoslovakia, Poland, Bulgaria, Romania, Albania, and East Germany.

16. Dana Adams Schmidt, "U.S. Backs Spain in Western Role," *New York Times*, March 24, 1960, p. 4.

17. See *Report of the Special Committee on the Problem of Hungary*. New York: United Nations General Assembly. Official Records: Eleventh Session, Supplement 18 (A/3592), 1957; and "The 1956 Hungarian Revolution: A History in Documents," George Washington University, The National Security Archive.

18. At the time, Lebanon was dominated by the Christian Phalangists.

19. Schoultz, *Beneath the United States*, pp. 212–219.

20. Schoultz, *Beneath the United States*, p. 346. In his *Empire's Workshop* (p. 50) Grandin says the U.S. merely paved the way.

21. It is alleged that he declared war to take the properties of German landholders.

22. See "The OAS: Trying to Hold the Americas Together," *Time*, May 14, 1965.

23. Somoza García was murdered by poet and musician Rigoberto López Pérez, who was also killed.

24. See, for instance, "Trujillo Appeals to Americas Unit," *New York Times*, January 1, 1950, p. 10.

25. "Trujillo Signs Nationalizing Bill," *New York Times*, January 1, 1955, p. 3.

26. Schoultz, *Beneath the United States*, p. 348.

27. The Remón-Eisenhower Treaty.

28. McPherson, *Yankee No!*, pp. 92–93.

29. "A Dangerous Person," *Time*, August 27, 1951.

30. While the White House was being renovated, Truman stayed at Blair House. On November 1, 1950, during a shootout, one of the assassins and a police officer were killed. President Truman was unharmed. Although a would-be assassin was captured, convicted and sentenced for execution, Truman commuted the sentence rather than make him a martyr. Kris Hollington, *Wolves, Jackals, and Foxes: The Assassins Who Changed History* (New York: Macmillan, 2008), pp. 6–11.

31. "Puerto Rico Is Not Free," *Time*, March 8, 1954; "Aftermath," *Time*, March 15, 1954. In 1953, he was paroled by Puerto Rican governor Muñoz Marín, whom he had tried to murder. However, after the attack on the Capitol, the pardon was revoked.

32. Szulc, *Fidel: A Critical Portrait*, p. 364.

33. "Aftermath."

34. "Plain Talk," *Time*, May 12, 1958.

35. John Vinocur, "A Republic of Fear," *New York Times Magazine*, September 23, 1984, pp. 21–23. Nixon's briefing must also have noted the number of political prisoners in Paraguay and the reports of torture of political prisoners. One obituary reported that the specialty of Stroessner's chief torturer, Pastor Coronel, was to conduct

interviews with the subject immersed in a bath of human excrement. If, after that, the subject still resisted, Coronel would administer further encouragement with an electric cattle prod, administered from behind. "Alfredo Stroessner, 93, Old-Style Military Dictator of Paraguay," *The Daily Telegraph*, August 17, 2006. See also Diana Jean Schemo, "Stroessner, Paraguay's Enduring Dictator, Dies, *New York Times*, August 16, 2006.

36. According to Pérez's obituary, it was run by Pedro Estrada, whom Hubert Herring in *The History of Latin America from the Beginnings to the Present* called "as vicious a manhunter as Hitler ever employed." Larry Rohter, "Marcos Pérez Jiménez, 87, Venezuelan Ruler," *New York Times*, September 22, 2007.

37. Ibid.

38. Alan McPherson, *Yankee No!*, pp. 9–37. A report states: "A mob surrounded his car and began rocking it back and forth, trying to turn it over and chanting 'Death to Nixon.'" Protected by only twelve Secret Service agents, the procession was forced to wait for the Venezuelan military to clear a path of escape. But by that time, the car had been nearly demolished and the vice president had seen his fill of South America. President Eisenhower sent a naval squadron to the Venezuelan coast in case they needed to rescue the vice president, but Nixon quietly left the country the next day. He returned to Washington to a hero's welcome. Over 15,000 people met him at the airport, including President Eisenhower and the entire cabinet. Over the next few days, politicians of both parties throughout the nation praised Nixon's courage, and congratulations poured in by the thousands. It was Nixon's shining moment, but the respect was more the result of Americans rallying behind their vice president than any change in Nixon's standing." "Richard M. Nixon, 36th Vice President (1953–1961)," United States Senate, http://www.senate.gov/artandhistory/history/common/generic/VP_Richard_Nixon.htm.

39. "Point 4 Pact Signed with Cuba," *New York Times*, June 21, 1951; p. 11.

40. "Soft and Hard," *New York Times*, March 29, 1953, p. E1.

41. "A Country by Country Survey of the Free World Communist Bloc Trading," *New York Times*, July 7, 1958, p. 7.

42. Tad Szulc, "Nixon to Propose New Latin Policy," *New York Times*, May 16, 1958, p. 12.

43. "Governmental Stability in Cuba Impresses Nixon," *Washington Post and Times Herald*, February 9, 1955, p. 9; "Nixon Begins Talks on Cuban Problems," *New York Times*, February 8, 1955; p. 16. Anthony Summers and Robyn Swan claim in *The Arrogance of Power: The Secret World of Richard Nixon* (New York: Viking Press, 2000) that Nixon allegedly had ties with Batista from his days as a tourist at the Hotel Nacional in Havana, where he had sustained large gambling losses. Nixon's close friend Bebe Rebozo reportedly was involved in Lansky gambling operations in the Miami area and also in New Orleans.

44. Murat Halstead, *The Story of Cuba: Her Struggles for Liberty: The Cause, Crisis and Destiny* (Chicago: The Werner Company, 1896), p. 29; Montaner, *Journey to the Heart of Cuba*, pp. 23–36; Gott, *Cuba: A New History*, pp. 57–59.

45. Jefferson in a letter to President Monroe, October 24, 1823, said: "I candidly confess that I have ever looked on Cuba as the most interesting addition which could be made to our system of States." The Monroe Doctrine was not issued until 1823, but as early as 1783, John Adams,

later to become the second president (1797–1801), said that Cuba was a natural extension of the North American continent, and that annexation would eventually be necessary. See, generally, Gaddis, *The Last Years of the Monroe Doctrine*.

46. "United States Supreme Court — The Proposed Purchase of Cuba in 1846," *New York Times*, December 10, 1852, p. 10, reports that Pierre Soulé of Louisiana made the offer on behalf of President James Knox Polk. Later, Polk authorized Secretary of State James Buchanan and Ambassador to Spain Romulus Mitchell Saunders to pay $100 million for Cuba in 1848. In 1854, Buchanan, Soulé and John Y. Mason wrote the Ostend Manifesto, which recommended taking Cuba as a slave-holding territory. The price had risen to $120 million. But refusal of the offer justified America in "wresting" Cuba from Spain. Amos S. Hershey, "The Recognition of Cuban Belligerency," *Annals of the American Academy of Political and Social Science* 7 (May 1896), pp. 74–85.

47. Louis A. Pérez, *Essays on Cuban History: Historiography and Research* (Gainesville: University Presses of Florida, 1995), p. 38, quoting Theodore Roosevelt to Henry Cabot Lodge, July 21, 1899, *Roosevelt Papers*.

48. 1868–78. Described as a stalemate, it ended with the Treaty of Zanjón.

49. *The Times of Havana*, September 16, 1957, p. 1. Louis Pérez Jr. estimated that there were 6,500 Americans in Cuba, most of them living in Havana. *Cuba and the United States*, p. 220.

50. Barnet Nover, "Nazi 5th Column Woos Cuba with Help from Spaniards," *Washington Post*, July 28, 1940, p. 6; "Anti-Falangist Talk in Cuba Angers Spain," *New York Times*, December 26, 1940, p. 13.

51. *The Times of Havana*, October 11, 1957, p. 2, and October 21, 1957, p. 3.

52. Greene called it an "entertainment" rather than a novel.

53. "The Vengeful Visionary," *Time*, January 26, 1959; "Britain Praises Rebels," *New York Times*, January 7, 1959, p. 16, Bonsal, *Cuba, Castro and the United States*, pp. 98–99; Seymour Topping, "Europe Supplies Caribbean Arms Despite U.S. Curb," *New York Times*, November 1, 1959, p. 1.

54. See "Britain Grants Recognition," *New York Times*, January 8, 1959, p. 3. Greene said that the British Foreign Office had even failed to recognize that a civil war was ongoing in Cuba.

55. Similar to the account of Haydee Santamaria at the Moncada uprising in 1953.

56. *Time*, January 26, 1959.

57. Bonsal, *Cuba, Castro and the United States*, p. 15; R. Hart Phillips, *Cuba, Island of Paradox*, pp. 284–285. General Salas Canizares was shot during the incursion at the embassy. Ernestina Otero was a witness.

58. Ramón Barquín and the Puros. Thomas, *Cuba: Or, the Pursuit of Freedom*, pp. 784, 884; Montaner, *Journey to the Heart of Cuba*, p. 66.

59. "Not Afraid to Die," *Time*, March 25, 1957.

Chapter 6

1. "A Former Army Stenographer, Batista Ruled Twice over Cuba," *New York Times*, January 2, 1959, p. 7.

2. Ibid.

3. Quote from Luis A. Baralt, Cuban consul general to New York, "Freedom Called Cuban Stimulant," *New York Times*, March 1,1959, p. F1. During the revolution,

Baralt resigned from the Cuban Foreign Service and exiled himself to Pleasantville, New York. "I do not have a beard, but I worked for the Revolution," he told the *New York Times.*

4. De la Cova, *The Moncada Attack*, p. 3.

5. Although the Communist Party was suppressed by Batista in 1952, it remained a force in Cuban politics. In fact, although he closed other newspapers and censored the press, Batista did not disturb *Hoy*, the Communist daily newspaper.

6. Thomas, *Cuba: Or, the Pursuit of Freedom*, p. 1026.

7. He is quoted by Carlos Franqui in *Diary of the Cuban Revolution* (New York: Viking Press, 1980): "[T]he first of January was also a terrible day.... We were betrayed, and an attempt was made to snatch victory from the people. We had to act very swiftly." p. 495.

8. Earl E. T. Smith, *The Fourth Floor*, p. 187.

9. Thomas, *Cuba: Or, the Pursuit of Freedom*, pp. 1027–1030; Coltman, *The Real Fidel Castro*, p. 137; R. Hart Phillips, "Castro Moving to Take Power," *New York Times*, January 1, 1959, p. 1. Actually, Piedra knew that the other justices of the Supreme Court would not support him as president. Bonachea and San Martin, *The Cuban Insurrection 1952–1959*, pp. 314–315. Justices Julio Garcerón and Enrique Rodrigues Narezo issued a statement saying that "a victorious revolution has taken place," obviating normal constitutional secession.

10. Ibid.

11. Thomas, *Cuba: Or, the Pursuit of Freedom*, p. 1028; Earl E. T. Smith, *The Fourth Floor*, pp. 185–186, 200–201. Cantillo told Smith that Batista had left him a "dead army."

12. See Phillips, "Cuba May Have a Tourist Season," *New York Times*, January 11, 1959, p. X23. Although Phillips had initially reported that there was massive damage, she later reported that the only hotels with much damage were the Hotel Sevilla Biltmore and the Hotel Plaza. Although the Capri had some glass damage, the rest were all intact. Also see Peter Khiss, "Batista and Regime Flee Cuba," *New York Times*, January 2, 1959, p. 1; Herbert L. Matthews, "Castro Aims Reflect Character of Cubans," *New York Times*, January 18, 1959, p. E6. Matthews says that the reason there was little damage was that Castro's men were well disciplined. In *Cuba, Island of Paradox*, Phillips describes how there was little damage considering the expectations from the Machado era. pp. 395–397.

13. Earl E. T. Smith, *The Fourth Floor*, pp. 187, 189.

14. Thomas, *Cuba: Or, the Pursuit of Freedom*, p. 1032.

15. E. G. Coltman, *The Real Fidel Castro*, pp. 140–141; "Castro Decrees a Halt in Strike Paralyzing Cuba," *New York Times*, January 5, 1959, p. 1. Gott, *Cuba: A New History*, p. 167.

16. "Castro at Floodtide," January 3, 1959, p. A6.

17. R. Hart Phillips, "Havana Welcomes Castro at End of Triumphal Trip," *New York Times*, January 9, 1959, p. 1.

18. Hebert L. Matthews, "Castro Aims Reflect Character of Cubans," *New York Times*, January 18, 1959, p. E6.

19. Earl E. T. Smith, *The Fourth Floor*, pp. 190–191. M-7-26 was less reluctant to permit American airlines to ferry people, as it was afraid that public property would be smuggled out.

20. Joseph U. Hinshaw, "U.S. Prepared to Evacuate Americans from Havana," *Washington Post*, January 2, 1959, p. A7; Gardner Bridge, "U.S. Doubts Peril to Americans but Orders Precautions," *Washington Post*, January 3, 1959, p. A1.

21. Ibid.

22. "Cuban Rebels Shoot 75 Beside Grave; One Directs Own Execution for TV," *Washington Post and Times Herald*, January 13, 1959, p. A1.

23. Bonachea and San Martin, *The Cuban Insurrection 1952–1959*, p. 320.

24. Coltman, *The Real Fidel Castro*, p. 140; Geyer, *Guerrilla Prince*, pp. 198–199.

25. "Huber Matos, a Moderate in the Cuban Revolution," *PBS American Experience*, http://www.pbs.org /wgbh/amex/castro/peopleevents/e_moderates.html. Matos would later spend 20 years in prison for treason after he submitted a letter of resignation in October 1959, citing his concern with the growing influence of Communists in Cuba's revolutionary government.

26. "An Idealistic Cuban," *New York Times*, January 3, 1959, p. 2. Thomas, *Cuba: Or, the Pursuit of Freedom*, p. 870; Gott, *Cuba: A New History*, p. 164; Bourne, *Fidel: A Biography*, p. 153.

27. Thomas, *Cuba: Or, the Pursuit of Freedom*, pp. 870, 1065. Bonachea and San Martin, *The Cuban Insurrection 1952–1959*, p. 321.

28. See Jules Dubois, *Operation America: The Communist Conspiracy in Latin America* (New York: Walker, 1963); Alan McPherson, *Yankee No!*; Herbert Matthews, "A New Chapter Opens in Latin America," *New York Times*, January 11, 1959, p. SM13.

29. Subsequent reports stated that President Eisenhower and Secretary of State Dulles had been given notice in October 1958 that Batista was "doomed" and that Castro would soon take power. "Congress Concerned," *New York Times*, January 12, 1959, p. 8.

30. State Department Dispatch 292.

31. Wayne S. Smith, *The Closest of Enemies: A Personal and Diplomatic Account of U.S.- Cuban Relations since 1957* (New York: W.W. Norton, 1987), p. 35. Ambassador Smith's version is Earl E. T. Smith, *The Fourth Floor*, pp. 164–187.

32. "Cuba in Dire Straits," p. 18.

33. "Cuba Releases U.S. Teachers," *Washington Post*, December 31, 1958, p. A4.

34. "Cuba Rebels Don't Want Mediation, Fidel Castro's Agent Here Declares," *Washington Post*, January 1, 1959, p. A4.

35. "Batista Sons Fly Here from Cuba," p. 1.

36. "Powder Magazines Explode," *New York Times*, December 31, 1958, p. 4.

37. Gott, *Cuba: A New History*, pp. 129–135; Pérez, *Cuba*, pp. 197–200; Thomas, *Cuba: Or, the Pursuit of Freedom*, pp. 209–216. .

38. *New York Times*, March 8, 1952, p. 4.

39. "Ike tells Russia to 'Live' Peace Hopes," Associated Press, January 2, 1959.

40. Batista, *The Cuban Republic*, p. 4. Batista said that sugar exports sank from more than $1 billion in 1920 to $45,256,000 in 1933.

41. Suchlicki, *University Students and Revolution in Cuba*, pp. 33–34.

42. Batista, *The Cuban Republic*, p. 4.

43. Gott, *Cuba: A New History*, pp. 136–137; Barry Carr, "Mill Occupations and Soviets: The Mobilisation of Sugar Workers in Cuba 1917–1933," *Journal of Latin American Studies* (February 1996), p. 129.

44. Taken from Helena, Montana, *Independent Record*, January 1, 1959.

45. Ibid., "Young Batista Tells Story of Family Fleeing."

46. Later revelations showed that Ruben had broken

with his father. A son of the first Batista marriage, Ruben reportedly confronted his father and called him a murderer to his face. Lloyd, "Batista's Trail of Blood," *Washington Post and Times Herald*, April 19, 1959, p. AW6.

47. See, for instance, Paterson, "Madhouse, Castro's Victory, Smith's Defeat," in *Contesting Castro*, pp. 226–227. Paterson cites Ruby Phillips and Herbert and Nancy Matthews to depict widespread looting and destruction. Similar stories were also reported by the wire services. However, the facts do not substantiate this. The police did not resist. There were some firefights, principally between M-7-26 and the Tigers, a private army run by Rolando Masferrer, an ally of Batista. The crowds did decapitate all the parking meters in Havana, and plate glass store windows were shattered. Some looters were shot. There was some rioting, but not much looting. Three casinos were trashed, but the rest had little or no damage. Paterson cited a story that actor George Raft had turned away "the mob" at the Capri Hotel, where he was working. However, this story is highly dubious. R. Hart Phillips's "Castro Moving to Take Power," *New York Times*, January 1, 1959, p. 1, in which she describes mass riots, is impeached in her book *Cuba, Isle of Paradise*, pp. 396–398, where she states that as soon as the "militia," members of the M-7-26 underground and *barbudos* appeared, order was restored.

48. "Castro Troops Move Rapidly into Havana," Associated Press, January 2, 1959.

49. Bonachea and San Martín, *The Cuban Insurrection 1952–1959*, p. 321.

50. Ibid.

51. Ibid., p. 48.

52. Thirty-five DR student members were killed, including almost all of the top members. Only five of Batista's guard were killed.

53. Bonachea and San Martín, *The Cuban Insurrection 1952–1959*, pp. 175–176, 185–187; Shetterly, *The Americano*, pp. 33, 38–40; Sweig, *Inside the Cuban Revolution*, pp. 106, 180. In order to avoid confusion, note that M-7-26 opened a "second front" in Oriente Province named after M-7-26 martyr Frank País in early 1958, under the command of Raúl Castro.

54. Bonachea and San Martín, *The Cuban Insurrection 1952–1959*, pp. 184–187; Thomas, *Cuba: Or, the Pursuit of Freedom*, pp. 979–981;

55. Bonachea and San Martín, *The Cuban Insurrection 1952–1959*, pp. 185 187.

56. Shetterly, *The Americano*, pp. 144–148. Castro named William Morgan, an American expatriate second in command to Gutiérrez Menoyo, as military governor of the city of Cienfuegos after Morgan and his men took the city on January 1, 1959.

57. Gardner Bridge. "U.S. Doubts Peril to Americans but Orders Precautions," *Washington Post*, January 3, 1959, p. A1. See also "Cuba Visitor Tells of Gang Suppression," *Washington Post and Times Herald*, January 7, 1959, p. A5, in which a traveler reported how M-7-26 members stopped the riots.

58. Francis L. McCarthy, "Castro Halts Cuba Strike; Shops Open," *Washington Post and Times Herald*, January 5, 1959, p. A1.

59. "A Cuban Dictator Falls," January 2, 1959, p. 24.

60. "A Symbol of Rebellion: Fidel Castro," *New York Times*, January 2, 1959, p. 6.

61. Ibid.

62. "Aftermath in Cuba," *New York Times*, January 3, 1959, p. 16.

63. Will Lissner, "Batista Asserts Army Ousted Him,"

New York Times, January 10, 1959, p. 1; "Batista Recounts Defection of Aides," *New York Times*, January 22, 1959, p. 7. Batista initially said that the joint chiefs asked him to resign because the army would not support him. The joint chiefs had been negotiating a truce with Castro and would install an interim government. He also said that he was told that his resignation would save lives. Paterson, *Contesting Castro*, pp. 204–205; Thomas, *Cuba: Or, the Pursuit of Freedom*, pp. 1022–1024, 1026. He later said that his key aides had defected. "Batista Recounts Defection of Aides," *New York Times*, January 22, 1959, p. 7.

64. "Three American Writers Seized," Associated Press, January 2, 1959. Actually two were writers, Larry Allen and George Kauffman. The third was A. P. Valentine, a photographer. The same day, Allen wrote "Battle in Havana Kills 40; Entry of Rebel Chiefs Put Off," *Washington Post*, January 2, 1959, p. A1. Allen described Havana as "bedraggled, still tense after a day of rioting."

65. R. Hart Phillips, "New Cuba Invites Tourists," *New York Times*, January 18, 1959, p. XX22.

66. R. Hart Phillips, "Castro Regime Strikes at Graft through Drastic Cuban Reform," *New York Times*, January 28, 1959, p. 1. The police could also put down bets without paying for them and received food and other items without cost as a matter of course.

67. Herbert S. Parmet, *Eisenhower and the American Crusades* (New York: Macmillan, 1972), p. 540.

68. Ibid., p. 561.

Chapter 7

1. Gott, *Cuba: A New History*, p. 162. Although he did not sign it, Pérez wrote most of it.

2. Some sources state that there were 124,000 Cubans living in the United States in 1959. See Clark, *The Exodus from Revolutionary Cuba, 1959–1974*, and "Cuban Immigration to the United States," culturalorientation.net, http://www.cal.org/co/cubans/IMMI.HTM. Also see "Analysis of the Opposition Movement to the Castro Regime," Foreign Service Dispatch, American Embassy, December 6, 1960, quoted in Maria de los Angeles Torres, *In the Land of Mirrors: Cuban Exile Politics in the United States* (Ann Arbor: University of Michigan Press, 2001), p. 205, footnote 1. The United States Census documented that by 1960, 79,150 Cubans were residing in the United States. United States Department of Commerce, Bureau of the Census, *Historical Statistics of the United States*, PC 80, S1–7.

3. Paterson, *Contesting Castro*, p. 216.

4. Sweig, *Inside the Cuban Revolution*, pp. 172–173.

5. Bonachea and San Martín, *The Cuban Insurrection 1952–1959*, pp. 238–240. Signatories to the pact were: Fidel Castro (M-7-26); Carlos Prío Socarrás (Auténticos); Enrique Rodríguez Loeches (Directorio Revolucionario); Justo Carrillo (Agrupación Montecristi); Manuel A. (Tony) de Varona (Partido Revolucionario Cubano Insurreccional); Angel Santos (Civic Resistance); Lincoln Rodón (Independent Democratic Party); David Salvador, Angel Cofiño, Pascasio Linares, Lauro Blanco, José M. Aguilera (Workers United); José Puente, Omar Fernández (FEU); and José Miró Cardona (the secretary-general of the conference).

6. Ibid.

7. Lissner, "Batista Asserts Army Ousted Him," *New York Times*, January 10, 1959, p. 1. Batista said that the joint chiefs asked him to resign because the army would not support him. The joint chiefs had been negotiating a

truce with Castro and would install an interim government. He also said that he was told that his resignation
would save lives. Ibid.; Batista, *Cuba Betrayed*, pp. 62–
66; Paterson, *Contesting Castro*, pp. 204–205; Thomas,
Cuba: Or, the Pursuit of Freedom, pp. 1022–1024, 1026.

8. "An Idealistic Cuban," *New York Times*, January 3,
1959, p. 2.

9. He is quoted by Carlos Franqui in *Diary of the
Cuban Revolution*: "[T]he first of January was also a terrible day.... We were betrayed, and an attempt was made
to snatch victory from the people. We had to act very
swiftly." p. 495.

10. Thomas, *Cuba: Or, the Pursuit of Freedom*, pp.
1027–1030; Paterson, *Contesting Castro*, pp. 216–217; Castro says that he met with "the operations chief," General
Cantillo, and although they had worked out a deal, the
army reneged. Betto, *Fidel and Religion*, pp. 260–261. See
also Batista, *Cuba Betrayed*, pp. 110–113 and Montaner,
Journey to the Heart of Cuba, p. 78.

11. Earl E. T. Smith, *The Fourth Floor*, p. 185.

12. Coltman, *The Real Fidel Castro*, p. 137; Earl E. T.
Smith, *The Fourth Floor*, p. 187.

13. Ibid.

14. Thomas, *Cuba: Or, the Pursuit of Freedom*, p. 1028;
Earl E. T. Smith, *The Fourth Floor*, pp. 185–186, 200–201.
Cantillo told Smith that Batista had left him a "dead
army."

15. "Fidel Castro Speaks to Citizens of Santiago," *Revolucion*, January 3, 4 and 5, 1959, Several sources include
University of Texas Castro Speech Archive, http://lanic.
utexas.edu/project/castro; the U.S. National Archive,
http://www.gwu.edu/~nsarchiv/bayofpigs/chron.html;
Bonachea and San Martín, *The Cuban Insurrection 1952–
1959*, p. 320. He initially stated that Santiago would be
the new capital of Cuba. "Santiago de Cuba has been the
strongest bulwark of the revolution, a revolution that is
beginning now. Our Revolution will be no easy task, but
a harsh and dangerous undertaking, particularly in the
initial phases. And in what better place could we establish
the Government of the Republic than in this fortress of
the Revolution." Residents of Havana would later say that
by elevating Santiago and Oriente Province, more than
600 miles from Cuba's major city, Castro wanted to dilute
their power in government.

16. Ibid.

17. Ibid.

18. Bonachea and San Martín, *The Cuban Insurrection
1952–1959*, p. 320.

19. Herbert L. Matthews, "Castro Decrees a Halt in
Strike Paralyzing Cuba," *New York Times*, January 5, 1959,
p. 1.

20. "Orderly Change of Power Sought," *New York
Times*, January 2, 1959, p. 6.

21. Ibid.

22. "Fleeing Batista Aides Force Airline Pilot at Gunpoint to Fly Them to New York," *New York Times*, January
2, 1959, p. 7.

23. Ibid.

24. Thomas, *Cuba: Or, the Pursuit of Freedom*, pp. 948,
976–977, 1196, 1204; Paterson, *Contesting Castro*, pp. 207,
248.

25. Lyman B. Kirkpatrick, Jr., *The Real CIA* (New
York: Macmillan, 1968), p. 182. This is substantiated by
Llerena in *The Unsuspected Revolution*, pp. 198–204, who
notes that despite pressure from Che Guevara and Raúl
Castro, who were Communists, Castro's political views
had not taken shape and he and Communism had a "marriage of convenience." See also, Montaner, *Journey to the

Heart of Cuba*; also Severando Gonzales, *The Secret Fidel
Castro*, p. 174, who claims Castro is actually a fascist.

26. Senate, *Executive Sessions*, 1958, p. 787.

27. Paterson, *Contesting Castro*, p. 221.

28. Herbert L. Matthews, "Top Castro Aide Denies
Red Tie; Leaders Say They 'Await Fidel,'" *New York Times*,
January 4, 1959, p. 7.

29. Castro is quoted as saying, "We are not only disposed to deport the gangsters, but to shoot them." Lacy,
Little Man, p. 262.

30. Paterson, *Contesting Castro*, pp. 234–235. See also
Bruce Brown, "Scouting 'Pelota Revolucionaria': Cuban
Baseball," *Atlantic Monthly*, July 1984. In the midst of all
of the excitement over the revolution and the establishment of the new government, foreign relations and national security, and economics, Castro was often preoccupied with baseball. On January 5, Castro met Buck
Cannell, a sports broadcaster in Matanzas, on his trek to
Havana. Castro and Cannel spent 15 minutes arguing
about a controversial call that an umpire had made in a
game between the Chicago Cubs and Boston Red Sox that
had been broadcast several months earlier by Cannell.
Bourne, *Fidel: A Biography*, p. 163.

31. Ibid.

32. Urrutia Lleó, *Fidel Castro & Company*, p. 35.

33. See Bonsal, *Cuba, Castro and the United States*, p.
101.

34. "Heavy Liquor Taxes Are Imposed in Cuba," *New
York Times*, September 17, 1959, p. 39.

35. Matthews, "Castro Criticizes U.S. Military Aid,"
New York Times, January 11, 1959, p. 32.

36. Ibid.

37. "3 U.S. Military Missions in Cuba to Be Recalled,"
New York Times, January 28, 1959, p. 14.

38. Jean White, "Castro Backers Take Over Embassy
Here as Cuban Envoy Resigns," *Washington Post*, pp. A1,
A5; Paterson, *Contesting Castro*, p. 227; Thomas, *Cuba:
Or, the Pursuit of Freedom*, p. 1030, note 43.

39. Thomas, *Cuba: Or, the Pursuit of Freedom*, pp. 947–
948, 1026. See also Gardner's testimony before the Senate
Judiciary Committee, August 27 and 30, 1960,
http://www.latinamericanstudies.org/us-cuba/gardner-
smith.htm. According to Gardner, the Eisenhower administration "pulled the rug" from under Batista. He accused the State Department of "Castro worship. "

40. For example, Hector de Ayala in France. "Cuban
Envoys Back Regime of Castro," *New York Times*, January
2, 1959, p. 6.

41. White, "Castro Backers Take Over Embassy Here
as Cuban Envoy Resigns."

42. Batista, *Cuba Betrayed*, p. 50; English, *Havana
Nocturne*, pp. 180–181.

43. Sweig, *Inside the Cuban Revolution*, pp. 85–86.

44. White, "Castro Backers Take Over Embassy Here
as Cuban Envoy Resigns."

45. His name was Angel Saavedra. "Embassy Aide Is
Rebel," *New York Times*, January 3, 1959, p. 2; "Castro
Had Spy at Embassy," *Washington Post*, January 3, 1959,
p. A3.

46. R. Hart Phillips, "Americans Speed Taxes to Aid
Cuba," *New York Times*, January 17, 1959, p. 1.

47. R. Hart Phillips, "Castro Heads Cuba's Armed
Forces; Regime Is Sworn In," *New York Times*, January 4,
1959, p. 1; Francis L. McCarthy, "Urrutia Takes Over
Cuban Rule: President Names Cabinet Members; Castro
Army Head." *Washington Post*, January 4, 1959, p. A1.

48. Phillips, "Castro Heads Cuba's Armed Forces;
Regime Is Sworn In."

49. McCarthy,"Urrutia Takes Over Cuban Rule: President Names Cabinet Members; Castro Army Head."

50. Ibid.

51. See R. Hart Phillips, "Castro Asks Labor Not to Strike Now," *New York Times*, February 8, 1959, p. 1; "Castro's New Role Reflects His Power," *New York Times*, February 22, 1959, p. E4.

52. See R. Hart Phillips, "Urrutia Will Let 300 Foes Depart," *New York Times*, January 8, 1959, p. 3.

53. Kenworthy, "U.S. Recognizes New Cuba Regime; Voices Goodwill," *New York Times*, January 8, 1959, p. 1.

54. "Top Castro Aide Denies Red Tie; Leaders Say They 'Await Fidel,'" *New York Times*, January 4, 1959, p. 7.

55. R. Hart Phillips, "Castro Eligible for Presidency," *New York Times*, February 11, 1959, p. 1.

56. "Moscow Is Told of Aid to Castro'" *New York Times*, February 1, 1959, p. 22. If Aguerre had anything to do with M-7-26, there is no record.

57. Paterson, *Contesting Castro*, p. 234.

58. Ibid. Quoting several sources including Jules Dubois. Typically, Cubans do not use the term *gringo*. Paterson says that Castro fully expected the United States to reject him and his revolution. However, he later said the same thing publicly. R. Hart Phillips, "Castro Says Cuba Wants Good Ties with Washington," *New York Times*, January 16, 1959, p. 1.

59. Phillips, "Castro Says Cuba Wants Good Ties with Washington," *New York Times*, January 16, 1959, p. 1. The same report in the *Washington Post* was inflammatory: "Keep Out, Cuba Rebel Warns U.S.," by Stanford Bradshaw, January 16, 1959, p. A1.

60. R. Hart Phillips, "Castro Charges U.S. Interference," *New York Times*, February 21, 1959, p. 8.

61. "Castro to Let Tourists Gamble," *Washington Post and Times Herald*, January 11, 1959, p. A5.

62. R. Hart Phillips, "Castro Regrets Delay in Arrival," *New York Times*, January 5, 1959, p. 3; Francis L. McCarthy, "Castro Halts Cuba Strike; Shops Open," *Washington Post and Times Herald*, January 5, 1959, p. A1; "Cuban Students Yield Their Arms," *New York Times*, January 11, 1959, p. 33. The naval officer was Pelayo García Olayon of the maritime police and the army officer was Colonel Castillas Lumpuy, head of the garrison at Santa Clara.

63. Ibid.

64. Francis L. McCarthy, "Castro Halts Cuba Strike; Shops Open," *Washington Post and Times Herald*, January 5, 1959, p. A1.

65. R. Hart Phillips, "Urrutia Will Let 300 Foes Depart," *New York Times*, January 8, 1959, p. 3.

66. Ibid.

67. "2 Americans Get Posts," *New York Times*, January 5, 1959, p. 3.

68. Also see Aran Shetterly, *The Americano: Fighting for Freedom in Castro's Cuba*; "A Fighter with Castro," *New York Times*, August 15, 1959, p. 4; Michael D. Sallah, "Cuba's Yankee Comandante," *Toledo Blade*, March 3, 2002.

69. Escalante, *The Cuba Project: CIA Covert Operations 1959–62*, p. 17.

70. "Flier from Miami Arrested in Cuba," *New York Times*, March 31, 1959, p. 3. The *Times* spelled the name "Spiritu."

71. See Department of State Operations Memorandum dated April 27, 1959.

72. See *Marks v. Esperdy*, 203 F.Supp. 389, 315 F.2d 673, *affirmed* 377 U.S. 214 (1964). Esperdy was director of the Immigration and Naturalization Service. See also "Executioner Is Ex-Convict," *New York Times*, March 31, 1959, p. 3; Anderson, *Che Guevara: A Revolutionary Life*, pp. 320, 341, 347, 387. In Guevara's diary Marks was described as a fearless fighter who was literally crazy and who had a "predilection" for executions. Orlando Borrego, Guevara's protégé and close friend, described Marks as "sadistic."

73. "U.S. Deserter Gives Up," *New York Times*, October 17, 1959, p. 5.

74. "Pilots for Hire," April 4, 1960.

75. Anderson, *Che Guevara: A Revolutionary Life*, p. 335.

76. E. W. Kenworthy, "United States Foresees No Obstacle to Early Recognition of the Castro Regime," *New York Times*, January 3, 1959, p. 3. See also "An Idealistic Cuban," p. 3.

77. "Cuba in Transition," January 6, 1959, p. 32.

78. "Castro Offers U.S. 'Respectful' Ties, *New York Times*, January 5, 1959, p. 3.

79. William L. Ryan, "Reds Yield to Rebels, Havana Clash Averted," *Washington Post and Times Herald*, January 5, 1959, p. A1; R. Hart Phillips, "Castro Regrets Delay in Arrival," *New York Times*, January 5, 1959, p. 3.

80. Ira Wolfer, quoted by Francis L. McCarthy in "Castro Halts Cuba Strike; Shops Open," *Washington Post and Times Herald*, January 5, 1959, p. A1.

81. Ryan, "Reds Yield to Rebels, Havana Clash Averted."

82. Phillips, "Urrutia Will Let 300 Foes Depart," *New York Times*, January 8, 1959, p. 3.

83. Ryan, "Rebels Execute Batista Aides," *Washington Post and Times Herald*, January 8, 1959, p. A7. Attributed to a reporter from the *Diario de la Marina*.

84. "Britain Praises Rebels," *New York Times*, January 7, 1959, p. 16. Any resemblance between the headline and the body of the article is merely a coincidence.

85. "Britain Grants Recognition," *New York Times*, January 8, 1959, p. 3. Despite obtaining British cooperation, Roberto Agramonte, the new foreign minister, continued to accuse the British of having supplied Batista with offensive weapons. On the same day, Argentina, Brazil, Chile, Nicaragua and the United Arab Republic also recognized Cuba. E. W. Kenworthy, "U.S. Recognizes New Cuba Regime; Voices Goodwill," *New York Times*, January 8, 1959, p. 1.

86. Herbert L. Matthews, "Castro Criticizes U.S. Military Aid," *New York Times*, January 11, 1959, p. 32.

87. McCarthy,"Urrutia Takes Over Cuban Rule: President Names Cabinet Members; Castro Army Head."

88. "Decree Rule for 18 Months," *New York Times*, January 7, 1959, p. 16.

89. R. Hart Phillips, "Urrutia Takes Up Duties in Havana; Names a Premier," *New York Times*, January 6, 1959, p. 1.

90. Paterson, *Contesting Castro*, p. 232.

91. Bardach, *Cuba Confidential*, pp. 245–246; Paterson, *Contesting Castro*, p. 233. The show was *The Toast of the Town*. Castro was interviewed in Santa Clara. Sullivan noticed that Castro wore a cross and asked him about it. Castro reportedly stated that one can be a Communist and wear a cross.

92. "Cuban Rivals Heed Castro Peace Appeal," *New York Times*, January 10, 1959, p. A4.

93. Phillips, "Urrutia Takes Up Duties in Havana; Names a Premier," *New York Times*, January 6, 1959, p. 1. Note that Chomón is referred to as "Chaumont," his family name, in the article.

94. Thomas, *Cuba: Or, the Pursuit of Freedom*, pp. 926–929.

95. Bonachea and San Martín, *The Cuban Insurrection 1952–1959*, pp. 185–186. Within the DR, Gutiérrez Menoyo and Rolando Cubela had vied to assume the co-mandante position. Chomón as secretary of the DR had initially sided with Cubela and charged Gutiérrez Menoyo with treason, but was later forced to accept Gutiérrez Menoyo as military leader.

96. Macaulay, *A Rebel in Cuba: An American's Memoir*, p. 37.

97. Ibid., pp. 159–162; "Cuban Rivals Heed Castro Peace Appeal," *New York Times*, January 10, 1959, p. A4.

98. R. Hart Phillips, "Rebels Dissolve Cuban Congress; Officials Ousted," *New York Times*, January 7, 1959, p. 1.

99. "Cuban Rivals Heed Castro Peace Appeal," *New York Times*, January 10, 1959, p. A4.

100. Thomas calls the era *l'illusion lyrique*, a lyric period, when nearly all observers on the scene were impressed "by the nobility, vigour and charm of the revolutionaries." Thomas, *Cuba: Or, the Pursuit of Freedom*, p. 1090.

101. "Cuban Students Yield Their Arms," *New York Times*, January 11, 1959, p. 33.

102. Ibid.

103. Ibid.

104. Thomas, *Cuba: Or, the Pursuit of Freedom*, pp. 1074–1075; Paterson, *Contesting Castro*, p. 232. Smith later said that the *barbudos* reminded him of John Dillinger's gang.

105. Kenworthy, "U.S. Recognizes New Cuba Regime; Voices Goodwill," *New York Times*, January 8, 1959, p. 1.

106. Ibid.

107. Geyer, *Guerrilla Prince*, pp. 134–135; R. Hart Phillips, "Urrutia Takes Up Duties in Havana; Names a Premier," *New York Times*, January 6, 1959, p. 1.

108. Paterson, *Contesting Castro*, p. 231.

109. Bonachea and San Martín, *The Cuban Insurrection 1952–1959*, p. 66.

110. Thomas, *Cuba: Or, the Pursuit of Freedom*, pp. 1065–1066.

111. Ibid., p. 1066.

112. Montaner, *Journey to the Heart of Cuba*, p. 83; Thomas, *Cuba: Or, the Pursuit of Freedom*, pp. 1063, 1066.

113. "Cuba Ousts Judges Who Scored Army," *New York Times*, June 13, 1958, p. 3.

114. Phillips, "Urrutia Will Let 300 Foes Depart," *New York Times*, January 8, 1959, p. 3.

115. Ryan, "Rebels Execute Batista Aides," *Washington Post and Times Herald*, January 8, 1959, p. A7.

116. Larry Allen, "Cuba Continues Executions as Toll Hits 180," *Washington Post and Times Herald*, January 15, 1959, p. A8.

117. R. Hart Phillips, "Castro Says Cuba Wants Good Ties with Washington," *New York Times*, January 16, 1959, p. 1.

118. For example, R. Hart Phillips, "Cuba to Try 1,000 for 'War Crimes,'" *New York Times*, January 20, 1959, p. 1; "Cuba Continues Quick Trials," *Washington Post and Times Herald*, January 19, 1959, p. A6; "One Man Court," *Time*, March 16, 1959; "Castro Threatens Death Penalty for Theft of Government Funds," *New York Times*, March 13, 1959, p. 8; R. Hart Phillips, "Racketeers Face Execution in Cuba," *New York Times*, March 27, 1959, p. 7.

119. Paterson, *Contesting Castro*, p. 233.

120. Phillips, "Urrutia Will Let 300 Foes Depart," *New York Times*, January 8, 1959, p. 3; Paterson, *Contesting Castro*, p. 232.

121. Ryan, "Rebels Execute Batista Aides," *Washington Post and Times Herald*, January 8, 1959, p. A7.

122. Phillips, "Urrutia Will Let 300 Foes Depart," *New York Times*, January 8, 1959, p. 3.

123. Francis L. McCarthy, "Havana Cheers Castro as Hero," *Washington Post and Times Herald*, January 9, 1959, p. A6.

124. Phillips, "Havana Welcomes Castro at End of Triumphal Trip," *New York Times*, January 9, 1959, p. 1.

125. McCarthy, "Havana Cheers Castro as Hero," *Washington Post and Times Herald*, January 9, 1959, p. A6.

126. "Castro, on TV, Predicts Arms Will Be Given Up," *New York Times*, January 10, 1959, p. 2. Apparently, he appeared on CBS twice that day, as he also appeared on the Sunday news program *Face the Nation*. "Castro to Let Tourists Gamble," *Washington Post and Times Herald*, January 11, 1959, p. A5.

127. "Castro, on TV, Predicts Arms Will Be Given Up," *New York Times*, January 10, 1959, p. 2.

128. "Cuban Rivals Heed Castro Peace Appeal," *New York Times*, January 10, 1959, p. A4.

129. Ibid. The article noted that there were an estimated 8,000 to 10,000 Communists in Cuba.

130. Matthews, "Castro Criticizes U.S. Military Aid," *New York Times*, January 11, 1959, p. 32.

131. "Cuban Students Yield Their Arms," *New York Times*, January 11, 1959, p. 33.

132. "Castro to Let Tourists Gamble," *Washington Post and Times Herald*, January 11, 1959, p. A5.

133. Ibid.

134. Matthews, "Castro Criticizes U.S. Military Aid," *New York Times*, January 11, 1959, p. 32. See also R. Hart Phillips, "Cuba May Have a Tourist Season," *New York Times*, January 11, 1959, p. X23.

135. "Congress Concerned," *New York Times*, January 12, 1959, p. 8.

136. "Aftermath in Cuba," *Washington Post and Times Herald*, January 10, 1959, p. A12.

137. "Cuban Rivals Heed Castro Peace Appeal," *Washington Post and Times Herald*, January 10, 1959, p. A4. The police chief was Cornelio Rojas.

138. "Cuba Course Unclear under Castro Regime," *New York Times*, January 11, 1959, p. E6.

139. Ibid.

140. Ibid.

141. Ibid.

142. Ibid.

143. R. Hart Phillips, "Military Court in Cuba Dooms 14 for 'War Crimes,'" *New York Times*, January 13, 1959, p. 1; "Cuban Rebels Shoot 75 Beside Grave; One Directs Own Execution for TV," *Washington Post and Times Herald*, January 13, 1959, p. A1.

144. Ibid.

145. "Congress Concerned," *New York Times*, January 12, 1959, p. 8; "Castro Denies Executions without Trials," *Washington Post and Times Herald*, January 12, 1959, p. A8.

146. "Cuban Rebels Shoot 75 Beside Grave; One Directs Own Execution for TV," *Washington Post and Times Herald*, January 13, 1959, p. A1; Phillips, "Military Court in Cuba Dooms 14 for 'War Crimes,'" *New York Times*, January 13, 1959, p. 1; "Executions in Cuba Protested," *New York Times*, January 13, 1959, p. 46. Letter from John Billi.

147. Phillips, op cit.; "Morse Asks Cuba to End 'Blood Baths,'" *Washington Post and Times Herald*, January 13, 1959, p. A4.

148. See Paterson, *Contesting Castro*, p. 134. He may

have been a little paranoid about it; but maybe not, as intervention remained on the table.

149. "Castro Denies Executions without Trials," *Washington Post and Times Herald*, January 12, 1959, p. A8.

150. Ibid.

151. Phillips, "Military Court in Cuba Dooms 14 for 'War Crimes,'" *New York Times*, January 13, 1959, p. 1.

152. Phillips asserted that almost every Cuban had a friend or loved one tortured or killed during the "Batista terror" and that the underground had been keeping a list of those who should be charged with war crimes.

153. R. Hart Phillips, "Castro Declares Trials Will Go On," *New York Times*, January 14, 1959, p. 1.

154. Ibid.

155. R. Hart Phillips, "100 Face Death in Trials About to Begin at Havana," *New York Times*, January 15, 1959, p. 1.

156. Phillips, "Castro Says Cuba Wants Good Ties with Washington," *New York Times*, January 16, 1959, p. 1; Bradshaw, "Keep Out, Cuba Rebel Warns U.S.," *Washington Post*, January 16, 1959, p. A1.

157. R. Hart Phillips, "Batista Said to Send Arms to Holdouts in Mountains," *New York Times*, January 18, 1959, p. 1.

158. Phillips, "100 Face Death in Trials About to Begin at Havana," *New York Times*, January 15, 1959, p. 1.

159. Larry Allen, "Cuba Continues Executions as Toll Hits 180," *Washington Post and Times Herald*, January 15, 1959, p. A8.

160. Phillips, "Americans Speed Taxes to Aid Cuba," *New York Times*, January 17, 1959, p. 1.

161. Allen, "Cuba Continues Executions as Toll Hits 180," *Washington Post and Times Herald*, January 15, 1959, p. A8.

162. R. Hart Phillips, "Castro Outlines Sweeping Plans," *New York Times*, February 4, 1959, p. 10.

163. "Castro Won't Run for Presidency," *New York Times*, January 13, 1959, p. 12.

164. One was Representative Adam Clayton Powell of New York. Herbert W. Cheshire, "Envoy Smith Resigns after Castro Protests," *Washington Post and Times Herald*, January 11, 1959, p. A1. The other congressman who demanded resignation was Charles O. Porter of Oregon.

165. Mooney, "Smith Quits Post as Envoy to Cuba," *New York Times*, January 11, 1959, p. 1.

166. John D. Morriss, "U.S. Will Speed Envoy to Havana," *New York Times*, January 16, 1959, p. 1; Phillips, "Castro's Cabinet off at Full Speed," *New York Times*, February 18, 1959, p. 16.

167. "Patience with Castro," *Washington Post and Times Herald*, January 22, 1959, p. A16.

168. "Castro to Let Tourists Gamble," *Washington Post and Times Herald*, January 11, 1959, p. A5.

169. "Castro Gives Gambling Go-Ahead on Tight Rein," *New York Times*, January 14, 1959, p. 4.

170. Bradshaw, "Keep Out, Cuba Rebel Warns U.S.," *Washington Post*, January 16, 1959, p. A1.

171. "Warships to Avoid Cuba," *New York Times*, January 16, 1959, p. 3.

172. R. Hart Phillips, "Americans Speed Taxes to Aid Cuba," *New York Times*, January 17, 1959, p. 1; "Cuba Gives Safe Conduct to Followers of Batista," *Washington Post and Times Herald*, February 21, 1959, p. A4.

173. Thomas, *Cuba: Or, the Pursuit of Freedom*, pp. 1084–1085.

174. Ibid., p. 1086.

175. Warren Duffee, "U.N. Inquiry Asked on Cuba," *Washington Post and Times Herald*, January 16, 1959, p. A4; John D. Morriss, "U.S. Will Speed Envoy to Havana," *New York Times*, January 16, 1959, p. 1.

176. Duffee, "U.N. Inquiry Asked on Cuba," *Washington Post and Times Herald*, January 16, 1959, p. A4.

177. "Fidel Castro's Cuba," *New York Times*, January 18, 1959, p. E12.

178. "The World," *New York Times*, January 18, 1959, p. E1.

179. "Rabbi Deplores Castro Revenge," *New York Times*, January 18, 1959, p. 78. The rabbi was William Rosenthal of Temple Israel in New York, who also compared Castro to Juan Perón, deposed dictator of Argentina.

180. "The World," *New York Times*, January 18, 1959, p. E1.

181. R. Hart Phillips, "Castro's Troops Pursue Diehards," *New York Times*, January 19, 1959, p. 4.

182. Ibid.

183. For example, Phillips, "Cuba to Try 1,000 for 'War Crimes,'" *New York Times*, January 20, 1959, p. 1; "Cuba Continues Quick Trials," *Washington Post and Times Herald*, January 19, 1959, p. A6.

184. Ibid.

185. Szulc, *Fidel: A Critical Portrait*, p. 534; Paterson, *Contesting Castro*, p. 2. Although Castro sometimes publicly took the position that the United States could not reinstate "Plattism," or that he was not afraid of intervention by the United States, he protested too much. His biographers note that he had a love/hate relationship with the United States all of his life. Montaner says that in Castro's mind anti–Americanism was necessary to make him a preeminent Latin American leader. Carlos Alberto Montaner, *Fidel Castro and the Cuban Revolution*, p. 10.

186. Fell Belair, Jr., "Castro Defended by," *New York Times*, January 20, 1959, p. 10. Muñoz Marín was a governor of Puerto Rico who defended Castro and the call for executions of war criminals.

187. Stanford Bradshaw, "Havana Cheers Castro at Rally," *Washington Post and Times Herald*, January 22, 1959, p. A6; R. Hart Phillips, "Castro Deplores His Critics Here," *New York Times*, January 22, 1959, p. 1; "The World," *New York Times*, January 25, 1959, p. E1.

188. Ibid.

189. Sorí Marín was minister of agriculture, but later immigrated to the United States. He returned to Cuba as an insurgent and was captured and tried. He was shot by a firing squad in 1961. See Thomas, *Cuba: Or, the Pursuit of Freedom*, p. 985n.

190. Captain Pino del Río prosecuted and Aristedes Acosta (a.k.a. d'Acosta, DaCosta or Dacosta) was for the defense.

191. Bonachea and San Martín, *The Cuban Insurrection 1952–1959*, pp. 104, 192; Thomas, *Cuba: Or, the Pursuit of Freedom*, p. 985.

192. R. Hart Phillips, "Cuban Show Trial of Batista Aides Opens in Stadium," *New York Times*, January 23, 1959, p. 1; R. Hart Phillips, "Batista Major Condemned in Havana Stadium Trial," *New York Times*, January 24, 1959, p. 1; "The World," *New York Times*, January 25, 1959, p. E1.

193. Lloyd, "Batista's Trail of Blood," *Washington Post and Times Herald*, April 19, 1959, p. AW6.

194. See Thomas, *Cuba: Or, the Pursuit of Freedom*, pp. 1084–1085.

195. Thomas, *Cuba: Or, the Pursuit of Freedom*, pp. 1088–1089; "The World," *New York Times*, January 25, 1959, p. E1. Szulc points out that the press never noted the difference between the American system of justice and the Cuban prosecutorial system based on the Napoleonic

Code. In the United States, an accused has a presumption of innocence and the prosecution bears the burden of proof. The Cubans had it the other way. Szulc, *Fidel: A Critical Portrait*, pp. 532–534.

196. "Castro Urges U.S. to Revise Policy," *New York Times*, January 26, 1959, p. 1.

197. "The World," *New York Times*, January 25, 1959, p. E1.

198. "Our Cuban Policy Queried," *New York Times*, January 25, 1959, p. E10.

199. "Cubans Call Off Stadium Trials," *New York Times*, January 27, 1959, p. 17.

200. Phillips, "Cuban Show Trial of Batista Aides Opens in Stadium," *New York Times*, January 23, 1959, p. 1; "Batista Major Condemned in Havana Stadium Trial," *New York Times*, January 24, 1959, p. 1; "Castro Asks Move to Curb Dictators," *New York Times*, January 25, 1959, p. 12; "The World," *New York Times*, January 25, 1959, p. E1; Thomas, *Cuba: Or, the Pursuit of Freedom*, pp. 1088–1089.

201. Thomas, *Cuba: Or, the Pursuit of Freedom*, pp. 1089–1090; "Hero's Welcome Given to Castro at Caracas," *New York Times*, January 24, 1959, p. 3; "Wild Ovation Given Castro in Caracas," *Washington Post and Times Herald*, January 24, 1959, p. A4; "Castro Urges Revolts in 3 Latin Nations," *Washington Post and Times Herald*, January 25, 1959, p. A7; "Castro Urges US. to Revise Policy," *New York Times*, January 26, 1959, p. 1.

202. Paterson, *Contesting Castro*, p. 257; Thomas, *Cuba: Or, the Pursuit of Freedom*, p. 1090; Bourne, *Fidel: A Biography*, pp. 170–171.

203. "Cuba Gives Safe Conduct to Followers of Batista," *Washington Post and Times Herald*, February 21, 1959, p. A4. Porfirio Rubirosa, ambassador from the Dominican, said that his presence in Havana was the best demonstration of good relations between the two countries.

204. "Castro Said to Regret Trials," *New York Times*, January 25, 1959, p. 12.

205. "Cubans Call Off Stadium Trials," *New York Times*, January 27, 1959, p. 17.

206. Jules Dubois, "Doomed Cuban Gets Retrial," *Washington Post and Times Herald*, January 28, 1959, p. A7; Szulc, *Fidel: A Critical Portrait*, pp. 532–534. Szulc says the show trial was Castro's biggest mistake.

207. "Prelate Appeals to Castro," *New York Times*, February 2, 1959, p. 5. He said that Cuba's punishments to date had not exceeded punishments given in other countries in analogous circumstances.

208. Thomas, *Cuba: Or, the Pursuit of Freedom*, p. 1196.

209. See R. Hart Phillips, "Civil Prisoners Jam Cuban Jails," *New York Times*, February 20, 1959, p. 10; Thomas, *Cuba: Or, the Pursuit of Freedom*. Thomas notes that they were more preoccupied by gambling than civil liberties.

210. Manuel Urrutia Lleó, *Fidel Castro & Company: Communist Tyranny in Cuba* (New York: Frederick A. Praeger, 1964), pp. 35–37; Thomas, *Cuba: Or, the Pursuit of Freedom*, pp. 1084–1086, 1197. Urrutia later said that his plan would have offered government compensation to casino workers and others who had lost jobs.

211. R. Hart Phillips, "Castro Eligible for Presidency," *New York Times*, February 11, 1959, p. 1; Thomas, *Cuba: Or, the Pursuit of Freedom*, p. 1197.

212. R. Hart Phillips, "Castro to Become Premier in Shift of Cuba's Regime," *New York Times*, February 14, 1959, p. 1.

213. Szulc, *Fidel: A Critical Portrait*, pp. 525–526.

214. Thomas, *Cuba: Or, the Pursuit of Freedom*, p. 1197.

Luis Orlando Rodríguez had been an Auténtico and had not been particularly allied with Castro, but he lobbied Urrutia insisting that Castro was the logical candidate.

215. Phillips, "Castro to Become Premier in Shift of Cuba's Regime," *New York Times*, February 14, 1959, p. 1. It is interesting that Castro does not discuss this appointment in his autobiography.

216. Urrutia Lleó, *Fidel Castro & Company*, pp. 38–39; Thomas, *Cuba: Or, the Pursuit of Freedom*, p. 1197.

217. "Castro Gets Cuban Reins as Premier," *Washington Post and Times Herald*, February 14, 1959, p. A1.

218. Phillips, "Castro to Become Premier in Shift of Cuba's Regime," *New York Times*, February 14, 1959, p. 1.

219. Paul P. Kennedy, "Nicaragua Fears Leftist Attacks," *New York Times*, February 15, 1959, p. 4.

220. Juan de Onis, "Paraguay Police Battle Students," *New York Times*, February 18, 1959, p. 16.

221. "Castro Begins Job as Premier," *Washington Post*, February 17, 1959, p. A6.

222. R. Hart Phillips, "Castro Takes Oath as Premier of Cuba," *New York Times*, February 17, 1959, p. 1.

223. "Castro Begins Job as Premier," *Washington Post and Times Herald*, February 17, 1959, p. A6.

224. "Castro Gets Cuban Reins as Premier," *Washington Post*, February 14, 1959, p. A1; Phillips, "Castro Takes Oath as Premier of Cuba," *New York Times*, February 17, 1959, p. 1.

225. "Fidel Castro Takes the Helm," *New York Times*, February 17, 1959, p. 30.

226. "Castro Begins Job as Premier," *Washington Post and Times Herald*, February 17, 1959, p. A6.

227. Phillips, "Castro Takes Oath as Premier of Cuba," *New York Times*, February 17, 1959, p. 1.

228. "Sosa Blanco Convicted 2d Time," *Washington Post and Times Herald*, February 18, 1959, p. A6; "Castro Begins Job as Premier," *Washington Post*, February 17, 1959, p. A6; R. Hart Phillips, "Castro's Cabinet Off at Full Speed," *New York Times*, February 18, 1959, p. 16.

229. "Cuban Executed after New Trial," *New York Times*, February 19, 1959, p. 9.

230. Among those held were Joaquín Martinez Saenz, former president of the Cuban National Bank; Emetrio Santovenia, former head of the Agricultural and Industrial Development Bank; labor leader Francisco Aguierre, delegate to the International Labor Organization; and Edward Klawans, an American and a naturalized Cuban lawyer, who was held by the army. Phillips, "Civil Prisoners Jam Cuban Jails," *New York Times*, February 20, 1959, p. 10.

231. "Executions in Cuba Rise to 483 Total," *New York Times*, March 20, 1959, p. 8.

232. "Castro's New Role Reflects His Power," *New York Times*, February 22, 1959, p. E4.

233. Perez, *Cuba*, p. 230. Pérez cites the magazine *Carteles*, May 26, 1957. *Revolución* reported that *Bohemia*, *Prensa Libre* and *The Times of Havana* had been included in Batista government records documenting bribes, but there is some question about the authenticity of the documents. Furthermore, even if they were authentic, there is a question whether the bribes worked. See Richard Cole, *Communication in Latin America* (Lanham, MD: Rowman & Littlefield, 1996), p. 143.

234. "Cuban Elections Two Years Away," *New York Times*, March 1, 1959, p. 11.

235. Frank H. Bartholomew, "Widespread Caribbean War Is Seen Up to Castro," *Washington Post and Times Herald*, March 10, 1959, p. A6; Paul P. Kennedy, "Nicaragua Fears Leftist Attacks," *New York Times*, Feb-

ruary 15, 1959, p. 4; "Caribbean Brews Political Storms," *New York Times*, March 13, 1959, p. 8. Among the countries affected were Honduras, Guatemala and British Honduras, Panama, the Dominican Republic, Haiti, Jamaica, Nicaragua, Costa Rica, Venezuela and, of course, Cuba.

236. Drew Pearson, "Some Relatives Earn Capitol Pay," *Washington Post and Times*, February 28, 1959 p. B11. The fund raiser was William McNally.

237. "Cuban Elections Two Years Away," *New York Times*, March 1, 1959, p. 11.

238. Miret had been a civil engineer before he joined the rebels. He was also soft-spoken and came across as an academic. Marie Smith, "Whiskered Conquerors of Cuba Here," *Washington Post and Times*, February 26, 1959, p. A1.

239. Ibid. Ms. Smith probably did not consider that Cienfuegos was careful to avoid poisoning.

240. "Castro to Visit U.S. Next Month," *New York Times*, March 4, 1959, p. 1.

241. "43 Fliers Acquitted by Tribunal in Cuba," *New York Times*, March 3, 1959, p. 8; "One Man Court," *Time*, March 16, 1959.

242. "Castro Assails Acquittals," *New York Times*, March 4, 1959, p. 11; "Castro to Act on Verdict Freeing Fliers," *Washington Post*, March 4, 1959, p. A7; "Castro Warns of Counter-Revolutionary Activities," *New York Times*, March 7, 1959, p. 10.

243. "Retrial of Airmen Troubling Cubans," *New York Times*, March 6, 1959, p. 5.

244. "The Justice of Cuba," *New York Times*, March 7, 1959, p. 20.

245. "Castro Charges Foes Openly Buy U.S. Arms," *Washington Post and Times Herald*, March 7, 1959, p. A5.

246. Ibid.; "One Man Court," *Time*, March 16, 1959.

247. Ibid.

248. Ibid.; "Cuba Execution Toll Tops 400," *Washington Post and Times Herald*, March 8, 1959, p. A13.

249. "Cuba Execution Toll Tops 400," *Washington Post and Times Herald*, March 8, 1959, p. A13.

250. "Fastest Gun in Havana," March 23, 1959; R. Hart Phillips, "Castro Threatens Death Penalty for Theft of Government Funds," *New York Times*, March 13, 1959, p. 8.

251. Phillips, "Castro Charges U.S. Interference," *New York Times*, February 21, 1959, p. 8.

252. "One Man Court," *Time*, March 16, 1959.

253. Phillips, "Castro Charges U.S. Interference," *New York Times*, February 21, 1959, p. 8.

254. Phillips, "Castro Threatens Death Penalty for Theft of Government Funds," *New York Times*, March 13, 1959, p. 8; "Fastest Gun in Havana," *Time*, March 23, 1959.

255. "6 from U.S. Held in Cuba on Pesos," *New York Times*, March 14, 1959, p. 3. One, Mike McLaney, was a casino operator at the Hotel Nacional in Havana. Another, retired lieutenant colonel Edward Solomon, was detained with 159,000 pesos. McLaney was held for a week, but later was released with a personal apology from Castro. R. Hart Phillips, "Cuba Admonished Out Executions," *New York Times*, March 24, 1959, p. 2.

256. "Executions in Cuba Rise to 483 Total," *New York Times*, March 20, 1959, p. 8; "End Executions, Cuba Paper Asks," *Washington Post and Times Herald*, March 20, 1959, p. A4.

257. Paterson, *Contesting Castro*, p. 114.

258. June 9, 1958; Paterson, *Contesting Castro*, p. 151; quoted at length: http://yawiki.org/proc/Jos%C3%A9_Figueres_Ferrer.

259. Thomas, *Cuba: Or, the Pursuit of Freedom*, p.

1204; R. Hart Phillips, "Castro Bars Pledge to Join U.S. in War," *New York Times*, March 23, 1959, p. 1; E. W. Kenworthy, "U.S. to Protect Castro on Visit," *New York Times*, March 28, 1959, p. 5.

260. Kenworthy, "U.S. to Protect Castro on Visit," *New York Times*, March 28, 1959, p. 5.

261. Thomas, *Cuba: Or, the Pursuit of Freedom*, p. 1204; "Cuba Admonished Out Executions," *New York Times*, March 24, 1959, p. 2.

262. "Invasion Threat Seen by Castro," *Washington Post*, March 24, 1959, p. A7.

263. Ibid.

264. "Jose Figueres Ferrer Is Dead at 83; Led Costa Ricans to Democracy," *New York Times*, June 9, 1990, p. 29. "At the time, I was conspiring against the Latin American dictatorships and wanted help from the United States," he recalled. "I was a good friend of Allen Dulles... But I never participated in espionage."

265. "Invasion Threat Seen by Castro," March 24, 1959, p. A7.

266. In "Letters to the Editor: Letter of Sam Crutchfield, Jr.," *Washington Post*, March 23, 1959, p. A12.

267. For example, Drew Pearson's "Washington Merry-Go-Round: Panama Canal Threat Pictured," *Washington Post*, March 25, 1959, p. D13. The columns of Andrew Russell (Drew) Pearson (1897–1969) were syndicated in over 600 newspapers and had an estimated 60 million readers. He had syndicated television and radio shows, also called *Washington-Merry-Go-Round*. Pearson had been a correspondent in Cuba in the 1930s, when he witnessed the fall of Machado and the rise of Batista.

268. Jules Dubois, "3 Invasion Plans Hit Cuban Snags," *Washington Post and Times Herald*, March 29, 1959, p. A5. Dubois reported that within anti–Somoza and Trujillo groups, subgroups of Communists and anti–Communists were dividing the opposition.

269. "Castro Is Linked to Colombia Plot," *Washington Post and Times Herald*, April 1, 1959, p. D9.

270. Ibid. He also referred to deposed Latin American dictators as our friends.

271. "Batista Assails Castro as Killer," *Washington Post and Times Herald*, April 3, 1959, p. D1; Pearson, "Perón Looks Back at 2 Big Errors," *Washington Post and Times Herald*, April 9, 1959, p. B15. After Pearson accused Castro's father of being a thief and who had stolen from warehouses he was supposed to be supervising, E. S. Whitman, vice president of United Fruit, wrote a letter to the *Washington Post* stating that everything Pearson had said about Angel Castro was a lie. "Letters to the Editor," *Washington Post and Times Herald*, February 28, 1960, p. E4.

272. Phillips, "Racketeers Face Execution in Cuba: Castro Warns Gambling and Narcotics Offenders — Says U.S. Aids Foes," *New York Times*, March 27, 1959, p. 7.

273. For example, Dubois, "3 Invasion Plans Hit Cuban Snags," *Washington Post and Times Herald*, March 29, 1959, p. A5. See also "Executioner Is Ex-Convict," *New York Times*, March 31, 1959, p. 3. Westbrook Pegler also wrote a column depicting Marks as a criminal. "Killer Mars 'Democracy' in Cuba," King Features Syndicate, April 28, 1959.

274. "Sugar and the Revolution," *New York Times*, April 3, 1959, p. 26.

275. R. Hart Phillips, "Castro Attacks U.S. Sugar Quota," *New York Times*, April 4, 1959, p. 1; George Auerbach, "Cuba's Sugar Problem," *New York Times*, April 8, 1959, p. 5.

276. See Joseph W. Dunn, "Cuban Disorders Buoy Sugar Price," *New York Times*, August 16, 1959, p. F1.

277. "Marijuana Seller Gets Death in Cuba," *New York Times*, April 9, 1959, p. 2.

278. "Cuba Aide Found Dead," *New York Times*, April 15, 1959, p. 16.

279. "Haitian Rebels Seize Airliner, Kill Pilot, Force Cuba Landing," *Washington Post and Times Herald*, April 11, 1959, p. A4.

280. "Castro Sees Threat by Foes," *New York Times*, April 11, 1959, p. 6.

281. Ibid.

282. E. W. Kenworthy, "Castro Will Meet Nixon on U.S. Trip," *New York Times*, April 11, 1959, p. 1.

283. Ibid.; "Del Pino Is U.S. Citizen," *New York Times*, July 26, 1959, p. 27.

284. "Castro Makes a Pitch," *New York Times*, April 15, 1959, p. 38.

285. "Castro Plans 'Truth Operation,'" *New York Times*, April 16, 1959, p. 6.

286. "Rodriguez Homer Gives Leafs 6–4 Win over Cubans," United Press International, April 15, 1959. The "Leafs" were the Toronto Maple Leafs. Cuban player Hector Rodriguez was on the Toronto team for many years. He died in Mexico in 2003.

287. "Restore Rights, Cubans Appeal," *Washington Post and Times Herald*, April 14, 1959, p. A6.

Chapter 8

1. R. Hart Phillips, "Grenade Kills 3 at Fete in Cuba," *New York Times*, February 2, 1959, p. 5.

2. "Anti-Castro Plot Laid to Chicagoan," *New York Times*, February 3, 1959, p. 1; R. Hart Phillips, "Cuba Says Indianan Admits Castro Plot," *New York Times*, February 6, 1959, p. 1; "Cuban Police Say Former Navy Flier Confessed Castro Assassination Plot," *Washington Post and Times Herald*, February 6, 1959, p. A4. His Miami contact was Daniel Vazques, husband of actress Marisol Alba. Nye reportedly said he cooperated because Batista must "hope … that I was dead," but he later denied that he was an assassin. R. Hart Phillips, "Indiana Flier Denies Plot to Kill Castro," *New York Times*, February 7, 1959, p. 1; "U.S. Flier Denies Plot to Kill Cuban Leader," *Washington Post and Times Herald*, February 7, 1959, p. A7; "Ex-Navy Airman Denies Plotting to Kill Castro," *Washington Post and Times Herald*, April 3, 1959, p. A4.

3. The soldier was José Duany Cobas, stationed in Santiago de Cuba. "Anti-Castro Plot Laid to Chicagoan," *New York Times*, February 3, 1959, p. 1.

4. R. Hart Phillips, "Racketeers Face Execution in Cuba," *New York Times*, March 27, 1959, p. 7.

5. Szulc, *Fidel: A Critical Portrait*, p. 313.

6. Thomas, *Cuba: Or, the Pursuit of Freedom*, pp. 797, 867; Szulc, *Fidel: A Critical Portrait*, p. 348. Jorge Agostini, head of Prío's secret police, returned from exile after the amnesty that released the Castro brothers was put into place. Juan Manuel Marquez, another opposition leader, had been picked up and beaten by the police.

7. Thomas, *Cuba: Or, the Pursuit of Freedom*, p. 877; Szulc, *Fidel: A Critical Portrait*, pp. 383–384, 391–392. Two Cuban military intelligence men disguised in Mexican police uniforms were supposed to do the deed. He later was arrested by genuine Mexican authorities on a visa violation. Paterson, *Contesting Castro*, p. 32.

8. Thomas, *Cuba: Or, the Pursuit of Freedom*, pp. 914–918, 923; Szulc, *Fidel: A Critical Portrait*, pp. 434–439.

9. Thomas, *Cuba: Or, the Pursuit of Freedom*, p. 967;

Bonachea and San Martín, *The Cuban Insurrection 1952–1959*, p. 105.

10. Coltman, *The Real Fidel Castro*, p. 109.

11. "Batista Denounces 'Barbarism' in Cuba," *New York Times*, January 16, 1959, p. 3. He later stated in an interview with Ruth Lloyd, "I didn't kill anyone. Castro's men tortured the civilians and blamed it on me. It wasn't 20,000; it was only 10,000." "Batista's Trail of Blood," *Washington Post and Times Herald*, April 19, 1959, p. AW6.

12. R. Hart Phillips, "Americans Speed Taxes to Aid Cuba," *New York Times*, January 17, 1959, p. 1.

13. Ibid. The driver's name was Consuegra.

14. "Trujillo Arming Legion for Defense of Haiti," *Washington Post and Times Herald*, March 6, 1959, p. C11.

15. "Warning to Aggressors Is Sounded by Trujillo," *New York Times*, March 12, 1959, p. 15; "5 Seized in 'Plot' Opposing Castro," *Washington Post and Times Herald*, March 12, 1959, p. A10.

16. Phillips, "Batista Said to Send Arms to Holdouts in Mountains," *New York Times*, January 18, 1959, p. 1; Phillips, "Castro's Troops Pursue Diehards," *New York Times*, January 19, 1959, p. 4.

17. John Scall, "Trujillo's Air Force Reported Buying 12 Jet Fighter Planes in Canada," *Washington Post and Times Herald*, January 26, 1959, p. A6.

18. Ibid.

19. Dubois, "Doomed Cuban Gets Retrial," *Washington Post and Times Herald*, January 28, 1959, p. A7.

20. "2 Condemned Cubans Make Escape as Firing Squad Pauses to Reload," *Washington Post and Times Herald*, March 6, 1959, p. A7.

21. "Castro Charges Foes Openly Buy U.S. Arms," *Washington Post and Times Herald*, March 7, 1959, p. A5.

22. "Figueres in Havana as Castro's Guest," *New York Times*, March 21, 1959, p. 14.

23. R. Hart Phillips, "Nye Goes on Trial as 'Plotter' in Cuba," *New York Times*, April 12, 1959, p. 1; "Nye and 5 Others Go on Trial in Castro Assassination Plot," *Washington Post and Times Herald*, April 12, 1959, p. A8; R. Hart Phillips, "Cuba Sentences Nye to Death as Plotter but Lets Him Leave," *New York Times*, April 13, 1959, p. 1; "Testimony Traces Arms," *New York Times*, April 13, 1959, p. 13; "Cuba Frees Condemned U.S. Pilot," *Washington Post and Times Herald*, April 13, 1959, p. A1. Nye's first lawyer had been Eloy Marino Brito. Nye was also convicted of setting fire to three airplanes in Miami that were to have been trans-shipped to M-7–26 in 1958.

Chapter 9

1. Phillips, "Castro Outlines Sweeping Plans," *New York Times*, February 4, 1959, p. 10.

2. Jacques Nevard, "Castro to Foster Private Shipping," *New York Times*, February 14, 1959, p. 42.

3. R. Hart Phillips, "Cuba's Bid for Visitors," *New York Times*, February 22, 1959, p. X25. Among the marchers were American, Cuban and Vezuelan schoolchildren. Among the bands were an American Legion drum and bugle corps, the University of Miami and Miami Jackson High School, and a band from a segregated all-black school.

4. R. Hart Phillips, "2 U.S. Companies Face Cuban Study," *New York Times*, February 24, 1959, p. 12.

5. R. Hart Phillips, "New Cuban Government Faces Huge Economic Problems," *New York Times*, January 25, 1959, p. E8.

6. Ibid.

7. George Auerbach, "Sugar Prices off on Shift in Cuba," *New York Times*, February 8, 1959, p. F1.

8. Ibid.

9. Phillips, "Castro Charges U.S. Interference," *New York Times*, February 21, 1959, p. 8.

10. Phillips, "New Cuban Government Faces Huge Economic Problems," *New York Times*, January 25, 1959, p. E8.

11. Thomas, *Cuba: Or, the Pursuit of Freedom*, p. 1068.

12. Phillips, "2 U.S. Companies Face Cuban Study," *New York Times*, February 24, 1959, p. 12.

13. R. Hart Phillips, "Castro Regime Strikes at Graft through Drastic Cuban Reform," *New York Times*, January 28, 1959, p. 1.

14. Ibid.

15. Phillips, "Civil Prisoners Jam Cuban Jails," *New York Times*, February 20, 1959, p. 10.

16. "Currency Market Shuns Cuban Peso," *New York Times*, February 20, 1959, p. 5; Frank Kelley, "Cuba Halts Conversion of Pesos," *Washington Post and Times Herald*, February 20, 1959, p. A4. At the time, Cuban currency was printed by the American Bank Note Company and Thomas de Larue and Company, London.

17. R. Hart Phillips, "Reforms in Cuba Cramp Economy," *New York Times*, March 21, 1959, p. 25. The rule had been that exporters exchanged 30 percent of their receipts for pesos, but under Batista the amount had been raised to 75 percent because the Batista government had also come under pressure.

18. See Jones, "Freedom Called Cuban Stimulant," *New York Times*, March 1, 1959, p. F1.

19. Ibid.

20. Phillips, "Americans Speed Taxes to Aid Cuba," *New York Times*, January 17, 1959, p. 1. Among the companies listed were: First National Bank of Boston, International Harvester Company, First National Bank of New York, United Fruit Company, and Crusellas Company, a subsidiary of Colgate Palmolive Company. Nicaro Nickel, owned by the United States government, made an advance payment of $375,000. In addition, many sugar mills also paid in advance.

21. Paterson, *Contesting Castro*, p. 232.

22. Thomas, *Cuba: Or, the Pursuit of Freedom*, p. 1065.

23. For example, Phillips, "New Cuba Invites Tourists," *New York Times*, January 18, 1959, p. XX22; P.J.C.F. [sic], "Midwinter Vacations 1959," *New York Times*, January 18, 1959, p. XX1.

24. "Opening of 8 Colonial Homes Set," *Washington Post and Times Herald*, January 18, 1959, p. C10.

25. Paterson, *Contesting Castro*, p. 44.

26. Gene Smith, "Utilities in Cuba Await Their Fate," *New York Times*, January 18, 1959, p. F1. *Time* reported that Castro called for nationalization of utilities in Cuba, land reform and industrial profit-sharing in 1953, but "he now calls these 'radical ideas not good for Cuba.'" "They Beat Batista," *Time*, January 12, 1959.

27. Paterson, *Contesting Castro*, p. 45.

28. Smith, "Utilities in Cuba Await Their Fate."

29. Paterson, *Contesting Castro*, p. 233; Phillips, "Castro Outlines Sweeping Plans," *New York Times*, February 4, 1959, p. 10.

30. Phillips, "Castro Regime Strikes at Graft through Drastic Cuban Reform," *New York Times*, January 28, 1959, p. 1; Phillips, "2 U.S. Companies Face Cuban Study," *New York Times*, February 24, 1959, p. 12; "Cuban Elections Two Years Away," *New York Times*, March 1, 1959, p. 11.

31. R. Hart Phillips, "Cuba to Try 1,000 for 'War Crimes,'" *New York Times*, January 20, 1959, p. 1.

32. Phillips, "Castro Outlines Sweeping Plans," *New York Times*, February 4, 1959, p. 10.

33. Castro and Ramonet, *Fidel Castro: My Life*, p. 243.

34. Phillips, "Castro Outlines Sweeping Plans," *New York Times*, February 4, 1959, p. 10.

35. Ibid.

36. See Phillips, "Castro Eligible for Presidency," *New York Times*, February 11, 1959, p. 1.

37. Nevard, "Castro to Foster Private Shipping," *New York Times*, February 14, 1959, p. 42.

38. R. Hart Phillips, "Castro Asks Labor Not to Strike Now," *New York Times*, February 8, 1959, p. 1.

39. "Castro Begins Job as Premier," *Washington Post*, February 17, 1959, p. A6; Phillips, "Castro's Cabinet Off at Full Speed," *New York Times*, February 18, 1959, p. 16.

40. Ibid.; "Sosa Blanco Convicted 2d Time," *Washington Post and Times Herald*, February 18, 1959, p. A6.

41. Phillips, "Castro Threatens Death Penalty for Theft of Government Funds," *New York Times*, March 13, 1959, p. 8.

42. Adverse possession gives ownership to people who have cared for land, even if they do not hold title to it. In the United States, most states protect similar rights, a tradition which stems from English common law. In Cuba, many of these properties were titled by Spanish land grants to absentee owners.

43. See, for instance, statements of Luis A. Baralt in Brendan M. Jones, "Freedom Called Cuban Stimulant," *New York Times*, March 1, 1959, p. F1.

44. "U.S. Envoys Ran Cuba, Castro Says," *Washington Post and Times Herald*, February 4, 1959, p. A8. It would be reasonable to expect that the landowners of excess property would be paid the price they had established for ad valorum tax purposes as "just compensation."

45. R. Hart Phillips, "Castro to Begin Giving Out Land," *New York Times*, January 30, 1959, p. 7; Francis L. McCarthy, "Land Gifts to Cubans Start Feb. 2," *Washington Post and Times Herald*, January 30, 1959, p. A5.

46. Urrutia Lleó, *Fidel Castro & Company*, p. 43; Phillips, "Castro Outlines Sweeping Plans," *New York Times*, February 4, 1959, p. 10; R. Hart Phillips, "Castro's New Role Reflects His Power," *New York Times*, February 22, 1959, p. E4. Urrutia said that this act was meant to undermine the communists, who had encouraged the *precaristas*. Castro had reportedly told Sorí Marín that he "wanted nothing to do with the Reds."

47. Phillips, "Reforms in Cuba Cramp Economy," *New York Times*, March 21, 1959, p. 25.

48. "Cuban Law Forces Sale of Idle Land," *New York Times*, March 22, 1959, p. 31.

49. Phillips, "Reforms in Cuba Cramp Economy," *New York Times*, March 21, 1959, p. 25.

50. "Cuban Farmers Given 7150 Acres as Land-Distribution Task Begins," *Washington Post and Times Herald*, March 3, 1959, p. A7.

51. See Helen Osieja, Economic Sanctions as an Instrument of U.S. Foreign Policy: The Case of the U.S. Embargo on Cuba. Boca Raton, FL: Dissertation.com, 2005, pp. 53–54. Mexico also had the Carranza Doctrine of 1918, which stated that foreign nationals should not be treated any differently than citizens of the host country.

52. Ibid. Calvo was an Argentine lawyer who devised the clause.

53. See Szulc, *Fidel: A Critical Portrait*, pp. 93–96; Bourne, *Fidel: A Biography*, pp. 19–20. For Castro, United Fruit Company was symbolic of the disparity between rich landowners versus poor *precaristas*. For a discussion regarding the cultural and political aspects of United Fruit's

Oriente holdings see Pérez, *On Becoming Cuban*, pp. 220–222, 228–231.

54. Árbenz resigned and was succeeded by Carlos Enrique Díaz. However, two days later, the army under Colonel Elfego Monzón deposed Díaz in a military junta. On July 2, 1954, Carlos Castillo Armas joined the ruling junta. Six days later, on July 8, Castillo succeeded Monzón as president. See database, The Council on Hemispheric Affairs, http://www.coha.org/. See also Greg Grandin, *Empire's Workshop*, pp. 42–45.

55. Koeppel, *Banana*, pp. 127–128. See also Schoultz, *Beneath the United States*, pp. 337–339. John Foster Dulles had been a partner in the law firm Sullivan and Cromwell, and represented the company. The company president was Thomas Dudley Cabot, brother of John Moors Cabot, assistant secretary of state for Latin America. Ed Whitman was married to Ann Whitman.

56. Grandin, *Empire's Workshop*, pp. 42–45. The phantom organization, "Organization of Militant Godless," never existed, but the CIA had hired psychologists and others, including "father of public relations" Edward Bernays (Sigmund Freud's nephew), to set up a disinformation program.

57. Matthews, "Top Castro Aide Denies Red Tie; Leaders Say They 'Await Fidel,'" *New York Times*, January 4, 1959, p. 7; Thomas, *Cuba: Or, the Pursuit of Freedom*, pp. 879–880. Although some reports state that Guevara had been officially involved with the Árbenz government, he was merely working in Guatemala, although he asked for and received amnesty in the Argentine embassy and had to go Mexico.

58. McCarthy, "Land Gifts to Cubans Start Feb. 2," *Washington Post and Times Herald*, January 30, 1959, p. A5.

59. Phillips, "2 U.S. Companies Face Cuban Study," *New York Times*, February 24, 1959, p. 12. Although Oltulsky spoke English and was a graduate of the University of Miami, the *Times* misspelled Oltulsky's name repeatedly.

60. "Anti-Castro Plot Laid to Chicagoan," *New York Times*, February 3, 1959, p. 1. Dean Angel Pérez Andre was replaced by Armando Ruiz Leiro. R. Hart Phillips, "Student Rebels Seize Havana U," *New York Times*, February 5, 1959, p. 7.

61. "2 Condemned Cubans Make Escape as Firing Squad Pauses to Reload," *Washington Post and Times Herald*, March 6, 1959, p. A7. Grau and his successors, including Batista, had tried agrarian reform themselves. See Russell B. Porter, "Gomez Promises Freedom in Cuba," *New York Times*, July 4, 1936, p. 1.

62. For an explanation of state "intervention," see Harry Schwartz, "Cuba Fashioning an Economic Web," *New York Times*, February 28, 1960, p. F1.

63. Alexander, *A History of Organized Labor in Cuba*, p. 60.

64. "Cuba Takes Over Phone Company," *New York Times*, March 5, 1959, p. 6.

65. "Cuba Slashes Rents," *New York Times*, March 7, 1959, p. 2.

66. "5 Seized in 'Plot' Opposing Castro," *Washington Post and Times Herald*, March 12, 1959, p. A10.

67. R. Hart Phillips, "Castro's Nationalism Disturbs Some Cubans," *New York Times*, April 5, 1959, p. E4.

68. Phillips, "Reforms in Cuba Cramp Economy," *New York Times*, March 21, 1959, p. 25.

69. "Cuba Plans Works to Build Up Oriente," *New York Times*, March 12, 1959, p. 5. The project costs would total $5,442,000.

70. Phillips, "Racketeers Face Execution in Cuba: Castro Warns Gambling and Narcotics Offenders — Says U.S. Aids Foes," *New York Times*, March 27, 1959, p. 7.

71. "Racketeers Face Execution in Cuba: Castro Warns Gambling and Narcotics Offenders — Says U.S. Aids Foes," *New York Times*, March 27, 1959, p. 7.

72. R. Hart Phillips, "Castro Cautions Industry in Cuba," *New York Times*, March 30, 1959, p. 6.

73. Phillips, "Castro's Nationalism Disturbs Some Cubans," *New York Times*, April 5, 1959, p. E4.

74. Ibid.

75. Auerbach, "Cuba's Sugar Problem," *New York Times*, April 8, 1959, p. 5.

76. Shetterly, *The Americano*, p. 158.

77. Shetterly, *The Americano*, pp. 162–164.

78. Macauley, *A Rebel in Cuba*, pp. 180–181.

Chapter 10

1. "Castro Plans 'Truth Operation,'" *New York Times*, April 16, 1959, p. 6.

2. Coltman, *The Real Fidel Castro*, p. 156. The Provisional Government paid the New York firm of Bernard Relin and Associates $72,000 per year. "Castro Regime Purges 26 Top Air Officers," *Washington Post and Times Herald*, June 19, 1959, p. A6. Thomas spells the name Relling. *Cuba: Or, the Pursuit of Freedom*, p. 1208.

3. A. H. Raskin, "Castro Rebuffed by Union Leaders," *New York Times*, April 29, 1959, p. 11. Moreover, although the Cuban Confederation of Labor asked the AFL/CIO to send a delegation to Cuba for a May Day celebration, they declined.

4. Geyer, *Guerrilla Prince*, p. 222. Geyer's principal sources were Pepin Bosch and Felipe Pazos.

5. Farber, *Origins Reconsidered*, p. 100, citing top secret records of the NSC.

6. E. W. Kenworthy, "Castro Due in Capital Today; Maximum Guard Unit Assigned," *New York Times*, April 15, 1959, p. 1; "Castro Plans 'Truth Operation,'" *New York Times*, April 16, 1959, p. 6; "Crowd Hails Castro as He Reaches U.S. for an 11-Day Visit," *New York Times*, April 16, 1959, p. 1.

7. "Crowd Hails Castro as He Reaches U.S. for an 11-Day Visit," *New York Times*, April 16, 1959, p. 1.

8. Richard E. Welch, *Response to Revolution: The United States and the Cuban Revolution, 1959–1961* (Chapel Hill: University of North Carolina Press, 1985), p. 34, citing U.S. Department of State Press Bulletin Number 90, March 16, 1959; Paterson, *Contesting Castro*, p. 256. Paterson says that Eisenhower deliberately snubbed Castro.

9. Thomas, *The Cuban Revolution*, p. 428. Thomas's chief sources are José Pepin Bosch, head of Bacardi, and Felipe Pazos, president of the National Bank, who took the flight with him.

10. Coltman, *The Real Fidel Castro*, p. 155.

11. "Panama Complains of Plotting in Cuba," *New York Times*, April 16, 1959, p. 7.

12. "Fidel Castro's Visit," *New York Times*, April 15, 1959, p. 32.

13. Drew Pearson, "Washington Merry-Go-Round: Former Buddy Opposes Castro," *Washington Post and Times Herald*, April 16, 1959, p. B15. Del Pino also accused Castro of causing the 1948 Bogotazo and being a thief.

14. Geyer, *Guerrilla Prince*, pp. 224–225; Coltman, *The Real Fidel Castro*, p. 156.

15. Wayne Smith, *The Closest of Enemies*, p. 47.

16. Rabe, *Eisenhower and Latin America*, pp. 123–124.

17. Phil Casey, "A Lesson for the Future, Castro Calls

Post-Revolution Cuban Executions," *Washington Post and Times Herald*, April 17, 1959, p. A1. He also insisted that an "embezzler should lose what he owned as well as what he stole," authorized confiscation of all personal property of Batista and hundreds of officials connected with him — including all congressmen, mayors, governors, Supreme Court justices, and all armed-forces officers who supported Batista's 1952 coup. "One Man Court," *Time*, March 16, 1959.

18. Ibid.

19. E. W. Kenworthy, "Castro Declares Regime Is Free of Red Influence," *New York Times*, April 18, 1959, p. 1.

20. Ibid.; Edward T. Folliard, "Red Label Is Rejected by Castro," *Washington Post and Times Herald*, April 18, 1959, p. A1.

21. Ibid.

22. "The Other Face," *Time*, April 27, 1959.

23. Ibid.

24. Szulc, *Fidel: A Critical Portrait*, pp. 537–539.

25. Phil Casey, "Castro Promises Cuba Will Honor Agreements," *Washington Post and Times Herald*, April 20, 1959, p. A1.

26. "The Other Face," *Time*, April 27, 1959; E. W. Kenworthy, "Castro Declares Regime Is Free of Red Influence," *New York Times*, April 18, 1959, p. 1; E. W. Kenworthy, "Castro Visit Leaves Big Question Mark," *New York Times*, April 19, 1959, p. E7.

27. "Castro Hails Newsmen," *New York Times*, April 19, 1959, p. 4.

28. Casey, "Castro Promises Cuba Will Honor Agreements," *Washington Post and Times Herald*, April 20, 1959, p. A1. For excerpts, see NBC Archives. http://www.news-desk.umd.edu/experts/hottopic_EDS.cfm?hotlist_id=88. Castro was also interviewed on *Meet the Press* in February 1959. http://www.msnbc.com/modules/cubavideo/meet-thepress.asp.

29. Dana Adams Schmidt, "Castro Rules Out Role as Neutral; Opposes the Reds," *New York Times*, April 20, 1959, p. 1; Casey, "Castro Promises Cuba Will Honor Agreements," *Washington Post and Times Herald*, April 20, 1959, p. A1; Phil Casey, "Castro Says Cuba Will 'Legally' Expropriate Land," *Washington Post and Times Herald*, April 21, 1959, p. A7.

30. Casey, "Castro Says Cuba Will 'Legally' Expropriate Land," *Washington Post and Times Herald*, April 21, 1959, p. A7.

31. Casey, "Castro Promises Cuba Will Honor Agreements," *Washington Post and Times Herald*, April 20, 1959, p. A1.

32. Philip Benjamin, "Police Increase Guard on Castro in Fear of Plot," *New York Times*, April 24, 1959, p. 1.

33. Thomas, *The Cuban Revolution*, p. 430; Schmidt, "Castro Rules Out Role as Neutral; Opposes the Reds," *New York Times*, April 20, 1959, p. 1; Casey, "Castro Promises Cuba Will Honor Agreements," *Washington Post and Times Herald*, April 20, 1959, p. A1.

34. Paterson, *Contesting Castro*, p. 241.

35. See also Richard Pearson, "Charles 'Bebe' Rebozo, 85, Dies," *Washington Post*, May 10, 1998, p. B8. According to detractors, Meyer Lansky ran the casino at the Hotel Nacional, and "comped" Nixon, giving him the Presidential Suite. Don Fulsom, "The Mob's President: Richard Nixon's Secret Ties to the Mafia," *Crime Magazine*, February 5, 2006.

36. Lacy, *Little Man*, pp. 281–283; Lowinger and Fox, *Tropicana Nights*, pp. 229–230; English, *Havana Nocturne*, pp. 94–100. The fund raiser was Dana Smith, allegedly also involved in a political slush fund that led to Nixon's "Checkers speech." Nixon had been accused of

being on the take. He went on national television to say all that he had received was his dog, Checkers, and he would not give him up.

37. See FBI memorandum from A. Rosen to the Home Loan Bank Board, dated April 16, 1969. http://foiafbi.gov/rebozo_charles_g/rebozo_charles_g_part02.pdf.

38. For instance, a memorandum dated January 9, 1959, regarding "Cuban Internal Revolutionary Activities" lists Rebozo as having "fronted for the Italian money [invested in Cuba] and was also influential at the Presidential palace between Ambassador Smith and former President Batista." According to the memo, Rebozo had served in the navy with Nixon in World War II and was his advisor on investments in Cuba, and Nixon stayed with Rebozo in Miami. Whether Nixon and Rebozo held joint investments is unclear. http://foia.fbi.gov/rebozo_charles_g/rebozo_charles_g_part04.pdf.

39. See Teletype dated February 9, 1959, FBI Communications Section. http://foia.fbi.gov/rebozo_charles_g/rebozo_charles_g_part05.pdf.

40. "Guns Guard Nixon; He Sees Batista," *Washington Post*, February 8, 1955, p. 2.

41. Ibid.; "Governmental Stability in Cuba Impresses Nixon," *Washington Post*, February 9, 1955, p. 9. See also Szulc, *Fidel: A Critical Portrait*, pp. 480,488.

42. Stephen G. Rabe, *Eisenhower and Latin America*, pp. 100–107; Alan McPherson, *Yankee No!*, pp. 9–37; Lars Schoultz, *Beneath the United States*, pp. 351–354. A report states: "A mob surrounded his car and began rocking it back and forth, trying to turn it over and chanting 'Death to Nixon.' Protected by only 12 Secret Service agents, the procession was forced to wait for the Venezuelan military to clear a path of escape. But by that time, the car had been nearly demolished and the vice president had seen his fill of South America. President Eisenhower sent a naval squadron to the Venezuelan coast in case they needed to rescue the vice president, but Nixon quietly left the country the next day. He returned to Washington to a hero's welcome. Over 15,000 people met him at the airport, including President Eisenhower and the entire cabinet. Over the next few days, politicians of both parties throughout the nation praised Nixon's courage, and congratulations poured in by the thousands. It was Nixon's shining moment, but the respect was more the result of Americans rallying behind their vice president than any change in Nixon's standing." "Richard M. Nixon, 36th Vice President (1953–1961)," United States Senate, http://www.senate.gov/artandhistory/history/common/generic/VP_Richard_Nixon.htm.

43. Schoultz, *Beneath the United States*, p. 352.

44. Thomas, *Cuba: Or, the Pursuit of Freedom*, p. 1210.

45. Ibid.

46. "Nixon Advises Castro," United Press International, April 26, 1959; Bourne, *Fidel: A Biography*, p. 175.

47. Geyer, *Guerrilla Prince*, pp. 225–226.

48. See Jeffrey J. Safford, "The Nixon-Castro Meeting of 19 April 1959," *Diplomatic History* 4 (Fall 1980), pp. 425–431. See also *Bay of Pigs Declassified*, pp. 7, 267; Paterson, *Contesting Castro*, p. 257 and Thomas, *The Cuban Revolution*, pp. 430–431.

49. See Jon Lee Anderson, *Che Guevara: A Revolutionary Life* (New York: Grove Press, 1997), p. 419; Szulc, *Fidel: A Critical Portrait*, p. 364.

50. *Diplomatic History* 4 (Fall 1980), pp. 425–431. Quoted in Paterson, *Contesting Castro*, p. 257. Marquis Childs used the precise language when describing the meeting. "On Sending Arms to Latin America," *Washington Post and Times Herald*, April 24, 1959, p. A18.

51. Richard M. Nixon, *Six Crises* (New York: Simon & Schuster, 1990), pp. 351–352.

52. Nixon, *Six Crises*; Thomas, *Cuba: Or, the Pursuit of Freedom*, p. 1210; Theodore Draper, *Castro's Revolution, Myths and Realities* (New York: Frederick A. Praeger, 1962), p. 62; Bourne, *Fidel: A Biography*, p. 175; Haynes Johnson, Manuel Artime, José Pérez San Roman, Erneido Oliva, Enrique Ruiz-Williams, *Bay of Pigs: The Leaders' Story of Brigade 2506* (New York: Dell Publishing Company, 1964), p. 27. Farber, in *The Origins of the Cuban Revolution*, p. 78, states that Nixon would later arrive at this position, but alleged in April he was "on to" Castro in early 1959 as an election tactic in his presidential campaign.

53. Thomas, *Cuba: Or, the Pursuit of Freedom*, p. 1211. He also said the same to Rufo López Fresquet.

54. Geyer, *Guerrilla Prince*, p. 232; Thomas, *Cuba: Or, the Pursuit of Freedom*, p. 1211.

55. Anderson refers to Bender as "Garry Dracher."

56. Paterson, *Contesting Castro*, p. 236.

57. "Upper Classmen v. Freshman," *Time*, April 27, 1959. The upperclassmen included Figueres, but the article depicted how Castro had turned on Figueres and aligned himself with the head of the Costa Rican opposition Communist Party. In a speech to veterans of the Costa Rican Revolution, Figueres is quoted: "In every American country there exists a Communist nucleus that backs a demagogue's leadership. 'Demagoguery, No! Communism, No!' Roared the veterans: 'Down with Fidel Castro!'"

58. Ibid. In an earlier article, *Time* pointed out that Castro had executed a marijuana peddler as a "social benefit" to society as a whole. "The First 100 Days," *Time*, April 20, 1959. However, within a few days the sentence was rescinded. R. Hart Phillips, "Castro Deplores Panama Landing," *New York Times*, April 29, 1959, p. 11. *Time* did not report the rescission.

59. "Humanist Abroad," *Time*, May 4, 1959.

60. Paul Sanders, "Will Castro Crack Down on Commies?" Associated Press, April 26, 1959.

61. R. Hart Phillips, "Nicaragua Rebels Arrested in Cuba," *New York Times*, April 20, 1959, p. 1. Later reports were that an anti–Panamanian army had left Cuba, led by Dr. Roberto Arias, a former Panamanian diplomat and husband of Dame Margot Fonteyn, the British actress. See "Panama Holds 3 in Rebel Landing," *New York Times*, April 27, 1959, p. 1. The U.S. had a treaty with Panama called the Mutual Security Act, and supplied small arms to the Panamanian government through the Canal Zone. The "force" turned out to consist of about five people, who immediately surrendered without bloodshed. "Invasion Force in Panama Yields to Americas Unit," *New York Times*, May 2, 1959, p. 1. Ambassador Bonsal called the expedition a "comic opera." Bonsal, *Cuba, Castro and the United States*, p. 66.

62. "Guatemala Will Fight Revolts in Her Sphere," *New York Times*, April 19, 1959, p. 4. The Guatemalan president was Miguel Ydigoras Fuentes.

63. "Invasion Intent Denied," *New York Times*, April 21, 1959; "Cuba Holds American in Invasion Plot," *Washington Post and Times Herald*, April 22, 1959, p. A9, p. 12. Hall was actually Loren Hall, who would later be part of anti–Castro activities.

64. "Cuba Bars a Role as Invasion Base," *New York Times*, April 22, 1959, p. 14.

65. Dana Adams Schmidt, "Castro Stresses Land Reform Aim," *New York Times*, p. 1.

66. "Castro Reaches Princeton," *New York Times*, April 21, 1959, p. 12; "Castro Vows He'll Aid Anti-Trujillo

Forces," *Long Island Newsday*, April 21, 1959; "Princeton Gives Castro Uproarious Reception," *Trenton Times*, April 21, 1959.

67. "Students Get Advice on Languages from Expert," *New York Times*, April 26, 1959, p. E9.

68. Phillip Benjamin, "Leader Tells of Hopes for Better Cuba," *New York Times*, April 22, 1959, p. 1.

69. E. W. Kenworthy, "Cuba Considers New Import Law," *New York Times*, April 22, 1959, p. 14.

70. Benjamin, "Leader Tells of Hopes for Better Cuba," *New York Times*, April 22, 1959, p. 1.

71. Ibid.

72. E. W. Kenworthy, "'Austerity' Held Near for Castro," *New York Times*, April 23, 1959, p. 2.

73. Ibid.

74. Clayton Knowles, "Castro Aide Sees Cuba's Best Year," *New York Times*, April 24, 1959, p. 6; "Rebellion's Financier," *New York Times*, April 24, 1959, p. 6.

75. "Tax Warning to Cubans," *New York Times*, May 4, 1959, p. 13.

76. Lindsay Parrott, "Castro Defends Election Delay," *New York Times*, April 23, 1959, p. 1.

77. Bruce W. Munn, "8 U.S. Gunmen Are Sought in Plot to Assassinate Castro," *Washington Post and Times Herald*, April 24, 1959, p. A3; Philip Benjamin, "Police Increase Guard on Castro in Fear of Plot," *New York Times*, April 24, 1959, p. 1.

78. Farber, *The Origins of the Cuban Revolution*, pp. 60–61; Fursenko and Naftali, *"One Hell of a Gamble": Khrushchev, Castro and Kennedy, 1958–1964* (New York: W.W. Norton, 1998), pp. 18, 359.

79. Fursenko and Naftali, *"One Hell of a Gamble,"* p. 11, citing an internal document from the Central Committee of the Communist Party of the Soviet Union.

80. R. Hart Phillips, "Reds' Alleged Role in Castro's Regime Alarming Havana," *New York Times*, April 24, 1959, p. 1. Among those Communists who had returned were Blas Roca and Lazaro Peña, who had been prominent labor leaders during the first Batista and Grau San Martín regimes.

81. Ibid.

82. William L. Ryan, "Castro Wins Good Will but Leaves Doubts," Associated Press, April 27, 1959.

83. "Man with a Bomb Seized Near Castro at Rally in Park," *New York Times*, April 25, 1959, p. 1.

84. Ibid. The man, John Gregory Feller, age 23, had been discharged as a master sergeant from the United States Air Force. Ingredients for a second bomb were found in his room. He told the police that he had nothing against Castro and just wanted to set off the bomb "for kicks." The police took him to Bellevue Hospital to be evaluated for mental disorder. Also see Phillip Benjamin, "Castro Departs to Joy of Police," *New York Times*, April 26, 1959, p. 3.

85. "Havana to Retain Baseball Berth," Associated Press, April 25, 1959.

86. "Roundup," Associated Press, April 21, 1959.

87. E. W. Kenworthy, "Cuba's Problems Pose Tests for U.S. Policy," *New York Times*, April 26, 1959, p. E7.

88. "Boston Mobilizes to Protect Castro," Associated Press, April 24, 1959; "Boston Braces after Bomb Incident," Associated Press, April 25, 1959.

89. Fursenko and Naftali, *"One Hell of a Gamble,"* pp. 10–11.

90. For instance, "Castro Justifies Mass Killings," United Press International, April 26, 1959; Jim Mc Laughlin, "Castro Defends Executions," *Lowell Sunday Sun*, April 26, 1959, p. 1.

91. "Castro Turning U.S. Enemies into Friends," Associated Press, April 26, 1959.

92. "New Death Threats Made against Fidel," United Press International, April 27, 1959.

93. Raymond Daniell, "Montreal Greets Castro as a Hero," *New York Times*, April 27, 1959, p. 3.

94. "Panama Holds 3 in Rebel Landing," *New York Times*, April 27, 1959, p. 1.

95. "Castro to Advise Cuba from Plane," *New York Times*, April 28, 1959, p. 18; "Castro Likes Texas," Associated Press, April 28. 1959. The oilman J. B. Ferguson gave Castro the colt, valued at about $10,000.

96. "Castro to Advise Cuba from Plane," *New York Times*, April 28, 1959, p. 18; R. Hart Phillips, "Castro Deplores Panama Landing," *New York Times*, April 29, 1959, p. 11; "Castro Men Seek Peace in Panama," *Washington Post and Times Herald*, April 29, 1959, p. A1.

97. Phillips, "Castro Deplores Panama Landing," *New York Times*, April 29, 1959, p. 11.

98. Herbert L. Matthews, *The Cuban Story*, p. 237.

99. Juan de Onis, "American Lands Will Meet Today," *New York Times*, April 28, 1959, p. 19.

100. Juan de Onis, "Castro Calls on U.S. for More Latin Aid," *New York Times*, May 3, 1959, p. 1.

101. Juan de Onis, "Castro Calls on U.S. for More Latin Aid," *New York Times*, May 3, 1959, p. 1.

102. "U.S. Foregoes Reply to Castro Aid Talk," *New York Times*, May 5, 1959, p. 11.

103. "Cuba Withdraws Plan for U.S. Aid," *New York Times*, May 8, 1959, p. 1.

104. Bonsal, *Cuba, Castro and the United States*, p. 65.

105. Bonsal, *Cuba, Castro and the United* States, p. 67; López Fresquet, *My Fourteen Months with Castro*, p. 177.

105. Thomas, *Cuba: Or, the Pursuit of Freedom*, p. 1210.

106. Bonsal, *Cuba, Castro and the United* States, p. 67; López Fresquet, *My Fourteen Months with Castro*, p. 177.

Chapter 11

1. "Cuban Workers Submit Demands," *New York Times*, May 3, 1959, p. 42.

2. Ibid.

3. Herbert L. Matthews, "Questions for Castro," *New York Times*, May 3, 1959, p. SM10.

4. "Cuba Called Communist Beachhead," *Washington Post and Times Herald*, May 4, 1959, p. A5.

5. "Castro Scoffs at Story of Red Role in Cuba," *Washington Post and Times Herald*, May 5, 1959, p. A7.

6. *Washington Post*, p. A7.

7. "City Labor Group Honors Figueres," *New York Times*, May 8, 1959, p. 8.

8. "Cuban Throng Hails Castro on Return," *New York Times*, May 9, 1959, p. 3.

9. Urrutia Lleó, *Fidel Castro & Company*, p. 44.

10. R. Hart Phillips, "Havana Classes Resume Monday," *New York Times*, May 10, 1959, p. 14.

11. R. Hart Phillips, "Castro Calling Halt in Military Trials," *New York Times*, May 12, 1959, p. 1.

12. "Prio Group in Cuba Urges Civil Rights," *New York Times*, May 16, 1959, p. 3.

13. R. Hart Phillips, "Castro Bars Role for 'Extremists,'" *New York Times*, May 23, 1959, p. 1; Jules Dubois, "Castro Assails Communists for Cuban Labor Difficulties," *Washington Post and Times Herald*, May 23, 1959, p. A4.

14. *New York Times*, May 12, 1959, p. 34.

15. R. Hart Phillips, "Castro's Newspaper Scores Communists," *New York Times*, May 17, 1959, p. 1.

16. "Communist Trend in Cuba Is Denied," *New York Times*, May 18, 1959, p. 8; "Cubans Deny Red Influence," *Washington Post and Times Herald*, May 18, 1959, p. A10. Appearing were Ernesto Dihigo, Cuban ambassador to the United States, Manuel Bisbé y Alberni, Cuban ambassador to the United Nations, and Carlos M. Lechuga, alternate U.N. delegate. Also appearing were Representative Porter and Leo Cherne, head of the Research Institute of America. Only Cherne maintained that Cuba was becoming a communist beachhead.

17. "Transition in Cuba," *Washington Post and Times Herald*, May 19, 1959, p. A20.

18. Phillips, "Castro Bars Role for 'Extremists,'" *New York Times*, May 23, 1959, p. 1.

19. Jules Dubois, "Castro Assails Communists for Cuban Labor Difficulties," *Washington Post and Times Herald*, May 23, 1959, p. A4.

20. George Auerbach, "Raw Sugar Price Climbing Sharply," *New York Times*, May 10, 1959, p. F1.

21. R. Hart Phillips, "Property Seizure Persists in Cuba," *New York Times*, May 11, 1959, p. 13.

22. "Castro Foes Lose Holdings in Cuba," *New York Times*, May 14, 1959, p. 10.

23. R. Hart Phillips, "Cuban Farm Law Imperils U.S. Sugar Concerns' Land," *New York Times*, May 19, 1959, p. 1.

24. Thomas, *Cuba. Or, the Pursuit of Freedom*, pp. 1215–1218.

25. "Sugar Mill Owners Ask for Meeting," Associated Press, May 23, 1959.

26. Thomas, *Cuba: Or, the Pursuit of Freedom*, pp. 1215–1216.

27. Thomas, *Cuba: Or, the Pursuit of Freedom*, pp. 1216–1217.

28. Geyer, *Guerrilla Prince*, p. 234.

29. In 1950 Japan, Mitsui, Mitsubishi, Sumitomo and Yasuda were preeminent in industry, commerce, and finance, conducted approximately a third of Japan's foreign trade, and held many small farmers in serfdom.

30. McPherson, *Yankee No!*, pp. 53–54.

31. See McPherson, p. 56. Lincoln established the Homestead Act of 1862 which provided free land to farmers who would agree to work their plots. Castro referenced Lincoln's "of the people, by the people and for the people" from the Gettysburg Address.

32. "Cuba's Agrarian Reform," *New York Times*, May 20, 1959, p. 34.

33. Phillips, "Castro Bars Role for 'Extremists,'" *New York Times*, May 23, 1959, p. 1.

34. Ibid.

35. At four cents per pound. The rate at the time was approximately 2.87 cents per pound. See R. Hart Phillips, "Land Seizure Act in Effect in Cuba," *New York Times*, June 5, 1959, p. 3, and R. Hart Phillips, "Society News Tax Is Dropped in Cuba," *New York Times*, June 6, 1959, p. 1; "U.S. Weighs Law Extension," *New York Times*, June 6, 1959, p. 6.

36. Antonio Núñez Jiménez, formerly a professor at Santa Clara University.

37. R. Hart Phillips, "Cuban Land Reform Adds to Uncertainty," *New York Times*, May 24, 1959, p. E4.

38. R. Hart Phillips, "Cuba Will Take Over Airlines; Charges Batista Men Own Them," *New York Times*, May 24, 1959, p. 1.

39. R. Hart Phillips, "40% Profits Tax Planned in Cuba," *New York Times*, May 31, 1959, p. 8.

40. "The Cuban Land Reform," *New York Times*, June 10, 1959, p. 36.

41. R. Hart Phillips, "Land Seizure Act in Effect in Cuba," *New York Times*, June 5, 1959, p. 3.

42. R. Hart Phillips, "Castro Opposes Alien Ownership," *New York Times*, June 11, 1959, p. 14.

43. Ibid.

44. "Communist Gives Castro Warning," *New York Times*, May 27, 1959, p. 1.

45. R. Hart Phillips, "Communists in Cuba Pose a Big Problem," *New York Times*, May 31, 1959, p. E4.

46. Phillips, "40% Profits Tax Planned in Cuba," *New York Times*, May 31, 1959,
p. 8. Phillips also ridiculed a proposed tax on people whose names appeared in newspaper society columns. Phillips continued to ridicule the tax in "Society-News Tax? Cuban Editors Shocked," June 2, 1959, p. 16. However, she noted that society editors were the best-paid journalists in Cuba, and claimed that the highest paid was Luis de Posada, of the *Diario de la Marina*. "Prior to the victory of the Castro Revolution," she said, "it was not uncommon for rich Cubans to spend up to $75,000 on a party. However, if the party was not reported by Luis de Posada, from a social point of view, it simply had not taken place." By June 5, the society news tax was dropped. R. Hart Phillips, "Society News Tax Is Dropped in Cuba," *New York Times*, June 6, 1959, p. 1. Although the premise of the tax, if it ever was seriously considered, was preposterous; note that the *Times* ran the story as front page news.

47. For the period 1954–1963, the highest tax rate was subject to a maximum effective rate limitation equal to 87 percent of statutory "taxable income." Robert A. Wilson and David E. Jordan, "Personal Exemptions and Individual Income Tax Rates, 1913–2002" (Rev. 6–02), in Internal Revenue Service, Statistics of Income Bulletin (Publication 1136), Spring 2002, pp. 216–225. In 1959 corporate taxes were about 25% of total government revenue. Steve Maguire, "Average Effective Corporate Tax Rates: 1959–2002," Congressional Research Service, September 5, 2003; Joel Friedman, "The Decline of Corporate Income Tax Revenues," Center on Budget and Policy Priorities, October 24, 2003. http://www.cbpp. org/10–16–03tax.htm.

48. William J. Jorden, "Americas Vote Nicaragua Study," *New York Times*, June 5, 1959, p. 1.

49. Tad Szulc, "Danger Signals Flare in Latin America," *New York Times*, June 7, 1959, p. E3.

50. "Castro Condemns Blows at Cubans," *New York Times*, June 7, 1959, p. 1.

51. "Miami Restaurant Attacked," *New York Times*, June 5, 1959, p. 28.

52. "7 Indicted in Miami in Arms Smuggling," *New York Times*, June 6, 1959, p. 6.

53. "Anti-Castro Rebels Seized," *New York Times*, June 6, 1959, p. 6.

54. Bonsal, *Cuba, Castro and the United States*, pp. 84–85.

55. "Batista Predicts Castro's Fall," *New York Times*, May 12, 1959, p. 4.

56. Bourne, *Fidel: A Biography of Fidel Castro*. "When this war is over," Castro wrote to Celia Sanchez in 1958, "a much wider and bigger war will commence for me: the war that I am going to wage against [the Americans]." At the time he had no more than 2,000 men, no navy and no air force.

57. Safford, "The Nixon-Castro Meeting," pp. 428–429.

58. Parnet, *Eisenhower and the American Crusades*, p. 561.

59. Paterson, *Contesting Castro*, p. 257.

60. Safford, "The Nixon-Castro Meeting," pp. 428–429.

61. See "Curbs posted on Cuban Sugar," *Wall Street Journal*, July 22, 1957, p. 16.

62. Jules Dubois, "Hear 1,000 Face Death after Trials: Charge Batista Got Fortune of 400 Millions," *Chicago Daily Tribune*, January 14, 1959, p. 1.

63. For example, see Report by Cuba on Resolution 60/12 of the United Nations General Assembly: "Necessity of ending the economic, commercial and financial blockade imposed by the United States of America against Cuba," United Nations, August 2006. The allegation is that the funds in American banks were only part of the Cuban treasury stolen by Batista and his allies.

Chapter 12

1. Bonsal, *Cuba, Castro and the United States*, p. 73.

2. Thomas, *Cuba: Or, the Pursuit of Freedom*, pp. 1215–1233; R. Hart Phillips, "Cuba Rebuffs U.S. on Land Payment," *New York Times*, June 16, 1959, p. 1.

3. Sweig, *Inside the Cuban Revolution*, p. 181. Thomas points out that the Sorí Marín plan was more conservative than many others in force: the European plans of the 1920s went much farther. *Cuba: Or, the Pursuit of Freedom*, p. 1217.

4. Thomas, *Cuba: Or, the Pursuit of Freedom*, pp. 1216–1217.

5. Geyer, *Guerrilla Prince*, pp. 234–235; Szulc, *Fidel: A Critical Portrait*, pp. 84–85, 499.

6. Ibid. In essence, INRA had the power of condemnation, to take property as long as the owners received just compensation. Because INRA could require membership in cooperative farms with the grant of ownership to the grantees, the concept is not the same as the Israeli kibbutz system, which are entirely voluntary. Israel also has another form of collective called *moshav shitufi*, in which production and services are managed collectively and individual households make their own decisions. In the United States, four states, Massachusetts, Virginia, Pennsylvania and Kentucky, are "commonwealths," based on similar concepts. The second paragraph of the preamble to the Constitution of Massachusetts states: "The body politic is formed by a voluntary association of individuals: it is a social compact, by which the whole people covenants with each citizen, and each citizen with the whole people, that all shall be governed by certain laws for the common good." http://www.mass.gov/legis/const.htm. The concept is that power in a commonwealth is derived from the people and, in the language of Abraham Lincoln, is "by the people and for the people." In theory the Commonwealth held an interest in all land, especially to "commons" such as Boston Common, park property open for use to any citizen.

7. Matthews, *The Cuban Story*, p. 233.

8. Castro and Ramonet, *Fidel Castro: My Life*, pp. 242–243.

9. Ibid., p. 243.

10. Gustavo Peña Monte, "Havana Bishop Endorses Castro Plan to Break Up Cuba's Larger Estates," *The Voice*, June 5, 1959, p. 9.

11. Castro and Ramonet, *Fidel Castro: My Life*, pp. 245–246.

12. Ibid., p. 246.

13. Bonsal, *Cuba, Castro and the United States*, p. 73.

14. See "News Summary and Index," *New York Times*, June 12, 1959, p. 29; R. Hart Phillips, "Land Law Splits Castro's Regime," *New York Times*, June 13, 1959, p. 1.

15. "Cuba's Political Crisis," *New York Times*, June 13, 1959, p. 20.

16. Phillips, "Land Law Splits Castro's Regime," *New York Times*, June 13, 1959, p. 1.

17. "Cuba's Political Crisis," *New York Times*, June 13, 1959, p. 20.

18. Castro and Ramonet, *Fidel Castro: My Life*, p. 242.

19. Urrutia Lleó, *Fidel Castro & Company*, pp. 45–48.

20. *Revolucion*, July 2, 1959, cited in Thomas, *Cuba: Or, the Pursuit of Freedom*, pp. 1230–1231, and in Urrutia Lleó, *Fidel Castro & Company*, p. 49.

21. Thomas, *Cuba: Or, the Pursuit of Freedom*, p. 1275.

22. *Bay of Pigs Declassified*, pp. 67–68. The DRE, led by Alberto Muller, Manuel Salvat and Luis Fernández Rocha, led anti–Castro student protests. Enrique Encinosa, *Unvanquished: Cuba's Resistance to Fidel Castro* (Los Angeles: Pureplay Press, 2004), p. 16.

23. Ibid. Also see Anderson, *Che Guevara: A Revolutionary Life*, p. 471.

24. Jesús Arboleya, *The Cuban Counter Revolution* (Athens, Ohio: Center for International Studies, 2000), p. 64, citing internal police records. The Cubans say that as a protégé of Sorí Marín , he was given a commission in the Rebel Army without having seen any combat, and was a Jesuit agent all along. Arboleya reports that Artime was directly tied to Angel Fernández Varela, a CIA agent who had been the head of the Falange in Cuba. Although he spoke no English, he was later named to head the CIA insurgent force Brigade 2506. There are also reports that after things went sour at the Bay of Pigs, his stock dropped and he was no longer trusted by the CIA and was eventually placed under surveillance. Dick Russell, *The Man Who Knew Too Much*. 2nd ed. (New York: Carroll & Graf, 2003), p. 507.

25. Johnson, Artime, et al., *Bay of Pigs: The Leader's Story of Brigade 2506*, p. 26.

26. Ibid.

27. Anderson, *Che Guevara: A Revolutionary Life*, p. 471.

28. Tad Szulc, "Cubans Denounce Eisenhower View as Hypocritical," *New York Times*, April 10, 1960, p. 1.

29. Wayne Smith, *The Closest of Enemies*, pp. 47–48.

30. Montaner, *Journey to the Heart of Cuba*, p. 88.

31. Bonsal, *Cuba, Castro and the United States*, p. 124.

32. Thomas, *Cuba: Or, the Pursuit of Freedom*, p. 1218.

33. "Cuba to Take Over Large Ranches Now," *New York Times*, June 24, 1959, p. 63.

34. See United Fruit Historical Society, "Jacobo Árbenz," 2006, http://www.unitedfruit.org/arbenz.htm. Árbenz and his foreign minister, Guillermo Toriello, owned properties that were expropriated.

35. Matthews, *The Cuban Story*, pp. 174–175; Thomas, *Cuba: Or, the Pursuit of Freedom*, pp. 1215–1233; Rabe, *Eisenhower and Latin America*, pp. 124–125.

36. Bonsal, *Cuba, Castro and the United States*, p. 74.

37. Phillips, "Cuba Rebuffs U.S. on Land Payment," *New York Times*, June 16, 1959, p. 1.

38. Wayne Smith, *The Closest of Enemies*, p. 48.

39. Ibid.; Bonsal, *Cuba, Castro and the United States*, pp. 70–77.

40. Ibid.

41. Castro and Ramonet, *Fidel Castro: My Life*, pp. 242–243; Pérez, *Cuba*, pp. 245–246; Bourne, *Fidel: A Biography*, pp. 180–181; Coltman, *The Real Fidel Castro*, p. 160.

42. "Castro Upbraids Foes of Land Plan," *New York Times*, June 14, 1959, p. 32.

43. Bonsal, *Cuba, Castro and the United States*, p. 89.

44. R. Hart Phillips, "Castro to Spend $134,500,000 on Public Works to Aid Jobless," *New York Times*, June 30, 1959, p. 9. The Provisional Government determined that it needed to avoid any company involved in graft under the Batista administration, and required companies to provide a history of all negotiations they may have had with the prior regime to determine whether they were worthy of participating in the stimulus program. "Contractors Must Report," *New York Times*, July 9, 1959, p. 8. The Provisional Government was also interested in recovering lost tax receipts and wanted to fine those who had participated in graft. Those who failed to present their records would be prosecuted.

45. Alexander, "Castro Seems Really to Be Tackling Cuba's Ills," *Washington Post and Times Herald*, June 21, 1959, p. E1.

46. López Fresquet, *My Fourteen Months with Castro*, pp. 116–121.

47. Bonsal, *Cuba, Castro and the United States*, p. 79.

48. Thomas, *Cuba: Or, the Pursuit of Freedom*, p. 1228.

49. Anderson, *Che Guevara: A Revolutionary Life*, pp. 426–433.

50. "Protestant Aide to Castro Here," *New York Times*, June 13, 1959, p. 11.

51. "Castro Regime Purges 26 Top Air Officers," *Washington Post and Times Herald*, June 19, 1959, p. A6.

52. "Cuba's Air Chief Quits; His Arrest Is Ordered," *Washington Post and Times Herald*, July 1, 1959, p. A6.

53. Thomas, *Cuba: Or, the Pursuit of Freedom*, p. 1231. Also escaped with Díaz Lanz and his brother, Sergio, was Frank Sturgis, chief of Cuban air force security. Coltman, *The Real Fidel Castro*, p. 161.

54. "Cuba to Take Over Large Ranches Now," *New York Times*, June 24, 1959, p. 63.

55. Phillips, "Anti-Castro Acts Spreading in Cuba," *New York Times*, July 3, 1959, p. 1; Francis L. McCarthy, "Castro Warns OAS against Intervention," *Washington Post and Times Herald*, July 4, 1959, p. A1.

56. The reports stated that two landing craft had been destroyed offshore, but no rebels had reached the Dominican mainland. There was also a contemporaneous episode in which Dominican émigrés were lured from Puerto Rico by a Dominican espionage agent, Juan de Dios Ventura Simó, who delivered 65 men to Trujillo. For his efforts, Ventura was promoted and given a medal. At the ceremony, he was congratulated by the U.S. ambassador to the Dominican Republic, Joseph S. Farland. A picture was taken. The Trujillo regime sent that picture to every news service to show how close the United States government was to Trujillo. See Herbert L. Matthews, "Trujillo Now Center of Caribbean Unrest," *New York Times*, June 28, 1959, p. E4. The next day, there were reports that Trujillo had Ventura executed for reasons unknown.

57. Bonsal, *Cuba, Castro and the United States*, pp. 76–77. He also says that Castro launched similar failed expeditions against Nicaragua and Haiti.

58. Thomas, *Cuba: Or, the Pursuit of Freedom*, p. 1228.

59. "Trujillo Reported to Crush Invasion Backed by Cuba," *New York Times*, June 24, 1959, p. 1; "Cuba Seeks to Buy Ships," *New York Times*, June 26, 1959, p. 6. The report stated that Castro had simulated a break with the Communists to hide from the United States a tacit alliance with the Soviets. See also Thomas J. Hamilton, "Domini-

cans Link Castro and Reds," *New York Times*, June 30, 1959, p. 9.

60. "Havana Informs O.A.S.," *New York Times*, June 27, 1959, p. 4.

61. "Cuba Breaks Ties with Trujillo Regime, Charges Killing of Defenseless Civilians," *Washington Post and Times Herald*, June 27, 1959, p. A4; R. Hart Phillips, "Cuban Regime Cuts Ties with Trujillo," *New York Times*, June 27, 1959, p. 1; Matthews, "Trujillo Now Center of Caribbean Unrest," *New York Times*, June 28, 1959, p. E4.

62. "Hoffa Is Linked to an Arms Plot," *New York Times*, July 1, 1959, p. 19; Edward T. Folliard, "Teamster Official Tied to Cuban Arms," *Washington Post and Times Herald*, July 1, 1959, p. A8. According to Shetterly, Hoffa's man in Miami and Havana was Domenick Bartone, aka Barton, who was later linked also to William Morgan in Havana. *Americano*, pp. 160–162, 167. The contacts with Morgan, Gutiérrez Menoyo and Trujillo are substantiated in a statement Batrone gave to the FBI on June 6, 1963. http:// www.maryferrell.org/mffweb/archive/viewer/showDoc.do ?docId=72173&relPageId=2. Bartone pleaded guilty with the Dominican consul in Miami to conspiracy to smuggle arms to anti–Castro groups. "Cuba Dominican Consul Guilty," *New York Times*, December 12, 1959, p. 48. The consul, Augusto Ferrando, also pleaded guilty to bribing customs officials and eventually was sentenced to five years' probation. Bartone was fined $10,000, and Joseph Liquori, a former Miami policeman also involved, was fined $250 and given two years' probation. "Consul on Probation," *New York Times*, December 31, 1959, p. 8. Arboleya describes Morgan as the foster son of Mafioso Dominic Bartoni, and names him as an associate of Meyer Lansky and Santos Trafficante. *The Cuban Counter-Revolution*, p. 306.

63. R. Hart Phillips, "Anti-Castro Acts Spreading in Cuba," *New York Times*, July 3, 1959, p. 1.

64. Kennett Love, "Wide Arms Deals Laid to Trujillo," *New York Times*, July 3, 1959, p. 6.

65. Tad Szulc, "Trujillo Faces Biggest Threat of His 30-Year Dictatorship," *New York Times*, July 5, 1959, p. 1; Tad Szulc, "Unrest Troubles Trujillo Regime," *New York Times*, July 6, 1959, p. 1; Tad Szulc, "Ciudad Trujillo Full of Rumors," *New York Times*, July 7, 1959, p. 18; Tad Szulc, "Dominican Affair Stirs the Caribbean Area," *New York Times*, July 12, 1959, p. E3.

66. See Drew Pearson, "U.S. Neglect of Latins Charged," *Washington Post and Times Herald*, August 12, 1959, p. D11.

67. Tad Szulc, "Radio War Rages in the Caribbean," *New York Times*, July 9, 1959, p. 9.

68. Matthews, *The Cuban Story*, p. 192; Castro and Ramonet, *Fidel Castro: My Life*, p. 293. Castro confuses the date, but explains that Trujillo had aided Batista during the Revolution and had given him sanctuary afterward, and "armed actions" were being launched against Cuba from the Dominican Republic.

69. Homer Bigart, "Dominican Rebels Recruit Puerto Rican Troops Here," *New York Times*, August 9, 1959, p. 1.

70. "Cuba's Air Chief Quits; His Arrest Is Ordered," *Washington Post and Times Herald*, July 1, 1959, p. A6. Three Americans and one British citizen were arrested, including Captain Paul Hughes, who had been an advisor to the Cuban air force.

71. Bonsal, *Cuba, Castro and the United States*, pp. 78–79.

72. "Castro Regime Purges 26 Top Air Officers," *Washington Post and Times Herald*, June 19, 1959, p. A6.

73. R. Hart Phillips, "Castro Rules Out Any Foreign Hand in Cuban Affairs," *New York Times*, July 4, 1959, p. 1; McCarthy, "Castro Warns OAS against Intervention," *Washington Post and Times Herald*, July 4, 1959, p. A1.

74. Emilio Cordero Michel, who called his own government "repulsive." *New York Times*, July 12, 1959, p. E2.

75. Urrutia Lleó, *Fidel Castro & Company*, pp. 50–51. The television interviewer on both occasions was Luis Conte Agüero.

76. Bonsal, *Cuba, Castro and the United States*, pp. 79–80.

77. Allen Drury, "Ex-Aide Calls Castro a Red at Hearing of Senate Unit," *New York Times*, July 15, 1959, p. 1; "Cuban's Testimony Arouses Senators," *New York Times*, July 14, 1959, p. 1; James Clayton, "Bomb Scare Disrupts Hearing of Former Castro Air Chief," *Washington Post and Times Herald*, p. A3. Díaz Lanz said that Castro wanted to use Cuba as a base to spread Communism. Communist indoctrination was part of military training. He named David Salvador and Armando Hart as leading communists. Burke also said that the threat had been great that Egypt and the entire Middle East would have become communist and noted that the Communist Party was the largest in Indonesia. Burke also spoke to reserve officers, stating that the Communist threat was also grave in Afghanistan and Honduras. "Burke Fears Red Seizure of Cuba Helm," *Washington Post and Times Herald*, July 14, 1959, p. A4. Another speaker was Henry Kissinger, of the Harvard Center for International Affairs, who said that a truce with the Soviets on Berlin would be "a major defeat for the West."

78. Drury, "Ex-Aide Calls Castro a Red at Hearing of Senate Unit," *New York Times*, July 15, 1959, p. 1.

79. Bonsal, *Cuba, Castro and the United States*, p. 80.

80. R. Hart Phillips, "Urrutia Criticizes U.S.," *New York Times*, July 14, 1959, p. 2. Urrutia would later apologize to Díaz Lanz for his statements about him. Urrutia Lleó, *Fidel Castro & Company*, pp. 67–68.

81. Coltman, *The Real Fidel Castro*, p. 161.

82. Thomas, *Cuba: Or, the Pursuit of Freedom*, p. 1232; "Eisenhower Says U.S. Has Made No Red Charge against Castro," *New York Times*, July 16, 1959, p. 2. Eisenhower's statements on Cuba were made during a discussion on Berlin, which during the Cold War seemed far more important than Cuba. "We Won't Retreat on Berlin, Ike Says," *Washington Post and Times Herald*, July 16, 1959, p. A7. He also commented on an impending Nixon trip to the Soviet Union. "News Conference in Brief," *New York Times*, July 16, 1959, p. 8.

83. "Cuba Has a One-Man Rule and It Is Called Non-Red," *New York Times*, July 16, 1959, p. 1.

84. "Cuba Near the Boiling Point," *Washington Post and Times Herald*, July 12, 1959, p. E5.

85. "Contractors Must Report," *New York Times*, July 9, 1959, p. 8. Deported with him were Lawrence Hall, implicated in the Panama invasion attempt, and Charles Saavedra, formerly of the Capri Hotel.

86. "Cuba Stays Deportation of Hoodlum," *Washington Post and Times Herald*, August 22, 1959, p. A3.

87. Phillips, "Urrutia Criticizes U.S.," *New York Times*, p. 2.

88. Franqui, *Family Portrait with Fidel*, pp. 42–44. Also see Geyer, *Guerrilla Prince*, pp. 236–237. The technique was to make the "people" think that they had made the decision to remove Urrutia. Also see Coltman, *The Real Fidel Castro,* pp. 161–162. Castro told Franqui, then a trusted associate, "I'm not going to resort to the usual Latin American style coup. I'm going directly to the people, because the people will know what to do." Franqui,

Family Portrait with Fidel, p. 42. Castro did not inform Raúl Castro about the plot, and Raúl attacked Franqui and tried to take over the newspaper. p. 43.

89. Urrutia Lleó, *Fidel Castro & Company*, pp. 53–57.

90. Loosely translated as "near treason." See also "Urrutia Accused by a Castro Aide," *New York Times*, July 19, 1959, p. 3. Urrutia also accused the aide, Antonio Núñez Jiménez, head of INRA, of being a Communist, and he too denied it.

91. Bonsal called them "menacing and hardly spontaneous mobs led by Castroite thugs." *Cuba, Castro and the United States*, p. 81.

92. "Cuban Crisis," *New York Times*, July 19, 1959, p. E1; Urrutia Lleó, *Fidel Castro & Company*, pp. 57–71; Thomas, *Cuba: Or, the Pursuit of Freedom*, pp. 1232–1233; Coltman, *The Real Fidel Castro*, p. 162; Szulc, *Fidel: A Critical Portrait*, pp. 555–557; R. Hart Phillips, "Castro Assails Cuban President, Forcing Him Out," *New York Times*, July 18, 1959, p. 1. Thomas says that Conrado Bécquer, of the sugar workers' union, initially publicly called for Urrutia's resignation.

93. Castro and Ramonet, *Fidel Castro: My Life*, pp. 243–244.

94. Ibid., p. 577. One allegation that Castro had made was that his wife was too fashion conscious and frequented expensive shops. Others commented that he was arrogant and vain. See Coltman, *The Real Fidel Castro*, p. 262.

95. Franqui says that Urrutia naively thought that Castro would renounce his brother Raúl as a communist. *Family Portrait with Fidel*, p. 43.

96. Geyer, *Guerrilla Prince*, p. 237.

97. Franqui, *Family Portrait with Fidel*, p. 43.

98. Marinello was the same man who attacked Castro's letter to the editor condemning government intrusion into education.

99. Coltman, *The Real Fidel Castro*, p. 162; Szulc, *Fidel: A Critical Portrait*, pp. 512–513; Thomas, *Cuba: Or, the Pursuit of Freedom*, p. 1085; "Tireless Revolutionary," *New York Times*, July 20, 1959, p. 2; "New Cuban Chief Is a Bookish Rebel," *Washington Post and Times Herald*, July 19, 1959, p. A6. Thomas says that Dorticós Torrado was actually the most bourgeois member of the cabinet. See also R. Hart Phillips, "Castro's Cabinet Bids Him Remain as Cuba's Ruler," *New York Times*, July 19, 1959, p. 1.

100. Bonsal, *Cuba, Castro and the United States*, p. 81.

101. However, within days, a private suit alleging treason was brought by José M. Gómez Quintero. Tad Szulc, "Cuban Labor Joins in Pressing Castro to Return as Premier," *New York Times*, July 23, 1959, p. 10. The government denied it had anything to do with it.

102. Phillips, "Castro's Cabinet Bids Him Remain as Cuba's Ruler," *New York Times*, July 19, 1959, p. 1; Robert D. Clark, "Castro Return to Duty 'Demanded' by Cabinet," *Washington Post and Times Herald*, July 19, 1959, p. A1.

103. "Castro's Choice," *Washington Post and Times Herald*, July 20, 1959, p. A14.

104. Szulc, *Fidel: A Critical Portrait*, pp. 509–526; Montaner, *Journey to the Heart of Cuba*, pp. 84–86. Montaner says that on January 1, 1959, the Communists had no idea that they had won the Revolution. Geyer says that she interviewed Alfredo Guevara, Fabio Grobart and Blas Roca, then heads of the Communist Party, and no secret meetings ever occurred. *Guerrilla Prince*, p. 235.

105. Tad Szulc, "Cuba Halts Work in Plea to Castro," *New York Times*, July 24, 1959, p. 1; "Pro-Castro 1-Hour Strike of Million Set," *Washington Post and Times Herald*, July 23, 1959, p. A7; "1-Hour Strike Ties Up Cuba," *Washington Post and Times Herald*, July 24, 1959, p. A7.

106. Tad Szulc, "Castro Foe Caught as Plane Is Downed," *New York Times*, July 26, 1959, p. 1. A photograph of Castro in uniform appeared with the article.

107. "Plot for Invasion of Cuba Charged," *New York Times*, July 18, 1959, p. 1; "State Department Absolved," *New York Times*, July 18, 1959, p. 3. Accused of fixing the sugar quota were Allen J. Ellender, Democrat of Louisiana, James O. Eastland, Democrat of Mississippi and Henry Capehart of Indiana.

108. George Auerbach, "Forecast Is Sour for World Sugar," *New York Times*, July 19, 1959, p. F1.

109. "Batista's Escape to U.S. Prevented," *New York Times*, July 18, 1959, p. 3.

110. Tad Szulc, "Batista Denies Trying to Flee from Dominican Haven to U.S.," *New York Times*, July 19, 1959, p. 2; Fabian Escalante, *The Cuba Project: CIA Covert Operations 1959–62*, pp. 23–24. This organization was led initially by Renaldo Blanco Navarro and Claudio Medel.

111. Tad Szulc, "Havana Crowds Wait for Castro," *New York Times*, July 21, 1959, p. 3. The Cuban White Rose is not to be confused with the German anti–Nazi organization of the same name.

112. Szulc, "Castro Foe Caught as Plane Is Downed," *New York Times*, July 26, 1959, p. 1; "Del Pino Is U.S. Citizen," *New York Times*, July 26, 1959, p. 27; "Top Castro Foe Caught in Cuba," *Washington Post and Times Herald*, July 26, 1959, p. A5; "Castro Denies Unrest in Caribbean," *Washington Post and Times Herald*, July 28, 1959, p. A8.

113. R. Hart Phillips, "Firm on Bonds for Land," *New York Times*, July 28, 1959, p. 2.

114. R. Hart Phillips, "Castro Resumes the Premiership," *New York Times*, July 27, 1959, p. 1; Tad Szulc, "Gay Cubans Hail Castro's Triumph," *New York Times*, July 27, 1959, p. 3; Harold K. Milks, "Castro Tells Cuba Crowd He'll Return," *Washington Post and Times Herald*, July 27, 1959, p. A1.

115. Tad Szulc, "Castro Accuses U.S. 'Monopolies,'" *New York Times*, July 28, 1959, p. 2.

116. "Game Called: Gunfire; Opposing Players Hit," *Washington Post and Times Herald*, July 27, 1959, p. A16; Szulc "Gay Cubans Hail Castro's Triumph," *New York Times*, July 27, 1959, p. 3.

117. Ibid.

118. Thomas, *Cuba: Or, the Pursuit of Freedom*, p. 1256.

119. Huber Matos, *Cómo Llegó la Noche*; Bosch, *American Experience: Fidel Castro*, Matos interview.

120. "Castro Aide Linked to Nicaraguan Raid," *New York Times*, July 28, 1959, p. 2.

121. "Castro Denies Unrest in Caribbean," *Washington Post and Times Herald*, July 28, 1959, p. A8.

122. "Cuban Protests O.A.S. Decision," *New York Times*, July 31, 1959, p. 4. The Cuban delegate was Levi Marrero. John C. Dreier, representing the United States, said he was afraid the resolution would open the door to a "broad and technical" discussion of Latin America's economic troubles.

123. Tad Szulc, "Cuba Formulates 'New Democracy,'" *New York Times*, July 29, 1959, p. 12; R. Hart Phillips, "Castro Reaches 95% of Cubans with Radio-TV Exhortations," *New York Times*, August 6, 1959, p. 9.

124. R. Hart Phillips, "Castro Movement of Children Rises," *New York Times*, August 7, 1959, p. 6.

125. "Today a Cuban Holiday," *New York Times*, July 30, 1959, p. 6.

126. "A Church Backs Castro," *New York Times*, August 4, 1959, p. 12.

Chapter 13

1. Montaner, *Journey to the Heart of Cuba*, p. 96.
2. Coltman, *The Real Fidel Castro*, p. 168. Also see R. Hart Phillips, "Castro's Brother Is Sent to Inter-American Parley," *New York Times*, August 17, 1959, p. 1.
3. R. Hart Phillips, "Cuba Said to Hold 4,500 as Plotters," *New York Times*, August 12, 1959, p. 1; R. Hart Phillips, "Castro Directing Fighting in Cuba," *New York Times*, August 13, 1959, p. 1; Joseph A. Taylor, "Raul Castro Escapes Assassin," *Washington Post and Times Herald*, August 11, 1959, p. A1; Joseph A. Taylor, "Cuba Foils Invasion, Reports Say," *Washington Post and Times Herald*, August 10, 1959, p. A1; "Cuba Arrests 1,000 in Smashing a Plot," *New York Times*, August 11, 1959, p. 1; "Army Is Alerted in Cuban Unrest," *New York Times*, August 10, 1959, p. 9; "Raúl Castro Denies Rebels Enter Cuba," *New York Times*, August 9, 1959, p. 10. Among those arrested initially were Roman Maestre Gutiérrez, who had been elected to the Cuban Congress as a member of the Free People's Party of Marquez Sterling; former Senator Arthur Hernández Tallaheche; and cattleman Arnaldo Caines Milanes.
4. Shetterly, *The Americano*, pp. 165–167. The consul was Augusto Ferrando.
5. Shetterly, *The Americano*, p. 192. See also Phillips, "Castro's Brother Is Sent to Inter-American Parley," *New York Times*, August 17, 1959, p. 1; R. Hart Phillips, "Castro Is Lionized for Tricking Foes; American Is Hailed," *New York Times*, August 16, 1959, p. 1; Chalmers M. Roberts, "Santiago Delegates Draft 'Declaration,'" *Washington Post and Times Herald*, August 15, 1959, p. A1.
6. Shetterly, *The Americano*, pp. 193–194.
7. Bonsal, *Cuba, Castro and the United States*, p. 84. Bonsal did not discuss his part in the episode and, more remarkably, did not discuss any role played by Gutiérrez Menoyo.
8. Thomas, *Cuba: Or, the Pursuit of Freedom*, p. 1238; Szulc, *Fidel: A Critical Portrait*, pp. 550–551; Phillips, "Castro Is Lionized for Tricking Foes; American Is Hailed," *New York Times*, August 16, 1959, p. 1; Roberts, "Santiago Delegates Draft 'Declaration,'" *Washington Post and Times Herald*, August 15, 1959, p. A1. R. Hart Phillips, "Cubans Capture Invasion Plane; Accuse Trujillo," *New York Times*, August 15, 1959, p. 1; "Castro Marks 33d Birthday Leading Fight against Threat in Las Villas," *Washington Post and Times Herald*, August 14, 1959, p. A1; R. Hart Phillips, "Castro Reports Revolt Crushed," *New York Times*, August 14, 1959, p. 2; Joseph A. Taylor, "Agents Seize Anti-Castro Ringleaders," *Washington Post and Times Herald*, August 12, 1959, p. A1. The pilot was Lieutenant Colonel Antonio Soto. In the Morgan/ Gutiérrez Menoyo version, Gutiérrez Menoyo got the drop on four of the conspirators, the government in waiting, at Morgan's house in Trinidad, as Castro entered. Shetterly, *The Americano*, pp. 189–197. Although the priest's name was spelled "Velasco" by Ruby Phillips and the *New York Times*, it is elsewhere spelled "Velazco." Caiñas Mílanés would soon be released after a hearing on a writ of habeas corpus. "Writ Frees Cuban Held as Plotter," *New York Times*, August 18, 1959, p. 11.
9. Bonsal, *Cuba, Castro and the United States*, p. 84.
10. Also known as the Christian Democrats. See Montaner, *Journey to the Heart of Cuba*, p. 97. Rasco, then

a professor at St. Thomas Villanueva University, had been head of the National Liberation Movement, and had been on the trip to the United States and Canada with Castro. Thomas, *Cuba: Or, the Pursuit of Freedom*, pp. 1212–1213.
11. "Communist Threat to the United States through the Caribbean," U.S. Senate Subcommittee to Investigate the Administration of the Internal Security Act and Other Internal Security Laws, Committee on the Judiciary, May 3, 1960. See also Juan Clark, "Religious Repression in Cuba at the Time of the Pope's Visit to the Island," Cuban Research Institute, Florida International University Archives, January 22, 1998. http://www.fiu.edu/~fcf/clark 12298.html.
12. "Castro Testifies in Matos Trial," *Washington Post and Times Herald*, December 15, 1959, p. A4.
13. "Cuban Priest Replies," *New York Times*, December 16, 1959, p. 16.
14. Tad Szulc, "Caribbean Clash Causes an Uproar at Americas Talk," *New York Times*, August 14, 1959, p. 1; Roberts, "Santiago Delegates Draft 'Declaration,'" *Washington Post and Times Herald*, August 15, 1959, p. A1.
15. Phillips, "Cubans Capture Invasion Plane; Accuse Trujillo," *New York Times*, August 15, 1959, p. 1; Szulc, "Caribbean Clash Causes an Uproar at Americas Talk," *New York Times*, August 14, 1959, p. 1.
16. Roberts, "Santiago Delegates Draft 'Declaration,'" *Washington Post and Times Herald*, August 15, 1959, p. A1; Szulc, "Caribbean Clash Causes an Uproar at Americas Talk," *New York Times*, August 14, 1959, p. 1; "Castro Brands Foreign Ministers Parley as Farce, Criticizes Herter," *Washington Post and Times Herald*, August 15, 1959, p. A1.
17. Thomas, *Cuba: Or, the Pursuit of Freedom*, p. 1239.
18. Ibid., p. 1239. Colonel Glawe, air attaché in Mexico.
19. Ibid.
20. "Latin Red Leaders Meeting in Chile," *Washington Post and Times Herald*, August 20, 1959, p. A4.
21. "Soviet Agent Tied to Reds in Havana," *New York Times*, August 22, 1959, p. 2. This information was supplied by General C. P. Cabell, speaking to the American Legion committee. He alleged the agent was Vadim Kotchergin, sent as part of a scheme to undermine government throughout Latin America.
22. Tad Szulc, "Caribbean Area Still Big Headache for U.S.," *New York Times*, August 23, 1959, p. E4.
23. Dunn, "Cuban Disorders Buoy Sugar Price," *New York Times*, August 16, 1959, p. F1.

Chapter 14

1. Rabe, *Eisenhower and Latin America*, p. 127; Bonsal, *Cuba, Castro and the United States*, p. 93.
2. Bonsal, Cuba, *Castro and the United States*, p. 84.
3. R. Hart Phillips, "U.S. Envoy, Castro Meet for 6 Hours," *New York Times*, September 5, 1959, p. 4.
4. Rabe, *Eisenhower and Latin America*, pp. 127–128, quoting a State Department memorandum signed by President Eisenhower. Rabe says that Herter was not "explicitly" calling for the overthrow of Castro.
5. Bonsal, *Cuba, Castro and the United States*, p. 93; Nixon, *Six Crises*, p. 379.
6. "Invaders Cuban, Haiti Maintains," *New York Times*, August 25, 1959, p. 13.
7. "Cuba's Embassy in Haiti Is Closed," *New York Times*, August 30, 1959, p. 13. The ambassador, Antonio Rodríguez Echazabal, had lived in Haiti for 20 years. He

turned over the embassy to the Mexican government. Inside were five Haitians whom he had granted asylum.

8. "Cuban Scores U.S. in Rift with Haiti," *New York Times*, September 2, 1959, p. 6.

9. "Assassination of Prisoners in Haiti," *Revolución*, September 1, 1959, pp. 1, 19.

10. "Cuba Said to Aid Nicaragua Reds," *New York Times*, August 23, 1959, p. 33. The source of the information was Chester Lacayo, a Nicaraguan civil engineer who had attended the University of California and Tulane University.

11. R. Hart Phillips, "Castro Bids Cuba Fight to Survive," *New York Times*, August 29, 1959, p. 6.

12. Shetterly, *The Americano*, pp. 209–214; "American Fighter for Castro Is Deprived of U.S. Citizenship," *New York Times*, September 4, 1959, p. 6. Removal of citizenship was initiated by Congressman Francis E. Walter, Democrat of Pennsylvania.

13. Shetterly, *The Americano*, pp. 213–214.

14. "Morgan, Cuban Aide, Will Renounce U.S." *New York Times*, September 22, 1959, p. 11.

15. Bonsal, *Cuba, Castro and the United States*, pp. 89–91; Phillips, "U.S. Envoy, Castro Meet for 6 Hours," *New York Times*, September 5, 1959, p. 4.

16. Bonsal, *Cuba, Castro and the United States*, pp. 98–99; Seymour Topping, "Europe Supplies Caribbean Arms Despite U.S. Curb," *New York Times*, November 1, 1959, p. 1.

17. "Britain Scored in Cuba," *New York Times*, September 15, 1959, p. 55.

18. Topping, "Europe Supplies Caribbean Arms Despite U.S. Curb," *New York Times*, November 1, 1959, p. 1.

19. Bonsal called them "terroristic incidents." *Cuba, Castro and the United States*, p. 97.

20. Montaner, *Journey to the Heart of Cuba*, p. 97.

21. "Cuba Arrests 40 in New Anti-Castro Plot," *Washington Post and Times Herald*, September 23, 1959, p. A8; "30 Reported Captured in West Cuba Battle," *Washington Post and Times Herald*, September 25, 1959, p. A14.

22. Thomas, *Cuba: Or, the Pursuit of Freedom*, p. 1243.

23. "Cuba Imposes Curb as Plane Is Seized," *New York Times*, October 4, 1959, p. 65; "Cuban Mill Is Bombed," *New York Times*, October 11, 1959, p. 28. Bonsal asserts that although it was assumed that the planes that did the bombings came from the United States, they could have come from inside Cuba. Bonsal, *Cuba, Castro and the United States*, p. 98. Encinosa says that the bombings were the work of White Rose or the Movement of Democratic Recuperation (MRD). Encinosa, *Unvanquished*, pp. 10–11.

24. Thomas, *Cuba: Or, the Pursuit of Freedom*, p. 1240, note 14. The editorial was written by Euclides Vásquez Candela.

25. Hal Hendrix, "Castro's Rule Seen Growing Shaky as Cuban Dissatisfaction Increases," *Washington Post and Times Herald*, September 28, 1959, p. B9. Hendrix was a staff reporter for the *Miami Daily News* who had spent a lot of time reporting from Cuba. He reported that the political parties that could not openly oppose Batista could not openly oppose Castro.

26. "Parachuted Arms Cuban Rebels Seized," *Washington Post and Times Herald*, September 28, 1959, p. B9; R. Hart Phillips, "Anti-Castro Acts Persist in Cuba," *New York Times*, October 14, 1959, p. 19. The Phillips articles are essentially restatements of her July piece titled "Anti-Castro Acts Spreading in Cuba," *New York Times*, July 3, 1959, p. 1.

27. R. Hart Phillips, "Castro Says Cuba Can Build Alone," *New York Times*, September 30, 1959, p. 14; Pérez, *On Becoming Cuban*, p. 482. Castro said he hoped that American manufactures of these products would invest in Cuba to produce them domestically. pp. 482–483.

28. "Castro Charges Dubois Leads Anti-Cuba Drive," *Washington Post and Times Herald*, September 30, 1959, p. A8. Eventually, in 1960, the *Diario* was outlawed.

29. "The Hemispheric Press," *New York Times*, October 12, 1959, p. 18.

30. p. 168. Also cited in Higgins, *The Perfect Failure*, pp. 58–59, and Schlesinger, *A Thousand Days*, pp. 224–225.

31. Schwartz, *Pleasure Island*, p. 161; English, *Havana Nocturne*, pp. 210–211.

32. Paterson, *Contesting Castro*, p. 52; English, *Havana Nocturne*, pp. 210–211.

33. Rufo López Fresquet, *My Fourteen Months with Castro* (New York: World Publishing Company, 1966), p. 114.

34. *Bay of Pigs Declassified*, p. 267; *Politics of Illusion*, pp. 159; Taylor, *Report*, pp. 3–4; Peter Wyden, *The Bay of Pigs: The Untold Story* (New York: Simon and Schuster, 1979), pp. 28–29.

35. Ibid.

36. *Bay of Pigs Declassified*, p. 25.

37. For instance, R. Hart Phillips, "Cuba Convention," *New York Times*, October 11, 1959, p. X27.

38. "Waifs Aided by Cuba," *New York Times*, October 16, 1959, p. 8.

39. R. Hart Phillips, "Cuba Moves Fast on Land Reform," *New York Times*, July 9, 1959, p. 8.

40. R. Hart Phillips, "Cuba Revamping School System," *New York Times*, July 26, 1959, p. 26.

41. Phillips, "Firm on Bonds for Land," *New York Times*, July 28, 1959, p. 2.

42. Jules Dubois, "Uncertainty on Cuba's Land Reform Has Investors Shivering on the Brink," *Washington Post and Times Herald*, August 6, 1959, p. A12; E. W. Kenworthy, "Cuba Seen Facing Crisis in Economy," *New York Times*, August 9, 1959, p. 16.

43. Gene Smith, "Castro Believed More Amenable," *New York Times*, August 9, 1959, p. F1.

44. Phillips, "Castro Says Cuba Can Build Alone," *New York Times*, September 30, 1959, p. 14.

45. Harold K. Milks, "Concern for Future Grips American Companies in Cuba," *Washington Post and Times Herald*, October 30, 1959, p. A12. Also see R. Hart Phillips, "Cuba Suspends Habeas Corpus to Quell Plots," *New York Times*, October 30, 1959, p. 1.

46. Phillips, "Castro Directing Fighting in Cuba," *New York Times*, August 13, 1959, p. 1. The Soviets bought 442,914 tons in 1955; 206,361 in 1956; 347,673 in 1957; 182,148 in 1958; and only 170,000 in 1959.

47. "Heavy Liquor Taxes Are Imposed in Cuba," *New York Times*, September 17, 1959, p. 39.

48. "Taxes on Imports Imposed by Cuba," *New York Times*, September 25, 1959, p. 44; "Stringent Levies by Cuba Backed," *New York Times*, September 26, 1959, p. 7; "Stiff New Controls Imposed by Cuba," *Washington Post and Times Herald*, September 25, 1959, p. C7; "Belt-Tightening in Cuba," *New York Times*, September 26, 1959, p. 22; "Monetary Fund Approves Cuban Exchange Action," *Washington Post and Times Herald*, September 26, 1959, p. D17.

49. Bonsal, *Cuba, Castro and the United States*, pp. 97–98.

50. Thomas, *Cuba: Or, the Pursuit of Freedom*, p. 1240;

"Stringent Levies by Cuba Backed," *New York Times*. September 26, 1959, p. 7. Roa said that politically and historically, Cuba belonged to the western group of nations, but that did not mean it would automatically vote with the western bloc in the UN, as it was neutral and nonaligned.

51. "Cuban Bond Issue for Land Decreed," *New York Times*, September 27, 1959, p. 22.

52. For example, former premier Georgy Malenkov became manager of a power station in Kazakhstan, and former foreign secretary Vyacheslav Molotov became ambassador to Mongolia.

53. On November, 4, 1956, a large Soviet force invaded Hungary. Over 2,500 Hungarians and 700 Soviet troops were killed in the conflict, and 200,000 Hungarians fled as refugees. *Time*'s "Man of the Year" for 1956 was the Hungarian freedom fighter. See also Report of the Special Committee On the Problem of Hungary. New York: United Nations General Assembly Official Records: Eleventh Session, Supplement 18 (A/3592), 1957.

54. Edwin A. Lahey, "Cuba Is Warned on Confiscation," *Washington Post and Times Herald*, October 15, 1959, p. A16.

55. Thomas, *Cuba: Or, the Pursuit of Freedom*, pp. 1242–1243.

56. R. Hart Phillips, "Shake-up in Cuba Laid to Unrest," *New York Times*, October 18, 1959, p. 1; Harold K. Milks, "Castro Names Raúl Army Czar," *Washington Post and Times Herald*, October 18, 1959, p. A5.

57. Ibid.

58. The arms shipment may have been generated by the CIA.

59. Bonachea and San Martin, *The Cuban Insurrection 1952–1959*, p. 289; Montaner, *Journey to the Heart of Cuba*, pp. 75–76. "There were five of us who led the revolution," Matos told the *Miami Herald*. The other four were the Castro brothers, Che Guevara, and Cienfuegos. Luisa Yanez, "Former Rebel Remembers Promise, Betrayal of Cuban Revolution," *Miami Herald*, January 9, 2009. http://www.miamiherald.com/news/americas/cuba/v-fullstory/843341.html.

60. Thomas, *Cuba: Or, the Pursuit of Freedom*, p. 1072.

61. Matos said, "But every time I brought it up to Fidel, he would say, 'No, no, no, I will not betray my commitment to Cuban history.'" Adriana Bosch, "Huber Matos, a Moderate in the Cuban Revolution," *American Experience: Fidel Castro*, Public Broadcasting System, December 31, 2004. http://www.pbs.org/wgbh/amex/castro/peopleevents/e_moderates.html.

62. Bourne, *Fidel: A Biography*, p. 190; Coltman, *The Real Fidel Castro*, pp. 162–163; Szulc, *Fidel: A Critical Portrait*, p. 557. Szulc says that the confluence of events made Castro think that Matos had conspired with Lanz and White Rose.

63. Bonsal, *Cuba, Castro and the United States*, p. 101.

64. Ibid.

65. "Anti-Castro Planes 'Raid' Cuba Capital," *Washington Post and Times Herald*, October 22, 1959, p. A1. Bonsal, *Cuba, Castro and the United States*, p. 98. See also R. Hart Phillips, "Castro Arrests Aide Who Quit after Charging Red Infiltration," *New York Times*, October 22, 1959, p. 1. Some reports list as many as 45 killed. R. Hart Phillips, "Cuban Crowds Assail U.S. after Attack by Terrorists," *New York Times*, October 23, 1959, p. 1.

66. Peter Kihss, "Ex-Brother-in-Law of Castro Leads Effort to Overthrow Him," *New York Times*, October 21, 1959, p. 1.

67. See Franqui, *Family Portrait with Fidel: A Memoir*, trans. by Alfred MacAdam (New York: Random House, 1984), pp. 52–55.

68. R. Hart Phillips, "Castro's Course Still a Puzzle," *New York Times*, February 7, 1960, p. E5.

69. Matos, *Cómo Llegó la Noche* (How the Night Fell) (Barcelona: Tusquets Editor, 2004); Bosch, *Fidel Castro*, Matos interview. See also Phillips, "Castro Arrests Aide Who Quit after Charging Red Infiltration," *New York Times*, October 22, 1959, p. 1.

70. Quoted in R. Hart Phillips, "Cuban Crowds Assail U.S. after Attack by Terrorists," *New York Times*, October 23, 1959, p. 1. See also Bonsal, *Cuba, Castro and the United States*, pp. 101–104. However, the published text of the letter does not include these passages. Thomas, *Cuba: Or, the Pursuit of Freedom*, p. 1244.

71. Franqui, pp. 53–54. Both Franqui and Thomas discuss Jorge Enrique Mendoza, a *Radio Rebelde* radio personality under Franqui (and the head of Radio Rebelde) and was the editor of *Revolucion*, the M-7-26 paper. Franqui infers that Mendoza tried to connect him with Matos's "plot." Thomas points out that Mendoza was a formoer Ortodoxo and law student who was appointed head of INRA in Camagüey. He later would be named editor of *Granma*, the Communist newspaper.

72. Bonsal, *Cuba, Castro and the United States*, p. 103.

73. Thomas relates that Castro went to Camagüey and personally made the arrest. Thomas, *Cuba: Or, the Pursuit of Freedom*, p. 1245. Joaquín Agramonte, the head of M-7–26 in Camagüey, was also arrested as a conspirator.

74. Matos, *Cómo Llegó la Noche*; Bosch, *Fidel Castro*, Matos interview. See also Phillips, "Castro Arrests Aide Who Quit after Charging Red Infiltration," *New York Times*, October 22, 1959, p. 1.

75. López Fresquet, *My Fourteen Months*, p. 130; Thomas, *The Cuban Revolution*, p. 1244.

76. Phillips, "Cuban Crowds Assail U.S. after Attack by Terrorists," *New York Times*, October 23, 1959, p. 1.

77. "F.B.I. Names Cuban Flier," *New York Times*, October 24, 1959, p. 4; Thomas, *Cuba: Or, the Pursuit of Freedom*, pp. 1245–1246. A subsequent investigation determined that Díaz Lanz flew a B-25 from Miami to Cuba and was met with antiaircraft fire, which killed three people and wounded 40. After he returned to Miami, Díaz Lanz was arrested. Bonsal, Cuba, *Castro and the United States*, pp. 104–105.

78. R. Hart Phillips, "Castro Charges Planes from U.S. Bombed Havana," *New York Times*, October 24, 1959, p. 1.

79. "Cuba Makes Charge at U.N.," *New York Times*, October 24, 1959, p. 4.

80. R. Hart Phillips, "Castro's Troubles and Washington's Reaction," *New York Times*, October 25, 1959, p. E4. The United States would later ask the OAS to "investigate" the Cuban exile community in the United States. E. W. Kenworthy, "U.S. Invites Unit of O.A.S. to Survey Cuba Refugees," *New York Times*, October 25, 1959, p. 1; R. Hart Phillips, "European Loans Reported in Cuba," *New York Times*, December 5, 1959, p. 12.

81. Phillips, "Castro Charges Planes from U.S. Bombed Havana," *New York Times*, October 24, 1959, p. 1.

82. Bonsal, *Cuba, Castro and the United States*, pp. 106–107; R. Hart Phillips, "300,000 Rally to Back Castro; He Condemns 'Raids' from U.S.," *New York Times*, October 27, 1959, p. 1; "Castro Blames U.S. for Raids," *Washington Post and Times Herald*, October 27, 1959, p. A4. Bonsal said Castro "shook his fist, roared defiance at the northern sky, foamed at the mouth and in every way comported

himself in a manner most reminiscent of Hitler at his most hysterical and most odious. Castro seemed indeed to have taken leave of his senses." p. 106.

83. Ibid.

84. "Castro Blames U.S. for Raids," *Washington Post and Times Herald*, October 27, 1959, p. A4.

85. Bonsal, *Cuba, Castro and the United States*, p. 107.

86. Rabe, *Eisenhower and Latin America*, pp. 126–127, quoting a State Department memorandum and a memorandum from President Eisenhower's son John of a meeting with Secretary Herter and Livingston Merchant, another State Department officer, dated October 27, 1959.

87. Franqui, *Family Portrait with Fidel*, p. 54.

88. Thomas, *Cuba: Or, the Pursuit of Freedom*, pp. 1246–1247; López Fresquet, *Fourteen Months*, p. 59.

89. R. Hart Phillips, "Cuba Takes Land of Ramon Castro," *New York Times*, October 19, 1959, p. 2.

90. McPherson, *Yankee No!* p. 57; Draper, *The Runaway Revolution*, p. 17; R. Hart Phillips, "Oil Companies' Files Are Sealed by Cuba," *New York Times*, October 31, 1959, p. 1.

91. McPherson, *Yankee No!* pp. 57–58.

92. Peter B. Bart, "Flow of Nickel from Cuba Halts," *New York Times*, December 16, 1959, p. 63.

93. Ibid.

94. R. Hart Phillips, "Cuba Takes Role in Mineral Sales," *New York Times*, December 22, 1959, p. 12.

95. Phillips, "Cuba Takes Land of Ramon Castro," *New York Times*, October 19, 1959, p. 2.

96. Franklyn Waltman, Jr., "Cuba's Choice — Rapid Social Reform or Complete Chaos and Terror," *Washington Post*, January 27, 1935, p. B1.

97. Thomas, *Cuba: Or, the Pursuit of Freedom*, p. 1147.

98. Thomas, *Cuba: Or, the Pursuit of Freedom*, pp. 1147–1148.

99. Thomas, Cuba: Or, the Pursuit of Freedom, pp. 1148–1150; "Sugar King," *Time*, July 28, 1958.

100. The property was held by Administración de Negocios Azucarreros. Thomas, *Cuba: Or, the Pursuit of Freedom*, p. 1150.

101. Pérez, *On Becoming Cuban*, p. 485.

102. Corse, "Presbyterians in the Revolution," In *Cuban Studies 31*, Lisandro Pérez, and Uva de Aragon, eds. Pittsburgh: Center for Latin American Studies, University of Pittsburgh Press, 1980.

103. Phillips, "Cuba Takes Land of Ramon Castro," *New York Times*, October 19, 1959, p. 2.

104. "Castro in Bid to Nasser," *New York Times*, October 18, 1959, p. 1.

105. R. Hart Phillips, "Castro Actions Suit the Communists' Aims," *New York Times*, November 29, 1959, p. E3.

106. Tad Szulc, "U.S. the Target Again," *New York Times*, November 5, 1959, p. 3.

107. "Castro Summons Envoy in Caracas," *New York Times*, November 8, 1959, p. 34.

108. Jack Raymond, "Pentagon Warns Cuba on Base; Says Rights Are Not Revocable," *New York Times*, October 28, 1959, p. 4. The text of the letter is provided in "Text of U.S. Statement on Envoy's Protest against Accusations by Premier Castro," *New York Times*, October 28, 1959, p. 4.

109. Ibid.

110. Bonsal, *Cuba, Castro and the United* States, p. 109.

111. William J. Jorden, "U.S. Protest Says Charges by Cuba Peril Relations," *New York Times*, October 28, 1959, p. 1.

112. Stewart Hensley, "Castro Attack Is Denounced in

U.S. Plea," *Washington Post and Times Herald*, October 28, 1959, p. A1.

113. "Ike Puzzled by Castro's Bitterness," *Washington Post and Times Herald*, October 29, 1959, p. A18; William J. Jorden, "Eisenhower Acts to Bar Illegal Flights — Castro Enmity Puzzles Him," *New York Times*, October 29, 1959, p. 1; "Transcript of President's News Conference on Foreign and U.S. Matters," *New York Times*, October 29, 1959, p. 19.

114. For example, Jorden, "Eisenhower Acts to Bar Illegal Flights — Castro Enmity Puzzles Him," *New York Times*, October 29, 1959, p. 1.

115. "Troubled Air," *Washington Post and Times Herald*, October 30, 1959, p. A18.

116. "U.S. Holds Plane Used in Leaflet Hop to Cuba," *Washington Post and Times Herald*, October 31, 1959, p. A7. Fiorini is the real name of Frank Sturgis, whose name became synonymous with political intrigue. Although he had been accused of having been a CIA contract agent since the mid-1950s, the U.S. president's commission on CIA activities within the United States, known as the Rockefeller Commission, determined that he never had been a CIA agent. He also was investigated for involvement in the Kennedy assassination and was convicted for conspiracy, burglary and wiretapping in the Watergate break-in that led to the resignation of President Nixon. He died in 1993.

117. Anthony Lewis, "U.S. Acts to Stop Flights to Cuba by Castro's Foes," *New York Times*, November 2, 1959, p. 1; Endre Marton, "U.S. Watch Kept on All Cuba Flights," *Washington Post and Times Herald*, November 2, 1959, p. A1.

118. Bonsal, Cuba, *Castro and the United States*, p. 108. In his book, the chapter is titled "Castro Slams the Door."

119. Phillips, "Cuba Suspends Habeas Corpus to Quell Plots," *New York Times*, October 30, 1959, p. 1. See also Milks, "Concern for Future Grips American Companies in Cuba," *Washington Post and Times Herald*, October 30, 1959, p. A12.

120. Phillips, "Cuba Suspends Habeas Corpus to Quell Plots," *New York Times*, October 30, 1959, p. 1.

121. Franqui, *Family Portrait with Fidel*, p. 55.

122. Cienfuegos was Fidel Castro's catcher when the barbudos' baseball team played exhibition games.

123. Franqui, *Family Portrait with Fidel*, pp. 55–58. Franqui speculates that although Cienfuegos was not a "true believer," Cienfuegos was following "FIDELity," loyalty to Fidel Castro. He also speculated that it was Cienfuegos' destiny to die at a young age.

124. "Castro Broadcast Assails U.S. Again," *New York Times*, November 13, 1959, p. 9. In *The Devil to Pay*, Jack Youngblood asserts that Cienfuegos was active member of the counter-revolution.

125. Peter Khiss, "Trujillo Regime Confirms Arming," *New York Times*, October 31, 1959, p. 1.

126. "Moscow Breaks Silence on Events in Cuba," *Washington Post and Times Herald*, October 31, 1959, p. A7; E. W. Kenworthy, "Moscow Echoes the Castro Line," *New York Times*, November 12, 1959, p. 12.

127. "Castro to Address Cubans Tonight," *Washington Post and Times Herald*, November 12, 1959, p. A9. Reportedly, Cuba had sent Victor Penza Cardoza to Europe to negotiate arms sales.

128. "Castro's Ex-aide Jailed in Florida," *New York Times*, November 5, 1959, p. 1.

129. R. Hart Phillips, "Assassins Attack Cuba Aide's Home," *New York Times*, November 6, 1959, p. 9.

130. Tad Szulc, "Cuba's Rebel City Proud but Uneasy,"

New York Times, November 25, 1959, p. 11. "It's not nice being called traitor for saying what you think," an unnamed source was quoted as saying.

131. "Ramon Castro Assailed," *New York Times*, November 25, 1959, p. 11.

132. R. Hart Phillips, "U.S. Note 'False,' Cubans Are Told," *New York Times*, November 11, 1959, p. 17.

133. "U.S. Note 'False,' Cubans Are Told," *New York Times*, November 11, 1959, p. 17.

134. David Sentner, "Washington Window," November 12, 1959.

135. Batista had invited the Hearst papers to Cuba in 1957 in an attempt to restore his credibility after Batista had declared Castro dead. The very much alive Castro was later shown on CBS News. Paterson, *Contesting Castro*, p. 85. David Sentner, who followed Cuba for Hearst, was the same man who had interviewed Batista at that time, and among his sources was Emilio Núñez-Portuondo, former Cuban UN ambassador under Batista. Also see Robert Traber, "Castro's Cuba," *The Nation*, January 23, 1960.

136. McPherson, *Yankee No!* p. 59.

137. Franqui, *Family Portrait with Fidel*, pp. 88–89; Thomas, *Cuba: Or, the Pursuit of Freedom*, pp. 1250–1251; "Castro Backers Win in Cuba Labor Vote," *New York Times*, November 10, 1959, p. 3.

138. "Revolution's Captives," *Washington Post and Times Herald*, November 24, 1959, p. A14; R. Hart Phillips, "Cuban Reds Beaten in Labor Union Vote," *New York Times*, November 24, 1959, p. 1; R. Hart Phillips, "Reds Frozen Out by Cuban Unions," *New York Times*, November 21, 1959, p. 1; Thomas, *Cuba: Or, the Pursuit of Freedom*, pp. 1250–1251, Franqui, *Family Portrait with Fidel*, pp. 61–63; Tad Szulc, "Politics Embroil Havana Meetings," *New York Times*, November 18, 1959, p. 18; "Cuban Labor Joins in Attacks on U.S.," *New York Times*, November 19, 1959, p. 21; R. Hart Phillips, "Castro Foes to Lose Properties in Cuba," *New York Times*, November 20, 1959, p. 1.

139. Thomas, *Cuba: Or, the Pursuit of Freedom*, pp. 1066, 1083.

140. Thomas, *Cuba: Or, the Pursuit of Freedom*, pp. 1250–1251, Franqui, *Family Portrait with Fidel*, pp. 61–63; Tad Szulc, "Politics Embroil Havana Meetings," *New York Times*, November 18, 1959, p. 18; "Cuban Labor Joins in Attacks on U.S.," *New York Times*, November 19, 1959, p. 21; R. Hart Phillips, "Castro Foes to Lose Properties in Cuba," *New York Times*, November 20, 1959, p. 1.

141. R. Hart Phillips, "Cuban Labor Cuts Inter-America Tie with Foes of Reds," *New York Times*, November 23, 1959, p. 1. The CTC called the Inter-American Regional Organization of Labor an agency of American imperialism. It set up the Confederation of Revolutionary Workers of Latin America. See also "Cuban Labor and the U.S.," *New York Times*, p. 36. See also Phillips, "Cuban Reds Beaten in Labor Union Vote," *New York Times*, November 24, 1959, p. 1; Phillips, "Reds Frozen Out by Cuban Unions," *New York Times*, November 21, 1959, p. 1.

142. "Cuba Unions Rebuff Plea by Castro," *Washington Post and Times Herald*, November 24, 1959, p. A1.

143. R. Hart Phillips, "Leftist Named President of Cuba's National Bank," *New York Times*, November 27, 1959, p. 1.

144. Phillips, "Cuban Reds Beaten in Labor Union Vote," *New York Times*, November 24, 1959, p. 1.

145. "Press Unit Scores Cuba," *New York Times*, November 24, 1959, p. 15.

146. "Castro to Address Cubans Tonight," *Washington Post and Times Herald*, November 12, 1959, p. A9.

147. R. Hart Phillips, "Cuba Plans Issue of Savings Bonds," *New York Times*, November 26, 1959, p. 2; Harold K. Milks, "Guevara Gets Key Post in Cuba Cabinet Shift," *Washington Post and Times Herald*, November 27, 1959, p. A5.

148. Karl E. Meyer, "Brazil's President Scolds U.S. for 'Indifference,'" *Washington Post and Times Herald*, November 13, 1959, p. A8. Brazil had 64 million people at the time. Cuba had about 7 million. The Brazilian foreign minister, Horatio Lafer, had until this time been considered a close ally.

149. "Castro Rips U.S. in Long TV Talk," *Washington Post and Times Herald*, November 13, 1959, p. A1; "Castro's Reply to U.S. Is Near," *Washington Post and Times Herald*, November 13, 1959, p. A9; "Castro Broadcast Assails U.S. Again," *New York Times*, November 13, 1959, p. 9; R. Hart Phillips, "Havana Rejects Protest by U.S. on Propaganda," *New York Times*, November 14, 1959, p. 1.

150. "Text of Cuban Note Rejecting Protest and Calling for a Change in U.S. Policy," *New York Times*, November 14, 1959, p. 8; Phillips, "Havana Rejects Protest by U.S. on Propaganda," *New York Times*, November 14, 1959, p. 1; "Cuba Tells U.S. to Reconsider Policy toward Castro Regime," *Washington Post and Times Herald*, November 14, 1959, p. A4.

151. For example, King Features syndicated columnist George E. Sokolsky called Castro a "petty little tyrant who employs anti–Yanquiism to keep himself in power." "These Days…" *Washington Post and Times Herald*, November 14, 1959, p. A7.

152. "Stakes High in Sugar Beet Race," *New York Times*, November 14, 1959, p. 25.

153. Jules Dubois, "Castro Is Regarded as Red Robin Hood," *Washington Post and Times Herald*, November 22, 1959, p. A11.

154. "Hate-U.S. Drive Tied to Censorship," *Washington Post and Times Herald*, November 23, 1959, p. A10; Jules Dubois, "Red Offensive Gains in Latin America," *Washington Post and Times Herald*, November 24, 1959, p. A7; Jules Dubois, "Moscow, Peking Efforts Linked in Latin America," *Washington Post and Times Herald*, November 25, 1959, p. A4.

155. Dubois, "Moscow, Peking Efforts Linked in Latin America," *Washington Post and Times Herald*, November 25, 1959, p. A4; Jules Dubois, "Kremlin Makes Havana Base for Drive in Latin America," *Washington Post and Times Herald*, November 26, 1959, p. A8. Vilma Espin, Raúl Castro's wife, attended a Communist women's conference in Chile. Dubois also alleged that Guantánamo was the target for Communist intervention.

156. "An Interview with 'El Che,'" *Washington Post and Times Herald*, November 14, 1959, p. A6. Meyer felt that Guevara was myopic about the United States, as he seemed to feel that the entire country was like Miami. He neglected to tell Meyer that he had actually visited Miami on his travels. Although he had visited the Middle East, Africa and the Far East ans a Cuban emissary, when asked whether he would like to visit Washington, he told Mayer that he would not feel comfortable, as he did not know the English language.

157. *New York Times*, November 23, 1959, p. 12.

158. Harold K. Milks, "Rally Opens as Castro Sees Plot to Turn Church against Him," *Washington Post and Times Herald*, November 29, 1959, p. 9; R. Hart Phillips, "Castro Censures Catholic Parley," *New York Times*, November 29, 1959, p. 19; R. Hart Phillips, "Cuban Catholics

Counter Red Aim," *New York Times*, November 30, 1959, p. 12.

159. "Cardinal Says Cuba Took Church Funds," *New York Times*, November 23, 1959, p. 12. The cardinal was Richard Cardinal Cushing. He also noted a shortage of priests throughout Latin America.

160. "Puerto Ricans Assail U.S.," *New York Times*, November 23, 1959, p. 22.

161. "Castro Ordered Jailed in Dominican Republic," *New York Times*, November 26, 1959, p. 2.

162. Phillips, "Leftist Named President of Cuba's National Bank," *New York Times*, November 27, 1959, p. 1; Milks, "Guevara Gets Key Post in Cuba Cabinet Shift," *Washington Post and Times Herald*, November 27, 1959, p. A5.

163. Bonsal, *Cuba, Castro and the United States*, p. 93.

164. López Fresquet, *My Fourteen Months with Castro*, pp. 60–61.

165. R. Hart Phillips, "Cuban Student Brigades March to Honor Eight Martyrs of 1871," *New York Times*, November 28, 1959, p. 11.

166. Ibid.; "Castro Links Marching Students to 'Human Wall' Defending Regime," *Chicago Tribune*, November 28, 1959, p. A4.

167. November 29, 1959, p. E3. Phillips also noted that the Provisional Government was intent on forming a nonaligned voting bloc and that Cuba had voted "for the first time" against the western bloc by abstaining rather than voting to seat Communist China in the United Nations.

168. Bonsal, *Cuba, Castro and the United States*, pp. 115–116.

169. "Castro Links Marching Students to 'Human Wall' Defending Regime," *Chicago Tribune*, November 28, 1959, p. A4.

170. In records from the George Washington University National Security Archives, Artíme quotes Castro as defining democracy as "this: a meeting of a group of men who know the road on which to take the people, that freely discuss the things they are going to do, having in their hands all the power of the State to do it." Castro also decides that the state will take possession of all land holdings, eliminating private property. At this point the campesinos were not told of these plans, according to Artíme's notes. Artíme stresses that the leadership intends to deceive the Cuban public about the plans of the revolution. The meeting of this "criollo Kremlin," according to Artíme, provides the catalyst for the "beginning of my rebellion." (Artíme, *Traición!*, pp. 3–16). Also see http://www.gwu.edu/~nsarchiv/bayofpigs.htm.

171. Tad Szulc, "Two Americans on Trial in Cuba," *New York Times*, December 1, 1959, p. 18; R. Hart Phillips, "3 U.S. Citizens Get Long Terms in Cuba," *New York Times*, December 9, 1959, p. 1; "3 American Pilots Get Long Terms in Cuba," *Washington Post and Times Herald*, December 9, 1959, p. A5.

172. Enrique Encinosa, *Unvanquished*, p. 10. Encinosa refers to Lamberton as Lawton.

173. "3 American Pilots Get Long Terms in Cuba," *Washington Post and Times Herald*, December 9, 1959, p. A5; Phillips, "3 U.S. Citizens Get Long Terms in Cuba," *New York Times*, December 9, 1959, p. 1. See also Eliot Kleinberg, *Palm Beach Past* (Charleston, SC: The History Press, 2006), pp. 77–80.

174. Phillips, "3 U.S. Citizens Get Long Terms in Cuba," *New York Times*, December 9, 1959, p. 1; "3 American Pilots Get Long Terms in Cuba," *Washington Post and Times Herald*, December 9, 1959, p. A5.

175. Ibid.

176. "American Escapes from Cuban Prison Day after Sentence," *New York Times*, December 10, 1959, p. 1; Eliot Kleinberg, *Palm Beach Past*, pp. 77–80.

177. "The World," *New York Times*, December 13, 1959, p. E2; "Raul Castro States He Is No Communist," *New York Times*, December 14, 1959, p. 6.; Kleinberg, *Palm Beach Past*, p. 80.

178. "Cuba Rejects Plea to Free U.S. Reporter," *Washington Post and Times Herald*, December 17, 1959, p. A15; R. Hart Phillips, "Castro Says Bloody Invasions Are Inevitable in Cuba in 1960," *New York Times*, December 17, 1959, p. 4; "U.S. Reporter Upheld," *New York Times*, December 17, 1959, p. 9.

179. R. Hart Phillips, "Reporter Convicted and Ousted by Cuba," *New York Times*, December 23, 1959, p. 1; "Havana Deports Miami Reporter," *New York Times*, December 24, 1959, p. 9.

180. E. W. Kenworthy, "U.S. Seizes Bombs Headed for Cuba," *New York Times*, December 2, 1959, p. 1.

181. E. W. Kenworthy, "Guatemala Accuses Cuba of Aiding Plot," *New York Times*, December 6, 1959, p. 1; Karl E. Meyer, "Guatemala Expects Invasion from Cuba," *Washington Post and Times Herald*, December 9, 1959, p. B16.

182. "Cuba Denounces U.S. over Failure of Jet Deal," *Washington Post and Times Herald*, December 4, 1959, p. A7; "Cuba Paper Labels Ike 'Hypocrite,'" *Washington Post and Times Herald*, December 5, 1959, p. A4.

183. R. Hart Phillips, "European Loans Reported in Cuba," *New York Times*, December 5, 1959, p. 12.

184. "Havana Tightens Dollar Controls," *New York Times*, December 10, 1959, p. 14.

185. For example, at the University of Pennsylvania, an Ivy League school, graduate students' tuition for academic year 1959–60 was less than $1,500. "Educational Costs (1960–1969)," University Archives and Records Center, University of Pennsylvania, http://www.archives.upenn.edu/histy/features/tuition/1960.html. At the University of Minnesota, a public university, tuition for out-of-state graduate students was $540 per year. University of Minnesota Annual Tuition Rates: 1960–61 to 2008–09, Office of Institutional Research, http://www.irr.umn.edu/tuition/TuitionUMNTC.pdf. Others in 1960: University of California at Berkeley, $0; Columbia University, $1,460; University of Georgia, $195; Harvard University, $1,520; Massachusetts Institute of Technology, $1,500; Michigan State University, $279; Northwestern University, $1,200; Pennsylvania State University, $480; University of Texas, $100.

186. Joseph Newman, "Roa Urges a New Cuban-U.S. Trade Accord," *Washington Post and Times Herald*, December 10, 1959, p. A5; Thomas J. Hamilton, "Dr. Roa Says Cuba Is Ready for Talk," *New York Times*, December 11, 1959, p. 9; E. W. Kenworthy, "Herter Reports U.S.–Cuban Ties Have Worsened," *New York Times*, December 11, 1959, p. 1.

187. "Cuba Seeks Racing," *New York Times*, December 13, 1959, p. S5.

188. "Cubans Are Pleased by U.S. Sugar Action," *New York Times*, December 20, 1959, p. 18.

189. "Paraguay Reports Crushing a Revolt," *New York Times*, December 13, 1959, p. 1.

190. "Paraguayan Rebels Still Holding Out," *New York Times*, December 14, 1959, p. 16; "Some Firing Still Heard in Paraguay," *Washington Post and Times Herald*, December 14, 1959, p. A13.

191. "Paraguay Charges Cuba Aided Rebels," *New York Times*, December 21, 1959, p. 14.

192. "Ex-Hero Gets 20 Years; 2 Other Cubans to Die," *Washington Post and Times Herald*, December 16, 1959, p. A4; "Raul Castro States He Is No Communist," *New York Times*, December 14, 1959, p. 6; "Castro Testifies in Matos Trial," *Washington Post and Times Herald*, December 15, 1959, p. A4; Thomas, *Cuba: Or, the Pursuit of Freedom*, pp. 1255–1256.

193. Thomas, *Cuba: Or, the Pursuit of Freedom*, p. 1255–1256; "Castro Testifies in Matos Trial," *Washington Post and Times Herald*, December 15, 1959, p. A4; R. Hart Phillips, "Ex-Castro Aide Draws 20 Years," *New York Times*, December 16, 1959, p. 1. See also Tad Szulc, "A Super-Cabinet Rules Over Cuba," *New York Times*, December 18, 1959, p. 1.

194. "2 Who Served Batista Are Executed in Cuba," *Washington Post and Times Herald*, December 20, 1959, p. B5; "The Firing Squads Resuming in Cuba," *New York Times*, December 20, 1959, p. 18; "Ex-Hero Gets 20 Years; 2 Other Cubans to Die," *Washington Post and Times Herald*, December 16, 1959, p. A4; R. Hart Phillips, "Cuban Military Court Sentences U.S. Engineer to 13-Year Term," *New York Times*, December 19, 1959, p. 4; Thomas, *Cuba: Or, the Pursuit of Freedom*, p. 1256. The executed counterinsurgents were Luis Lara Crespo and José Antonio Vincente Morfi Reyes, both former members of Batista's army. Lara had been sentenced to die previously, but had escaped, only to be captured and retried.

195. Ibid; "Santiago Trials Scheduled," *New York Times*, December 13, 1959, p. 28.

196. R. Hart Phillips, "Cuban Military Court Sentences U.S. Engineer to 13-Year Term," *New York Times*, December 19, 1959, p. 4; "American Businessman Is Given 13 Years as Anti-Castro Agent," *Washington Post and Times Herald*, December 19, 1959, p. A1.

197. Thomas, *Cuba: Or, the Pursuit of Freedom*, p. 1257.

198. Tad Szulc, "A Year of Castro Rule in Cuba: Leftists Speeding Vast Reforms," *New York Times*, December 17, 1959, p. 1; Tad Szulc, "A Super-Cabinet Rules Over Cuba," *New York Times*, December 18, 1959, p. 1.

199. Szulc, "A Year of Castro Rule in Cuba: Leftists Speeding Vast Reforms," *New York Times*, December 17, 1959, p. 1; Tad Szulc, "Cuba Exploiting Discord with U.S." *New York Times*, December 20, 1959, p. 1.

200. Pérez, *On Becoming Cuban*, pp. 489–491; Szulc, "Cuba Exploiting Discord with U.S.," *New York Times*, December 20, 1959, p. 1; Bonsal, *Cuba, Castro and the United States*, pp. 115–116.

201. "The Problem of Cuba," *New York Times*, December 21, 1959, p. 26.

202. Perez, *On Becoming Cuban*, pp. 485–486; Thomas, *Cuba: Or, the Pursuit of Freedom*, pp 1257–1258.

203. Traditionally celebrated by cooking a pig on a spit in a hole dug for the occasion. Presents are traditionally exchanged on Epiphany.

204. Ibid.; "Don Feliciano, a Native, Replaces Santa in Cuba," *New York Times*, December 21, 1959, p. 9. Pérez reports that when Santa Claus was depicted in Cuba, his beard was black to make him look like a *barbudo*. He also says that while treats from northern countries were discouraged, it was permitted to import traditional Spanish candies, consistent with the traditional Cuban observance of Christmas. By that time, however, the Provisional Government had broken relations with Spain. The *Times* describes the Don wearing a drooping mustache and a beard divided into two strands. He wears a straw hat, brim turned up, a guayabera, baggy trousers and leggings. Apparently children did not identify with him and did not revere him like they might Santa Claus.

205. Phillips, "Castro Says Bloody Invasions Are Inevitable in Cuba in 1960," *New York Times*, December 17, 1959, p. 4.

206. Ibid.

207. "Cuba Police Arrest 13 in 2 Plots," *Washington Post and Times Herald*, December 25, 1959, p. A6.

208. R. Hart Phillips, "U.S. Cleric Finds Cuba Friendly; Urges Washington to Be Patient," *New York Times*, December 18, 1959, p. 12.; Corse, "Presbyterians in the Revolution," in *Cuban Studies 31*, p. 11.

209. Kenneth Dole, "News of the Churches," *Washington Post and Times Herald*, December 19, 1959, p. B3. Dole cites Reverend Clair Hutchens of Colonia, New Jersey.

210. See Phillips, "Castro's Course Still a Puzzle," *New York Times*, February 7, 1960, p. E5.

211. Ibid.

212. R. Hart Phillips, "Castro Asks Cubans to Inform On All Who Oppose Revolution," *New York Times*, December 21, 1959, p. 1; "Castro Sets Up Informer System to Find Revolution's Enemies," *Washington Post and Times Herald*, December 22, 1959, p. A8. In the *Post* version, there is some question whether the headline is accurate, as Castro is not quoted as saying that Cuba had already established an informant system. The Batista regime relied on spies (*chivatos*) who were systematically paid for information. Although Cuba would eventually establish Committees for the Defense of the Revolution throughout Cuba to fulfill that role, as of December 1959, it may be that Castro was quoted inaccurately and was referring to the Batista organization. The word for "goat" was not translated properly in the *Post* version. American newspapers found it ironic that Castro gave the speech mainly to beauticians and barbers, when he was bearded and probably needed some grooming.

213. James Buchanan, "Neighbor Spies Help Jail Castro Critics," *Washington Post and Times Herald*, December 28, 1959, p. A11; James Buchanan, "Havana Teen-Agers Are Agents for Castro's New Secret Police," *Washington Post and Times Herald*, December 29, 1959, p. A9.

214. Ibid. Buchanan described how a theater owner was arrested and lost his property when a waiter accused him of anti-revolutionary activities for carrying a copy of *Avance*, which by late 1959 was considered an opposition newspaper. He also alleged that there were as many as 150 DIER agents working in Miami and New York.

215. Henequen plants are primarily used to make rope.

216. Phillips, "Castro Asks Cubans to Inform On All Who Oppose Revolution," *New York Times*, December 21, 1959, p. 1.

217. R. Hart Phillips, "Cuba Celebrates Year of Castro," *New York Times*, January 1, 1960, p. 6.

218. "Sentences Suspended," *New York Times*, December 22, 1959, p. 12. Others included Juan A. Orta and Juan Henriques, Prío's brother-in-law.

219. "Invasion of Cuba Called Imminent," *New York Times*, December 29, 1959, p. 8; R. Hart Phillips, "Cuba Arrests 45 as Conspirators," *New York Times*, December 30, 1959, p. 4; "3 Plots Foiled, Castro Agents Say," *Washington Post and Times Herald*, December 30, 1959, p. A4.

220. "Cuban High Schools Get Army Program," *New York Times*, January 7, 1960, p. 10.

221. "More Tourists in Cuba," *New York Times*, December 31, 1959, p. 3.

222. Phillips, "Cuba Celebrates Year of Castro," *New York Times*, January 1, 1960, p. 6; "Castro Gracious in New Year Role," *New York Times*, January 2, 1960, p. 3.

223. Ibid.; and Franqui, *Family Portrait with Fidel*, pp.

65–66. Franqui sat at Fidel Castro's table. Other than the Louises and the French authors, Franqui didn't report on the other invitees.

224. "Cuban High Schools Get Army Program," *New York Times*, January 7, 1960, p. 10.

225. "Cuba Promoting '3d Bloc' Parley," *New York Times*, January 3, 1960, p. 7.

Chapter 15

1. R. Hart Phillips, "Economic Revolution Casts Cloud of Doubt over Cuba," *New York Times*, January 13, 1960, p. 49.

2. Bonsal, *Cuba, Castro and the United States*, p. 118; Dana Adams Schmidt, "Land Seizures Evaluated," *New York Times*, January 12, 1960, p. 11.

3. R. Hart Phillips, "Cuba Turns Down Complaint by U.S. on Land Seizures," *New York Times*, January 12, 1960, p. 11.

4. Rabe, *Eisenhower and Latin America*, p. 128.

5. Rabe, *Eisenhower and Latin America*, p. 128, quoting from the Church Committee, *Alleged Assassination Plots*, 92–93. Rabe says that Dulles was acting on a recommendation by J. C. King, head of the CIA's Western Hemisphere Division.

6. Fabian Escalante, *The Cuba Project: CIA Covert Operations 1959–62* (New York: Ocean Press, 2004), p. 43.

7. Rabe, *Eisenhower and Latin America*, p. 128. It is interesting that an article written by E. W. Kenworthy restates the same reservation. Kenworthy stated that the note delivered by Ambassador Bonsal had actually been directed to other Latin American countries to show them that the United States would not tolerate similar actions by other Latin American countries. The argument that the United States would not penalize the Cuba people was repeated. "U.S. Goes Slow," *New York Times*, January 17, 1960, p. E7.

8. Escalante, *The Cuba Project: CIA Covert Operations 1959–62*, p. 43; see also J. Hawkins, *Record of Paramilitary Action against the Castro Government of Cuba* (Central Intelligence Agency, May 5, 1961); Wyden, *The Bay of Pigs: The Untold Story*, pp. 28–29; Maxwell Taylor, *Paramilitary Study Group Report* (CIA, June 13, 1961), pp. 3–4.

9. Escalante, *The Cuba Project*, p. 43.

10. Ibid., 43–44.

11. Also known as Branch 4. *Bay of Pigs Declassified*, pp. 25, 267; James G. Blight and Peter Kornbluh, Editors, *Politics of Illusion: The Bay of Pigs Invasion Reexamined* (Boulder, CO: Lynne Rienner Publications, 1998, 1999), pp. 159–160. Esterline would become the head of Branch 4.

12. Warren Unna, "U.S. to Seek Damages Despite Cuban Rebuff," *Washington Post and Times Herald*, January 13, 1960, p. A5.

13. "U.S. Technical Aid Pressed in Cuba," *New York Times*, January 13, 1960, p. 70; "Cuba's Hungry Aided by U.S. Surplus Food," *New York Times*, January 13, 1960, p. 69.

14. George E. Sokolsky, "These Days ... Sugar and Coffee," *Washington Post and Times Herald*, January 14, 1960, p. A23. As in previous columns, Sokolsky refers to Cuba and Castro as "enemies."

15. Carroll Kilpatrick, "Nixon Calls Ike Strong President," *Washington Post and Times Herald*, January 17, 1960, p. A1; "Nixon Warns Cuba on Alienating U.S.," *New York Times*, January 17, 1960, p. 31.

16. R. Hart Phillips, "Castro Criticizes Nixon's Comment," *New York Times*, January 19, 1960, p. 14; "Castro Calls Nixon Speech 'Insolent,'" *Washington Post and Times Herald*, January 19, 1960, p. A5.

17. R. Hart Phillips, "Tread of Militia Resounds in Cuba," *New York Times*, January 17, 1960, p. 1. The union working for the Havana newspaper *Información* wanted to add that although they were publishing it, the Smith allegation was not true.

18. "Cuba Begins Taking Sugar-Cane Lands," *New York Times*, January 15, 1960, p. 4.

19. Phillips, "Castro Criticizes Nixon's Comment," *New York Times*, January 19, 1960, p. 14.

20. Francis L. McCarthy, "New Trujillo 'Truce' with Cuba Is Puzzler," *Washington Post and Times Herald*, January 21, 1960, p. A7.

21. "Hands-Off Policy in Cuba," *New York Times*, January 29, 1960, p. 5.

22. "U.S. Doubts O.A.S. Power to Halt Trujillo's Arrests," *New York Times*, February 7, 1960, p. 1. Also see "De Gaulle Cracks Down," *New York Times*, February 7, 1960, p. E1.

23. "Cuban Publisher Refugee in Miami," *New York Times*, January 21, 1960, p. 13. Jorge Zayas, also chairman of the Inter-American Press Association's Committee on Press Freedom, said he wouldn't return without a personal guarantee from Castro as to freedom of the press.

24. "Castro Is Accused of Stifling Press," *New York Times*, January 24, 1960, p. 9. Zayas admitted that he had conferred with the United States State Department before writing some of his columns.

25. Bonsal, *Cuba, Castro and the United States*, pp. 118–120; Thomas, *Cuba: Or, the Pursuit of Freedom*, pp. 1262–1263; Anderson, *Che Guevara: A Revolutionary Life*, pp. 460–461; R. Hart Phillips, "Castro, in Clash, Ousts Spain's Aide," *New York Times*, January 21, 1960, p. 1; Harold K. Milks, "Castro Ousts Spanish Ambassador after Envoy Interrupts TV Speech," *Washington Post and Times Herald*, January 21, 1960, p. A1. Castro recounted that the Spanish ambassador was a "bull." Castro and Ramonet, *Fidel Castro: My Life*, pp. 404–495.

26. R. Hart Phillips, "Cubans Support Ouster," *New York Times*, January 22, 1960, p. 6.

27. See E. W. Kenworthy, "U.S. Sees Castro Dropping Charge," *New York Times*, February 25, 1960, p. 1. The person referenced in the letter who needed help to escape from Cuba was Manuel Artime Buesa, M.D., a former Rebel Army officer and INRA official who would later become a principal anti–Castro leader.

28. William Blair, "Herter Charges Castro Insulted U.S. in TV Speech," *New York Times*, January 22, 1960, p. 1; Bonsal, *Cuba, Castro and the United States*, p. 118; E. W. Kenworthy, "Senators Assail Castro's Actions," *New York Times*, January 23, 1960, p. 1.

29. "In the Maelstrom," *Washington Post and Times Herald*, January 23, 1960, p. A10.

30. Thomas, *Cuba: Or, the Pursuit of Freedom*, p. 1262.

31. Ibid.

32. Drew Pearson, "Bonsal's Return to Cuba Is Held Up," *Washington Post and Times Herald*, January 30, 1960, p. D11. Ambassador Bonsal would state later that the Cuban government did not have direct evidence to charge him with having aided or enabled opposition groups. Bonsal, *Cuba, Castro and the United States*, p. 127.

33. "Cubans Accuse U.S. of Propaganda Act," *New York Times*, January 26, 1960, p. 17. USIS was the United States Information Service.

34. Bonsal, *Cuba, Castro and the United States*, pp. 121–

124; "News Conference in Brief," *New York Times*, January 27, 1960, p. 14; "Text of the Statement by Eisenhower on Cuba," *New York Times*, January 27, 1960, p. 10; "Transcript of Eisenhower's News Conference on Foreign and Domestic Matters," *New York Times*, January 27, 1960, p. 14.

35. Ibid.; E. W. Kenworthy, "President Rules Out Reprisals on Cuba," *New York Times*, January 27, 1960, p. 1; Warren Unna, "Ike, 'Perplexed' by Cuba, Opposes Any Reprisals," *Washington Post and Times Herald*, January 27, 1960, p. A1.

36. Ibid. Also E. W. Kenworthy, "U.S. Gaining Hope in Cuban Dispute," *New York Times*, February 1, 1960, p. 17.

37. R. Hart Phillips, "Cuba's President Puts Onus on U.S.," *New York Times*, January 28, 1960, p. 9. Ambassador Bonsal said that the Argentinean ambassador to Cuba spoke to Fidel Castro, and that Castro agreed to tone down his anti–American statements. However, there were allegations that the Argentinean ambassador also told Castro that the United States was willing to aid Cuba in financing land reform. However, according to Ambassador Bonsal, this allegation was false and had it been true would have amounted to "appeasement." Bonsal, *Cuba, Castro and the United States*, pp. 125–126.

38. Letter of Robert Hugh Reed, "Understanding Cuba," *New York Times*, January 28, 1960, p. 30. Reed was pastor of the First Presbyterian Church in Long Branch, New Jersey, and was the secretary of the Council of Churches for Long Branch and the vicinity.

39. "Sugar Import Cut Urged to Curb Cuba," *New York Times*, February 3, 1960, p. 9.

40. Testimony regarding the Fair Play for Cuba Committee before the Senate Judiciary Subcommittee to Investigate the Administration of the Internal Security Act and Other Security Laws, May 5, 1960.

41. "Attacks upon U.S. by Cubans Cease," *New York Times*, January 29, 1960, p. 5; Kenworthy, "U.S. Gaining Hope in Cuban Dispute," *New York Times*, February 1, 1960, p. 17.

42. "Central Park Ceremony for Cuban Hero Erupts into Riot Over Castro," *New York Times*, January 29, 1960, p. 1.

43. Thomas, *Cuba: Or, the Pursuit of Freedom*, p. 1264.

44. Ibid.

45. "Mikoyan to Open Exhibit in Cuba," *New York Times*, February 1, 1960, p. 1.

46. "Castro Welcomes Mikoyan in Cuba," *New York Times*, February 5, 1960, p. 1.

47. R. Hart Phillips, "3 Shot in Havana Rioting as Mikoyan Opens Exhibit," *New York Times*, February 6, 1960, p. 1; James Reston, "Mr. Mikoyan Comes to the Caribbean," *New York Times*, February 7, 1960, p. E8. Reston said that as soon as shots were fired, Mikoyan "disappeared before you could say 'peaceful coexistence.'"

48. Bonsal, *Cuba, Castro and the United States*, pp. 130–132.

49. Peter Jackson, "Soviet Pledges Aid to Havana," *Washington Post and Times Herald*, February 12, 1960, p. A5.

50. R. Hart Phillips, "Mikoyan Offers Planes to Cuba," *New York Times*, February 13, 1960, p. 1; R. Hart Phillips, "Soviet Gives Cuba 100 Million Credit on Sale of Sugar," *New York Times*, February 14, 1960, p. 1; James Reston, "The New Sugar Daddy from Moscow," *New York Times*, February 14, 1960, p. E8; Harold K. Milks, "Mikoyan and Castro Sign Soviet Trade Pact," *Washington Post and Times Herald*, February 14, 1960, p. A8.

51. "News Summary and Index," *New York Times*, February 14, 1960, p. 95.

52. E. W. Kenworthy, "U.S. Declines Brazil Offer to Seek Better Cuban Ties," *New York Times*, February 5, 1960, p. 1.

53. R. Hart Phillips, "Cuba Says Soviet Will Keep Sugar," *New York Times*, February 16, 1960, p. 10.

54. "Soviet-Cuban Pact Spurs World Sugar in Active Trading," *New York Times*, February 16, 1960, p. 51.

55. Harry Schwartz, "Soviet Will Send Cuba Vital Goods," *New York Times*, February 19, 1960, p. 6.

56. Phillips, "3 Shot in Havana Rioting as Mikoyan Opens Exhibit," *New York Times*, February 6, 1960, p. 1.

57. Draper, *Castroism: Theory and Practice*, pp. 142–143.

58. Kenworthy, "U.S. Declines Brazil Offer to Seek Better Cuban Ties," *New York Times*, February 5, 1960, p. 1.

59. Paul P. Kennedy, "Nicaragua to End Rift with Cuba," *New York Times*, February 14, 1960, p. 27.

60. Milks, "Mikoyan and Castro Sign Soviet Trade Pact," *Washington Post and Times Herald*, February 14, 1960, p. A8.

61. Manuel Artime Buesa, *Idearío: Puntos Basicos in Traición! Gritan 20,000 Tumbas Cubanas* (Mexico City: Editorial Jus, 1960); *Bay of Pigs Declassified*, p. 268.

62. See James Reston, "Anti-U.S. Gesture by Castro Is Seen," *New York Times*, February 15, 1960, p. 1.

63. James Reston, "Capital Considers a Tougher Policy on Castro Regime," *New York Times*, February 18, 1960, p. 1.

64. "Ex-aide Says Cuba Got 12 Czech MiG's," *New York Times*, February 18, 1960, p. 2. The ex-aide was Batista's former ambassador to the United Nations, Emilio Núñiez-Portuondo; "Castro Bitter in Comment," *New York Times*, February 20, 1960, p. 4.

65. Ibid.

66. For example, Drew Pearson, "Halleck to Back Pollution Bill Veto," *Washington Post and Times Herald*, February 18, 1960, p. B15; James Reston, "Cuba's Drift to the Left," *New York Times*, February 19, 1960, p. 6.

67. "Fidel Seen Outsmarted on Soviet Sugar Deal," *Washington Post and Times Herald*, March 3, 1960, p. B17. The article cites research by B. W. Dwyer and Company.

68. R. Hart Phillips, "Soviet Exhibition Havana's Top Hit," *New York Times*, February 25, 1960, p. 12.

69. "Castro Accuses Americans," *New York Times*, February 19, 1960, p. 6; William Jorden, "U.S. Sends Castro Apology on Plane Wrecked in Cuba," *New York Times*, February 20, 1960, p. 1; Lewis Gulick, "Apology Given Cuba," *Washington Post and Times Herald*, February 20, 1960, p. A1.

70. "U.S. Acts to Curb Latin Gunrunning," *New York Times*, February 19, 1960, p. 1.

71. Jorden, "U.S. Sends Castro Apology on Plane Wrecked in Cuba," *New York Times*, February 20, 1960, p. 1; Gulick, "Apology Given Cuba," *Washington Post and Times Herald*, February 20, 1960, p. A1; A. H. Raskin, "U.S. Officials Doubt an Effective Check on Flights to Cuba," *New York Times*, February 21, 1960, p. 1.

72. "Apology Seen as Cuban 'Victory,'" *New York Times*, February 21, 1960, p. 3.

Chapter 16

1. R. Hart Phillips, "Cuba Unions Oust Anti-red Leaders," *New York Times*, January 25, 1960, p. 1.

2. Alexander, *A History of Organized Labor in Cuba,* pp. 202–203.

3. Ibid., p. 205.

4. Ibid., pp. 206–207; "Anti-Red Labor Leader in Cuba Faces Ouster," *Washington Post and Times Herald,* April 22, 1960, p. A4.

5. See, generally, Alexander, *A History of Organized Labor in Cuba.*

6. R. Hart Phillips, "Castro's Regime Puts All Trade under Controls," *New York Times,* February 21, 1960, p. 1.

7. R. Hart Phillips, "Castro Calls for U.S. Talks to Settle Disagreements," *New York Times,* February 23, 1960, p. 1; Thomas J. Hamilton, "Cuba Seeks Seat on Council of U.N.," *New York Times,* February 23, 1960, p. 1.

8. Felix Belair, Jr., "Eisenhower Hails Puerto Rico Gains as He Begins Tour," *New York Times,* February 23, 1960, p. 1.

9. "Washington Aides Receptive," *New York Times,* February 23, 1960, p. 3.

10. Tad Szulc, "City Is Thronged," *New York Times,* February 25, 1960, p. 1.

11. Charles A. Santos-Busch, "Relations with Cuba," *New York Times,* February 25, 1960, p. 28.

12. Kenworthy, "U.S. Sees Castro Dropping Charge," *New York Times,* February 25, 1960, p. 1.

13. "Castro Threatens Curbs on Foreign Investment," *Washington Post and Times Herald,* February 25, 1960, p. A4; R. Hart Phillips, "Foreign Capital Curbed by Castro," *New York Times,* February 26, 1960, p. 7.

14. Harry Schwartz, "Cuba Fashioning an Economic Web," *New York Times,* February 28, 1960, p. F1; R. Hart Phillips, "Cubans Will Base Economy on System of Co-operatives," *New York Times,* February 28, 1960, p. 1.

15. Ibid.

16. "Castro Threatens Curbs on Foreign Investment," *Washington Post and Times Herald,* February 25, 1960, p. A4.

17. "13% of Cuba's Cane Bombed, Union Says," *New York Times,* February 27, 1960; p. 3.

18. "Cuba's Economic Development," *New York Times,* February 27, 1960, p. 18. The editorial relied on studies published by German researcher Walter Frielingsdorf, who had just published *Reformas Sociales y Desarrollo Economico* (Havana: Editorial Lex, 1960). Frielingsdorf pointed out that the development of the United States economy was made possible by foreign investment. The *Times* also ran articles, such as Cabell Phillips, "Concern over Cuba's Course Mounts," *New York Times,* February 28, 1960, p. E4, which reiterated fears of chaos in Cuba. The article reported that the wealthy class had been labeled as "enemies" and had been imprisoned or fled.

19. "Castro Plans a Court-Martial," *New York Times,* February 26, 1960, p. 6.

20. Kenworthy, "Senators Accuse Pentagon on Aid," *New York Times,* February 26, 1960, p. 1. The Mutual Security Act of 1959 required the same amount spent in 1959 to be spent in 1960, but the Pentagon increased it. The senators were Wayne Morse, Democrat of Oregon, and George Aiken, Republican of Vermont.

21. Warren Unna, "Cubans, Dominicans Get $719,000 in U.S. Aid," *Washington Post and Times Herald,* February 26, 1960, p. 12.

22. "U.S. Note Bids Cuba Drop Parley Curb," *New York Times,* March 1, 1960, p. 1; Harold K. Milks, "U.S. Welcomes Talks with Cuba but Refuses Pledge of No Reprisals," *Washington Post and Times Herald,* March 1, 1960, p. A4.

23. "Reply to Cuba," *New York Times,* March 1, 1960,

p. 32;" ...under our Constitution the Executive can not bind the Legislative branch."

24. A president can enter into treaties with the advice and consent of the Senate. U.S. Constitution, Article II, Section 2, Clause 2; *State of Missouri V. Holland,* 252 U.S. 416 (1920).

25. George Sokolsky, "These Days ... Peace Is Wonderful," *Washington Post and Times Herald,* March 1, 1960, p. A11.

26. Carroll Kilpatrick, "Castro Gets U.S. Protest on Attacks," *Washington Post and Times Herald,* March 16, 1960, p. A1.

27. See R. Hart Phillips, "Vituperation against U.S. Rises in Cuba after Herter Criticism," *New York Times,* March 10, 1960, p. 3.

28. "France, Italy File Protests with Cuba," *Washington Post and Times Herald,* March 2, 1960, p. A9.

29. "Our Man in Miami," *Time,* November 7, 1960.

30. English, *Havana Nocturne,* pp. 100–101, 130–132; Cirules, *The Mafia in Havana,* pp. 15–17, 160–163. Originally, Barletta's Banco Atlántico was the principal financier of gambling interests, but after BANDES was established, the bank was reorganized. Cirules reports that during the war, Barletta alleged that he had been a double agent. pp. 15–16.

31. Juan de Onis, "Eisenhower Rides through Tear Gas in Uruguay Clash," *New York Times,* March 3, 1960, p. 1; Murrey Marder, "Ike Meets Outbreaks in Uruguay," *Washington Post and Times Herald,* March 3, 1960, p. A1.

32. Tad Szulc, "Latin Hosts Back U.S. Cuban Policy," *New York Times,* March 3, 1960, p. 7.

33. "Eisenhower's Tour," *New York Times,* March 6, 1960, p. E1; Tad Szulc, "Crowds' Acclaim Viewed as Index," *New York Times,* March 4, 1960, p. 8; Tad Szulc, "Eisenhower Tour: The Promises and the Expectations," *New York Times,* March 6, 1960, p. E6.

34. Murrey Marder, "Ike's Trip Uncovers Skepticism About U.S," *Washington Post and Times Herald,* March 4, 1960, p. A1. Marder said there was more skepticism than outright hostility, but the examples given sound more hostile than that. See also "Eisenhower's Tour," *New York Times,* March 6, 1960, p. E1.

35. Ibid.

36. For example, Paul S. Kennedy, "Cuban Aides Woo Central America," *New York Times,* March 20, 1960, p. 14.

37. "Land Seizure Expected," *New York Times,* March 3, 1960, p. 9.

38. Szulc, "Latin Hosts Back U.S. Cuban Policy," *New York Times,* March 3, 1960, p. 7.

39. R. Hart Phillips, "75 Die in Havana as Munitions Ship Explodes at Dock," *New York Times,* March 5, 1960, p. 1.

40. R. Hart Phillips, "Castro Links U.S. to Ship 'Sabotage'; Denial Is Swift," *New York Times,* March 6, 1960, p. 1; Harold K. Milks, "Castro Lays Blast to U.S. Interests," *Washington Post and Times Herald,* March 6, 1960, p. A1.

41. "U.S. Denies Insinuation," *New York Times,* March 6, 1960, p. 3; "Chapman in Miami," *New York Times,* March 8, 1960, p. 18; Milton Carr, "Cuba Frees American in Ship Blast," *Washington Post and Times Herald,* March 7, 1960, p. A1; "Cuba Releases American Held in Harbor Blast," *St. Petersburg Times,* March 7, 1960, p. 1. "Nebraskan Freed," *New York Times,* March 7, 1960, p. 2. Chapman was arrested briefly a second time and asked about his whereabouts on January 1, 1959, but was released when he showed that he was not in Cuba at that time. "Cubans

Arrest Chapman Again, Free Him to Catch Next Plane," *Washington Post and Times Herald*, March 8, 1960, p. A4.

42. "Explosions in Havana," *New York Times*, March 6, 1960, p. E10.

43. "Tragedy in Havana," *Washington Post and Times Herald*, March 7, 1960, p. A12.

44. Bonsal, *Cuba, Castro and the United States*, pp. 133–134.

45. Dana Adams Schmidt, "Herter Upbraids Cuban on Charge in Ship Explosion," *New York Times*, March 8, 1960, pp. 1, 16. The Cuban official was the chargé d'affaires officer Enrique Patterson.

46. R. Hart Phillips, "Cuba Rejects U.S. Protest; Calls Herter 'Aggressive,'" *New York Times*, March 9, 1960, p. 1; "Cuba Rejects Herter's Protest," *Washington Post and Times Herald*, March 9, 1960, p. A1.

47. "Accord Held Far Off," *New York Times*, March 9, 1960, p. 14.

48. E. W. Kenworthy, "Herter Hopes That Breach with Cuba Can Be Healed," *New York Times*, March 10, 1960, p. 1,6.

49. E. V. Jones, "Dockworker Set Ship Blast in Havana, American Claims," *Miami Herald*, March 7, 1960, p. 1.

50. Ibid. "As soon as they were gone, I went down and hurried to Morgan's home where I picked up my clothes, then went to the airport. I got aboard the next plane for Miami." Asked if he thought Morgan was in on the sabotage plot, Evans replied: "No, I don't think so. He probably knew nothing about it."

51. Ibid. When questioned, Morgan stated: "The kid has to be out of his mind to say a thing like that. It's crazy." Morgan told the press that Evans had come to Cuba two weeks earlier looking for a job "to help the revolution. He said Evans stayed at his home and he helped him get a job with the National Institute of Agrarian Reform — which administers Castro's land redistribution program — but the young Oklahoman was in no way connected with his own staff."

52. "Cuba Rejects Herter's Protest," *Washington Post and Times Herald*, March 9, 1960, p. A1. The attaché, Felipe Vidal Santiago, told the press that the heat was largely generated by a nearby electric plant.

53. Escalante, *The Cuba Project: CIA Covert Operations 1959–62*, pp. 45–46. According to Escalante, this was effectuated by Operation 40.

54. Ibid.

55. "Herter's Hopes Branded New 'Threat' by Cubans," *Washington Post and Times Herald*, March 10, 1960, p. A5; Phillips, "Vituperation against U.S. Rises in Cuba after Herter Criticism," *New York Times*, March 10, 1960, p. 3.

56. Drew Pearson, "Americans Urged to Quit Cuba," *Washington Post and Times Herald*, March 13, 1960, p. E5; "Cuba 'Intervenes' in 3 American Sugar Mills," *Washington Post and Times Herald*, March 12, 1960, p. A5.

57. "War Games Started," *Washington Post and Times Herald*, March 9, 1960, p. A9.

58. Fursenko and Naftali, *One Hell of a Gamble*, p. 41.

59. R. Hart Phillips, "Castro Restates View in Ship Case," *New York Times*, March 13, 1960, p. 27.

60. R. Hart Phillips, "Castro Stresses 'Aggression' Fear," *New York Times* , March 14, 1960, p. 8.

61. *Bay of Pigs Declassified*, p. 269.

62. López Fresquet, *My Fourteen Months with Castro*, pp. 155–156, 174–174; Thomas, *Cuba: Or, the Pursuit of Freedom*, pp. 1270–1271. In *American Policy Failures in Cuba*, Lazo admitted that he was not a U.S. embassy of-

ficial, had absolutely no authority to broker a deal, and alleged that he had acted alone. pp. 224–225.

63. Dana Adams Schmidt, "Dominicans Told to Return B-26's," *New York Times*, March 17, 1960, p. 14.

64. Ibid.

65. E. W. Kenworthy, "Cuban Aide in U.S Quits in Protest," *New York Times*, March 18, 1960, p. 1.

66. "Pons Called Traitor," *New York Times*, March 19, 1960, p. 5.

67. Anderson, *Che Guevara: A Revolutionary Life*, p. 406.

68. Thomas, *The Cuban Revolution*, p. 1271.

69. López Fresquet, *My Fourteen Months with Castro*, p. 176. López found this out only after he had already defected, but stated that it would not have made any difference in his decision to do so. Also see Mario Lazo, *American Policy Failures in Cuba: Dagger in the Heart* (New York: Twin Circle Publishing, 1968, 1970), pp. 224–225.

70. Kenworthy, "Cuban Aide in U.S Quits in Protest," *New York Times*, March 18, 1960, p. 1; Warren Unna, "3 More Cuban Aides Quit Castro's Regime," *Washington Post and Times Herald*, March 18, 1960, p. A1.

71. Unna, "3 More Cuban Aides Quit Castro's Regime," *Washington Post and Times Herald*, March 18, 1960, p. A1.

72. Jack Raymond, "Cuba Says Attaché Who Quit in Washington Stole $110,000," *New York Times*, March 20, 1960, p. 1; Leslie Whitten, "Cuba Sues Defector for $110,000," *Washington Post and Times Herald*, March 20, 1960, p. A8; Warren Unna, "U.S. Sending Bonsal Back to Havana Post," *Washington Post and Times Herald*, March 19, 1960, p. A1. The attaché, Miguel Pons Guizueta, a delegate to the OAS, accused Castro of being a Communist, and accused the Cuban government of being anti–Semitic. "Pons Called Traitor," *New York Times*, March 19, 1960, p. 5.

73. "Cuban's Ouster Barred," *New York Times*, March 12, 1960, p. 7. The judge was Joseph Lieb.

74. "Nebraskan Freed," *New York Times*, March 7, 1960, p. 2.

75. R. Hart Phillips, "Cuba Continues Seizing Business," *New York Times*, March 11, 1960, p. 6; "$100 Million Takeovers Set in Cuba," *Washington Post and Times Herald*, March 11, 1960, p. A4.

76. Ibid.

77. R. Hart Phillips, "New Town Rising in Cuban Fields," *New York Times*, March 3, 1960, p. 9.

78. Ibid.

79. R. Hart Phillips, "Tobacco Grower Adjusts in Cuba," *New York Times*, March 4, 1960, p. 10.

80. Ibid. Sharecroppers of Cuban Land and Leaf Company could keep as much as 80 percent of their crop.

81. "Cuba 'Intervenes' in 3 American Sugar Mills," *Washington Post and Times Herald*, March 12, 1960, p. A5.

82. "Trujillo Said to Bar Retirement; Terms Leaders of U.S. Hostile," *New York Times*, March 18, 1960, p. 2. Some of Trujillo's remarks were also relayed by Senator George Smathers, Democrat of Florida, who visited the Dominican Republic and gave a press conference.

83. E. W. Kenworthy, "U.S. Envoy to Cuba to Resume Post; Senators Divided," *New York Times*, March 19, 1960, p. 1.

84. Bonsal, *Cuba, Castro and the United States*, pp. 134–135.

85. Rabe, *Eisenhower and Latin America*, pp. 162–164; Bonsal, *Cuba, Castro and the United States*, p. 135; Howard Jones, *The Bay of Pigs* (New York: Oxford University Press, 2004), pp. 18–20; *Politics of Illusion*, p. 160. Interestingly,

Bonsal cites Eisenhower's *Waging Peace* and Nixon's *Six Crises*. Apparently, he was not involved in making the decision.

86. Jones, *The Bay of Pigs*, pp. 18–20.

87. Escalante, *The Cuba Project: CIA Covert Operations 1959–62*, p. 48.

88. Rabe, *Eisenhower and Latin America*, p. 17.

89. Wyden, *The Bay of Pigs: The Untold Story*, pp. 22–23.

90. *Bay of Pigs Declassified*, pp. 210, 270. E. Howard Hunt and Greg Aunapu, *American Spy: My Secret History in the CIA, Watergate and Beyond* (Hoboken, NJ: John Wiley and Sons, 2007), pp. 74–75.

91. Hunt, *American Spy*, pp. 74–76.

92. Wyden, *The Bay of Pigs: The Untold Story*, pp. 20–23; Hunt, *American Spy*, p. 23.

93. See Joan Didion, *Miami* (New York: Simon and Schuster, 1987), p. 81.

94. Ibid. Didion estimates that at its peak, the CIA employed 120,000 agents reporting to its Miami operations center. See also Carlos Lechuga, *Cuba and the Missile Crisis* (New York: Ocean Press, 2001), p. 18.

95. Hunt, *American Spy*, p. 115.

96. *Bay of Pigs Declassified*, pp. 268–269. Rivas Vasquez would eventually become the head of Venezuelan state security. "Obituary: Rafael Rivas Vázquez y Galdos," *Miami Herald*, November 25, 2000.

97. R. Hart Phillips, "Cuba's Bank Chief Views U.S. as Foe in Economic Fight," *New York Times*, March 21, 1960, p. 1.

98. "Guevara Renews Attack on U.S. as Bonsal Returns to Cuba Post," *Washington Post and Times Herald*, March 21, 1960, p. A5.

99. Phillips, *New York Times*, March 21, 1960, p. 1.

100. R. Hart Phillips, "American Fliers Downed by Cuba," *New York Times*, March 22, 1960, p. 1. Howard Lewis Runquist and William J. Shergales, were held for attempting to help Damasco Montesino and his family. Montesino had been head of the motor patrol in Havana during the Batista regime.

101. "Planes That Raid Cuba," *New York Times*, March 24, 1960, p. 32.

102. "Castro's Overthrow Predicted," *New York Times*, March 26, 1960, p. 4.

103. Tad Szulc, "Castro Resumes Talk of Invasion," *New York Times*, March 28, 1960, p. 10.

104. Tad Szulc, "Pro Communists in Havana Battle Foes in Street," *New York Times*, March 26, 1960, p. 1.

105. Tad Szulc, "Cuba Takes Over Fifth TV Station," *New York Times*, March 27, 1960, p. 30.

106. R. Hart Phillips, "Youth of Cuba Collecting Funds for Arms against 'Aggressor,'" *New York Times*, March 27, 1960, p. 32; Szulc, "Castro Resumes Talk of Invasion," *New York Times*, March 28, 1960, p. 10.

107. Tad Szulc, "Cuba: Revolutionary Fervor Mounts," *New York Times*, March 27, 1960, p. E5.

108. "Orioles Shun Havana, Cuba Writers Protest," *Washington Post and Times Herald*, March 29, 1960, p. A18.

109. Tad Szulc, "Castro Warns U.S. to Modify Policy," *New York Times*, March 29, 1960, p. 16.

110. "Cuba Denies Planning to End U.S. Base Pact," *Washington Post and Times Herald*, March 29, 1960, p. A5.

111. E. W. Kenworthy, "President Voices Concern on Cuba," *New York Times*, March 31, 1960, p. 3.

112. Szulc, "Cuba: Revolutionary Fervor Mounts," *New York Times*, March 27, 1960, p. E5.

113. Tad Szulc, "Brazilian to Shorten Cuba Visit over 'Misquotation' about U.S.," *New York Times*, April 1, 1960, p. 12.

114. Ed Cony, "Lean Days Begin in Castro's Utopia," *Washington Post and Times Herald*, March 31, 1960, p. A20.

115. "Santiago Cools toward Castro; City Was Once His Stronghold," *New York Times*, April 1, 1960, p. 1.

116. Phillips, "Castro Increasing Pressure on U.S. Sugar Mills in Cuba," *New York Times*, April 2, 1960, p. 8.

117. "Cuba Plans United Fruit Seizure," *Washington Post and Times Herald*, April 8, 1960, p. B10.

118. "Communism in Cuba," *New York Times*, April 1, 1960, p. 32.

119. Arthur Krock, "Propaganda Brake on Our Cuban Policy," *New York Times*, April 1, 1960, p. 32.

120. "Poland Set to Supply Jet Planes to Castro," *Washington Post and Times Herald*, April 2, 1960, p. A4; Tad Szulc, "Cubans and Poles Sign Trade Treaty," *New York Times*, April 2, 1960, p. 1.

121. "Pole Denies Cuba to Get Army Planes," *Washington Post and Times Herald*, April 7, 1960, p. A6. The Pole was Deputy Prime Minister Piotr Jaroszowicz, who was visiting the United States.

122. Jack Anderson, "U.S. Weapons Smuggled to Castro," *Washington Post and Times Herald*, April 2, 1960, p. B19.

123. Warren Unna, "Open Defiance Perils Future Role of OAS," *Washington Post and Times Herald*, April 6, 1960, p. A7.

124. "$100 Million Takeovers Set in Cuba," *Washington Post and Times Herald*, March 11, 1960, p. A4.

125. "Press Reports on Cuba Assailed as 'Sophistry,'" *Washington Post and Times Herald*, April 7, 1960, p. A6. Testimony regarding the Fair Play for Cuba Committee before the Senate Judiciary Subcommittee to Investigate the Administration of the Internal Security Act and Other Security Laws, May 5, 1960. Also see De Palma, *The Man Who Invented Fidel*, pp. 227–228.

126. "Castro Worse Than Batista, Cuban Envoy Says in Quitting," *Washington Post and Times Herald*, April 8, 1960, p. A7.

127. Macaulay, *A Rebel in Cuba: An American's Memoir*, pp. 180–192.

128. "Drive on Anti-Reds in Cuba 'Disturbs' U.S.," *Washington Post and Times Herald*, April 9, 1960, p. A5; E. W. Kenworthy, "Letter Is Issued," *New York Times*, April 9, 1960, p. 1.

129. Murrey Marder, "Ike Cautions Latins against Cuba's Path," *Washington Post and Times Herald*, April 9, 1960, p. A1.

130. "Ike's Letter Denounced in Cuba," *Washington Post and Times Herald*, April 10, 1960, p. A7; Szulc, "Cubans Denounce Eisenhower View as Hypocritical," *New York Times*, April 10, 1960, p. 1.

131. Szulc, "Cubans Denounce Eisenhower View as Hypocritical," *New York Times*, April 10, 1960, p. 1.

132. Ibid.

133. "Former Backers of Castro Urge Anti-Red Rising," *New York Times*, April 11, 1960, p. 1.

134. Alexander, *A History of Organized Labor in Cuba*, p. 207.

135. Tad Szulc, "U.S. Notes to Cuba Link Castro Rule to Rising Tension," *New York Times*, April 12, 1960, p. 1.

136. Ronald Kessler, *Inside the CIA: Revealing the Secrets of the World's Most Powerful Spy Agency* (New York: Pocket Books, 1992), p. 80; Rabe, *Eisenhower and Latin America*, p. 139.

137. "Crisis in the Cold War," *New York Times*, May 9, 1960, p. 28.

138. Felix Belair, Jr., "President Asserts Secrecy of Soviet Justifies Spying," *New York Times*, May 12, 1960, p. 1.

139. Perret, *Eisenhower*, p. 583.

140. Hunt, *American Spy*, pp. 116–117.

141. Ibid. It would later be asserted that Hunt had also recommended that the CIA assassinate Castro at the time of invasion. Gus Russo, *Live by the Sword: The Secret War against Castro and the Death of JFK* (Baltimore: Bancroft Press, 1998), p. 446, citing a 1967 investigation by Jack Anderson.

142. "Castro Says Cuba Fired On U.S. Ship," *New York Times,* May 14, 1960, p. 1.

143. Rabe, *Eisenhower and Latin America*, p. 139; Perret, *Eisenhower*, p. 584.

144. *Bay of Pigs Declassified*, p. 272.

145. Alexander, A *History of Organized Labor in Cuba*, p. 207; Montaner, *Journey to the Heart of Cuba*, p. 98; Encinosa, *Unvanquished*, p. 17. Encinosa says that Salvador was able to recruit hundreds of followers.

146. Thomas, *Cuba: Or, the Pursuit of Freedom*, p. 1286.

147. Montaner, *Journey to the Heart of Cuba*, p. 98.

148. Arboleya, *The Cuban Counterrevolution*, p. 67.

149. Encinosa, *Unvanquished*, pp. 17–18.

150. Ibid. Bosch was head of Movimiento Insurreccional de Recuperacion Revolucionaria (MIRR). See also Arboleya, *The Cuban Counterrevolution*, p. 151.

151. Thomas, *Cuba: Or, the Pursuit of Freedom*, p 1288.

152. Daniel Rubiera Zim, "Straining the Special Relationship: British and U.S. Policies toward the Cuban Revolution, 1959–1961," in *Cuban Studies 33*. Lisandro Pérez, Uva De Aragon, Editors (Pittsburgh: University of Pittsburgh. Center for Latin American Studies, University of Pittsburgh Press, 1980), pp. 84–86. See also Bonsal, *Cuba, Castro and the United States*, p. 149.

153. Bonsal, *Cuba, Castro and the United States*, p. 149.

154. "Havana Expels 2 U.S. Attachés," *Washington Post and Times Herald*, June 17, 1960, p. A13; R. Hart Phillips, "Two U.S. Attachés Ousted by Havana on a Plot Charge," *New York Times*, June 17, 1960, p. 1. Raúl Castro would later allege that they were Nazis because World War II items were found on them. Friedemann and Sweet would allege that they were "trophies." "Major Castro Calls Them Spies," *New York Times*, August 6, 1960, p. 6; "U.S. Says Cubans Plot to Show 2 Ousted F.B.I. Men as 'Nazis,'" *New York Times*, August 6, 1960, p. 1.

155. John D. Morris, "2 Aides of Castro Expelled by U.S.; Spying Is Charged," *New York Times*, June 19, 1960, p. 1. The aides were Carlos Sánchez y Basquet of the Miami consulate and Dr. Berta Pia y Badia of the New York consulate.

156. "Cuba Ousts 3d Embassy Employee," *Washington Post and Times Herald*, September 24, 1960, p. A6; R. Hart Phillips, "Cuba Seizes Aide of U.S. Embassy," *New York Times*, September 16, 1960, p. 1; "Cuba Frees Embassy Secretary," *Washington Post and Times Herald*, September 17, 1960, p. A4; Marjorie Lennox was secretary to Leonard H. Price, First Embassy Secretary, and Caroline O. Stacy was a general secretary.

157. The Hilton was owned by the Hotel and Restaurant Workers' Federation. Phillips, "Two U.S. Attachés Ousted by Havana on a Plot Charge," *New York Times*, June 17, 1960, p. 1.

158. E. W. Kenworthy, "Cuba: Shift in U.S. Policy," *New York Times*, June 26, 1960, p. E4.

159. See Bonsal, *Cuba, Castro and the United States*, p. 145. Actually, there had been an oil strike in 1954 near

Camagüey. Current estimates by the U.S. Geological Survey place Cuba's potential deep-water reserves at 4.6 billion barrels of oil and 9.8 trillion cubic feet of natural gas. Nick Miroff, "Cuba's Undersea Oil Could Help Thaw Trade with U.S.," *Washington Post*, May 16, 2009.

160. Tad Szulc, "Last 2 Refineries Seized by Castro; Oil Supplies Low," *New York Times*, July 2, 1960, p. 1.

161. R. Hart Phillips, "Havana Rejects Seizure Protest," *New York Times*, July 9, 1960, p. 3.

162. William J. Jorden, "U.S. Studies Step On Cuba Seizures," *New York Times*, July 2, 1960, p. 2.

163. Bonsal, *Cuba, Castro and the United States*, pp. 145–153; Thomas, *Cuba: Or, the Pursuit of Freedom*, pp. 1288–1289; Domínguez, *To Make a World Safe for Revolution*, pp. 24–25; Wayne Smith, *The Closest of Enemies*, p. 57.

164. Ibid.; "Eisenhower Bars a Red Cuba, Tells Russians Not to Meddle; Khrushchev Warns of Rockets," *New York Times*, July 10, 1960, p. 1; Felix Belair, Jr., "President Is Firm," *New York Times*, July 10, 1960, p. 1.

165. "The News of the Week in Review," *New York Times*, July 24, 1960, p. E1.

166. Ibid.; "The News of the Week in Review," *New York Times*, July 31, 1960, p. E1.

167. *Bay of Pigs Declassified*, p. 273.

168. Ibid.; *Politics of Illusion*, p. 160.

169. "Havana Will Lose Its Baseball Club," *New York Times*, July 8, 1960, p. 24; "Shaughnessy Pulls Club," *Washington Post and Times Herald*, July 8, 1960, p. 50.

170. Bjarkman, *A History of Cuban Baseball*, p. 409.

171. "Havana Team Shift Called 'Big Mistake,'" *Washington Post and Times Herald*, July 9, 1960, p. A13.

172. Ibid. Maduro stated that one reason for the move of the team to Jersey City the threat of the Continental League, the International League placed the value of franchises too high and the Toronto and Buffalo franchises were threatening to jump to the new league. He was personally in debt and would lose everything.

173. "Guards Assigned Nap Reyes after 'Traitor' Charge," *Washington Post and Times Herald*, July 17, 1960, p. C3.

174. Macaulay, *A Rebel in Cuba: An American's Memoir*, pp. 192–194.

175. Ibid., pp. 186–188.

176. Theron Corse, "Presbyterians in the Revolution: An American Missionary Church in Cuba, 1959–1970," in *Cuban Studies 31* (Pittsburgh, University of Pittsburgh Press, 2001), p. 14.

177. Ibid.

178. *Bay of Pigs Declassified*, pp. 273–274.

179. Ibid., p. 274, citing the CIA Inspector General's Report on Efforts to Assassinate Fidel Castro, pp. 3, 14; *Politics of Illusion*, p. 160; Kessler, *Inside the CIA*, pp. 42–43; Jones, *The Bay of Pigs*, pp. 22–23.

180. Wyden, *The Bay of Pigs: The Untold Story*, pp. 45–46; *Bay of Pigs Declassified*, p. 274. The story's author was David Kraslow.

181. *Bay of Pigs Declassified*, p. 274.

182. Wyden, *The Bay of Pigs: The Untold Story*, p. 30; *Politics of Illusion*, p. 161.

183. Bonsal, Cuba, *Castro and the United States*, pp. 161–163; Domínguez, *To Make a World Safe for Revolution*, p. 26; *Bay of Pigs Declassified*, p. 274.

184. W. H. Lawrence, "Kennedy Declares Castro Is Enemy; Sees U.S. Arms Lag," *New York Times*, August 27, 1960, p. 1.

185. *Bay of Pigs Declassified*, p. 275.

186. Corse, "Presbyterians in the Revolution," in

Cuban Studies 31, p. 11, citing an article in *Christianity Today.*

187. "The News of the Week in Review," *New York Times*, September 25, 1960, p. E1.

188. Jack Raymond, "President Calls Pair Traitorous," *New York Times*, September 7, 1960, p. 1. Burton F. Mitchell and William H. Martin defected in Moscow. Both were "mathematicians."

189. "Cuban Asks Asylum; Tells of Spy Ring," *New York Times*, September 27, 1960; p. 21.

190. "Castro Moves Out of Hotel in Huff, Takes His Party to One in Harlem," *Washington Post and Times Herald*, September 20, 1960, p. A1.

191. Max Frankel, "Cuban Puts Case," *New York Times*, September 27, 1960, p. 1; "Castro Vowed Brevity and Spoke 4 1/2 Hours," *New York Times*, September 27, 1960, p. 21. All of the allegations were later refuted. "U.S. Accusation Lists Castro's 'Half-Truths' and 'Distortions' about Controversy," *New York Times*, October 15, 1960, p. 6.

192. Note that Ambassador Bonsal knew or had reason to know that the CIA had been infiltrated by double agents by that time. Bonsal, *Cuba, Castro and the United States*, p. 164.

193. "Two Say Cuban Ties Led to Loss of Jobs," *New York Times*, September 23, 1960, p. 17.

194. "Castro Returns Home in Plane Borrowed from Soviet Union," *Washington Post and Times Herald*, September 29, 1960, p. A6.

195. Inspector General's Report on Efforts to Assassinate Fidel Castro, p. 1:98; *Bay of Pigs Declassified*, p. 275; *Politics of Illusion*, p. 161.

196. Ibid.

197. "Cuba Ousts 3d Embassy Employe," *Washington Post and Times Herald*, September 24, 1960, p. A6.

198. Anderson, *Che Guevara: A Revolutionary Life*, p. 482.

199. Wayne Smith, *The Closest of Enemies*, p. 57.

200. Leo Egan, "Kennedy Assails Nixon over Cuba," *New York Times*, October 7, 1960, p. 1; Julius Duscha, "Kennedy Hits Nixon's Cuba Role," *Washington Post and Times Herald*, October 7, 1960, p. A1. Candidate Kennedy insinuated that the problem would have been diffused early on had the Eisenhower administration offered "the hand of American friendship" to thwart Communism.

201. See "U.S. Jury Indicts a Batista Backer," *New York Times*, April 11, 1961, p. 1; "Former Batista Aide Is Indicted at Miami," *Washington Post and Times Herald*, April 11, 1961, p. A6. The Americans executed were Allan D. Thompson, Anthony Zarba, and Robert O. Fuller.

202. Anthony Salvard.

203. George Washington University National Security Archives, October 12, 1960.

204. *Bay of Pigs Declassified*, p. 276.

205. Jones, *The Bay of Pigs*, pp. 28–29.

206. R. Hart Phillips, "Havana Arrests U.S. Expatriate," *New York Times*, October 22, 1960; p. 1; "Cuba Seizes Man Who Gave Up U.S.," *New York Times*, October 22, 1960, p. 4. Shetterly reports that Trujillo had placed a bounty on Morgan's head and that the FBI was involved in an assassination conspiracy directed at Morgan. *The Americano*, p. 213.

207. Geyer, *Guerrilla Prince*, p. 195. Geyer quotes Lazaro Ascensio, another veteran from the Escambray campaign, who alleged that Castro also accused Che Guevara and even his brother Raúl of being no more than mercenaries.

208. Bernard D. Nossiter, "Cuba Trade Embargoed by U.S.," *Washington Post and Times Herald*, October 20, 1960, p. A1.

209. Bonsal, *Cuba, Castro and the United States*, pp. 165–166.

210. Peter Kihss, "Berle Backs Kennedy's Policy of Aid for Anti-Castro Forces," *New York Times*, October 26, 1960, p. 25. Kennedy's advisor, Adolph A. Berle, Jr., stated that there was hard evidence that Cuba was supporting communist infiltration in other Latin American countries, which was a violation of the Rio Treaty, among others.

211. Tad Szulc, "Cuba Mediation Urged in Brazil," *New York Times*, October 26, 1960, p. 27.

212. R. Hart Phillips, "Hope of U.S. Shift Voiced by Castro," *New York Times*, November 29, 1960, p. 19.

213. "Attack Fear Activates Cuba Force," *Washington Post and Times Herald*, November 9, 1960, p. A8.

214. Thomas, *Cuba: Or, the Pursuit of Freedom*, p. 1296.

215. Evan Thomas, *The Very Best Men: Four Who Dared* (New York: Simon and Schuster, 1996), pp. 205–206. Droller called Hunt "Popsy" and "Boychick." Most commentators say that Droller was intensely disliked. Jones, *Bay of Pigs*, p. 73.

216. Ibid., p. 1296–1297; Shetterly, *The Americano*, pp. 256–258.

217. Shetterly, *The Americano*, p. 256.

218. Ibid.

219. Alexander, *A History of Organized Labor in Cuba*, p. 207; "Ex-Aide of Castro Seized in Flight," *New York Times*, November 6, 1960, p. 24; "Attack Fear Activates Cuba Force," *Washington Post and Times Herald*, November 9, 1960, p. A8; "Cuba Grabs Fleeing Labor Chief," *Washington Post and Times Herald*, November 6, 1960, p. A6.

220. pp. 378–379.

221. Katrina vanden Heuvel, "Suppressing News: Déjà Vu," *The Nation*, February 25, 2007. Vanden Heuvel reports that Kennedy pressured the *New York Times* not to report the imminent invasion. Later, Kennedy was quoted as saying, "If you had printed more about the [Bay of Pigs] operation, you would have saved us from a colossal mistake."

222. Morley, *Imperial State and Revolution*, p. 137.

223. Coise, "Presbyterians in the Revolution," in *Cuban Studies 31*, pp. 11–12.

224. Ibid., p. 13.

Chapter 17

1. "Castro Repeats Charge," *New York Times*, January 2, 1961, p. 2; R. Hart Phillips, "Castro Tells U.S. Staff in Embassy Must Be Slashed," *New York Times*, January 3, 1961, p. 1.

2. Bonsal, *Cuba, Castro and the United States*, p. 175.

3. "Castro Repeats Charge," *New York Times*, January 2, 1961, p. 2.

4. Bonsal, *Cuba, Castro and the United States*, p. 176.

5. "Memorandum of Meeting with the President," George Washington University National Security Archives, January 3, 1961. Morley states that the president predicted that the invasion would occur in March. *Imperial State and Revolution*, p. 125.

6. Sam Pope Brewer, "Cuba Aides of U.S. Arrive in Miami," *New York Times*, January 5, 1961, p. A1.

7. García, *Havana USA*, pp. 24–25; also see de los Angeles Torres, *In the Land of Mirrors*, p. 50.

8. Castro and Ramonet, *Fidel Castro: My Life*, pp. 236–239.

9. R. Hart Phillips, "U.S. Aides Start Leaving Havana," *New York Times*, January 5, 1961, p. 1.

10. Ibid.

11. "CIA, Memorandum For Chief WH/4, Policy Decisions Required for Conduct of Strike Operations Against Government of Cuba," George Washington University National Security Archives, January 4, 1961.

12. Ibid. The CIA's Tracy Barnes later outlined problems: "Most importantly ... contrary to views expressed at a January 3 meeting, the operation is unable to house or train more than 750 strike force members. Further, he argues that the operation 'should' have a U.S. base for resupply following the strike landing." "CIA, Material for the 5 January Special Group Meeting, Memorandum for Director of Central Intelligence," George Washington University National Security Archives, January 5, 1961.

13. Max Frankel, "In Cuba: U.S. Action Appears to Have Been a Surprise to Havana," *New York Times*, January 8, 1961, p. E3.

14. "The Break with Cuba," *New York Times*, January 5, 1961, p. 30.

15. "Summary of Editorial Comment on United States Break in Relations with Cuba," *New York Times*, January 5, 1961, p. 10.

16. Robert E. Baker, "Britons Criticize Ike on Cuba, Laos," *Washington Post and Times Herald*, January 6, 1961, p. A14.

17. "3 Americans Sentenced," *New York Times*, January 11, 1961, p. 10. The Americans were Eustice Brunet, Edmund Taranske, Daniel Carswell, and Mario Nordio, a naturalized citizen who was deported.

18. Lindesay Parrott, "Cuba Fails to Get U.N. Vote on 'Plot' by U.S. to Invade," *New York Times*, January 6, 1961, p. 1; "Cuban Urges U.N. Bar U.S. 'Invasion,'" *New York Times*, January 1, 1961, p. 15.

19. "U.S. Denies Invasion Charge," *New York Times*, January 3, 1961, p. 5.

20. "Kennedy Picketed Here," *New York Times*, January 5, 1961, p. 6.

21. Peter Kihss, "Anti-Castro Group Is Termed 'Almost Ready' to Invade Cuba," *New York Times*, January 5, 1961, p. 6.

22. "U.S. Pro-Castro Unit Asks Inquiry on C.I.A.," *New York Times*, January 6, 1961, p. 3.

23. Kihss, "Anti-Castro Group Is Termed 'Almost Ready' to Invade Cuba," *New York Times*, January 5, 1961, p. 6.

24. Richard Valeriani, "Cuba Presses Arrest of Foes," *Washington Post and Times Herald*, January 9, 1961, p. A7; "U.S. Carrier at Guantánamo," *New York Times*, January 10, 1961, p. 10.

25. John G. Norris, "U.S. Carrier Stirs Up New Cuba Invasion Cry," *Washington Post and Times Herald*, January 10, 1961, p. A8.

26. Marquis Childs, "Cuban Dilemma Threatens U.S.," *Washington Post and Times Herald*, January 6, 1961, p. A18.

27. Robert Berrellez, "Cuba Places All Available Arms, Hopes for Changes by Kennedy," *Washington Post and Times Herald*, January 6, 1961, p. A9.

28. Ibid.

29. Valeriani, "Cuba Presses Arrest of Foes," *Washington Post and Times Herald*, January 9, 1961, p. A7; R. Hart Phillips, "Cubans Arrest Ten in 'Invasion' Tension," *New York Times*, January 9, 1961, p. 1.

30. Ibid.

31. Phillips, "Cubans Arrest Ten in 'Invasion' Tension," *New York Times*, January 9, 1961, p. 1.

32. Berrellez, "Cuba Places All Available Arms, Hopes for Changes by Kennedy," *Washington Post and Times Herald*, January 6, 1961, p. A9.

33. R. Hart Phillips, "6 Americans Get 30 Years in Cuba," *New York Times*, February 1, 1961, p. 4. The six were: Alford E. Gibson, 32, Durham, North Carolina; Leonard L. Schmidt, 21, Chicago; George R. Beck, 24, Taunton, Massachusetts; Tommy L. Baker, 28, Dothan, Alabama; Donald J. Green, 28, a naturalized citizen from Montreal; and James B. Beane, Cedar Falls, North Carolina. Later records would list Green as Donald Joe Greene of Clover, South Carolina, and Beane as Beans.

34. "Cuba Said to Aid 'Fair Play' Group," *New York Times*, January 11, 1961, p. 10; Ben F. Meyer, "Quiz Told Cuban Paid Bulk of Castro Ad Cost," *Washington Post and Times Herald*, January 11, 1961, p. A12.

35. Max Frankel, "Castro and Trujillo Call Truce, Diplomats in Caribbean Believe," *New York Times*, January 5, 1961, p. 13.

36. "JCS, Chronology of JCS Participation in Bumpy Road," George Washington University National Security Archives, January 11, 1961.

37. "Evaluation of Possible Military Courses of Action in Cuba," Defense Department Memorandum, George Washington University National Security Archives, January 16, 1961.

38. "Ydigoras Denies Invasion Plan," *New York Times*, January 11, 1961, p. 11; Jack Raymond, "Guatemala Calls Forces Defensive," *New York Times*, January 11, 1961, p. 1.

39. "Cuban Invasion Scare Is Traced to 'Trainee' of Guatemalan Camp," *Washington Post and Times Herald*, January 11, 1961, p. A12.

40. R. Hart Phillips, "Cuba's Mobilization Limits Cane Harvest," *New York Times*, January 12, 1961, p. 1.

41. R. Hart Phillips, "Cuba Opens Drive for Cane Cutters," *New York Times*, January 30, 1961, p. 10.

42. "*Informe Especial*: 1961," George Washington University National Security Archives, January 12, 1961.

43. Sam Pope Brewer, "Exiles Say Military Resistance to Castro Is Growing inside Cuba," *New York Times*, January 14, 1961, p. 1.

44. "The White House, Meeting in the Cabinet Room, 9:45 A.M., January 19, 1961," George Washington University National Security Archives, January 19, 1961.

Chapter 18

1. John Fitzgerald Kennedy, Inaugural Address, January 20, 1961.

2. Phillips, "6 Americans Get 30 Years in Cuba," *New York Times*, February 1, 1961, p. 4.

3. R. Hart Phillips, "Castro Suggests Amity with U.S.," *New York Times*, January 21, 1961, p. 1; "Castro Suspends Trials in Kennedy Peace Bid," *Washington Post and Times Herald*, January 21, 1961, p. A13.

4. E. W. Kenworthy, "Latins' Progress Is Kennedy Goal," *New York Times*, January 26, 1961, p. 1.

5. McGeorge Bundy, "Memorandum of Discussion on Cuba, Cabinet Room, January 28, 1961," George Washington University National Security Archives, January 28, 1961.

6. John Fitzgerald Kennedy, State of the Union Address, 1961, Washington, DC, January 30, 1961.

7. Wyden, *The Bay of Pigs: The Untold Story*, pp. 89–90. Also reported in George Washington University National Security Archives.

8. "Chairman L. L. Lemnitzer, Memorandum for the

Secretary of Defense, Military Evaluation of the CIA Para-military Plan, Cuba," George Washington University National Security Archives, February 3, 1961.

9. McGeorge Bundy, Memorandum from the President's Special Assistant for National Security Affairs to President Kennedy, in George Washington University National Security Archives, February 8, 1961. Bundy and National Security Advisor Richard Goodwin "join in believing that there should certainly not be an invasion adventure without careful diplomatic soundings" which are likely to support the position of the State Department.

10. Ibid.

11. McGeorge Bundy, "Memorandum of Meeting with President Kennedy, White House, Washington, February 8, 1961," George Washington University National Security Archives, February 8, 1961.

12. "Costa Rica Expels Anti-Castro Exiles," *New York Times*, March 5, 1961, p. 32.

13. Johnson, Artime, et al., *Bay of Pigs: The Leader's Story of Brigade 2506*, p. 61; Also reported in George Washington University National Security Archives. The men were transported to Peten, in the jungles of Northern Guatemala. "Frank" was Gerry Droller, aka Frank Bender.

14. Max Frankel, "Guatemala Irate in U.N. over Cuba," *New York Times*, March 21, 1961, p. 14. The ambassador, Carlos Alejos, accused Cuba of aiding Guatemalan Communist ex-president Jacobo Arbenz, who was in exile in Havana.

15. "Death of Cuban Ambassador to U.N. Delays General Assembly Debate," *Washington Post and Times Herald*, March 21, 1961, p. A10.

16. McGeorge Bundy, "Memorandum to JFK," in George Washington University National Security Archives, February 18, 1961.

17. "Santa Maria Case Linked to a Cuban," *New York Times*, February 11, 1961, p. 7. In the Santa Maria affair, January 22, 1961, an alleged plot was uncovered to commandeer a Portuguese ship, take it to Angola and initiate a revolution against Portugal.

18. "Castro Aide Asks Asylum," *New York Times*, January 28, 1961; p. 2; Sam Pope Brewer, "Cuban Exiles Ask U.S. to Release 13," *New York Times*, June 1, 1961, p. 15. See also Shetterly, *The Americano*, pp. 268–270.

19. Shetterly, *The Americano*, pp. 269–270.

20. Ibid., pp. 272–273; R. Hart Phillips, "Morgan Is Shot as Cuba 'Traitor.'" *New York Times*, March 12, 1961, p. 32; Martin P. Houseman, "Firing Squad Executes U.S. Turncoat in Cuba," *Washington Post and Times Herald*, March 12, 1961, p. A10. According to Shetterly, Morgan should not have been given a death sentence. However, Morgan had embarrassed Trujillo so much that Trujillo demanded the death of Morgan as part of the deal to end the confrontation between Cuba and the Dominican Republic. Castro acquiesced. *The Americano*, pp. 280–281. Shetterly cites a CIA document as substantiation. Interestingly, he was given the Catholic last rites.

21. "American in Havana Gets 30-year Term," *New York Times*, April 16, 1964, p. 9.

22. Milton Besser, "U.S. Intensifies Plot, Cuba Charges in U.N.," *Washington Post and Times Herald*, March 16, 1961, p. D11; "U.S. Accused Again by Cuba in the U.N.," *New York Times*, March 16, 1961, p. 8.

23. Phillips, "Cubans Urged to Sharpen Vigil Against Enemies of Revolution," *New York Times*, March 19, 1961, p. 31.

24. See George Washington University National Security Archives. Also cited in Molina, *Diario de Girón*, pp. 56–57.

25. Peter Kihss, "U.S. Asks Court Bar Questions on Castro Foes in Miami Area," *New York Times*, March 24, 1961, p. 3.

26. "Molina Guilty in Girl's Death; Convicted of 2d-Degree Murder," *New York Times*, April 8, 1961, p. 2. Eventually, Molina's lawyers lost all appeals. Cuba had agreed to accept Molina as part of a bargain for trade during the prisoner exchange after the Bay of Pigs, but the court and the U.S. government would not accept the deal. "Molina Given 20 Years to Life as Court Rejects Cuban Offer," *New York Times*, June 30, 1961, p. 8; "Appeals Court Bars Review for Molina," *New York Times*, May 1, 1964, p. 10.

27. "Soviet Asked to Clarify Its Cease-Fire Position," *Washington Post and Times Herald*, April 18, 1961, p. A1; Wallace Carroll, "President Is Firm," *New York Times*, April 19, 1961, p. 1.

28. James Reston, "Top U.S. Advisers in Dispute on Aid to Castro's Foes," *New York Times*, April 11, 1961, p. 1.

29. McGeorge Bundy, Memorandum for the President, March 15, 1961, in *Politics of Illusion*, pp. 220–221.

30. Arthur Schlesinger, Jr., Memorandum for the President, March 15, 1961, in *Politics of Illusion*, pp. 222–223.

31. "U.S. Jury Indicts a Batista Backer," *New York Times*, April 11, 1961, p. 1; "Former Batista Aide Is Indicted at Miami," *Washington Post and Times Herald*, April 11, 1961, p. A6. The Americans executed were Allan D. Thompson, Anthony Zarba, and Robert Fuller.

32. R. Hart Phillips, "Cubans Urged to Sharpen Vigil against Enemies of Revolution," *New York Times*, March 19, 1961, p. 31.

33. R. Hart Phillips, "Castro Sees Help of All Americas," *New York Times*, March 26, 1961, p. 31; "Cardenas Backs Stand on Castro," *New York Times*, April 1, 1961, p. 4.

34. R. Hart Phillips, "Castro Tightens His Hold on Cubans," *New York Times*, March 26, 1961, p. E8.

35. Ibid.

36. "Text of the State Department's Document Denouncing Castro Regime in Cuba," *New York Times*, April 4, 1961, p. 14.

37. Peter Kihss, "Castro Minister Says U.S. Wages Undeclared War," *New York Times*, April 6, 1961, p. 1.

38. Arboleya, *The Cuban Counterrevolution*, pp. 89–90.

39. Tania Long, "Anti-Castro Units Trained to Fight at Florida Bases," *New York Times*, April 7, 1961, p. 1; E. W. Kenworthy, "Leader of Anti-Castro Cubans Tells Aims to U.S.," *New York Times*, April 7, 1961, p. 2; Sam Pope Brewer, "Castro Foe Says Uprising Is Near," *New York Times*, April 8, 1961, p. 1.

40. Tad Szulc, "Rivalries Beset Top Cuban Exiles," *New York Times*, April 9, 1961, p. 1.

41. Arboleya, *The Cuban Counterrevolution*, p. 88.

42. Tad Szulc, "C.I.A. Is Accused by Bitter Rebels," *New York Times*, April 22, 1961, p. 1.

43. "Castro's Foes Reported Moving to Invade Cuba," *Washington Post and Times Herald*, April 8, 1961, p. C15.

44. "Overthrowing Revolutions," *New York Times*, April 14, 1961, p. 28.

45. "Cuban Policy Criticized," *New York Times*, April 12, 1961, p. 40.

46. Johnson, Artime, et al., *Bay of Pigs: The Leader's Story of Brigade 2506*, p. 77.

47. Gabriel Molina, *Diario de Girón* (Havana, Cuba: Política, 1983), p. 113.

48. George Washington University National Security Archives, April 13, 1961.

49. Martin P. Houseman, "3 Cuban Areas Torn by Rebels," *Washington Post and Times Herald*, April 12, 1961, p. A1.

50. "Transcript of President Kennedy's News Conference," *Washington Post*, April 13, 1961, p. A10; Johnson, Artime, et al., *Bay of Pigs: The Leader's Story of Brigade 2506*, p. 72.

51. Wyden, *The Bay of Pigs: The Untold Story*, p. 170: "I believe the president did not realize that the air strike was an integral part of the operational plan he had approved." Richard Bissell, Jr., *Reflections of a Cold Warrior: From Yalta to the Bay of Pigs*. With contributions by Jonathan E. Lewis and Frances T. Pudlo (New Haven, CT: Yale University Press, 1996), p. 183.

52. R. Hart Phillips, "Arms Depot Hit," *New York Times*, April 16, 1961, p. 1; Sam Pope Brewer, "Castro Foes Call Cubans to Arms; Predict Uprising," *New York Times*, April 9, 1961, p. 1.

53. Phillips, "Arms Depot Hit," *New York Times*, April 16, 1961, p. 1.

54. Harold K. Milks, "7 Are Reported Dead in Havana; U.S. Is Blamed," *Washington Post and Times Herald*, April 16, 1961, p. A1.

55. Johnson, Artime, et al., *Bay of Pigs: The Leader's Story of Brigade 2506*, pp. 90–91; Wyden, *The Bay of Pigs: The Untold Story*, p. 185. Fidel Castro later quipped that not even Hollywood would try to convince anyone with that story.

56. Johnson, Artime, et al., *Bay of Pigs: The Leader's Story of Brigade 2506*, p. 86.

57. McCandlish Phillips, "Miro Says Cuba Air Raiders Were in 'Contact' with Exiles," *New York Times*, April 16, 1961, p. 5.

58. "U.S. Seeking Data on Raids in Cuba," *New York Times*, April 16, 1961, p. 1.

59. Johnson, Artime, et al., *Bay of Pigs: The Leader's Story of Brigade 2506*, pp. 83–86; Arboleya, *The Cuban Counterrevolution*, p. 85; "Sequence of Events," George Washington University National Security Archives, May 3, 1961.

60. Arboleya, *The Cuban Counterrevolution*, pp. 85–86.

61. Thomas, *Cuba: Or, the Pursuit of Freedom*, p. 1365.

62. "27 Held as Plotters against Castro's Life," *Washington Post and Times Herald*, April 19, 1961, p. A9.

63. Thomas, *Cuba: Or, the Pursuit of Freedom*, p. 1365.

64. Molina, *Diario de Girón*, p. 127.

65. Wayne Smith, *The Closest of Enemies*, p. 53.

66. Wyden, *The Bay of Pigs: The Untold Story*, pp. 198–210. Bissell would later state that he made "a major mistake. For the record, we should have spoken to the president and made as strong a case as possible on behalf of the operation and the welfare of the brigade." *Reflections of a Cold Warrior*, p. 184. See also Chambers M. Roberts and Murrey Marder, "President Decided on Cuba Venture on Advice of Joint Chiefs and CIA," *Washington Post and Times Herald*, April 22, 1961, p. A1.

67. "Invasion of Cuba Reported Begun by a Rebel Force," *New York Times*, April 17, 1961, p. 1.

68. Using Thomas's figures in *Cuba: Or, the Pursuit of Freedom*, p. 1370.

69. Wyden, *The Bay of Pigs: The Untold Story*, pp. 264–265, 273–288.

70. Ibid., 294.

71. George Washington University National Security Archives.

72. Tad Szulc, "Anti-Castro Units Land in Cuba; Report Fighting at Beachhead," *New York Times*, April 18, 1961, p. 1.

73. Jack V. Fox, "Insurgents Hit Cuba in 4 Provinces," *Washington Post and Times Herald*, April 18, 1961, p. A1.

74. Thomas J. Hamilton, "Roa Charges U.S. Armed Invaders," *New York Times*, April 18, 1961, p. 1; Johnson, Artime, et al., *Bay of Pigs: The Leader's Story of Brigade 2506*, pp. 92–93.

75. James Reston, "Rusk Declares Sympathy of Nation for Castro Foes," *New York Times*, April 18, 1961, p. 1.

76. Milton Besser, "Reds Press for Speedy U.N. Action," *Washington Post and Times Herald*, April 19, 1961, p. A1.

77. "27 Held as Plotters against Castro's Life," *Washington Post and Times Herald*, April 19, 1961, p. A9; Tad Szulc, "Rebels Hopeful," *New York Times*, April 21, 1961, p. 1.

78. "Sori Marin is Ex-Castro Aide," *New York Times*, April 20, 1961, p. 10.

79. Richard Cohen, "Prisoners of Castro — In Cuba and Here," *Washington Post*, July 26, 1986 p. 1.

80. Jack V. Fox, "Cuban Invasion Appears to Be Crushed by Castro's Red-Supplied Jets, Arms," *Washington Post and Times Herald*, April 20, 1961, p. A1.

81. Wyden, *The Bay of Pigs: The Untold Story*, p. 319. Wyden cites Goodwin, who states that President Kennedy was detached, measuring and considering everything that was presented to him, in the manner it was presented, and trusted his advisors.

82. Tad Szulc, "C.I.A. Is Accused by Bitter Rebels," *New York Times*, April 22, 1961. The report accused Bissell and Barnes of "playing it by ear" by setting up an "anarchic and disorganized" command structure for the operation. The planning was described as "frenzied." Kirkpatrick accused Bissell of misleading the president by failing to say that "success had become dubious." The report concluded that "'plausible deniability' had become a pathetic illusion." Thus the title of *The Politics of Illusion*. The report is also contained and summarized in George Washington University National Security Archives.

83. Kessler, *Inside the CIA*, p. 67.

84. Dom Bonafede, "Miami Refugees Puzzle Over Why Attack Went Sour," *Washington Post and Times Herald*, April 21, 1961, p. A13.

85. Trumbull Higgins, *The Perfect Failure: Kennedy, Eisenhower and the CIA at the Bay of Pigs* (New York: W.W. Norton, 1987), p. 119.

86. Szulc, "C.I.A. Is Accused by Bitter Rebels," *New York Times*, April 22, 1961, p. 1. Ray was a graduate of the University of Utah.

87. Ibid.

88. Higgins says that it never had a chance. *The Perfect Failure*, p. 167.

Chapter 19

1. Perez, *On Becoming Cuban*, pp. 493–494. Perez says that Secretary of State Herter said the same about Fidel Castro: in English, he was reasonable; in Spanish "he became voluble, excited and somewhat 'wild'" (citing a memorandum of a conference with President Eisenhower, April 18, 1959). Pérez also cited a 1955 history of *I Love Lucy*.

2. "Radio: Lucy's $8,000,000," *Time*, March 2, 1953.

3. "Show Business: Desiloot," *Time*, November 16, 1962.

4. After Desi was bought out, it also produced *The Andy Griffith Show, The Jack Benny Program, I Spy, Mannix, Gomer Pyle, USMC, Mission: Impossible,* and *That Girl.*

5. Coyne Steven Sanders, and Tom Gilbert, *Desilu: The Story of Lucille Ball and Desi Arnaz* (New York: Quill, 1993), pp. 115–118. Arnaz was accused of infidelity in magazines such as *Confidential,* with articles such as "Does Desi Really Love Lucy?"

6. "People, March 14, 1960," *Time,* March 14, 1960.

7. Meyers, *Hemingway: A Biography,* p. 518.

8. "Castro Praised by Hemingway," *Arizona Republic,* April 26, 1959, p. 2.

9. "Hemingway Back in Cuba," *New York Times,* November 6, 1959, p. 9. J. R. Topping of the American embassy reported that Hemingway wanted to be considered a Cuban, and opposed American policy initiatives. Meyers, *Hemingway: A Biography,* p. 519.

10. *How It Was,* pp. 592–593.

11. For example, see Report by Cuba on Resolution 60/12 of the United Nations General Assembly: "Necessity of ending the economic, commercial and financial blockade imposed by the United States of America against Cuba," United Nations, August 2006. The allegation is that the funds in American banks were only part of the Cuban treasury stolen by Batista and his allies.

12. After the Castro government began to nationalize businesses, President Eisenhower announced an embargo on trade. Exceptions were agricultural products and medicines. "Embargo Plan Is Eisenhower's," *New York Times,* October 14, 1960, p. 13. The embargo went into effect on October 19.

13. In legal parlance, the tort of alienation of affections is an anachronistic concept wherein the jilted party sues the "other party" for intruding on the marriage. In concept, the wronged party seeks redress not against the spouse, but against the intruder. In this analogy, the civil wrong would have been committed by the Soviet Union. Instead of accusing the Soviet Union of interference, the U.S. fixed its attention on a less imposing former ally, Cuba. Although Castro now says that he was a Communist, most credible American historians now say that instead of the Communists infiltrating the Provisional Government, Castro infiltrated the Communist Party, put his men in control and removed the old party leaders from power. See, for instance, Rabe, *Eisenhower and Latin America,* pp. 131–132; Richard E. Welch, Jr. *Response to Revolution,* p. 10. To others, the ascension of a Cuban dictatorship is as if some of the gangster groups from the University of Havana seized power. They merely use the name "Communism." See, for instance, Thomas, *The Cuban Revolution,* p. 1486.

14. See James Reston, "Cuba's Drift to the Left," *New York Times,* February 19, 1960, p. 6. Even friends of the U.S. said that we were too obsessed in trying to identify Communists and "beat down" our critics rather than trying to correct the situations which caused criticism. Murrey Marder, "Ike's Trip Uncovers Skepticism about U.S.," *Washington Post and Times Herald,* March 4, 1960, p. A1. American skeptics considered the Cuban Revolution a vehicle for the Soviet Union to make the United States intervene, in the same way that it had intervened to smash a popular uprising in Hungary. See, for instance, Marquis Childs, "A Greek Tragedy Unfolds in Cuba," *Washington Post and Times Herald,* March 18, 1960, p. A14. However, Childs said that intervention would be disastrous, and would further the strategy to eventually take over Brazil, which is huge compared to tiny Cuba. He noted that some

"professional anti–Communists" had been "playing" with the worst "corruptionists and butchers" of the Batista regime, and said the Eisenhower administration needed to proceed with caution.

15. According to Shetterly, one of the conditions of reproachment was that Castro execute William Morgan. *The Americano,* pp. 280–281.

16. Szulc, *Fidel: A Critical Portrait,* pp. 169, 175–181; Bourne, *Fidel: A Biography,* p. 46. Castro's trip was paid for by Perón. Thomas, *Cuba: Or, the Pursuit of Freedom,* p. 814.

17. Rabe, *Eisenhower and Latin America,* pp. 19–20. Perón's "third ideological position, *justalisimo,* had a number of similar policies later expressed in 'Castroism.'" The United States had also actively opposed Perón's election in 1946. Schoultz, *Beneath the United States,* pp. 321–325.

18. See William J. Jorden, "Foreign Aid: What Is Involved," *New York Times,* February 21, 1960, p. E5.

19. Theodore Draper, *Castroism: Theory and Practice* (New York: Frederick A. Praeger, 1965), p. 142.

20. Milks, "Mikoyan and Castro Sign Soviet Trade Pact," *Washington Post and Times Herald,* February 14, 1960, p. A8.

21. "The News of the Week in Review," *New York Times,* January 10, 1960, p. E1.

22. Ibid.

23. John Prados, *Safe for Democracy: The Secret Wars of the CIA* (Chicago: Ivan Dee, 2006), pp. 344–346.

24. Starting in 1958, the U.S. planned Project Tiger to infiltrate South Vietnamese special forces units into North Vietnam. CIA officers were in close contact with both sides during an attempted coup in 1960. Ibid., pp. 340–341.

25. The Congo would become independent of Belgium in July 1960. For a more complete discussion of CIA activities in the Congo, see Ambrose, *Ike's Spies,* pp. 298–303.

26. "The News of the Week in Review," *New York Times,* February 14, 1960, p. E1.

27. "The News of the Week in Review," *New York Times,* January 31, 1960, p. E1.

28. James Reston, "President Warns Soviet on Berlin," *New York Times,* April 28, 1960, p. 1. See also: "West May Seek to Revive Berlin Plan Soviet Barred," *New York Times,* December 21, 1959, p. 1. The "Western Big Four" agreed it would be better to "phase in" unification of Germany.

29. "The News of the Week in Review," *New York Times,* January 10, 1960, p. E1.

30. Reston, "Cuba's Drift to the Left," *New York Times,* February 19, 1960, p. 6.

31. For example, Belgian rifles shipped on *La Coubre* exploded in Havana Harbor, March 4, 1960, had cost twice as much as the going rate. E. W. Kenworthy, "Heavy Cuban Arms Buying Slashes Foreign Reserves," *New York Times,* March 11, 1960, p. 1.

32. "Fidel Seen Outsmarted on Soviet Sugar Deal," *Washington Post and Times Herald,* March 3, 1960, p. B17. The article cites research by B. W. Dwyer and Company.

33. Rabe also points out that Batista sold a half-million tons of sugar to the Soviets and the 1960 deal was for a million tons. This was about a sixth of the total Cuban sugar production capacity for 1960. This would have left plenty of sugar for the United States market. He says that the U.S. was too focused on the communist issue to deal. *Eisenhower and Latin America,* p. 130. See also Phillips, "Castro Directing Fighting in Cuba," *New York Times,* August 13, 1959, p. 1. The Soviets bought 442,914 tons

from Batista in 1955; 206,361 in 1956; 347,673 in 1957; 182,148 in 1958, and only 170,000 in 1959.

34. "U.S. Acts to Curb Latin Gunrunning," *New York Times*, February 19, 1960, p. 1.

35. See Rabe, *Eisenhower and Latin America*, p. 151, citing a Senate executive session transcript.

36. After the U.S. implemented a trade embargo designed to starve Cuba, it retaliated by expropriating American-owned companies.

37. See López Fresquet, *My Fourteen Months with Castro*.

38. Ibid., pp. 41–56.

39. Rabe, *Eisenhower and Latin America*, p. 77.

40. Schoultz, *Beneath the United States*, pp. 316–326.

41. Rabe, *Eisenhower and Latin America*, pp. 36–38, 85–86, 93–94.

42. *Fidel Castro and the Cuban Revolution: Age, Position, Character, Destiny, Personality and Ambition* (New Brunswick, NJ: Transaction Publishers, 2007), p. 167.

43. Bourne, *Fidel: A Biography*, p. 175.

44. Ibid., p. 165.

45. See Zim, "Straining the Special Relationship: British and U.S. Policies toward the Cuban Revolution, 1959–1961," p. 72. However, Britain had a "special relationship" with the United States and leaned heavily in our favor.

46. Smith, *The Closest of Enemies*, pp. 49–54. Some also note that he had an obsession with historical figures such as Alexander the Great. Coltman, *The Real Fidel Castro*, pp. 9, 220. See Castro and Ramonet, *Fidel Castro: My Life*, p. 40. Although he did not publicly admit it, he also deeply admired Franco. Geyer, *Guerrilla Prince*, p. 332. Geyer says Castro saw himself as the third youngest "conqueror" in history after Alexander and Franco.

47. Arboleya, *The Cuban Counter Revolution*, pp. 31–34. Also see Testimony of Arthur Gardner, Ambassador to Cuba, 1953–1957, before U.S. Senate Subcommittee to Investigate the Administration of the Internal Security Act and Other Internal Security Laws, of the Committee on the Judiciary, May 3, 1960. Second Session, Part 9, August 27, 1960.

48. Wayne Smith, *The Closest of Enemies*, p. 48; Bonsal, *Cuba, Castro and the United States*, pp. 70–77.

49. Wayne Smith, *The Closest of Enemies*, p. 51.

50. Ibid.

51. "Castro Makes a Pitch," *New York Times*, April 15, 1959, p. 38.

52. "Havana to Retain Baseball Berth," Associated Press, April 25, 1959.

53. Tad Szulc, "Castro Foe Caught as Plane Is Downed," *New York Times*, July 26, 1959, p. 1. A photograph of Castro winding up in uniform appeared with the article.

54. Thornley, "Minneapolis Millers, 1959 Junior World Series vs. Havana."

55. Bjarkman, *A History of Cuban Baseball*, p. 409.

56. "Havana Team Shift Called 'Big Mistake,'" *Washington Post and Times Herald*, July 9, 1960, p. A13.

57. The Continental League was a proposed eight-team professional baseball league announced on July 27, 1959, and scheduled to begin play in the 1961 season, designed to compete with major league baseball. After the New York Giants and Brooklyn Dodgers had moved to California, teams were planned for Denver, Houston, Minneapolis–St. Paul, New York City, Toronto, Montreal, Atlanta, Buffalo, and Dallas/Fort Worth. Honolulu, Mexico City and Jersey City, the new home of the Sugar Kings, were considered. Although there were congressional hearings and support from potential investors, by August 1960,

the Continental League was dissolved and soon baseball would expand. See Dick Young, "National League Votes Expansion to 10 Clubs," *Washington Post and Times Herald*, July 19, 1960, p. A15; Joseph M. Sheehan, "Baseball Men from 3 Leagues to Confer Today on Expansion," *New York Times*, August 2, 1960, p. 32.

58. For example, "Rodriguez Homer Gives Leafs 6–4 Win over Cubans," *Kittaning News-Leader*, April 15, 1959, p. 12.

59. Each party received approximately $10 million worth of Desilu stock. Ball accused Arnaz of exhibiting "fits of temper" in front of "everyone." See "Tearful Lucille Ball Divorces Desi Arnaz," *Los Angeles Times*, May 5, 1960, p. B1; "Lucille Ball Wins Divorce from Arnaz," *New York Times*, May 5, 1960, p. 40; "Lucy Divorces 'Jekyll-and-Hyde' Desi," *Washington Post and Times Herald*, May 5, 1960, p. C26.

60. Alan McPherson in *Yankee No!* remarked that actual U.S. policy toward Cuba "oscillated between near paralysis and gunboat diplomacy." p. 38.

61. "Former Backers of Castro Urge Anti-Red Rising," *New York Times*, April 11, 1960, p. 1.

62. In fact, Castro tried to enlist leaders like Nasser and Sukarno to support him in objecting to American threats to Cuba. See, for instance, "Provocations Decried," *New York Times*, May 14, 1960, p. 10.

63. *Underhill v. Hernandez*, 168 U.S. 250 (1897). In an action for wrongful detention in Venezuela, the Court stated: "Every sovereign state is bound to respect the independence of every other sovereign state, and the courts of one country will not sit in judgment on the acts of the government of another, done within its own territory."

64. Dan Koeppel, *Banana*, p. 170. According to Koeppel, two of the boats were named *Barbara* and *Houston*, after George Herbert Walker Bush's wife, Barbara, and his adopted hometown, Houston, Texas.

65. Bonsal, *Cuba, Castro and the United States*, pp. 268–269; Richard E. Welch, Jr., *Response to Revolution*, pp. 36–38.

66. Castro alleged that sufficient funds to pay for the properties were held in United States banks in the name of Batista and his followers. With that money, the government would not have had to issue bonds. Phillips, "Firm on Bonds for Land," *New York Times*, July 28, 1959, p. 2.

67. For example, under an earlier version of repatriation of properties, Hershey had sold its Cuban holdings by 1946.

68. The Inter-American Treaty of Reciprocal Assistance of 1947 was an anti–Soviet pact, and all signatories were to rise to the defense of any country if attacked. Although the Soviets had not attacked, during the Cold War "interference" was close enough. Although all countries were supposed to work together through OAS, the United States did not seek OAS sanction to intervene in Guatemala in 1954. Cuba had tried, without success, to invoke the Rio Treaty when it was threatened by the Dominican Republic in August 1959. In August 1969, however, Cuba walked out on the OAS in San José , Costa Rica, when the OAS condemned intervention "or the threat of intervention" obviously directed toward Cuba and the Soviet Union. Domínguez, *To Make a World Safe for Revolution*, pp. 26–27.

69. Testimony of retired army chief of staff Maxwell Taylor before the Senate Preparedness Subcommittee, cited in *New York Times*, February 5, 1960, p. 1.

70. "News Summary and Index;" *New York Times*, February 5, 1960, p. 29.

71. "Papers Assail U.S.," *New York Times*, May 25, 1960, p. 6.

72. Warren Unna, "Cubans, Dominicans Get $719,000 in U.S. Aid," *Washington Post and Times Herald*, February 26, 1960, p. 12; E. W. Kenworthy, "Senators Accuse Pentagon on Aid," *New York Times*, February 26, 1960, p. 1.

73. Donald H. May, "Cuba Seizures of U.S. Property Are Put in Excess of $1.2 Billion," *Washington Post and Times Herald*, January 16, 1965, p. A11.

74. "Cuba Calls In Foreign Money for Exchange," *Washington Post and Times Herald*, May 7, 1961, p. A12. Although some of the real estate losses were deemed questionable for tax purposes by the Internal Revenue Service, they were eventually approved. Robert T. Metz, "Approved. Taxes May Be Bar to Foreign Deals," *New York Times*, March 5, 1961, p. F1.

75. "G.E. Net Income Fell 29% in 1960," *New York Times*, February 3, 1961, p. 31.

76. Robert T. Metz, "Tax Relief Sought by Mining Industry for Expropriation," *New York Times*, February 18, 1962, p. F1.

77. Edward Hudson, "Air and Sea Links to Cuba Decrease," *New York Times*, November 12, 1960, p. 42.

78. See Jean White, "U.S. Experts Baffled by Hijacking Problem," *Washington Post and Times Herald*, February 6, 1969, p. A4. Although Cuban officials returned the hijackers at first, after the Cuban Missile Crisis they no longer did.

79. "Half of 7,000 U.S. Residents Thought to Have Left as Departures Continue," *New York Times*, July 10, 1960, p. 5.

80. Ibid. However, the Presbyterians might have been the exception. See Corse, "Presbyterians in the Revolution," in *Cuban Studies 31*, pp. 11–13.

81. "Cuba Nationalizes Yule; Santa Claus Is Banned," *New York Times*, October 8, 1959, p. 17.

82. "Don Feliciano, a Native, Replaces Santa in Cuba," *New York Times*, December 21, 1959, p. 9.

83. See Phillips, "Cubans Arrest Ten in 'Invasion' Tension," *New York Times*, January 9, 1961, p. 1.

84. Ibid.

85. See Pérez, *On Becoming Cuban*, pp. 484–486.

86. William C. Baggs, "The Other Miami — City of Intrigue," *New York Times*, March 13, 1960, p. SM25. By the mid 1970s, the sabotage and terror of Havana would be transplanted to Miami, when members of anti–Castro groups under investigation by the U.S. government bombed the Miami office of the FBI, the Dade County State's Attorney's Office, the Miami-Dade Police Department and Miami International Airport. Controversial figures such as Batista ally Rolando Masferrer were gunned down in a period of violence that extended to the 1980s, when accusations were made that the same groups had entered into the illicit drug trade to finance their anti–Castro activities. "Miami Police Widen Investigation into 4 Slayings at Official's Home," *New York Times*, December 17, 1980, p. A26. In April 1974, a small group composed mainly of members of the Cuban Nationalist Movement (CNM), a Falangist-oriented organization, Zero, took credit for the murder of exile leader José Elias de la Torriente and Masferrer, who had helped fund Alpha 66, another prominent anti–Castro paramilitary organization. From 1974 to 1976, 10 prominent Miami Cubans were murdered and 200 bombings occurred, all reportedly due to warfare among exile groups. "Legacy of Terror," *New York Times*, July 16, 1978, p. SM8. In 1980 a Cuban employee of the United Nations was assassinated in New York by an anti–Castro group called Omega 7, which had been named by the FBI as the most dangerous terrorist organization in the United States. Arnold H. Lubasch, "Judge Sentences Omega 7 Leader to Life in Prison," *New York Times*, November 10, 1984. p. 1. "[Juan] Arocena organized Omega 7 on Sept. 11, 1974, for the purpose of carrying out terrorist murders and bombings exclusively within the United States," the prosecutors said in a sentencing memorandum. The group was also charged with 14 bombings in New York. In Antonio Prohías' *Mad Magazine's* "Spy vs. Spy" cartoon, the intrigue and violence parallels *Spy vs. Spy*, life imitated art as readers could not tell one character from another. See *Spy Vs Spy Complete Casebook* (New York: Watson-Guptill, 2001). Prohías was born in Cienfuegos, Cuba, in 1921, and passed away in Miami in 1998.

87. Tad Szulc, "U.S. Investigating Cubans in Florida," *New York Times*, April 27, 1960, p. 11.

88. "Exile Leader Accuses President of Breaking Vow to Invade Cuba," *New York Times*, April 16, 1963, p. 1.

89. See de los Angeles Torres, *In the Land of Mirrors*, pp. 100–102.

90. Seventy-nine thousand people passed through Key West in 1960. Bean, et al., *The Hispanic Population of the United States*, p. 26.

91. "Cuba's Refugees," *New York Times*, January 28, 1962, p. 140.

92. Ibid.

93. Number 17 on the Billboard Hot 100 for nine weeks in the period April–June 1963.

94. Corse, "Presbyterians in the Revolution," in *Cuban Studies 31*, p. 2.

95. Ibid., pp. 14–15.

96. Sam Pope Brewer, "Exiles Say Military Resistance to Castro Is Growing Inside Cuba," *New York Times*, January 14, 1961, p. 1.

97. "Cuban Exiles in Miami Mark Tradition of Miracles," *New York Times*, September 10, 1975, p. 34.

98. See the village website, http://www.oyotunji-africanvillage.org/?id=1.

99. Followers observe Santa Barbara as Chango, although Santa Barbara was decanonized by the Catholic Church.

100. "Tourist Barren Cuba Sours 'Sugar King,'" *Washington Post and Times Herald*, August 8, 1960, p. B6.

101. Bean, et al., *The Hispanic Population of the United States*, p. 27. Bean et al. do not accept this assessment but merely report it, citing several other studies.

102. "Senators Subdue Athletics, 8–3, with Help from a Triple Play," *New York Times*, July 24, 1960, p. S3.

103. Bjarkman, *A History of Cuban Baseball*, pp. 25–38. Bjarkman calls Dihigo baseball's least known Hall of Famer, a "versatile Cuban pitcher-infielder-outfielder who stands head and shoulders above his Latin countrymen." González does not agree. Dihigo played for the Cuban Stars (1923–1927), Homestead Grays (1928), Philadelphia Hilldales (1929, 1931), Stars of Cuba (1930), Baltimore Black Sox (1931), and New York Cubans (1935–1936, 1945) in the black major leagues. He also played in Cuba (1922–1947), Venezuela (1933) and Mexico (1937–1940, 1944). He is also in the Cuban, Mexican and Venezuelan halls of fame.

104. See Milton H. Jamail, *Full Count: Inside Cuban Baseball* (Carbondale: Southern Illinois University Press, 2000), p. 15, and Bruce Brown, "Scouting 'Pelota Revolucionaria': Cuban Baseball," *Atlantic Monthly*, July 1984. See also Martin Dihigo, "Desde El Grand Stand," *Hoy*, February 6, 1950; Alfredo Santana Alonso, *El Inmortal Del Béisbol* (Havana: Instituto Cubano Del Libro, 1998).

105. See "Cuban Baseball Has Own Style," *Washington Post and Times Herald*, January 30, 1966, p. C3.

106. Richard Welch, Jr., says the idea that Castro was a communist is "a lie." *Response to Revolution*, p. 10. Even many of Castro's most ardent enemies agreed. Rafael Díaz Balart, formerly Castro's best friend and brother-in-law and later head of White Rose, an anti–Castro underground organization, was quoted as saying, "Fidel is not a communist. Fidel is simply for himself. During his student days, he admired Mussolini and quoted Hitler. If he had gained power twenty years earlier, he would have worn a swastika. Two centuries ago, he would have crowned himself emperor." Quoted in Encinosa, *Unvanquished*, p. 6. Moreover, Soviet premier Nikita Khrushchev told President John F. Kennedy in about 1962, "Castro is no Communist, but you are turning him into one." Quoted in Ben Corbett, *This Is Cuba: An Outlaw Culture Survives* (Cambridge, MA: Westview Press, 2004), p. 174; also quoted in many other places, as, for example in Draper, *Castro's Revolution, Myths and Realities* (New York: Frederick A. Praeger, 1962): "[T]hose who insist that Castro has led a Communist revolution from the start have never thought through the implications of their position." p. 75. Van Gosse points out that Communists in the United States considered Castro to be a middle-class intellectual without benefit of the "base" of communist support, the working class. *Where the Boys Are: Cuba, Cold War America and the Making of the New Left* (London: Verso, 1993), pp. 124–125.

107. Thomas, "Cuba: the United States and Batista, 1952–58," p. 172; Paterson, *Contesting Castro*, pp. 120, 184–186. Batista made this allegation, as did some U.S. ambassadors, but it was never proven. Another theme, since disproved over time, was that Castro was not originally a communist but either a dupe or a "captive" to the communists. There is some evidence that Castro's expenses for the 1948 Bogota Conference were paid by the communists, and when he was arrested by the Mexican police in 1956, he was reported to be a member of the Communist Party in an article in *Bohemia*, a Cuban news magazine. However, this evidence is questionable, and there is also more evidence to show that the communists considered Castro to be a "Putschist." There is undisputable evidence that they rejected his leadership until late 1958. See, for instance, Draper, *Castroism: Theory and Practice*, pp. 27–29. The *Bohemia* article was written by Luis Dam and published July 8, 1956, p. 87.

108. See Enrique Encinosa, *Unvanquished*, p. 6.

109. See Leslie Dewart, *Christianity and Revolution: The Lesson of Cuba* (New York: Herder and Herder, 1963), p. 24.

110. In Theodore Draper's view the communists and Castro "walked toward each other, each with his eyes open, each filling a need in the other." Draper, *Castro's Revolution: Myths and Realities*, p. 105. This is seconded by many other historians. Draper notes that there are two stages. In the first the communists became allied with Castro in late 1958. In the second, there was a fusion, probably beginning in late 1959. See Draper, *Castroism: Theory and Practice*, pp. 34–40. There is a minority opinion that Castro had a shadow government as early as April 1959, as expressed by Tad Szulc and Carlos Alberto Montaner, but only flimsy evidence has been produced.

111. Gonzalez, *The Pride of Havana*, p. 220.

112. "'Down with Batista!' Shout 15,000 Cubans; Opposition Speakers Cheered in Attacks on Official Candidate," *New York Times*, January 30, 1940, p. 16. Protesters accused Batista of being a lackey for the Soviets, and connected them to Nazi Germany.

113. Batista, *The Cuban Republic*, pp. 15–16; Thomas, *The Cuban Revolution*, p. 299. Batista later rationalized that Cuba was at war against Germany and he asked all anti–Nazi parties to join in the fight. *The Cuban Republic*, pp. 15–16.

114. Cited in F. Lennox Campello,"The Cuban Communist Party's Anti-Castro Activities," http://members. tripod.com/~Campello/castro.html (1987).

115. Del Aguila, *Cuba, Dilemmas of a Revolution*, p. 31.

116. "Our triumph would have meant the immediate ascent to power of Orthodoxy [to the views of José Martí], first provisionally, and later by means of general elections." Fidel Castro, 1955, quoted in Robert E. Quirk, *Fidel Castro*, p. 53. Quirk says that at the time Castro was more concerned with winning a position of power for himself than with formulating an ideological position.

117. Del Aguila, Cuba, *Dilemmas of a Revolution*, p. 37.

118. José Luis Llovio-Menéndez. *Insider: My Hidden Life as a Revolutionary in Cuba*. Translated by Edith Grossman. (New York: Bantam Books, 1988), p. 54.

119. As told to Jules Dubois, quoted in Quirk, *Fidel Castro*, p. 189.

120. July 15, 1956; Szulc, *Fidel: A Critical Portrait*, pp. 391–395; Draper, *Castroism: Theory and Practice*, pp. 27–29.

121. Draper, *Castroism: Theory and Practice*, pp. 29–30.

122. Ibid., 30–31; Matthews, *The Cuban Story*, pp. 51–52. The letter is now in the Columbia University library. This letter was written in the wake of the assassination attempt on Batista by students form the University of Havana.

123. Del Aguila, *Cuba, Dilemmas of a Revolution*, p. 37.

124. Dewart, *Christianity and Revolution*, p. 118, citing Carlos Rafael Rodríguez.

125. Castro later maintained that there were over 100,000.

126. Geyer, *Guerrilla Prince*, p. 164.

127. For example, see Thomas, *The Cuban Revolution*, p. 208–209. Sweig, in *Inside the Cuban Revolution*, describes how there was a lack of coordination between the M-7-26 leadership in Havana, particularly Faustino Pérez, head of the underground, and the PSP, pp. 124–131. After the April 1957 general strike failed, and after at least 100 supporters were killed and several hundred arrested, Castro charged that the communists had "sabotaged the strike to promote the downfall of the [26 of July] Movement." Later, Castro was to say in an interview to *Look* that "the Cuban Communists ... have never opposed Batista, for whom they have seemed to feel a closer friendship. " Quoted in Szulc, *Fidel: A Critical Portrait*, p. 488, and F. Lennox Campello, "The Cuban Communist Party's Anti-Castro Activities," http://members.tripod.com/~Campello/castro.html (1987). During that same period, the United States investigated but could never confirm that Castro was a communist. Paterson, *Contesting Castro*, pp. 71–72.

128. Enrique Meneses, *Fidel Castro*, translated by J. Halco Ferguson (New York: Taplinger, 1966), p. 62.; also quoted in Paterson, *Contesting Castro*, p. 120; discussed in Quirk, *Fidel Castro*, pp. 158–161.

129. Del Aguila, *Cuba, Dilemmas of a Revolution*, p. 51.

130. Anderson, *Che Guevara: A Revolutionary Life*, p. 338. By this time Gutiérrez Menoyo's group, SNFE, had split from the group led by Faure Chomón.

131. See Thomas, *Cuba: Or, the Pursuit of Freedom*, p. 1251.

132. Besides Father Sardiñas, who was a comandante of the Rebel Army and later a cabinet member in the Provisional Government, others were Father Francisco Beristaín, Father Antonio Rivas, Father Angel Rivas, Father Lucas Iruretagoyena, Father Cipriano Cabero, Father Juan Ramón O'Farrill, and Father Jorge Bez Chabebe. Another was Father Modesto Amo, priest of Yaguajay, who served in the Máximo Gómez Column, the Communist guerrilla group in the Escambray. Thomas, *The Cuban Revolution*, p. 230; Kirk, *Between God and the Party*, p. 49. In Havana, Father Moisés Arrechea, chaplain of the Colón Cemetery, recruited young Catholics for the Sierra. Also in the capital, Monsignor Eduardo Boza Masvidal and his assistant Father Madrigal hid revolutionaries, as did Father Manuel Rodríguez Rozas. Catholic lay leaders Antonio Fernández, president of the youth wing of Acción Católica, and Enrique Canto, former president of Acción Católica in Santiago, actively opposed Batista. John M. Kirk, *Between God and the Party: Religion and Politics in Revolutionary Cuba* (Tampa: University of South Florida Press, 1989), p. 49. Father Rosario Maxilliano Perez alleged that he was a member of M-7-26 in "Communist Threat to the United States through the Caribbean," U.S. Senate Subcommittee to Investigate the Administration of the Internal Security Act and Other Internal Security Laws, of the Committee on the Judiciary, May 3, 1960. Father Javier Arzuaga, a Basque Franciscan priest, served as chaplain of La Cabana during the executions, but he was not part of the Rebel Army. From the transcript of El Programa Radial Magazine Cubano, a radio show, aired December 17, 2006, San Juan, Puerto Rico. Transcript at www.contactocuba.com/art2037.htm. And *barbudo* priest Father Francisco Guzmán helped draft the unconditional surrender proclamation on January 1, 1959.

133. R. Hart Phillips, "Castro's Newspaper Scores Communists," *New York Times*, May 17, 1959, p. 1. Fidel Castro described the Revolution as "humanist" and opposed to dictators of the right and the left. At the same time, *Hoy*, the Communist daily, praised Castro for pursuing a "neutral" foreign policy.

134. Del Aguila, *Cuba, Dilemmas of a Revolution*, p. 50.

135. Lyman B. Kirkpatrick, Jr., *The Real CIA* (New York: Macmillan, 1968), pp. 168–169. This is substantiated by Llerena in *The Unsuspected Revolution*, pp. 198–204, who notes that despite pressure from Che Guevara and Raúl Castro, who were communists, Fidel Castro's political views had not taken shape and he and Communism had a "marriage of convenience." Peter G. Bourne, psychiatrist/biographer, subjects Fidel Castro to "psychoanalysis," and in essence finds a narcissistic personality moved by circumstances to choose Soviet influence as a least restrictive alternative. According to this analysis, the U.S. may not have pushed Cuba into the Soviet sphere of influence, because Castro had a long-standing hatred and resentment for the United States, but Castro also is a megalomaniac who has trouble separating his and Cuba's identities.

136. Szulc, *Fidel: A Critical Portrait*, p. 469; Anderson, *Che Guevara: A Revolutionary Life*, p. 273.

137. See Anderson, *Che Guevara: A Revolutionary Life*, p. 235. Guevara felt that Pérez, who would eventually become a high-ranking Communist, was bound by his middle-class upbringing.

138. Fursenko and Naftali, *"One Hell of a Gamble,"* p. 11.

139. López Fresquet, *My Fourteen Months with Castro*, p. 152.

140. Eisenhower, *Waging Peace*, p. 533.

141. *Bay of Pigs Declassified*, p. 267; Taylor, *Paramilitary Study Group Report*, pp. 3–4.; Wyden, *The Bay of Pigs: The Untold Story*, pp. 28–29.

142. See Jones, *The Bay of Pigs*, p. 18. Jones notes that as a military commander, Eisenhower was hard nosed and hot tempered. After he returned to civilian life, his image did not reflect his real personality.

143. "Castro Repeats Charge," *New York Times*, January 2, 1961, p. 2.

144. See Jules R. Benjamin, "Interpreting the U.S. Reaction to the Cuban Revolution, 1959–1960," in *Cuban Studies* 19, edited by Carmelo Mesa-Lago (Pittsburgh: University of Pittsburgh Press, 1989), pp. 157–161. Also see Jules R. Benjamin, *The United States and the Origins of the Cuban Revolution* (Princeton, NJ: Princeton University Press, 1990).

145. Escalante, *The Cuba Project: CIA Covert Operations 1959–62*, pp. 22–23. See also FBI file 2–1423–9TH NR 36, which states that as of May 5, 1959, Trujillo was close to acting. The sources listed were: "1) General Manuel Benitez, head of National Police of Cuba from 1940 to 1944 and member of Cuban Legislature from 1948 to 1958; (2) Frank Perez Perez, a source of Miami Office who is aligned with General Benitez and Rolando Masferrer, former Cuban Senator and newspaperman who maintained a private army of hoodlums while Batista was in power and who has been described as a bandit and gangster; (3) I. Irving Davidson, registered agent of Israeli and Nicaraguan Governments who talked with Batista in the Dominican Republic on 4/29/59."

146. Grayston L. Lynch, *Decision for Disaster: Betrayal at the Bay of Pigs* (Dulles, Va.: Brassey's Inc., 1998), pp. 15–16; Kessler, *Inside the CIA*, pp. 35–38. Kessler says that his fact came to light after defections by two highly placed Cuban intelligence agents in 1987–1988. Lynch says that many of the "assets" or contract agents were unqualified and that the anti-Castro organizations were riddled with members of G-2, the Cuban version of the KGB. He also noted that Cubans, in his estimation, are gregarious and by nature cannot keep a secret. p. 15.

147. Thomas, *Cuba: Or, the Pursuit of Freedom*, pp. 725–726; "Troops Guard Batista; Nip Revolt," *Washington Post*, February 4, 1941, p. 1; Arthur E. L. Monroe, "Batista Exiles 4 as Leaders of Revolt Plot," *Washington Post*, February 5, 1941, p. 1. By May 1942, Pedraza had returned to Cuba. "Ousted Staff Chief Back in Cuba," *New York Times*, May 5, 1942, p. 11.

148. Thomas, *Cuba: Or, the Pursuit of Freedom*, p. 746.

149. "Fleeing Batista Aides Force Airline Pilot at Gunpoint to Fly Them to New York," *New York Times*, January 2, 1959, p. 7.

150. "Cubans Ask Arrest of 8 by Dominicans," *New York Times*, February 27, 1959, p. 8.

151. Casey, "A Lesson for the Future, Castro Calls Post-Revolution Cuban Executions," *Washington Post and Times Herald*, April 17, 1959, p. A1.

152. "The World," *New York Times*, April 19, 1959, p. E1.

153. Perez, *Cuba and the United States*, p. 250; Ambrose, *Eisenhower the President*, p. 499; Rabe, *Eisenhower and Latin America*, p. 168; McPherson, *Yankee No!* p. 66; Morley, *Imperial State and Revolution*, p. 95.

154. Richard E. Welch, *Response to Revolution*, p. 192.

155. R. Hart Phillips, "Castro Proposes 'Deal' on Captives," *New York Times*, May 18, 1961, p. 8.

156. Castro also threatened to use the prisoners as forced labor to defend the island against the United States. Ibid.

157. Philip J. Bigger, *Negotiator: The Life and Career of James B. Donovan* (Allentown, Pa.: Lehigh University Press, 2006); "Dr. James B. Donovan, 53, Dies; Lawyer Arranged Spy Exchange," *New York Times*, January 20, 1970, p. 43. Donovan kept negotiating and by 1964 had brought more than 9,700 Cubans and Americans to the United States. In 1960, Donovan was not the only person who could have lessened American losses in Cuba. Mikoyan visited Hemingway at his *finca*. After Heming-

way died, his widow asked if she could help negotiate as she knew Castro. Kennedy asked her whether he had read Katherine Ann Porter's *Ship of Fools*, and told her that she was politically unreliable. Mary Hemingway, *How It Was*, p. 153.

158. "Donovan Inquiry Asked in House," *New York Times*, June 12, 1963, p. 17.

159. Arthur Schlesinger, Jr., *A Thousand Days: John F. Kennedy in the White House* (New York: Houghton Mifflin Harcourt, 2002), pp. 766–767.

160. Tom Wicker, "Kennedy's Speech Stirs Cuba Exiles," *New York Times*, December 31, 1962, p. 3.

Bibliography

"AAA," *New York Times*, March 9, 1952, p. xxi.

Aadland, Florence, and Ted Tomey. *The Big Love*. New York: Lance Books, 1961.

Aarons, George A. "The Lucayans: The People Whom Columbus Discovered in the Bahamas." *Five Hundred Magazine*, April 1990, Vol. 2, No. 1, pp. 6–7.

"Accord Held Far Off," *New York Times*, March 9, 1960, p. 14.

Adams, Taylor. "Overthrowing Revolutions," letter to the Editor. *New York Times*, April 14, 1961, p. 28.

Addie, Robert. "Pascual 'Persuaded' to Forget Winter Ball," *Washington Post*, November 6, 1957, p. A18.

_____. "Lane Ready to Ask for Winter Ball Ban," *Washington Post*, February 23, 1958.

"Aftermath," *Time*, March 15, 1954.

"Aftermath in Cuba," *New York Times*, January 3, 1959, p. 16.

"Aftermath in Cuba," *Washington Post*, January 10, 1959, p. A12.

Agreement between the United States and Cuba for the Lease of Lands for Coaling and Naval Stations. February 23, 1903.

Agrupación Católica Universitaria, *Encuesta de Trabajadores Rurales, 1956–57*, reprinted in Economia y Desarrollo, University of Havana, 1972, pp. 188–122. Also quoted in other sources.

Alexander, Charles. *Ty Cobb*. New York: Oxford University Press, 1984.

Alexander, Robert J. *A History of Organized Labor in Cuba*. Westport, Conn.: Praeger, 2002.

_____. "Castro Seems Really to Be Tackling Cuba's Ills," *Washington Post and Times Herald*, June 21, 1959, p. E1.

_____. "Cuban Election Unlikely Before Mid–1960," *Washington Post and Times Herald*, June 22, 1959, p. A6.

"Alfredo Stroessner, 93, Old-Style Military Dictator of Paraguay," *The Daily Telegraph*, August 17, 2006.

"Alien Labor Bar Urged," *New York Times*, July 15, 1950, p. 17.

Allen, Larry. "Battle in Havana Kills 40; Entry of Rebel Chiefs Put Off," *The Washington Post*, January 2, 1959, p. A1.

_____. "Cuba Continues Executions as Toll Hits 180," *Washington Post and Times Herald*, January 15, 1959, p. A8.

Altman, Ida. *Emigrants and Society: Extremadura and Spanish America in the Sixteenth Century*. Berkeley: University of California Press, 1989.

Alvarez, Manuel A. "A History of Cuban Broadcasting," www.oldradio.com/archives.

Amber, Jane Francis. *Christopher Columbus's Jewish Roots*. Northvale, NJ: Jason Aronson, 1991.

Ambrose, Stephen E. *Eisenhower the President*. New York: Simon and Schuster, 1984.

_____. *Ike's Spies: Eisenhower and the Espionage Establishment*. Jackson: University Press of Mississippi, 1999.

_____. *Nixon: The Triumph of a Politician, 1962–1972*. New York: Simon and Schuster, 1989.

"American *Barbudos* Put an End to Looting," *The Times of Havana*, January 8, 1959, p. 16. "American Businessman Is Given 13 Years as Anti-Castro Agent," *Washington Post*, December 19, 1959, p. A1.

"American Fighter for Castro Is Deprived of U.S. Citizenship," *New York Times*, September 4, 1959, p. 6.

"American in Havana Gets 30-Year Term," *New York Times*, April 16, 1964, p. 9.

Anderson, Jack. "U.S. Weapons Smuggled to Castro," *Washington Post and Times Herald*, April 2, 1960, p. B19.

Anderson, John Lee. *Che Guevara: A Revolutionary Life*. New York: Grove Press, 1997.

"Anti-Castro Planes 'Raid' Cuba Capital," *Washington Post*, October 22, 1959, p. A1.

"Anti-Castro Plot Laid to Chicagoan," *New York Times*, February 3, 1959, p. 1.

"Anti-Castro Rebels Seized," *New York Times*, June 6, 1959, p. 6.

"Anti-Falangist Talk in Cuba Angers Spain," *New York Times*, December 26, 1940, p. 13.

"Anti-Red Labor Leader in Cuba Faces Ouster," *Washington Post*, April 22, 1960, p. A4.

"Apology Seen as Cuban 'Victory,'" *New York Times*, February 21, 1960, p. 3.

"Appeals Court Bars Review for Molina," *New York Times*, May 1, 1964, p. 10.

Arboleya, Jesús. *The Cuban Counter Revolution*. Athens, OH: Center for International Studies, 2000.

"Are We Training Cuban Guerrillas?" *The Nation*, November 19, 1960, pp. 378–379.

Argote Freyre, Frank. *Fulgencio Batista: From Revolutionary to Strongman*. New Brunswick, NJ: Rutgers University Press, 2006.

"Army Is Alerted in Cuban Unrest," *New York Times*, August 10, 1959, p. 9.

"Army Tightens Grip on Cuban Province," *Washington Post*, January 3, 1932, p. M3.

Arrington, Vanessa. "A Life of Close Calls for Cuban Leader," Associated Press, August 3, 2006.

Arroyo, Anita. "Three Kings," *Diario de la Marina*, January 8, 1959.

Arteaga y Betancourt, Manuel. Obituary. *Time*, March 29, 1963.

Artime Buesa, Manuel. *Idearios: Puntos Basicos*. February 1 & 13, 1960.

_____. *Traición! Gritan 20,000 Tumbas Cubanas*. Mexico City: Editorial Jus, 1960.

"Asks for New Policy," *Washington Post*, December 17, 1914, p. 11.

"Asks Senate Try Batista," *New York Times*, December 13, 1943, p. 13.

Associated Press. "Boston Braces after Bomb Incident," April 25, 1959.

_____. "Boston Mobilizes to Protect Castro," April 24, 1959.

_____. "Castro Likes Texas," April 28, 1959.

_____. "Castro Turning U.S. Enemies into Friends," April 26, 1959.

_____. "Havana to Retain Baseball Berth," April 25, 1959.

_____. "Ike tells Russia to 'Live' Peace Hopes," January 2, 1959.

_____. "Three American Writers Seized," January 2, 1959.

"Astounding Intelligence," *New York Times*, March 30, 1861, p. 1.

"Attack Fear Activates Cuba Force," *Washington Post*, November 9, 1960, p. A8.

"Attacks upon U.S. by Cubans Cease," *New York Times*, January 29, 1960, p. 5.

Auerbach, George. "Sugar Prices off on Shift in Cuba," *New York Times*, February 8, 1959, p. F1.

_____. "Cuba's Sugar Problem," *New York Times*, April 8, 1959, p. 5.

_____. "Raw Sugar Price Climbing Sharply," *New York Times*, May 10, 1959, p. F1.

_____. "Forecast Is Sour for World Sugar," *New York Times*, July 19, 1959, p. F1.

Austin, O. P. *Commercial Cuba in 1905*. Washington, DC: Bureau of Statistics. Department of Commerce and Labor, 1905.

Auténtico Party website. http://www.autentico.org/oa09253.php.

Ayorinde, Christine. *Afro-Cuban Religiosity, Revolution, and National Identity*. Gainesville: University Press of Florida, 2005.

Baggs, William C. "The Other Miami: City of Intrigue," *New York Times*, March 13, 1960, p. SM25.

Bak, Richard. *Ty Cobb: His Tumultuous Life and Times*. Dallas, TX: Taylor, 1994.

Baker, Robert E. "Britons Criticize Ike on Cuba, Laos," *Washington Post and Times Herald*, January 6, 1961, p. A14.

Baker, Russell. "Batista Is in Peril, U.S. Aide Reports," *New York Times*, January 1, 1959, p. 1.

"Banana Pants, Rainbow Shoes Latest Florida Fads for Males," *Washington Post*, November 20, 1951, p. B4.

Bardach, Ann Louise. *Cuba Confidential: Love and Vengeance in Miami and Havana*. New York: Random House, 2003.

_____. "Our Man's in Miami: Patriot or Terrorist?" *Washington Post*, April 17, 2005, p. B3.

Bardach, Ann Louise, and Larry Rohter. "A Bomber's Tale: Taking Aim at Castro; Key Cuba Foe Claims Exiles' Backing." *New York Times,* July 12, 1998, sec. 1, p. 1.

Bart, Peter B. "Flow of Nickel from Cuba Halts," *New York Times*, December 16, 1959, p. 63.

Bartholomew, Frank H. "Widespread Caribbean War Is Seen Up to Castro," *Washington Post and Times Herald*, March 10, 1959, p. A6.

Baseball Hall of Fame website, http://www.baseballhallof-fame.org.

"Baseball Men to Quit Havana," *New York Times*, October 13, 1959, p. 49.

"Baseball Players and the Antitrust Laws," *Columbia Law Review*, pp. 242–258 (1953).

Batista, Fulgencio. *Cuba Betrayed*. New York: Vantage Press, 1962.

_____. *The Growth and Decline of the Cuban Republic*. New York: Devin-Adair, 1964.

Batista, Ruben. "Young Batista Tells Story of Family Fleeing," Associated Press, January 1, 1959.

"Batista Claimed Credit for Reform," *New York Times*, March 11, 1952, p. 13.

"Batista Decrees Cubans May Kill Strike Inciters," *New York Times*, April 4, 1958, p. 1.

"Batista Denounces 'Barbarism' in Cuba," *New York Times*, January 16, 1959, p. 3.

"Batista Gives Prío One-Way Pass to Mexico," *Washington Post*, March 13, 1952, p. 6.

"Batista Is Accused of Having Red Aides," *New York Times*, August 28, 1940, p. 4.

"Batista Police Attack Cuban Bar Association Protesters," *New York Times*, August 1, 1957, p. 8.

"Batista Predicts Castro's Fall," *New York Times*, May 12, 1959, p. 4.

"Batista Recounts Defection of Aides," *New York Times*, January 22, 1959, p. 7.

"Batista Seeking Absolute Power," *New York Times*, December 8, 1958, p. 1.

"Batista's Escape to U.S. Prevented," *New York Times*, July 18, 1959, p. 3.

"Batista Sons Fly Here from Cuba," *New York Times*, December 31, 1958, p. 1.

Battles, Ford Lewis. *Analysis of the Institutes of the Christian Religion of John Calvin*. Phillipsburg, NJ: P & R Publishing, 2001.

Beale, Calvin. "American Triracial Isolates," *Eugenics Quarterly*, December 1957.

Bean, Frank D., and Marta Tienda, National Committee for Research on the 1980 Census. *The Hispanic Population of the United States*. New York: Russell Sage Foundation, 1987.

Beevor, Anthony. *The Battle for Spain: The Spanish Civil War 1936–1939*. New York: Penguin Books, 2001.

Beezley, William H., and Judith Ewell, eds. *The Human Tradition in Latin America: The Twentieth Century*. Wilmington, DE: Scholarly Resources, 1987, pp. 231–244.

Belair, Felix, Jr. "Castro Defended by Muñoz Marín," *New York Times*, January 20, 1959, p. 10.

_____. "Eisenhower Hails Puerto Rico Gains as He Begins Tour," *New York Times*, February 23, 1960, p. 1.

_____. "President Asserts Secrecy of Soviet Justifies Spying," *New York Times*, May 12, 1960, p. 1.

_____. "President Is Firm," *New York Times*, July 10, 1960, p. 1.

Bellegarde-Smith, Patrick. *Fragments of Bone: Neo-African Religions in a New World*. Urbana: University of Illinois Press, 2005.

"Belt-Tightening in Cuba," *New York Times*, September 26, 1959, p. 22.

Benjamin, Jules R. "Interpreting the U.S. Reaction to the Cuban Revolution, 1959–1960." In *Cuban Studies 31*, Lisandro Pérez, and Uva de Aragon, eds. Pittsburgh: Center for Latin American Studies, University of Pittsburgh Press, 1980.

_____. *The United States and the Origins of the Cuban Revolution*. Princeton, NJ: Princeton University Press, 1990.

Benjamin, Philip. "Castro Departs to Joy of Police," *New York Times*, April 26, 1959, p. 3.

_____. "Leader Tells of Hopes for Better Cuba," *New York Times*, April 22, 1959, p. 1.

_____. "Police Increase Guard on Castro in Fear of Plot," *New York Times*, April 24, 1959, p. 1.

Bergman, Jerry. "Why President Eisenhower Hid His Jehovah's Witness Upbringing," *JW Research Journal* 6, no. 2 (July–December 1999).

Berrellez, Robert. "Cuba Places All Available Arms, Hopes for Changes by Kennedy," *Washington Post and Times Herald*, January 6, 1961, p. A9.

Besser, Milton. "Reds Press for Speedy U.N. Action," *Washington Post and Times Herald*, April 19, 1961, p. A1.

_____. "U.S. Intensifies Plot, Cuba Charges in U.N.," *Washington Post and Times Herald*, March 16, 1961, p. D11.

"Best Seat in the House," *Time*, October 14, 1957.

Bethell, Leslie. *Cuba: A Short History*. London: Cambridge University Press, 1993.

Betto, Frei. *Fidel and Religion: Castro Talks on Revolution and Religion with Frei Bretto*. New York: Simon and Schuster, 1987.

Beutke, Allyson A. *Behind Closed Doors: The Dark Legacy of the Johns Committee*. Documentary film, 1999. http://www.behindcloseddoorsfilm.com/index2.htm.

Bigart, Homer. "Dominican Rebels Recruit Puerto Rican Troops Here," *New York Times*, August 9, 1959, p. 1.

_____. "Rebel Chief Offers Batista Plan to End Cuban Revolt," *New York Times*, February 26, 1958, p. 1.

Bigger, Philip J. *Negotiator: The Life and Career of James B. Donovan*. Allentown, PA: Lehigh University Press, 2006.

Billi, John. "Executions in Cuba Protested," letter to the Editor. *New York Times*, January 13, 1959, p. 46.

Binder, David. "Cuban Exile Admits Bombing an Airliner Killing 73 Aboard," *New York Times*, October 19, 1976, p. 2.

Bissell, Richard, Jr. *Reflections of a Cold Warrior: From Yalta to the Bay of Pigs*. New Haven, CT: Yale University Press, 1996.

Bjarkman, Peter C. *A History of Cuban Baseball, 1864–2006*. Jefferson, NC: McFarland, 2007.

Black, Jan Knippers. *Area Handbook for Cuba* 2nd ed. Washington: American University Foreign Area Studies, 1971.

Blair, William. "Herter Charges Castro Insulted U.S. in TV Speech," *New York Times*, January 22, 1960, p. 1.

Blight, James G., and Peter Kornbluth, eds. *Politics of Illusion: The Bay of Pigs Invasion Reexamined*. Boulder, CO: Lynne Reinner Publications, 1999.

Bogenschild, Thomas E. "Dr. Castro's Princeton Visit, April 20–21, 1959," Program in Latin American Studies, http://www.princeton.edu/~plas/publications/Essays/castro.html.

"The Bogota Conference," Editorial, *New York Times*, May 2, 1948, p. 120.

Bonachea, Ramon L., and Marta San Martin. *The Cuban Insurrection 1952–1959*. New Brunswick, NJ: Transaction Books, 1974.

Bonafede, Dom. "Miami Refugees Puzzle Over Why Attack Went Sour," *Washington Post and Times Herald*, April 21, 1961, p. A13.

Bonsal, Philip W. *Cuba, Castro and the United States*. Pittsburgh: University of Pittsburgh Press, 1971.

Bosch, Adriana. "Huber Matos, a Moderate in the Cuban Revolution," *American Experience: Fidel Castro*, Public Broadcasting System, December 31, 2004. http://www.pbs.org/wgbh/amex/castro/peopleevents/e_moderates.html.

Boswell, Thomas D., and James R. Curtis. *The Cuban-American Experience*. Totowa, NJ: Rowman and Allanheld, 1985.

Bourne, Peter G. *Fidel: A Biography of Fidel Castro*. New York: Dodd, Mead, 1986.

Bowen, Wayne H. *Spain during World War II*. Columbia: University of Missouri Press, 2006.

Bowles, Chester. "Our Cuban Policy Queried," letter to the Editor. *New York Times*, January 25, 1959, p. E10.

Bracker, Milton. "Bogota Frees 12 Communists Held 16 Days; Court Finds No Proof of Complicity in Riot," *New York Times*, April 30, 1948, p. 9.

_____. "3 U.S. Lads Take Cuba Rebel Oath," *New York Times*, March 24, 1957, p. 43.

Bradshaw, Stanford. "Havana Cheers Castro at Rally," *Washington Post and Times Herald*, January 22, 1959, p. A6.

_____. "Keep Out, Cuba Rebel Warns U.S.," *Washington Post*, January 16, 1959, p. A1.

Brady, Kathleen. *Lucille: The Life of Lucille Ball*. New York: Billboard Books, 2001.

Brandon, George. *Santería from Africa to the New World: The Dead Sell Memories*. Bloomington: Indiana University Press, 1993.

"The Break with Cuba," *New York Times*, January 5, 1961, p. 30.

Brewer, Roy. "The Use of Habanera Rhythm in Rockabilly Music," *American Music* 17, pp. 300–317 (1999).

Brewer, Sam Pope. "Castro Foe Says Uprising Is Near," *New York Times*, April 8, 1961, p. 1.

_____. "Castro Foes Call Cubans to Arms; Predict Uprising," *New York Times*, April 9, 1961, p. 1.

_____. "Cuban Aides of U.S. Arrive in Miami," *New York Times*, January 5, 1961, p. 6.

_____. "Cuban Exiles Ask U.S. to Release 13," *New York Times*, June 1, 1961, p. 15.

_____. "Exiles Say Military Resistance to Castro Is Growing inside Cuba," *New York Times*, January 14, 1961, p. 1.

Bridge, Gardner. "U.S. Doubts Peril to Americans but Orders Precautions," *Washington Post*, January 3, 1959, p. A1.

"Britain Grants Recognition," *New York Times*, January 8, 1959, p. 3.

"Britain Praises Rebels," *New York Times*, January 7, 1959, p. 16.

"Britain Scored in Cuba," *New York Times*, September 15, 1959, p. 55.

Bronner, Stephen Eric. *Twentieth Century Political Theory: A Reader*. 2nd ed. Florence, KY: Routledge, 2006.

Brown, Bruce. "Scouting 'Pelota Revolucionaria': Cuban Baseball," *Atlantic Monthly*, July 1984.

Browne, Donald R. "Review of *Radio and Television in Cuba: The Pre-Castro Era*," *Historical Journal of Film, Radio and Television*, Vol. 14, 1994, p. 92.

Buchanan, James. "Havana Teen-Agers Are Agents for Castro's New Secret Police," *Washington Post and Times Herald*, December 29, 1959, p. A9.

_____. "Neighbor Spies Help Jail Castro Critics," *Washington Post and Times Herald*, December 28, 1959, p. A11.

"The Budget: Deficit Up," *Time*, June 16, 1958.

Buhle, Paul. "The Last of the Hollywood Ten," *The Progressive* 65, January 2001, p. 24.

Bulmer-Thomas, V., John H. Coatsworth, and Roberto Cortés Conde. *The Cambridge Economic History of Latin*

America: The Colonial Era and the Short Nineteenth Century. Cambridge, UK: Cambridge University Press, 2006.

Bundy, McGeorge. "Memorandum of Discussion on Cuba, Cabinet Room, January 28, 1961," George Washington University National Security Archives, January 28, 1961.

Bunning, James Paul, and Ralph Bernstein. *The Story of Jim Bunning*. Philadelphia: J.B. Lippincott, 1965.

Burk, Robert F. *Much More Than a Game: Players, Owners, and American Baseball since 1921*. Chapel Hill: University of North Carolina Press, 2002.

"Burke Fears Red Seizure of Cuba Helm," *Washington Post*, July 14, 1959, p. A4.

Butler, Edward F. *Spain's Involvement in the American Revolutionary War*, http://www.sar.org/mxssar/spinvo-1.htm.

"The Butler Expedition; The Troops on Board the *Constitution* to Disembark and Go into Camp," *New York Times*, January 11, 1862, p. 8.

Cabrera, Lydia. *El Monte*. Miami: Ediciónes Universal, 1982. Originally published in Havana, 1954.

Cabrera Infante, Guillermo. *Mea Cuba*. New York: Farrar, Straus and Giroux, 1993.

Caldwell, Robert G. *The Lopez Expeditions to Cuba, 1848–1851*. Princeton, NJ: Princeton University Press, 1915.

Campbell, Joseph. *The Hero with a Thousand Faces*. Princeton, NJ: Princeton University Press, 1968.

Campello, F. Lennox. "The Cuban Communist Party's Anti–Castro Activities," (1987), http://members.tripod.com/~Campello/castro.html.

Campello, Lenny. "The First Black in Baseball." (2004), http://blogcritics.org/archives/2004/08/25/122255.php.

Campion, James. "Castro, Baseball, and the Great Divide," *Aquarian Weekly* (April 26, 2000), http://www.jamescampion.com/chekcuba.html.

Cancio Isla, Wilfredo. "Manuel M. Fraginals, Cuban Scholar," *Miami Herald*, May 11, 2001.

"Candidate & Bishops," *Time*, April 27, 1959.

Canizares, Raúl. *Cuban Santería: Walking with the Night*. Rochester, VT: Dorchester Books, 1999.

"Cardinal Says Cuba Took Church Funds," *New York Times*, November 23, 1959, p. 12.

"Caribbean Bloc Urged by Nixon," *New York Times*, March 5, 1955, p. 1.

Carr, Barry. "Mill Occupations and Soviets: The Mobilisation of Sugar Workers in Cuba 1917–1933," *Journal of Latin American Studies*, February 1996, p. 129.

Carr, Milton. "Cuba Frees American in Ship Blast," *Washington Post and Times Herald*, March 7, 1960, p. A1.

Carroll, Wallace. "President Is Firm," *New York Times*, April 19, 1961, p. 1.

Casey, Phil. "Castro Promises Cuba Will Honor Agreements," *Washington Post and Times Herald*, April 20, 1959, p. A1.

_____. "Castro Says Cuba Will 'Legally' Expropriate Land," *Washington Post and Times Herald*, April 21, 1959, p. A7.

_____. "A Lesson for the Future, Castro Calls Post-Revolution Cuban Executions," *Washington Post and Times Herald*, April 17, 1959, p. A1.

Castañeda, Jorge G. *Campañero: The Life and Death of Che Guevara*. Translated by Marina Castañeda. New York: Vintage Books, 1998.

Castro, Fidel. Letter, *Bohemia Magazine,* July 15, 1956.

Castro, Fidel. Speech archives. Several sources include University of Texas Castro Speech Archive, http://lanic.

utexas.edu/project/castro; National Security Archive, http://www.gwu.edu/~nsarchiv/bayofpigs/chron.html.

Castro, Fidel, with Arturo Alape, "Fidel Castro Reveals Role in 9 April 1948 Colombian Uprising," *El Siglo*, April 11, 1982, pp. 6–7 English translation available at http://lanic.utexas.edu/la/cb/cuba/castro/1982/19820411.

Castro, Fidel, with Ignacio Ramonet. *Fidel Castro: My Life*. Translated by Andrew Hurley. New York: Scribner, 2007.

"Castro Accuses Americans," *New York Times*, February 19, 1960, p. 6.

"Castro Aide Asks Asylum," *New York Times*, January 28, 1961, p. 2.

"Castro Aide Linked to Nicaraguan Raid," *New York Times*, July 28, 1959, p. 2.

"Castro Aides Halt and Search Autos," *New York Times*, February 28, 1959.

"Castro Asks Move to Curb Dictators," *New York Times*, January 25, 1959, p. 12.

"Castro Assails Acquittals," *New York Times*, March 4, 1959, p. 11.

"Castro at Floodtide," *Washington Post*, January 3, 1959, p. A6.

"Castro Backers Win in Cuba Labor Vote," *New York Times*, November 10, 1959, p. 3.

"Castro Begins Job As Premier," *Washington Post*, February 17, 1959, p. A6.

"Castro Bitter in Comment," *New York Times*, February 20, 1960, p. 4.

"Castro Blames U.S. for Raids," *Washington Post*, October 27, 1959, p. A4.

"Castro Blasts Chaumont; Militia Giving Up Arms," *The Times of Havana*, January 16, 1959, p. 1.

"Castro Brands Foreign Ministers Parley as Farce, Criticizes Herter," *Washington Post*, August 15, 1959, p. A1.

"Castro Broadcast Assails U.S. Again," *New York Times*, November 13, 1959, p. 9.

"Castro Calls Nixon Speech 'Insolent,'" *Washington Post*, January 19, 1960, p. A5.

"Castro Charges Dubois Leads Anti-Cuba Drive," *Washington Post*, September 30, 1959, p. A8.

"Castro Charges Foes Openly Buy U.S. Arms," *Washington Post*, March 7, 1959, p. A5.

"Castro Condemns Blows at Cubans," *New York Times*, June 7, 1959, p. 1.

"Castro Denies Executions without Trials," *Washington Post*, January 12, 1959, p. A8.

"Castro Denies Unrest in Caribbean," *Washington Post*, July 28, 1959, p. A8.

"Castro Foes Lose Holdings in Cuba," *New York Times*, May 14, 1959, p. 10.

"Castro Forms New Church," *Washington Post*, January 27, 1967, p. B5.

"Castro Gets Cuban Reins As Premier," *Washington Post*, February 14, 1959, p. A1.

"Castro Gives Gambling Go-Ahead on Tight Rein," *New York Times*, January 14, 1959, p. 4.

"Castro Gracious in New Year Role," *New York Times*, January 2, 1960, p. 3.

"Castro Had Spy at Embassy," *Washington Post*, January 3, 1959, p. A3.

"Castro Hails Newsmen," *New York Times*, April 19, 1959, p. 4.

"Castro in Bid to Nasser," *New York Times*, October 18, 1959, p. 1.

"Castro Is Accused of Stifling Press," *New York Times*, January 24, 1960, p. 9.

"Castro Justifies Mass Killings," United Press International, April 26, 1959.

"Castro Links Marching Students to 'Human Wall' Defending Regime," *Chicago Tribune,* November 28, 1959, p. A4.

"Castro Makes a Pitch," *New York Times,* April 15, 1959, p. 38.

"Castro Marks 33d Birthday Leading Fight against Threat in Las Villas," *Washington Post,* August 14, 1959, p. A1.

"Castro Men Seek Peace in Panama," *Washington Post,* April 29, 1959, p. A1.

"Castro Movement Approaches Victory after Many Defeats," *New York Times,* January 2, 1959, p. 6.

"Castro Moves Out of Hotel in Huff, Takes His Party to One in Harlem," *Washington Post,* September 20, 1960, p. A1.

"Castro Offers U.S. 'Respectful' Ties," *New York Times,* January 5, 1959, p. 3.

"Castro, on TV, Predicts Arms Will Be Given Up," *New York Times,* January 10, 1959, p. 2.

"Castro Ordered Jailed in Dominican Republic," *New York Times,* November 26, 1959, p. 2.

"Castro Plans a Court-Martial," *New York Times,* February 26, 1960, p. 6.

"Castro Plans 'Truth Operation,'" *New York Times,* April 16, 1959, p. 6.

"Castro Praised by Hemingway," United Press International, April 26, 1959.

"Castro Reaches Princeton," *New York Times,* April 21, 1959, p. 12.

"Castro Regime Purges 26 Top Air Officers," *Washington Post,* June 19, 1959, p. A6.

"Castro Rejects 'Threats,'" *New York Times,* May 28, 1960, p. 8.

"Castro Repeats Charge," *New York Times,* January 2, 1961, p. 2.

"Castro Returns Home in Plane Borrowed from Soviet Union," *Washington Post,* September 29, 1960, p. A6.

"Castro Rips U.S. in Long TV Talk," *Washington Post,* November 13, 1959, p. A1.

"Castro Said to Regret Trials," *New York Times,* January 25, 1959, p. 12.

"Castro Says Cuba Fired on U.S. Ship," *New York Times,* May 14, 1960, p. 1.

"Castro's Choice," *New York Times,* July 20, 1959, p. A14.

"Castro Scoffs at Story of Red Role in Cuba," *Washington Post,* May 5, 1959, p. A7.

"Castro Seeking U.S. Talks on Cuban Political Issues," *New York Times,* December 11, 1958, p. 1.

"Castro Sees Threat by Foes," *New York Times,* April 11, 1959, p. 6.

"Castro Sets Up Informer System to Find Revolution's Enemies," *Washington Post,* December 22, 1959, p. A8.

"Castro's Ex-aide Jailed in Florida," *New York Times,* November 5, 1959, p. 1.

"Castro's Foes Reported Moving to Invade Cuba," *Washington Post,* April 8, 1961, p. C15.

"Castro's Overthrow Predicted," *New York Times,* March 26, 1960, p. 4.

"Castro's Reply to U.S. Is Near," *Washington Post,* November 13, 1959, p. A9.

"Castro Summons Envoy in Caracas," *New York Times,* November 8, 1959, p. 34.

"Castro Suspends Trials in Kennedy Peace Bid," *Washington Post,* January 21, 1961, p. A13.

"Castro Testifies in Matos Trial," *Washington Post,* December 15, 1959, p. A4.

"Castro Threatens Curbs on Foreign Investment," *Washington Post,* February 25, 1960, p. A4.

"Castro to Act on Verdict Freeing Fliers," *Washington Post,* March 4, 1959, p. A7.

"Castro to Address Cubans Tonight," *Washington Post,* November 12, 1959, p. A9.

"Castro to Advise Cuba from Plane," *New York Times,* April 28, 1959, p. 18.

"Castro to Let Tourists Gamble," *Washington Post,* January 11, 1959, p. A5.

"Castro to Visit U.S. Next Month," *New York Times,* March 4, 1959, p. 1.

"Castro Upbraids Foes of Land Plan," *New York Times,* June 14, 1959, p. 32.

"Castro Urges Revolts in 3 Latin Nations," *Washington Post,* January 25, 1959, p. A7.

"Castro Urges U.S. to Revise Policy," *New York Times,* January 26, 1959, p. 1.

"Castro Vowed Brevity and Spoke 4 1/2 Hours," *New York Times,* September 27, 1960, p. 21.

"Castro Vows He'll Aid Anti-Trujillo Forces," *Long Island Newsday,* April 21, 1959.

"Castro Warns of Counter-Revolutionary Activities," *New York Times,* March 7, 1959, p. 10.

"Castro Welcomes Mikoyan in Cuba," *New York Times,* February 5, 1960, p. 1.

"Castro Worse than Batista, Cuban Envoy Says in Quitting," *Washington Post,* April 8, 1960, p. A7.

The Catholic Encyclopedia. General reference. Charles George Herbermann, ed. New York: R. Appleton, 1907.

Central Intelligence Agency. Foreign and Domestic Influences on the Colombian Communist Party, 1957–1963.

Central Intelligence Agency. Report on Plots to Assassinate Fidel Castro. April 25, 1967; cover memorandum by the Inspector General dated 23 May 1967.

"Central Park Ceremony for Cuban Hero Erupts into Riot over Castro," *New York Times,* January 29, 1960, p. 1.

Cepeda, Rafael. "The Church in Cuba." *Reformed and Presbyterian World,* 27, no. 6 (June 1963), pp. 261–270.

"Chapman in Miami," *New York Times,* March 8, 1960, p. 18.

Cheshire, Herbert W. "Envoy Smith Resigns after Castro Protests," *Washington Post and Times Herald,* January 11, 1959, p. A1.

"Chief Executioner," *Time,* April 13, 1959.

Childs, Marquis. "Cuban Dilemma Threatens U. S.," *Washington Post and Times Herald,* January 6, 1961, p. A18.

_____. "A Greek Tragedy Unfolds in Cuba," *Washington Post and Times Herald,* March 18, 1960, p. A14

_____. "On Sending Arms to Latin America," *Washington Post and Times Herald,* April 24, 1959, p. A18.

Childs, Matt D. *The 1812 Aponte Rebellion in Cuba and the Struggle against Atlantic Slavery.* Envisioning Cuba series. Chapel Hill: University of North Carolina Press, 2006.

"A Church Backs Castro," *New York Times,* August 4, 1959, p. 12.

"The Church in Cuba," LiceoCubao.com, December 17, 2007, http://www.liceocubano.com/Spn/Circular/Edicion_I/Aporte2.asp.

Cirules, Enrique. *The Mafia in Havana.* Melbourne: Ocean Press, 2004.

"City Labor Group Honors Figueres," *New York Times,* May 8, 1959, p. 8.

Clark, Juan. "Religious Repression in Cuba, At the Time of the Pope's Visit to the Island," Cuban Research Institute, Florida International University Archives, January 22, 1998. http://www.fiu.edu/~fcf/clark12298.html.

Clark, Juan M. "The Exodus from Revolutionary Cuba, 1959–1974: A Sociological Analysis." Gainesville, Florida (Ph.D. Dissertation, University of Florida), 1975.

Clark, Robert D. "Castro Return to Duty 'Demanded' by Cabinet," *Washington Post and Times Herald*, July 19, 1959, p. A1.

Clayton, James. "Bomb Scare Disrupts Hearing of Former Castro Air Chief," *Washington Post and Times Herald*, p. A3.

Clune, John James. "A Cuban Convent in the Age of Enlightened Reform: The Observant Franciscan Community of Santa Clara of Havana, 1768–1808," *The Americas* 57, no. 3 (January 2001) pp. 309–327.

Cluster, Dick, and Hernández, Rafael. *The History of Havana*. New York: Palgrave Macmillan, 2008.

Cohen, Richard. "Prisoners of Castro — In Cuba and Here," *Washington Post*, July 26, 1986, p. 1.

Cole, Richard. *Communication in Latin America*. Lanham, MD: Rowman & Littlefield, 1996.

"Colombia Breaks Off Relations with Soviet," *New York Times*, May 4, 1948, p. 1.

Coltman, Leycester. *The Real Fidel Castro*. New Haven, CT: Yale University Press, 2003.

Columbus, Christopher. *Journal of First Voyage to America*. New York: Albert & Charles Boni, 1924.

Committee on Foreign Relations, Review of Foreign Policy, 1958, Part 1, 85th Congress, 2nd Session, February-March, 1958. Washington, DC: U.S. Government Printing Office, 1958.

"Communism in Cuba," *New York Times*, April 1, 1960, p. 32.

"Communist Gives Castro Warning," *New York Times*, May 27, 1959, p. 1.

"Communist Trend in Cuba Is Denied," *New York Times*, May 18, 1959, p. 8.

Como, Perry. "A Hit Is Born: The Story of 'Papa Loves Mambo,'" *Coronet Magazine*, February 1955.

"Congress Called 'Duty Bound' by Celler to Help New League," *New York Times*, July 28, 1959, p. 30.

"Congress Concerned," *New York Times*, January 12, 1959, p. 8.

"Consul on Probation," *New York Times*, December 31, 1959, p. 8.

"Contractors Must Report," *New York Times*, July 9, 1959, p. 8.

Conway, Christopher. "The Limits of Analogy: José Martí and the Haymarket Martyrs," *A Contra Corriente* 2, no. 1 (Fall 2004).

_____. "The Silent Hero," *A Contra Corriente* 4, no. 1 (Fall 2006), pp. 155–162.

Cony, Ed. "A Chat on a Train: Dr. Castro Describes His Plans for Cuba," *Wall Street Journal*, April 22, 1959.

_____. "Lean Days Begin in Castro's Utopia," *Washington Post and Times Herald*, March 31, 1960, p. A20.

Corbett, Ben. *This Is Cuba: An Outlaw Culture Survives*. Cambridge, MA: Westview Press, 2004.

Corse, Theron. "Presbyterians in the Revolution: An American Missionary Church in Cuba, 1959–1970." In *Cuban Studies 31*. Lisandro Pérez, and Uva de Aragon, eds. Pittsburgh: Center for Latin American Studies, University of Pittsburgh Press, 1980.

"Costa Rica Expels Anti-Castro Exiles," *New York Times*, March 5, 1961, p. 32.

Council on Hemispheric Affairs website. http://www.coha.org.

"A Country-by-Country Survey of the Free World–Communist Bloc Trading," *New York Times*, July 7, 1958, p. 7.

Country Profile: Cuba. Washington, DC: Library of Congress. Federal Research Division, 2006.

Cox, Harvey Gallagher. "Fidel and Religion: Thoughts on the Church and Cuba," *The Nation*, May 9, 1987.

Crahan, Margaret R. "Cuba: Religion and Revolutionary Institutionalization," *Journal of Latin American Studies* 17 (1985).

_____. "Salvation through Christ or Marx: Religion in Revolutionary Cuba," *Journal of Interamerican Studies and World Affairs*, February 1979.

Crankshaw, Joe. "Prío Left Memories, Papers; Dead Cuban Leader Had No Property," *Miami Herald*, May 24, 1977.

"Crisis in the Cold War," *New York Times*, May 9, 1960, p. 28.

Critchlow, Donald T. *Enemies of the State: Personal Stories from the Gulag*. Chicago: Ivan R. Dee, 2002.

"Crowd Hails Castro as He Reaches U.S. for an 11-Day Visit," *New York Times*, April 16, 1959, p. 1.

"Crowds Hail Castro on Trip to Havana," *Washington Post*, January 6, 1959, p. A6.

"Cuba Aide Found Dead," *New York Times*, April 15, 1959, p. 16.

Cuba and the Rule of Law. Geneva: International Commission of Jurists, 1962.

"Cuba and U.S. in Arms Pact," *New York Times*, March 8, 1952, p. 4.

"Cuba Arrests 40 in New Anti-Castro Plot," *Washington Post*, September 23, 1959, p. A8.

"Cuba Arrests 1,000 in Smashing a Plot," *New York Times*, August 11, 1959, p. 1.

"Cuba Bars a Role as Invasion Base," *New York Times*, April 22, 1959, p. 14.

"Cuba Begins Taking Sugarcane Lands," *New York Times*, January 15, 1960, p. 4.

"Cuba Breaks Ties with Trujillo Regime, Charges Killing of Defenseless Civilians," *Washington Post*, June 27, 1959, p. A4.

"Cuba Called Communist Beachhead," *Washington Post*, May 4, 1959, p. A5.

"Cuba Calls in Foreign Money for Exchange," *Washington Post*, May 7, 1961, p. A12.

"Cuba Continues Quick Trials," *Washington Post*, January 19, 1959, p. A6.

"Cuba Denies Planning to End U.S. Base Pact," *Washington Post*, March 29, 1960, p. A5.

"Cuba Denounces U.S. over Failure of Jet Deal," *Washington Post*, December 4, 1959, p. A7.

"Cuba Dominican Consul Guilty," *New York Times*, December 12, 1959, p. 48.

"Cuba Elects Prío as Next President," *New York Times*, June 3, 1948, p. 13.

"Cuba Execution Toll Tops 400," *Washington Post*, March 8, 1959, p. A13.

"Cuba Frees Condemned U.S. Pilot," *Washington Post*, April 13, 1959, p. A1.

"Cuba Frees Embassy Secretary," *Washington Post*, September 17, 1960, p. A4.

"Cuba Gives Safe Conduct to Followers of Batista," *Washington Post*, February 21, 1959, p. A4.

"Cuba Grabs Fleeing Labor Chief," *Washington Post*, November 6, 1960, p. A6.

"Cuba Halts Trials for Easter Week," *New York Times*, March 25, 1959, p. 13.

"Cuba Holds American in Invasion Plot," *Washington Post*, April 22, 1959, p. A9, p. A12.

"Cuba Imposes Curb as Plane Is Seized," *New York Times*, October 4, 1959, p. 65.

"Cuba in Dire Straits," *New York Times*, December 31, 1958, p. 18.

"Cuba 'Intervenes' in 3 American Sugar Mills," *Washington Post*, March 12, 1960, p. A5.

"Cuba in Transition," *New York Times*, January 6, 1959, p. 32.

"Cuba Makes Charge at U.N.," *New York Times*, October 24, 1959, p. 4.

"Cuba Nationalizes Yule; Santa Claus Is Banned," *New York Times*, October 8, 1959, p. 17.

"Cuba Ousts Judges Who Scored Army," *New York Times*, June 13, 1958, p. 3.

"Cuba Ousts 3d Embassy Employee," *Washington Post*, September 24, 1960, p. A6.

"Cuba Paper Labels Ike 'Hypocrite,'" *Washington Post*, December 5, 1959, p. A4.

"Cuba Plans United Fruit Seizure," *Washington Post*, April 8, 1960, p. B10.

"Cuba Plans Works to Build Up Oriente," *New York Times*, March 12, 1959, p. 5.

"Cuba Police Arrest 13 in 2 Plots," *Washington Post*, December 25, 1959, p. A6.

"Cuba Political Tension High after Shooting," *Washington Post*, April 23, 1947, p. 12.

"Cuba Promoting '3d Bloc' Parley," *New York Times*, January 3, 1960, p. 7.

"Cuba Rebels Don't Want Mediation, Fidel Castro's Agent Here Declares," *Washington Post*, January 1, 1959, p. A4.

"Cuba Rejects Herter's Protest," *Washington Post*, March 9, 1960, p. A1.

"Cuba Rejects Plea to Free U.S. Reporter," *Washington Post*, December 17, 1959, p. A15.

"Cuba Releases U.S. Teachers," *Washington Post*, December 31, 1958, p. A4.

"Cuba Said to Aid 'Fair Play' Group," *New York Times*, January 11, 1961, p. 10.

"Cuba Said to Aid Nicaragua Reds," *New York Times*, August 23, 1959, p. 33.

"Cuba Seeks Racing," *New York Times*, December 13, 1959, p. S5.

"Cuba Seeks to Buy Ships," *New York Times*, June 26, 1959, p. 6.

"Cuba Seizes Man Who Gave Up U.S.," *New York Times*, October 22, 1960, p. 4.

"Cuba Slashes Rents," *New York Times*, March 7, 1959, p. 2.

"Cuba Stays Deportation of Hoodlum," *Washington Post*, August 22, 1959, p. A3.

"Cuba Takes Over Phone Company," *New York Times*, March 5, 1959, p. 6.

"Cuba Tells U.S. to Reconsider Policy toward Castro Regime," *Washington Post*, November 14, 1959, p. A4.

"Cuba: The Archbishop Speaks," *Time*, May 30, 1960.

"Cuba Thwarts Plot to Seize Army Camp," *Washington Post*, May 18, 1946, p. 3.

"Cuba to Take Over Large Ranches Now," *New York Times*, June 24, 1959, p. 63.

"Cuba to Resume Summary Trials: Three Courts-Martial Will Be Formed in Havana to Handle Batista Men," *New York Times*, January 25, 1959, p. 12.

"Cuba Urged to End Franco Tie," *New York Times*, December 20, 1944, p. 8.

"Cuba Visitor Tells of Gang Suppression," *Washington Post*, January 7, 1959, p. A5.

"Cuba Withdraws Plan for U.S. Aid," *New York Times*, May 8, 1959, p. 1.

"Cuban Asks Asylum; Tells of Spy Ring," *New York Times*, September 27, 1960, p. 21.

"Cuban Baseball Has Own Style," *Washington Post*, January 30, 1966, p. C3.

"Cuban Bond Issue for Land Decreed," *New York Times*, September 27, 1959, p. 22.

"Cuban Candidate Shoots Himself," *New York Times*, August 6, 1951, p. 1.

"Cuban Crisis," *New York Times*, July 19, 1959, p. E1.

"A Cuban Dictator Falls," *New York Times*, January 2, 1959, p. 24.

Cuban Economic Research Project. *A Study on Cuba.* Coral Gables, FL: University of Miami Press, 1965.

"Cuban Elections Two Years Away," *New York Times*, March 1, 1959, p. 11.

"Cuban Envoys Back Regime of Castro," *New York Times*, January 2, 1959, p. 6.

"Cuban Executed after New Trial," *New York Times*, February 19, 1959, p. 9.

"Cuban Exile Seized in Bombing of Ship," *New York Times*, December 17, 1965, p. 29.

"Cuban Exiles Fasting in Jail," *New York Times*, June 15, 1965, p. 12.

"Cuban Exiles Guilty in Ship Conspiracy," *New York Times*, November 16, 1968, p. 29.

"Cuban Exiles in Miami Mark Tradition of Miracles," *New York Times*, September 10, 1975, p. 34.

"Cuban Farmers Given 7150 Acres As Land-Distribution Task Begins," *Washington Post*, March 3, 1959, p. A7.

"Cuban High Schools Get Army Program," *New York Times*, January 7, 1960, p. 10.

"Cuban Immigration to the United States," culturalorientation.net, http://www.cal.org/co/cubans/IMMI.HTM.

"Cuban Invasion Scare Is Traced to 'Trainee' of Guatemalan Camp," *Washington Post*, January 11, 1961, p. A12.

"Cuban Labor Group Moves to Oust Reds," *New York Times*, April 1, 1947.

"Cuban Labor Joins in Attacks on U.S.," *New York Times*, November 19, 1959, p. 21.

"The Cuban Land Reform," *New York Times*, June 10, 1959, p. 36.

"Cuban Law Forces Sale of Idle Land," *New York Times*, March 22, 1959, p. 31.

"Cuban League Recognized by American Pro Baseball," *Christian Science Monitor*, July 11, 1947, p. 13.

"Cuban Mill Is Bombed," *New York Times*, October 11, 1959, p. 28.

"Cuban Party Leader Sentenced," *New York Times*, April 28, 1949, p. 3.

"Cuban Police Say Former Navy Flier Confessed Castro Assassination Plot," *Washington Post*, February 6, 1959, p. A4.

"Cuban Policy Criticized," *New York Times*, April 12, 1961, p. 40. Letters from Raymond D. Higgins and Martin B. Travis.

"Cuban Priest Replies," *New York Times*, December 16, 1959, p. 16.

"Cuban Protests O.A.S. Decision," *New York Times*, July 31, 1959, p. 4.

"Cuban Publisher Refugee in Miami," *New York Times*, January 21, 1960, p. 13.

"Cuban Rebel Chief Slain in Skirmish," *New York Times*, June 28, 1912, p. 5.

"Cuban Rebels Shoot 75 Beside Grave; One Directs Own Execution for TV," *Washington Post*, January 13, 1959, p. A1.

"Cuban Rivals Heed Castro Peace Appeal," *Washington Post*, January 10, 1959, p. A4.

"Cuban Scores U.S. in Rift with Haiti," *New York Times*, September 2, 1959, p. 6.

"Cuban Senate Crisis Results from Brawl; Group of Minority Demands Guarantees," *New York Times*, August 6, 1941, p. 6.

"Cuban Senator Hurt in Duel," *New York Times*, April 19, 1945, p. 3.

"Cuban Senator Scores Regime, Shoots Himself," *Washington Post*, August 7, 1951, p. A9.

"Cuban Senator Slashed in Duel with Colleague," *Washington Post*, October 27, 1946, p. M1.

"Cuban Senators Fight Duel with Sabers," *Washington Post*, July 14, 1947, p. 1.

"Cuban Senators in Duel," *New York Times*, March 28, 1947, p. 5.

"Cuban Signs Rio Pact," *New York Times*, December 10, 1948, p. 13.

"Cuban Slaves Set Free," *New York Times*, June 18, 1886, p. 3.

"Cuban Students Yield Their Arms," *New York Times*, January 11, 1959, p. 33.

"Cuban Terrorist Gets 10 Years for Firing on Vessel in Miami," *New York Times*, December 14, 1968, p. 16.

"Cuban Throng Hails Castro on Return," *New York Times*, May 9, 1959, p. 3.

"Cuban Urges U.N. Bar U.S. 'Invasion,'" *New York Times*, January 1, 1961, p. 15.

"Cuban Vote Count of House in Doubt," *New York Times*, June 3, 1950, p. 5.

"A Cuban Way of Styles," *Life*, May 5, 1958.

"Cuban Workers Submit Demands," *New York Times*, May 3, 1959, p. 42.

"Cubans Accuse U.S. of Propaganda Act," *New York Times*, January 26, 1960, p. 17.

"Cubans Are Pleased by U.S. Sugar Action," *New York Times*, December 20, 1959, p. 18.

"Cubans Arrest Chapman Again, Free Him to Catch Next Plane," *Washington Post*, March 8, 1960, p.A4.

"Cubans Ask Arrest of 8 by Dominicans," *New York Times*, February 27, 1959, p. 8.

"Cubans Call Off Stadium Trials," *New York Times*, January 27, 1959, p. 17.

"Cubans Deny Red Influence," *Washington Post*, May 18, 1959, p. A10.

"Cubans Duel to Draw," *New York Times*, February 18, 1947, p. 16.

"Cuban's Ouster Barred," *New York Times*, March 12, 1960, p. 7.

"Cuban's Testimony Arouses Senators," *New York Times*, July 14, 1959, p. 1.

"Cuba's Agrarian Reform," *New York Times*, May 20, 1959, p. 34.

"Cuba's Air Chief Quits; His Arrest Is Ordered," *Washington Post*, July 1, 1959, p. A6.

"Cuba's Economic Development," *New York Times*, February 27, 1960, p. 18.

"Cuba's Embassy in Haiti Is Closed," *New York Times*, August 30, 1959, p. 13.

"Cuba's Hungry Aided by U.S. Surplus Food," *New York Times*, January 13, 1960, p. 69.

"Cuba's Political Crisis," *New York Times*, June 13, 1959, p. 20.

"Cuba's Premier Resigns; Some in Cabinet May Quit," *New York Times*, March 8, 1952, p. 4.

"Cuba's Refugees," *New York Times*, January 28, 1962, p. 140.

Cunningham, James. "Casino Gambling Nixed: No Dice, Dice Urrutia," *The Times of Havana*, January 8, 1959, p. 1.

Cunningham, James F. "Castro Urges Mobilization to Halt Foreign Invasion: Premier Says Foreign Press behind Move," *The Times of Havana*, March 21, 1959, pp. 1, 3.

"Curbs Posted on Cuban Sugar," *The Wall Street Journal*, July 22, 1957, p. 16.

"Currency Market Shuns Cuban Peso," *New York Times*, February 20, 1959, p. 5.

"A Dangerous Person," *Time*, August 27, 1951.

Daniell, Raymond. "Montreal Greets Castro as a Hero," *New York Times*, April 27, 1959, p. 3.

D'Antonio, Michael. *Hershey: Milton S. Hershey's Extraordinary Life of Wealth, Empire, and Utopian Dreams*. New York: Simon & Schuster, 2006.

"Dawn of Election Year Finds 'Ike' Still Leading the Pack," *Washington Post*, January 2, 1952, p. 9.

"Day Decreed in Cuba," *New York Times*, November 28, 1952, p. 15.

"Death for Two Cubans Upheld in Revolt Plot," *Washington Post*, August 24, 1934, p. 5.

"Death of Cuban Ambassador to U.N. Delays General Assembly Debate," *Washington Post*, March 21, 1961, p. A10.

"Decree Rule for 18 Months," *New York Times*, January 7, 1959, p. 16.

"Defeat for Castro," *Time*, September 5, 1960.

"De Gaulle Cracks Down," *New York Times*, February 7, 1960, p. E1.

De la Cova, Antonio Rafael. "Filibusters and Freemasons: The Sworn Obligation," *Journal of the Early Republic* 17, no. 1 (Spring 1997), pp. 95–120.

_____. *The Moncada Attack*. Columbia: University of South Carolina Press, 2007.

Del Aquila, Juan M. *Cuba:Dilemmas of a Revolution*. 3rd ed. Boulder, CO: Westview Press, 1994.

De Las Casas, Bartolomeo. Ed. Nigel Griffin. *A Short Account of the Destruction of the Indies*. New York: Penguin, 1992. Originally published 1542.

_____. *The Devastation of the Indies*. Baltimore: Johns Hopkins University Press, 1992. Originally published 1542.

De la Torre, Miguel. *Santería: The Beliefs and Rituals of a Growing Religion in America*. Grand Rapids, MI: William B. Eerdmans, 2004.

De La Torre, Miguel A. *La Lucha for Cuba: Religion and Politics on the Streets of Miami*. Berkeley: University of California Press, 2003.

De los Angeles Torres, Maria. *In the Land of Mirrors: Cuban Exile Politics in the United States*. Ann Arbor: University of Michigan Press, 2001.

"Del Pino Is U.S. Citizen," *New York Times*, July 26, 1959, p. 27.

De Onis, Juan. "American Lands Will Meet Today," *New York Times*, April 28, 1959, p. 19.

_____. "Anti-Castro Extremists Tolerated, If Not Encouraged, by Some Latin American Nations," *New York Times*, November 15, 1976, p. 10.

_____. "Anti-Nixon Drive Found Concerted," *New York Times*, May 10, 1958, p. 1.

_____. "Castro Calls on U.S. for More Latin Aid," *New York Times*, May 3, 1959, p. 1.

_____. "Eisenhower Rides through Tear Gas in Uruguay Clash," *New York Times*, March 3, 1960, p. 1.

_____. "Paraguay Police Battle Students," *New York Times*, February 18, 1959, p. 16.

De Palma, Anthony. *The Man Who Invented Fidel: Castro Cuba and Hernert L. Matthews of* The New York Times. New York: Public Affairs Press, 2006.

_____. "Vilma Espin, Rebel and Wife of Raúl Castro, Dies at 77," *New York Times*, June 30, 2007.

Dewart, Leslie. *Christianity and Revolution: The Lesson of Cuba.* New York: Herder and Herder, 1963.

Didion, Joan. *Miami.* New York: Simon and Schuster, 1987.

DiEugenio, James, *Destiny Betrayed: JFK, Cuba, and the Garrison Case.* New York: Sheridan Square Press, 1992.

Dihigo, Martin. "Desde El Grand Stand." *Hoy,* February 6, 1950.

Dinges, John, and Saul Landau. *Assassination on Embassy Row.* London: Writers and Readers, 1981.

"Diplomatic Intervener," *New York Times*, February 20, 1960, p. 12.

Dole, Kenneth. "News of the Churches," *Washington Post and Times Herald*, December 19, 1959, p. B3.

Domínguez, Jorge I. *Cuba: Order and Revolution.* Cambridge, MA: Belknap Press of Harvard University Press, 1978.

Domínguez, Jorge I. *To Make a World Safe for Revolution: Cuba's Foreign Policy.* Cambridge, MA: Harvard University Press, 1989.

Dominguez, Maria Finn, ed. *Cuba in Mind.* New York: Vintage, 2004.

"Don Feliciano, a Native, Replaces Santa in Cuba," *New York Times,* December 21, 1959, p. 9.

"Donovan Inquiry Asked in House," *New York Times*, June 12, 1963, p. 17.

"'Down with Batista!' Shout 15,000 Cubans; Opposition Speakers Cheered in Attacks on Official Candidate," *New York Times,* January 30, 1940, p. 16.

Draper, Theodore. *Abuse of Power.* New York: Viking Press, 1967.

_____. *Castroism: Theory and Practice.* New York: Praeger, 1965.

_____. *Castro's Revolution, Myths and Realities.* New York: Praeger, 1962.

"Dr. Chibas, Cuban Senator, Dies of Wounds Self-Inflicted as He Ended Radio Broadcast," *New York Times,* August 17, 1951, p. 8.

"Drive on Anti-Reds in Cuba 'Disturbs' U.S.," *Washington Post,* April 9, 1960, p. A5.

"Dr. James B. Donovan, 53, Dies; Lawyer Arranged Spy Exchange," *New York Times,* January 20, 1970, p. 43.

"Dr. Paxton Talks of Cuba," *Washington Post,* March 17, 1898, p. 4.

Drury, Allen. "Ex-Aide Calls Castro a Red at Hearing of Senate Unit," *New York Times,* July 15, 1959, p. 1.

Drye, Willie. "Evidence of 16th-Century Spanish Fort in Appalachia?" *National Geographic News,* November 22, 2004.

Dubois, Jules. "Castro Assails Communists for Cuban Labor Difficulties," *Washington Post and Times Herald,* May 23, 1959, p. A4.

_____. "Castro Is Regarded as Red Robin Hood," *Washington Post and Times Herald,* November 22, 1959, p. A11.

_____. "Doomed Cuban Gets Retrial," *Washington Post and Times Herald,* January 28, 1959, p. A7.

_____. *Fidel Castro: Rebel-Liberator or Dictator?* Indianapolis: Bobbs-Merrill, 1959.

_____. "Hate-U.S. Drive Tied to Censorship," *Washington Post and Times Herald,* November 23, 1959, p. A10.

_____. "Hear 1,000 Face Death after Trials: Charge Batista

Got Fortune of 400 Millions," *Chicago Daily Tribune,* January 14, 1959, p. 1.

_____. "Kremlin Makes Havana Base for Drive in Latin America," *Washington Post and Times Herald,* November 26, 1959, p. A8.

_____. "Moscow, Peking Efforts Linked in Latin America," *Washington Post and Times Herald,* November 25, 1959, p. A4.

_____. *Operation America: The Communist Conspiracy in Latin America.* New York: Walker and Company, 1963.

_____. "Red Offensive Gains in Latin America," *Washington Post and Times Herald,* November 24, 1959, p. A7.

_____. "Red Power in Cuba Held Exaggerated," *Washington Post,* May 7, 1959, p. A7.

_____. "3 Invasion Plans Hit Cuban Snags," *Washington Post and Times Herald,* March 29, 1959, p. A5.

_____. "Uncertainty on Cuba's Land Reform Has Investors Shivering on the Brink," *Washington Post and Times Herald,* August 6, 1959, p. A12.

Duffee, Warren. "U.N. Inquiry Asked on Cuba," *Washington Post and Times Herald,* January 16, 1959, p. A4.

Dugan, George. "TV Sponsors Ask for Billy Graham," *New York Times,* March 3, 1955, p. 37.

Dulles, Allen W. *The Craft of Intelligence: America's Legendary Spy Master on the Fundamentals of Intelligence Gathering for a Free World.* Guilford, CT: Lyons, 2006.

Dulles, John Foster. *The Spiritual Legacy of John Foster Dulles.* Philadelphia: Westminster Press, 1960.

_____. *War or Peace.* New York: Macmillan, 1950.

Dunlap, David W. "Raul Roa of Cuba Dies at 75; Foreign Minister for 17 Years," *New York Times,* July 8, 1982, p. B16.

Dunn, Joseph W. "Cuban Disorders Buoy Sugar Price," *New York Times,* August 16, 1959, p. F1.

Durling, Henry. "Gambling Mecca of the New World," *Cabaret Magazine,* December 1956.

Duscha, Julius. "Kennedy Hits Nixon's Cuba Role," *Washington Post and Times Herald,* October 7, 1960, p. A1.

Eckstein, Susan Eva. *Back from the Future: Cuba under Castro.* 2nd ed. New York: Routledge, 2003.

Effrat, Louis. "Kubek's Homecoming Something Milwaukee Fans Will Find Hard to Forget," *New York Times,* October 6, 1957, p. 206.

Egan, Leo. "Kennedy Assails Nixon over Cuba," *New York Times,* October 7, 1960, p. 1.

Eisenhower, Dwight David. Inaugural Address. Washington, DC, January 20, 1953. http://www.eisenhower.archives.gov/speeches/1953_inaugural_address.html.

_____. Presidential Executive Order 10631—Code of Conduct for Members of the Armed Forces of the United States, August 17, 1955.

_____. *Waging Peace.* New York: Doubleday, 1960.

"Eisenhower Bars a Red Cuba, Tells Russians Not to Meddle; Khrushchev Warns of Rockets," *New York Times,* July 10, 1960, p. 1.

"Eisenhower Says U.S. Has Made No Red Charge against Castro," *New York Times,* July 16, 1959, p. 2.

"Eisenhower's Tour," *New York Times,* March 6, 1960, p. E1. "Ex-aide Says Cuba Got 12 Czech MiGs," *New York Times,* February 18, 1960, p. 2.

"Embargo Plan Is Eisenhower's," *Time,* October 14, 1960, p. 13.

"Embassy Aide Is Rebel," *New York Times,* January 3, 1959, p. 2.

Encinosa, Enrique. *Unvanquished: Cuba's Resistance to Fidel Castro.* Los Angeles: Pureplay Press, 2004.

Enders, Eric. "Armando Marsáns," The Baseball Biogra-

phy Project, http://bioproj.sabr.org/bioproj.cfm?a=v&
   v=l&pid=8838&bid=971.
"End Executions, Cuba Paper Asks," *Washington Post*,
   March 20, 1959, p. A4.
"End of the Nye Case," *Time*, April 20, 1959.
English, T. E. *Havana Nocturne: How the Mob Owned
   Cuba and Then Lost It to the Revolution*. New York:
   William Morrow, 2008.
"Epilogue to a Failure," *Time*, July 26, 1963.
Escalante, Fabian. *The Cuba Project: CIA Covert Operations
   1959–62*. New York: Ocean Press, 2004.
_____. *The Secret War: CIA Covert Operations against Cuba,
   1959–62*. New York: Ocean Press, 1995.
Espinosa, Gastón, Virgilio P. Elizondo, and Jesse Miranda,
   eds. *Latino Religions and Civic Activism in the United
   States*. New York: Oxford University Press, 2005.
"Ex-Aide of Castro Seized in Flight," *New York Times*,
   November 6, 1960, p. 24.
"Ex-Allies Seized by Cuban Regime; Plot Laid to ABC,"
   New York Times, October 4, 1933, p. 1.
"Executioner Is Ex-Convict," *New York Times*, March 31,
   1959, p. 3.
"Executions in Cuba Rise to 483 Total," *New York Times*,
   March 20, 1959, p. 8.
"Ex-Hero Gets 20 Years; 2 Other Cubans to Die," *Wash-
   ington Post*, December 16, 1959, p. A4.
"Exile Leader Accuses President of Breaking Vow to Invade
   Cuba," *New York Times*, April 16, 1963, p. 1.
"Ex-Navy Airman Denies Plotting to Kill Castro," *Wash-
   ington Post*, April 3, 1959, p. A4.
"Explosions in Havana," *New York Times*, March 6, 1960,
   p. E10.
"Ex-Senator Johnson Named New League," *New York
   Times*, July 28, 1959, p. 30.
"Ex-Senator Pardoned in Cuba," *New York Times*, June 2,
   1949, p. 16.
Falcoff, Mark. *Cuba the Morning After: Confronting Cas-
   tro's Legacy*. Washington, DC: American Enterprise In-
   stitute, 2003.
Falkenberg, Claudia, and Andrew Solt, eds. *A Really Big
   Show: A Visual History of the Ed Sullivan Show*. Text by
   John Leonard. New York: Viking Studio Books, 1992.
Farber, Samuel. *The Origins of the Cuban Revolution Re-
   considered*. Chapel Hill: University of North Carolina
   Press, 2006.
_____. *Revolution and Reaction in Cuba 1933–1960*. Mid-
   dletown, CT: Wesleyan University Press, 1976.
Faria, Miguel. *Cuba in Revolution: Escape from a Lost Par-
   adise*. New York: Hacienda Publishing, 2002.
Farr, Jory. *Rites of Rhythm: The Music of Cuba*. New York:
   Regan Books, 2003.
"Fastest Gun in Havana," *Time*, March 23, 1959.
FBI files from the FBI Freedom of Information Act Read-
   ing Room, http://foia.fbi.gov:
   Desi Arnaz, http://foia.fbi.gov/foiaindex/arnaz.htm
   Lucille Ball, http://foia.fbi.gov/foiaindex/ball.htm
   Ernest Hemingway, http://foia.fbi.gov/foiaindex/
      ernesthemingway.htm
   Frank Sinatra, http://foia.fbi.gov/foiaindex/sinatra.
      htm
"FBI Links Cuban Exile to 25 Terror Acts," *Boston Globe*,
   December 28, 1983, pg. 1.
"F.B.I. Names Cuban Flier," *New York Times*, October 24,
   1959, p. 4.
Federal Register. Hearings before the Subcommittee on
   Antitrust and Monopoly. Committee on the Judiciary.
   U.S. Senate, 85th Cong., 2nd. Sess. July 1958.
_____. Hearings before the U.S. Senate Subcommittee to
Investigate the Administration of the Internal Security
   Act and Other Internal Security Laws. Committee on
   the Judiciary, 1st Sess., May 3, 1960. Second Session
   Part 9, August 27, 1960.
_____. Hearings of United States House of Representatives
   Select Committee on Assassinations, Anti-Castro Ac-
   tivities and Organizations, Etc. March 1979.
Feeley, Connie. "Peale, President Address FBI Class,"
   Washington Post, November 9, 1957, p. C1.
Fernández, Damian J. *Cuba and the Politics of Passion*.
   Austin: University of Texas Press, 2000.
Ferrer, Ada. *Insurgent Cuba: Race Nation and Revolution,
   1868–1898*. Chapel Hill: University of North Carolina
   Press, 1999.
"Fidel Castro Addressed 1871 Gathering," Speech on Sta-
   tion COQQ in Cuba, November 28, 1959.
"Fidel Castro's Cuba," *New York Times*, January 18, 1959,
   p. E12.
"Fidel Castro Speaks to Citizens of Santiago," *Revolución*,
   January 3–5, 1959.
"Fidel Castro's Visit," *New York Times*, April 15, 1959, p.
   32.
"Fidel Castro Takes the Helm," *New York Times*, February
   17, 1959, p. 30.
"Fidel's Cuba," *PBS NewsHour with Jim Lehrer*, January
   1, 1999.
"Fidel Seen Outsmarted on Soviet Sugar Deal," *Washing-
   ton Post*, March 3, 1960, p. B17.
"A Fighter with Castro," *New York Times*, August 15, 1959,
   p. 4.
Figueredo, Jorge S. *Cuban Baseball: A Statistical History,
   1878–1961*. Jefferson, NC: McFarland, 2003.
"Figueres in Havana as Castro's Guest," *New York Times*,
   March 21, 1959, p. 14.
Finney, John W. "Castro Will Get Tractor Pledge," *New
   York Times*, May 23, 1961.
"5th Column Curb Urged," *New York Times*, November
   13, 1940, p. 12.
"The Firing Squads Resuming in Cuba," *New York Times*,
   December 20, 1959, p. 18.
"The First 100 Days," *Time*, April 20, 1959.
"500 U.S. Refugees Arrive in Florida," *New York Times*,
   January 4, 1959, p. 9.
"5 Seized in 'Plot' Opposing Castro," *Washington Post*,
   March 12, 1959, p. A10.
"Fla. Death Linked to Voodooism," *Washington Post*, Oc-
   tober 16, 1973, p. D16.
"Fleeing Batista Aides Force Airline Pilot at Gunpoint to
   Fly Them to New York," *New York Times*, January 2,
   1959, p. 7.
"Flier from Miami Arrested in Cuba," *New York Times*,
   March 31, 1959, p. 3.
Florida Legislative Investigation Committee Records, 1954–
   1965, Series S 1486.
Folliard, Edward T. "Red Label Is Rejected by Castro,"
   Washington Post and Times Herald, April 18, 1959, p. A1.
_____. "Teamster Official Tied to Cuban Arms," *Wash-
   ington Post and Times Herald*, July 1, 1959, p. A8.
Fontova, Humberto E. *Fidel: Hollywood's Favorite Tyrant*.
   Washington, DC: Regnery, 2005.
"A Former Army Stenographer, Batista Ruled Twice over
   Cuba," *New York Times*, January 2, 1959, p. 7.
"Former Batista Aide Is Indicted at Miami," *Washington
   Post*, April 11, 1961, p. A6.
"43 Fliers Acquitted by Tribunal in Cuba," *New York
   Times*, March 3, 1959, p. 8.
"14,500 Subversive Aliens in United States," *Washington
   Post*, July 21, 1955, p. 20.

Fox, Jack V. "Cuban Invasion Appears to Be Crushed by Castro's Red-Supplied Jets, Arms," *Washington Post and Times Herald*, April 20, 1961, p. A1.

_____. "Insurgents Hit Cuba in 4 Provinces," *Washington Post and Times Herald*, April 18, 1961, p. A1.

"France, Italy File Protests with Cuba," *Washington Post*, March 2, 1960, p. A9.

Frankel, Max. "Castro and Trujillo Call Truce, Diplomats in Caribbean Believe," *New York Times*, January 5, 1961, p. 13.

_____. "Cuban Puts Case," *New York Times*, September 27, 1960, p. 1.

_____. "Guatemala Irate in U.N. over Cuba," *New York Times*, March 21, 1961, p. 14.

_____. "In Cuba: U.S. Action Appears to Have Been a Surprise to Havana," *New York Times*, January 8, 1961, p. E3.

Franqui, Carlos. *Diary of the Cuban Revolution*. New York: Viking Press, 1980.

_____. *Family Portrait with Fidel: A Memoir*, trans. by Alfred MacAdam. New York: Random House, 1984.

"Freedom's Missionary," *Time*, June 1, 1959.

Friedlander, Paul J. C. "Castro's Cuba and Tourism," *New York Times*, November 1, 1959, p. XX25.

Friedman, Joel. "The Decline of Corporate Income Tax Revenues," *Center on Budget and Policy Priorities*, October 24, 2003. http://www.cbpp.org/10-16-03tax.htm.

Frielingsdorf, Walter. *Reformas Sociales y Desarrollo Economico*. Havana: Editorial Lex, 1960.

Fuentes, Norberto. *The Autobiography of Fidel Castro*. Translated from the Spanish by Anna Kushner. New York: W. W. Norton, 2010.

"Fugitive Slaves Going South," *New York Times*, October 27, 1861, p. 4.

Fulsom, Don. "The Mob's President: Richard Nixon's Secret Ties to the Mafia," *Crime Magazine*, February 5, 2006.

Fursenko, Aleksandr, and Timothy J. Naftali. *"One Hell of a Gamble": Khrushchev, Castro and Kennedy, 1958–1964*. New York: W. W. Norton, 1998.

Gaddis, John Lewis. *The Cold War: A New History*. New York: Penguin, 2005.

_____. *The Last Years of the Monroe Doctrine, 1945–1993*. New York: Macmillan, 1995.

_____. *Strategies of Containment: A Critical Appraisal of Postwar National Security Policy*. New York: Oxford University Press, 1982.

Galvez, Wenceslao. *El Beisbol en Cuba*. Havana, 1898.

"Gamblers in Cuba Face Dim Future," *New York Times*, January 4, 1959, p. 6.

"Game Called: Gunfire; Opposing Players Hit," *Washington Post*, July 27, 1959, p. A16.

"A Game of Casino," *Time*, January 20, 1958.

García, Maria Cristina. *Havana USA: Cuban Americans and Cuban Exiles in South Florida, 1959–1994*. Berkeley: University of California Press, 1996.

"G.E. Net Income Fell 29% in 1960," *New York Times*, February 3, 1961, p. 31.

"Gen. Lee Predicts Trouble for Cuba," *New York Times*, July 8, 1902, p. 1.

Gerth, Jeff. *Nixon and the Mafia*. New York: Sun Dance, 1972.

Geyer, Georgie Anne. *Guerrilla Prince: The Untold Story of Fidel Castro*. Kansas City: Andrews McMeel, 2003.

_____. "The Unexpected Lives of Fidel Castro," *World and I* 16 (May 2001).

Goethals, Henry. "Revolution Comes to the Cuban Capitol," *The Times of Havana*, January 4, 1959, p. 8.

Gómez Treto, Raúl. *The Church and Socialism in Cuba*. Maryknoll, NY: Orbis Books, 1988.

González Echevarría, Roberto. *The of Havana: A History of Cuban Baseball*. New York: Oxford University Press, 1999.

González, Servando. *The Secret Fidel Castro: Deconstructing the Symbol*. Oakland, CA: Inteli Books, 2001.

González-Wippler, Migene. *Rituals and Spells of Santería*. New York: Original Publications, 1984.

_____. *Santería: The Religion, Faith, Rites, Magic*. St. Paul: Llewellyn, 1994.

Gosse, Van. *Where the Boys Are: Cuba, Cold War America and the Making of the New Left*. London: Verso, 1993.

Gott, Richard. *Cuba: A New History*. New Haven, CT: Yale University Press, 1964.

"Governmental Stability In Cuba Impresses Nixon," *Washington Post*, February 9, 1955, p. 9.

"Government Property; Florida Channel Fortifications, Lights, &c. Shall They Be Surrendered?" *New York Times*, January 9, 1861, p. 2.

Grace, Roger M. "U.S. Draws Suit over Taxation of Coca-Cola as Medicine," *Metropolitan News-Enterprise* (Los Angeles), Thursday, January 26, 2006, p. 16.

Grandin, Greg. *Empire's Workshop: Latin America, the United States, and the Rise of Imperialism*. New York: Metropolitan Books/Henry Holt, 2007.

Greer, Harold E. "Leoncio Veguilla," in *The Human Tradition in Latin America: The Twentieth Century*. William H. Beezley and Judith Ewell, eds. Wilmington, DE: Scholarly Resources, 1987, pp. 231–244.

Gruson, Sydney. "West May Seek to Revive Berlin Plan Soviet Barred," *New York Times*, December 21, 1959, p. 1.

"Guards Assigned Nap Reyes after 'Traitor' Charge," *Washington Post*, July 17, 1960, p. C3.

"Guatemala Will Fight Revolts in Her Sphere," *New York Times*, April 19, 1959, p. 4.

"Guevara Renews Attack on U.S. as Bonsal Returns to Cuba Post," *Washington Post*, March 21, 1960, p. A5.

Gulick, Lewis. "Apology Given Cuba," *Washington Post and Times Herald*, February 20, 1960, p. A1.

"Gunmen Fire on Capitol at Havana," *Washington Post*, April 22, 1947, p. 1.

"Guns Guard Nixon; He Sees Batista," *Washington Post*, February 8, 1955, p. 2.

Gurian, Waldemar, and M. A. Fitzsimons, eds. *The Catholic Church in World Affairs*. Notre Dame, IN: University of Notre Dame Press, 1954.

Guyol, Edwin Warren. "Palma's Clear Field," *Washington Post*, February 9, 1902, p. 26.

"Haitian Rebels Seize Airliner, Kill Pilot, Force Cuba Landing," *Washington Post*, April 11, 1959, p. A4.

Halberstam, David. *The Fifties*. New York: Random House, 1993.

"Half of 7,000 U.S. Residents Thought to Have Left as Departures Continue," *New York Times*, July 10, 1960, p. 5.

Halperin, Maurice. *The Rise and Decline of Fidel Castro: An Essay in Contemporary History*. Berkeley: University of California Press, 1972.

Halsall, Paul. "Modern History Sourcebook: Benito Mussolini: What Is Fascism, 1932." http://www.fordham.edu/halsall/mod/mussolini-fascism.html.

Halstead, Murat. *The Story of Cuba: Her Struggles for Liberty: The Cause, Crisis and Destiny*, Chicago: The Werner Company, 1896.

Hamilton, Thomas J. "Cuba Seeks Seat on Council of U.N.," *New York Times*, February 23, 1960, p. 1.

_____. "Dominicans Link Castro and Reds," *New York Times*, June 30, 1959, p. 9.

_____. "Dr. Roa Says Cuba Is Ready for Talk," *New York Times*, December 11, 1959, p. 9.

_____. "Roa Charges U.S. Armed Invaders," *New York Times*, April 18, 1961, p. 1.

Hand, Jack. "Majors See Possibility in Future, *Washington Post*, December 12, 1947, p. B7.

"'Hands-Off' Policy in Cuba," *New York Times*, January 29, 1960, p. 5.

"Havana Deports Miami Reporter," *New York Times*, December 24, 1959, p. 9.

"Havana Expels 2 U.S. Attachés," *Washington Post*, June 17, 1960, p. A13.

"Havana Informs O.A.S.," *New York Times*, June 27, 1959, p. 4.

"Havana Team Shift Called 'Big Mistake,'" *Washington Post*, July 9, 1960, p. A13.

"Havana, 3–2 Victor, Takes Series, 4–3," *New York Times*, October 7, 1959, p. 54.

"Havana Tightens Dollar Controls," *New York Times*, December 10, 1959, p. 14.

"Havana Will Lose Its Baseball Club," *New York Times*, July 8, 1960, p. 24.

Hawkins, J. Record of Paramilitary Action against the Castro Government of Cuba, Central Intelligence Agency, May 5, 1961.

Hayes, Evelyn. "Debut for Designer from Cuba," *Washington Post*, May 3, 1955, p. 31.

"Heavy Liquor Taxes Are Imposed in Cuba," *New York Times*, September 17, 1959, p. 39.

Helg, Aline. *Our Rightful Share: The Afro-Cuban Struggle for Equality, 1886–1912.* Chapel Hill: University of North Carolina Press, 1994.

Hemingway, Ernest. "The Shot," *True: The Men's Magazine*, April 1951, pp. 25–28.

Hemingway, Gregory. *Papa: A Personal Memoir.* New York: Houghton Mifflin, 1976.

Hemingway, Hilary, and Carlene Brennan. *Hemingway in Cuba.* New York: Ruggedland, 2005.

Hemingway, Leicester. *My Brother Ernest Hemingway.* New York: World Publishing Company, 1962.

Hemingway, Mary Welsh. *How It Was.* New York: Alfred A. Knopf, 1976.

"Hemingway Back in Cuba," *New York Times*, November 6, 1959, p. 9.

"The Hemispheric Press," *New York Times*, October 12, 1959, p. 18.

Hendrix, Hal. "Castro's Rule Seen Growing Shaky as Cuban Dissatisfaction Increases," *Washington Post and Times Herald*, September 28, 1959, p. B9.

Hensley, Stewart. "Castro Attack Is Denounced in U.S. Plea," *Washington Post and Times Herald*, October 28, 1959, p. A1.

"Hero's Welcome Given to Castro at Caracas," *New York Times*, January 24, 1959, p. 3.

Herring, Hubert. *The History of Latin America from the Beginnings to the Present.* New York: Knopf, 1968.

Hershey, Amos S. "The Recognition of Cuban Belligerency," *Annals of the American Academy of Political and Social Science* 7 (May 1896) p. 74–85.

Herter, Christian. Press Conference, March 9, 1960. *New York Times*, March 10, 1960, p. 6.

"Herter's Hopes Branded New 'Threat' by Cubans," *Washington Post*, March 10, 1960, p. A5.

Higgins, Trumbull. *The Perfect Failure: Kennedy, Eisenhower and the CIA at the Bay of Pigs.* New York: W.W. Norton, 1987.

Higham, Charles. *Errol Flynn: The Untold Story.* New York: Doubleday, 1980.

"High Church Fights Pan-Protestantism," *New York Times*, September 24, 1915, p. 5.

"High Tribunal Reverses Batista Fliers' Acquittal," *New York Times*, March 8, 1959, p. 10.

Hill, Gladwin. "Peons Net Farmer a Fabulous Profit," *New York Times*, March 26, 1951, p. 25.

Hills, George. *Franco: The Man and His Nation.* New York: Macmillan, 1967.

Hinshaw, Joseph U. "U.S. Prepared to Evacuate Americans from Havana," *Washington Post*, January 2, 1959, p. A7.

"History of Cuba," *Boston University Theology Archives*, http://sthweb.bu.edu/archives/index.php?option=com_awiki&view=mediawiki&article=History_of_Cuba.

"Hoffa Is Linked to an Arms Plot," *New York Times*, July 1, 1959, p. 19.

Hollington, Kris. *Wolves, Jackals, and Foxes: The Assassins Who Changed History.* New York: Macmillan, 2008.

Holloway, J. E. *Africanisms in America: Blacks in the Diaspora.* Bloomington: Indiana University Press, 1991.

"Honolulu Vetoed by Third League," *New York Times*, October 10, 1959, p. 16.

Hoopes, Townsend. *The Devil and John Foster Dulles.* Boston: Little, Brown, 1973.

Horowitz, Irving Louis. *Cuban Communism, 1959–1995.* New Brunswick, NJ.: Transaction, 1995.

Horstman, Barry M. "Powell Crosley, Jr.: Innovator, Sportsman Dreamed Big." *Cincinnati Post*, April 8, 1999.

Houseman, Martin P. "Firing Squad Executes U.S. Turncoat in Cuba," *Washington Post and Times Herald*, March 12, 1961, p. A10.

House of Representatives. Hearings before the Antitrust Subcommittee, Committee on the Judiciary, United States House of Representatives, 85th Cong., 1st Sess. Part 2, August 7, 1957.

"Huber Matos, a Moderate in the Cuban Revolution," *PBS American Experience*, http://www.pbs.org/wgbh/amex/castro/peopleevents/e_moderates.html

Hudson, Edward. "Air and Sea Links to Cuba Decrease," *New York Times*, November 12, 1960, p. 42.

Huff, Russell J. "The Family Crisis in Latin America," *Ave Maria* 95, no. 1 (January 6, 1962), p. 5.

"Humanist Abroad," *Time*, May 4, 1959.

Hunt, E. Howard. *Give Us This Day.* New Rochelle, NY: Arlington House, 1973.

_____, and Greg Aunapu. *American Spy: My Secret History in the CIA, Watergate and Beyond.* Hoboken, NJ: John Wiley and Sons, 2007.

"An Idealistic Cuban," *New York Times*, January 3, 1959, p. 2.

"Ike Is Urged to Set Up 'Rights' Machinery," *Washington Post*, September 1, 1957, p. A2.

"Ike Puzzled by Castro's Bitterness," *Washington Post*, October 29, 1959, p. A18.

"Ike's Letter Denounced in Cuba," *Washington Post*, April 10, 1960, p. A7.

Immerman, Richard H. *John Foster Dulles: Piety, Pragmatism and Power in U.S. Foreign Policy.* Wilmington, DE: Scholarly Resources Books, 1999.

"Immigrant Population of Cuba," *The Times of Havana*, September 16, 1957, p. 1.

"Important Arrest of Slavers; Appleton Oaksmith's Case Made Doubly Sure," *New York Times*, January 19, 1862, p. 5.

"Integration Delayed," *Time*, December 31, 1956.

"In the Maelstrom," *Washington Post*, January 23, 1960, p. A10.

"Invaders Cuban, Haiti Maintains," *New York Times*, August 25, 1959, p. 13.

"Invasion Force in Panama Yields to Americas Unit," *New York Times*, May 2, 1959, p. 1.

"Invasion Intent Denied," *New York Times*, April 21, 1959, p. 12.

"Invasion of Cuba Called Imminent," *New York Times*, December 29, 1959, p. 8.

"Invasion of Cuba Reported Begun by a Rebel Force," *New York Times*, April 17, 1961, p. 1.

"Invasion Threat Seen by Castro," *Washington Post*, March 24, 1959, p. A7.

Jackson, Peter. "Soviet Pledges Aid to Havana," *Washington Post and Times Herald*, February 12, 1960, p. A5.

Jamail, Milton H., *Full Count: Inside Cuban Baseball*. Carbondale: Southern Illinois University Press, 2000.

James, George. "R. Hart Phillips, Times Reporter Who Covered Castro's Revolution," *New York Times*, p. D27.

"A Job at the Palace," *Time*, June 14, 1948.

John Birch Society. *Blue Book*. Belmont, MA: John Birch Society, 1958.

Johnson, Haynes, Artime, Manuel, Pérez San Román, José, et al. *Bay of Pigs: The Leaders' Story of Brigade 2506*. New York: Dell, 1964.

Jones, Brendan M. "Freedom Called Cuban Stimulant," *New York Times*, March 1, 1959, p. F1.

Jones, E. V. "Dockworker Set Ship Blast in Havana, American Claims," *Miami Herald*, March 7, 1960, p. 1.

Jones, Howard. *The Bay of Pigs*. New York: Oxford University Press, 2004.

Jorden, William J. "Americas Vote Nicaragua Study," *New York Times*, June 5, 1959, p. 1.

_____. "Eisenhower Acts to Bar Illegal Flights: Castro Enmity Puzzles Him," *New York Times*, October 29, 1959, p. 1.

_____. "Foreign Aid: What Is Involved," *New York Times*, February 21, 1960, p. E5.

_____. "Peiping Attacks Eisenhower Trip," *New York Times*, February 25, 1960, p. 10.

_____. "U.S. Protest Says Charges by Cuba Peril Relations," *New York Times*, October 28, 1959, p. 1.

_____. "U.S. Sends Castro Apology on Plane Wrecked in Cuba," *New York Times*, February 20, 1960, p. 1.

_____. "U.S. Studies Step on Cuba Seizures," *New York Times*, July 2, 1960, p. 2.

"José Figueres Ferrer Is Dead at 83; Led Costa Ricans to Democracy," *New York Times*, June 9, 1990, p. 29.

"The Justice of Cuba," *New York Times*, March 7, 1959, p. 20.

Kaplan, Dana Evan. "Fidel Castro the Jew?" Society for Crypto-Judaic Studies, http://www.cryptojews.com/Highlights_of_SCJS_MiamiBeach_Conference.htm.

Kaplan, Morris. "9 Cuban Exiles Held in 6 Bombings Here," *New York Times*, October 24, 1968, p. 1.

Kelley, Frank. "Cuba Halts Conversion of Pesos," *Washington Post and Times Herald*, February 20, 1959, p. A4.

Kemp, Kathryn W. *God's Capitalist: Asa Candler of Coca-Cola*. Macon, GA: Mercer University Press, 2002.

Kendrick, Alexander. *Prime Time: The Life of Edward R. Murrow*. Boston: Little, Brown, 1969.

Kennedy, John Fitzgerald. Inaugural Address. Washington, DC, January 20, 1961.

_____. State of the Union Address, 1961. Washington, DC, January 30, 1961.

Kennedy, John Fitzgerald, and Allan Nevins. *The Strategy of Peace*. New York: Harper, 1960.

Kennedy, Paul P. "Caribbean Brews Political Storms," *New York Times*, March 13, 1959, p. 8.

_____. "Cuban Aides Woo Central America," *New York Times*, March 20, 1960, p. 14.

_____. "Nicaragua to End Rift with Cuba," *New York Times*, February 14, 1960, p. 27.

_____. "Nicaragua Fears Leftist Attacks," *New York Times*, February 15, 1959, p. 4.

_____. "U.S. Helps Train an Anti-Castro Force at Secret Guatemalan Air-Ground Base," *New York Times*, January 10, 1961, p. 1.

"Kennedy Picketed Here," *New York Times*, January 5, 1961, p. 6.

Kenworthy, E. W. "'Austerity' Held Near for Castro," *New York Times*, April 23, 1959, p. 2.

_____. "Castro Declares Regime Is Free of Red Influence," *New York Times*, April 18, 1959, p. 1.

_____. "Castro Due in Capital Today; Maximum Guard Unit Assigned," *New York Times*, April 15, 1959, p. 1.

_____. "Castro Visit Leaves Big Question Mark," *New York Times*, April 19, 1959, p. E7.

_____. "Castro Will Meet Nixon on U.S. Trip," *New York Times*, April 11, 1959, p. 1.

_____. "Cuba Seen Facing Crisis in Economy," *New York Times*, August 9, 1959, p.16.

_____. "Cuba: Shift in U.S. Policy," *New York Times*, June 26, 1960, p. E4.

_____. "Cuban Aide in U.S. Quits in Protest," *New York Times*, March 18, 1960, p. 1.

_____. "Cuba's Problems Pose Tests for U. S. Policy," *New York Times*, April 26, 1959, p. E7.

_____. "Guatemala Accuses Cuba of Aiding Plot," *New York Times*, December 6, 1959, p. 1.

_____. "Heavy Cuban Arms Buying Slashes Foreign Reserves," *New York Times*, March 11, 1960, p. 1.

_____. "Herter Hopes That Breach with Cuba Can Be Healed," *New York Times*, March 10, 1960, p. 1.

_____. "Herter Reports U.S.-Cuban Ties Have Worsened," *New York Times*, December 11, 1959, p. 1.

_____. "Latins' Progress Is Kennedy Goal," *New York Times*, January 26, 1961, p. 1.

_____. "Leader of Anti-Castro Cubans Tells Aims to U.S.," *New York Times*, April 7, 1961, p. 2.

_____. "Letter Is Issued," *New York Times*, April 9, 1960, p. 1.

_____. "Moscow Echoes the Castro Line," *New York Times*, November 12, 1959, p.12.

_____. "President Rules Out Reprisals on Cuba," *New York Times*, January 27, 1960, p. 1.

_____. "President Voices Concern on Cuba," *New York Times*, March 31, 1960, p. 3.

_____. "Senators Accuse Pentagon on Aid," *New York Times*, February 26, 1960, p. 1.

_____. "Senators Assail Castro's Actions," *New York Times*, January 23, 1960, p. 1.

_____. "United States Foresees No Obstacle to Early Recognition of the Castro Regime," *New York Times*, January 3, 1959, p. 3.

_____. "U.S. Declines Brazil Offer to Seek Better Cuban Ties," *New York Times*, February 5, 1960, p. 1.

_____. "U.S. Envoy to Cuba to Resume Post; Senators Divided," *New York Times*, March 19, 1960, p. 1.

_____. "U.S. Goes Slow," *New York Times*, January 17, 1960, p. E7.

_____. "U.S. Gaining Hope in Cuban Dispute," *New York Times*, February 1, 1960, p. 17.

_____. "U.S. Invites Unit of O.A.S. to Survey Cuba Refugees," *New York Times*, October 25, 1959, p. 1.

_____. "U.S. Puts Embargo on Goods to Cuba; Curbs Ship Deals," *New York Times*, October 20, 1960, p. 1.

_____. "U. S. Recognizes New Cuba Regime; Voices Goodwill," *New York Times*, January 8, 1959, p. 1.

_____. "U.S. Sees Castro Dropping Charge," *New York Times*, February 25, 1960, p. 1.

_____. "U. S. Seizes Bombs Headed for Cuba," *New York Times*, December 2, 1959, p. 1.

_____. "U.S. to Protect Castro on Visit," *New York Times*, March 28, 1959, p. 5.

Kessler, Ronald. *Inside the CIA: Revealing the Secrets of the World's Most Powerful Spy Agency.* New York: Pocket Books, 1992.

Kihss, Peter. "Anti-Castro Group Is Termed 'Almost Ready' to Invade Cuba," *New York Times*, January 5, 1961, p. 6.

_____. "Batista and Regime Flee Cuba," *New York Times*, January 2, 1959, p. 1.

_____. "Berle Backs Kennedy's Policy of Aid for Anti-Castro Forces," *New York Times*, October 26, 1960, p. 25.

_____. "Castro Minister Says U.S. Wages Undeclared War," *New York Times*, April 6, 1961, p. 1.

_____. "Ex-Brother-in-Law of Castro Leads Effort to Overthrow Him," *New York Times*, October 21, 1959, p. 1.

_____. "Pro-Castro Body Reports U.S. Gain," *New York Times*, November 20, 1960, p. 30.

_____. "Trujillo Regime Confirms Arming," *New York Times*, October 31, 1959, p. 1.

_____. "U.S. Asks Court Bar Questions on Castro Foes in Miami Area," *New York Times*, March 24, 1961, p. 3.

Kilgallen, Dorothy. "Judy Keeps Bodyguards Busy," *Washington Post*, March 25, 1958, p. B8.

Kimball, Richard B. *Cuba and the Cubans.* New York: G.P. Putnam, 1850.

Kirk, John M. *Between God and the Party: Religion and Politics in Revolutionary Cuba.* Tampa: University of South Florida Press, 1989.

_____. *José Martí, Mentor of the Cuban Nation.* Tampa: University of South Florida Press, 1982.

Kilpatrick, Carroll. "Castro Gets U.S. Protest on Attacks," *Washington Post and Times Herald*, March 16, 1960, p. A1.

_____. "Nixon Calls Ike Strong President," *Washington Post and Times Herald*, January 17, 1960, p. A1.

Kirkpatrick, Lyman B., Jr. *The Real CIA.* New York: Macmillan, 1968.

Kleber, John E., ed. *The Kentucky Encyclopedia.* Lexington: University Press of Kentucky, 1992.

Kleinberg, Eliot. *Palm Beach Past.* Charleston, SC: The History Press, 2006.

Knowles, Clayton. "Castro Aide Sees Cuba's Best Year," *New York Times*, April 24, 1959, p. 6.

Koeppel, Dan. *Banana: The Fate of the Fruit That Changed the World.* New York: Hudson Street Press, 2008.

Kornbluh, Peter, ed. *Bay of Pigs Declassified: The Secret CIA Report on the Invasion of Cuba* New York: The New Press, 1998.

Krock, Arthur. "Propaganda Brake on Our Cuban Policy," *New York Times*, April 1, 1960, p. 32.

Lacy, Robert. *Little Man: Meyer Lansky and the Gangster Life.* New York: Little Brown, 1991.

LaFarelle, Lorenzo G. *Bernardo de Gálvez: Hero of the American Revolution.* Austin, TX: Eakin Press, 1992.

Lahey, Edwin A. "Cuba Is Warned on Confiscation," *Washington Post and Times Herald*, October 15, 1959, p. A16.

_____. "Gamblers Find Cuban Paradise," *Chicago Daily News*, January 9, 1958.

Landau, Saul. "No Más Canosa," *Monthly Review*, March 1999, p. 22.

"Land for 'Serfs,'" *Washington Post*, August 7, 1953, p. 4.

"Land Seizure Expected," *New York Times*, March 3, 1960, p. 9.

"Latin America Is Cool toward U.S., *Washington Post*, March 11, 1917, p. 5.

"Latin Red Leaders Meeting in Chile," *Washington Post*, August 20, 1959, p. A4.

Lawrence, W. H. "Kennedy Declares Castro Is Enemy; Sees U.S. Arms Lag," *New York Times*, August 27, 1960, p. 1.

Lazo, Mario. *American Policy Failures in Cuba: Dagger in the Heart.* New York: Twin Circle, 1970.

Lazo, Rodrigo. *Writing to Cuba: Filibustering and Cuban Exiles in the United States.* Chapel Hill: University of North Carolina Press, 2005.

Lechuga, Carlos. *Cuba and the Missile Crisis.* New York: Ocean Press, 2001.

Lecuona Zanetti, Oscar, Alejandro García, Franklin W. Knight, and Mary Todd. *Sugar & Railroads: A Cuban History, 1837–1959.* Chapel Hill: University of North Carolina Press, 1998.

"Legacy of Terror," *New York Times*, July 16, 1978, p. SM8.

Leonard, Thomas M. *Encyclopedia of Cuban–United States Relations.* Jefferson, NC: McFarland, 2004.

_____. *Fidel Castro: A Biography.* Westport, CT: Greenwood, 2004.

"Letters to the Editor: Letter from E. S. Whitman," *Washington Post*, February 28, 1960, p. E4.

"Letters to the Editor: Letter from Sam Crutchfield, Jr.," *Washington Post*, March 23, 1959, p. A12.

Levander, Caroline. "Confederate Cuba," *American Literature* 78, no. 4 (December 2006), pp. 821–839.

Levine, Robert M. *Secret Missions to Cuba: Fidel Castro, Bernardo Benes and Cuban Miami* New York: Palgrave, 2001.

Lewis, Anthony. "U.S. Acts to Stop Flights to Cuba by Castro's Foes," *New York Times*, November 2, 1959, p. 1.

Lewis, Norman. *A View of the World.* London: Eland, 1986.

Lewis, Paul. "Felipe Pazos, 88, Economist; Cuban Split Early with Castro." *New York Times,* March 7, 2001.

Library of Congress, Federal Research Division. *Country Profile: Cuba.* Washington, DC: September 2006.

Lindsay, J. O. *The New Cambridge Modern History.* London: Cambridge University Press, 1957.

Liss, Sheldon B. *Roots of Revolution: Radical Thought in Cuba.* Lincoln: University of Nebraska Press, 1987.

Lissner, Will. "Batista Asserts Army Ousted Him," *New York Times*, January 10, 1959, p.1.

Llerena, Mario. *The Unsuspected Revolution: The Birth and Rise of Castroism.* Ithaca, NY: Cornell University Press, 1978.

Llovio-Menéndez, José Luis. *Insider: My Hidden Life as a Revolutionary in Cuba.* Translated by Edith Grossman. New York: Bantam Books, 1988.

Lloyd, Ruth. "Batista's Trail of Blood," *Washington Post and Times Herald*, April 19, 1959, p. AW6.

Long, Tania. "Anti-Castro Units Trained to Fight at Florida Bases," *New York Times*, April 7, 1961, p. 1.

López Fresquet, Rufo. *My Fourteen Months with Castro.* New York: World, 1966.

Love, Kennett. "Wide Arms Deals Laid to Trujillo," *New York Times*, July 3, 1959, p. 6.

"Low-Flying Byrd," *Time*, July 22, 1957.

Lowinger, Rosa, and Ofelia Fox. *Tropicana Nights: The Life and Times of the Legendary Cuban Nightclub.* Orlando, FL: Harcourt, 2005.

Lubasch, Arnold H., "Judge Sentences Omega 7 Leader to Life in Prison," *New York Times*, November 10, 1984, p. 1.

"Lucille Ball Wins Divorce from Arnaz," *New York Times*, May 5, 1960, p. 40.

"'Lucky' Leaves a Souvenir; Face Slap and Cuban Duel," *Washington Post*, March 28, 1947, p. 13.

"Lucy Divorces 'Jekyll-and-Hyde' Desi," *Washington Post*, May 5, 1960, p. C26.

Luis, William. *Culture and Customs of Cuba.* Westport, CT: Greenwood Press, 2001.

Lynch, Grayston L. *Decision for Disaster: Betrayal at the Bay of Pigs.* Washington, DC: Brassey's, 1998.

"Major Castro Calls Them Spies," *New York Times*, August 6, 1960, p. 6.

Matibag, Eugenio. *Afro-Cuban Religious Experience.* Gainesville: University of Florida Press, 1996.

Macaulay, Alex. Citadel Presidential Inaugural Celebration (April 20, 2006), http://www3.citadel.edu/symposium-macaulay.

Macaulay, Neill. *A Rebel in Cuba: An American's Memoir.* Chicago: Quadrangle Books, 1970.

MacGaffey, Wyatt, and Clifford R. Barnett. *Twentieth Century Cuba: The Background of the Castro Revolution.* Garden City, NY: Doubleday, 1965.

"Machado Foe Here from Death Cell," *New York Times*, October 28, 1932, p. 21.

Machiavelli, Nicolo. *The Prince.* Westport, CT: Greenwood Press, 1975.

Magnusen, Karl O., and Leonardo Rodriguez. "Cuba, Labor, and Change." *Labor Studies Journal* 23, no. 2 (Summer 1998), p. 21.

Maguire, Steve. "Average Effective Corporate Tax Rates: 1959–2002," *Congressional Research Service*, September 5, 2003.

"Major Religions of the World Ranked by Number of Adherents," Adherents.com, http://www.adherents.com/Religions_By_Adherents.html, 2005.

Mann, Woodrow, and Anthony Lewis. "Washington Studies Little Rock Dispute," *New York Times*, September 4, 1957, p. 1.

"Man of the Year: Dulles, Man of 1954," *Time*, January 3, 1955.

"Man with a Bomb Seized Near Castro at Rally in Park," *New York Times*, April 25, 1959, p. 1.

Marder, Murrey. "Ike Cautions Latins against Cuba's Path," *Washington Post and Times Herald*, April 9, 1960, p. A1.

_____. "Ike Meets Outbreaks in Uruguay," *Washington Post and Times Herald*, March 3, 1960, p. A1.

_____. "Ike's Trip Uncovers Skepticism About U.S," *Washington Post and Times Herald*, March 4, 1960, p. A1.

"Marijuana Seller Gets Death in Cuba," *New York Times*, April 9, 1959, p. 2.

Marina, Gloria, and Arnold Markowitz. "Fiery Bosch Courts Terrorist Label," *Miami Herald*, November 8, 1976.

Maris, Gary L. "International Law and Guantánamo," *The Journal of Politics* 29, no. 2 (1967), p. 263.

Marks v. Esperdy, 377 U.S. 214 (1964).

Marshall, William J. *Baseball's Pivotal Era, 1945–1951.* Lexington: University of Kentucky Press, 1999.

Martí, José. *José Martí: Selected Writings*, ed. and trans. Esther Allen. New York: Penguin, 2002.

Martino, John V. *I Was Castro's Prisoner.* New York: Devin-Adair, 1963.

Marton, Endre. "U.S. Watch Kept on All Cuba Flights," *Washington Post and Times Herald*, November 2, 1959, p. A1.

Marty, Martin E. *Pilgrims in Their Own Land: 500 Years of Religion in America.* New York, Penguin, 1984.

Matibag, Eugenio. *Afro-Cuban Religious Experience.* Gainesville: University of Florida Press, 1996.

Matos, Huber. *Cómo Llegó la Noche (How the Night Fell).* Barcelona: Tusquets Editor, 2004.

Matthews, Herbert L. "Castro Aims Reflect Character of Cubans," *New York Times*, January 18, 1959, p. E6.

_____. "Castro Criticizes U.S. Military Aid," *New York Times*, January 11, 1959, p. 32.

_____. "Castro Decrees a Halt in Strike Paralyzing Cuba," *New York Times*, January 5, 1959, p. 1.

_____. "Castro Won't Run for Presidency," *New York Times*, January 13, 1959, p. 12.

_____. "Cuba Course Unclear under Castro Regime," *New York Times*, January 11, 1959, p. E6.

_____. "Cuba Has a One-Man Rule and It Is Called Non-Red," *New York Times*, July 16, 1959, p. 1.

_____. "Cuban Rebel Is Visited in Hideout," *New York Times*, February 24, 1957, p. 1.

_____. *The Cuban Story.* New York: George Braziller, 1961.

_____. "Havana Swarms with Rebel Units," *New York Times*, January 3, 1959, p. 1.

_____. "Mobs Riot and Loot in Havana," *New York Times*, January 2, 1959, p. 1.

_____. "A New Chapter Opens in Latin America," *New York Times*, January 11, 1959, p. SM13.

_____. "Now Castro Faces the Harder Fight," *New York Times*, March 8, 1959, p. SM22.

_____. "Old Order in Cuba Is Threatened by Forces of an Internal Revolt," *New York Times*, February 26, 1957, p.13.

_____. "Questions for Castro," *New York Times*, May 3, 1959, p. SM10.

_____. "Rebel Strength Gaining in Cuba, but Batista Has the Upper Hand," *New York Times*, February 25, 1957, p. 1.

_____. "Soviet Exit Marks New Cuban Policy," *New York Times*, April 9, 1952, p. 12.

_____. "Top Castro Aide Denies Red Tie; Leaders Say They 'Await Fidel,'" *New York Times*, January 4, 1959, p. 7.

_____. "Trujillo Now Center of Caribbean Unrest," *New York Times*, June 28, 1959, p. E4.

_____. "Why Latin America Is Vital to Us," *New York Times*, April 26, 1959, p. SM17.

May, Donald H. "Cuba Seizures of U.S. Property Are Put in Excess of $1.2 Billion," *Washington Post and Times Herald*, January 16, 1965, p. A11.

"McCarran and the Alien," *New York Times*, August 23, 1951, p. 21.

McCarthy, Francis L. "Castro Halts Cuba Strike; Shops Open," *Washington Post and Times Herald*, January 5, 1959, p. A1.

_____. "Castro Warns OAS against Intervention," *Washington Post and Times Herald*, July 4, 1959, p. A1.

_____. "Cuba Seeks Fugitives in Asylum; New Charges Filed, Three Sentenced," *Washington Post and Times Herald*, February 9, 1959, p. A11.

_____. "Havana Cheers Castro as Hero," *Washington Post and Times Herald*, January 9, 1959, p. A6.

_____. "Land Gifts to Cubans Start Feb. 2," *Washington Post and Times Herald*, January 30, 1959, p. A5.

_____. "New Trujillo 'Truce' with Cuba Is Puzzler," *Washington Post and Times Herald*, January 21, 1960, p. A7.

_____. "Urritia Takes over Cuban Rule: President Names Cabinet Members; Castro Army Head." *Washington Post*, January 4, 1959, p. A1.

McFadden, Robert D., "Cuban Attache at U.N. Is Slain from Ambush on Queens Road," *New York Times*, September 12, 1980, p. A1.

McLaughlin, Jim. "Castro Defends Executions," *Lowell Sunday Sun*, April 26, 1959, p. 1.

McLendon, Winzola. "His 'Sexy Styles' Are 'Good Taste,'" *Washington Post*, October 2, 1957, p. D3.

McPherson, Alan. *Yankee No! Anti-Americanism in U.S.–Latin American Relations*. Cambridge, MA: Harvard University Press, 2003.

Mecham, J. Lloyd. *The United States and Inter-American Security, 1889–1960*. Austin: University of Texas Press, 1961.

Meeting, Phillip. "Cultural Imperialism, Afro-Cuban Religion and Santiago's Failure in Hemingway's *The Old Man and the Sea*." *The Hemingway Review* 26, no. 1 (2006), pp. 6–24.

Melanson, Richard A., and David Mayers, eds. *Reevaluating Eisenhower: American Foreign Policy in the 1950s*. Urbana: University of Illinois Press, 1987.

Mellow, James R. *Hemingway: A Life without Consequences*. Reading, MA: Addison-Wesley, 1992.

Meneses, Enrique. *Fidel Castro*. Trans. by J. Halco Ferguson. New York: Taplinger, 1966.

Metz, Robert T. "Approved, Taxes May Be Bar to Foreign Deals," *New York Times*, March 5, 1961, p. F1.

_____. "Tax Relief Sought by Mining Industry for Expropriation," *New York Times*, February 18, 1962, p. F1.

Meyer, Ben F. "Quiz Told Cuban Paid Bulk of Castro Ad Cost," *Washington Post and Times Herald*, January 11, 1961, p. A12.

Meyer, Karl E. "Brazil's President Scolds U.S. for 'Indifference,'" *Washington Post and Times Herald*, November 13, 1959, p. A8.

_____. "Guatemala Expects Invasion from Cuba," *Washington Post and Times Herald*, December 9, 1959, p. B16.

_____. "How It Looked from the Inside," *Washington Post and Times Herald*, May 14, 1961, p. E4.

_____. "The Long Shadow Cast by a Cuban," *Washington Post and Times Herald*, December 29, 1959, p. A8.

_____. "Neutrality Difficult in Castro's Revolt," *Washington Post and Times Herald*, September 19, 1958, p. A5.

Meyers, Jeffrey. *Hemingway: A Biography*. New York: Harper and Row, 1999.

"Miami Police Widen Investigation into 4 Slayings at Official's Home," *New York Times*, December 17, 1980, p. A26.

"Miami Restaurant Attacked," *New York Times*, June 5, 1959, p. 28.

Midelfort, H. C. Erik. *A History of Madness in Sixteenth-Century Germany*. Stanford, CA: Stanford University Press, 1999.

"Mikoyan to Open Exhibit in Cuba," *New York Times*, February 1, 1960, p. 1.

"Military Visits Batista's Military," *The Times of Havana*, October 17, p. 2.

Milks, Harold K. "Castro Lays Blast to U.S. Interests," *Washington Post and Times Herald*, March 6, 1960, p. A1.

_____. "Castro Names Raúl Army Czar," *Washington Post and Times Herald*, October 18, 1959, p. A5.

_____. "Castro Ousts Spanish Ambassador after Envoy Interrupts TV Speech," *Washington Post and Times Herald*, January 21, 1960, p. A1.

_____. "Castro Tells Crowd He'll Return: Circus Atmosphere, Shootings Mark Revolt Birthday," *Washington Post*, July 27, 1959, p. A1.

_____. "Concern for Future Grips American Companies in Cuba," *Washington Post and Times Herald*, October 30, 1959, p. A12.

_____. "Guevara Gets Key Post in Cuba Cabinet Shift," *Washington Post and Times Herald*, November 27, 1959, p. A5.

_____. "Mikoyan and Castro Sign Soviet Trade Pact," *Washington Post and Times Herald*, February 14, 1960, p. A8.

_____. "Rally Opens as Castro Sees Plot to Turn Church against Him," *Washington Post and Times Herald*, November 29, 1959, p. 9.

_____. "7 Are Reported Dead in Havana; U.S. Is Blamed," *Washington Post and Times Herald*, April 16, 1961, p. A1.

_____. "U.S. Welcomes Talks with Cuba but Refuses Pledge of No Reprisals," *Washington Post and Times Herald*, March 1, 1960, p. A4.

Miller, Ivor L. "Religious Symbolism in Cuban Political Performance," *The Drama Review (TDR)* 44, no. 2 (Summer 2000), pp. 30–55.

Mills, C. Wright. *Listen Yankee: The Revolution in Cuba*. New York: McGraw-Hill, 1960.

Miroff, Nick. "Cuba's Undersea Oil Could Help Thaw Trade with U.S.," *Washington Post*, May 16, 2009.

Molina, Gabriel. *Diario de Giron*. Havana: Política, 1983.

"Molina Given 20 Years to Life As Court Rejects Cuban Offer," *New York Times*, June 30, 1961, p. 8.

"Molina Guilty in Girl's Death; Convicted of 2d-Degree Murder," *New York Times*, April 8, 1961, p. 2.

Mooney, Richard E. "Smith Quits Post as Envoy to Cuba," *New York Times*, January 11, 1959, p. 1.

Monahan, James, and Kenneth O. Gilmore, *The Great Deception: The Inside Story of How the Kremlin Took Over Cuba*. New York: Farrar, Straus, 1963.

"Monetary Fund Approves Cuban Exchange Action," *Washington Post*, September 26, 1959, p. D17.

Monroe, Arthur F. L. "Batista Exiles 4 as Leaders of Revolt Plot," *Washington Post*, February 5, 1941, p.1.

Montaner, Carlos Alberto. *Cuba, Castro and the Caribbean*. New Brunswick, NJ: Transaction, 1985.

_____. *Fidel Castro and the Cuban Revolution: Age, Position, Character, Destiny, Personality and Ambition*. New Brunswick, NJ: Transaction, 2007.

_____. *Journey to the Heart of Cuba: Life as Fidel Castro*. New York: Algora, 2001.

_____. *"Quiere Castro Abandonar a los Sovíticos?"* *La Estrella de Panamá*, February 22, 1985.

Moore, Carlos. *Castro, the Blacks and Africa*. Los Angeles: Center for African American Studies, UCLA, 1988.

Morales, Ed. *The Latin Beat: The Rhythms and Roots of Latin Music from Bosa Nova to Salsa and Beyond*. Cambridge, MA: Da Capo, 2003.

Morelock, Bill. "Conscience vs. McCarthy: the Political Aaron Copland," Minnesota Public Radio, May 3, 2005. http://news.minnesota.publicradio.org/features/2005/05/03_morelockb_unamerican.

"More Slave-traders Arrested in New Bedford," *New York Times*, January 19, 1862, p. 8.

"More Tourists in Cuba," *New York Times*, December 31, 1959, p. 3.

Morgan, Kay Summersby. *Past Forgetting: My Love Affair with Dwight D. Eisenhower*. New York: Simon & Schuster, 1977.

"Morgan, Cuban Aide, Will Renounce U.S.," *New York Times*, September 22, 1959, p. 11.

Morley, Morris H. *Imperial State and Revolution: The United States and Cuba, 1952–1986*. New York: Cambridge University Press, 1987.

Morris, John D. "2 Aides of Castro Expelled by U.S.; Spying Is Charged," *New York Times*, June 19, 1960, p. 1.

_____. "U.S. Will Speed Envoy to Havana," *New York Times*, January 16, 1959, p. 1.

"Morse Asks Cuba to End 'Blood Baths,'" *Washington Post*, January 13, 1959, p. A4.

"Moscow Breaks Silence on Events in Cuba," *Washington Post*, October 31, 1959, p. A7.

"Moscow Is Told of Aid to Castro," *New York Times*, February 1, 1959, p. 22.

Munn, Bruce W. "8 U.S. Gunmen Are Sought in Plot to Assassinate Castro," *Washington Post and Times Herald*, April 24, 1959, p. A3.

Murphy, Joseph M. *Santería: African Spirits in America*. Boston: Beacon, 1988.

Murphy, Robert. *Diplomat among Warriors*. Garden City, NY: Doubleday, 1964.

Murray, David. *Odious Commerce: Britain, Spain and the Abolition of the Cuban Slave Trade*. Cambridge, UK: Cambridge University Press, 1980.

National Security Archive. "Bay of Pigs 40 Years After: Chronology." http://www.gwu.edu/~nsarchiv/bayof pigs/chron.html.

"Nebraskan Freed," *New York Times*, March 7, 1960, p. 2.

"Negroes Win in Havana," *New York Times*, January 4, 1910, p. 4.

Nevard, Jacques. "Castro to Foster Private Shipping," *New York Times*, February 14, 1959, p. 42.

"New Cuban Chief Is a Bookish Rebel," *Washington Post*, July 19, 1959, p. A6.

"New Death Threats Made against Fidel," United Press International, April 27, 1959.

"The New Diplomacy," *Time*, September 19, 1960.

Newman, Joseph. "Roa Urges a New Cuban-U.S. Trade Accord," *Washington Post and Times Herald*, December 10, 1959, p. A5.

"New Public Works Projects of the Batista Regime," *Gente Magazine* (American Edition), January 5, 1958.

"News Conference In Brief," *New York Times*, July 16, 1959, p. 8.

"News Conference in Brief," *New York Times*, January 27, 1960, p. 14.

"News of the Day: The Rebellion," *New York Times*, January 3, 1862, p. 8.

"The News of the Week in Review," *New York Times*, January 10, 1960, p. E1.

"The News of the Week in Review," *New York Times*, January 31, 1960, p. E1.

"The News of the Week in Review," *New York Times*, February 14, 1960, p. E1.

"The News of the Week in Review," *New York Times*, July 24, 1960, p. E1.

"The News of the Week in Review," *New York Times*, July 31, 1960, p. E1.

"The News of the Week in Review," *New York Times*, September 25, 1960, p. E1.

"News Summary and Index," *New York Times*, June 12, 1959, p. 29.

"News Summary and Index," *New York Times*, February 5, 1960, p. 29.

"News Summary and Index," *New York Times*, February 14, 1960, p. 95.

"Night Club in the Sky: Cubana Airlines' Tropicana Special," *Cabaret Magazine*, January 1957.

"The 1956 Hungarian Revolution: A History in Documents," National Security Archive. Washington, DC: George Washington University, 2008.

Nixon, Richard M. *Six Crises*. New York: Simon & Schuster, 1990.

"Nixon Advises Castro," United Press International, April 26, 1959.

"Nixon Begins Talks on Cuban Problems," *New York Times*, February 8, 1955, p. 16.

"Nixon Warns Cuba on Alienating U.S.," *New York Times*, January 17, 1960, p. 31.

"Nonviolent Resistance," *Time*, September 24, 1956.

Nossiter, Bernard D. "Cuba Trade Embargoed by U.S.," *Washington Post and Times Herald*, October 20, 1960, p. A1.

"Not Afraid to Die," *Time*, March 25, 1957.

Nover, Barnet. "Nazi 5th Column Woos Cuba with Help From Spaniards," *Washington Post*, July 28, 1940, p. 6.

"Nye and 5 Others Go on Trial in Castro Assassination Plot," *Washington Post*, April 12, 1959, p. A8.

"The OAS: Trying to Hold the Americas Together," *Time*, May 14, 1965.

"Obituary: Rafael Rivas Vázquez y Galdos," *Miami Herald*, November 25, 2000.

"Obituary: Rev. Jorge J. Sardiña," *Miami Herald*, February 12, 2008.

O'Farril, the Reverend Juan Raymond. Testimony before U.S. Senate Subcommittee to Investigate the Administration of the Internal Security Act and Other Internal Security Laws. Committee on the Judiciary, May 4, 1960.

Omang, Joanne. "Cuban Exile Bosch Defends Violence, Critical of CIA, FBI," *Washington Post*, April 3, 1977, p. 146.

"1-Hour Strike Ties Up Cuba," *Washington Post*, July 24, 1959, p. A7.

"$100 Million Takeovers Set in Cuba," *Washington Post*, March 11, 1960, p. A4.

"One Man Court," *Time*, March 16, 1959.

Onigman, Marc. "Cuba vs. the Major Leagues: Game Is No Longer the Same," *New York Times*, March 19, 1978, p. S2.

"Opening of 8 Colonial Homes Set," *Washington Post*, January 18, 1959, p. C10.

"Opinion of the Week: At Home and Abroad," *New York Times*, February 28, 1960, p. E11.

"Orderly Change of Power Sought," *New York Times*, January 2, 1959, p. 6.

"Orioles Shun Havana, Cuba Writers Protest," *Washington Post*, March 29, 1960, p. A18.

Ortíz, Francisco. *Contrapunteo Cubano del Tabaco y el Azúcar* (Cuban Counterpoint: Tobacco and Sugar). Trans. Harriet De Onis. 1940. Reprint, Durham, NC: Duke University Press, 1995.

Osieja, Helen. "Economic Sanctions as an Instrument of U.S. Foreign Policy: The Case of the U.S. Embargo on Cuba." Boca Raton, FL: Dissertation.com, 2005.

"The Other Face," *Time*, April 27, 1959.

Otulski, Enrique. *Vida Clandestina: My Life In the Revolution*. New York: John Wiley and Sons, 2002.

"Our Man in Miami," *Time*, November 7, 1960.

"Ousted Staff Chief Back in Cuba," *New York Times*, May 5, 1942, p. 11.

Pack, Richard. "Report from Havana," *New York Times*, April 28, 1946, p. X7.

"Palma Elected by Default," *Washington Post*, January 2, 1902, p. 1.

"Palma Is Cuba Bound," *Washington Post*, April 17, 1902, p. 3.

Pappas, Doug. "Spring 1999, Looking Back." *SABR Business of Baseball Committee Newsletter*. 1999.

Page, Joseph A. *Perón: A Biography*. New York: Random House, 1983.

"Panama Complains of Plotting in Cuba," *New York Times*, April 16, 1959, p. 7.

"Panama Holds 3 in Rebel Landing," *New York Times*, April 27, 1959, p. 1.

"Papers Assail U.S.," *New York Times*, May 25, 1960, p. 6.

"Parachuted Arms Cuban Rebels Seized," *Washington Post*, September 28, 1959, p. B9.

"Paraguayan Rebels Still Holding Out," *New York Times*, December 14, 1959, p. 16.

"Paraguay Charges Cuba Aided Rebels," *New York Times*, December 21, 1959, p. 14.

"Paraguay Reports Crushing a Revolt," *New York Times*, December 13, 1959, p. 1.

Parmet, Herbert S. *Eisenhower and the American Crusades*. New York: Macmillan, 1972.

"Parr, Jack," The Museum of Broadcast Communication. http://www.museum.tv/archives/etv/P/htmlP/paarjack/paarjack.htm.

Parrott, Lindsay. "Castro Defends Election Delay," *New York Times*, April 23, 1959, p. 1.

_____. "Cuba Fails to Get U.N. Vote on 'Plot' by U.S. to Invade," *New York Times*, January 6, 1961, p.1.

Paterson, Thomas G. *Contesting Castro: The United States and the Triumph of the Cuban Revolution*. New York: Oxford University Press, 1995.

"Patience with Castro," *Washington Post*, January 22, 1959, p. A16.

Peale, Norman Vincent. "Prayers Saved President's Leg," *Washington Post*, June 19, 1954, p. 16.

"Pearl of the Antilles," *Time*, January 26, 1959.

Pearson, Drew. "Washington Merry-Go-Round: Americans Urged to Quit Cuba," *Washington Post and Times Herald*, March 13, 1960, p. E5.

_____. "Washington Merry-Go-Round: Batista Assails Castro as Killer," *Washington Post and Times Herald*, April 3, 1959, p. D1.

_____. "Washington Merry-Go-Round: Bonsal's Return to Cuba Is Held Up," *Washington Post and Times Herald*, January 30, 1960, p. D11.

_____. "Washington Merry-Go-Round: Castro Is Linked to Colombia Plot," *Washington Post and Times Herald*, April 1, 1959, p. D9.

_____. "Washington Merry-Go-Round: Cuba Near the Boiling Point," *Washington Post and Times Herald*, July 12, 1959, p. E5.

_____. "Washington Merry-Go-Round: Former Buddy Opposes Castro," *Washington Post and Times Herald*, April 16, 1959, p. B15.

_____. "Washington Merry-Go-Round: Halleck to Back Pollution Bill Veto," *Washington Post and Times Herald*, February 18, 1960, p. B15.

_____. "Washington Merry-Go-Round: Ike Ponders Trip to Latin America," *Washington Post*, November 20, 1952, p. 51.

_____. "Washington Merry-Go-Round: Panama Canal Threat Pictured," *Washington Post*, March 25, 1959, p. D13.

_____. "Washington Merry-Go-Round: Perón Looks Back at 2 Big Errors," *Washington Post and Times Herald*, April 9, 1959, p. B15.

_____. "Washington Merry-Go-Round: Some Relatives Earn Capitol Pay," *Washington Post and Times*, February 28, 1959, p. B11.

_____. "Washington Merry-Go-Round: U.S. Neglect of Latins Charged," *Washington Post and Times Herald*, August 12, 1959, p. D11.

_____. "Washington Merry-Go-Round," *Washington Post and Times Herald*, February 7, 1960, p.E5.

Pegler, Westbrook. "Killer Mars 'Democracy' in Cuba," King Features Syndicate, April 28, 1959.

Peña Monte, Gustavo. "Havana Bishop Endorses Castro Plan to Break Up Cuba's Larger Estates," *The Voice*, June 5, 1959, p. 9.

"People, Mar. 14, 1960," *Time*, March 14, 1960.

Perez, Louis A., Jr. *Cuba and the United States: Ties of Singular Intimacy*, 2nd ed. Athens: University of Georgia Press, 1990.

_____. *Cuba: Between Reform and Revolution*. New York: Oxford University Press, 2006.

_____. *Essays on Cuban History: Historiography and Research*. Gainesville: University Press of Florida, 1995.

_____. *On Becoming Cuban: Identity, Nationality, and Culture*. New York: The Ecco Press, 1999.

_____. *To Die in Cuba: Suicide and Society*. Chapel Hill: University of North Carolina Press, 2005.

Pérez Serates, Enrique. "Nueva Cuba," *La Quincena*, January, 1959, p. 18.

Perret, Geoffrey, *Eisenhower*. Holbrook, MA: Adams Media Corporation, 1999.

"Peso Holds Its Value," *The Times of Havana*, January 24, 1959, p. 14.

Phillips, Cabell. "Concern over Cuba's Course Mounts," *New York Times*, February 28, 1960, p. E4.

Phillips, David Atlee. *The Night Watch*. New York: Atheneum, 1977.

Phillips, McCandlish. "Miro Says Cuba Air Raiders Were in 'Contact' with Exiles," *New York Times*, April 16, 1961, p. 5.

Phillips, R[uby] Hart. "American Fliers Downed by Cuba," *New York Times*, March 22, 1960, p. 1.

_____. "Americans Speed Taxes to Aid Cuba," *New York Times*, January 17, 1959, p. 1.

_____. "Anti-Castro Acts Persist in Cuba," *New York Times*, October 14, 1959, p. 19.

_____. "Anti-Castro Acts Spreading in Cuba," *New York Times*, July 3, 1959, p. 1.

_____. "Arms Depot Hit," *New York Times*, April 16, 1961, p. 1.

_____. "Assassins Attack Cuba Aide's Home," *New York Times*, November 6, 1959, p. 9.

_____. "Batista in Power after Cuban Coup," *New York Times*, March 11, 1952, p. 1.

_____. "Batista Major Condemned in Havana Stadium Trial," *New York Times*, January 24, 1959, p. 1.

_____. "Batista Said to Send Arms to Holdouts in Mountains," *New York Times*, January 18, 1959, p. 1.

_____. "Candidate in Cuba Bars Army Abroad," *New York Times*, February 16, 1952, p. 6.

_____. "Cardenas Backs Stand on Castro," *New York Times*, April 1, 1961, p. 4.

_____. "Carnival in Cuba," *New York Times*, March 5, 1952, p. 111.

_____. "Castro Actions Suit the Communists' Aims," *New York Times*, November 29, 1959, p. E3.

_____. "Castro Arrests Aide Who Quit after Charging Red Infiltration," *New York Times*, October 22, 1959, p. 1.

_____. "Castro Asks Cubans to Inform On All Who Oppose Revolution," *New York Times*, December 21, 1959, p. 1.

_____. "Castro Asks Labor Not to Strike Now," *New York Times*, February 8, 1959, p. 1.

_____. "Castro Assails Cuban President, Forcing Him Out," *New York Times*, July 18, 1959, p. 1.

_____. "Castro Assaults Cuban Army Post: Rebel Unit Raids Evacuated Headquarters and Flees," *New York Times*, July 28, 1957, p. 1.

_____. "Castro Attacks U.S. Sugar Quota," *New York Times*, April 4, 1959, p. 1.

_____. "Castro Bars Pledge to Join U.S. in War," *New York Times*, March 23, 1959, p. 1.

_____. "Castro Bars Role for 'Extremists,'" *New York Times*, May 23, 1959, p. 1.

_____. "Castro Bids Cuba Fight to Survive," *New York Times*, August 29, 1959, p. 6.

_____. "Castro Calling Halt in Military Trials," *New York Times*, May 12, 1959, p. 1.

_____. "Castro Calls for U.S. Talks to Settle Disagreements," *New York Times*, February 23, 1960, p. 1.

_____. "Castro Cautions Industry in Cuba: Capital, Notably Sugar Mill Ownership, Must Aid the Revolution, He Asserts," *New York Times*, March 30, 1959, p. 6.

_____. "Castro Censures Catholic Parley," *New York Times*, November 29, 1959, p. 19.

_____. "Castro Charges Planes from U.S. Bombed Havana," *New York Times*, October 24, 1959, p. 1.

_____. "Castro Charges U.S. Interference," *New York Times*, February 21, 1959, p. 8

_____. "Castro Criticizes Nixon's Comment," *New York Times*, January 19, 1960, p. 14.

_____. "Castro Declares Trials Will Go On," *New York Times*, January 14, 1959, p. 1.

_____. "Castro Deplores His Critics Here," *New York Times*, January 22, 1959, p. 1.

_____. "Castro Deplores Panama Landing," *New York Times*, April 29, 1959, p. 11.

_____. "Castro Directing Fighting in Cuba," *New York Times*, August 13, 1959, p. 1.

_____. "Castro Eligible for Presidency; New Law Also Clears Way for Aide, an Argentine," *New York Times*, February 11, 1959, p. 1.

_____. "Castro Foes to Lose Properties in Cuba," *New York Times*, November 20, 1959, p. 1.

_____. "Castro Heads Cuba's Armed Forces; Regime Is Sworn In," *New York Times*, January 4, 1959, p. 1.

_____. "Castro, in Clash, Ousts Spain's Aide, *New York Times*, January 21, 1960, p. 1.

_____. "Castro Increasing Pressure on U.S. Sugar Mills in Cuba," *New York Times*, April 2, 1960, p. 8.

_____. "Castro Is Lionized for Tricking Foes; American Is Hailed," *New York Times*, August 16, 1959, p. 1.

_____. "Castro Links U.S. to Ship 'Sabotage'; Denial Is Swift," *New York Times*, March 6, 1960, p. 1.

_____. "Castro Movement of Children Rises," *New York Times*, August 7, 1959, p. 6.

_____. "Castro Moving to Take Power," *New York Times*, January 1, 1959, p. 1.

_____. "Castro Names President as Rebels Enter Havana; Street Clashes Continue," *New York Times*, January 3, 1959, p. 1.

_____. "Castro Opposes Alien Ownership," *New York Times*, June 11, 1959, p. 14.

_____. "Castro Outlines Sweeping Plans," *New York Times*, February 4, 1959, p. 10.

_____. "Castro Proposes 'Deal' on Captives," *New York Times*, May 18, 1961, p. 8.

_____. "Castro Reaches 95% of Cubans with Radio-TV Exhortations," *New York Times*, August 6, 1959, p. 9.

_____. "Castro Regime Strikes at Graft through Drastic Cuban Reform," *New York Times*, January 28, 1959, p. 1.

_____. "Castro Regrets Delay in Arrival," *New York Times*, January 5, 1959, p. 3.

_____. "Castro Reports Revolt Crushed," *New York Times*, August 14, 1959, p. 2.

_____. "Castro Restates View in Ship Case," *New York Times*, March 13, 1960, p. 27.

_____. "Castro Resumes the Premiership," *New York Times*, July 27, 1959, p. 1.

_____. "Castro Rules Out Any Foreign Hand in Cuban Affairs," *New York Times*, July 4, 1959, p. 1.

_____. "Castro Says Bloody Invasions Are Inevitable in Cuba in 1960," *New York Times*, December 17, 1959, p. 4.

_____. "Castro Says Cuba Can Build Alone," *New York Times*, September 30, 1959, p. 14.

_____. "Castro Says Cuba Wants Good Ties with Washington," *New York Times*, January 16, 1959, p. 1.

_____. "Castro Stresses 'Aggression' Fear," *New York Times*, March 14, 1960, p. 8.

_____. "Castro Suggests Amity with U.S.," *New York Times*, January 21, 1961, p. 1.

_____. "Castro's Brother Is Sent to Inter-American Parley," *New York Times*, August 17, 1959, p. 1.

_____. "Castro's Cabinet Bids Him Remain as Cuba's Ruler," *New York Times*, July 19, 1959, p. 1.

_____. "Castro's Cabinet Off at Full Speed," *New York Times*, February 18, 1959, p. 16.

_____. "Castro's Course Still a Puzzle," *New York Times*, February 7, 1960, p. E5.

_____. "Castro Sees Help of All Americas," *New York Times*, March 26, 1961, p. 31.

_____. "Castro Takes Oath As Premier of Cuba," *New York Times*, February 17, 1959, p. 1.

_____. "Castro Tells U.S. Staff in Embassy Must Be Slashed," *New York Times*, January 3, 1961, p. 1.

_____. "Castro Threatens Death Penalty for Theft of Government Funds; Accused Aide Is Suicide after Warning By Premier — Had Been Questioned on Release of Seized Account," *New York Times*, March 13, 1959, p. 8.

_____. "Castro Tightens His Hold on Cubans," *New York Times*, March 26, 1961, p. E8.

_____. "Castro to Become Premier in Shift of Cuba's Regime," *New York Times*, February 14, 1959, p. 1.

_____. "Castro to Begin Giving Out Land," *New York Times*, January 30, 1959, p. 7.

_____. "Castro to Spend $134,500,000 on Public Works to Aid Jobless," *New York Times*, June 30, 1959, p. 9.

_____. "Castro's Nationalism Disturbs Some Cubans," *New York Times*, April 5, 1959, p. E4.

_____. "Castro's New Role Reflects His Power," *New York Times*, February 22, 1959, p. E4.

_____. "Castro's Newspaper Scores Communists," *New York Times*, May 17, 1959, p. 1.

_____. "Castro's Regime Puts All Trade under Controls," *New York Times*, February 21, 1960, p. 1.

_____. "Castro's Troops Pursue Diehards," *New York Times*, January 19, 1959, p. 4.

_____. "Castro's Troubles and Washington's Reaction," *New York Times*, October 25, 1959, p. E4.

_____. "Chinese in Cuba Plan Red Paper," *New York Times*, July 10, 1959, p. 8.

[Phillips, Ruby Hart.] "Civil Prisoners Jam Cuban Jails," *New York Times*, February 20, 1959, p. 10.

_____. "Communists in Cuba Pose a Big Problem," *New York Times*, May 31, 1959, p. E4.

_____. "Cuba Admonished Out Executions," *New York Times*, March 24, 1959, p. 2.

_____. "Cuba Arrests 45 as Conspirators," *New York Times*, December 30, 1959, p. 4.

_____. "Cuba Celebrates Year of Castro," *New York Times*, January 1, 1960, p. 6.

_____. "Cuba Continues Seizing Business," *New York Times*, March 11, 1960, p. 6.

_____. "Cuba Convention," *New York Times*, October 11, 1959, p. X27.

_____. *Cuba, Island of Paradise*. New York: Astor-Honor, 1960.

_____. *Cuba, Island of Paradox*. New York: McDowell, Obolensky, 1959.

_____. "Cuba May Have a Tourist Season," *New York Times*, January 11, 1959, p. X23.

_____. "Cuba Moves Fast on Land Reform," *New York Times*, July 9, 1959, p. 8.

_____. "Cuba Opens Drive for Cane Cutters," *New York Times* January 30, 1961, p. 10.

_____. "Cuba Rebuffs U.S. on Land Payment," *New York Times*, June 16, 1959, p. 1.

_____. "Cuba Recovering from Brief Rising: Round-Up of Batista Foes Is Under Way — Regime Drops Idea of Partial Election," *New York Times*, March 15, 1957, p. 11.

_____. "Cuba Rejects U.S. Protest; Calls Herter 'Aggressive,'" *New York Times*, March 9, 1960, p. 1.

_____. "Cuba Revamping School System," *New York Times*, July 26, 1959, p. 26.

_____. "Cuba Said to Hold 4,500 as Plotters," *New York Times*, August 12, 1959, p. 1.

_____. "Cuba Says Indianan Admits Castro Plot," *New York Times*, February 6, 1959, p. 1.

_____. "Cuba Says Soviet Will Keep Sugar," *New York Times*, February 16, 1960, p. 10.

_____. "Cuba Seizes Aide of U.S. Embassy," *New York Times*, September 16, 1960, p. 1.

_____. "Cuba Sentences Nye to Death as Plotter but Lets Him Leave," *New York Times*, April 13, 1959, p. 1.

_____. "Cuba Suspends Habeas Corpus to Quell Plots," *New York Times*, October 30, 1959, p. 1.

_____. "Cuba Takes Land of Ramón Castro," *New York Times*, October 19, 1959, p. 2.

_____. "Cuba to Try 1,000 for 'War Crimes,'" *New York Times*, January 20, 1959, p. 1.

_____. "Cuba Turns Down Complaint by U.S. on Land Seizures," *New York Times*, January 12, 1960, p. 1.

_____. "Cuba Unions Oust Anti-red Leaders," *New York Times*, January 25, 1960, p. 1.

_____. "Cuba Will Take Over Airlines; Charges Batista Men Own Them," *New York Times*, May 24, 1959, p. 1.

_____. "Cuban Catholics Counter Red Aim," *New York Times*, November 30, 1959, p. 12.

_____. "Cuban Civic Units Oppose Carnival," *New York Times*, June 22, 1957, p. 6.

_____. "Cuban Crowds Assail U.S. after Attack by Terrorists," *New York Times*, October 23, 1959, p.1.

_____. "Cuban Farm Law Imperils U.S. Sugar Concerns' Land," *New York Times*, May 19, 1959, p. 1.

_____. "Cuban Labor Cuts Inter-america Tie with Foes of Reds," *New York Times*, November 23, 1959, p. 1.

_____. "Cuban Land Reform Adds to Uncertainty," *New York Times*, May 24, 1959, p. E4.

_____. "Cuban Military Court Sentences U.S. Engineer to 13-Year Term," *New York Times*, December 19, 1959, p. 4.

_____. "Cuban Reds Beaten in Labor Union Vote," *New York Times*, November 24, 1959, p. 1.

_____. "Cuban Regime Cuts Ties with Trujillo," *New York Times*, June 27, 1959, p. 1.

_____. "Cuban Show Trial of Batista Aides Opens in Stadium," *New York Times*, January 23, 1959, p. 1.

_____. "Cuban Student Brigades March to Honor Eight Martyrs of 1871," *New York Times*, November 28, 1959, p. 11.

_____. "Cuban Voting Set Amid Wide Curbs," *The New York Times*, October 26, 1958, p. 17.

_____. "Cubans Arrest Ten in 'Invasion' Tension," *New York Times*, January 9, 1961, p. 1.

_____. "Cubans Capture Invasion Plane; Accuse Trujillo," *New York Times*, August 15, 1959, p. 1.

_____. "Cubans Support Ouster," *New York Times*, January 22, 1960, p. 6.

_____. "Cubans Urged to Sharpen Vigil Against Enemies of Revolution," *New York Times*, March 19, 1961, p. 31.

_____. "Cubans Will Base Economy on System of Cooperatives," *New York Times*, February 28, 1960, p. 1.

_____. "Cuba's Bank Chief Views U.S. As Foe in Economic Fight," *New York Times*, March 21, 1960.

_____. "Cuba's Bid for Visitors," *New York Times*, February 22, 1959, p. X25.

_____. "Cuba's Mobilization Limits Cane Harvest," *New York Times*, January 12, 1961, p. 1.

_____. "Cuba's President Puts Onus on U.S.," *New York Times*, January 28, 1960, p. 9.

_____. "Democracy Saved, Batista Tells Cuba," *New York Times*, February 5, 1941, p. 1.

_____. "Economic Revolution Casts Cloud of Doubt over Cuba," *New York Times*, January 13, 1960, p. 49.

_____. "European Loans Reported in Cuba," *New York Times*, December 5, 1959, p. 12.

_____. "Ex-Castro Aide Draws 20 Years," *New York Times*, December 16, 1959, p. 1.

_____. "Firm on Bonds for Land," *New York Times*, July 28, 1959, p. 2.

_____. "Foreign Capital Curbed by Castro," *New York Times*, February 26, 1960, p. 7.

_____. "40% Profits Tax Planned in Cuba," *New York Times*, May 31, 1959, p. 8.

_____. "Grenade Kills 3 at Fete in Cuba," *New York Times*, February 2, 1959, p. 5.

_____. "Havana Arrests U.S. Expatriate," *New York Times*, October 22, 1960; p. 1.

_____. "Havana Classes Resume Monday," *New York Times*, May 10, 1959, p. 14.

_____. "Havana Rejects Protest by U.S. on Propaganda," *New York Times*, November 14, 1959, p. 1.

_____. "Havana Rejects Seizure Protest," *New York Times*, July 9, 1960, p. 3.

_____. "Havana Welcomes Castro at End of Triumphal Trip," *New York Times*, January 9, 1959, p. 1.

_____. "Hope of U.S. Shift Voiced by Castro," *New York Times*, November 29, 1960, p. 19.

_____. "Incipient Revolt Quashed in Cuba," *New York Times*, March 17, 1945, p. 9.

_____. "Indiana Flier Denies Plot to Kill Castro," *New York Times*, February 7, 1959, p. 1.

_____. "Land Law Splits Castro's Regime," *New York Times*, June 13, 1959, p. 1.

_____. "Land Seizure Act in Effect in Cuba," *New York Times*, June 5, 1959, p. 3.

_____. "Leftist Named President of Cuba's National Bank," *New York Times*, November 27, 1959, p. 1.

_____. "Military Court in Cuba Dooms 14 for 'War Crimes,'" *New York Times*, January 13, 1959, p. 1.

_____. "Morgan Is Shot as Cuba 'Traitor.'" *New York Times*, March 12, 1961, p. 32.

_____. "New Cuba Invites Tourists," *New York Times*, January 18, 1959, p. XX22.

_____. "New Cuban Government Faces Huge Economic Problems," *New York Times*, January 25, 1959, p. E8.

_____. "New Town Rising in Cuban Fields," *New York Times*, March 3, 1960, p. 9.

_____. "Nicaragua Rebels Arrested in Cuba," *New York Times*, April 20, 1959, p. 1.

_____. "Nye Goes on Trial As 'Plotter' in Cuba," *New York Times*, April 12, 1959, p. 1.

_____. "Oil Companies' Files Are Sealed by Cuba," *New York Times*, October 31, 1959, p. 1.

_____. "100 Face Death in Trials About to Begin at Havana," *New York Times*, January 15, 1959, p. 1.

_____. "Property Seizure Persists in Cuba," *New York Times*, May 11, 1959; p. 13.

_____. "Racketeers Face Execution in Cuba: Castro Warns Gambling and Narcotics Offenders — Says U.S. Aids Foes," *New York Times*, March 27, 1959, p. 7.

_____. "Rebels Dissolve Cuban Congress; Officials Ousted," *New York Times*, January 7, 1959, p. 1.

_____. "Reds' Alleged Role in Castro's Regime Alarming Havana," *New York Times*, April 24, 1959, p. 1.

_____. "Reds' Cuban Base Reported Crushed," *New York Times*, September 27, 1953, p. 32.

_____. "Reds Frozen Out by Cuban Unions," *New York Times*, November 21, 1959, p. 1.

_____. "Reforms in Cuba Cramp Economy," *New York Times*, March 21, 1959, p. 25.

_____. "Reporter Convicted and Ousted by Cuba," *New York Times*, December 23, 1959, p. 1.

_____. "Santiago Cools toward Castro; City Was Once His Stronghold," *New York Times*, April 1, 1960, p. 1.

_____. "75 Die in Havana as Munitions Ship Explodes at Dock," *New York Times*, March 5, 1960, p. 1.

_____. "Shake-up in Cuba Laid to Unrest," *New York Times*, October 18, 1959, p. 1.

_____. "6 Americans Get 30 Years in Cuba," *New York Times*, February 1, 1961, p. 4.

_____. "Society-News Tax? Cuban Editors Shocked," *New York Times*, June 2, 1959, p. 16.

_____. "Society News Tax Is Dropped in Cuba," *New York Times*, June 6, 1959, p. 1.

_____. "Soviet Exhibition Havana's Top Hit," *New York Times*, February 25, 1960, p. 12.

_____. "Soviet Gives Cuba 100 Million Credit on Sale of Sugar," *New York Times*, February 14, 1960, p. 1.

_____. "Student Rebels Seize Havana U.," *New York Times*, February 5, 1959, p. 7.

_____. "300,000 Rally to Back Castro; He Condemns 'Raids' from U.S.," *New York Times*, October 27, 1959, p. 1.

_____. "3 Shot in Havana Rioting as Mikoyan Opens Exhibit," *New York Times*, February 6, 1960, p. 1.

_____. "3 U.S. Citizens Get Long Terms in Cuba," *New York Times*, December 9, 1959, p. 1.

_____. "Tobacco Grower Adjusts in Cuba," *New York Times*, March 4, 1960, p. 10.

_____. *The Tragic Island: How Communism Came to Cuba.* Englewood Cliffs, N.J.: Prentice-Hall, 1961.

_____. "Tread of Militia Resounds in Cuba," *New York Times*, January 17, 1960, p. 1.

_____. "2 U.S. Companies Face Cuban Study," *New York Times*, February 24, 1959, p. 12.

_____. "Two U.S. Attachés Ousted by Havana on a Plot Charge," *New York Times*, June 17, 1960, p. 1.

_____. "Urrutia Criticizes U.S.," *New York Times*, July 14, 1959, p. 2.

_____. "Urrutia Takes Up Duties in Havana; Names a Premier," *New York Times*, January 6, 1959, p. 1.

_____. "Urrutia Will Let 300 Foes Depart," *New York Times*, January 8, 1959, p. 3.

_____. "U.S. Aides Start Leaving Havana," *New York Times*, January 5, 1961, p. 1.

_____. "U.S. Cleric Finds Cuba Friendly; Urges Washington to Be Patient," *New York Times*, December 18, 1959, p. 12.

_____. "U.S. Envoy, Castro Meet for 6 Hours," *New York Times*, September 5, 1959, p. 4.

_____. "U.S. Note 'False,' Cubans Are Told," *New York Times*, November 11, 1959, p. 17.

_____. "Vituperation against U.S. Rises in Cuba after Herter Criticism," *New York Times*, March 10, 1960, p. 3.

_____. "Youth of Cuba Collecting Funds for Arms against 'Aggressor,'" *New York Times*, March 27, 1960, p. 32.

Pierson, Peter. *The History of Spain.* Westport, CT: Greenwood Press, 1999.

Pile, John. *A History of Interior Design.* 3rd ed. Hoboken, NJ: John Wiley and Sons, 2005.

P. J. C. F. [sic]. "Midwinter Vacations 1959," *New York Times,* January 18, 1959, p. XX1.

"Plain Talk," *Time* magazine, May 12, 1958.

"Planes That Raid Cuba," *New York Times*, March 24, 1960, p. 32.

"Plot for Invasion of Cuba Charged," *New York Times*, July 18, 1959, p. 1.

"Plot to Kill Castro Is Revealed," *The Times of Havana*, January 16, 1959, p. 1.

"Plot to Shoot Envoy of U.S. in Cuba Fails," *Washington Post*, November 9, 1935, p. 1.

"Plot to Slay President of Cuba Foiled," *Washington Post*, March 18, 1945, p. M1.

"Point 4 Pact Signed with Cuba," *New York Times*, June 21, 1951, p. 11.

"Poland Set to Supply Jet Planes to Castro," *Washington Post*, April 2, 1960, p. A4.

"Police Leader Is Jailed," *New York Times*, March 9, 1948, p. 11.

"Police Mobilized for Broadcast," *Washington Post*, February 18, 1951, p. M8.

"Political Row Besets Cuba over Dominican Republic Plot," *Washington Post*, October 1, 1947, p. 1.

Pollack, Howard. *Aaron Copland: The Life and Work of an Uncommon Man.* Champaign: University of Illinois Press, 2000.

"Pons Called Traitor," *New York Times*, March 19, 1960, p. 5.

Porter, Russell B. "Gomez Promises Freedom in Cuba," *New York Times*, July 4, 1936, p. 1.

Povich, Shirley. "This Morning: Cubans Demonstrate at the World Series," *Washington Post*, October 7, 1958.

_____. "This Morning: Homesick Cuban Players," *Washington Post*, August 1, 1948.

"Powder Magazines Explode," *New York Times*, December 31, 1958, p. 4.

"Power Plant at Habanilla Falls," *The Times at Havana*, August 29, 1957, p. 3.

Prados, John. *Safe for Democracy: The Secret Wars of the CIA.* Chicago: Ivan R. Dee, 2006.

"Prelate Appeals to Castro," *New York Times*, February 2, 1959, p. 5.

"Presidential Candidates Speak Out for Religion," *Washington Post*, May 3, 1952, p. 1.

"Press Reports on Cuba Assailed as 'Sophistry,'" *Washington Post*, April 7, 1960, p. A6.

"Press Unit Scores Cuba," *New York Times*, November 24, 1959, p. 15.

Preussen, Ronald W. *John Foster Dulles: The Road to Power*. New York: The Free Press, 1982.

"Princeton Gives Castro Uproarious Reception," *Trenton Times*. April 21, 1959.

"Prío Backs Castro and the Revolution," *Miami News*, December 30, 1960, p. 3.

"Prío Group in Cuba Urges Civil Rights," *New York Times*, May 16, 1959, p. 3.

"The Problem of Cuba," *New York Times*, December 21, 1959, p. 26.

"Pro-Castro 1-Hour Strike of Million Set," *Washington Post*, July 23, 1959, p. A7.

"Protestant Aide to Castro Here," *New York Times*, June 13, 1959, p. 11.

"Provocations Decried," *New York Times*, May 14, 1960, p. 10.

"Puerto Ricans Assail U.S.," *New York Times*, November 23, 1959, p. 22.

"Puerto Rico Is Not Free," *Time*, March 8, 1954.

Quirk, Robert E. *Fidel Castro*. New York: W.W. Norton, 1995.

"Rabbi Deplores Castro Revenge," *New York Times*, January 18, 1959, p. 78.

Rabe, Stephen G. *Eisenhower and Latin America: The Foreign Policy of Anti-Communism*. Chapel Hill: University of North Carolina Press, 1968.

"Radio: Lucy's $8,000,000," *Time*, March 2, 1953.

"Ramón Castro Assailed," *New York Times*, November 25, 1959, p. 11.

Ramos, Marcos A. *Protestantism and Revolution in Cuba*. Miami: The University of Miami, North-South Center for the Research Institute for Cuban Studies, 1989.

Ranzal, Edward. "U.S. Indicts Prio As Cuban Plotter: Ex-President and 8 Others Said to Prepare Attack," *New York Times*, February 14, 1958, p. 1.

Rasco, José Ignacio. "Semblanza de Fidel Castro," in Efrén Córdova, ed., *40 Años de Revolución: El Legado de Castro*. Miami: Ediciones Universal, 1999, pp. 411–444.

Raskin, A. H. "Castro Rebuffed by Union Leaders," *New York Times*, April 29, 1959, p. 11.

"Raúl Castro Attacks U.S.," *New York Times*, February 25, 1960, p. 12.

"Raúl Castro Denies Rebels Enter Cuba," *New York Times*, August 9, 1959, p. 10.

"Raúl Castro States He Is No Communist," *New York Times*, December 14, 1959, p. 6.

Raymond, Jack. "Cuba Says Attaché Who Quit in Washington Stole $110,000," *New York Times*, March 20, 1960, p.1.

_____. "Guatemala Calls Forces Defensive," *New York Times*, January 11, 1961, p.1.

_____. "Pentagon Warns Cuba on Base; Says Rights Are Not Revocable," *New York Times*, October 28, 1959, p. 4.

_____. "President Calls Pair Traitorous," *New York Times*, September 7, 1960, p.1.

"Rebellion's Financier," *New York Times*, April 24, 1959, p. 6.

"Rebel Munitions Seized," *The Times of Havana,* October 14, 1957, p. 3.

"The Rebel Steamer *Victoria* Leaves Havana. Secession Sympathizers in Havana; a United States Officer Traduced. Experimental Gunnery," *New York Times*, February 28, 1862, p. 2.

"Red Embrace in Cuba," *New York Times*, May 12, 1959, p. 34.

"Red Voters in Cuba Gain Some Ground," *New York Times*, October 26, 1947, p. 21.

Reed, Robert Hugh. "Understanding Cuba," letter to the Editor. *New York Times*, January 28, 1960, p. 30.

"Remember the Maine"—The Beginnings of War," Library of Congress, http://memory.loc.gov/ammem/saw html/sawsp2.html.

"Reply to Cuba," *New York Times*, March 1, 1960, p. 32.

Report by Cuba on Resolution 60/12 of the United Nations General Assembly. "Necessity of Ending the Economic, Commercial and Financial Blockade Imposed by the United States of America against Cuba," United Nations, August 2006.

"Reporting a Revolution," *Time*, February 9, 1959.

Report of the Special Committee on the Problem of Hungary. New York: United Nations General Assembly. Official Records: Eleventh Session, Supplement 18 (A/3592), 1957.

Research Initiative on Cuban Agriculture, www.cuba nag.ifas.ufl.edu.

Reston, James. "Anti-U.S. Gesture by Castro Is Seen," *New York Times*, February 15, 1960, p. 1.

_____. "Capital Considers a Tougher Policy on Castro Regime," *New York Times*, February 18, 1960, p. 1.

_____. "Cuba's Drift to the Left," *New York Times*, February 19, 1960, p. 6.

_____. "Mr. Mikoyan Comes to the Caribbean," *New York Times*, February 7, 1960, p. E8.

_____. "The New Sugar Daddy from Moscow," *New York Times*, February 14, 1960, p. E8.

_____. "President Warns Soviet on Berlin," *New York Times*, April 28, 1960, p. 1.

_____. "Rusk Declares Sympathy of Nation for Castro Foes," *New York Times*, April 18, 1961, p. 1.

_____. "Top U.S. Advisers in Dispute on Aid to Castro's Foes," *New York Times*, April 11, 1961, p. 1.

"Retrial of Airmen Troubling Cubans," *New York Times*, March 6, 1959, p. 5.

"Return of the Firing Squad," *Time*, October 24, 1960.

"Assassination of Prisoners in Haiti," *Revolución*, September 1, 1959, pp. 1, 19.

"Revolution's Captives," *Washington Post*, November 24, 1959, p. A14.

Rice, Diana. "What the Trip Will Cost," *New York Times*, April 13, 1958, p. xx17.

"Richard M. Nixon, 36th Vice President (1953–1961)," United States Senate, http://www.senate.gov/artandhistory/history/common/generic/VP_Richard_Nixon.htm.

Richards, John F. *The Unending Frontier: An Environmental History of the Early Modern World*. Berkeley: University of California Press, 2003.

"A Ridiculous Invention," *New York Times*, June 2, 1862.

Rigdon, Susan. "Limitations on the Use of Culture as an Explanatory Concept: The Case of Long-term Poverty," in Katherine A. Rhoades and Anne Statham, eds., *Speaking Out: Women, Poverty, and Public Policy*. University of Wisconsin System Women's Studies Consortium, October 29–31, 1998.

"Rioting Breaks Out in Havana, *Washington Post*, January 2, 1959, p. A6.

Rippel, Joel A. *75 Memorable Moments in Minnesota*

Sports. Minneapolis: Minnesota Historical Society Press, 2003.

Roberts, Chalmers M. "50 Years Ago, Cuba's Rebels Took Control," *Miami Herald*, December 31, 2008. http://www.miamiherald.com/news/americas/cuba/v-fullstory/story/832180.html.

_____. "Santiago Delegates Draft 'Declaration,'" *Washington Post and Times Herald*, August 15, 1959, p. A1.

Roberts, Chalmers M., and Murrey Marder. "President Decided on Cuba Venture on Advice of Joint Chiefs and CIA," *Washington Post and Times Herald*, April 22, 1961, p. A1.

Roberts, John Storm. *The Latin Tinge: The Impact of Latin American Music on the United States*. 2nd ed. New York: Oxford University Press, 1999.

Robinson, Eugene. *Last Dance in Havana: The Final Days of Fidel and the Start of the New Cuban Revolution*. New York: Free Press, 2004.

Robles, Frances. "Cuba's Revolution at 50: Gains Fade, Despair Endures," *Miami Herald*, December 14, 2008. http://www.miamiherald.com/news/americas/cuba/v-fullstory/story/811777.html.

Rock, David. *Authoritarian Argentina: The Nationalist Movement, Its History and Its Impact*. Berkeley: University of California Press, 1993.

"Rodriguez Homer Gives Leafs 6–4 Win over Cubans," United Press International, April 15, 1959.

Rodríguez-Mangual, Edna M. *Lydia Cabrera and the Construction of an Afro-Cuban Cultural Identity*. Chapel Hill: University of North Carolina Press, 2004.

Rohter, Larry. "Cuba Eager for Tourist Dollars, Dusts Off Its Vacancy Sign," *New York Times*, October 19, 1995.

_____. "Marcos Pérez Jiménez, 87, Venezuelan Ruler," *New York Times*, September 22, 2007.

Ross, Ciro Bianchi. "Graham Greene's Cuban Time," Cuba Now.Net, July 24, 1996, http://www.cubanow.net/pages/articulo.php?sec=17&t=2&item=1246.

Rossi, John P. *The National Game: Baseball and American Culture*. Chicago: Ivan R. Dee, 2000.

Rucker, Mark, and Peter Bjarkman. *Smoke: The Romance and Lore of Cuban Baseball*. New York: Total Sports Illustrated, 1999.

Russell, Dick. *The Man Who Knew Too Much*. 2nd ed. New York: Carroll & Graf, 2003.

Russo, Gus. *Live by the Sword: The Secret War against Castro and the Death of JFK*. Baltimore, MD: Bancroft Press, 1998.

Ryan, William L. "Agonizing Hour Has Come for Cuba after 50 Years," Associated Press, January 1, 1959.

_____. "American Citizens Not Endangered, White House Says," *Washington Post*, January 2, 1959, p. A1.

_____. "Castro Wins Good Will but Leaves Doubts," Associated Press, April 27, 1959.

_____. "Rebels Execute Batista Aides," *Washington Post and Times Herald*, January 8, 1959, p. A7.

_____. "Reds Yield to Rebels, Havana Clash Averted," *Washington Post and Times Herald*, January 5, 1959, p. A1.

Sachar, Howard M. *Farewell España: The World of the Sephardim Remembered*. New York: Alfred A. Knopf, 1994.

Safford, Jeffrey J. "The Nixon-Castro Meeting of 19 April 1959," *Diplomatic History* 4 (Fall 1980), pp. 425–431.

Sallah, Michael D. "Cuba's Yankee Comandante," *Toledo Blade*, March 3, 2002.

"Salsa Queen Cruz Remembered," *New York Times*, July 19, 2003.

Salwen, Michael B. *Radio and Television in Cuba: The Pre–Castro Era*. Ames: Iowa State University Press, 1994.

Sanchez, Máximo. "Dodgers Edge Reds, 3 to 2, at Havana's Gran Stadium," *The Times of Havana*, March 21, 1959, p. 13.

Sanchez, Máximo. "Reds Blank Blues, Take First." *The Havana Times*, October 24, 1957, p. 16.

Sanders, Coyne Steven, and Tom Gilbert. *Desilu: The Story of Lucille Ball and Desi Arnaz*. New York: Quill, 1993.

Sanders, Paul. "Will Castro Crack Down on Commies?" Associated Press, April 26, 1959.

Sands, Robert R. *Anthropology, Sport and Culture*. Westport, CT: Bergin & Garvey, 1999. "Santa Maria Case Linked to a Cuban," *New York Times*, February 11, 1961, p. 7.

Santana Alonso, Alfredo. *El Inmortal Del Beisbol*. Havana: Instituto Cubano Del Libro, 1998.

"Santiago Trials Scheduled," *New York Times*, December 13, 1959, p. 28.

Santos-Busch, Charles A. "Relations with Cuba," *New York Times*, February 25, 1960, p. 28.

Scall, John. "Trujillo's Air Force Reported Buying 12 Jet Fighter Planes in Canada," *Washington Post and Times Herald*, January 26, 1959, p. A6.

"Scene of Revolt Is a Lush Green Island, Largest and Most Populous of Antilles," *New York Times*, January 2, 1959, p. 7.

Schemo, Diana Jean. "Stroessner, Paraguay's Enduring Dictator, Dies," *New York Times*, August 16, 2006.

Schipani, Andres. "The Final Triumph of Saint Che," *The Observer*, September 23, 2007.

Schlesinger, Arthur M., Jr., ed. *The Almanac of American History*. Greenwich, CT: Barnes & Noble Books, 1993.

_____. Memorandum, Document 0355, June 9, 1961. Cuban Information Archives, http://cuban-exile.com/doc_351–375/doc0355.html.

_____. *A Thousand Days: John F. Kennedy in the White House*. New York: Houghton Mifflin Harcourt, 2002.

Schmidt, Dana Adams. "Castro Rules Out Role as Neutral; Opposes the Reds," *New York Times*, April 20, 1959, p. 1.

_____. "Castro Stresses Land Reform Aim," *New York Times*, April 21, 1959, p. 1.

_____. "Dominicans Told to Return B-26's," *New York Times*, March 17, 1960, p. 14.

_____. "Dulles Applauds Caracas Results," *New York Times*, March 15, 1954, p. 1.

_____. "Herter Upbraids Cuban on Charge in Ship Explosion," *New York Times*, March 8, 1960, p. 1.

_____. "Land Seizures Evaluated," *New York Times*, January 12, 1960, p. 11.

_____. "U.S. Aides Wary on Cuba's Future," *New York Times*, January 2, 1959, p. 1.

_____. "U.S. Backs Spain in Western Role," *New York Times*, March 24, 1960, p. 4.

Schoenberg, Nara. "The Son Also Falls," *Chicago Tribune*, November 19, 2001.

Schoultz, Lars. *Beneath the United States*. Cambridge, Mass.: Harvard University Press, 1998.

Schwartz, Harry. "Cuba Fashioning an Economic Web," *New York Times*, February 28, 1960, p. F1.

_____. "Soviet Will Send Cuba Vital Goods," *New York Times*, February 19, 1960, p. 6.

Schwartz, Rosalie. *Pleasure Island: Tourism and Temptation in Cuba*. Lincoln: University of Nebraska Press, 1997.

Semillas de Fuego: Compilación Sobre La Lucha Clandestina en La Capital. Prologue by Faustino Pérez. Epilogue by

Melba Hernández. Havana: Editorial de Ciencias Sociales, 1989.

"Senator from Daytona," *Time*, April 12, 1948.

"Senators Subdue Athletics, 8–3, with Help from a Triple Play," *New York Times*, July 24, 1960, p. S3.

"Sentences Suspended," *New York Times*, December 22, 1959, p. 12.

Sentner, David. "Washington Window," Hearst Headline Service, November 12, 1959.

Server, Lee. *Ava Gardner: "Love Is Nothing."* London: St. Martin's Press, 2008.

"7 Indicted in Miami in Arms Smuggling," *New York Times*, June 6, 1959, p. 6.

"Shaughnessy Pulls Club," *Washington Post*, July 8, 1960, p. 50.

Sheehan, Joseph M. "Baseball Men from 3 Leagues to Confer Today on Expansion," *New York Times*, August 2, 1960, p. 32.

Shelden, Michael. *Graham Greene: The Enemy Within*. New York: Random House, 1994.

Sherry, Norman. *The Life of Graham Greene, Volume II*. New York: Viking Books, 2004.

Shetterly, Aran. *The Americano: Fighting for Freedom in Castro's Cuba*. New York: Algonquin Books, 2007.

"Show Business: Desiloot," *Time*, November 16, 1962.

Shurmaitis, Dawn. "Life with Papa." *New Jersey Monthly*, September 2005.

Shute, Nancy. "Haven't Got a Clue? Maybe DNA Will Do; Regular Folks and History Buffs Play Detective." *U.S. News and World Report*, July 24, 2000.

Sierra, J. A. The History of Cuba. www.historyofcuba.com.

"6 Anti-Castro Cubans Freed after U.S. Drops Charges," *New York Times*, January 3, 1968, p. 45.

"6 from U.S. Held in Cuba on Pesos," *New York Times*, March 14, 1959, p. 3.

"The Slave-trade," *New York Times*, January 17, 1861, p. 6.

Smith, Earl E. T. *The Fourth Floor: An Account of the Castro Communist Revolution*. Washington, DC: Selous Foundation, 1962, 1987.

Smith, Gaddis. *The Last Years of the Monroe Doctrine, 1945–1993*. New York: Hill and Wang, 1994.

Smith, Gene. "Castro Believed More Amenable," *New York Times*, August 9, 1959, p. F1.

_____. "Utilities in Cuba Await Their Fate," *New York Times*, January 18, 1959, p. F1.

Smith, Lois M., and Alfred Padula. *Sex and Revolution: Women in Socialist Cuba*. New York: Oxford University Press, 1996.

Smith, Marie. "Whiskered Conquerors of Cuba Here," *Washington Post and Times*, February 26, 1959, p. A1.

Smith, Robert F. *The United States and Cuba: Business and Diplomacy, 1917–1960*. New York: Bookman Associates, 1960.

Smith, Wayne S. *The Closest of Enemies: A Personal and Diplomatic Account of U.S.-Cuban Relations since 1957*. New York: W.W. Norton, 1987.

Smylie, James H. *A Brief History of the Presbyterians*. Louisville, KY: Geneva Press, 1996.

Snyder, Brad. *A Well Paid Slave: Curt Flood's Fight for Free Agency in Professional Sports*. New York: Viking, 2006.

Sokolsky, George E. "These Days...." *Washington Post and Times Herald*, November 14, 1959, p. A7.

_____. "These Days ... Peace is Wonderful," *Washington Post and Times Herald*, March 1, 1960, p. A11.

_____. "These Days ... Sugar and Coffee," *Washington Post and Times Herald*, January 14, 1960, p. A23.

_____. "These Days ... That Cuban Ad," *Washington Post and Times Herald*, April 21, 1960, p. A23.

"Some Firing Still Heard in Paraguay," *Washington Post*, December 14, 1959, p. A13.

"Sorí Marín Is Ex-Castro Aide," *New York Times*, April 20, 1961, p. 10.

"Sosa Blanco Convicted 2d Time," *Washington Post*, February 18, 1959, p. A6.

"Soviet Agent Tied to Reds in Havana," *New York Times*, August 22, 1959, p. 2.

"Soviet Asked to Clarify Its Cease-Fire Position," *Washington Post and Times Herald*, April 18, 1961, p. A1.

"Soviet-Cuban Pact Spurs World Sugar in Active Trading," *New York Times*, February 16, 1960, p. 51.

"Soviet Will Get Cuban Sugar," *New York Times*, August 8, 1953, p. 3.

Spargo, Mary. "Mere 14 Million Communists Are Altering Globe," *Washington Post*, May 23, 1948, p. B1.

Spence, Terry. "Ernest Hemingway's Son Gregory Dies." Associated Press, October 4, 2001. "Stakes High in Sugar Beet Race," *New York Times*, November 14, 1959, p. 25.

Stang, Allen. *The Actor: The True Story of John Foster Dulles, Secretary of State, 1953–1959*. Boston, MA: Western Islands, 1968.

"State Department Absolved," *New York Times*, July 18, 1959, p. 3.

Staten, Clifford L. *The History of Cuba*. New York: Palgrave Macmillan, 2005.

Stein, Lisa. "Did Columbus Bring Syphilis to Europe?" *Scientific American*, January 15, 2008.

"Steps Taken to Prevent Hot Pesos: One Person Can Bring in Only 50 Pesos," *The Times of Havana*, January 29, 1959, p. 1.

St. George, Andrew. "Cuban Rebels," *Look*, February 4, 1958, p. 30.

"Stiff New Controls Imposed by Cuba," *Washington Post*, September 25, 1959, p. C7.

Strauss, Neil. "The Indestructible Beat of Bo Diddley," *Rolling Stone*, August 11, 2005.

"Stringent Levies by Cuba Backed," *New York Times*, September 26, 1959, p. 7.

"Students Get Advice on Languages from Expert," *New York Times*, April 26, 1959, p. E9.

Stump, Al. *Cobb: A Biography*. Chapel Hill, NC: Algonquin, 1994.

"A Success Story in Necklines: Luis Estévez Is a One-Year Wonder," *Life*, April 2, 1956.

Suchlicki, Jaime. *Cuba: From Columbus to Castro and Beyond*. Washington, DC: Brassey's, 2002.

_____. *University Students and Revolution in Cuba, 1920–1968*. Coral Gables, FL: University of Miami Press, 1969.

"Sugar and the Revolution," *New York Times*, April 3, 1959, p. 26.

"Sugar Import Cut Urged to Curb Cuba," *New York Times*, February 3, 1960, p. 9.

"Sugar King," *Time*, July 28, 1958.

"Summary of Editorial Comment on United States Break in Relations with Cuba," *New York Times*, January 5, 1961, p. 10.

Summers, Anthony, and Robyn Swan. *The Arrogance of Power: The Secret World of Richard Nixon*. New York: Viking Press, 2000.

_____. *Sinatra: The Life*. New York, Alfred A. Knopf, 2005.

Sun Tzu. *The Art of War*. http://www.gutenberg.org/etext/132.

Suro, Federico. "Shopping for Witches Brew," *Americas* (English Edition) 43 (September-October 1991), p. 1.

Sweig, Julia E. *Inside the Cuban Revolution: Fidel Castro and the Cuban Underground.* Cambridge, MA: Harvard University Press, 2002.

"A Symbol of Rebellion: Fidel Castro," *New York Times*, January 2, 1959, p. 6.

Symmes, Patrick. *The Boys from Dolores: Fidel Castro's Classmates from Revolution to Exile.* New York: Pantheon, 2007.

Szulc, Tad. "Anti-Castro Units Land in Cuba; Report Fighting at Beachhead," *New York Times*, April 18, 1961, p. 1.

_____. "As Castro Speaks: 'The Wall! The Wall!'" *New York Times*, December 13, 1959, p. SM11.

_____. "Batista Denies Trying to Flee from Dominican Haven to U. S.," *New York Times*, July 19, 1959, p. 2.

_____. "Brazilian to Shorten Cuba Visit over 'Misquotation' About U.S.," *New York Times*, April 1, 1960, p.12.

_____. "British Capture 17 Cuban Exiles and Raiding Boat," *New York Times*, April 2, 1963, p. 1.

_____. "Caribbean Area Still Big Headache for U.S.," *New York Times*, August 23, 1959, p. E4. _____. "Caribbean Clash Causes an Uproar at Americas Talk," *New York Times*, August 14, 1959, p. 1.

_____. "Castro Accuses U.S. 'Monopolics,'" *New York Times*, July 28, 1959, p. 2.

_____. "Castro Foe Caught as Plane Downed," *New York Times*, July 25, 1959, pp. 1, 27.

_____. "Castro Resumes Talk of Invasion," *New York Times*, March 28, 1960, p. 10.

_____. "Castro Warns U.S. to Modify Policy," *New York Times*, March 29, 1960, p. 16.

_____. "C.I.A. Is Accused by Bitter Rebels," *New York Times*, April 22, 1961, p. 1.

_____. "City Is Thronged," *New York Times*, February 25, 1960, p. 1.

_____. "Ciudad Trujillo Full of Rumors," *New York Times*, July 7, 1959, p. 18.

_____. "Crowds' Acclaim Viewed as Index," *New York Times*, March 4, 1960, p. 8.

_____. "Cuba Exploiting Discord with U.S." *New York Times*, December 20, 1959, p. 1.

_____. "Cuba Formulates 'New Democracy,'" *New York Times*, July 29, 1959, p. 12.

_____. "Cuba Halts Work in Plea to Castro," *New York Times*, July 24, 1959, p. 1.

_____. "Cuba Mediation Urged in Brazil," *New York Times*, October 26, 1960, p. 27.

_____. "Cuban Labor Joins in Pressing Castro to Return as Premier," *New York Times*, July 23, 1959, p. 10.

_____. "Cubans and Poles Sign Trade Treaty," *New York Times*, April 2, 1960, p. 1.

_____. "Cubans Denounce Eisenhower View as Hypocritical," *New York Times*, April 10, 1960, p. 1.

_____. "Cuba: Revolutionary Fervor Mounts," *New York Times*, March 27, 1960, p. E5.

_____. "Cuba's Rebel City Proud but Uneasy," *New York Times*, November 25, 1959, p. 11.

_____. "Cuba Takes Over Fifth TV Station," *New York Times*, March 27, 1960, p. 30.

_____. "Danger Signals Flare in Latin America," *New York Times*, June 7, 1959, p. E3.

_____. "Dominican Affair Stirs the Caribbean Area," *New York Times*, July 12, 1959, p. E3.

_____. "Eisenhower Tour: the Promises and the Expectations," *New York Times*, March 6, 1960, p. E6.

_____. *Fidel: A Critical Portrait.* New York: William Morrow and Company, 1986.

_____. "Former Backers of Castro Urge Anti-Red Rising," *New York Times*, April 11, 1960, p. 1.

_____. "Gay Cubans Hail Castro's Triumph," *New York Times*, July 27, 1959, p. 3.

_____. "Havana Crowds Wait for Castro," *New York Times*, July 21, 1959, p. 3.

_____. "Last 2 Refineries Seized by Castro; Oil Supplies Low," *New York Times*, July 2, 1960, p. 1.

_____. "Latin Hosts Back U.S. Cuban Policy," *New York Times*, March 3, 1960, p. 7.

_____. "Nixon to Propose New Latin Policy," *New York Times*, May 16, 1958, p. 12.

_____. "Politics Embroil Havana Meetings," *New York Times*, November 18, 1959, p. 18.

_____. "Pro-Communists in Havana Battle Foes in Street," *New York Times*, March 26, 1960, p. 1.

_____. "Radio War Rages in the Caribbean," *New York Times*, July 9, 1959, p. 9.

_____. "Rebels Hopeful," *New York Times*, April 21, 1961; p. 1.

_____. "Rivalries Beset Top Cuban Exiles," *New York Times*, April 9, 1961, p. 1.

_____. "A Super-Cabinet Rules Over Cuba," *New York Times*, December 18, 1959, p. 1.

_____. "Trujillo Faces Biggest Threat of His 30-Year Dictatorship," *New York Times*, July 5, 1959, p. 1.

_____. "Two Americans on Trial in Cuba," *New York Times*, December 1, 1959, p. 18.

_____. "Unrest Troubles Trujillo Regime," *New York Times*, July 6, 1959, p. 1.

_____. "U.S. Investigating Cubans in Florida," *New York Times*, April 27, 1960, p. 11.

_____. "U.S. Notes to Cuba Link Castro Rule to Rising Tension," *New York Times*, April 12, 1960, p. 1.

_____. "A Year of Castro Rule in Cuba: Leftists Speeding Vast Reforms," *New York Times*, December 17, 1959, p. 1.

Tapper, Jake. "The Ghost of Terror Past," *Salon*, January 11, 2002.

"Taxes on Imports Imposed by Cuba," *New York Times*, September 25, 1959, p. 44

"Tax Warning to Cubans," *New York Times*, May 4, 1959, p. 13

Taylor, Joseph A. "Agents Seize Anti-Castro Ringleaders," *Washington Post and Times Herald*, August 12, 1959, p. A1.

_____. "Cuba Foils Invasion, Reports Say," *Washington Post and Times Herald*, August 10, 1959, p. A1.

_____. "Raúl Castro Escapes Assassin," *Washington Post and Times Herald*, August 11, 1959, p. A1.

Taylor, Maxwell. *Paramilitary Study Group Report.* Washington, DC: Central Intelligence Agency, June 13, 1961.

"Tearful Lucille Ball Divorces Desi Arnaz," *Los Angeles Times*, May 5, 1960, p. B1.

"Terrorism Charged to Cubans in Testimony by Miami Police," *New York Times*, August 23, 1976, p. 12.

"Terrorist Unit Says It Killed Exile," *Washington Post*, November 5, 1975, p. A4.

"Testimony Traces Arms," *New York Times*, April 13, 1959, p. 13.

"Text of Address by President Eisenhower at Pan American Union," *New York Times*, April 13, 1953, p. 13.

"Text of Cuban Note Rejecting Protest and Calling for a Change in U.S. Policy," *New York Times*, November 14, 1959, p. 8.

"Text of the State Department's Document Denouncing

Bibliography

Castro Regime in Cuba," *New York Times*, April 4, 1961, p. 14.

"Text of the Statement by Eisenhower on Cuba," *New York Times*, January 27, 1960, p. 10.

"Text of U.S. Statement on Envoy's Protest against Accusations by Premier Castro," *New York Times*, October 28, 1959, p. 4. "The Text of Two Bogota Accords," May 1, 1948, p. 7.

"Their Man in Havana," *Time*, January 19, 1959.

"The Theoretical Transfer," *Washington Post*, March 29, 1902, p. 6.

"They Beat Batista," *Time*, January 12, 1959.

"13% of Cuba's Cane Bombed, Union Says," *New York Times*, February 27, 1960, p. 3.

"30 Reported Captured in West Cuba Battle," *Washington Post*, September 25, 1959, p. A14.

Thomas, Evan. *The Very Best Men: Four Who Dared*. New York, Simon and Schuster, 1996.

Thomas, Hugh. *Cuba; Or the Pursuit of Freedom*. New York: Harper & Row, 1971.

_____. *The Cuban Revolution*. NY: Harper & Row, 1971.

_____. "Cuba: the United States and Batista, 1952–58," *World Affairs* 149 (1987), pp.160–176.

Thomas, Tony. *Errol Flynn: The Spy Who Never Was*. New York: Citadel, 1990.

Thornley, Stew. "Minneapolis Millers, 1959 Junior World Series vs. Havana," http://stewthornley.net/millers_havana.html.

"3 American Pilots Get Long Terms in Cuba," *Washington Post*, December 9, 1959, p. A5.

"3 Americans Sentenced," *New York Times*, January 11, 1961, p. 10.

"342 Americans Due in Cuba for Tour," *New York Times*, December 25, 1960, p. 6.

"3 Plots Foiled, Castro Agents Say," *Washington Post*, December 30, 1959, p. A4.

"3 U.S. Military Missions in Cuba to Be Recalled," *New York Times*, January 28, 1959, p. 14.

"3 U.S. Youths Reported in Cuban Rebel Ranks, *Washington Post*, March 9, 1957, p. A4.

"Tireless Revolutionary," *New York Times*, July 20, 1959, p. 2.

Tivnan, Edward. "Voodoo That New Yorkers Do," *New York Times*, December 2, 1979, p. SM46.

"Today a Cuban Holiday," *New York Times*, July 30, 1959, p. 6.

Toot, Peter T. *Armando Marsans: A Cuban Pioneer in the Major Leagues*. Jefferson, NC: McFarland, 2004.

"Top Castro Foe Caught in Cuba," *Washington Post*, July 26, 1959, p. A5.

Topping, Seymour. "Europe Supplies Caribbean Arms Despite U.S. Curb," *New York Times*, November 1, 1959, p. 1.

Torbitt, William. *Nomenclature of an Assassination Cabal*, self-published, http://scribblguy.50megs.com/torbitt.htm (1970).

"Tourist-Barren Cuba Sours 'Sugar King,'" *Washington Post*, August 8, 1960, p. B6.

Traber, Robert. "Castro's Cuba," *The Nation*, January 23, 1960.

"Trade Not Aid," *Time*, January 5, 1953.

"Tragedy in Havana," *Washington Post*, March 7, 1960, p. A12.

"Transcript of Eisenhower's News Conference on Foreign and Domestic Matters," *New York Times*, January 27, 1960, p. 14.

"Transcript of President Kennedy's News Conference," *Washington Post*, April 13, 1961, p. A10.

"Transcript of President's News Conference on Foreign and U.S. Matters," *New York Times*, October 29, 1959, p. 19.

"Transition in Cuba," *Washington Post*, May 19, 1959, p. A20.

"Troops Guard Batista; Nip Revolt," *Washington Post*, February 4, 1941, p.1.

"Troops in Readiness as Cuba Votes Today," *New York Times*, June 1, 1950, p. 11.

"Tropicana Bombed," *New York Times*, January 2, 1957, p. 4.

"Troubled Air," *Washington Post*, October 30, 1959, p. A18.

"The True Life of Rebel Castro," *Gente Magazine* (American Edition) 1, no. 1 (January 5, 1958).

"Trujillo Appeals to Americas Unit," *New York Times*, January 1, 1950, p. 10.

"Trujillo Arming Legion for Defense of Haiti," *Washington Post*, March 6, 1959, p. C11.

"Trujillo Reported to Crush Invasion Backed by Cuba," *New York Times*, June 24, 1959, p. 1. "Trujillo Said to Bar Retirement; Terms Leaders of U.S. Hostile," *New York Times*, March 18, 1960, p. 2.

"Trujillo Signs Nationalizing Bill," *New York Times*, January 1, 1955, p. 3.

Trussell, C. P. "Eisenhower Scores Attack on Clergy; M'-Carthy Aide Out," *New York Times*, July 10, 1953, p. 1.

Tuckner, Howard M. "Honolulu Group Hopes to Enter a Team in Third Major League," *New York Times*, August 20, 1959, p. 16.

_____. "Third Major League Is Formed in Baseball," *New York Times* July 28, 1959, p. 1.

Turner, Frederick C. *Catholicism and Political Development in Latin America*. Chapel Hill: University of North Carolina Press, 1971.

"27 Held as Plotters against Castro's Life," *Washington Post*, April 19, 1961, p. A9.

"2 Americans Get Posts," *New York Times*, January 5, 1959, p. 3.

"2 Anti-Castro Chiefs Freed at Extortion Trial in Miami," *New York Times*, December 19, 1966, p. 47.

"2 Condemned Cubans Make Escape As Firing Squad Pauses to Reload," *Washington Post*, March 6, 1959, p. A7.

"2 Cuban Refugees Held as Extorters," *New York Times*, November 26, 1965, p. 44.

"Two Say Cuban Ties Led to Loss of Jobs," *New York Times*, September 23, 1960, p. 17.

"Two Suspects Accused of Planning Attacks," *The Times of Havana*, October 11, 1957, p. 13.

"2 Who Served Batista Are Executed in Cuba," *Washington Post*, December 20, 1959, p. B5.

"Underrating the Cuban Patriots," *Washington Post*, April 3, 1902, p. 6.

"Unhappy Doctor," *Time*, June 9, 1947.

United Fruit Historical Society, http://www.unitedfruit.org/arbenz.htm.

U.N. Statistical Yearbook, 1958. New York: United Nations, 1958.

United States Central Intelligence Agency. "An Appraisal of the Cuban Sugar Industry," CIA (March 1961). Published internally by the CIA. Available in the Library of Congress and at George Washington University Library.

United States Department of Commerce. Bureau of the Census. "Historical Statistics of the United States," PC 80, S1–7, 2001.

United States Department of State, Office of Electronic

Information, Bureau of Public Affairs, http://www.state.gov/r/pa/ho/time/ip/16324.htm (2007). Multiple references.

    Central Files: E.G. in telegram 152 to Havana, September 10, 1957. Aid., 737.00/9–1057.

    Rubottom Files: Lot 59 D 573, Cuba. Secret. Drafted by Wieland and Leonhardy, December 23, 1957.

    Press Bulletin Number 90, March 16, 1959.

    Operations Memorandum dated April 27, 1959 Treaties.

    42 United States Department of State Bulletin, p. 158.

    43 United States Department of State Bulletin, pp. 141–142 (nationalization of oil companies); pp. 603–604 (nationalization of banks).

United States Senate. "Communist Threat to the United States through the Caribbean," Hearings before the Subcommittee to Investigate the Administration of the Internal Security Act and Other Internal Security Laws, Committee on the Judiciary, United States Senate, Eighty-sixth Congress. Testimony: Major Pedro L. Díaz Lanz, July 14, 1959, General C. P. Cabell, November 5, 1959; Father Eduardo Aguirre, May 3, 1960; Father Rosario Maxilliano Pérez, May 3, 1960; Rafael Díaz-Balart, May 3, 1960; Manuel Antonio Ugalde Carrillo, May 3 and 4, 1960; Andres Jose Rivero Agüero, May 4, 1960; Father Juan Ramón O'Farril, May 4, 1960; Francisco J. Tabernilla, May 6, 1960; Salvador Díaz-Verson, May 6, 1960; Ambassador Arthur Gadner, August 27, 1960; Ambassador Earl E. T. Smith, August 30, 1960.

United States Senate. Hearings "Fair Play for Cuba Committee" before the Senate Judiciary Subcommittee to Investigate the Administration of the Internal Security Act and Other Security Laws, May 5, 1960.

"United States Supreme Court — The Proposed Purchase of Cuba in 1846," *New York Times*, December 10, 1852, p. 10.

Unna, Warren. "Cubans, Dominicans Get $719,000 in U.S. Aid," *Washington Post and Times Herald*, February 26, 1960, p. 12.

_____. "Ike, 'Perplexed' by Cuba, Opposes Any Reprisals," *Washington Post and Times Herald*, January 27, 1960, p. A1.

_____. "Open Defiance Perils Future Role of OAS," *Washington Post and Times Herald*, April 6, 1960, p. A7.

_____. "3 More Cuban Aides Quit Castro's Regime," *Washington Post and Times Herald*, March 18, 1960, p. A1.

_____. "U.S. Sending Bonsal Back to Havana Post," *Washington Post and Times Herald*, March 19, 1960, p. A1.

_____. "U.S. to Seek Damages Despite Cuban Rebuff," *Washington Post and Times Herald*, January 13, 1960, p. A5.

"Upper Classmen v. Freshman," *Time*, April 27, 1959.

"Uranium Strike in Pinar del Río," *The Times of Havana*, October 11, 1957, p. 2, and October 21, 1957, p. 3.

Urban, C. Stanley. "The Africanization of Cuba Scare, 1853–1855," *The Hispanic American Historical Review* 37, no. 1 (February 1957), pp. 29–45.

Urrutia Lleó, Manuel. *Fidel Castro & Company: Communist Tyranny in Cuba*. New York: Frederick A. Praeger, 1964.

"Urrutia Accused by a Castro Aide," *New York Times*, July 19, 1959, p. 3.

"U.S. Accusation Lists Castro's 'Half-Truths' and 'Distortions' About Controversy," *New York Times*, October 15, 1960, p. 6.

"U.S. Accused Again by Cuba in the U.N.," *New York Times*, March 16, 1961, p. 8.

"U.S. Acts to Curb Latin Gunrunning," *New York Times*, February 19, 1960, p. 1.

"U.S. Carrier at Guantánamo," *New York Times*, January 10, 1961, p. 10.

"U.S. Denies Invasion Charge," *New York Times*, January 3, 1961, p. 5.

"U.S. Deserter Gives Up," *New York Times*, October 17, 1959, p. 5.

"U.S. Doubts O.A.S. Power to Halt Trujillo's Arrests," *New York Times*, February 7, 1960, p. 1.

"U.S. Envoys Ran Cuba, Castro Says," *Washington Post*, February 4, 1959, p. A8.

"U.S. Experts Baffled by Hijacking Problem," *Washington Post and Times Herald*, February 6, 1969, p. A4.

"U.S. Flier Denies Plot to Kill Cuban Leader," *Washington Post*, February 7, 1959, p. A7.

"U.S. Foregoes Reply to Castro Aid Talk," *New York Times*, May 5, 1959, p. 11.

"U.S. Holds Plane Used in Leaflet Hop to Cuba," *Washington Post*, October 31, 1959, p. A7.

"U.S. Jury Acquits 4 Foes of Castro," *New York Times*, June 5, 1966, p. 56.

"U.S. Jury Indicts a Batista Backer," *New York Times*, April 11, 1961, p. 1.

"U.S. Note Bids Cuba Drop Parley Curb," *New York Times*, March 1, 1960, p. 1.

"U.S. Officials Doubt an Effective Check on Flights to Cuba," *New York Times*, February 21, 1960, p. 1.

"U.S. Pro-Castro Unit Asks Inquiry on C.I.A.," *New York Times*, January 6, 1961, p. 3.

"U.S. Reporter Upheld," *New York Times*, December 17, 1959, p. 9.

"U.S. Says Cubans Plot to Show 2 Ousted F.B.I. Men as 'Nazis,'" *New York Times*, August 6, 1960, p. 1.

"U.S. Seeking Data on Raids in Cuba," *New York Times*, April 16, 1961, p. 1.

"U.S. Technical Aid Pressed in Cuba," *New York Times*, January 13, 1960, p. 70.

"U.S. Weighs Law Extension," *New York Times*, June 6, 1959, p. 6.

Valeriani, Richard. "Cuba Presses Arrest of Foes," *Washington Post and Times Herald*, January 9, 1961, p. A7.

Valls, Jorge. *Twenty Years and Forty Days: Life in a Cuban Prison*. New York: Americas Watch, 1986.

Vanden Heuvel, Katrina. "Suppressing News: Déjà Vu," *The Nation*, February 23, 2007.

"Vatican Wary on Cuba," *New York Times*, January 4, 1959, p. 4.

Velie, Lester. "Suckers in Paradise: How Americans Lose Their Shirts in Caribbean Gambling Joints," *Saturday Evening Post*, March 28, 1953.

"The Vengeful Visionary," *Time* magazine, January 26, 1959.

Vinocur, John. "A Republic of Fear," *New York Times Magazine*, September 23, 1984, pp. 21–23.

Volsky, George. "In Castro's Gulag," *New York Times Magazine*, October 18, 1987.

"Waifs Aided by Cuba," *New York Times*, October 16, 1959, p. 8.

Waldor, Milton A. *Peddlers of Fear: The John Birch Society*. Newark, NJ: Lynnross, 1966.

Waltman, Franklyn, Jr. "Cuba's Choice — Rapid Social Reform or Complete Chaos and Terror," *Washington Post*, January 27, 1935, p. B1.

"War Games Started," *Washington Post*, March 9, 1960, p. A9.

"Warning to Aggressors Is Sounded by Trujillo," *New York Times*, March 12, 1959, p. 15.

"Warships to Avoid Cuba," *New York Times*, January 16, 1959, p. 3.

"Washington Aides Receptive," *New York Times*, February 23, 1960, p. 3.

"We Won't Retreat on Berlin, Ike Says," *Washington Post*, July 16, 1959, p. A7.

Weber, David J. *The Spanish Frontier in North America.* New Haven, CT: Yale University Press, 1992.

Weisbord, Albert. "Perspectives of the Cuban Revolution," *La Parola del Popolo*, January 1962.

Welch, Richard E. *Response to Revolution: The United States and the Cuban Revolution, 1959–1961.* Chapel Hill: University of North Carolina Press, 1985.

Welch, Robert. *The Blue Book of the John Birch Society.* Belmont, MA: Self-published, 1959.

_____. *The Politician: A Look at the Forces That Propelled Dwight David Eisenhower to the Presidency.* Belmont, MA: Self-published, 1954, reprinted 1961.

Wendel, Tim. *Castro's Curveball.* New York: Ballantine Books, 1999.

White, Jean. "Castro Backers Take Over Embassy Here as Cuban Envoy Resigns," *Washington Post*, January 2, 1959, pp. A1, A5.

Whitten, Leslie. "Cuba Sues Defector for $110,000," *Washington Post and Times Herald*, March 20, 1960, p. A8.

Wiesenthal, Simon. *Sails of Hope: The Secret Mission of Columbus.* New York: Macmillan, 1973.

"Wild Ovation Given Castro in Caracas," *Washington Post*, January 24, 1959, p. A4.

Williams, Ian. "The Secret History of Rum," *The Nation*, November 22, 2005.

Williams, Mary Louise. "Colonyites and the Revolution: Excitement Minus the Damage," *The Times of Havana*, January 8, 1959, p. 6.

Wilson, Robert A., and David E. Jordan. "Personal Exemptions and Individual Income Tax Rates, 1913–2002" (Rev. 6–02), in *Internal Revenue Service Statistics of Income Bulletin* (Publication 1136), Spring 2002, pp. 216–225.

Wilson, Samuel M. "Columbus, My Enemy," *Natural History*, December 1990, pp. 44–49.

Winston, Paul. "America Not Yet Ready for Running of the Bulls," *Business Insurance*, July 23, 2007, p. 30.

"Wizard at Work," *Time*, March 20, 1950.

"The World," *New York Times*, January 18, 1959, p. E1.

"The World," *New York Times*, January 25, 1959, p. E1.

"The World," *New York Times*, April 19, 1959, p. E1.

"The World," *New York Times*, December 13, 1959, p. E2.

The World of 1898: The Spanish American War. Washington, DC: Library of Congress, 1998. http://www.loc.gov/rr/hispanic/1898/intro.html.

"Worried over the Prospect of Possible Injury to U.S. Visiting or Resident Baseball Players, the International League Took Steps to Transfer the Franchise of the Triple A Havana Sugar Kings to Jersey City," *Time*, July 18, 1960.

Wright, Irene A. *The Early History of Cuba, 1492–1586.* New York: Macmillan, 1916.

"Writ Frees Cuban Held as Plotter," *New York Times*, August 18, 1959, p. 11.

Wyden, Peter. *The Bay of Pigs: The Untold Story.* New York: Simon and Schuster, 1979.

Yanez, Luisa. "Former Rebel Remembers Promise, Betrayal of Cuban Revolution," *Miami Herald*, January 9, 2009. http://www.miamiherald.com/news/americas/cuba/v-fullstory/story/843341.html.

Yaremko, Jason M. *U.S. Protestant Missions in Cuba: From Independence to Castro.* Gainesville: University Press of Florida, 2000.

"Ydigoras Denies Invasion Plan," *New York Times*, January 11, 1961, p. 11.

Young, Dick. "National League Votes Expansion to 10 Clubs," *Washington Post and Times Herald*, July 19, 1960, p. A15.

Youngblood, Jack, and Robin Moore. *The Devil to Pay.* New York: Coward-McCann, 1961.

Zim, Daniel Rubeira. "Straining the Special Relationship: British and U.S. Policies toward the Cuban Revolution, 1959–1961," in *Cuban Studies 33*. Lisandro Pérez and Uva De Aragon, eds. Pittsburgh: Center for Latin American Studies, University of Pittsburgh Press, 1980.

Zoglin, Richard. "Lucille Ball: The First Lady of Comedy Brought Us Laughter as Well as Emotional Truth," *Time*, June 8, 1998.

Zoumaras, Thomas. "Eisenhower's Foreign Economic Policy: The Case of Latin America," in R. A. Melanson and D. A. Mayers, eds. *Reevaluating Eisenhower.* Urbana: University of Illinois Press, 1987, pp. 155–191.

Index